Lecture Notes in Computer Science 2895

Edited by G. Goos, J. Hartmanis, and J. van Leeuwen

T0254419

Springer
Berlin
Heidelberg
New York
Hong Kong
London
Milan
Paris
Tokyo

Atsushi Ohori (Ed.)

Programming Languages and Systems

First Asian Symposium, APLAS 2003
Beijing, China, November 27-29, 2003
Proceedings

 Springer

Series Editors

Gerhard Goos, Karlsruhe University, Germany
Juris Hartmanis, Cornell University, NY, USA
Jan van Leeuwen, Utrecht University, The Netherlands

Volume Editor

Atsushi Ohori
Japan Advanced Institute of Science and Technology
School of Information Science
Tatsunokuchi, Ishikawa 923-1292, Japan
E-mail: ohori@jaist.ac.jp

Cataloging-in-Publication Data applied for

A catalog record for this book is available from the Library of Congress.

Bibliographic information published by Die Deutsche Bibliothek
Die Deutsche Bibliothek lists this publication in the Deutsche Nationalbibliografie;
detailed bibliographic data is available in the Internet at <http://dnb.ddb.de>.

CR Subject Classification (1998): D.3, D.2, F.3, D.4, D.1, F.4.1

ISSN 0302-9743
ISBN 3-540-20536-5 Springer-Verlag Berlin Heidelberg New York

Springer-Verlag is a part of Springer Science+Business Media

springeronline.com

© Springer-Verlag Berlin Heidelberg 2003
Printed in Germany

Typesetting: Camera-ready by author, data conversion by PTP-Berlin, Protago-TeX-Production GmbH
Printed on acid-free paper   SPIN: 10969830   06/3142   5 4 3 2 1 0

Foreword

With warm-hearted and friendly promotion by our Japanese friends Prof. Atsushi Ohori, Prof. Tetsuo Ida, and Prof. Zhenjiang Hu, and other distinguished professors and scholars from countries and regions such as Japan, South Korea, Singapore, and Taiwan, the 1st Asian Symposium on Programming Languages and Systems (APLAS 2003) took place in Beijing. We received 76 papers, among which 24 were selected for the proceedings after serious evaluation, which fully demonstrates the high quality of the collected papers. I hereby, on behalf of the Program Committee and the Organization Committee of the symposium, would like to extend the warmest welcome and hearty thanks to all colleagues who attended the symposium, all scholars who generously contributed their papers, and all those who were actively dedicated to the organization of this symposium.

Over the past decade, the Asian economy has undergone rapid development. Keeping pace with this accelerated economic growth, Asia has made great headway in software, integrated circuits, mobile communication and the Internet. All this has laid a firm material foundation for undertaking theoretical research on computer science and programming languages. Therefore, to meet the increasing demands of the IT market, great opportunities and challenges in advanced research in these fields. I strongly believe that in the coming future, with the persistent efforts of our colleagues, the Asian software industry and research on computer science will be important players in the world economy, on an equal footing with their counterparts in the United States and Europe.

I am of the opinion that, to enhance Asian computer science research, much more attention should be paid to the new issues and technical problems brought with the development of the software industry in the world, particularly in Asia, and accordingly, we should advance computer science research in Asia to a position with distinctive features and great prospects. In the course of the Asian economic development over the past 10 years, the pursuit of highly reliable software and efficient software development processes has created urgent demands for basic research on computer science. In addition, theoretical guidelines are required to solve the problems of congestion, waste and security generated in the storage, transmission and processing of massive information on the Internet. Under such circumstances, it is expected that a new discipline, namely Information Physics, will be born in the near future.

Dear colleagues, as leading theorists of computer science in Asia, we should take up this task and put all our efforts into achieving creative breakthroughs in the fields mentioned above, and promoting our ongoing contacts and cooperation with our European and American colleagues, and thus turn Asia into a promising land of research on computer science and technology, and make a historical contribution to the progress of mankind as a whole.

September 2003   Wei Li

Preface

This volume contains the proceedings of APLAS 2003, the 1st Asian Symposium on Programming Languages and Systems, held in Beijing, China, November 27–29, 2003, sponsored by the Asian Association for Foundation of Software (AAFS) and Beihang University.

The symposium was devoted to foundational issues in programming languages and systems, covering (but not limited to) the following areas:

- concurrency and parallelism,
- language implementation and optimization,
- mobile computation and security,
- program analysis and verification,
- program transformation and calculation,
- programming paradigms and language design,
- programming techniques and applications,
- semantics, categorical and logical foundations,
- tools and environments, and
- type theory and type systems.

In response to the call for papers, 76 papers were submitted by authors from Australia, Austria, China, Denmark, France, India, Italy, Japan, Korea, Portugal, Singapore, Spain, Taiwan, the United Arab Emirates, the UK, and the USA. Each paper was reviewed by at least three program committee members with the help of external expert reviewers. The program committee meeting was conducted electronically from August 5 through August 15th. The competition was very tough and the deliberation was a difficult process. After careful and thorough discussion, the program committee selected 24 papers. I would like to sincerely thank all the members of the APLAS 2003 Program Committee for their excellent job, and all the external reviewers for their invaluable contribution. The submission and review process was managed using the CyberChair system.

In addition to the 24 contributed papers, the symposium also included talks by three invited speakers: Thomas A. Henzinger (University of California at Berkeley, USA), Simon Peyton Jones (Microsoft Research, UK), and Wen-tsun Wu (Academia Sinica, China). I am grateful to the three invited speakers.

Many people helped in the effort to establish this new Asian-based conference series, APLAS, as a high-quality forum to serve the worldwide programming languages community. Without their help and enthusiastic support, APLAS 2003 would not have happened. My special thanks to our general chair, Wei Li, whose initiative and efforts made the first APLAS in Beijing possible. I would like to thank Shilong Ma. In addition to his hard work as a program committee member, he helped us to solve numerous problems we encountered during our planning, and during APLAS 2003, itself. The AAFS steering committee provided advice and suggestions. I would particularly like to thank Tetsuo Ida, who provided advice and suggestions at several critical moments.

September 2003   Atsushi Ohori

Organization

General Chair

Wei Li   Beihang University, China

Program Chair

Atsushi Ohori   Japan Advanced Institute of Science and Technology, Japan

Program Committee

Manuel Chakravarty	University of New South Wales, Australia
Wei Ngan Chin	National University of Singapore, Singapore
Tyng-Ruey Chuang	Academia Sinica, Taiwan
Yuxi Fu	Shanghai Jiaotong University, China
Masahito Hasegawa	Kyoto University, Japan
Kohei Honda	Queen Mary and Westfield College, UK
Zhenjiang Hu	University of Tokyo, Japan
Peter Lee	Carnegie Mellon University, USA
Shilong Ma	Beihang University, China
Martin Odersky	École Polytechnique de Lausanne, Switzerland
Don Sannella	University of Edinburgh, UK
Zhong Shao	Yale University, USA
Kwangkeun Yi	Seoul National University, Korea
Taiichi Yuasa	Kyoto University, Japan

Referees

Philippe Altherr	Florin Craciun
Hugh Anderson	Vincent Cremet
Stefan Andrei	Pascal Cuoq
David Aspinall	Neil D. Jones
Martin Berger	Kyung-goo Doh
Lennart Beringer	Burak Emir
Andrew Bernard	Kai Engelhardt
Johannes Borgstroem	Hyunjoon Eo
Patricia Bouyer	Lin Gao
Chiyan Chen	Maria Garcia de la Banda
Kwanghoon Choi	Samir Genaim
Williamd D Clinger	Stephen Gilmore

Robert Glück
Katsuhiko Gondow
Makoto Hamana
Nadeem Abdul Hamid
Hwansoo Han
Yasushi Hayashi
Nevin Heintze
Fritz Henglein
Ralf Hinze
Kunihiko Hiraishi
Kathrin Hoffmann
Haruo Hosoya
Chunnan Hsu
Ralf Huuck
Atsushi Igarashi
Kyriakos Kalorkoti
Hyun-Gu Kang
Hyun-gu Kang
Gabriele Keller
Siau-Cheng Khoo
Iksoon Kim
Tsuneyasu Komiya
Jaejin Lee
Oukseh Lee
James Leifer
Hans-Wolfgang Loidl
Kenneth MacKenzie
Sergio Maffeis
Sebastian Maneth
Julio Mariño-Carballo
Olga Marroquin Alonso
Andrew McCreight
Francois Metayer
Aart Middeldorp
Nikolay Mihaylov
Alberto Momigliano
Stefan Monnier
Soo-Mook Moon
Shin-ichiro Mori
Shin-Cheng Mu
Masaki Murakami
Keisuke Nakano
Zhaozhong Ni
Mizuhito Ogawa
Yasuo Okabe
Mitsu Okada

Vincent van Oostrom
Yunheung Paek
Emir Pasalic
Leaf Petersen
Frank Pfenning
Corneliu Popeea
Riccardo Pucella
Femke van Raamsdonk
Julian Rathke
Andrei Sabelfeld
Amr Sabry
Sean Seefried
Emil Sekerinski
Sunae Seo
Qin Shengchao
Sangmin Shim
Nigel Smart
Harald Sondergaard
Ian Stark
Erik Stenman
Donald Stewart
Yuefei Sui
Martin Sulzmann
Kenjiro Taura
Jennifer Tenzer
Valery Trifonov
Kazunori Ueda
Joe Vanderwaart
Rene Vestergaard
Bow-Yaw Wang
Yongjun Wang
Adam Wiggins
Simon Winwood
Mark Wotton
Hongwei Xi
Dana Xu
Ke Xu
Jingling Xue
Hongseok Yang
Masahiro Yasugi
Ching-Long Yeh
Shoji Yuen
Patryk Zadarnowski
Matthias Zenger
Li Zhang
Sheng Zhong

Table of Contents

Invited Talk 2

Session 4

Session 5

Session 6

Invited Talk 3

Session 7

On a Method of Global Optimization
Invited Talk

Wen-tsun Wu[1]

Institute of Systems Science, Academia Sinica, Beijing 100080, China

The usual optimization problem, in eventually introducing some further new variables, may be put in the following form: **Optimization Problem O**. Let $f, g_j, (j = 1, \cdots, m)$ be infinitely differentiable real functions in variables $X = \{x_1, x_2, \cdots, x_n\}$ in a domain D of $\mathbf{R}^n(X), \mathbf{R}$ being the real field. To find *optimal* (maximum or minimum) value(s) of f for $X \in D$ under the constraint conditions

$$g_j = 0, j = 1, 2, \cdots, m.$$

Various known methods for the solving of Problem O give usually only optimal values of *local* character which are in general not unique. On the other hand if the functions f, g_j are all *polynomial* ones, then we have discovered some method which will give the *unique global* optimal (greatest or least) value of the Problem, so far it is known to exist. In fact, we have the following

Theorem. For the Optimization Problem O with f, g_j all *polynomials* there is a *finite* set of real values **K** such that: If the *global* optimal (greatest or least) value of f in D does exist, then this optimal value is equal to the optimal (greatest or least) value of the *finite* set **K**.

We call the finite set **K** in the theorem the **Finite Kernel Set** of Problem O. It can be algorithmically determined by means of some package due to D.K.Wang of our Institute. Various kinds of problems like non-linear programming, geometric and trigonometric inequalities-proving, definiteness of polynomials, traffic control, etc. have been solved by means of the above method.

A. Ohori (Ed.): APLAS 2003, LNCS 2895, p. 1, 2003.

Observing Asymmetry and Mismatch

Xiaoju Dong and Yuxi Fu*

Department of Computer Science, Shanghai Jiaotong University,
Shanghai 200030, China
{dong-xj,fu-yx}@cs.sjtu.edu.cn

Abstract. The chi calculus is studied in the framework incorporating
two constructions widely useful in applications: asymmetric communication and mismatch condition. The barbed bisimilarity is used to give a
general picture of how the two constructions affect the observational theory. Both the operational properties and the algebraic properties of the
enriched calculus are investigated to support an improved understanding
of the bisimulation behaviors of the model.

1 Introduction

We study the asymmetric χ-calculus with mismatch. The background of this
investigation is as follows:

- The χ-calculus was independently proposed by Fu in [2,3] and by Parrow and
  Victor in [15]. Fu was motivated to simplify the π-calculus and to provide a
  proof theoretical interpretation of concurrent computation ([5]). Parrow and
  Victor shared the motivation on simplification. They were also trying to give
  a more direct interpretation of concurrent constraint programming ([17]).
  The model they proposed, called Fusion Calculus, is actually the polyadic
  χ-calculus. The χ-calculus is symmetric in the sense that the input and output prefixes are of the same form and that communications are symmetric.
  Theoretical investigations on Fusion Calculus are carried out in [16]. More
  fundamental studies on χ-calculus are done in [4,6,8]. The important results in [4,6,8] are the introduction of L-bisimilarities, the classification of
  L-bisimilarities using bisimulation lattice, and the characterizations of L-
  bisimilarities in terms of open style bisimilarities.
- Symmetry of communications is a beautiful thing to have in theory. In programming practice however there is a need for asymmetric communications.
  The symmetry introduces extra uncertainty. This nondeterministic feature

---

* The author is supported by the National Distinguished Young Scientist Fund
of NNSFC (60225012), the Shanghai Science and Technology Development Fund
(025115032), the Young Scientist Research Fund and the University Scholar Funding Scheme. He is also supported by BASICS, Center of Basic Studies in Computing Science, sponsored by Shanghai Education Commission. BASICS is affiliated to
the Department of Computer Science of Shanghai Jiaotong University.

A. Ohori (Ed.): APLAS 2003, LNCS 2895, pp. 2–19, 2003.

is not always welcome by users. In reality we often come across with situations in which we favor a command that always acts as an output instruction in whatever environments it resides. In other words we really need a command set that draws a line between an input command and an output command. Therefore it is necessary to pay as much attention to the asymmetric χ-calculus as to the symmetric one. Parrow and Victor have studied the asymmetric χ-calculus, which they called Update Calculus, in [14]. A more systematic investigation into the asymmetry is reported in [7]. It turns out that the theory of the asymmetric χ-calculus is much richer than the theory of the symmetric χ-calculus. The barbed bisimilarity of the asymmetric χ-calculus for example reveals some aspects of process identity for the first time. Some of the equivalence properties are beyond our intuition at first sight. But they are very reasonable from an observational viewpoint.

– A familiar programming construct is the binary *if B then C_1 else C_2* command. One could say that this command is behind all the 'intelligent behaviors' of computer programs. In calculi of mobile processes the command *if B then C_1 else C_2* can be coded up by a process like $[x=y]P + [x \neq y]Q$. Here the mismatch plays a crucial role. Now the binary command *if B then C_1 else C_2* could be simulated by two consecutive unary commands *if B then C_1; if ¬B then C_2*. The negation operator appeared here implies that if we would translate the program *if B then C_1; if ¬B then C_2* into a process in some calculus of mobile processes we would have to use the mismatch. One could argue that the positive match operator $[x=y]$ suffices in a lot of cases. This is true at the expanse that programs so constructed are unnecessarily complex since a lot of coding-up is applied. It should be pointed out that these cases are restricted to the applications where computation flows depend on enumerations of finite numbers of names. Of course the calculus can be extended with other constructs like infinite sum. However that would give rise to a model more abstract and less real. Motivated by applications, the mismatch operator turns out to be very important in theory. Some of the results in process algebra are valid only in the presence of this operator. In the framework of the χ-calculus, the mismatch operator has been studied in [9,10,11]. It is demonstrated in these papers that the mismatch could be extremely subtle. Even the definitions of bisimulations call for extra care! The hyperequivalence studied in [16] for example is not even observational in the presence of mismatch. See [11] for counter examples.

In this paper we study the interplay between the asymmetry and the mismatch in the framework of the χ-calculus. Both features are motivated by applications. And both are significant in theory. Based upon previous work on the asymmetry and the mismatch, we will show, both operationally and algebraically, how one-step actions of the asymmetric χ-calculus with mismatch are simulated by observationally equivalent sequences of actions. We will achieve this by looking at the barbed bisimilarity. We omit the proofs and some intermediate lemmas. One could find a detailed account in the full paper [1]. In the rest of the paper we will refer to 'asymmetric χ-calculus with mismatch' as 'χ-calculus'.

2   Asymmetric Chi Calculus with Mismatch

Let $\mathcal{N}$ be the set of names ranged over by small case letters and $\overline{\mathcal{N}}$ the set $\{\overline{x} \mid x \in \mathcal{N}\}$ of co-names. The Greek letter α ranges over $\mathcal{N} \cdot \overline{\mathcal{N}}$, where the dot $\cdot$ denotes set union. For $\alpha \in \mathcal{N} \cdot \overline{\mathcal{N}}$, let $\overline{\alpha}$ be defined as a if $\alpha = \overline{a}$ and as $\overline{a}$ if $\alpha = a$. The χ-processes are defined by the following abstract grammar:

$$P := \mathbf{0} \mid \alpha x.P \mid P \mid P \mid (x)P \mid [x{=}y]P \mid [x{\neq}y]P \mid P{+}P$$

Let λ range over the set of transition labels $\{ax, \overline{a}x, a(x), \overline{a}(x), y/x, (y)/x \mid a, x, y \in \mathcal{N}\} \cdot \{\tau\}$ and γ over $\{ax, \overline{a}x, a(x), \overline{a}(x) \mid a, x \in \mathcal{N}\} \cdot \{\tau\}$. In $(y)/x$ and y/x, x and y must be different. The free and bound names are defined as usual. We use the notation $fn(\_)$, $bn(\_)$ and $n(\_)$ in their standard meaning. We write $P\{y/x\}$ for the result of substituting y for x throughout P. We will assume that a bound name is distinct from any other name in all environments.

In the following labelled transition system, symmetric rules have been systematically omitted.

Sequentialization

$$\overline{\alpha x.P \xrightarrow{\alpha x} P}$$

Composition

$$\frac{P \xrightarrow{\gamma} P'}{P \mid Q \xrightarrow{\gamma} P' \mid Q} \qquad \frac{P \xrightarrow{y/x} P'}{P \mid Q \xrightarrow{y/x} P' \mid Q\{y/x\}} \qquad \frac{P \xrightarrow{(y)/x} P'}{P \mid Q \xrightarrow{(y)/x} P' \mid Q\{y/x\}}$$

Communication

$$\frac{P \xrightarrow{a(x)} P' \quad Q \xrightarrow{\overline{a}y} Q'}{P \mid Q \xrightarrow{\tau} P'\{y/x\} \mid Q'} \qquad \frac{P \xrightarrow{a(x)} P' \quad Q \xrightarrow{\overline{a}(x)} Q'}{P \mid Q \xrightarrow{\tau} (x)(P' \mid Q')} \qquad \frac{P \xrightarrow{ax} P' \quad Q \xrightarrow{\overline{a}x} Q'}{P \mid Q \xrightarrow{\tau} P' \mid Q'}$$

$$\frac{P \xrightarrow{ax} P' \quad Q \xrightarrow{\overline{a}y} Q' \quad x \neq y}{P \mid Q \xrightarrow{y/x} P'\{y/x\} \mid Q'\{y/x\}} \qquad \frac{P \xrightarrow{ax} P' \quad Q \xrightarrow{\overline{a}(y)} Q'}{P \mid Q \xrightarrow{(y)/x} P'\{y/x\} \mid Q'\{y/x\}}$$

Localization

$$\frac{P \xrightarrow{\lambda} P' \quad x \notin n(\lambda)}{(x)P \xrightarrow{\lambda} (x)P'} \qquad \frac{P \xrightarrow{\alpha x} P' \quad x \notin \{\alpha, \overline{\alpha}\}}{(x)P \xrightarrow{\alpha(x)} P'}$$

$$\frac{P \xrightarrow{y/x} P'}{(x)P \xrightarrow{\tau} P'} \qquad \frac{P \xrightarrow{y/x} P'}{(y)P \xrightarrow{(y)/x} P'} \qquad \frac{P \xrightarrow{(y)/x} P'}{(x)P \xrightarrow{\tau} (y)P'}$$

Condition and Selection

$$\frac{P \xrightarrow{\lambda} P'}{[x{=}x]P \xrightarrow{\lambda} P'} \qquad \frac{P \xrightarrow{\lambda} P'}{[x{\neq}y]P \xrightarrow{\lambda} P'} \qquad \frac{P \xrightarrow{\lambda} P'}{P{+}Q \xrightarrow{\lambda} P'}$$

Here are some examples of communication admissible by the operational semantics:

$$(x)(R \,|\, (\bar{a}y.P \,|\, ax.Q)) \xrightarrow{\tau} R\{y/x\} \,|\, (P\{y/x\} \,|\, Q\{y/x\}), \text{ where } y \neq x$$
$$(x)\bar{a}x.P \,|\, (y)ay.Q \xrightarrow{\tau} (z)(P\{z/x\} \,|\, Q\{z/y\}), \text{ where } z \text{ is fresh}$$

Communications of this language are asymmetric because one has

$$\bar{a}y.P \,|\, (x)ax.Q \xrightarrow{\tau} P \,|\, Q\{y/x\}$$

but not

$$(y)\bar{a}y.P \,|\, ax.Q \xrightarrow{\tau} P\{x/y\} \,|\, Q$$

For more about the operational semantics, see [7,8,9,10,11].

In addition to the prefix αx, we need some auxiliary prefixes:

$$\alpha(x).P \overset{\text{def}}{=} (x)\alpha x.P, \qquad \text{bound prefix}$$
$$\langle y/x \rangle.P \overset{\text{def}}{=} (a)(\bar{a}y \,|\, ax.P), \quad \text{update prefix}$$
$$(y/x).P \overset{\text{def}}{=} (y)\langle y/x \rangle.P, \qquad \text{bound update prefix}$$
$$\tau.P \overset{\text{def}}{=} (a)\langle a/a \rangle.P, \qquad \text{tau prefix}$$

where $x \notin \{\alpha, \bar{\alpha}\}$, $x \neq y$ and a is fresh. The set of all prefixes will also be ranged over by λ.

We will write ϕ and ψ, called conditions, to stand for sequences of match and mismatch combinators concatenated one after another, and δ for a sequence of mismatch operators. The notation $\phi \Rightarrow \psi$ says that ϕ logically implies ψ and $\phi \Leftrightarrow \psi$ that ϕ and ψ are logically equivalent. The concatenation of ψ and ϕ is denoted by $\psi\phi$.

A substitution σ respects ψ if $\psi \Rightarrow x{=}y$ implies $\sigma(x) = \sigma(y)$ and $\psi \Rightarrow x{\neq}y$ implies $\sigma(x) \neq \sigma(y)$. Dually ψ respects σ if $\sigma(x) = \sigma(y)$ implies $\psi \Rightarrow x{=}y$ and $\sigma(x){\neq}\sigma(y)$ implies $\psi \Rightarrow x{\neq}y$. The substitution σ agrees with ψ, and ψ agrees with σ, if they respect each other. The substitution σ is induced by ψ if it agrees with ψ and $n(\sigma) \subseteq n(\psi)$.

Let V be a finite set of names. We say that ϕ is complete on V if $n(\phi) = V$ and for each pair x, y of names in V it holds that either $\phi \Rightarrow x = y$ or $\phi \Rightarrow x \neq y$.

A sequence of names $x_1, \ldots, x_n$ will be abbreviated as $\boldsymbol{x}$. Suppose Y is a finite set $\{y_1, \ldots, y_n\}$ of names. The notation $[y{\notin}Y]P$ will stand for $[y{\neq}y_1] \ldots [y{\neq}y_n]P$.

Let $\Longrightarrow$ be the reflexive and transitive closure of $\xrightarrow{\tau}$. We will write $\overset{\widehat{\lambda}}{\Longrightarrow}$ for $\Longrightarrow\xrightarrow{\lambda}\Longrightarrow$. We will also write $\overset{\widehat{\lambda}}{\Longrightarrow}$ for $\overset{\lambda}{\Longrightarrow}$ if $\lambda \neq \tau$ and for $\Longrightarrow$ otherwise.

In the rest of this paper we often come across with situations where we have to deal with a sequence of actions. The principal case is this:

$$P \overset{(y_1)/x(y_2)/y_1}{\Longrightarrow} \ldots \overset{(y_n)/y_{n-1}}{\Longrightarrow} P'$$

When $n = 0$ we shall understand that the above sequence denotes $P \Longrightarrow P'$ and that y_n denotes x.

3   Barbed Bisimulation

It has now become a routine to look at the barbed bisimilarity [13] when one investigates a new process calculus. For a channel based process calculus, the barbed approach often gives rise to the weakest bisimulation equivalence for the calculus.

Definition 1. *A process P is strongly barbed at a, notation $P \downarrow a$, if $P \xrightarrow{\alpha(x)} P'$ or $P \xrightarrow{\alpha x} P'$ for some P' such that $a \in \{\alpha, \overline{\alpha}\}$. P is barbed at a, written $P \Downarrow a$, if some P' exists such that $P \Longrightarrow P' \downarrow a$. A binary relation $\mathcal{R}$ is barbed if $\forall a \in \mathcal{N}$, $P \Downarrow a \Leftrightarrow Q \Downarrow a$ whenever $P\mathcal{R}Q$.*

The notation of context is also important to the semantic investigation. Contexts are defined inductively as follows: (i) $[]$ is a context; (ii) If $C[]$ is a context then $\alpha x.C[]$, $C[] \mid P$, $P \mid C[]$, $(x)C[]$ and $[x{=}y]C[]$ are contexts. Full contexts satisfy additionally: (iii) if $C[]$ is a context then $C[] + P$, $P + C[]$ and $[x{\neq}y]C[]$ are contexts. We are now ready to define barbed bisimulation.

Definition 2. *Let $\mathcal{R}$ be a barbed symmetric relation closed under context. The relation $\mathcal{R}$ is a barbed bisimulation if whenever $Q\mathcal{R}P \xrightarrow{\tau} P'$ then $Q \Longrightarrow Q'\mathcal{R}P'$ for some Q'. The barbed bisimilarity $\approx_b$ is the largest barbed bisimulation.*

In the presence of the asymmetry and the mismatch operator, the barbed bisimilarity is extremely complex. Let's take a look at three simple examples:

– The first is concerned with (bound) updates. The process $(z/x).\langle y/z\rangle.Q$ is barbed bisimilar to $(z/x).\langle y/z\rangle.Q + [x{\neq}y]\langle y/x\rangle.Q\{x/z\}$. For either process to have any effect on an environment the name x must be bound, in which case both processes would have the same effect on the environment. The following internal communication for instance

$$(x)(((z/x).\langle y/z\rangle.Q + [x{\neq}y]\langle y/x\rangle.Q\{x/z\}) \mid P) \xrightarrow{\tau} Q\{x/z\}\{y/x\} \mid P\{y/x\}$$

is simulated by two consecutive communications

$$(x)((z/x).\langle y/z\rangle.Q \mid P) \xrightarrow{\tau} (z)(\langle y/z\rangle.Q\{z/x\} \mid P\{z/x\})$$
$$\xrightarrow{\tau} Q\{z/x\}\{y/z\} \mid P\{z/x\}\{y/z\}$$

Notice that in order for the component $[x{\neq}y]\langle y/x\rangle.Q\{x/z\}$ to invoke a communication it must be placed in an environment in which x is localized.

– The second is about free input actions. One could argue that

$$ax.[x{\neq}y]\tau.Q\{x/z\} + (z/x).ay.\langle y/z\rangle.Q + [x{\neq}y]ax.Q\{x/z\}$$

is barbed bisimilar to $ax.[x{\neq}y]\tau.Q\{x/z\} + (z/x).ay.\langle y/z\rangle.Q$. There are two main situations in which the component $[x{\neq}y]ax.Q\{x/z\}$ may participate in an internal communication. If x is instantiated by some name different from y then the component $ax.[x{\neq}y]\tau.Q\{x/z\}$ can simulate the action since the mismatch $x{\neq}y$ would be valid as long as x is replaced by some name that is not y. Otherwise the component $(z/x).ay.\langle y/z\rangle.Q$ does the job.

– The third is about bound output actions. The process

$$\overline{a}(z).[z{\neq}y](x/z).Q + (z/y).\overline{a}z.(x/z).Q + \overline{a}(x).Q\{x/z\}$$

is barbed bisimilar to $\overline{a}(z).[z{\neq}y](x/z).Q + (z/y).\overline{a}z.(x/z).Q$. For instance

$$(y)(ay.P \,|\, (\overline{a}(z).[z{\neq}y](x/z).Q + (z/y).\overline{a}z.(x/z).Q + \overline{a}(x).Q\{x/z\}))$$
$$\xrightarrow{\tau} (x)(P\{x/y\} \,|\, Q\{x/z\}\{x/y\})$$

is simulated by

$$(y)(ay.P \,|\, (\overline{a}(z).[z{\neq}y](x/z).Q + (z/y).\overline{a}z.(x/z).Q))$$
$$\xrightarrow{\tau} (z)(az.P\{z/y\} \,|\, \overline{a}z.(x/z).Q\{z/y\})$$
$$\xrightarrow{\tau} (z)(P\{z/y\} \,|\, (x/z).Q\{z/y\})$$
$$\xrightarrow{\tau} (x)(P\{z/y\}\{x/z\} \,|\, Q\{z/y\}\{x/z\})$$

It should be obvious from the above examples that, from the viewpoint of the barbed bisimilarity, a non-tau action of a process could be simulated by several sequences of non-tau actions of a bisimilar process. An action could be simulated by different sequences of actions in different environments. Different actions are simulated by different sequences of actions. And these sequences of actions are of different shapes.

A more interesting aspect of the barbed bisimilarity is to figure out in what manners a given action could be simulated. Let's see an example. Suppose $P \approx_b Q$ and $P \xrightarrow{ax} P'$. For the barbed bisimilarity the free input action is not directly observable. What an observer can do is to observe the consequences of the action by putting P in an environment. By doing that the observer gets to know the effects of the action on the environment. Therefore in order to see how Q might simulate P we need to put them in the same environments and analyze the operational behaviours of Q. There are two major cases:

– Case one:
  • Consider first the context $\_ \,|\, \overline{a}x.b(u)$ for fresh b, u. Then $P \,|\, \overline{a}x.b(u) \xrightarrow{\tau} P' \,|\, b(u) \xrightarrow{b(u)} P' \,|\, \mathbf{0}$. Suppose it is simulated by $Q \,|\, \overline{a}x.b(u) \overset{b(u)}{\Longrightarrow} Q' \,|\, \mathbf{0} \approx_b P' \,|\, \mathbf{0}$. This sequence of actions can be factorized in two manners: Either

$$Q \,|\, \overline{a}x.b(u) \Longrightarrow Q_1 \,|\, \overline{a}x.b(u) \xrightarrow{\tau} Q_2 \,|\, b(u) \xrightarrow{b(u)} Q_2 \,|\, \mathbf{0} \Longrightarrow Q' \,|\, \mathbf{0}$$

  or

$$Q \,|\, \overline{a}x.b(u) \Longrightarrow Q_1 \,|\, \overline{a}x.b(u) \xrightarrow{\tau} Q''\{x/z\} \,|\, b(u) \xrightarrow{b(u)} Q''\{x/z\}|\mathbf{0} \Longrightarrow Q'|\mathbf{0}$$

  In the first case, $Q \overset{ax}{\Longrightarrow} Q' \approx_b P'$. In the second case, $Q \overset{a(z)}{\Longrightarrow} Q''$ and $Q''\{x/z\} \Longrightarrow Q' \approx_b P'$.

- Consider now the context $(x)(\_ \mid \bar{a}z.\bar{b}x)$ for fresh b, z. Then

$$(x)(P \mid \bar{a}z.\bar{b}x) \xrightarrow{\tau} P'\{z/x\} \mid \bar{b}z \xrightarrow{\bar{b}z} P'\{z/x\} \mid \mathbf{0}$$

This sequence of actions can be matched up by $(x)(Q \mid \bar{a}z.\bar{b}x) \overset{\bar{b}z}{\Longrightarrow} Q' \mid \mathbf{0}$, which can be factorized in two ways: Either

$$(x)(Q \mid \bar{a}z.\bar{b}x) \Longrightarrow (y_n)(Q_1 \mid \bar{a}z.\bar{b}y_n)$$
$$\xrightarrow{\tau} Q_2 \mid \bar{b}z$$
$$\xrightarrow{\bar{b}z} Q_2 \mid \mathbf{0}$$
$$\Longrightarrow Q' \mid \mathbf{0}$$

or

$$(x)(Q \mid \bar{a}z.\bar{b}x) \Longrightarrow (y_n)(Q_1 \mid \bar{a}z.\bar{b}y_n)$$
$$\Longrightarrow (y_n)(Q_2 \mid \bar{b}y_n)$$
$$\Longrightarrow Q_3 \mid \bar{b}z$$
$$\xrightarrow{\bar{b}z} Q_3 \mid \mathbf{0}$$
$$\Longrightarrow Q' \mid \mathbf{0}$$

In the former case

$$Q \overset{(y_1)\!\langle x(y_2)/y_1}{\Longrightarrow} \cdots \overset{(y_n)/y_{n-1} \, ay_n}{\Longrightarrow} Q_2\{y_n/z\} \Longrightarrow Q'\{y_n/z\}$$

and $Q'\{y_n/z\}\{x/y_n\} \approx_b P'$ for some $y_1, \ldots, y_n$, where $n \geq 0$. In the latter case

$$Q \overset{(y_1)\!\langle x(y_2)/y_1}{\Longrightarrow} \cdots \overset{(y_n)/y_{n-1} \, a(z) \, (z_1)/y_n \, (z_2)/z_1}{\Longrightarrow} \cdots \overset{(z_m)/z_{m-1} \, z/z_m}{\Longrightarrow} Q'$$

and $Q'\{x/z\} \approx_b P'$ for some $z, y_1, \ldots, y_n, z_1, \ldots, z_m$, where $n \geq 0$ and $m \geq 0$.

- Case two: For each y distinct from x one has

$$(x)(P \mid \bar{a}y.[x{=}y]b(u)) \xrightarrow{\tau} P'\{y/x\} \mid [y{=}y]b(u) \xrightarrow{b(u)} P'\{y/x\} \mid \mathbf{0}$$

for fresh names b and u. It follows from $P \approx_b Q$ that $(x)(Q \mid \bar{a}y.[x{=}y]b(u))$ $\overset{b(u)}{\Longrightarrow} Q' \mid \mathbf{0} \approx_b P'\{y/x\} \mid \mathbf{0}$, which can be factorized in five different fashions:

- The first factorization is

$$(x)(Q \mid \bar{a}y.[x{=}y]b(u)) \Longrightarrow (y_n)(Q_1 \mid \bar{a}y.[y_n{=}y]b(u))$$
$$\xrightarrow{\tau} Q_2\{y/y_n\} \mid [y{=}y]b(u)$$
$$\xrightarrow{b(u)} Q_2\{y/y_n\} \mid \mathbf{0}$$
$$\Longrightarrow Q' \mid \mathbf{0}$$

Obviously

* $Q \xrightarrow{(y_1)/x(y_2)/y_1} \cdots \xrightarrow{(y_n)/y_{n-1}} Q_1$ for some $y_1, \ldots, y_n$, where $n \geq 0$;
* $Q_1 \xrightarrow{ay_n} Q_2$;
* $Q_2\{y/y_n\} \Longrightarrow Q'$.

- The second factorization is

$$(x)(Q \mid \bar{a}y.[x{=}y]b(u)) \Longrightarrow (y_n)(Q_1 \mid \bar{a}y.[y_n{=}y]b(u))$$
$$\xrightarrow{\tau} (y_n)(Q_2\{y/z\} \mid [y_n{=}y]b(u))$$
$$\Longrightarrow Q_3 \mid [y{=}y]b(u)$$
$$\xrightarrow{b(u)} Q_3 \mid \mathbf{0}$$
$$\Longrightarrow Q' \mid \mathbf{0}$$

Then
* $Q \xrightarrow{(y_1)/x(y_2)/y_1} \cdots \xrightarrow{(y_n)/y_{n-1}} Q_1$ for some $y_1, \ldots, y_n$, where $n \geq 0$;
* $Q_1 \xrightarrow{a(z)} Q_2$ for some z;
* $Q_2\{y/z\} \xrightarrow{(z_1)/y_n(z_2)/z_1} \cdots \xrightarrow{(z_m)/z_{m-1}y/z_m} Q_3$ for some $z_1, \ldots, z_m$, where $m \geq 0$;
* $Q_3 \Longrightarrow Q'$.

- The third factorization is

$$(x)(Q \mid \bar{a}y.[x{=}y]b(u)) \Longrightarrow (y_n)(Q_1 \mid \bar{a}y.[y_n{=}y]b(u))$$
$$\xrightarrow{\tau} (y_n)(Q_2 \mid [y_n{=}y]b(u))$$
$$\Longrightarrow Q_3 \mid [y{=}y]b(u)$$
$$\xrightarrow{b(u)} Q_3 \mid \mathbf{0}$$
$$\Longrightarrow Q' \mid \mathbf{0}$$

Clearly
* $Q \xrightarrow{(y_1)/x(y_2)/y_1} \cdots \xrightarrow{(y_n)/y_{n-1}} Q_1$ for some $y_1, \ldots, y_n$, where $n \geq 0$;
* $Q_1 \xrightarrow{ay} Q_2$;
* $Q_2 \xrightarrow{(z_1)/y_n(z_2)/z_1} \cdots \xrightarrow{(z_m)/z_{m-1}y/z_m} Q_3$ for some $z_1, \ldots, z_m$, where $m \geq 0$;
* $Q_3 \Longrightarrow Q'$.

- The fourth factorization is

$$(x)(Q \mid \bar{a}y.[x{=}y]b(u)) \Longrightarrow Q_1 \mid \bar{a}y.[y{=}y]b(u)$$
$$\xrightarrow{\tau} Q_2 \mid [y{=}y]b(u)$$
$$\xrightarrow{b(u)} Q_2 \mid \mathbf{0}$$
$$\Longrightarrow Q' \mid \mathbf{0}$$

Then
* $Q \xrightarrow{(y_1)/x(y_2)/y_1} \cdots \xrightarrow{(y_n)/y_{n-1}y/y_n} Q_1$ for some $y_1, \ldots, y_n$, where $n \geq 0$;
* $Q_1 \xrightarrow{ay} Q_2$;
* $Q_2 \Longrightarrow Q'$.

- The fifth factorization is

$$(x)(Q \mid \bar{a}y.[x{=}y]b(u)) \Longrightarrow Q_1 \mid \bar{a}y.[y{=}y]b(u)$$
$$\xrightarrow{\tau} Q_2\{y/z\} \mid [y{=}y]b(u)$$
$$\xrightarrow{b(u)} Q_2\{y/z\} \mid \mathbf{0}$$
$$\Longrightarrow Q' \mid \mathbf{0}$$

It follows that

* $Q \xRightarrow{(y_1)\langle x(y_2)/y_1} \Longrightarrow \cdots \xRightarrow{(y_n)/y_{n-1}y/y_n} Q_1$ for some $y_1, \ldots, y_n$, where $n \geq 0$;
* $Q_1 \xrightarrow{a(z)} Q_2$ for some z;
* $Q_2\{y/z\} \Longrightarrow Q'$

The above analysis suffices to show that the barbed bisimilarity is very tricky. In order to obtain a full picture, one needs to make sure that the barbed bisimilar processes are compared in *all* possible environments with consideration to *all* possible operational behaviours.

In the remaining part of the section we will establish six lemmas, each of which describes the simulation properties for one kind of actions, bearing in mind that there are altogether six kinds of non-tau actions in the χ-calculus.

Lemma 3. *Suppose $P \approx_b Q$ and $P \xrightarrow{a(x)} P'$. Then $Q \xRightarrow{a(x)} Q' \approx_b P'$ for some Q' and, for each y distinct from x, at least one of the following properties holds:*

1. *$Q \Longrightarrow \xrightarrow{a(z)} Q''$ and $Q''\{y/z\} \Longrightarrow Q' \approx_b P'\{y/x\}$ for some Q', Q'', z;*
2. *$Q \xRightarrow{ay} Q' \approx_b P'\{y/x\}$ for some Q'.*

Lemma 4. *Suppose $P \approx_b Q$ and $P \xrightarrow{ax} P'$. Then either $Q \xRightarrow{ax} Q'$ for some Q' or both the following properties hold:*

1. *$Q \Longrightarrow \xrightarrow{a(z)} Q''$ and $Q''\{x/z\} \Longrightarrow Q' \approx_b P'$ for some Q', Q'', z;*
2. *at least one of the following properties holds:*
   - *$Q \xRightarrow{(y_1)\langle x(y_2)/y_1} \cdots \xRightarrow{(y_n)/y_{n-1} ay_n} Q'$ and $Q'\{x/y_n\} \approx_b P'$ for some Q', $y_1, \ldots, y_n$, where $n \geq 1$;*
   - *$Q \xRightarrow{(y_1)\langle x(y_2)/y_1} \cdots \xRightarrow{(y_n)/y_{n-1} a(z)} \xRightarrow{(z_1)/y_n (z_2)/z_1} \cdots \xRightarrow{(z_m)/z_{m-1} z/z_m} Q'$ and $Q'\{x/z\} \approx_b P'$ for some Q', z, $y_1, \ldots, y_n, z_1, \ldots, z_m$, where $n \geq 0$ and $m \geq 0$.*

And, for each y distinct from x, at least one of the following properties holds:

1. *$Q \xRightarrow{(y_1)\langle x(y_2)/y_1} \cdots \xRightarrow{(y_n)/y_{n-1} ay_n} Q''$ and $Q''\{y/y_n\} \Longrightarrow Q' \approx_b P'\{y/x\}$ for some Q', Q'', $y_1, \ldots, y_n$, where $n \geq 0$;*
2. *$Q \xRightarrow{(y_1)\langle x(y_2)/y_1} \cdots \xRightarrow{(y_n)/y_{n-1} a(z)} Q''$ and $Q''\{y/z\} \xRightarrow{(z_1)/y_n (z_2)/z_1} \cdots \xRightarrow{(z_m)/z_{m-1} y/z_m} Q' \approx_b P'\{y/x\}$ for some Q', Q'', $z, y_1, \ldots, y_n, z_1, \ldots, z_m$, where $n \geq 0$ and $m \geq 0$;*

3. $Q \xrightarrow{(y_1)\langle x(y_2)/y_1} \Rightarrow \cdots \xrightarrow{(y_n)/y_{n-1}} \xrightarrow{ay} \xrightarrow{(z_1)/y_n(z_2)/z_1} \Rightarrow \cdots \xrightarrow{(z_m)/z_{m-1}y/z_m} \Rightarrow Q' \approx_b P'\{y/x\}$
for some Q', $y_1, \ldots, y_n$, $z_1, \ldots, z_m$, where $n \geq 0$ and $m \geq 0$;

4. $Q \xrightarrow{(y_1)\langle x(y_2)/y_1} \Rightarrow \cdots \xrightarrow{(y_n)/y_{n-1}y/y_n} \xrightarrow{ay} \Rightarrow Q' \approx_b P'\{y/x\}$ for some Q', $y_1, \ldots, y_n$, where $n \geq 0$;

5. $Q \xrightarrow{(y_1)\langle x(y_2)/y_1} \Rightarrow \cdots \xrightarrow{(y_n)/y_{n-1}y/y_n} \xrightarrow{a(z)} Q''$ and $Q''\{y/z\} \Longrightarrow Q' \approx_b P'\{y/x\}$ for some Q', Q'', z, $y_1, \ldots, y_n$, where $n \geq 0$.

Lemma 5. *Suppose* $P \approx_b Q$ *and* $P \xrightarrow{\bar{a}(x)} P'$. *Then* $Q \xrightarrow{\bar{a}(x)} \xrightarrow{(y_1)\langle x(y_2)/y_1} \Rightarrow \cdots \xrightarrow{(y_n)/y_{n-1}}$ Q' *and* $Q'\{x/y_n\} \approx_b P'$ *for some* Q', $y_1, \ldots, y_n$, *where* $n \geq 0$. *And, for each* y *distinct from* x, *at least one of the following properties holds:*

1. $Q \xrightarrow{(y_1)\langle y(y_2)/y_1} \Rightarrow \cdots \xrightarrow{(y_n)/y_{n-1}\bar{a}(z)} Q''$ *and* $Q''\{z/y_n\} \xrightarrow{(z_1)\langle z(z_2)/z_1} \Rightarrow \cdots \xrightarrow{(z_m)/z_{m-1}}$ Q' *and* $Q'\{x/z_m\} \approx_b P'\{x/y\}$ *for some* Q', Q'', z, $y_1, \ldots, y_n$, $z_1, \ldots, z_m$, *where* $n \geq 0$ *and* $m \geq 0$;

2. $Q \xrightarrow{(y_1)\langle y(y_2)/y_1} \Rightarrow \cdots \xrightarrow{(y_n)/y_{n-1}\bar{a}y_n} \xrightarrow{(z_1)/y_n(z_2)/z_1} \Rightarrow \cdots \xrightarrow{(z_m)/z_{m-1}} Q'$ *and* $Q'\{x/z_m\} \approx_b P'\{x/y\}$ *for some* Q', $y_1, \ldots, y_n$, $z_1, \ldots, z_m$, *where* $n \geq 0$ *and* $m \geq 0$.

Lemma 6. *Suppose* $P \approx_b Q$ *and* $P \xrightarrow{\bar{a}x} P'$. *Then* $Q \xrightarrow{\bar{a}x} Q' \approx_b P'$ *for some* Q' *and, for each* y *distinct from* x, *at least one of the following properties holds:*

1. $Q \xrightarrow{(y_1)\langle y(y_2)/y_1} \Rightarrow \cdots \xrightarrow{(y_n)/y_{n-1}x/y_n} \xrightarrow{\bar{a}x} Q' \approx_b P'\{x/y\}$ *for some* Q', $y_1, \ldots, y_n$, *where* $n \geq 0$;

2. $Q \xrightarrow{(y_1)\langle y(y_2)/y_1} \Rightarrow \cdots \xrightarrow{(y_n)/y_{n-1}\bar{a}x} Q''$ *and* $Q''\{x/y_n\} \Longrightarrow Q' \approx_b P'\{x/y\}$ *for some* Q', Q'', $y_1, \ldots, y_n$, *where* $n \geq 0$;

3. $Q \xrightarrow{(y_1)\langle y(y_2)/y_1} \Rightarrow \cdots \xrightarrow{(y_n)/y_{n-1}\bar{a}y_n} \xrightarrow{(z_1)/y_n(z_2)/z_1} \Rightarrow \cdots \xrightarrow{(z_m)/z_{m-1}x/z_m} Q' \approx_b P'\{x/y\}$
for some Q', $y_1, \ldots, y_n, z_1 \ldots, z_m$, where $n \geq 0$ and $m \geq 0$;

4. $Q \xrightarrow{(y_1)\langle y(y_2)/y_1} \Rightarrow \cdots \xrightarrow{(y_n)/y_{n-1}\bar{a}(z)} Q''$ *and* $Q''\{z/y_n\} \xrightarrow{(z_1)\langle z(z_2)/z_1} \Rightarrow$ $\cdots \xrightarrow{(z_m)/z_{m-1}x/z_m} Q' \approx_b P'\{x/y\}$ *for some* Q', Q'', $z, y_1, \ldots, y_n, z_1, \ldots, z_m$, *where* $n \geq 0$ *and* $m \geq 0$.

Lemma 7. *Suppose* $P \approx_b Q$ *and* $P \xrightarrow{(y)/x} P'$. *Then* $Q \xrightarrow{(y_1)\langle x(y_2)/y_1} \Rightarrow \cdots \xrightarrow{(y_n)/y_{n-1}}$ Q' *and* $Q'\{y/y_n\} \approx_b P'$ *for some* Q', $y_1, \ldots, y_n$, *where* $n \geq 0$.

Lemma 8. *Suppose* $P \approx_b Q$ *and* $P \xrightarrow{y/x} P'$. *Then* $Q \xrightarrow{(y_1)\langle x(y_2)/y_1}$ $\cdots \xrightarrow{(y_n)/y_{n-1}y/y_n} Q' \approx_b P'$ *for some* Q', $y_1, \ldots, y_n$, *where* $n \geq 0$.

So there is a trade off for the simplicity of the definition of the barbed bisimilarity: The dependency of $\approx_b$ on contexts makes it difficult to understand. What the above lemmas achieve is to establish some context-free properties of the internal behaviors of the barbed bisimulation. The question of to what extent these context free properties shape the behaviors of $\approx_b$ is to be answered in the next section.

4   Open Barbed Bisimulation

The purpose of this section is to give a context free characterization of the barbed bisimilarity. We now make use of Lemma 3 through Lemma 8 to give alternative characterizations of $\approx_b$. The results established in these lemmas are turned into defining properties in the following definition.

Definition 9. *Let $\mathcal{R}$ be a binary symmetric relation closed under substitution. It is called an open barbed bisimulation if the followings hold whenever $P\mathcal{R}Q$:*

1. *If $P \xrightarrow{\tau} P'$ then $Q \Longrightarrow Q'\mathcal{R}P'$ for some Q'.*
2. *If $P \xrightarrow{a(x)} P'$ then $Q \overset{a(x)}{\Longrightarrow} Q'\mathcal{R}P'$ for some Q' and, for each y distinct from x, at least one of the following properties holds:*
   - $Q \Longrightarrow \xrightarrow{a(z)} Q''$ and $Q''\{y/z\} \Longrightarrow Q'\mathcal{R}P'\{y/x\}$ for some Q', Q'', z;
   - $Q \overset{ay}{\Longrightarrow} Q'\mathcal{R}P'\{y/x\}$ for some Q'.
3. *If $P \xrightarrow{ax} P'$ then either $Q \overset{ax}{\Longrightarrow} Q'\mathcal{R}P'$ for some Q' or both the following properties hold:*
   - $Q \Longrightarrow \xrightarrow{a(z)} Q''$ and $Q''\{x/z\} \Longrightarrow Q'\mathcal{R}P'$ for some Q', Q'', z.
   - *at least one of the following properties holds:*
     - $Q \overset{(y_1)/x(y_2)/y_1}{\Longrightarrow} \cdots \overset{(y_n)/y_{n-1}\,ay_n}{\Longrightarrow} Q'$ and $Q'\{x/y_n\}\mathcal{R}P'$ for some Q', $y_1,\ldots,y_n$, where $n \geq 1$;
     - $Q \overset{(y_1)/x(y_2)/y_1}{\Longrightarrow} \cdots \overset{(y_n)/y_{n-1}\,a(z)}{\Longrightarrow} \overset{(z_1)/y_n(z_2)/z_1}{\Longrightarrow} \cdots \overset{(z_m)/z_{m-1}\,z/z_m}{\Longrightarrow} Q'$ and $Q'\{x/z\}\mathcal{R}P'$ for some Q', z, $y_1,\ldots,y_n$, $z_1,\ldots,z_m$, where $n \geq 0$ and $m \geq 0$.

   And, for each y distinct from x, at least one of the following properties holds:
   - $Q \overset{(y_1)/x(y_2)/y_1}{\Longrightarrow} \cdots \overset{(y_n)/y_{n-1}\,ay_n}{\Longrightarrow} Q''$ and $Q''\{y/y_n\} \Longrightarrow Q'\mathcal{R}P'\{y/x\}$ for some Q', Q'', $y_1,\ldots,y_n$, where $n \geq 0$;
   - $Q \overset{(y_1)/x(y_2)/y_1}{\Longrightarrow} \cdots \overset{(y_n)/y_{n-1}\,a(z)}{\Longrightarrow} Q''$ and $Q''\{y/z\} \overset{(z_1)/y_n(z_2)/z_1}{\Longrightarrow} \cdots \overset{(z_m)/z_{m-1}\,y/z_m}{\Longrightarrow} Q'\mathcal{R}P'\{y/x\}$ for some Q', Q'', z, $y_1,\ldots,y_n$, $z_1,\ldots,z_m$, where $n \geq 0$ and $m \geq 0$;
   - $Q \overset{(y_1)/x(y_2)/y_1}{\Longrightarrow} \cdots \overset{(y_n)/y_{n-1}\,ay\,(z_1)/y_n(z_2)/z_1}{\Longrightarrow} \cdots \overset{(z_m)/z_{m-1}\,y/z_m}{\Longrightarrow} Q'\mathcal{R}P'\{y/x\}$ for some Q', $y_1,\ldots,y_n$, $z_1,\ldots,z_m$, where $n \geq 0$ and $m \geq 0$;
   - $Q \overset{(y_1)/x(y_2)/y_1}{\Longrightarrow} \cdots \overset{(y_n)/y_{n-1}\,y/y_n\,ay}{\Longrightarrow} Q'\mathcal{R}P'\{y/x\}$ for some Q', $y_1,\ldots,y_n$, where $n \geq 0$;
   - $Q \overset{(y_1)/x(y_2)/y_1}{\Longrightarrow} \cdots \overset{(y_n)/y_{n-1}\,y/y_n\,a(z)}{\Longrightarrow} Q''$ and $Q''\{y/z\} \Longrightarrow Q'\mathcal{R}P'\{y/x\}$ for some Q', Q'', z, $y_1,\ldots,y_n$, where $n \geq 0$.
4. *If $P \xrightarrow{\bar{a}(x)} P'$ then $Q \overset{\bar{a}(x)(y_1)/x(y_2)/y_1}{\Longrightarrow} \cdots \overset{(y_n)/y_{n-1}}{\Longrightarrow} Q'$ and $Q'\{x/y_n\}\mathcal{R}P'$ for some Q', $y_1,\ldots,y_n$, where $n \geq 0$. And for each y distinct from x at least one of the following properties holds:*
   - $Q \overset{(y_1)/y(y_2)/y_1}{\Longrightarrow} \cdots \overset{(y_n)/y_{n-1}\,\bar{a}(z)}{\Longrightarrow} Q''$ and $Q''\{z/y_n\} \overset{(z_1)/z(z_2)/z_1}{\Longrightarrow} \cdots \overset{(z_m)/z_{m-1}}{\Longrightarrow} Q'$ and $Q'\{x/z_m\}\mathcal{R}P'\{x/y\}$ for some Q', Q'', z, $y_1,\ldots,y_n$, $z_1,\ldots,z_m$, where $n \geq 0$ and $m \geq 0$;

$$- Q \xrightarrow{(y_1)\langle y(y_2)/y_1} \Longrightarrow \cdots \xrightarrow{(y_n)/y_{n-1}\,\bar{a}y_n} \xrightarrow{(z_1)/y_n(z_2)/z_1} \Longrightarrow \cdots \xrightarrow{(z_m)/z_{m-1}} \Longrightarrow Q' \text{ and}$$

$Q'\{x/z_m\}\ \mathcal{R}P'\{x/y\}$ for some Q', $y_1, \ldots, y_n$, $z_1, \ldots, z_m$, where $n \geq 0$ and $m \geq 0$.

5. If $P \xrightarrow{\bar{a}x} P'$ then $Q \overset{\bar{a}x}{\Longrightarrow} Q'\mathcal{R}P'$ for some Q' and, for each y distinct from x, at least one of the following properties holds:

  - $Q \xrightarrow{(y_1)\langle y(y_2)/y_1} \Longrightarrow \cdots \xrightarrow{(y_n)/y_{n-1}x/y_n} \overset{\bar{a}x}{\Longrightarrow} Q'\mathcal{R}P'\{x/y\}$ for some Q', $y_1, \ldots, y_n$, where $n \geq 0$;

  - $Q \xrightarrow{(y_1)\langle y(y_2)/y_1} \Longrightarrow \cdots \xrightarrow{(y_n)/y_{n-1}} \overset{\bar{a}x}{\Longrightarrow} Q''$ and $Q''\{x/y_n\} \Longrightarrow Q'\mathcal{R}P'\{x/y\}$ for some Q', Q'', $y_1, \ldots, y_n$, where $n \geq 0$;

  - $Q \xrightarrow{(y_1)\langle y(y_2)/y_1} \Longrightarrow \cdots \xrightarrow{(y_n)/y_{n-1}\,\bar{a}y_n} \xrightarrow{(z_1)/y_n} \Longrightarrow \cdots \xrightarrow{(z_m)/z_{m-1}x/z_m} \Longrightarrow Q'\mathcal{R}P'\{x/y\}$ for some Q', $y_1, \ldots, y_n, z_1 \ldots, z_m$, where $n \geq 0$ and $m \geq 0$;

  - $Q \xrightarrow{(y_1)\langle y(y_2)/y_1} \Longrightarrow \cdots \xrightarrow{(y_n)/y_{n-1}\bar{a}(z)} \Longrightarrow Q''$ and $Q''\{z/y_n\} \xrightarrow{(z_1)/z(z_2)/z_1} \Longrightarrow \cdots \xrightarrow{(z_m)/z_{m-1}\ x/z_m} \Longrightarrow Q'\mathcal{R}P'\{x/y\}$ for some Q', Q'', $z, y_1, \ldots, y_n, z_1, \ldots, z_m$, where $n \geq 0$ and $m \geq 0$.

6. If $P \xrightarrow{(y)/x} P'$ then $Q \xrightarrow{(y_1)\langle x(y_2)/y_1} \Longrightarrow \cdots \xrightarrow{(y_n)/y_{n-1}} \Longrightarrow Q'$ and $Q'\{y/y_n\}\mathcal{R}P'$ for some Q', $y_1, \ldots, y_n$, where $n \geq 0$.

7. If $P \xrightarrow{y/x} P'$ then $Q \xrightarrow{(y_1)\langle x(y_2)/y_1} \Longrightarrow \cdots \xrightarrow{(y_n)/y_{n-1}y/y_n} \Longrightarrow Q'\mathcal{R}P'$ for some Q', $y_1, \ldots, y_n$, where $n \geq 0$.

The open barbed bisimilarity $\approx_b^o$ is the largest open barbed bisimulation.

The above definition is correct in the sense of the following theorem.

Theorem 10. *The two relations $\approx_b$ and $\approx_b^o$ coincide.*

Proof. By Lemma 3 through Lemma 8, $\approx_b$ is an open barbed bisimilarity. Thus $\approx_b \subseteq \approx_b^o$. For the reverse inclusion we need to prove that $\approx_b^o$ is closed under context and is barbed. The barbedness is clear from Definition 9. Closure under context can be proved in a routine manner. Let's take a look at one case. Suppose $P \approx_b^o Q$ and we want to show that $(x)P \approx_b^o (x)Q$. If $(y)P \xrightarrow{(y)/x} P'$ is caused by $P \xrightarrow{y/x} P'$ then $Q \xrightarrow{(y_1)\langle x(y_2)/y_1} \Longrightarrow \cdots \xrightarrow{(y_n)/y_{n-1}y/y_n} \Longrightarrow Q' \approx_b^o P'$ for some Q', $y_1, \ldots, y_n$, where $n \geq 0$. It follows that $(y)Q \xrightarrow{(y_1)\langle x(y_2)/y_1} \Longrightarrow \cdots \xrightarrow{(y_n)/y_{n-1}(y)/y_n} \Longrightarrow Q' \approx_b^o P'$. $\square$

The equivalence $\approx_b^o$ is not closed under the choice combinator and the mismatch operator. The largest congruence relation $\simeq_b^o$ contained in $\approx_b^o$ is defined in the following standard manner.

Definition 11. *We say P and Q are open barbed congruent, notation $P \simeq_b^o Q$, if $P \approx_b^o Q$ and, for each substitution σ, the following properties hold:*

(i) *If $P\sigma \xrightarrow{\tau} P'$ then $Q\sigma \overset{\tau}{\Longrightarrow} Q' \approx_b^o P'$ for some Q'.*

(ii) *If $P\sigma \xrightarrow{(y)/x} P'$ then $Q\sigma \xrightarrow{(y_1)\langle x(y_2)/y_1} \Longrightarrow \cdots \xrightarrow{(y_n)/y_{n-1}} \Longrightarrow Q'$ and $Q'\{y/y_n\} \approx_b^o P'$ for some Q', $y_1, \ldots, y_n$, where $n \geq 0$, such that the length of $\xrightarrow{(y_1)\langle x(y_2)/y_1} \Longrightarrow \cdots \xrightarrow{(y_n)/y_{n-1}} \Longrightarrow$ is nonzero.*

(iii) *The symmetric statements of (i) and (ii).*

L1	$(x)\mathbf{0} = \mathbf{0}$	
L2	$(x)\alpha y.P = \mathbf{0}$	$x \in \{\alpha, \overline{\alpha}\}$
L3	$(x)\alpha y.P = \alpha y.(x)P$	$x \notin \{y, \alpha, \overline{\alpha}\}$
L4	$(x)(y)P = (y)(x)P$	
L5	$(x)[y{=}z]P = [y{=}z](x)P$	$x \notin \{y, z\}$
L6	$(x)[x{=}y]P = \mathbf{0}$	$x \neq y$
L7	$(x)(P{+}Q) = (x)P{+}(x)Q$	
L8	$(x)\langle y/z\rangle.P = \langle y/z\rangle.(x)P$	$x \notin \{y, z\}$
L9	$(x)\langle y/x\rangle.P = \tau.P\{y/x\}$	$x \neq y$
L10	$(x)\tau.P = \tau.(x)P$	
M1	$\phi P = \psi P$	$\phi \Leftrightarrow \psi$
M2	$[x{=}y]P = [x{=}y]P\{y/x\}$	
M3	$\psi(P{+}Q) = \psi P{+}\psi Q$	
M4	$P = [x{=}y]P{+}[x{\neq}y]P$	
M5	$[x{\neq}x]P = \mathbf{0}$	
S1	$P{+}\mathbf{0} = P$	
S2	$P{+}Q = Q{+}P$	
S3	$P{+}(Q{+}R) = (P{+}Q){+}R$	
S4	$P{+}P = P$	
U1	$\langle y/x\rangle.P = \langle y/x\rangle.[x{=}y]P$	
U2	$\langle x/x\rangle.P = \tau.P$	
U3	$\tau.P = \tau.P + \langle y/x\rangle.P$	$y \notin fn(P)$

Fig. 1. The Axiomatic System AS

5   Completeness

The advantage of the context free characterizations of the barbed congruence is that it allows one to use an inductive method in proofs concerning the barbed congruence. In particular the inductive approach can be applied to establish the completeness of an axiomatic system with respect to the barbed congruence. The equational system AS is given in Fig. 1. Parrow and Victor have studied in [14] almost the same system. The difference is that theirs lacks of U3.

The parallel composition operator can be removed by the expansion law. Let π_i and π_j range over $\{\tau\}\cdot\{\alpha x, \langle y/x\rangle \mid x, y \in \mathcal{N}\}$. The expansion law is:

$$P \mid Q = \sum_{i \in I} \psi_i(\boldsymbol{x})\pi_i.(P_i \mid Q) + \sum_{\substack{\pi_i = a_i x_i \\ \pi_j = \overline{b_j} y_j}} \psi_i \varphi_j(\boldsymbol{x})(\boldsymbol{y})[a_i{=}b_j]\langle y_j/x_i\rangle.(P_i \mid Q_j)$$

$$+ \sum_{j \in J} \varphi_j(\boldsymbol{y})\pi_j.(P \mid Q_j) + \sum_{\substack{\pi_i = \overline{a_i} x_i \\ \pi_j = b_j y_j}} \psi_i \varphi_j(\boldsymbol{x})(\boldsymbol{y})[a_i{=}b_j]\langle x_i/y_j\rangle.(P_i \mid Q_j)$$

where P is $\sum_{i \in I} \psi_i(\boldsymbol{x})\pi_i.P_i$, Q is $\sum_{j \in J} \varphi_j(\boldsymbol{y})\pi_j.Q_j$ and $\{\boldsymbol{x}\} \cap \{\boldsymbol{y}\} = \emptyset$.

We write $AS \vdash P = Q$ to mean that the equality $P = Q$ can be derived from the axioms of AS, the expansion law and the laws for the congruence relation. If additional laws $A_1, \ldots, A_n$ are also used we write $AS \cdot \{A_1, \ldots, A_n\} \vdash P = Q$.

T1	$\alpha x.\tau.P = \alpha x.P$
T2	$\tau.P = P + \tau.P$
T3	$\alpha x.(P + \delta \tau.Q) = \alpha x.(P + \delta \tau.Q) + [x \notin n(\delta)]\delta \alpha x.Q$
T4	$\tau.P = \tau.(P + \psi(y/x).P)$ $\qquad\qquad\qquad\qquad y \notin fn(P)$
T5	$TT5 = TT5 + [x \notin Y_3 \cup \cdots \cup Y_7][x \notin n(\delta)]\delta \bar{a}x.Q\{x/z\}\{x/v\}$ $\quad z, v \notin n(\delta)$
T6	$TT6 = TT6 + [x \notin Y_2 \cup \cdots \cup Y_7][x \notin n(\delta)]\delta ax.Q\{x/z\}\{x/v\}$ $\quad z, v \notin n(\delta)$
T7	$TT7 = TT7 + [x \notin Y_2 \cup \cdots \cup Y_7][x \notin n(\delta)]\delta ax.Q\{x/z\}\{x/v\}$ $\quad z, v \notin n(\delta)$
T8	$(z/x).(P + \delta \langle y/z \rangle.Q) = (z/x).(P + \delta \langle y/z \rangle.Q) + [x \neq y]\delta \langle y/x \rangle.Q\{y/z\}$ $\quad z \notin n(\delta)$

Fig. 2. The tau laws

In addition to the basic laws some very complex axioms are also necessary. These laws, called tau laws, are about the tau and the update prefixes. The complexity of the tau laws is anticipated by Definition 9. Figure 2 contains the tau laws used in this paper. T5 through T7 are so complicated that some abbreviations have to be used. Let's explain the tau laws:

- T1 and T2 are Milner's first and second tau laws.
- T3 is more general than Milner's third law.
- T4 deals with the bound update prefixes. It is equivalent to the more general form $\tau.P = \tau.(P + \sum_{i \in I} \phi_i \tau.P)$ as proved in [12].
- T5 is concerned with the free output prefixes, in which TT5 stands for

$$\bar{a}x.(P + [x \notin Y]\delta \tau.Q\{x/z\}\{x/v\})$$

$$+ \sum_{y \in Y_1} \langle x/y \rangle.(P_y + \delta \, \bar{a}x.(P'_y + \delta \tau.Q\{x/z\}\{x/v\}))$$

$$+ \sum_{y \in Y_2} \bar{a}x.(P_y + \delta[x=y]\tau.Q\{x/z\}\{x/v\})$$

$$+ \sum_{y \in Y_3} (z/y).(P_y + [x \notin n(\delta)]\delta \, \bar{a}x.(P'_y + \delta[x=y]\tau.Q\{x/v\}))$$

$$+ \sum_{y \in Y_4} \bar{a}y.(P_y + [x \notin n(\delta)]\delta \langle x/y \rangle.Q\{x/z\}\{x/v\})$$

$$+ \sum_{y \in Y_5} (z/y).(P_y + [x \notin n(\delta)]\delta \bar{a}y.(P'_y + [x \notin n(\delta)]\delta \langle x/y \rangle.Q\{x/v\}))$$

$$+ \sum_{y \in Y_6} \bar{a}(z).(P_y + [x \notin n(\delta)]\delta[y=z]\langle x/y \rangle.Q\{x/v\})$$

$$+ \sum_{y \in Y_7} (z/y).(P_y + [x \notin n(\delta)]\delta \bar{a}(v).(P'_y + [x \notin n(\delta)]\delta[y=v]\langle x/y \rangle.Q))$$

This complicated law is an equational interpretation of the simulating properties of the free output actions prescribed in Definition 9. The first component $\bar{a}x.(P + [x \notin Y]\delta \tau.Q\{x/z\}\{x/v\})$ corresponds to the simulation $Q \overset{\bar{a}x}{\Longrightarrow} Q'$. The other seven summands correspond to the rest of the simulating properties for the free output actions.

- T6 is about the free input prefixes, where TT6 abbreviates

$$ax.(P+[x\notin Y]\delta\tau.Q\{x/z\}\{x/v\})$$
$$+ \sum_{y\in Y_1} ax.(P_y+\delta[x=y]\tau.Q\{x/z\}\{x/v\})$$
$$+ \sum_{y\in Y_2} (z/x).(P_y+[x\notin n(\delta)]\delta ax.(P'_y+\delta[x=y]\tau.Q\{x/v\}))$$
$$+ \sum_{y\in Y_3} a(z).(P_y+[x\notin n(\delta)]\delta[z=y]\langle z/x\rangle.Q\{x/v\})$$
$$+ \sum_{y\in Y_4} (z/x).(P_y+[x\notin n(\delta)]\delta a(v).(P'_y+[x\notin n(\delta)]\delta[v=y]\langle v/x\rangle.Q))$$
$$+ \sum_{y\in Y_5} ay.(P_y+[x\notin n(\delta)]\delta\langle y/x\rangle.Q\{x/z\}\{x/v\})$$
$$+ \sum_{y\in Y_6} (z/x).(P_y+[x\notin n(\delta)]\delta ay.(P'_y+[x\notin n(\delta)]\delta\langle y/x\rangle.Q\{x/v\}))$$
$$+ \sum_{y\in Y_7} \langle y/x\rangle.(P_y+\delta a(z).(P'_y+\delta[z=y]\tau.Q\{x/v\}))$$
$$+ \sum_{y\in Y_8} \langle y/x\rangle.(P_y+\delta ay.(P'_y+\delta\tau.Q\{x/z\}\{x/v\}))$$

- T7 is also about the free input prefixes, where TT7 is for

$$a(z).(P+[z\notin Y][x\notin n(\delta)]\delta[z=x]\tau.Q) + TTT7$$
$$+ \sum_{y\in Y_1} ax.(P_y+\delta[x=y]\tau.Q\{x/z\}\{x/v\})$$
$$+ \sum_{y\in Y_2} (z/x).(P_y+[x\notin n(\delta)]\delta ax.(P'_y+\delta[x=y]\tau.Q\{x/v\}))$$
$$+ \sum_{y\in Y_3} a(z).(P_y+[x\notin n(\delta)]\delta[z=y]\langle z/x\rangle.Q\{x/v\})$$
$$+ \sum_{y\in Y_4} (z/x).(P_y+[x\notin n(\delta)]\delta a(v).(P'_y+[x\notin n(\delta)]\delta[v=y]\langle v/x\rangle.Q))$$
$$+ \sum_{y\in Y_5} ay.(P_y+[x\notin n(\delta)]\delta\langle y/x\rangle.Q\{x/z\}\{x/v\})$$
$$+ \sum_{y\in Y_6} (z/x).(P_y+[x\notin n(\delta)]\delta ay.(P'_y+[x\notin n(\delta)]\delta\langle y/x\rangle.Q\{x/v\}))$$
$$+ \sum_{y\in Y_7} \langle y/x\rangle.(P_y+\delta a(z).(P'_y+\delta[z=y]\tau.Q\{x/v\}))$$
$$+ \sum_{y\in Y_8} \langle y/x\rangle.(P_y+\delta ay.(P'_y+\delta\tau.Q\{x/z\}\{x/v\}))$$

where TTT7 is one of the following processes:

- $(z/x).(P+[z\notin Y][x\notin n(\delta)]\delta ax.(P'+[x\notin n(\delta)]\delta\tau.Q\{x/v\}))$
- $a(z).(P+[z\notin Y][x\notin n(\delta)]\delta[z\neq x]\langle z/x\rangle.Q\{x/v\})$
- $(z/x).(P+[z\notin Y][x\notin n(\delta)]\delta a(v).(P'+[v\notin Y][x\notin n(\delta)]\delta[v\neq x]\langle v/x\rangle.Q))$

– T8 deals with consecutive update actions. What it says is that the global effect of some consecutive updates is the same as that of a single update.

We have provided enough laws to construct a complete axiomatic system for the barbed congruence. We need the notion of normal form in the proof of completeness.

Definition 12. *P is in normal form on $V \supseteq fn(P)$ if it is of the form:*

$$\sum_{i\in I_1}\phi_i\alpha_i x_i.P_i + \sum_{i\in I_2}\phi_i\alpha_i(x).P_i + \sum_{i\in I_3}\phi_i\langle z_i/y_i\rangle.P_i + \sum_{i\in I_4}\phi_i(y/x_i).P_i$$

such that the following conditions are satisfied:

- $\{x,y\} \cap fn(P) = \emptyset$;
- I_1, I_2, I_3, I_4 *are pairwise disjoint finite indexing sets;*
- ϕ_i *is complete on V for each $i \in I_1 \cup I_2 \cup I_3 \cup I_4$;*
- P_i *is in normal form on V for $i \in I_1 \cup I_3$;*
- P_i *is in normal form on $V \cup \{x\}$ for $i \in I_2$;*
- P_i *is in normal form on $V \cup \{y\}$ for $i \in I_4$.*

Using the notion of normal form one can establish the saturation properties.

Lemma 13 (saturation). *Suppose Q is in normal form on V, ϕ is complete on V, and σ is a substitution induced by ϕ. Then the following properties hold, where AS_w denotes $AS\cdot\{T1,T2,T3\}$:*

(i) If $Q\sigma \stackrel{\tau}{\Longrightarrow} Q'$ then $AS_w \vdash Q = Q+\phi\tau.Q'$.

(ii) If $Q\sigma \stackrel{\alpha x}{\Longrightarrow} Q'$ then $AS_w \vdash Q = Q+\phi\alpha x.Q'$.

(iii) If $Q\sigma \stackrel{\alpha(x)}{\Longrightarrow} Q'$ then $AS_w \vdash Q = Q+\phi\alpha(x).Q'$.

(iv) If $Q\sigma \stackrel{y/x}{\Longrightarrow} Q'$ then $AS_w \vdash Q = Q+\phi\langle y/x\rangle.Q'$.

(v) If $Q\sigma \stackrel{(y)/x}{\Longrightarrow} Q'$ then $AS_w \vdash Q = Q+\phi\langle y/x\rangle.Q'$.

(vi) If $Q\sigma \stackrel{\tau}{\Longrightarrow} Q'$ then $AS_w\cdot\{T4\} \vdash Q = Q + \phi\langle y/x\rangle.Q'$.

(vii) If $Q\sigma \stackrel{(y_1)/x}{\Longrightarrow}\stackrel{(y_2)/y_1}{\Longrightarrow} \ldots \stackrel{(y_n)/y_{n-1}}{\Longrightarrow}\stackrel{(y)/y_n}{\Longrightarrow} Q'$, where $n \geq 1$, then $AS_w\cdot\{T8\} \vdash Q = Q + \phi\langle y/x\rangle.Q'$.

(viii) If $Q\sigma \stackrel{(y_1)/x}{\Longrightarrow}\stackrel{(y_2)/y_1}{\Longrightarrow} \ldots \stackrel{(y_n)/y_{n-1}}{\Longrightarrow}\stackrel{y/y_n}{\Longrightarrow} Q'$, where $n \geq 1$, then $AS_w\cdot\{T8\} \vdash Q = Q + \phi\langle y/x\rangle.Q'$.

By exploiting the saturation properties, we could prove the completeness using structural induction. The proof is carried out in two steps. First a special case of completeness is established by induction on processes of special forms. This takes the following form: If $\tau.P \simeq_b^o \tau.Q$ then $AS_b^o \vdash \tau.P = \tau.Q$, where AS_b^o is AS extended with all the tau laws. Then the full completeness is proved using the partial completeness result.

Theorem 14 (completeness). *If $P \simeq_b^o Q$ then $AS_b^o \vdash P = Q$.*

6   Final Remarks

The asymmetric version was first studied by Parrow and Victor in [14], where they called it Update Calculus. They have studied the simplest bisimulation equivalence: the strong open bisimilarity. It is important to notice that the strong barbed bisimilarity is different from the strong open bisimilarity. One has that $(y/x).P+\tau.P\{x/y\}$ is strongly barbed bisimilar to $\tau.P\{x/y\}$. But it is obvious that they are not strongly open bisimilar. If the operational semantics does not identify x/x to τ, then $\langle x/x \rangle.P+\tau.P$ is also strongly barbed bisimilar to $\tau.P$. The χ-calculus is a good example to show the subtlety of the barbed equivalence. Even the strong barbed bisimilarity has something to tell us!

The main achievement of this paper is a 'complete' understanding of the barbed congruence on finite processes of the asymmetric χ-calculus with mismatch. In view of the complex laws proposed in this paper, one could argue whether the understanding offered here is so complete. T5, T6 and T7 involve processes with many summands. The question is if this is an intrinsic feature of the calculus. In other words, can T5, T6 and T7 be considerably simplified? Let's review a well known fact in the π-calculus. The early equivalence and the late equivalence of the π-calculus differ in the following equality:

$$a(x).P+a(x).Q \;=\; a(x).P+a(x).Q+a(x).([x{=}y]P+[x{\neq}y]Q)$$

It holds for the early equivalence but is invalid for the late equivalence. This is because in the late scenario the input action

$$a(x).([x{=}y]P+[x{\neq}y]Q) \xrightarrow{a(x)} [x{=}y]P+[x{\neq}y]Q$$

can be matched by neither $a(x).P$ nor $a(x).Q$. This example shows that in the presence of the mismatch operator, an input prefix could induce different descendants depending on different input names. The situation can not be improved because at the operational level $P \xrightarrow{\lambda} P'$ does not imply $P\sigma \xrightarrow{\lambda\sigma} P'\sigma$. For the open congruence the early and late dichotomy also exists. For the χ-calculus with mismatch all bisimulation congruences are of early nature. It is therefore expected that laws concerning the input prefix operator are involved. The situation is more complex than in the π-calculus due to the following reasons:

- The output prefixes can also 'input' names in a roundabout way. The symmetric communication $\bar{a}(x).P \mid ay.Q \xrightarrow{\tau} P\{y/x\} \mid Q$ could be imitated by

$$\bar{a}(x).P \mid a(z).(b)(bz \mid \bar{b}y.Q) \xrightarrow{\tau}\xrightarrow{\tau} P\{y/x\} \mid (b)(\mathbf{0} \mid Q)$$

  for fresh b, z. So even in the asymmetric χ-calculus the laws for the output prefixes are just as complex as for the input prefixes.
- For the barbed congruence an input (output) action could be simulated by many sequences of non-tau actions and combinations of those.

It is our personal belief that no fundamental simplification of T5, T6 and T7 is possible. But it is possible that the axiomatic system is equivalent to a simpler system.

References

1. X. Dong and Y. Fu: Algebraic Theory of Asymmetric Chi Calculus with Mismatch. Draft.
2. Y. Fu: The χ-Calculus. *Proceedings of the International Conference on Advances in Parallel and Distributed Computing*(IEEE Computer Society Press, 1997) 74–81.
3. Y. Fu: A Proof Theoretical Approach to Communications. *ICALP '97*, Lecture Notes in Computer Science **1256** (Springer, 1997) 325–335.
4. Y. Fu: Bisimulation Lattice of Chi Processes. *ASIAN '98*, Lecture Notes in Computer Science **1538** (Springer, 1998) 245–262.
5. Y. Fu: Reaction Graphs. *Journal of Computer Science and Technology*, **13** (1998) 510–530.
6. Y. Fu: Variations on Mobile Processes. *Theoretical Computer Science*, **221** (1999) 327–368.
7. Y. Fu: Open Bisimulations of Chi Processes. *CONCUR'99*, Lecture Notes in Computer Science **1664** (Springer, 1999) 304–319.
8. Y. Fu: Bisimulation Congruence of Chi Calculus. *Information and Computation*, **184** (2003) 201–226.
9. Y. Fu and Z. Yang: Chi Calculus with Mismatch. *CONCUR 2000*, Lecture Notes in Computer Science **1877** (Springer, 2000) 596–610.
10. Y. Fu and Z. Yang: The Ground Congruence for Chi Calculus. *FST&TCS 2000*, Lecture Notes in Computer Science **1974** (Springer, 2000) 385–396.
11. Y. Fu and Z. Yang: Understanding the Mismatch Combinator in Chi Calculus. *Theoretical Computer Science*, **290** (2003) 779–830.
12. Y. Fu and Z. Yang: Tau Laws for Pi Calculus. *Theoretical Computer Science*, to appear.
13. R. Milner and D. Sangiorgi: Barbed Bisimulation. *ICALP '92*, Lecture Notes in Computer Science **623** (Springer, 1992) 685–695.
14. J. Parrow and B. Victor: The Update Calculus. *AMAST '97*, Lecture Notes in Computer Science **1119** (Springer, 1997) 389–405.
15. J. Parrow and B. Victor: The Fusion Calculus: Expressiveness and Symmetry in Mobile Processes. *LICS '98* (IEEE Computer Society, 1998) 176–185.
16. J. Parrow and B. Victor: The Tau-Laws of Fusion. *CONCUR '98*, Lecture Notes in Computer Science **1466** (Springer, 1998) 99–114.
17. B. Victor and J. Parrow: Concurrent Constraints in the Fusion Calculus. *ICALP '98*, Lecture Notes in Computer Science **1443** (Springer, 1998) 455–469.

Expressive Synchronization Types for Inheritance in the Join Calculus

Qin Ma and Luc Maranget

Inria Rocquencourt, BP 105, 78153 Le Chesnay Cedex, France
{Qin.Ma,Luc.Maranget}@inria.fr

Abstract. In prior work, Fournet *et al.* proposed an extension of the join calculus with class-based inheritance, aiming to provide a precise semantics for concurrent objects. However, as we show here, their system suffers from several limitations, which make it inadequate to form the basis of a practical implementation.

In this paper, we redesign the static semantics for inheritance in the join calculus, equipping class types with more precise information. Compared to previous work, the new type system is more powerful, more expressive and simpler. Additionally, one runtime check of the old system is suppressed in the new design. We also prove the soundness of the new system, and have implemented type inference.

1 Introduction

Object-oriented programming is an attractive framework for taming the complexity of modern concurrent systems. In the standard approach, as in Java [11], ABCL/1 [20] or Obliq [4], objects represent agents that may exchange messages over a network. These languages usually model concurrency by threads and control synchronization behavior with locks (or some variant thereof). However, combining concurrency and object-oriented programming as if they were independent hinders incremental code development by inheritance [15]. Roughly, objects follow synchronization policies to keep their internal state consistent in the presence of concurrent method calls, but traditional inheritance is not sufficient to program these policies incrementally.

In [9], Fournet *et al.* address this issue. They define the *objective-join* calculus, aiming to provide a precise semantics for concurrent objects. Doing so, they follow many authors, who either enrich well-established object calculi with concurrency primitives [10,2,16], or extend process calculi with object-oriented features [19]. The base calculus of [9] is the *join calculus* [7], a simple name-passing calculus, related to the pi-calculus but with a functional flavor. Objects are introduced by the classical technique of objects-as-records (of names). This technique is particularly natural in the join calculus, where several names and their behavior with respect to synchronization are defined simultaneously, via *join-definitions*. Then, [9] introduces a class layer to support incremental programming and code reuse.

A. Ohori (Ed.): APLAS 2003, LNCS 2895, pp. 20–36, 2003.

However, there are several limitations to the theory presented in [9] which make it inadequate to form the basis of a practical implementation. At first glance, class types look close to their sequential counterparts, namely, lists of channel names with the types of the messages they accept. Although this information is sufficient for typing objects, whose basic operation is message receiving, it falls short in typing class-based inheritance of synchronization behavior. As a consequence, [9] in fact includes some extra information about synchronization behavior in class types. Unfortunately, the extra information is not expressive enough, leading to the following shortcomings: objects sometimes are not as polymorphic as they could; names flagged as abstract by typing may actually possess a definition; and, under particular conditions, a complicated runtime check on classes is necessary to guarantee program safety. The present paper solves these difficulties with a new type system for classes, of which the main contribution is the inclusion of complete synchronization behavior in class types.

The paper is organized as follows. We give a brief review of the object and class calculus in Sec. 2. Then, from Sec. 3 to Sec. 5, we illustrate the shortcomings of the former system, and meanwhile suggest possible remedies. Sec. 6 presents our solution —a new design of the static class semantics— and as well states the properties of subject reduction and type safety though omits the lengthy proofs (given in [14]). Finally, we conclude.

2   A Brief Review of the Objective-Join Calculus

2.1   Objects and Classes

Objects arise naturally in the join calculus when the join-definitions are named and lifted to be the values of the calculus. For instance, a one-place buffer object is defined as follows:

> obj $buffer =$
> $\quad put(n,r)$ & $Empty()$ ▷ $r.reply()$ & $buffer.Some(n)$
> or $get(r)$ & $Some(n)$ ▷ $r.reply(n)$ & $buffer.Empty()$
> init $buffer.Empty()$

The basic operation is still asynchronous message passing, but expressed by object-oriented dot notation. Here, the process $buffer.put(n,r)$ sends a $put(n,r)$ message to the object $buffer$. In the message, put is the $label$ and (n,r) is the $content$.

As in join, the labels defined in one object are organized by several $reaction$ $rules$ to specify how messages sent on these labels will be synchronized and processed. In the above $buffer$ object, four labels are defined and arranged in two reaction rules. Each reaction rule consists of a $join$-$pattern$ and a $guarded$ $process$, separated by ▷. When there are messages pending on all the labels in a given pattern, the object can react by consuming the messages and triggering the guarded process. Given this synchronization mechanism, $buffer$ will behave as follows:

- If *buffer* is empty (*i.e.* an *Empty*() message is pending), and a put attempt is made (by sending a *put*(*n*,*r*) message), then *buffer* will react by sending back an acknowledgement message on label *reply* of the continuation *r* and, concurrently, shifting itself into the *Some*(*n*) state.
- Symmetrically, the value *n* stored in *buffer* (*i.e.* a *Some*(*n*) message is pending) can be retrieved by *get*(*r*), and the buffer then returns to the empty state.
- Any *put* requests sent to a full buffer (or *get* request to an empty buffer) will be delayed until the object is changed into the complementary state by other messages.

Finally, the (optional) init part initializes *buffer* as an empty buffer. See [1] for a more implementation-oriented description of a similar example.

As we can see, the state of *buffer* is encoded as a message pending on *Empty* or on *Some*. To keep the one-place buffer consistent, there should be only one message pending on either of these two labels. This invariant holds as long as no message on these labels can be sent from outside, which can be guaranteed by the following a statically enforced privacy policy: Labels starting with an uppercase letter are *private* labels; messages can be sent on those labels only from within guarded processes (and from the init part as well). Other labels are unrestricted; they are called *public* labels and work as ports offered by the object to the external world.

Classes act as templates for sets of objects with the same behavior. For instance, the class defining the one-place buffer above looks like this:

> class $c\_buffer = \mathsf{self}(z)$
> $get(r)$ & $Some(n) \triangleright r.reply(n)$ & $z.Empty()$
> or $put(n,r)$ & $Empty() \triangleright r.reply()$ & $z.Some(n)$

The prefix self (z) explicitly binds the name z to the self reference in the class definition. And to instantiate an object from the class, we just do:

> obj $buffer = c\_buffer$ init $buffer.Empty()$

The calculus of [9] allows the derivation of new class definitions from existing ones. A class can be extended with new reaction rules, synchronizations among the labels of a class can be modified, and new processes can be added to the reaction rules of a class. These computations on classes finally yield classes solely made of *disjunctions* (or) of several reaction rules (as is the *c_buffer* class). Such classes are ready for being instantiated and are called *normal forms*.

2.2   Types

Types for classes and objects are inspired by the OCaml type system [18]. More precisely, typing is by structure; both class types and object types are sets of label names paired with the types of the messages they accept; object types only collect public labels, while class types include both private and public labels. Object types may end with a row variable, standing for more label-type pairs and such row variables provide a useful degree of polymorphism.

For instance, consider a simple synchronization object *join* with an internal counter:

> obj *join* = *sync1*(*r1*) & *sync2*(*r2*) & *Count*(*x*) ▷
>   *r1.reply*() & *r2.reply*() & *join.Count*(*x*+1)

The type of the object *join* is [*sync1* : (([*reply* : (); ϱ]); *sync2* : (([*reply* : (); ϱ'])]. The two row variables ϱ and ϱ' indicate that except for the *reply* label, there is no other constraints on the continuation objects sent to the *sync* labels. Furthermore, label *Count* does not show up because it is private. By contrast, the type of the corresponding *c_join* class contains all the labels:

> object
>   label *sync1*: ([*reply* : (); ϱ]) ; label *sync2*: ([*reply* : (); ϱ']) ;
>   label *Count*: (int)
> end

However, during the design of the type system of [9], it appeared that class types should include additional information. We introduce them in the next two sections using examples.

3 Polymorphism

3.1 Polymorphism and Synchronization

There are two kinds of type variables in the type system: ordinary type variables and row variables. As in the ML type system, polymorphism is parametric polymorphism, obtained essentially by generalizing the free type variables.

As in the join calculus, synchronizations impact on polymorphism [8,5]: two different labels are said to be *correlated* when they appear in the same join-pattern, and type variables that appear in the types of several correlated labels cannot be generalized. Consider, for instance, a synchronous buffer object:

> obj *sbuffer* = *get*(*r*) & *put*(*n,s*) ▷ *r.reply*(*n*) & *s.reply*()

The types of the two correlated labels *get* and *put* are (([*reply* : (θ); ϱ]) and (θ, [*reply* : (); ϱ']), respectively. Type variable θ is shared by their types, so it should not be generalized. Otherwise, the two occurrence of θ could be instantiated independently as, for instance, integer and string. This then might result in a runtime type error: attempting to deliver a string when an integer is expected. By contrast, the type variables ϱ and ϱ' can be generalized. Generalized row variable ϱ intuitively means that as long as the constraint on *reply* label is preserved, different messages sent on label *get* can take different continuation objects as *r*, and similarly for ϱ' with respect to label *put*.

However, the limitation on polymorphism is only object-level, not class-level, because two *get* or *put* labels of two different objects are completely independent *w.r.t.* synchronization. More concretely, consider the following class version of the synchronous buffer.

> class *c_sbuffer* = *get*(*r*) & *put*(*n,s*) ▷ *r.reply*(*n*) & *s.reply*()

Class *c_sbuffer* can be instantiated twice to two different objects, one dealing with integers, and the other with strings. As a consequence, all the free type variables in class types are generalized, but class types record the correlation amongst labels, in order to restrict polymorphism at object creation time. To collect this information, the type system of [9] abstracts the join-patterns of a class into a set of *coupled* labels W. The computation of coupled labels from reaction rules can be described as a two-phase process:

1. First, simplify join-patterns by removing labels accepting empty tuple (because correlating with this kind of labels does not cause type variable sharing) and remove join-patterns consisting of only one label.
2. Then, gather all the remaining labels into the set of coupled labels.

The set W is then kept in the class type, and referred to when an object is to be created: all the type variables shared by several labels in W are restricted to be monomorphic in the corresponding object type. As a result, the type of the synchronous buffer class is as follows:

> class *c_sbuffer*: $\forall \theta, \varrho, \varrho'$. object
>   label *get*: ($[\, reply: (\theta); \varrho]$) ;
>   label *put*: ($\theta, [\, reply: (); \varrho']$)
>   end $W = \{get,\ put\}$

Here labels *get* and *put* are coupled, and hence the type variable θ is not generalizable in object types.

3.2   More Polymorphism in Object Types

According to the previous section, the following object definition:

> obj *counter* =
>   *Value*(x) & *plus*(y,r) ▷ r.*reply*() & *counter.Value*(x+y)
>   or *Value*(x) & *incr*(r) ▷ *counter.Value*(x) & *counter.plus*(1,r)

correlates the labels *plus* and *Value* by the first join-pattern, and the labels *incr* and *Value* by the second join-pattern (but not the labels *plus* and *incr*).

The types of the labels of this object are *Value*: (int), *plus*: (int, $[\, reply : (); \varrho]$) and *incr*: ($[\, reply : (); \varrho]$). The free row variable ϱ appears in the types of both *plus* and *incr*, but since the two labels are not correlated, it can be generalized.

However, lifting the object definition *counter* into a class definition will yield the class *c_counter* with type:

> class *c_counter*: object ... end $W = \{\ Value,\ plus,\ incr\}$

Both *plus* and *incr* appear as coupled labels, which forbids the generalization of the shared free type variable ϱ in the type of the objects.

This undue restriction on polymorphism originates in the flat structure of the set W. Such a structure may couple labels that are not actually correlated, more precisely, the coupled label relation is the transitive closure of correlation amongst labels accepting non-empty tuples. In the *counter* example, labels *plus* and *incr* get "correlated" through *Value*.

However, if we replace the second step of the computation of the set W in Sec. 3.1 by collecting labels from different patterns in separate sets, thereby organizing W as the set of these sets, we may have a better solution. The criterion for restriction changes accordingly: for now, only those type variables shared by two labels coming from the same member set of W are non-generalizable. The new type of the class *c_counter* is

$$\text{class } \textit{c\_counter: object } \ldots \text{ end } W = \{\{\textit{Value, plus}\}, \{\textit{Value, incr}\}\}$$

We see that the labels *plus* and *incr* are separated in different member sets, so that the type variable ϱ can be polymorphic. More generally, the layered structure of the new W gets rid of the transitivity side-effect, and restores proper polymorphism. It is important to notice that the new W sets still abstract on the join-patterns: zero-arity labels and non-synchronized labels do not show up.

4   Selective Refinement and Abstract Labels

4.1   Semantics of Selective Refinement

Selective refinement is the only operator on classes that can modify the reaction rules. It can be understood by analogy with ML-style pattern matching. Selective refinement rewrites a class c into a new class c' by matching the reaction rules of c against a refinement sequence. A refinement sequence is an ordered list of refinement clauses, and refinement clauses are tried in that order. A refinement clause $K_1 \Rightarrow K_2 \triangleright Q$ consists of three parts: the selective pattern K_1, the refinement pattern K_2 and the refinement process Q. A refinement clause matches a reaction rule $J \triangleright P$ when K_1 is a sub-pattern of J, that is, when all the labels in K_1 also appear in J. Then, J can be written as $K_1 \,\&\, K$ and the matched reaction rule is refined into the new reaction $K \,\&\, K_2 \triangleright P \,\&\, Q$. As a consequence, a reaction rule is rewritten according to the first matching refinement clause if it exists. Otherwise, the reaction rule remains unchanged.

4.2   Abstract Labels after Selective Refinement

Now let us consider again the class *c_counter* of Sec. 3.2 and assume that, for debugging purpose, we wish to log each *plus* attempt on the terminal. This can be achieved by a two-step modification: First, the *plus* label is renamed into *unlogged_plus*, using selective refinement; then, the *plus* label is redefined:

```
class c_intermediate =
    match c_counter with
        plus(y,r) ⇒ unlogged_plus(y,r) ▷ 0
    end
class c_logged_counter = self(z)
    c_intermediate
    or plus(y,r) ▷ out.print_int(y) & z.unlogged_plus(y,r)
```

The type of the class *c_intermediate* is as follows:

> class *c_intermediate*: $\forall \varrho$. object
>   label *Value*: (int) ;
>   abstract label *plus*: (int , [*reply* : (); ϱ]) ;
>   label *incr*: ([*reply* : (); ϱ]) ;
>   label *unlogged_plus*: (int , [*reply* : (); ϱ])
>   end $W = \{...\}$

It is important to notice that this type is inferred at compile time, considering only the type of the class *c_counter* and the refinement clauses, without actually performing the selective refinement. We observe that the label *plus* is still present in the type of class *c_intermediate*. However, this label is now tagged as abstract. In fact, the normal form of class *c_intermediate* as computed at runtime looks like:

> class *c_intermediate* = self(z)
> $Value(x)$ & $unlogged\_plus(y,r) \triangleright r.reply()$ & $z.Value(x{+}y)$
>   or $Value(x)$ & $incr(r) \triangleright counter.Value(x)$ & $z.plus(1,r)$
>   or $\{plus\}$

The label *plus* does not appear in the patterns any more, but it still appears in the guarded process of the second reaction rule. This fact is accounted for by stating that *plus* is abstract in class *c_intermediate*, using the new construct $\{plus\}$. As in the ordinary sense of object-oriented programming, classes with abstract labels cannot be instantiated. Therefore, class *c_intermediate* is prevented from instantiation until a concrete and type compatible definition for *plus* is provided, as performed by the definition of class *c_logged_counter*. This constraint is reflected by the abstract tag in the class type.

4.3   Abstract or Maybe Abstract

We move on to another example: a machine creator (the class) which creates vendor machines (the objects) selling both tea and coffee.

> class *c_vendor* =
>   *two_euros*() & *tea*() $\triangleright$ *out.print_string*("tea")
>   or *two_euros*() & *coffee*() $\triangleright$ *out.print_string*(" coffee ")

Later, the price of tea decreases to one euro, so the machine creator should be modified. Such a modification is attempted by selective refinement:

> class *c_promo_vendor* =
>   match *c_vendor* with
>   *two_euros*() & *tea*() $\Rightarrow$ *one_euro*() & *tea*() $\triangleright$ 0
>   end

The normal form of class *c_promo_vendor* at runtime is:

> class *c_promo_vendor* =
>   *one_euro*() & *tea*() $\triangleright$ *out.print_string*("tea")
>   or *two_euros*() & *coffee*() $\triangleright$ *out.print_string*(" coffee ")

Unfortunately, the type of class *c_promo_vendor* tags *two_euros* as abstract:

    class *c_promo_vendor*: object
      abstract label *two_euros*: () ;
      label *tea* : () ; label *coffee* : () ; label *one_euro*: ()
    end $W = \{...\}$

And this will, in practice, prevent from creating any real new vendor machine objects from this class.

The discrepancy between the compile time type and the runtime normal form comes from the way selective refinement is typed. Since types do not include all synchronization information, the effect of selective refinement can only be approximated while typing. As regards labels that no more exist in the join-patterns of the resulting class, the approximation can be described as follows:

1. For each clause in the selective refinement $K_1 \Rightarrow K_2 \triangleright Q$, compute the set of labels that appear in K_1 but not in K_2.
2. Take the union of the differences calculated in 1.

As demonstrated by the refinement from *c_vendor* to *c_promo_vendor*, this approximation is not always exact. As an untimely consequence, the abstract qualifier in types significantly departs from its usual meaning: an abstract label is in fact a label that *may* lack a definition, while common sense and tradition suggest that abstract labels should be labels with no definition. Accordingly, the information conveyed by the abstract qualifier in types is significantly reduced.

This abstract as maybe abstract semantics is expressed by a "subsumption" rule Sub in the type system of [9]. Basically, this rule lifts abstract label set inclusion into subtyping. Such a subtyping is of little practical interest.

However, if selective refinement can be effectively carried out during typing, the type of compile time will be able to tell exactly which label is abstract in the runtime normal form. Then the expedient of the Sub rule can be withdrawn. It is certainly a more practical solution compared with the former type system.

5   New Labels during Selective Refinement

In the previous section, we saw that some labels in a class can lose their definitions during selective refinement. Symmetrically, selective refinement introduces new labels. Those new labels endanger the basic type safety property of avoiding "message not understood" errors. For instance, consider the following selective refinement.

    class *cc* = match *c* with *x*() & *y*() $\Rightarrow$ *z*() $\triangleright$ 0 end

We additionally assume that class *c* indeed possesses the two labels *x* and *y*, as shown by its type.

    class *c*: object label *x* : () ; label *y*: () end $W = \{...\}$

Then, label z is new to the class c, and by the typing of [9], the type of the resulting class cc will include the new label:

class cc: object
    abstract label x : () ;   abstract label y: () ;
    label z: () ;
end $W = \{...\}$

However, class c can be either of the following two definitions, because both of them have the type of class c given above.

class $c_1 = x() \ \& \ y() \rhd P_1$
class $c_2 = \ x() \rhd P_2 \text{ or } y() \rhd Q_2$

If c is c_1, the runtime normal form of class cc will effectively possess the new label z. But, if x and y are not synchronized (*i.e.* if c is c_2), then class cc does not provide a definition for label z. Obviously, if nothing is done for the latter case, basic type safety is broken. The solution adopted in [9] enforces the actual introduction of all new labels. In practice, a runtime check of the presence of some labels (in this example, label z) has to be performed after selective refinement. When some labels are missing, the running program fails with a specific *refinement error*. From a language design perspective, this solution is moderately acceptable.

1. It can be argued that programmers would design selective refinements with the intention to define some new labels.
2. Refinement error is by far more tolerable than the "message not understood" error. The former may only show up when building classes, while the latter may occur when using objects. Hence, refinement error occurs earlier, less frequently, and conveys properer information for easier correctness by programmers.

However, guaranteeing type safety at no runtime price is certainly a better solution. This can be achieved provided types are detailed enough, so that pattern matching on reaction rules can be performed while typing. Then, only effectively introduced new labels show up in the resulting type.

6   The New Type System

Based on the analysis in the previous three sections, we realize that the weak points of the system of [9] originates in the information deficiency in class types. As a consequence, this system fails to embody the semantics of synchronization behaviors and their inheritance. We now present our new type system, which elaborates on the former system of [9]. The main novelty lies in equipping each class type with the structure of all its join-patterns, but there are other differences. In our description, we mostly point out changes *w.r.t.* the former system. We do not include here the syntax of objects and classes, nor their semantics, since those are unchanged except for the suppression of one runtime check (see Sec. 5).

6.1   Type Algebra

The type algebra of the new type system appears in Fig.1. The class types are written as $\zeta(\rho)B^W$. As before, B lists the types of all the *declared* labels in the class and $[\rho]$ refers to the object type of self. By contrast, our *correlated* label set W replaces the coupled label set of [9]. Following the two-layer structure introduced in Sec. 3.2, W is a set of sets of labels, namely, $W \subseteq 2^{\mathcal{L}}$ ($\mathcal{L}$ collects all the labels in this calculus). Member sets of W are ranged over by π ($\pi \subseteq \mathcal{L}$), each π corresponding to one join-pattern, and the whole set W represents all the patterns of the class normal form. Our class types do not include a set of abstract labels, while the types of [9] did. The set of abstract labels can now be computed easily from class types as $dom(B) \setminus \overline{W}$, where $\overline{W}$ is the flattening of W (union of all member sets) and $dom(B)$ is the domain of B. Moreover, by contrast, the abstract labels computed in this manner are abstract in the ordinary sense (see Sec. 4.3)

$$
\begin{array}{lll}
\tau & ::= \theta \mid [\rho] & \textbf{Object type} \\
\rho & ::= \emptyset \mid \varrho \mid m : \widetilde{\tau}; \rho & \textbf{Row type} \\
\sigma & ::= \forall X.\tau & \textbf{Type scheme} \\[6pt]
\alpha & ::= \theta \mid \varrho & \textbf{Type Variable} \\
\widetilde{\tau} & ::= (\tau_i{}^{i \in I}) & \textbf{Tuple type} \\
B & ::= \emptyset \mid \ell : \widetilde{\tau}; B & \textbf{Internal type} \\[6pt]
\tau^c & ::= \zeta(\rho)B^W & \textbf{Class type} \\
\sigma^c & ::= \forall X.\tau^c & \textbf{Class type scheme} \\[6pt]
\tau^s & ::= B^F & \textbf{Refinement sequence type} \\
F & ::= \emptyset \mid \pi \Rightarrow W; F & \textbf{Refinement rules}
\end{array}
$$

Fig. 1. Syntax for the type algebra

The type B^F of a refinement sequence conveys the latter's whole structure, including refinement clause order. The system of [9] did not attach a particular type to a refinement sequence. Although such a type is not needed to type applications of selective refinement, our solution simplifies the typing rules and reflects our attempt to make selective refinement an autonomous operator.

Rules for object names and labels.

Object-Var
$$\dfrac{x : \forall X.\tau \in A}{A \vdash x : \tau\{\gamma_\alpha/\alpha^{\alpha\in X}\}}$$

Label
$$\dfrac{A \vdash x : [m : \tilde{\tau}; \rho]}{A \vdash x.m :: \tilde{\tau}}$$

Private-Label
$$\dfrac{x : \forall X.(f : \tilde{\tau}; B) \in A}{A \vdash x.f :: \tilde{\tau}\{\gamma_\alpha/\alpha^{\alpha\in X}\}}$$

Rules for processes.

Null
$$A \vdash 0$$

Send
$$\dfrac{A \vdash x.\ell :: (\tau_i{}^{i\in I}) \qquad (A \vdash x_i : \tau_i)^{i\in I}}{A \vdash x.\ell(x_i{}^{i\in I})}$$

Join Parallel
$$\dfrac{A \vdash x.M_1 \qquad A \vdash x.M_2}{A \vdash x.(M_1 \ \& \ M_2)}$$

Parallel
$$\dfrac{A \vdash P \qquad A \vdash Q}{A \vdash P \ \& \ Q}$$

Class
$$\dfrac{A \vdash C :: \zeta(\rho)B^W \qquad \rho = (B \upharpoonright \mathcal{M}); \varrho}{A + c : \forall \mathsf{Gen}\ (\rho, B, A).\zeta(\rho)B^W \vdash P}{A \vdash \mathsf{class}\ c = C\ \mathsf{in}\ P}$$

Object
$$\dfrac{\begin{array}{ll} A \vdash \mathsf{self}(x)\ C :: \zeta(\rho)B^W & \rho = B \upharpoonright \mathcal{M} \\ A + x : \forall X.[\rho], x : \forall X.(B \upharpoonright \mathcal{F}) \vdash P & dom(B) = \overline{W} \\ A + x : \forall X.[\rho] \vdash Q & X = \mathsf{Gen}\ (\rho, B, A) \setminus ctv(B^W) \end{array}}{A \vdash \mathsf{obj}\ x = C\ \mathsf{init}\ P\ \mathsf{in}\ Q}$$

Fig. 2. Typing rules for names, and processes

6.2 Typing Rules

Our system's typing judgments are as follows:

$A \vdash x : \tau$	object x has type τ in environment A;
$A \vdash x.\ell :: \tilde{\tau}$	label ℓ in object x has type $\tilde{\tau}$ in environment A;
$A \vdash P$	process P is well-typed in environment A;
$A \vdash K :: B$	join-pattern K has type B in environment A;
$A \vdash C :: \tau^c$	class C has type τ^c in environment A;
$A \vdash S :: \tau^s$	refinement sequence S has type τ^s in environment A.

Typing judgments rely on *type environments* A that bind class and object names to type schemes:

$$A ::= \emptyset \mid c : \sigma^c; A \mid x : \sigma; A \mid x : \forall X.B; A$$

An object x may have two complementary bindings in A, $x : \sigma$ (external scheme) for public labels, and $x : \forall X.B$ (internal scheme) for private labels.

The typing rules appear in Fig. 2 and 3. Before we have a close look at the rules, some auxiliary definitions should be mentioned.

– $\{\gamma_\alpha/\alpha^{\alpha\in X}\}$ expresses the substitution of type variables by types.

Rules for patterns.

Empty-Pattern
$$A \vdash 0 :: \emptyset$$

Message-Pattern
$$\frac{(x_i : \tau_i \in A)^{\,i \in I}}{A \vdash \ell(x_i{}^{\,i \in I}) :: (\ell : \tau_i{}^{\,i \in I})}$$

Synchronization
$$\frac{A \vdash J_1 :: B_1 \qquad A \vdash J_2 :: B_2}{A \vdash J_1 \,\&\, J_2 :: B_1 \oplus B_2}$$

Alternative
$$\frac{A \vdash J_1 :: B_1 \qquad A \vdash J_2 :: B_2}{A \vdash J_1 \text{ or } J_2 :: B_1 \oplus B_2}$$

Rules for classes.

Class-Var
$$\frac{c : \forall X. \zeta(\rho) B^W \in A}{A \vdash c :: (\zeta(\rho) B^W)\{\gamma_\alpha / \alpha^{\,\alpha \in X}\}}$$

Self-Binding
$$\frac{A + x : [\rho],\, x : (B \upharpoonright \mathcal{F}) \vdash C :: \zeta(\rho) B^W}{A \vdash \mathsf{self}(x)\, C :: \zeta(\rho) B^W}$$

Reaction
$$\frac{A' \vdash J :: B \qquad A + A' \vdash P \qquad dom(A') = fn(J)}{A \vdash J \triangleright P :: \zeta(\rho) B^{col(J)}}$$

Abstract
$$\frac{dom(B) = L}{A \vdash L :: \zeta(\rho) B^{\emptyset}}$$

Disjunction
$$\frac{A \vdash C_1 :: \zeta(\rho) B_1^{W_1} \qquad A \vdash C_2 :: \zeta(\rho) B_2^{W_2}}{A \vdash C_1 \text{ or } C_2 :: \zeta(\rho)(B_1 \oplus B_2)^{W_1 \cup W_2}}$$

Refinement
$$\frac{\begin{array}{c} A \vdash C :: \zeta(\rho) B^W \\ A \vdash S :: B'^{F} \\ \vdash W \text{ with } F :: W' \qquad B \uparrow B' \end{array}}{A \vdash \mathsf{match}\ C \text{ with } S \text{ end} :: \zeta(\rho)((B' \upharpoonright \overline{W'}) \oplus B)^{W'}}$$

Rules for refinement clauses.

Modifier-Clause
$$\frac{\begin{array}{cc} A' \vdash K :: B_1 & A \vdash S :: B^F \\ A' \vdash K' :: B_2 & col(K) = \{\pi\} \\ A + A' \vdash P & dom(A') = fn(K') \end{array}}{A \vdash K \Rightarrow K' \triangleright P \,\big|\, S :: (B_1 \oplus B_2 \oplus B)^{(\pi \Rightarrow col(K'))|F}}$$

Modifier-Empty
$$A \vdash \emptyset :: \emptyset^{\emptyset}$$

Rules for filters.

Apply
$$\vdash \pi \uplus \pi' \text{ with } \pi \Rightarrow W \,\big|\, F :: \{\pi' \uplus \pi_i \mid \pi_i \in W\}$$

End
$$\vdash \pi \text{ with } \emptyset :: \{\pi\}$$

Next
$$\frac{\pi_1 \not\subseteq \pi \qquad \vdash \pi \text{ with } F :: W}{\vdash \pi \text{ with } \pi_1 \Rightarrow W_2 \,\big|\, F :: W}$$

Or
$$\frac{(\vdash \pi_i \text{ with } F :: W_i)^{\,\pi_i \in W}}{\vdash W \text{ with } F :: \bigcup_{\pi_i \in W} W_i}$$

Fig. 3. Typing rules for patterns, classes, refinement clauses, and filters

- $dom(A)$ is the set of identifiers bound in A. $A + A'$ equals $(A \setminus dom(A')) \cup A'$, where $A \setminus X$ removes from A all the bindings of names in X and $A + x :$ $\forall X.[\rho], x : \forall X.B$ means $A \setminus \{x\} \cup x : \forall X.[\rho] \cup x : \forall X.B$.
- $B \upharpoonright L$ restricts B to the set of labels L. Labels $\ell \in \mathcal{L}$ are divided into *private labels* $f \in \mathcal{F}$ and *public labels* $m \in \mathcal{M}$.
- $ftv()$ is the set of free type variables occurring in various constructs.
- Gen (ρ, B, A) is the set of the type variables that occur free in row type ρ or in internal type B, but not in type environment A.
- $ctv(B^W)$ computes the subset of the free type variables in B that are shared by at least the types of two correlated labels according to W.

$$ctv(B^W) = \bigcup_{\pi_i \in W} ctv(B^{\{\pi_i\}})$$
$$ctv(B^{\{\pi\}}) = \bigcup_{l \in \pi, l' \in \pi, l \neq l'} ftv(B(l)) \cap ftv(B(l'))$$

- predicate $B_1 \uparrow B_2$ expresses that B_1 and B_2 coincide on their common labels.
- $B_1 \oplus B_2$ is written for the union of B_1 and B_2, provided $B_1 \uparrow B_2$ holds.
- $col(J)$ computes the correlated labels set from a join-pattern J.

$$col(\emptyset) = \emptyset$$
$$col(\ell(\widetilde{u})) = \{\{\ell\}\}$$
$$col(J \& J') = \{\pi_1 \uplus \pi_2 \mid \pi_1 \in col(J), \pi_2 \in col(J')\}$$
$$col(J \text{ or } J') = col(J) \cup col(J')$$

The symbol $\uplus$ means disjoint union, since patterns are required to be linear (or in patterns is a complication, which can be ignored in a first reading).

Processes. The Class rule differs from before by the additional condition $\rho = (B \upharpoonright \mathcal{M}); \varrho$ in the premise. This condition requires an early compatibility check to verify that the types (in B) of the public labels inferred from the patterns are compatible with those (in ρ) inferred from the messages sent to self. In the old system, this check was delayed until object instantiation, which in turn delayed the detection of some errors. Such a delay is particularly annoying in a separate compilation context.

For the Object rule, checking the absence of abstract labels is now performed by the equation $dom(B) = \overline{W}$. In spite of the new condition on public labels in the Class rule, we retain the condition $\rho = (B \upharpoonright \mathcal{M})$ of [9]. It is still needed for anonymous class definitions, and also has the effect of closing the object type ρ. However, the most significant change is the replacement of the imprecise coupled labels by our exact correlated labels in the computation of generalizable type variables.

Classes. All rules are simplified thanks to the disappearance of the explicit abstract labels component in class types. The bizarre Sub rule is not needed any more, as discussed in Sec. 4.3. Our precise correlated labels set is introduced in the rule Reaction, using the external definition $col(J)$,

The rules for typing selective refinement undergo significant changes. In match C with S end, the typing of class C and the typing of refinement sequence S were combined in [9] but are now independent. Compatibility checks between labels common to C and S are now performed explicitly by condition $B \uparrow B'$; furthermore, most of the construction of the resulting type is performed by the auxiliary judgment W with $F :: W'$, which computes the patterns of the resulting class. Finally, the effectively introduced new labels (compare to Sec. 5) are added by $B' \upharpoonright \overline{W'}$. There is a minor difference $w.r.t$ [9]: our system allows labels in the selective patterns of S that are not necessarily in class C. Such a requirement is no longer essential to type safety and we believe that imposing it on programmers is too restrictive. Of course, some warning (analogous to the "unused match case" of ML pattern-matching) can be issued.

Refinement clauses. Rule Modifier-Clause serves both to collect label-type pairs (in B) and to compute the refinement rules F. Processes of refinement clauses P are also typed.

Filters. The rules for typing a filter mimic the semantics of selective refinement which is in analogy with ML-style pattern matching, but the irrelevant management of abstract names is omitted. Rules Apply, Next, and End handle the matching of one π set by the refinement rule F, while rule Or collects the resulting partial W_i sets into the resulting correlated label set W'. Linearity of resulting patterns is now checked simply by the disjoint union $\pi' \uplus \pi_i$ used in the rule Apply. Thereby, we drop one cryptic premise in the Refinement rule of [9].

6.3   Subject Reduction and Safety

The typing is finally extended to chemical solutions in order to illustrate the properties of the type system. An additional judgment: $A \vdash \mathcal{D} \Vdash \mathcal{P}$ is used and the rules are as follows:

Chemical-Solution	Definition
$A = \cup_{\psi x \# D \in \mathcal{D}} A_x$	$A \vdash \text{self}(x)\, D :: \zeta(\rho) B^W$
$(A^\psi \setminus \{x\} \vdash D :: A_x)^{\psi x \# D \in \mathcal{D}}$	$X = \text{Gen}\,(\rho, B, A) \setminus ctv(B^W)$
$(A^\psi \vdash P)^{\psi \# P \in \mathcal{P}}$	$\rho = B \upharpoonright \mathcal{M} \qquad dom(B) = \overline{W}$
$\vdash \mathcal{D} \Vdash \mathcal{P}$	$A \vdash D :: x : \forall X.[\rho], x : \forall X.(B \upharpoonright \mathcal{F})$

For lack of space, and because this work focuses on type system design, we will not recall the semantics of the objective-join calculus, which can be found in [9][1]. However, we formally state the correctness of our system.

Theorem 1 (Subject reduction).

---

[1] In the class semantics, the premise $dl(S) \subseteq dl(C')$ can be erased from rule Match

1. *Chemical reduction preserves chemical typing:*
   Suppose $\vdash \mathcal{D} \Vdash \mathcal{P}$. *If* $\mathcal{D} \Vdash \mathcal{P} \equiv \mathcal{D}' \Vdash \mathcal{P}'$ *or* $\mathcal{D} \Vdash \mathcal{P} \longrightarrow \mathcal{D}' \Vdash \mathcal{P}'$, *then* $\vdash \mathcal{D}' \Vdash \mathcal{P}'$.
2. *Class rewriting preserves typing: if* $A \vdash P$ *and* $P \longmapsto P'$ *then* $A \vdash P'$.

Theorem 2 (Safety).   *Well-typed chemical solutions do not fail.*

Informally, the type system guarantees: no undefined class names or object names; no attempts to instantiate from abstract classes; no violations of privacy; and no "message not understood" errors. The formal definitions of failures appear in [14], so do the proofs.

This kind of safety meets the general requirements of a standard type system. Of course, richer system can be considered to provide more specific properties such as deadlock-freedom, *etc.* [12]

7   Conclusion and Future Work

Class types, also known as class interfaces or class signatures, should characterize the externally visible properties of classes. We claim that when concurrent objects are concerned, the synchronization behavior is one such critical property. Based on this idea, we redesigned the static semantics of the concurrent object calculus of [9], equipped class types with their join patterns, and came up with a simpler but more expressive type system. This new type system has more polymorphism, suppresses the runtime overhead that was essential to safety in the old system, and accepts more safe programs. Furthermore, it is easier for programmers to understand and use. We also implemented type inference adapting some of the efficient techniques from [17].

Future work. As putting whole join-patterns into class types compromises abstraction, whether and how we can regain it is an interesting question. We see that the current type system handles all class operations (instantiation, disjunction and selective refinement). If we impose some restrictions on the application of certain operators to certain classes, class types can then be more abstract. For example, when some class is tagged as *final*, the only required synchronization-related information is the set of non-generalizable type variables. So instead of keeping the join-patterns, we can record just this set of variables. More generally, different restrictions will require different amount of synchronization information, and we can eventually reach a multi-leveled framework of abstracting class types, in which a class type may be assigned different degrees of abstraction in different contexts.

Another way to introduce abstraction is by *hiding* labels defined in a class. Such labels do not show up in the class type, so are untouched by later inheritance and overriding. This will in turn cause significant changes in the semantics of the class operations, probably leading us to a more powerful calculus.

In the old type system [9], selective refinement is typed per application. It would be more interesting if we could make selective refinement an autonomous class-to-class operator. Giving each selective refinement an independent type as we have done in our current type system falls short of this goal: the description of the parameters accepted is missing, and it is impossible to infer the resulting class by looking at the type of selective refinement alone. We wish to integrate our work with current research on *mixins* [3,6] and hopefully make the selective refinement a mixin-like operator in the concurrent setting.

Our ultimate goal is to implement our object-oriented extension of join calculus as a concurrent object-oriented programming language. Since the JoCaml [13] implementation already incorporates the join calculus into OCaml, we will pursue our goal by extending JoCaml.

Acknowledgements. The authors wish to thank James Leifer and Pierre-Louis Curien for their comments on drafts of this paper.

References

1. N. Benton, L. Cardelli, and C. Fournet. Modern concurrency abstractions for $C^\#$. In *Proceedings of ECOOP 2002*, LNCS 2374, pages 415–440, 2002.
2. P. D. Blasio and K. Fisher. A calculus for concurrent objects. In *Proceedings of CONCUR '96*, LNCS 1119, pages 655–670, 1996.
3. G. Bracha and W. Cook. Mixin-Based Inheritance. In *Proceedings of OOP-SLA.ECOOP '90*, pages 303–311. ACM press, 1990.
4. L. Cardelli. Obliq: A language with distributed scope. *Computing Systems*, 8(1):27–59, 1995.
5. G. Chen, M. Odersky, C. Zenger, and M. Zenger. A functional view of join. Technical Report ACRC-99-016, University of South Australia, 1999.
6. M. Flatt, S. Krishnamurthi, and M. Felleisen. Classes and mixins. In *Proceedings of POPL '98*, pages 171–183. ACM press, 1998.
7. C. Fournet and G. Gonthier. The reflexive chemical abstract machine and the join-calculus. In *Proceedings of POPL '96*, pages 372–385. ACM press, 1996.
8. C. Fournet, C. Laneve, L. Maranget, and D. Rémy. Implicit typing à la ML for the join-calculus. In *Proceedings of CONCUR '97*, LNCS 1243, pages 196–212, 1997.
9. C. Fournet, L. Maranget, C. Laneve, and D. Rémy. Inheritance in the join calculus. *Journal of Logic and Algebraic Programming*. To appear, http://pauillac.inria.fr/~maranget/papers/ojoin.ps.gz.
10. A. D. Gordon and P. D. Hankin. A concurrent object calculus: reduction and typing. In *Proceedings of HLCL '98*, ENTCS 16(3), 1998.
11. B. J. James Gosling and G. Steele. *The Java Language Specification*. Addison Wesley Longman Inc., Reading, Mass., 1996.
12. N. KoBayashi. Type systems for concurrent programs. In *Proceedings of UNU/IIST 10th Anniversary Colloquium, Lisbon, Portugal*, 2002. To appear.
13. F. Le Fessant. The JoCaml system prototype. Software and documentation available from http://pauillac.inria.fr/jocaml, 1998.
14. Q. Ma and L. Maranget. Expressive synchronization types for inheritance in the join calculus. Rapport de recherche 4889, INRIA-Rocquencourt, http://pauillac.inria.fr/~ma/papers/oojoin-tr.ps, 2003.

15. S. Matsuoka and A. Yonezawa. Analysis of inheritance anomaly in object-oriented concurrent programming languages. In G. Agha, P. Wegner, and A. Yonezawa, editors, *Research Directions in Concurrent Object-Oriented Programming*, chapter 4, pages 107–150. The MIT Press, 1993.
16. O. Nierstrasz. Towards an object calculus. In *Proceedings of ECOOP '91 Workshop on Object-Based Concurrent Computing*, LNCS 612, pages 1–20, 1992.
17. D. Rémy. Extension of ML type system with a sorted equation theory on types. Rapport de recherche 1766, INRIA-Rocquencourt, 1992.
18. D. Rémy and J. Vouillon. Objective ML: An effective object-oriented extension to ML. *Theory And Practice of Object Systems*, 4(1):27–50, 1998.
19. V. T. Vasconcelos. Typed concurrent objects. In *Proceedings of ECOOP '94 Workshop on Object-Based Concurrent Computing*, LNCS 821, pages 100–117, 1994.
20. A. Yonezawa, J.-P. Briot, and E. Shibayama. Object-oriented concurrent programming in ABCL/1. In *Proceedings of OOPSLA '86*, ACM SIGPLAN Notices 21(11), pages 258–268, 1986.

Term Graph Rewriting for the π-Calculus*

Fabio Gadducci

Dipartimento di Informatica, Università di Pisa
via F. Buonarroti 2, I-56127 Pisa
gadducci@di.unipi.it

Abstract. We propose a graphical implementation for (possibly) recursive processes of the π-calculus, encoding each process into a term graph. Our implementation is sound and complete with respect to the standard structural congruence for the calculus: Two processes are equivalent if and only if they are mapped into isomorphic term graphs. Most importantly, the encoding allows for using standard graph rewriting mechanisms in modelling the reduction semantics of the calculus.

Keywords: Term graph rewriting, process calculi, reduction semantics.

1 Introduction

Historically, the theory of graph rewriting lies its roots on the late Sixties, as the conceptual extension of the theory of formal languages, dealing with structures more general than strings. The extension was motivated by a wide range of interests, from pattern recognition to data type specification. Nowadays, the emphasis has shifted from the generative aspects of the formalism, moving toward what could be called the "state transformation" view: A graph is considered as a data structure, on which a set of rewriting rules may implement local changes. An interest confirmed by the large diffusion of visual specification languages, such as the standard UML, and the use of graphical tools for their manipulation.

Term graph rewriting is an instance of graph transformation, dealing with efficient implementations of the term rewriting mechanism, which are obtained by performing reductions over suitable graphical structures, instead of using the standard representation of terms as trees. As it happened for graph transformation, the emphasis moved from considering the formalism as a technique for equational deduction, typical of e.g. the functional and datatype communities, to considering the reduction mechanism itself as expressing a basic computational paradigm, where terms describe the states of an abstract machine and rewrites express its possible evolutions [22].

* Research partially supported by the Italian MIUR project COMETA (*Computational Metamodels*); and by the EU within the FET - Global Computing Initiative, project AGILE IST-2001-32747 (*Architectures for Mobility*). The funding bodies are not responsible for any use that might be made of the results presented here.

A. Ohori (Ed.): APLAS 2003, LNCS 2895, pp. 37–54, 2003.

To some extent, this is also the intuition behind the introduction of process algebras, such as Milner's CCS [23]: They represent specification languages for concurrent systems, which are considered as structured entities interacting *via* some synchronisation mechanism. A (possibly distributed) system is just a term over a signature, under the hypothesis that each operator represents a basic feature of the system. The reduction mechanism (accounting for the interaction between distinct components of a system) is usually described operationally, according to the so-called SOS-style [30], where the rewriting steps are inductively defined by a set of inference rules, driven by the structure of terms. Novel extensions of the process algebras paradigm involved calculi with higher-order features such as process mobility. Here systems are terms, carrying a set of associated *names*, and usually provided with a *structural* congruence, expressing basic observational properties; the reduction mechanism may also change the topology of a system, which formally amounts to the change of the associated set of names.

Recent years have seen many proposals concerning the use of graph rewriting techniques for simulating reduction in process algebras, in particular for their mobile extensions. Typically, the use of graphs allows for getting rid of the problems concerning the implementation of reduction over the structural equivalence, such as e.g. the α-conversion of bound names. Most of these proposals follow the same pattern: At first, a suitable graphical syntax is introduced, and its operators used for implementing processes. After that, usually ad-hoc graph rewriting techniques are developed for simulating the reduction semantics. Most often, the resulting graphical structures are eminently hierarchical (that is, roughly, each node/edge is itself a structured entity, and possibly a graph). From a practical point of view, this is unfortunate, since the restriction to standard graphs would allows for the reuse of already existing theoretical techniques and practical tools.

Building on our work on the syntactical presentation of graphs and graph rewrites [6,7,13] (using formalisms adopted in the algebraic specification community for the modelling of flow graphs [10]), we propose an encoding of (possibly recursive) processes of the π-calculus into term graphs, proving its soundness and completeness with respect to the original reduction semantics. The use of unstructured (that is, non hierarchical) graphs allows for the reuse of standard graph rewriting theory and tools for simulating the reduction semantics of the calculus, such as the double-pushout (DPO) approach and the associated concurrent semantics (which allows for the simultaneous execution of independent reductions, thus implicitly defining a non-deterministic concurrent semantics [2]).

Our proposal is expressive enough to encode the full calculus, including also non-deterministic choices. In general, we consider our use of unstructured graphs as an advancement with respect to most of the other implementations of the π-calculus based on graph rewriting [20,28], as well as for those based on more general graphical formalisms, such as *pi-nets* [25] and *interaction diagrams* [29]. Similar considerations hold also for the efforts on the graphical presentation [18] of *action calculus* [26], an abstract formalism for capturing many features of calculi with process mobility, which, as argued in [19], represents an intuitive flow graph model for programming languages.

Our representation is reminiscent of the work on the CHARM [8] and on *process graphs* [33]. In the former, graphs are represented algebraically, with a term structure which is analogous to the normal form presentation of structurally congruent π-processes originally proposed by Milner (and rightly so, since they are both inspired by the seminal work of Berry and Boudol on the CHAM [4]). In the latter, an embedding of processes into non-hierarchical graphs is proposed, albeit in a context more reminiscent of interaction nets than of standard graph rewriting. The same considerations hold for *reaction graphs*, underlying the work on χ-calculus [12]; which in turn shares many assumptions with the *fusion calculus*. It is noteworthy that *solo diagrams* [21], the graphical formalism associated to the latter calculus, uses hyper-graphs techniques which are similar to ours: The main difference concerns the treatment of recursive processes, as well as our interest in capturing also non-determinism.

The paper has the following structure. In Section 2 we introduce the finite fragment of the calculus, its syntax and reduction semantics. Section 3 recalls some basic definitions about term graphs, introducing in particular two operations on them, *sequential* and *parallel composition*. These operators are needed in Section 4, where we present our encoding of finite processes into term graphs. Our presentation is purely set-theoretical, while its algebraic description, using the already mentioned results on the syntactical presentation of graphs (as surveyed in [5,6]) can be obtained along the lines of [15]. Section 5 briefly recalls some standard theory and tools of (term) graph rewriting, and then proves the main result of the paper; namely, that the reduction semantics can be simulated using the graph reduction mechanism on the set of graphs obtained by the encoding. Finally, Section 6 extends the encoding to recursive processes.

2   The Finite Fragment of the π-Calculus

This section shortly introduces the finite fragment of the π-calculus, its structural equivalence and the associated reduction semantics.

Definition 1 (processes). *Let $\mathcal{N}$ be a set of names, ranged over by $x, y, w, \ldots$. A process P is a term generated by the (mutually recursive) syntax*

$$P ::= M, \ (\nu x)P, \ P_1 \mid P_2$$

$$M ::= 0, \ \alpha.P, \ M_1 + M_2 \qquad for \ \alpha \in \{x(y), \overline{x}y\}$$

We let $P, Q, R, \ldots$ range over the set Proc of processes, and $M, N, O \ldots$ range over the set Sum of summations.

We assume the standard definitions for the set of free names of a process P, denoted by $fn(P)$. Similarly for α-convertibility, with respect to the *restriction* operators $(\nu y)P$ and the *input* operators $x(y).P$: In both cases, the name y is bound in P, and it can be freely α-converted. Using these definitions, the behaviour of a process P is described as a relation over *abstract processes*, i.e., a relation obtained by closing a set of basic rules under structural congruence.

Definition 2 (reduction semantics). *The reduction relation for processes is the relation $R_\pi \subseteq Proc \times Proc$, closed under the structural congruence $\equiv$ induced by the set of axioms in Figure 1, inductively generated by the following set of axioms and inference rules*

$$\frac{}{x(y).P + M \mid \overline{x}w.Q + N \to P\{^w/_y\} \mid Q}$$

$$\frac{P \to Q}{(\nu x)P \to (\nu x)Q} \qquad \frac{P \to Q}{P \mid R \to Q \mid R}$$

where $P \to Q$ means that $\langle P, Q \rangle \in R_\pi$.

The first rule denotes the communication between two processes, possibly occurring inside a non-deterministic context. The process $\overline{x}w.Q$ is ready to communicate the (possibly global) name w along the channel x; it then synchronises with process $x(y).P$, and the local name y is thus substituted by w on the residual process P. The two latter rules simply state the closure of the reduction relation with respect to the operators of restriction and parallel composition.

$$P \mid Q = Q \mid P \qquad P \mid (Q \mid R) = (P \mid Q) \mid R \qquad P \mid 0 = P$$

$$M + N = N + M \qquad M + (N + O) = (M + N) + O \qquad M + 0 = M$$

$$(\nu x)(\nu y)P = (\nu y)(\nu x)P \qquad (\nu x)(P \mid Q) = P \mid (\nu x)Q \ \text{ for } x \notin fn(P)$$

Fig. 1. The set of structural axioms.

The only difference with respect to the syntax and the operational semantics for the finite fragment of the calculus proposed in the initial chapter of [32] (see Definition 1.1.1, Table 1.1 and Table 1.3) is the lack of the prefix operator $\tau.P$ and of the structural axiom $(\nu x)0 = 0$. While the inclusion of τ would arise no difficulties, adding the axiom would have forced us to consider cumbersome rules for removing the occurrence of "useless" operators in the graphical encoding. We refer the reader to [14] for an alternative structural congruence for processes.

3   Graphs and Term Graphs

We open the section recalling the definition of (ranked) term graphs: We refer to [5,6] for a detailed introduction, as well as for a comparison with standard definitions such as those in [3,31]. In the following we assume a chosen signature (Σ, S), for Σ a set of operators, and S a set of sorts, such that the *arity* of an operator in Σ is a pair (ω, s), for $\omega \in S^*$ and $s \in S$ (with λ the empty string).

Definition 3 (graphs). *A labelled graph d (over (Σ, S)) is a five tuple $d = \langle N, E, l, s, t \rangle$, where N, E are the sets of nodes and edges; l is the pair of labelling functions $l_e : E \to \Sigma$, $l_n : N \to S$; $s : E \to N^*$ and $t : E \to N$ are the source and target functions; and such that for each edge $e \in E$, the arity of $l_e(e)$ is $(l_n^*(s(e)), l_n(t(e)))$, i.e., each edge preserves the arity of its label.*

With an abuse of notation, in the definition above we let l_n^* stand for the extension of the function l_n from nodes to strings of nodes. In the following, we denote the components of a graph d by N_d, E_d, l_d, s_d and t_d.

Definition 4 (graph morphisms). *Let d, d' be graphs. A (graph) morphism $f : d \to d'$ is a pair of functions $f_n : N_d \to N_{d'}$, $f_e : E_d \to E_{d'}$ that preserves the labelling, source and target functions.*

In order to inductively define an encoding for processes, we need to define some operations over graphs. The first step is to equip them with suitable "handles" for interacting with an environment, built out of other graphs.

Definition 5 ((ranked) term graphs). *Let d_r, d_v be graphs with no edges. A (d_r, d_v)-ranked graph (a graph of rank (d_r, d_v)) is a triple $g = \langle r, d, v \rangle$, for d a graph and $r : d_r \to d$, $v : d_v \to d$ the root and variable morphisms.*

Let g, g' be ranked graphs of the same rank. A ranked graph morphism $f : g \to g'$ is a graph morphism $f_d : d \to d'$ between the underlying graphs that preserves the root and variable morphisms.

Two graphs $g = \langle r, d, v \rangle$ and $g' = \langle r', d', v' \rangle$ of the same rank are isomorphic if there exists a ranked graph isomorphism $\phi : g \to g'$. A (d_r, d_v)-ranked term graph G is an isomorphism class of (d_r, d_v)-ranked graphs.

With an abuse of notation, we sometimes refer to the nodes in the image of the variable (root) morphism as variables (roots, respectively). Moreover, we often use the same symbols of ranked graphs to denote term graphs, Finally, $G : d_r \to d_v$ denotes a term graph of rank (d_r, d_v).

We now introduce two operations on ranked term graphs: They will be needed in the presentation of our encoding for processes.

Definition 6 (sequential and parallel composition). *Let $G = \langle r, d, v \rangle : d_i \to d_v$ and $H = \langle r', d', v' \rangle : d_r \to d_i$ be term graphs. Then, their sequential composition is the term graph $H \circ G = \langle r'', d'', v'' \rangle$ of rank (d_r, d_v), for d'' the disjoint union $d \uplus d'$, modulo the equivalence on nodes induced by $r(x) = v'(x)$ for all $x \in N_{d_i}$, and $r'' : d_r \to d''$, $v'' : d_v \to d''$ the uniquely induced arrows.*

Let $G = \langle r, d, v \rangle : d_r \to d_v$ and $H = \langle r', d', v' \rangle : d'_r \to d'_v$ be term graphs. Then, their parallel composition is the term graph $G \otimes H = \langle r'', d'', v'' \rangle$ of rank $(d_r \cup d'_r, d_v \cup d'_v)$, for d'' the disjoint union $d \uplus d'$, modulo the equivalence on nodes induced by $r(x) = r'(x)$ for all $x \in N_{d_r} \cap N_{d'_r}$ and $v(y) = v'(y)$ for all $y \in N_{d_v} \cap N_{d'_v}$, and $r'' : d_r \cup d'_r \to d''$, $v'' : d_v \cup d'_v \to d''$ the uniquely induced arrows.

Intuitively, the sequential composition $H \circ G$ is obtained by taking the disjoint union of the graphs underlying G and H, and gluing the roots of G with the corresponding variables of H. Similarly, the parallel composition $G \otimes H$ is obtained by taking the disjoint union of the graphs underlying G and H, and gluing the roots (variables) of G with the corresponding roots (variables) of H.

Note that the two operations are defined on "concrete" graphs. Nevertheless, the result is clearly independent of the choice of the representative (and this implies that e.g. both parallel and sequential composition are associative).

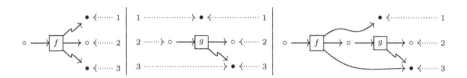

Fig. 2. Two term graphs, and their sequential composition

Example 1 (sequential composition). Let us consider the signature (Σ_e, S_e), for $S_e = \{s_p, s_n\}$ and $\Sigma_e = \{f : s_p s_n s_p \to s_n, g : s_n s_p \to s_n\}$. Two term graphs, built out of the signature (Σ_e, S_e), are shown in Figure 2. The nodes in the domain of the root (variable) morphism are depicted as a vertical sequence on the left (right, respectively); edges are represented by their label, from where arrows pointing to the source nodes leave, and to where the arrows from the target node arrive. The variable and root morphisms are represented by dotted arrows, directed from right-to-left and left-to-right, respectively.

The term graph on the left has rank $(\emptyset, \{1, 2, 3\})$, four nodes and one edge (labelled by f); the term graph on the middle has rank $(\{1, 2, 3\}, \{1, 2, 3\})$, four nodes and one edge (labelled by g). For graphical convenience, in the underlying graph the nodes of sort s_p are denoted by •, those of sort s_n by ∘.

Sequential composition of term graphs is performed by matching the roots of the second graph with the variables of the first one, as shown by the term graph on the right: It has rank $(\emptyset, \{1, 2, 3\})$, five nodes and two edges, and it is obtained by sequentially composing the other two.

A *(term graph) expression* is a term over the signature containing all ranked term graphs as constants, and parallel and sequential composition as binary operators. An expression is *well-formed* if all occurrences of both parallel and sequential composition are defined for the rank of the argument sub-expressions, according to Definition 6; the *rank* of an expression is then computed inductively from the rank of the term graphs appearing in it, and its *value* is the term graph obtained by evaluating all operators in it.

4   From Processes to Term Graphs

The first step in our simulation of the π-calculus is to encode processes into term graphs, built out of a suitable signature (Σ_π, S_π), and proving that the encoding preserves structural convertibility. Then, standard graph rewriting techniques will be used for simulating the reduction mechanism.

The set of sorts S_π contains $\{s_p, s_s, s_n\}$: Intuitively, a graph reachable from a node of sort s_p (of sort s_s) corresponds to a process (to a summation, respectively), whilst each node of sort s_n basically represents a name. The set of operators Σ_π contains $\{in, out : s_p s_n s_n \to s_s, \nu : s_n \to s_p, c : s_s \to s_p, go : \lambda \to s_p\}$. Clearly, the operators in and out simulates the input and output prefixes, respectively; and ν stands for restriction. There is no operator for simulating either parallel composition or non-deterministic choice. Instead, the operator c is a syntactical device for "coercing" the occurrence of a summation inside a process context (a standard device from algebraic specifications [17]). Finally, the operator go is another syntactical device for detecting the "entry" point of the computation, thus avoiding to perform any reduction below the outermost prefix operators: It is needed for modelling the reduction semantics in Section 5.

The second step is the characterisation of a class of graphs, such that all processes can be encoded into an expression containing only those graphs as constants, and parallel and sequential composition as binary operators. Thus, let us consider names $p, s \notin \mathcal{N}$: Our choice is depicted in Figure 3 and Figure 4, where the symbol $\diamond$ is now used to represent nodes of sort s_s.

Fig. 3. Term graphs $op_{x,y}$ (with $op \in \{in, out\}$), ν_x, c and go.

$$\circ \overset{x}{\longleftarrow} \quad x \longrightarrow \circ \overset{x}{\longleftarrow} \quad x \longrightarrow \circ \quad \Big| \quad p \longrightarrow \bullet \quad \Big| \quad s \longrightarrow \diamond$$

Fig. 4. Term graphs new_x, id_x, 0_x, 0_p and 0_s.

Now, for a set Γ of names, let us denote id_Γ and new_Γ as shorthands for $\bigotimes_{o \in \Gamma} id_o$ and $\bigotimes_{o \in \Gamma} new_o$, respectively: They are well-defined, since the $\otimes$ operator is associative. Finally, the encoding of processes into term graphs, mapping each finite process into a graph expression, is introduced in the definition below.

Definition 7 (encoding for processes). *Let P be a process, and let Γ be a set of names, such that $\mathbf{fn}(P) \subseteq \Gamma$. The (mutually recursive) encodings $[\![P]\!]^p_\Gamma$ and $[\![M]\!]^s_\Gamma$, mapping a process P into a term graph, are defined by structural induction according to the rules in Figure 5 (where we assume the standard definition for name substitution),*

$$
\begin{aligned}
[\![P]\!]^{go}_\Gamma &= [\![P]\!]^p_\Gamma \otimes go \\
[\![M]\!]^p_\Gamma &= \begin{cases} 0_p \otimes new_\Gamma & \text{if } \mathbf{fn}(M) = \emptyset \\ c \circ [\![M]\!]^s_\Gamma & \text{otherwise} \end{cases} \\
[\![(\nu y)P]\!]^p_\Gamma &= ([\![P\{^w/_y\}]\!]^p_{\{w\}\cup\Gamma} \otimes \nu_w) \circ (0_w \otimes id_\Gamma) \text{ for name } w \notin \Gamma \\
[\![P \mid Q]\!]^p_\Gamma &= [\![P]\!]^p_\Gamma \otimes [\![Q]\!]^p_\Gamma \\
[\![0]\!]^s_\Gamma &= 0_s \otimes new_\Gamma \\
[\![\overline{x}y.P]\!]^s_\Gamma &= out_{x,y} \circ ([\![P]\!]^p_\Gamma \otimes id_{\{x,y\}}) \\
[\![x(y).P]\!]^s_\Gamma &= in_{x,w} \circ ([\![P\{^w/_y\}]\!]^p_{\{w\}\cup\Gamma} \otimes id_{\{x,w\}}) \circ (0_w \otimes id_\Gamma) \text{ for name } w \notin \Gamma \\
[\![M + N]\!]^s_\Gamma &= [\![M]\!]^s_\Gamma \otimes [\![N]\!]^s_\Gamma
\end{aligned}
$$

Fig. 5. The graphical encodings for processes.

The mapping prefixes the term graph $[\![P]\!]^p_\Gamma$ with the occurrence of a "ready" tag, the go operator: It will denote the activating point for reduction, dictating the control flow for the reduction of the process. Note also the conditional rule for the mapping of $[\![M]\!]^p_\Gamma$. This is required by the use of 0 as the neutral element for both the parallel and the non-deterministic operator: In fact, the syntactical requirement $\mathbf{fn}(M) = \emptyset$ coincides with the semantical constraint $M \equiv 0$.

The mapping is well-defined, in the sense that the value of the resulting graph expression is independent from the choice of the name w in the rules for restriction and input prefix; moreover, given a set of names Γ, the encoding $[\![P]\!]^p_\Gamma$ of a process P is a term graph of rank $(\{p\}, \Gamma)$.

Example 2 (mapping a process). In order to give some intuition about the intended meaning of the previous rules, we show here the explicit construction of the encoding for the process $P = x(z).\overline{z}w.0 \mid \overline{x}x.0$, with respect to the set of names $\Gamma = \{x, w\}$. The denotation for term graph $[\![P]\!]^p_\Gamma$ is given below.

$$
\begin{aligned}
[\![P]\!]^p_\Gamma &= [\![x(z).\overline{z}w.0]\!]^p_\Gamma \otimes [\![\overline{x}x.0]\!]^p_\Gamma \\
&= [c \circ in_{x,v} \circ ([\![\overline{v}w.0]\!]^p_{\{v\}\cup\Gamma} \otimes id_{\{x,v\}}) \circ (0_v \otimes id_\Gamma)] \otimes \\
&\quad \otimes [c \circ out_{x,x} \circ ([\![0]\!]^p_\Gamma \otimes id_x)] \\
&= \{c \circ in_{x,v} \circ \{[c \circ out_{v,w} \circ (0_p \otimes new_{\{v\}\cup\Gamma} \otimes id_{\{v,w\}})] \otimes id_{\{x,v\}}\} \circ \\
&\quad \circ (0_v \otimes id_\Gamma)\} \otimes [c \circ out_{x,x} \circ (0_p \otimes new_\Gamma \otimes id_x)]
\end{aligned}
$$

We freely used the fact that both parallel and sequential compositions are associative. A simpler expression denoting the same term graph is given below.

$$
\{c \circ in_{x,v} \circ [(c \circ out_{v,w}) \otimes id_{\{x,v\}}] \circ (0_p \otimes 0_v \otimes id_\Gamma)\} \otimes [c \circ out_{x,x} \circ (0_p \otimes new_w \otimes id_x)]
$$

The equivalence between the two expressions can be proved by calculating the associated term graph, unique up-to isomorphism, represented in Figure 6.

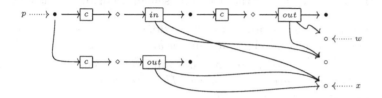

Fig. 6. The term graph $[\![x(z).\bar{z}w.0 \mid \bar{x}x.0]\!]_{\{x,w\}}$.

The equivalence could be proved also by exhibiting suitable properties of the parallel and sequential operators. We refer again the reader to [5,6] for the presentation of some algebraic laws for various graphical structures. With respect to our example, we simply remark that e.g. the equivalence between the different expressions for $[\![\bar{x}x.0]\!]_\Gamma^p$ (compare the right component of the topmost $\otimes$ operator in the two expressions) is obtained *via* the equality $new_x \otimes id_x = id_x$.

The mapping $[\![-]\!]_\Gamma^p$ is not surjective, since there are term graphs of rank $(\{p\}, \Gamma)$ that are not image of any process. Nevertheless, our encoding is sound and complete, as stated by the proposition below.

Proposition 1. *Let P, Q be processes, and let Γ be a set of names, such that $fn(P) \cup fn(Q) \subseteq \Gamma$. Then, $P \equiv Q$ if and only if $[\![P]\!]_\Gamma^p = [\![Q]\!]_\Gamma^p$.*

Note in particular how the occurrence of each restriction operator is linked to the process where it occurs, still preserving associativity, as shown by Figure 7.

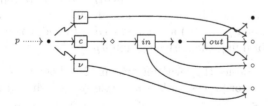

Fig. 7. Term graph encoding for both $(\nu x)(\nu y)x(z).\bar{z}y.0$ and $(\nu y)(\nu x)x(z).\bar{z}y.0$.

5   From Reductions to Graph Rewrites

We open the section recalling the basic tools of the double-pushout (DPO) approach to graph rewriting, as presented in [9,11]. We then provide a graph rewriting system $\mathcal{R}_\pi$ for modelling the reduction semantics of the π-calculus.

Definition 8 (graph production and derivation). *A graph production $p : \sigma$ is composed of a* production name p *and of a* span of graph morphisms $\sigma = (d_L \xleftarrow{l} d_K \xrightarrow{r} d_R)$. *A graph transformation system (or* GTS*) $\mathcal{G}$ is a set of productions, all with different names. Thus, when appropriate, we denote a production $p : \sigma$ using only its name p.*

A double-pushout diagram is like the diagram depicted in Figure 8, where top and bottom are spans and (1) and (2) are pushout squares in the category $\mathbf{G}_{\Sigma,S}$ of graphs and graph morphisms (over the signature (Σ, S)). Given a production $p : (d_L \xleftarrow{l} d_K \xrightarrow{r} d_R)$, a direct derivation from d_G to d_H via production p and triple $m = \langle m_L, m_K, m_R \rangle$ is denoted by $d_G \overset{p/m}{\Longrightarrow} d_H$.

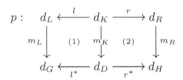

Fig. 8. A DPO direct derivation.

We let $d_G \Longrightarrow d_H$ denote the existence of a direct derivation between d_G and d_H, leaving unspecified the applied production and the chosen triple.

Operationally, the application of a production p to a graph d_G consists of three steps. First, the *match* $m_L : d_L \to d_G$ is chosen, providing an occurrence of d_L in d_G. Let us now assume that m_L is *edge-preserving* (i.e., that it is injective of edges). Then, all items of d_G matched by $d_L - l(d_K)$ are removed, and those nodes eventually identified by $l \circ m_L$ coalesced, leading to the *context graph* d_D. Finally, the items of $d_R - r(d_K)$ are added to d_D, further coalescing those nodes identified by r, obtaining the derived graph d_H.

We can now introduce the rewriting system $\mathcal{R}_\pi$, showing how it simulates the reduction semantics for processes. It is a simple system, since it contains just one rule, $p_\pi : (d_L^\pi \xleftarrow{l} d_K^\pi \xrightarrow{r} d_R^\pi)$, depicted in Figure 9: The graph on the left-hand side (center, right-hand side) is d_L^π (d_K^π and d_R^π, respectively). The action of the rule is described by the names of the nodes: As an example, the nodes identified by 1 and 2, distinct in d_L^π, are coalesced into 3 in d_R^π. The node identifiers are of course arbitrary: They correspond to the actual elements of the set of nodes, and they are used just to characterise the span of functions.

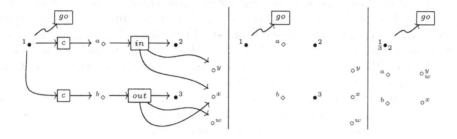

Fig. 9. The production rule p_π for $\mathcal{R}_\pi$.

It seems noteworthy that just one rule is needed to recast the reduction semantics for the π-calculus. First of all, the structural rules are taken care by the fact that graph morphisms allow for embedding a graph into a larger one, thus simulating the closure of reduction by context. Second, no distinct instance of the rule is needed: It is as if a particular process were chosen for representing the synchronisation, and graph isomorphism would take care of the closure with respect to structural congruence, as well as of the renaming of free names. Finally, we remark that, even if the search of a match can be considered a global operation, rule application itself is just a local operation, coalescing a few nodes and removing four edges.

Let us now introduce some notation. The symbol $\{|P|\}$ denotes the graph (that is, a representative of the equivalence class of isomorphic graphs) underlying the term graph $[\![P]\!]_\Gamma^{go}$, for $\Gamma = fn(P)$; the symbol $reach(d)$ denotes the sub-graph of d reachable from the node in the source of the only edge labelled by go. We can now state the main theorems of the paper, concerning the soundness and completeness of our encoding with respect to the reduction semantics.

Theorem 1 (encoding preserves reductions). *Let P, Q be processes. If $P \rightarrow Q$, then $\mathcal{R}_\pi$ entails a direct derivation $\{|P|\} \Longrightarrow d$ via an edge-preserving match, and $reach(d) = \{|Q|\}$.*

Intuitively, a reduction step is simulated by applying a rule on an enabled event, i.e., by finding a match covering a sub-graph with the go operator on top. The restriction to the reachable sub-graph is needed in order to remove all those items corresponding to the sub-processes which are discarded after the execution of the non-deterministic choices. In rewriting jargon, it would correspond to a "garbage collection" phase.

Theorem 2 (encoding does not add reductions). *Let P be a process. If $\mathcal{R}_\pi$ entails a direct derivation $\{|P|\} \Longrightarrow d$ via an edge-preserving match, then there exists a process Q such that $P \rightarrow Q$ and $\{|Q|\} = reach(d)$.*

As noted before, the correspondence holds since the presence of the go operator forces the match to be applied only to operators on top, thus forbidding the occurrence of a reduction inside the outermost prefix operators.

The restriction to edge-preserving matches is necessary in order to ensure that the two edges labelled by c can never be merged together. Intuitively, allowing for their coalescing would correspond to the synchronisation of two summations, i.e., as allowing for a reduction $x(y).P+\overline{x}w.Q \to P\{^{w}/_{y}\} \mid Q$. Instead, it is necessary to allow for the coalescing of nodes, in order to recover those synchronisations with output prefix $\overline{x}x$, as in Figure 10 below.

It has to be noted that the previous results extend to any sequence of rewrites: If a rule is applicable to a graph d, then all the items have to be contained in $reach(d)$, due to the unique occurrence of the edge labelled go.

Example 3 (rule application). Consider the term graph $[\![x(z).\overline{z}w.0 \mid \overline{x}x.0]\!]^{P}_{\{x,w\}}$, depicted in Figure 6, and the associated graph $\{\!|x(z).\overline{z}w.0 \mid \overline{x}x.0|\!\}$, represented on the left of Figure 10. The application of a rewriting step, resulting in the term graph on the right, simulates the transition $x(z).\overline{z}w.0 \mid \overline{x}x.0 \to \overline{x}w.0$. In fact, the reachable part of the graph on the right is isomorphic to $\{\!|\overline{x}w.0|\!\}$.

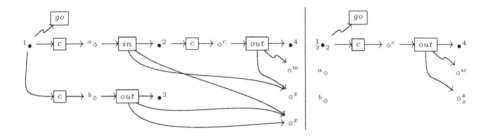

Fig. 10. A rewriting step, simulating the transition $x(z).\overline{z}w.0 \mid \overline{x}x.0 \to \overline{x}w.0$.

Remark 1 (on concurrent reductions). The role of the *interface* graph d_K in a graph rewriting rule (see Figure 8) is to characterise in the graph to be rewritten the items that are read but not consumed by a direct derivation. Such a distinction is important when considering *concurrent* derivations. Concurrent derivations are defined as equivalence classes of concrete derivations up-to so-called *shift equivalence* [9], identifying (as for the analogous, better-known *permutation equivalence* of the λ-calculus) those derivations which differ only for the scheduling of independent steps. Roughly, the equivalence states the interchangeability of two direct derivations $d_1 \Longrightarrow d_2 \Longrightarrow d_3$ if they act either on disjoint parts of d_1, or on parts that are in the image of the interface graphs.

Thus, our encoding may be exploited for defining a concurrent reduction semantics of the π-calculus. The presence of the operator go on the interface graph allows for the simultaneous execution of more than one reduction, since its sharing implies that more than one pair of (distinct) input and output resources may synchronise. The removal of the two edges labelled by c ensures that simultaneous reductions must not occur inside the same summation.

6 Dealing with Recursion

The introduction of a *replication* operator, denoted by !, is by now almost considered the standard approach for dealing with infinite processes. Intuitively, the behaviour of a process !P coincides with the behaviour of a (possibly) unbound number of instances of P itself, i.e., $P \mid P \mid \ldots$. Unfortunately, it seems a difficult task to describe within our graphical encoding the behaviour of processes including replication, since this operator implicitly represents a global operation, involving the duplication of necessarily unspecified sub-processes, and it is hence hard to model *via* graph rewriting, which is an eminently local process.

Nevertheless, it should be obvious that our framework allows for the modelling of *recursive* processes, that is, of processes defined using constant invocation, which is equivalent to the use of replication (as originally stated in [24], p. 212). Each process is compiled into a graph transformation system, adding to the production rule p_π in Figure 9 also new rules for simulating unfolding steps.

6.1 On Recursive Processes

In this section we present recursive processes and their reduction semantics. With minor variations, the reader may refer to [32], Section 3.2.

Definition 9 (recursive process expressions). *Let $\mathcal{N}$ be a set of names, ranged over by $x, y, w, \ldots$, and let $\mathcal{C}$ be a set of* process identifiers, *ranged over by $A, B, C, \ldots$. A (recursive) process expression P is a term generated by the (mutually recursive) syntax*

$$P ::= M, \ (\nu x)P, \ P_1 \mid P_2, \ A\langle x_1, \ldots, x_n \rangle$$

$$M ::= 0, \ \alpha.P, \ M_1 + M_2 \qquad \text{for } \alpha \in \{x(y), \overline{x}y\}$$

We let $P, Q, R, \ldots$ range over the set RProc of process expressions; and $M, N, O, \ldots$ over the set RSum of summation expressions.

We assume the standard definition for the set of free names of a process expression (just stating that $\mathit{fn}(A\langle x_1, \ldots, x_n \rangle) = \{x_1, \ldots, x_n\}$), as well as those of (capture avoiding) substitution and α-conversion.

Definition 10 (recursive processes). *Let $\mathcal{N}$ be a set of names, ranged over by $x, y, w, \ldots$, and let $\mathcal{C}$ be a set of process identifiers, ranged over by $A, B, C, \ldots$. A recursive process ϕ is a finite set of equations (at most one for each process identifier A) of the following kind*

$$A(x_1, \ldots, x_n) =_\phi P_A$$

for x_i's distinct names and P_A process expression with $\mathit{fn}(P_A) \subseteq \{x_1, \ldots, x_n\}$.

Intuitively, an equation corresponds to a procedure definition (introducing formal parameters within round brackets), and each identifier in a process expression represents a procedure invocation (actual parameters within angle brackets).

Definition 11 (recursive reduction semantics). *The reduction relation for recursive process ϕ is the relation $R^\phi_\pi \subseteq RProc \times RProc$, closed under the structural congruence $\equiv$ induced by the set of axioms in Figure 1, inductively generated by the following set of axioms and inference rules*

$$\overline{x(y).P + M \mid \overline{x}w.Q + N \to_\phi P\{^w/_y\} \mid Q}$$

$$\frac{P \to_\phi Q}{(\nu x)P \to_\phi (\nu x)Q} \qquad \frac{P \to_\phi Q}{P \mid R \to_\phi Q \mid R}$$

$$\frac{}{A\langle y_1, \ldots, y_n \rangle \to_\phi P_A\{^{y_1}/_{x_1}, \ldots, ^{y_n}/_{x_n}\}} \quad \textit{for } A(x_1, \ldots, x_n) =_\phi P_A$$

where $P \to_\phi Q$ means that $\langle P, Q \rangle \in R^\phi_\pi$.

6.2 From Recursive Processes to Term Graphs

In the definition of reductions semantics given in the previous section, we associated to each recursive process a different reduction system. It then seems natural, in order to encode recursive processes into term graphs, to associate a distinct graph transformation system to each process, for simulating its behaviour.

Let us first consider the signature (Σ^r_π, S_π): It extends (Σ_π, S_π) with an operator A_n for each equation identifier A and natural number n, with source the sort s_n repeated n-times and target s_p. The signature is infinite, of course, but the set of operators actually present in each recursive process is finite.

We must extend also the class of graphs to be used as constants, in order to simulate process expressions by graph expressions. Besides those graphs depicted in Figure 3 and Figure 4, we need also term graphs such as the one depicted on Figure 11, intuitively representing $A\langle x_1, \ldots, x_n \rangle$.

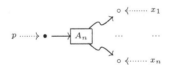

Fig. 11. The term graph $A_{x_1, \ldots, x_n}$.

Remember that id_Γ stands for $\bigotimes_{o \in \Gamma} id_o$, for a set of names Γ. The encoding of process expressions into term graphs is then introduced in the definition below.

Definition 12 (encoding for process expressions). *Let P be a process expression, and let Γ be a set of names, such that $fn(P) \subseteq \Gamma$. The encoding $[\![P]\!]^{go}_\Gamma$, mapping a process expression P into a term graph, is given by extending the encoding of Definition 7 with the following rule*

$$[\![A\langle x_1, \ldots, x_n \rangle]\!]^p_\Gamma = A_{x_1, \ldots, x_n} \otimes new_\Gamma$$

The mapping is well-defined, and, given a set of names Γ, the encoding $[\![P]\!]_\Gamma^{go}$ of a process expression P is a term graph of rank $(\{p\}, \Gamma)$. It is still sound and complete, as stated by the proposition below, extending Proposition 1.

Proposition 2. *Let P, Q be process expressions, and let Γ be a set of names, such that $fn(P) \cup fn(Q) \subseteq \Gamma$. Then, $P \equiv Q$ if and only if $[\![P]\!]_\Gamma^{go} = [\![Q]\!]_\Gamma^{go}$.*

6.3   From Recursive Processes to Graph Transformation Systems

Given a recursive process ϕ, we can now introduce the rewriting system $\mathcal{R}_\pi^\phi$, showing how it simulates the recursive reduction semantics. It extends $\mathcal{R}_\pi$, introduced in Section 5, adding an unfolding rule p_A^ϕ, depicted in Figure 12, for each equation $A(x_1, \ldots, x_n) =_\phi P_A$ in ϕ.

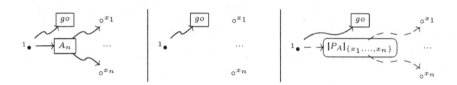

Fig. 12. The production rule p_A^ϕ for $A(x_1, \ldots, x_n) =_\phi P_A$.

In Figure 12 we represent the term graph $G = [\![P_A]\!]_{\{x_1, \ldots, x_n\}}$, of rank $(\{p\}, \{x_1, \ldots, x_n\})$, by circling the expression: The n dashed arrows leaving it originate from the variables (hence, from the nodes pointed by the x_i's) of G; the only dashed arrow reaching it points to the root of G.

Theorem 3 (encoding the reductions). *Let ϕ be a recursive process, and let P, Q be process expressions. If $P \rightarrow_\phi Q$, then $\mathcal{R}_\pi^\phi$ entails a direct derivation $\{\!|P|\!\} \Longrightarrow d$ via an edge-preserving match, and $reach(d) = \{\!|Q|\!\}$.*

Vice versa, let ϕ be a recursive process, and let P be a process expression. If $\mathcal{R}_\pi^\phi$ entails a direct derivation $\{\!|P|\!\} \Longrightarrow d$ via an edge-preserving match, then there exists a process expression Q such that $P \rightarrow_\phi Q$ and $\{\!|Q|\!\} = reach(d)$.

Example 4 (mapping a recursive process). Let us now consider the process expression $P = A\langle x\rangle \mid B\langle x\rangle$, for the process ϕ defined by

$$A(x) =_\phi x(y).A\langle y\rangle \qquad\qquad B(x) =_\phi \overline{x}x.B\langle x\rangle$$

The unfolding rule p_B^ϕ is presented in Figure 13.

How is the reduction $P \rightarrow_\phi P$ simulated? The graph on the left of Figure 14 represents $\{\!|P|\!\}$; the graph on the center represents the situation after the (possibly simultaneous) application of both the unfolding rules p_A^ϕ and p_B^ϕ; now, an application of the rule for synchronisation will do the trick, obtaining the graph on the right: Its reachable component is isomorphic to the initial state.

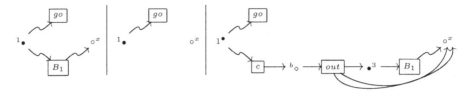

Fig. 13. The production rule p_B^ϕ for $B(x) =_\phi \overline{x}x.B\langle x\rangle$.

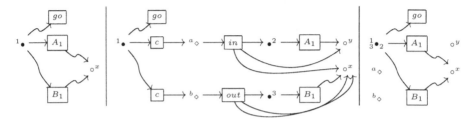

Fig. 14. Unfolding $\{\!| A\langle x\rangle \mid B\langle x\rangle |\!\}$ to $\{\!| x(y).A\langle y\rangle \mid \overline{x}x.B\langle x\rangle |\!\}$, then synchronising.

7 Conclusions and Further Work

In this paper we presented an encoding of (possibly recursive) processes of the π-calculus into term graphs, proving its soundness and completeness with respect to the original reduction semantics.

The key technical point is the use of nodes as place-holders for names, and in particular of a graph morphism for representing the free names occurring in a process. Our solution avoids the need of any encapsulation for encoding processes, and it allows for capturing the full extent of the calculus, including recursion and non-deterministic choice. Moreover, the use of unstructured graphs allows for the reuse of standard graph rewriting theory and tools for simulating the reduction semantics of the calculus. We consider this an advancement with respect to most of the other approaches for the graphical implementation of calculi with name mobility (such as Parrow's *interaction diagrams* [29], Gardner's *process frameworks* [16] or Milner's *bigraphs* [27]), where ad-hoc mechanisms for graph rewriting have to be developed.

Our presentation of the finite fragment of the π-calculus is reminiscent of the encoding for mobile ambients in [14]. This fact strengthens our belief that any calculus with name mobility may find a presentation within our formalism, along the line of the encodings in these two papers. The calculus should contain a parallel operator which is associative, commutative and with an identity; also, its operational semantics should be reduction-like (i.e., *via* unlabelled transitions), and the rules should not substitute a free name for another, so that name substitution be handled by node coalescing. The mechanism is reminiscent of *name fusion*, hence the resemblance of our graphical encoding with solo diagrams.

Our encoding of process reduction represents a starting point: we plan to test its efficiency by using it as a preprocessing step in one of the many existing tools for implementing graph rewriting. On the theoretical side, an interesting topic is the study of the observational equivalences induced on processes by the encoding, according e.g. to the bisimulation theory for graph grammars [1]. The results could be revealing since, as noted by one referee, "as there are term graphs which do not correspond to processes of the source calculus, the observational equivalence on the term graphs should not be the same as that on the π-calculus".

References

1. A. Baldan, P. Corradini and U. Montanari. Bisimulation equivalences for graph grammars. In W. Brauer, H. Ehrig, J. Karhumäki, and A. Salomaa, editors, *Formal and Natural Computing*, volume 2300 of *Lect. Notes in Comp. Sci.*, pages 158–190. Springer, 2002.
2. P. Baldan, A. Corradini, H. Ehrig, M. Löwe, U. Montanari, and F. Rossi. Concurrent semantics of algebraic graph transformation. In H. Ehrig, H.-J. Kreowski, U. Montanari, and G. Rozenberg, editors, *Handbook of Graph Grammars and Computing by Graph Transformation*, volume 3, pages 107–187. World Scientific, 1999.
3. H.P. Barendregt, M.C.J.D. van Eekelen, J.R.W. Glauert, J.R. Kennaway, M.J. Plasmeijer, and M.R. Sleep. Term graph reduction. In J.W. de Bakker, A.J. Nijman, and P.C. Treleaven, editors, *Parallel Architectures and Languages Europe*, volume 259 of *Lect. Notes in Comp. Sci.*, pages 141–158. Springer, 1987.
4. G. Berry and G. Boudol. The chemical abstract machine. *Theor. Comp. Sci.*, 96:217–248, 1992.
5. R. Bruni, F. Gadducci, and U. Montanari. Normal forms for algebras of connections. *Theor. Comp. Sci.*, 286:247–292, 2002.
6. A. Corradini and F. Gadducci. An algebraic presentation of term graphs, via gs-monoidal categories. *Applied Categorical Structures*, 7:299–331, 1999.
7. A. Corradini and F. Gadducci. Rewriting on cyclic structures: Equivalence between the operational and the categorical description. *Informatique Théorique et Applications/Theoretical Informatics and Applications*, 33:467–493, 1999.
8. A. Corradini, U. Montanari, and F. Rossi. An abstract machine for concurrent modular systems: CHARM. *Theor. Comp. Sci.*, 122:165–200, 1994.
9. A. Corradini, U. Montanari, F. Rossi, H. Ehrig, R. Heckel, and M. Löwe. Algebraic approaches to graph transformation I: Basic concepts and double pushout approach. In G. Rozenberg, editor, *Handbook of Graph Grammars and Computing by Graph Transformation*, volume 1. World Scientific, 1997.
10. V.-E. Căzănescu and Gh. Ştefănescu. A general result on abstract flowchart schemes with applications to the study of accessibility, reduction and minimization. *Theor. Comp. Sci.*, 99:1–63, 1992.
11. F. Drewes, A. Habel, and H.-J. Kreowski. Hyperedge replacement graph grammars. In G. Rozenberg, editor, *Handbook of Graph Grammars and Computing by Graph Transformation*, volume 1. World Scientific, 1997.
12. Y. Fu. Variations on mobile processes. *Theor. Comp. Sci.*, 221:327–368, 1999.
13. F. Gadducci, R. Heckel, and M. Llabrés. A bi-categorical axiomatisation of concurrent graph rewriting. In M. Hofmann, D. Pavlovič, and G. Rosolini, editors, *Category Theory and Computer Science*, volume 29 of *Electr. Notes in Theor. Comp. Sci.* Elsevier Science, 1999.

14. F. Gadducci and U. Montanari. A concurrent graph semantics for mobile ambients. In S. Brookes and M. Mislove, editors, *Mathematical Foundations of Programming Semantics*, volume 45 of *Electr. Notes in Theor. Comp. Sci.* Elsevier Science, 2001.
15. F. Gadducci and U. Montanari. Comparing logics for rewriting: Rewriting logic, action calculi and tile logic. *Theor. Comp. Sci.*, 285:319–358, 2002.
16. Ph. Gardner. From process calculi to process frameworks. In C. Palamidessi, editor, *Concurrency Theory*, volume 1877 of *Lect. Notes in Comp. Sci.*, pages 69–88. Springer, 2000.
17. J. Goguen and J. Meseguer. Order sorted algebra I: Equational deduction for multiple inheritance, overloading, exceptions and partial operations. *Theor. Comp. Sci.*, 105:217–273, 1992.
18. M. Hasegawa. *Models of Sharing Graphs*. PhD thesis, Department of Computer Science, University of Edinburgh, 1997.
19. A. Jeffrey. Premonoidal categories and a graphical view of programs. Technical report, School of Cognitive and Computing Sciences, University of Sussex, 1997. Available at http://www.cogs.susx.ac.uk/users/alanje/premon/.
20. B. König. Generating type systems for process graphs. In J. C. M. Baeten and S. Mauw, editors, *Concurrency Theory*, volume 1664 of *Lect. Notes in Comp. Sci.*, pages 352–367. Springer, 1999.
21. C. Laneve, J. Parrow, and B. Victor. Solo diagrams. In N. Kobayashi and B. Pierce, editors, *Theoretical Aspects of Computer Science*, volume 2215 of *Lect. Notes in Comp. Sci.*, pages 127–144. Springer, 2001.
22. J. Meseguer. Conditional rewriting logic as a unified model of concurrency. *Theor. Comp. Sci.*, 96:73–155, 1992.
23. R. Milner. *Communication and Concurrency*. Prentice Hall, 1989.
24. R. Milner. The polyadic π-calculus: A tutorial. In F.L. Bauer, W. Brauer, and H. Schwichtenberg, editors, *Logic and Algebra of Specification*, volume 94 of *Nato ASI Series F*, pages 203–246. Springer, 1993.
25. R. Milner. Pi-nets: A graphical formalism. In D. Sannella, editor, *European Symposium on Programming*, volume 788 of *Lect. Notes in Comp. Sci.*, pages 26–42. Springer, 1995.
26. R. Milner. Calculi for interaction. *Acta Informatica*, 33:707–737, 1996.
27. R. Milner. Bigraphical reactive systems. In K.G. Larsen and M. Nielsen, editors, *Concurrency Theory*, volume 2154 of *Lect. Notes in Comp. Sci.*, pages 16–35. Springer, 2001.
28. U. Montanari, M. Pistore, and F. Rossi. Modeling concurrent, mobile and co-ordinated systems via graph transformations: Concurrency, parallellism, and distribution. In H. Ehrig, H.-J. Kreowski, U. Montanari, and G. Rozenberg, editors, *Handbook of Graph Grammars and Computing by Graph Transformation*, volume 3, pages 189–268. World Scientific, 1999.
29. J. Parrow. Interaction diagrams. *Nordic Journal of Computing*, 2:407–443, 1995.
30. G. Plotkin. A structural approach to operational semantics. Technical Report DAIMI FN-19, Computer Science Department, Aarhus University, 1981.
31. D. Plump. Term graph rewriting. In H. Ehrig, G. Engels, H.-J. Kreowski, and G. Rozenberg, editors, *Handbook of Graph Grammars and Computing by Graph Transformation*, volume 2, pages 3–61. World Scientific, 1999.
32. S. Sangiorgi and D. Walker. *The π-calculus: A Theory of Mobile Processes*. Cambridge University Press, 2001.
33. N. Yoshida. Graph notation for concurrent combinators. In T. Ito and A. Yonezawa, editors, *Theory and Practice of Parallel Programming*, volume 907 of *Lect. Notes in Comp. Sci.*, pages 393–412. Springer, 1994.

Useless-Code Elimination and Program Slicing for the Pi-Calculus

Naoki Kobayashi

Department of Computer Science
Tokyo Institute of Technology
kobayasi@cs.titech.ac.jp

Abstract. In this paper, we study program transformations called *useless-code elimination* and *program slicing* in the context of the π-calculus. The aim of useless-code elimination and program slicing is to simplify a program by eliminating useless or unimportant part of the program. We define formal correctness criteria for those transformations, present a type-based transformation method, and prove its correctness.

1 Introduction

In this paper, we study useless-code elimination and program slicing[1] for the π-calculus [15, 21]. The purpose of *useless-code elimination* [3, 6, 11, 23] (UCE, in short) is to optimize a program by eliminating part of code that does not contribute to the observable program behavior. (It is more aggressive optimization than deadcode elimination in the sense that UCE may eliminate part of code that is executed in the original program, as long as that part does not affect the observable behavior.) *Program slicing* [19, 22] can be considered a generalization of UCE: It aims to eliminate part of code that does not contribute to a certain interesting part of the program behavior. Program slicing is useful for program optimization, debugging, verification, etc. For example, suppose that a concurrent program suffers from a race condition. To find the cause of the race, one may perform program slicing to obtain a simplified program that exhibits the same race condition, so that one can inspect the simplified program instead of the original program. As another example, suppose that one wants to verify that a concurrent program satisfies a certain property. Then, one may perform program slicing to extract a part of the code that is relevant to the property to be verified, and then perform verification.

Both UCE [3, 6, 11, 23] and program slicing [8, 19, 22] have been extensively studied for sequential programs, but they have been relatively unexplored for concurrent programs. There are some pieces of work on program slicing for concurrent programs [9, 14, 24], but the slicing algorithms are too specific to a particular language or a thread model, so that it is not clear whether they can be applied to other concurrent languages. Moreover, only a few of them [9] give

---

[1] There are several kinds of program slicing [8, 22]: Throughout this paper, we use the term program slicing to refer to the static, backward slicing.

A. Ohori (Ed.): APLAS 2003, LNCS 2895, pp. 55–72, 2003.

a formal correctness criterion. The aim of this paper is, therefore, to establish formal, general foundations for UCE and program slicing by using the π-calculus as a target of the study. By using the π-calculus, (i) we can reuse standard definitions of process equivalence and type theories for defining correctness criteria of UCE and program slicing and developing transformation algorithms, (ii) we hope that the techniques developed here can be used in a wide range of concurrent programming languages (since the π-calculus is general enough to model various concurrency primitives), and (iii) we hope that we can clarify the relationship between program slicing and information flow analysis for concurrent languages [10, 18], which are both instances of dependency analyses [2] but have been studied independently in the context of concurrent languages.

The main technical contributions of this paper are summarized as follows:

- We give a general, formal definition of the problems of UCE and program slicing for the π-calculus by using the idea of (weak) barbed congruence [21]. The idea of barbed congruence is to compare two processes by putting them into the same context and check whether they can simulate each other. Since correctness criteria of program slicing may vary depending on its purpose, we parameterize the barbed congruence with the set of contexts that processes can be put into, so that various criteria can be obtained by changing the set of contexts.

- We present a *type-based* method for UCE and program slicing, and prove its correctness. Thanks to the use of the type-based technique, we can separate the issue of *what is* a valid transformation and the issue of *how to obtain* a valid transformation: The former can be specified in a declarative manner by using rules similar to typing rules, and the latter can be reduced to the problem of type reconstruction. We can also use a standard proof technique for showing soundness of the transformation. A distinguishing feature of our *type-based* transformation is that it works for *untyped* programs. We enable an application of a type-based transformation to untyped programs by introducing a special type describing untyped values. We think that dealing with untyped programs is important for programs that run in open environments, where we cannot assume that an environment (in particular, a malicious one) respects types. Note that a transformation that is correct in the typed world may be incorrect in the untyped world: For example, although $x \sim y$ (which should be read "x and y are equivalent") holds under the assumption that both x and y have the same singleton type (hence having the same value), $x \sim y$ does not hold in the untyped world. For another example, **if** b **then** e **else** $e \sim e$ in the typed world, but **if** b **then** e **else** $e \nsim e$ in the untyped world, since b in the lefthand process may not be a boolean, in which case a run-time error is reported. We expect that the idea of our type-based transformation for untyped programs can be used for applying other type-based program analysis and transformation techniques to untyped programs.

The rest of this paper is structured as follows. Section 2 introduces the syntax and operational semantics of the language. Section 3 gives a formal definition of the problems of UCE and program slicing. Section 4 presents a type-based transformation method for UCE and program slicing. Section 5 discusses extensions of our method. Section 6 discusses related work and Section 7 concludes. Proofs and more examples are given in the full version of this paper, available from http://www.kb.cs.titech.ac.jp/~kobayasi/publications.html.

2   Language

2.1   Syntax

Definition 1. *The sets of* processes *and* values *are defined by:*

$$P \text{ (processes)} ::= \mathbf{0} \mid v![v_1, \ldots, v_n].\, P \mid v?[y_1, \ldots, y_n].\, P$$
$$\mid (P \mid Q) \mid (\nu x)\, P \mid *P \mid \textbf{if } v \textbf{ then } P \textbf{ else } Q$$
$$v \text{ (values)} \quad ::= x \mid \star \mid \textbf{true} \mid \textbf{false}$$

Process $\mathbf{0}$ does nothing. Process $v![v_1, \ldots, v_n].\, P$ sends a tuple $[v_1, \ldots, v_n]$ of values on channel v, and behaves like P after the tuple is received. Process $v?[y_1, \ldots, y_n].\, P$ waits to receive a tuple $[v_1, \ldots, v_n]$ of values, binds $y_1, \ldots, y_n$ to $v_1, \ldots, v_n$, and behaves like P. $P \mid Q$ runs P and Q in parallel. Process $(\nu x)\, P$ creates a fresh communication channel, binds x to it, and behaves like P. Process $*P$ runs infinitely many copies of P in parallel. Process **if** v **then** P **else** Q behaves like P if v is **true** and behaves like Q if v is **false**. A communication channel is represented by a variable. The value $\star$ denotes an empty value, corresponding to the null tuple in functional language ML [16] (the element of a singleton type **unit**). In examples, we will use other values such as strings and integers.

We assume that the input prefix $v?[y_1, \ldots, y_n]$ binds variables $y_1, \ldots, y_n$, and the ν-prefix (νx) binds x. The set of free variables (i.e., those that are not bound by any prefix) in P is denoted by $\mathbf{FV}(P)$. We assume that bound variables are implicitly renamed as necessary to ensure that bound variables are different from each other and free variables.

We give a higher precedence to prefixes and conditionals (**if**) than to the parallel composition, so that $(\nu y)\, x?[y].\, P \mid Q$ means $((\nu y)\, (x?[y].\, P)) \mid Q$. A sequence $v_1, \ldots, v_n$ is abbreviated to $\tilde{v}$. $(\nu \tilde{u})\, P$ is an abbreviated form of $(\nu u_1) \cdots (\nu u_n)\, P$. We often abbreviate $x![\tilde{v}].\, \mathbf{0}$ to $x![\tilde{v}]$.

2.2   Operational Semantics

Following the standard reduction semantics [21], we define the operational semantics by using a structural relation and a reduction relation. Unlike in the standard semantics, however, we do not require the structural relation to be a congruence relation, for the sake of technical convenience (see Remark 1 below).

Definition 2. *A structural preorder $\preceq$ is the least reflexive and transitive relation relation on processes closed under the rules in Figure 1. A reduction relation $\longrightarrow$ is the least relation closed under the rules in Figure 1.*

$$P \mid Q \preceq Q \mid P \qquad \text{(SP-Commut)} \qquad *P \preceq *P \mid P \qquad \text{(SP-Rep)}$$

$$P \mid (Q \mid R) \preceq (P \mid Q) \mid R \quad \text{(SP-Assoc)}$$

$$\frac{x \text{ is not free in } Q}{(\nu x)\,P \mid Q \preceq (\nu x)\,(P \mid Q)} \quad \text{(SP-New)}$$

$$\frac{P \preceq P' \qquad Q \preceq Q'}{P \mid Q \preceq P' \mid Q'} \quad \text{(SP-Par)}$$

$$\frac{P \preceq Q}{(\nu x)\,P \preceq (\nu x)\,Q} \quad \text{(SP-CNew)}$$

$$x![v_1, \ldots, v_n].\,P \mid x?[z_1, \ldots, z_n].\,Q \longrightarrow P \mid [v_1/z_1, \ldots, v_n/z_n]Q \quad \text{(R-Com)}$$

$$\frac{P \longrightarrow Q}{P \mid R \longrightarrow Q \mid R} \quad \text{(R-Par)}$$

$$\text{if true then } P \text{ else } Q \;\longrightarrow\; P \quad \text{(R-IfT)}$$

$$\frac{P \longrightarrow Q}{(\nu x)\,P \longrightarrow (\nu x)\,Q} \quad \text{(R-New)}$$

$$\text{if false then } P \text{ else } Q \;\longrightarrow\; Q \quad \text{(R-IfF)}$$

$$\frac{P \preceq P' \qquad P' \longrightarrow Q' \qquad Q' \preceq Q}{P \longrightarrow Q} \quad \text{(R-SP)}$$

Fig. 1. Structural Preorder and Reduction Relation

Intuitively, $P \longrightarrow Q$ means that P is reduced to Q in one step (by a communication or reduction of a conditional expression).

Remark 1. If the relation $\preceq$ were symmetric, allowing $*P \mid P \preceq *P$, then Theorem 2, one of the main theorems about the correctness of the transformation given later, would not hold.

Example 1. Let *CPoint* be the following process ("$\_$" denotes an unused bound variable):

$$
\begin{aligned}
(\nu state)\,(\nu cstate)\,(state![1,2] \mid cstate![\text{``}black\text{''}] \\
\mid *set?[x,y,c,r].\,state?[\_,\_].\,cstate?[\_].\,(state![x,y] \mid cstate![c] \mid r![]) \\
\mid *getxy?[r].\,(state?[x,y].\,(state![x,y] \mid r![x,y])) \\
\mid *getc?[r].\,(cstate?[c].\,(cstate![c] \mid r![c])))
\end{aligned}
$$

CPoint works as a colored point object that provides three kinds of services (called *methods* below) along channels *set*, *getxy*, and *getc*. The channel *state* is used to store the current coordinate, and the channel *cstate* is used to store the current color. The processes $*set?[x,y,c]. \cdots$, $*getxy?[r]. \cdots$, and $*getc?[r]. \cdots$ implement methods *set* (for updating the current state), *getxy* (for reading the current coordinate), and *getc* (for reading the current color) respectively. If *CPoint* receives a tuple of values $[x,y,c,r]$ along *set*, it invalidates the current coordinate and color (by $state?[\_,\_].\,cstate?[\_].$), sets its current coordinate and color to $[x,y]$ and c (by $state![x,y] \mid cstate![c]$), and sends a message to r to confirm that the update has completed. If *CPoint* receives a channel r along *getxy*, then it reads the current coordinate, and sends it to r.

3   Useless-Code Elimination and Program Slicing

In this section, we define the problems of UCE and program slicing.

A *context* is a term obtained by replacing a sub-process of a process with $\langle\rangle$. We write $\mathcal{C}$ for the set of all contexts. We write $C\langle P\rangle$ for the process obtained by replacing $\langle\rangle$ in C with P.

We say that a process Q is a *slice* of P, written $P \gg Q$, if Q is a process obtained by removing or replacing some sub-processes of P with $\mathbf{0}$, and replacing some values with $\star$. The formal definition is given below.

Definition 3 (slice). *A binary relation $P \gg Q$ on processes and a binary relation $v \gg_V v'$ on values are the least reflexive and transitive relations closed under the following rules:*

$$v \gg_V \star \qquad\qquad P \gg \mathbf{0} \qquad\qquad C\langle P\rangle \gg P$$

$$\frac{v \gg_V v' \qquad \forall i \in \{1,\dots,n\}.v_i \gg_V v'_i}{v![v_1,\dots,v_n].\,P \gg v'![v'_1,\dots,v'_n].\,P} \qquad \frac{v \gg_V v'}{v?[y_1,\dots,y_n].\,P \gg v'?[y_1,\dots,y_n].\,P}$$

$$\frac{v \gg_V v'}{\textbf{if } v \textbf{ then } P \textbf{ else } Q \;\gg\; \textbf{if } v' \textbf{ then } P \textbf{ else } Q}$$

$$\frac{P \gg Q}{C\langle P\rangle \gg C\langle Q\rangle}$$

The rule $P \gg \mathbf{0}$ allows elimination a sub-process, while $C\langle P\rangle \gg P$ allows elimination of a context. For example, the latter allows $x?[\,].\,y![\,]$ to be replaced by $y![\,]$.

The purpose of UCE and program slicing is to obtain slices that preserve a certain behavior of the original process. To define what behavior should be preserved, we adapt the barbed congruence [21]. The idea of the barbed congruence is to compare two processes by putting them into various contexts, and check whether they exhibit the same observational behavior. The contextual definition of the barbed congruence allows us to express slicing criteria in terms of the set of contexts in which processes are compared. We could instead use testing equivalence [17], another contextual definition of process equivalence. We have chosen the barbed congruence since it is stronger than the testing equivalence and also since the co-inductive definition of the equivalence is convenient for proving the correctness of the type-based transformation given in Section 4.

The usual definition of barbed congruence uses as observables (which are called *barbs* in the terminology of barbed congruence) information about on which channel a process may perform input or output. Since we are working on an untyped calculus, we also add a type error as an observable. We first define a predicate $P \Uparrow$, which means that a type error has occurred in P, and then define the set of barbs (observables) $Barbs(P)$.

Definition 4. *We write $P \Uparrow$ if one of the following conditions holds:*

- $P \preceq (\nu\tilde{u})\,(\textbf{if } v \textbf{ then } Q_1 \textbf{ else } Q_2 \mid R) \text{ with } v \notin \{\textbf{true}, \textbf{false}\}$
- $P \preceq (\nu\tilde{u})\,(v![\tilde{w}].\,Q \mid R) \text{ with } v \in \{\textbf{true}, \textbf{false}, \star\}$
- $P \preceq (\nu\tilde{u})\,(v?[\tilde{y}].\,Q \mid R) \text{ with } v \in \{\textbf{true}, \textbf{false}, \star\}.$
- $P \preceq (\nu\tilde{u})\,(x![v_1, \ldots, v_m].\,P \mid x?[y_1, \ldots, y_n].\,Q \mid R) \text{ with } m \neq n.$

Definition 5. *The (weak) barbs of P, written $Barbs(P)$, is defined by:*

$$Barbs(P) = \{x^! \mid P \longrightarrow^* \preceq (\nu\tilde{u})\,(x![v_1, \ldots, v_n].\,Q \mid R) \wedge x \notin \{\tilde{u}\}\}$$
$$\cup \{x^? \mid P \longrightarrow^* \preceq (\nu\tilde{u})\,(x?[y_1, \ldots, y_n].\,Q \mid R) \wedge x \notin \{\tilde{u}\}\}$$
$$\cup \{\textbf{error} \mid P \longrightarrow^* Q \wedge Q \Uparrow\}$$

Now we define process equivalence relations. Intuitively, processes P and Q are weakly barbed bisimilar if they can simulate each other. P and Q are weakly barbed congruent if they are bisimilar in any context. In the case of program slicing, we may not be interested in running processes P and Q in arbitrary contexts. We therefore introduce the notion of barbed S-congruence, which uses only contexts in S to compare two processes.

Definition 6 (barbed bisimulation, congruence). *A binary relation $\mathcal{R}$ on processes is a weak barbed bisimulation if the following conditions hold for any $(P, Q) \in \mathcal{R}$.*

1. *If $P \longrightarrow P'$, then there exists Q' such that $Q \longrightarrow^* Q'$ and $(P', Q') \in \mathcal{R}$.*
2. *If $Q \longrightarrow Q'$, then there exists P' such that $P \longrightarrow^* P'$ and $(P', Q') \in \mathcal{R}$.*
3. *$Barbs(P) = Barbs(Q)$.*

P and Q are weakly barbed bisimilar, written $P \overset{\bullet}{\approx} Q$, if $(P, Q) \in \mathcal{R}$ holds for some weak barbed bisimulation $\mathcal{R}$. Let S be a set of contexts. P and Q are weakly barbed S-congruent, written $P \approx_S Q$, if for any context $C \in S$, $C\langle P\rangle \overset{\bullet}{\approx} C\langle Q\rangle$ holds.

We can now define the criteria of UCE and program slicing.

Definition 7 (proper slice, program slicing, UCE). *Let S be a set of contexts. Q is a proper S-slice of P if $P \gg Q$ and $P \approx_S Q$. The problem of program slicing is, given a process P and a set S of contexts, to find a proper S-slice of P. The problem of useless-code elimination is, given a process P, to find a proper $\mathcal{C}$-slice of P.*

As defined above, the problem of UCE can be considered an instance of the program slicing problem. Conversely, a certain class of program slicing problems can be reduced to the problem of UCE.

- If one is interested in only the communication behavior of P on a certain set $\{\tilde{x}\}$ of channels, then one can perform program slicing by choosing the set of contexts: $\{C\langle(\nu\tilde{u})\,\langle\,\rangle\rangle \mid C \in \mathcal{C}\}$, where $\{\tilde{u}\} = \mathbf{FV}(P)\backslash\{\tilde{x}\}$. Alternatively, one can first modify a given process P into $(\nu\tilde{u})\,P$, perform UCE, and then remove the ν-prefixes $(\nu\tilde{u})$.

- If one is interested in the first argument of messages sent on x by a given process but not in the second argument, one can achieve program slicing by choosing the set of contexts: $\{C\langle(\nu x)\,(\langle\,\rangle \mid x?[y,z].\,w![y])\rangle \mid C \in \mathcal{C}\}$. Alternatively, one can first modify a given process P into $(\nu x)\,(P \mid x?[y,z].\,w![y])$, perform UCE, and then remove the context $(\nu x)\,(\langle\,\rangle \mid x?[y,z].\,w![y])$.

Some of the standard program slicing problems do not directly match the criterion given in Definition 7, but we can pre-process an input program so that those problems match our slicing criterion.

- Program slicing is often specified by a set of interesting program points, so that the behavior in those program points is preserved. Let us assume that a label is attached to each interesting program point, like $x?^l[y].\,P$. Then, before applying program slicing, we can transform $x?^l[y].\,P$ into $x?[y].\,(l![\,]\mid P)$. In this way, we can ensure that interesting program points are executed in the original program if and only if they are executed in a sliced program.
- If we want to ensure also that states are preserved at a set of interesting program points, we can pre-process a given program to replace a process of the form $x?^l[y].\,P$ with $x?[y].\,(l![\tilde{u}]\mid P)$, before performing program slicing. Here, $\{\tilde{u}\}$ is the set of live variables at l. This criterion roughly corresponds to the correctness criterion that Hatcliff et al. [9] used for slicing multi-threaded Java programs.

Example 2. Recall the process *CPoint* in Example 1. Suppose that every client is interested only in services *set* and *getxy* (in other words, no client accesses channel *getc*). Then, we let a set S of contexts be $\{C\langle(\nu getc)\,\langle\,\rangle\rangle \mid C \in \mathcal{C}\}$. The following process is a proper S-slice of *CPoint*:

$$(\nu state)\,(state![1,2]$$
$$\mid *set?[x,y,\_,r].\,state?[\_,\_].\,(state![x,y]\mid r![\,])$$
$$\mid *getxy?[r].\,(state?[x,y].\,(state![x,y]\mid r![x,y])))$$

In addition to the process $*getc?[r].\;\cdots$, communications on channel *cstate* has been removed above. How to perform this kind of optimization is discussed in the rest of this paper.

4   Type-Based Useless-Code Elimination

In this section, we present a type-based method for UCE. As discussed in Section 3, a certain class of program slicing problems can be turned into the problem of UCE, so that the method presented here can also be used for program slicing.

4.1   Basic Ideas

An idea of our type-based UCE comes from our earlier work on type-based UCE for a typed λ-calculus [11]. The aim of our UCE for the λ-calculus [11] was to replace sub-terms with the empty value $\star$, so that the value of the whole expression does not change. This can be reduced to the problem of replacing as many sub-terms as possible with $\star$ so that the resulting term has the same type as the original term. This is intuitively understood as follows: The only possibility that the evaluation result is changed by the replacement is that the replaced sub-terms are actually used during evaluation, so that the replacement of them with $\star$ introduces a run-time error. If the resulting term is well-typed, however, such a run-time error cannot happen.

The idea described above can be used in UCE for the π-calculus for replacing value expressions with $\star$. In addition, we need to address the following issues to deal with the (untyped) π-calculus:

– What is a sufficient criterion for replacing sub-processes with **0**? Unlike in the case of the λ-calculus, preservation of the well-typedness is not a sufficient condition. For example, if x is a channel that can be accessed by a context, replacing $x![\,]$ with **0** obviously changes the observable behavior.
– How to deal with untyped processes: Our previous type-based UCE for the λ-calculus [11] was for typed programs and it was only proved that the effect of the transformation cannot be observed by any *well-typed* context. As argued in Section 1, to optimize programs that are executed in open environments, one cannot assume that the environment respects typing.

For the first issue above, We distinguish between the type of processes that contain interesting communications and the type of processes that do not, and we enforce by transformation rules that if P contains interesting communications, input or output operations that guard execution of P are also considered interesting communications. For the second issue, following type systems for reasoning about security properties [1, 4, 7], we introduce a type **Un** describing untyped values, so that any process can be typed.

4.2   Types

Definition 8 (types). *The sets of* types *and* process types *are defined by:*

$$\tau \ (types) ::= \mathbf{Un} \mid \mathbf{bool} \mid [\tau_1, \ldots, \tau_n] \ \mathbf{chan} \mid \mathbf{unit}$$
$$I \ (process \ types) ::= \mathbf{N} \mid \mathbf{I}$$

Type **Un** describes untyped (or untrusted) values. For example, values provided by an unknown environment should be given this type. Type **bool** is the type of booleans, and $[\tau_1, \ldots, \tau_n]$ **chan** is the type of channels that are used for transmitting a tuple of values of types $\tau_1, \ldots, \tau_n$.

The process type **I** describes a process that is informative (may contain important communications) and **N** describes a process that is *non-informative* (contains no important communications).

Definition 9 (subtyping relation). *The subtyping relation $\tau_1 \leq \tau_2$ is the least reflexive relation satisfying the following laws:*

$$\textbf{unit} \leq \textbf{Un} \qquad\qquad \textbf{bool} \leq \textbf{Un} \qquad\qquad [\textbf{Un}, \ldots, \textbf{Un}] \textbf{ chan} \leq \textbf{Un}$$

The binary relation $I_1 \leq I_2$ on process types is the least reflexive relation satisfying the law: $\textbf{N} \leq \textbf{I}$.

A *type environment* is a mapping form a finite set of variables to types. We use meta-variables Γ and Δ to denote type environments. We write $\emptyset$ for the typing environment whose domain is empty, and write $dom(\Gamma)$ for the domain of Γ. When $x \notin dom(\Gamma)$, we write $\Gamma, x : \tau$ for the type environment obtained by extending the type environment Γ with the binding of x to τ. We abbreviate $(\cdots ((\emptyset, x_1 : \tau_1), x_2 : \tau_2), \cdots), x_n : \tau_n$ to $x_1 : \tau_1, x_2 : \tau_2, \ldots, x_n : \tau_n$.

4.3 Transformation Rules

We introduce a relation $\Gamma \vdash P : I \Longrightarrow P' \dashv \Gamma'$, which means that process P that is well-typed under Γ is transformed into process P that is well-typed under Γ'. We call Γ an *input type environment*, and Γ' an *output type environment*. For example, using the input type environment $x : [\textbf{bool}]\ \textbf{chan}$, we can transform the process $x![\textbf{true}]$ in one of the following ways.

$$x : [\textbf{bool}]\ \textbf{chan} \vdash x![\textbf{true}] : \textbf{I} \Longrightarrow x![\textbf{true}] \dashv x : [\textbf{bool}]\ \textbf{chan}$$
$$x : [\textbf{bool}]\ \textbf{chan} \vdash x![\textbf{true}] : \textbf{I} \Longrightarrow x![\star] \dashv x : [\textbf{unit}]\ \textbf{chan}$$
$$x : [\textbf{bool}]\ \textbf{chan} \vdash x![\textbf{true}] : \textbf{N} \Longrightarrow \textbf{0} \dashv x : \textbf{unit}$$

In the first transformation, x remains to be a channel for sending booleans, so that the process remains unchanged. In the second transformation, x is changed into a channel for sending an empty value, and the value $\textbf{true}$ is replaced by $\star$. In the third transformation, the output on x is judged to be unimportant, so that the type of x is replaced by $\textbf{unit}$ and the whole process is replaced by $\textbf{0}$. It depends on the output type environment which of the above transformations should be chosen.

The relation $\Gamma \vdash P : I \Longrightarrow Q \dashv \Delta$ is defined as the least relation closed under the transformation rules given in Figure 3. In the rules, we use an auxiliary relation $\Gamma \vdash v : \tau \Longrightarrow v' : \tau' \dashv \Gamma'$ given in Figure 2. It means that the value v that has type τ under Γ is transformed into the value v' that has type τ' under Γ'. When performing UCE, we are particularly interested in transformations of the form:

$$x_1 : \textbf{Un}, \cdots, x_n : \textbf{Un} \vdash P : I \Longrightarrow Q \dashv x_1 : \textbf{Un}, \cdots, x_n : \textbf{Un}.$$

Variables $x_1, \ldots, x_n$ are used as an interface with the environment. Since we cannot generally assume that the environment behaves in a well-typed manner, we transform a given process on the assumption that those variables have type $\textbf{Un}$. As is clear from the transformation rules, however, type environments other than $x_1 : \textbf{Un}, \cdots, x_n : \textbf{Un}$ may appear in intermediate steps of derivation.

We now explain transformation rules. The rules in Figure 2 are used for transformation of values. There are two kinds of rules: those whose name end with ELIM and the other rules. The former rules are used for replacing values with $\star$. The type of the resulting term is given type **unit**. The latter rules are used for preserving the value. The condition $\tau \neq$ **unit** in TRV-VAR ensures that a variable whose type is changed into **unit** does not appear in the result of transformation.

The rules in Figure 3 are used for transformation of processes. Again, there are two kinds of rules: those whose names end with ELIM and the other rules. The former class of rules are used for replacing the process with **0**, while the latter class of rules are used for preserving the outermost structure of the process. In the former class of rules (TR-OUTELIM, TR-INELIM, and TR-IFELIM), it is ensured that all the sub-processes have type **N** (so that no important process is eliminated) and that a value being accessed has an appropriate type (so that no process that may cause a run-time error is eliminated). The second condition is, for example, ensured by the condition $\Gamma(x) = [\tau_1, \ldots, \tau_n]$ **chan** in TR-OUTELIM. It ensures that x must be a communication channel.

In the latter class of rules, sub-processes are transformed using the same input and output type environments: For example, in TR-PAR, sub-processes P and Q are transformed using the same input type environment Γ and the same output type environment Γ'. This ensures that a process is transformed in a consistent manner: For example, there is no such case that x is judged to be important in one sub-process while it is judged to be unimportant and removed in another sub-process.

Note that the condition $[\tau_1, \ldots, \tau_n]$ **chan** $\leq \tau$ in TR-OUT allows τ to be type **Un** (and in this case, $\tau_1, \ldots, \tau_n$ must be **Un**). Thus, TR-OUT can be used to transform an ill-typed process like **true![false]**. In fact, we can derive $\emptyset \vdash$ **true![false]** $: \mathbf{I} \Longrightarrow$ **true![false]** $\dashv \emptyset$ from $\emptyset \vdash$ **true** $: \mathbf{Un} \Longrightarrow$ **true** $: \mathbf{Un} \dashv \emptyset$ and $\emptyset \vdash$ **false** $: \mathbf{Un} \Longrightarrow$ **false** $: \mathbf{Un} \dashv \emptyset$.

Remark 2. We did not include rules for eliminating (νx), $*$, and parallel composition, so that the output of transformation may contain redundant occurrences of those constructors. We leave elimination of such redundancy to a post-processing phase. For example, $(\nu x)\,(x![\,]\mid x?[\,].\,\mathbf{0})$ is transformed into $(\nu x)\,(\mathbf{0}\mid\mathbf{0})$. We can then clean up this code to obtain **0** in a post-processing phase.

Example 3. The process $(\nu x)\,(x![\mathbf{true},\mathbf{false}]\mid x?[z,w].\,y![z])$ can be transformed as follows.

$$y : \mathbf{Un} \vdash (\nu x)\,(x![\mathbf{true},\mathbf{false}]\mid x?[z,w].\,y![z]) : \mathbf{I} \Longrightarrow$$
$$(\nu x)\,(x![\mathbf{true},\star]\mid x?[z,w].\,y![z]) \dashv y : \mathbf{Un}$$

Example 4. Let us consider the following process:

$$y?[b,r].\,(\nu x)\,(x?[\,].\,\mathbf{0}\mid r![\,]\mid \mathbf{if}\ b\ \mathbf{then}\ x![\,]\ \mathbf{else}\ \mathbf{0}\ )$$

Let $\Gamma = y : \mathbf{Un}, b : \mathbf{Un}, r : \mathbf{Un}, x : [\,]$ **chan** and $\Delta = y : \mathbf{Un}, b : \mathbf{Un}, r : \mathbf{Un}, x : \mathbf{unit}$. Then, sub-processes are transformed as follows.

$$\Gamma \vdash x?[\,].\,\mathbf{0} : \mathbf{N} \Longrightarrow \mathbf{0} \dashv \Delta$$
$$\Gamma \vdash r![\,] : \mathbf{I} \Longrightarrow r![\,] \dashv \Delta$$
$$\Gamma \vdash \mathbf{if}\ b\ \mathbf{then}\ x![\,]\ \mathbf{else}\ \mathbf{0}\ : \mathbf{I} \Longrightarrow \mathbf{if}\ b\ \mathbf{then}\ \mathbf{0}\ \mathbf{else}\ \mathbf{0}\ \dashv \Delta$$

$$\frac{\mathbf{bool} \leq \tau \qquad b \in \{\mathbf{true}, \mathbf{false}\}}{\Gamma \vdash b : \tau \Longrightarrow b : \tau \dashv \Gamma'} \qquad (\text{TrV-Bool})$$

$$\frac{\mathbf{bool} \leq \tau \qquad b \in \{\mathbf{true}, \mathbf{false}\}}{\Gamma \vdash b : \tau \Longrightarrow \star : \mathbf{unit} \dashv \Gamma'} \qquad (\text{TrV-BoolElim})$$

$$\frac{\mathbf{unit} \leq \tau' \leq \tau}{\Gamma \vdash \star : \tau \Longrightarrow \star : \tau' \dashv \Gamma'} \qquad (\text{TrV-Unit})$$

$$\frac{\tau \neq \mathbf{unit}}{\Gamma, x : \tau \vdash x : \tau \Longrightarrow x : \tau' \dashv \Gamma', x : \tau'} \qquad (\text{TrV-Var})$$

$$\frac{\Gamma(x) = \tau}{\Gamma \vdash x : \tau \Longrightarrow \star : \mathbf{unit} \dashv \Gamma'} \qquad (\text{TrV-VarElim})$$

Fig. 2. Transformation Rules for Values

Using TR-PAR, TR-NEW, and TR-IN, we obtain:

$$y : \mathbf{Un} \vdash y?[b, r]. (\nu x) (x?[]. \mathbf{0} \mid r![] \mid \mathbf{if} \ b \ \mathbf{then} \ x![] \ \mathbf{else} \ \mathbf{0} \ ) : \mathbf{I} \Longrightarrow$$
$$y?[b, r]. (\nu x) (\mathbf{0} \mid r![] \mid \mathbf{if} \ b \ \mathbf{then} \ \mathbf{0} \ \mathbf{else} \ \mathbf{0} \ ) \dashv y : \mathbf{Un}$$

Note that **if** b **then** $x![]$ **else** $\mathbf{0}$ cannot be replaced by $\mathbf{0}$: Since y has type $\mathbf{Un}$, a non-boolean value may be assigned to b, so that replacing **if** b **then** $x![]$ **else** $\mathbf{0}$ with $\mathbf{0}$ changes the observable behavior. If it is guaranteed that y is used according to type $[\mathbf{bool}, [] \ \mathbf{chan}] \ \mathbf{chan}$ by the environment, then the if-expression can be removed as follows:

$$y : [\mathbf{bool}, [] \ \mathbf{chan}] \ \mathbf{chan} \vdash y?[b, r]. (\nu x) (x?[]. \mathbf{0} \mid r![] \mid \mathbf{if} \ b \ \mathbf{then} \ x![] \ \mathbf{else} \ \mathbf{0} \ ) : \mathbf{I}$$
$$\Longrightarrow y?[b, r]. (\nu x) (\mathbf{0} \mid r![] \mid \mathbf{0}) \dashv y : [\mathbf{bool}, [] \ \mathbf{chan}] \ \mathbf{chan}$$

Example 5. Let us consider the following, simplified version of *CPoint* in Example 1.

$$(\nu state) (\nu cstate) (state![1, 2] \mid cstate![\text{``black''}]$$
$$\mid *set?[x, y, c]. (state?[\_, \_]. state![x, y] \mid cstate?[c']. cstate![c])$$
$$\mid *getxy?[r]. (state?[x, y]. (state![x, y] \mid r![x, y]))$$
$$\mid *getc?[r]. (cstate?[c]. (cstate![c] \mid r![c])))$$

Here, we have omitted a reply of the method *set*: How to deal with the original version of *CPoint* is discussed in Section 5.

The above process is transformed into:

$$(\nu state) (\nu cstate) (state![1, 2] \mid \mathbf{0}$$
$$\mid *set?[x, y, \_]. (state?[x', y']. state![x, y] \mid \mathbf{0})$$
$$\mid *getxy?[r]. (state?[x, y]. (state![x, y] \mid r![x, y])) \mid \mathbf{0})$$

under the input type environment *set* : $\mathbf{Un}$, *getxy* : $\mathbf{Un}$, *getc* : $[[] \ \mathbf{chan}] \ \mathbf{chan}$ and the output type environment *set* : $\mathbf{Un}$, *getxy* : $\mathbf{Un}$, *getc* : $\mathbf{unit}$. If every client is

$$\Gamma \vdash \mathbf{0} : I \Longrightarrow \mathbf{0} \dashv \Gamma' \qquad \text{(Tr-Zero)}$$

$$\frac{\Gamma \vdash P : I_1 \Longrightarrow P' \dashv \Gamma' \qquad \Gamma \vdash Q : I_2 \Longrightarrow Q' \dashv \Gamma' \qquad I_1, I_2 \leq I}{\Gamma \vdash P \mid Q : I \Longrightarrow P' \mid Q' \dashv \Gamma'} \quad \text{(Tr-Par)}$$

$$\frac{\begin{array}{c} \Gamma \vdash P : I \Longrightarrow P' \dashv \Gamma' \qquad \Gamma \vdash v : \tau \Longrightarrow v' : \tau' \dashv \Gamma' \\ [\tau_1, \ldots, \tau_n]\ \mathbf{chan} \leq \tau \qquad [\tau_1', \ldots, \tau_n']\ \mathbf{chan} \leq \tau' \\ \Gamma \vdash v_i : \tau_i \Longrightarrow v_i' : \tau_i' \dashv \Gamma' \ (\text{for each } i \in \{1, \ldots, n\}) \end{array}}{\Gamma \vdash v![v_1, \ldots, v_n].\, P : \mathbf{I} \Longrightarrow v'![v_1', \ldots, v_n'].\, P' \dashv \Gamma'} \quad \text{(Tr-Out)}$$

$$\frac{\begin{array}{c} \Gamma \vdash P : \mathbf{N} \Longrightarrow P' \dashv \Gamma' \\ \Gamma(x) = [\tau_1, \ldots, \tau_n]\ \mathbf{chan} \qquad \Gamma'(x) = \mathbf{unit} \\ \Gamma \vdash v_i : \tau_i \Longrightarrow \star : \mathbf{unit} \dashv \Gamma' \ (\text{for each } i \in \{1, \ldots, n\}) \end{array}}{\Gamma \vdash x![v_1, \ldots, v_n].\, P : \mathbf{N} \Longrightarrow \mathbf{0} \dashv \Gamma'} \quad \text{(Tr-OutElim)}$$

$$\frac{\begin{array}{c} \Gamma, y_1 : \tau_1, \ldots, y_n : \tau_n \vdash P : I \Longrightarrow P' \dashv \Gamma', y_1 : \tau_1', \ldots, y_n : \tau_n' \\ \Gamma \vdash v : \tau \Longrightarrow v' : \tau' \dashv \Gamma' \\ [\tau_1, \ldots, \tau_n]\ \mathbf{chan} \leq \tau \qquad [\tau_1', \ldots, \tau_n']\ \mathbf{chan} \leq \tau' \end{array}}{\Gamma \vdash v?[y_1, \ldots, y_n].\, P : \mathbf{I} \Longrightarrow v'?[y_1, \ldots, y_n].\, P' \dashv \Gamma'} \quad \text{(Tr-In)}$$

$$\frac{\begin{array}{c} \Gamma, y_1 : \tau_1, \ldots, y_n : \tau_n \vdash P : \mathbf{N} \Longrightarrow P' \dashv \Gamma', y_1 : \mathbf{unit}, \ldots, y_n : \mathbf{unit} \\ \Gamma(x) = [\tau_1, \ldots, \tau_n]\ \mathbf{chan} \qquad \Gamma'(x) = \mathbf{unit} \end{array}}{\Gamma \vdash x?[y_1, \ldots, y_n].\, P : \mathbf{N} \Longrightarrow \mathbf{0} \dashv \Gamma'} \quad \text{(Tr-InElim)}$$

$$\frac{\begin{array}{c} \Gamma, x : \tau \vdash P : I \Longrightarrow P' \dashv \Gamma', x : \tau' \\ [\tau_1, \ldots, \tau_n]\ \mathbf{chan} \leq \tau \end{array}}{\Gamma \vdash (\nu x)\, P : I \Longrightarrow (\nu x)\, P' \dashv \Gamma'} \quad \text{(Tr-New)}$$

$$\frac{\Gamma \vdash P : I \Longrightarrow P' \dashv \Gamma'}{\Gamma \vdash *P : I \Longrightarrow *P' \dashv \Gamma'} \quad \text{(Tr-Rep)}$$

$$\frac{\begin{array}{c} \Gamma \vdash v : \tau \Longrightarrow v' : \tau' \dashv \Gamma' \qquad \mathbf{bool} \leq \tau, \tau' \\ \Gamma \vdash P : I_1 \Longrightarrow P' \dashv \Gamma' \qquad \Gamma \vdash Q : I_2 \Longrightarrow Q' \dashv \Gamma' \end{array}}{\Gamma \vdash \mathbf{if}\ v\ \mathbf{then}\ P\ \mathbf{else}\ Q : \mathbf{I} \Longrightarrow \mathbf{if}\ v'\ \mathbf{then}\ P'\ \mathbf{else}\ Q' \dashv \Gamma'} \quad \text{(Tr-If)}$$

$$\frac{\begin{array}{c} \Gamma \vdash v : \mathbf{bool} \Longrightarrow v' : \tau' \dashv \Gamma' \\ \Gamma \vdash P : \mathbf{N} \Longrightarrow P' \dashv \Gamma' \qquad \Gamma \vdash Q : \mathbf{N} \Longrightarrow Q' \dashv \Gamma' \end{array}}{\Gamma \vdash \mathbf{if}\ v\ \mathbf{then}\ P\ \mathbf{else}\ Q : \mathbf{N} \Longrightarrow \mathbf{0} \dashv \Gamma'} \quad \text{(Tr-IfElim)}$$

Fig. 3. Transformation Rules for Processes

interested only in the first component of the return value of the *getxy* method, the above process can be further transformed into

$$\begin{aligned} &(\nu state)\, (\nu cstate)\, (state![1, \star] \mid \mathbf{0} \\ &\quad \mid *set?[x, \_, \_].\, (state?[x', \_].\, state![x, \star] \mid \mathbf{0}) \\ &\quad \mid *getxy?[r].\, (state?[x, \_].\, (state![x, \star] \mid r![x, \star])) \\ &\quad \mid \mathbf{0}) \end{aligned}$$

by using the input type environment *set* : **Un**, *getxy* : [[**Un**, **int**] **chan**] **chan**, *getc* : [[] **chan**] **chan** and the output type environment:
set : **Un**, *getxy* : [[**Un**, **unit**] **chan**] **chan**, *getc* : [[] **chan**] **chan**.

4.4   Soundness of Transformation

The soundness of our type-based transformation is stated as follows.

Theorem 1. *Suppose that $\Gamma(x) = \mathbf{Un}$ for every $x \in dom(\Gamma)$. If $\Gamma \vdash P : I \Longrightarrow Q \dashv \Gamma$, then Q is a proper C-slice of P.*

We give a proof sketch below. A full proof is given in the full version of this paper. We first introduce a relation $P \equiv_0 Q$, which means intuitively that P and Q are equal except for garbage processes $\mathbf{0}$.

Definition 10. *A binary relation $\equiv_0$ on processes is the least congruence relation that satisfies the following rules:*

$$P \mid \mathbf{0} \equiv_0 P \qquad\qquad *\mathbf{0} \equiv_0 \mathbf{0} \qquad\qquad (\nu x)\,\mathbf{0} \equiv_0 \mathbf{0} \qquad\qquad \frac{P \preceq Q}{P \equiv_0 Q}$$

The following theorem, which corresponds to the subject reduction property of the usual type system, states that the transformation relation is preserved by reduction.

Theorem 2.

1. *If $\Gamma \vdash P : I \Longrightarrow Q \dashv \Delta$ and $P \longrightarrow P'$, then there exists Q' such that (i) $Q \equiv_0 Q'$ or $Q \longrightarrow Q'$, and (ii) $\Gamma \vdash P' : I' \Longrightarrow Q' \dashv \Delta$ with $I' \leq I$.*
2. *If $\Gamma \vdash P : I \Longrightarrow Q \dashv \Delta$ and $Q \longrightarrow Q'$, then there exists P' such that $P \longrightarrow P'$ and $\Gamma \vdash P' : I' \Longrightarrow Q' \dashv \Delta$ with $I' \leq I$.*

Definition 11. *The strong barbs of P, written $SBarbs(P)$, is defined by:*

$$SBarbs(P) = \{x^! \mid P \equiv (\nu\tilde{u})\,(x![v_1,\ldots,v_n].\,Q \mid R) \wedge x \notin \{\tilde{u}\}\}$$
$$\cup \{x^? \mid P \equiv (\nu\tilde{u})\,(x?[y_1,\ldots,y_n].\,Q \mid R) \wedge x \notin \{\tilde{u}\}\}$$
$$\cup \{\mathbf{error} \mid P \Uparrow\}$$

Theorem 3 (transformation preserves barbs). *If $\Gamma \vdash P : I \Longrightarrow Q \dashv \Delta$ and $\Gamma(x) = \mathbf{Un}$ for every $x \in dom(\Gamma)$, then $SBarbs(P) = SBarbs(Q)$.*

Theorems 2 and 3 imply that our transformation preserves the weak barbed bisimilarity.

Theorem 4. *Suppose that $\Gamma(x) = \mathbf{Un}$ for every $x \in dom(\Gamma)$. If $\Gamma \vdash P : I \Longrightarrow Q \dashv \Gamma$, then $P \overset{\bullet}{\approx} Q$.*

Lemma 1. *Suppose that $\Gamma(x) = \mathbf{Un}$ for every $x \in dom(\Gamma)$. If $\Gamma \vdash P : I \Longrightarrow Q \dashv \Gamma$ and C is a context, then $\Delta \vdash C\langle P \rangle : \mathbf{I} \Longrightarrow C\langle Q \rangle \dashv \Delta$ holds for Δ such that $\Delta(x) = \mathbf{Un}$ for every $x \in dom(\Delta)$.*

Theorem 4 and Lemma 1 imply the soundness of the transformation rules.

Proof of Theorem 1. Suppose that $\Gamma \vdash P$ and $\Gamma \vdash P : I \Longrightarrow Q \dashv \Gamma$ hold. $P \gg Q$ is trivial by the transformation rules. To show $P \approx_C Q$, it is sufficient to show that $C\langle P \rangle \overset{\bullet}{\approx} C\langle Q \rangle$ holds for any context C. By Lemma 1, $\Delta \vdash C\langle P \rangle : \mathbf{I} \Longrightarrow C\langle Q \rangle \dashv \Delta$ holds for Δ such that $\Delta(x) = \mathbf{Un}$ for every $x \in dom(\Delta)$. So, $C\langle P \rangle \overset{\bullet}{\approx} C\langle Q \rangle$ follows from Theorem 4. $\square$

4.5   How to Find Valid Transformations

Theorem 1 implies that we can perform UCE for a process P by finding Q such that $x_1 : \mathbf{Un}, \ldots, x_n : \mathbf{Un} \vdash P : I \Longrightarrow Q \dashv x_1 : \mathbf{Un}, \ldots, x_n : \mathbf{Un}$ holds. This can be carried out by performing type reconstruction in a demand-driven manner, in the same way as the type-based UCE for the λ-calculus [11]. For example, since TR-OUTELIM is preferred to TR-OUT, the type constraints required by TR-OUT are added only when it turns out to be impossible to apply TR-OUTELIM. We conjecture that a valid transformation can be obtained in time linear in the size of a given process as is the case for the type-based UCE for the λ-calculus [11].

5   Discussion

5.1   Extension of the Transformation Method

Using the type-based transformation described in Section 4 alone is actually insufficient in many cases, so that we need to combine it with other transformations. For example, consider the process $(\nu x)\, (x![\,]\, |\, x?[\,].\, y![\,])$. Although $y![\,]$ is a proper $\mathcal{C}$-slice, $y : \mathbf{Un} \vdash (\nu x)\, (x![\,]\, |\, x?[\,].\, y![\,]) : I \Longrightarrow y![\,] \dashv y : \mathbf{Un}$ does not hold: Rule TR-INELIM allows elimination of the input on x in $x?[\tilde{y}].\, P$ only when its continuation part P has type $\mathbf{N}$, so that we cannot replace $x?[\,].\, y![\,]$ with $y![\,]$. For the same reason, communications on channel $cstate$ in Example 1 cannot be eliminated by our type-based transformation, since in the method set, the continuation of the input on $cstate$ contains an important communication $r![\,]$. (In Example 5, we have omitted the communication on r, so that communications on $cstate$ could be eliminated.)

   The above problem can be solved by using type systems that can guarantee lock-freedom [12, 20]. For example, our type system for lock-freedom [12] can guarantee that for certain input or output processes, there are always corresponding output or input processes. If $x?[\,].\, (P\, |\, Q)$ is such a process (more precisely, if the input is annotated with the time limit 0 [12]) and if all the outputs on x are asynchronous (in the sense that the continuation part is $\mathbf{0}$), then $x?[\,].\, (P\, |\, Q)$ is equivalent to $(x?[\,].\, P)\, |\, Q$. Using this fact, the above process can be first replaced with $(\nu x)\, (x![\,]\, |\, x?[\,].\, \mathbf{0}\, |\, y![\,])$, and then it is replaced with $(\nu x)\, (\mathbf{0}\, |\, \mathbf{0}\, |\, y![\,])$ by the transformation in Section 4. In a similar manner, we can eliminate communications on $cstate$ from $CPoint$: See Appendix A.

5.2   Limitation of the Slicing Criteria

We think that our slicing criteria given in Section 3 (combined with some pre-processing) cover a wide range of program slicing problems, but they are by no means universal. For example, they are not sufficient for the purpose of finding the cause of a deadlock. Consider the deadlocked process: $(\nu x)\, (\nu y)\, (x?[\,].\, (P\, |\, y![\,])\, |\, y?[\,].\, (Q\, |\, x![\,]))$. If one wants to find the cause of the deadlock by looking at a slice of the process, $(\nu x)\, (\nu y)\, (x?[\,].\, y![\,]\, |\, y?[\,].\, x![\,])$

would be an ideal slice. According to the slicing criterion in Section 3, however, **0**, which is not useful for finding the cause of the deadlock, is also a proper slice. It is left for future work to find an appropriate criterion for this kind of program slicing. (Fortunately, our type-based transformation given in Section 3 does NOT transform $(\nu x)\,(\nu y)\,(x?[\,].\,(P\,|\,y![\,])\,|\,y?[\,].\,(Q\,|\,x![\,]))$ into **0**, but it is a coincidence, coming from the limitation of our type-based transformation.)

6   Related Work

There are recently several pierces of work on program slicing for concurrent programs [5, 9, 14, 24]. They use either a specific programming language (Java) or more restrictive thread models than the π-calculus. They describe slicing algorithms in a procedural manner, as opposed to our declarative specification using type-based transformation rules. As for the quality of sliced programs, our type-based method can eliminate less code than those based on flow graphs [5, 9], since our method does not take into account the direction of data flow. We can overcome the problem by using subtyping as in type-based UCE for functional languages [3, 6]. Hatcliff et al. [9] gave a formal correctness criterion of program slicing for multi-threaded Java programs, by using a variant of bisimulation. As mentioned in Section 3, we think that this criterion can be considered an instance of our general slicing criterion (modulo preprocessing).

Our type-based method for UCE is related with three lines of research. First, the idea of using types for eliminating useless expressions has its origin in type-based UCE for functional programs [3, 6, 11]. The main differences are that in the present work, we deal with concurrency primitives and untyped programs. Secondly, the idea of introducing a special type **Un** to deal with untrusted values has been used in type systems for reasoning about security properties [1, 4, 7]. Thirdly, our method is also related with type-based information flow analysis for the π-calculus [10, 18], since UCE, program slicing, and information flow analysis can all be considered instances of the dependency analysis [2]. In fact, UCE can be used for information flow analysis and vice versa: We can verify that information about some secret data is not leaked by a process P, by performing UCE on P and checking that the secret data are removed by UCE. Conversely, we can check that a certain term in a process P is unnecessary, by marking it as secret data and performing information flow analysis to check that information about the marked data is not leaked by P. An important difference between the present work and the type-based information flow analyses for the π-calculus is that the previous work on type-based information flow analyses restrict the environment of a process to well-typed environments, while we do not impose such restriction. Our type-based UCE described in Section 4 is not powerful enough to perform as accurate information flow analysis as Honda and Yoshida's type system [10], but with the extension sketched in Section 5, the accuracy of our analysis seems to become comparable to that of Honda and Yoshida's type system. Unlike Honda and Yoshida's type system, the extended analysis can be performed automatically without programmers' annotation [13].

7 Conclusion

We gave a formal definition of the problems of useless-code elimination and program slicing for the π-calculus and presented a type-based method that is applicable to untyped programs. We hope that this work serves as a basis for further formal studies of UCE and program slicing for concurrent programs.

Acknowledgment. We thank Atsushi Shiro for discussions on the subject, and Reynald Affeldt, Haruo Hosoya, and Atsushi Igarashi for comments on a draft of this paper.

References

1. M. Abadi. Secrecy by typing in security protocols. *Journal of the Association for Computing Machinery (JACM)*, 46(5):749–786, 1999.
2. M. Abadi, A. Banerjee, N. Heintze, and J. G. Rieck. A core calculus of dependency. In *Proceedings of ACM SIGPLAN/SIGACT Symposium on Principles of Programming Languages*, pages 147–169, 1999.
3. S. Berardi, M. Coppo, F. Damiani, and P. Giannini. Type-based useless-code elimination for functional programs. In *Proceedings of SAIG 2000*, volume 1924 of *Lecture Notes in Computer Science*, pages 172–189. Springer-Verlag, 2000.
4. L. Cardelli, G. Ghelli, and A. D. Gordon. Secrecy and group creation. In *Proceedings of CONCUR 2000*, volume 1877 of *Lecture Notes in Computer Science*, pages 365–379. Springer-Verlag, 2000.
5. J. Cheng. Slicing concurrent programs - a graph-theoretical approach. In *Automated and Algorithmic Debugging*, volume 749 of *Lecture Notes in Computer Science*, pages 223–240. Springer-Verlag, 1993.
6. F. Damiani. Useless-code detection and elimination for pcf with algebraic data types. In *Proceedings of TLCA'99*, volume 1581 of *Lecture Notes in Computer Science*, pages 83–97. Springer-Verlag, 1999.
7. A. D. Gordon and A. Jeffrey. Authenticity by typing for security protocols. In *Proceedings of the 14th IEEE Computer Security Foundations Workshop (CSFW 2001)*, pages 145–159. IEEE Computer Society Press, 2001.
8. M. Harman and R. M. Hierons. An overview of program slicing. *Software Focus*, 2(3):85–92, 2001.
9. J. Hatcliff, J. Corbett, M. Dwyer, S. Sokolowski, and H. Zheng. A formal stufy of slicing for multi-threaded programs with jvm concurrency primitives. In *Proceedings of SAS'99*, volume 1694 of *Lecture Notes in Computer Science*, pages 1–18. Springer-Verlag, 1999.
10. K. Honda and N. Yoshida. A uniform type structure for secure information flow. In *Proceedings of ACM SIGPLAN/SIGACT Symposium on Principles of Programming Languages*, pages 81–92, 2002.
11. N. Kobayashi. Type-based useless variable elimination. *Higher-Order and Symbolic Computation*, 14(2-3):221–260, 2001.
12. N. Kobayashi. A type system for lock-free processes. *Information and Computation*, 177:122–159, 2002.
13. N. Kobayashi. Type-based information flow analysis for the pi-calculus. submitted, 2003.

14. J. Krinke. Static slicing of threaded programs. In *Proc. ACM SIG-PLAN/SIGFSOFT Workshop on Program Analysis for Software Tools and Engineering (PASTE'98)*, pages 35–42, Montreal, Canada, June 1998. ACM SIGPLAN Notices 33(7).

15. R. Milner. *Communicating and Mobile Systems: the Pi-Calculus*. Cambridge University Press, 1999.

16. R. Milner, M. Tofte, R. Harper, and D. MacQueen. *The Definition of Standard ML (Revised)*. The MIT Press, 1997.

17. R. D. Nicola and M. C. B. Hennessy. Testing equivalence for processes. *Theoretical Computer Science*, 34:83–133, 1984.

18. F. Pottier. A simple view of type-secure information flow in the π-calculus. In *Proceedings of the 15th IEEE Computer Security Foundations Workshop*, pages 320–330, 2002.

19. T. Reps and T. Turnidge. Program specialization via program slicing. In *Proceedings of the Dagstuhl Seminar on Partial Evaluation*, volume 1110 of *Lecture Notes in Computer Science*, pages 409–429, 1996.

20. D. Sangiorgi. The name discipline of uniform receptiveness. *Theoretical Computer Science*, 221(1-2):457–493, 1999.

21. D. Sangiorgi and D. Walker. *The Pi-Calculus: A Theory of Mobile Processes*. Cambridge University Press, 2001.

22. F. Tip. A survey of program slicing techniques. *Journal of Programming Languages*, 3:121–181, 1995.

23. M. Wand and I. Siveroni. Constraint systems for useless variable elimination. In *Proceedings of ACM SIGPLAN/SIGACT Symposium on Principles of Programming Languages*, pages 291–302, 1999.

24. J. Zhao. Slicing concurrent Java programs. In *Proceedings of the 7th IEEE International Workshop on Program Comprehension*, pages 126–133, May 1999.

Appendix

A   Program Slicing for *CPoint* in Example 1

In this appendix, we show how to achieve program slicing for *CPoint* in Example 1, by using the transformation in Section 4 and the extension sketched in Section 5.

Suppose that every client is interested only in services *set* and *getxy*. Then, program slicing is achieved by performing UCE for $(\nu getc)\, CPoint$. By using the transformation in Section 4, $(\nu getc)\, CPoint$ is transformed into the following process (let *set* : **Un**, *getxy* : **Un** be the input and output type environment):

$$(\nu getc)\,(\nu state)\,(\nu cstate)\,(state![1,2] \mid cstate![\star]$$
$$\mid *set?[x,y,c,r].\,state?[\_,\_].\,cstate?[\_].\,(state![x,y] \mid cstate![\star] \mid r![\,])$$
$$\mid *getxy?[r].\,(state?[x,y].\,(state![x,y] \mid r![x,y]))$$
$$\mid *getc?[\_].\,(cstate?[\_].\,(cstate![\star] \mid \mathbf{0})))$$

The argument of channel *cstate* has been removed (replaced by $\star$) and a reply on channel *getc* has been removed, but communications on *cstate* have not been removed yet.

Now, as mentioned in Section 5, using the type system for lock-freedom [12], we can replace the above process with the following process:

$$(\nu getc)\,(\nu state)\,(\nu cstate)\,(state![1,2] \mid cstate![\star]$$
$$\mid *set?[x,y,\_,r].\,state?[\_,\_].\,(cstate?[\_].\,cstate![\star] \mid state![x,y] \mid r![\,])$$
$$\mid *getxy?[r].\,(state?[x,y].\,(state![x,y] \mid r![x,y]))$$
$$\mid *getc?[\_].\,(cstate?[\_].\,(state![\star] \mid \mathbf{0})))$$

Here, the sub-process $cstate?[\_].\,(state![x,y] \mid cstate![\star] \mid r![\,])$ has been replaced with $(cstate?[\_].\,cstate![\star]) \mid state![x,y] \mid r![\,]$, so that the dependency between communications on $cstate$ and r is removed.

Now, by applying the transformation in Section 4 again, we obtain the following optimized program:

$$(\nu getc)\,(\nu state)\,(\nu cstate)\,(state![1,2] \mid \mathbf{0}$$
$$\mid *set?[x,y,\_,r].\,state?[\_,\_].\,(\mathbf{0} \mid state![x,y] \mid r![\,])$$
$$\mid *getxy?[r].\,(state?[x,y].\,(state![x,y] \mid r![x,y]))$$
$$\mid \mathbf{0})$$

This is identical to the sliced program given in Example 2 modulo garbage processes $\mathbf{0}$ and ν-prefixes.

Constraint Functional Logic Programming for Origami Construction

Tetsuo Ida[1], Mircea Marin[2]*, and Hidekazu Takahashi[3]

[1] Institute of Information Sciences and Electronics
University of Tsukuba, Tsukuba, Japan
Tetsuo.Ida@acm.org
[2] Johann Radon Institute for Computational and Applied Mathematics
Johannes Kepler University, Linz, Austria
mircea.marin@oeaw.ac.at
[3] Kawase High School, Hikone, Shiga, Japan
hidezaku@pop.biwako.ne.jp

Abstract. We describe origami programming methodology based on constraint functional logic programming. The basic operations of origami are reduced to solving systems of equations which describe the geometric properties of paper folds. We developed two software components: one that provides primitives to construct, manipulate and visualize paper folds and the other that solves the systems of equations. Using these components, we illustrate computer-supported origami construction and show the significance of the constraint functional logic programming paradigm in the program development.

1 Introduction

Origami is a Japanese traditional art of paper folding. Recently, origami received wide range of interest among mathematicians, math educators and computer scientists, as well as origami artists, as origami proves helpful in understanding essence of fundamental geometrical problem solving. To computer scientists and mathematicians the interest lies largely in the integration of various modes of computing during the origami construction.

The purpose of this paper is twofold: to show origami construction as an application of constraint functional logic programming, and to show the effectiveness of origami construction in the math and computer science education. To show the former is the main objective, and to attain this we will use a constraint functional logic programming system called Open CFLP [1,2] and an origami construction environment [3]. The illustrative examples will serve as the concrete examples of pedagogical effectiveness of this approach.

In our scheme, computer origamists can perform an origami construction by invoking paper folding functions with parameters that determine the kind of the paper fold. Moreover, the final result, as well as the results of the intermediary

---

* Supported by the Austrian Academy of Sciences.

A. Ohori (Ed.): APLAS 2003, LNCS 2895, pp. 73–88, 2003.

steps, of these operations can be visualized and manipulated. The process of the computer origami construction is driven by the computation of constraint solving, where the constraints are on geometrical objects in Euclidean space. The constraints are internally represented as equations. It is, therefore, a challenging theme to study origami construction as an application of constraint functional logic programming, which is a programming paradigm of, in essence, solving equations over various domains. In particular, we will explore the capabilities of Open CFLP that can solve equations over specified domains, such as the domains of terms, of polynomials, and of reals.

In origami construction, the problem specifications are clear and explicit, as we will see later. The specifications are then reduced to those for solving equations with respect to a theory provided as a set of conditional rewrite rules. Writing a theory is the task of programmers, and computer origamists will focus on finding appropriate folds.

In the sequel we will show how the origami construction can be programmed. Section 2 introduces the basics of origami geometry and of constraint functional logic programming. We will fully develop the origami construction in constraint functional logic programming in the following sections with instructive examples. In section 6 we draw some conclusions and directions of further research.

2   Preliminaries

In this section we summarize basic notions and notations that are necessary for understanding the principles of our computer origami construction. We give the representation of point, line, plane, (line) segment and polygon in the following, assuming that those notions are understood.

We rely on the notation of *Mathematica* [12] to describe our program constructs since the systems we will be using are written in *Mathematica*. Notably, we deviate from the common notation of mathematics in that functions are represented as $f[a_1, \ldots, a_n]$ rather than $f(a_1, \ldots, a_n)$. In *Mathematica* when $f[a_1, \ldots, a_n]$ can not be reduced further, the value of $f[a_1, \ldots, a_n]$ is itself. This property is taken advantage of to define a new structure. Namely, when f is not defined to be a function, f is regarded as a constructor symbol. In this case, $f[a_1, \ldots, a_n]$ is interpreted as a structure whose name is f and which contains the values of $a_1, \ldots, a_n$.

Origami. The word *origami* is a combined word coming from *ori* (fold) and *kami* (paper). Traditionally, we use origami to mean sometimes a folding paper, act of paper folding or art of origami. As such, we also use the word origami in a flexible way depending on the context.

An origami is constructed in a stepwise manner, where in each construction a fold is made along a line. An origami at its i-th construction step is represented by a structure Origami[$i, planes, order$], where *planes* is a list of plane structures (see below) and *order* is the overlay relation between the planes that constitute the origami. Origamis are indexed by asserting $\mathtt{Origami}[i] = \mathtt{Origami}[i, planes, order]$ for quick access[1].

Plane. A plane is represented by a structure $\mathtt{Plane}[id, poly, nbrs, mpoints]$, where id is an integer identifying the plane, $poly = \mathtt{Polygon}[\{P_1, \dots, P_k\}]$ represents a polygon made of vertices $P_1, \dots, P_k$, $nbrs$ is a list of neighboring planes $\{o_1, \dots, o_k\}$, where o_j is the id of the plane that is adjacent to the edge $\overline{P_j P_{j+1}}$ (we let $P_{k+1} = P_1$), and $mpoints$ is a list of mark points (see below for the definition).

Polygon. Given a sequence of vertices $P_1, \dots, P_k$, ordered counter-clockwise, a polygon is represented by a structure $\mathtt{Polygon}[\{P_1, \dots, P_k\}]$.

Point and Mark Point. A point, whose x-, y- and z- coordinates are u, v and w respectively, is represented by a structure $\mathtt{Point}[u, v, w]$. The z- coordinate is omitted when we are working only in 2D on the plane $z = 0$. Internally, however, all points are represented in 3D. The translation from 2D to 3D is done automatically by the system. A mark point is a structure used to refer to a designated point on planes at some steps of the origami construction. It is represented by a pair of a point name and a point. For example, $\{\text{"M"}, \mathtt{Point}[1, 2]\}$. For short, we call this mark point "M".

Line and Segment. A segment $\overline{PQ}$ between points P and Q is represented by $\mathtt{Segment}[P, Q]$. A line $a\,x + b\,y + c = 0$ on the plane $z = 0$ is represented by $\mathtt{Line}[a, b, c]$. A line is said to extend the segment $\overline{PQ}$ if it passes through the points P and Q.

Constraint Functional Logic Program. A constraint functional logic program consists of a goal and a theory. The latter is given by a set of conditional rewrite rules of the form $f[args] \rightarrow r$ or $f[args] \rightarrow r \Leftarrow C$ where C is a list of boolean expressions which denotes their logical conjunction. The boolean expressions are equations over some domains. Note that any boolean expression can be turned to an equation by equating the expression to boolean value True, if necessary. $f[args]$ and r are called the left-hand and right-hand side of the rewrite rule, respectively. C is called the conditional part of the rewrite rule. Extra variables (*i.e.*, variables without occurrences on the left-hand side of the rewrite rule) are allowed in the conditional part, where they are supposed to be existentially quantified. A rewrite rule $f[args] \rightarrow r \Leftarrow C$ partially defines function f. It is used to reduce an instance $f[args]\theta$ to $r\theta$ if $C\theta$ holds, where θ is an arbitrary substitution. A function symbol which appears at the outermost position of the left-hand side of a rewrite rule is called *defined symbol*. The other function symbols are either *constructors* or *constraint operators*.

---

[1] Note that indexing this way is the feature of *Mathematica*.

Equations are expressions of the form $s \approx t$ or $s \triangleright t$. Their meaning is: $s \approx t$ if s and t are reduced to the value, and $s \triangleright t$ if s is reduced to t.

A goal is a list of boolean expressions. Solving a goal G with respect to a theory T is a computation of the constraint functional logic program. It yields a substitution θ such that $G\theta$ holds in the theory T. Logically speaking, solving a goal is proving an existential formula $\exists x_1...x_m.\,G$, where our concern is not only about the validity of $\exists x_1...x_m.\,G$, but about the substitutions θ over $x_1, ..., x_m$ that make $G\theta$ True.

3   Principles of Origami Construction

An origami is folded along a line called *crease*. The crease can be determined by the points it passes through or by the points (and/or lines) it brings together. The fold determined in the former is called *through* action (abbreviated to Th), and the latter *bring* action (abbreviated to Br). We can combine the two actions, and we have the following six basic fold operations formally stated as Origami Axioms [4,5] of Huzita. It is shown that by the six basic operations commanded by Origami Axioms we can construct 2D geometrical objects that can be constructed by a ruler and a compass. Actually, origami is more powerful than the ruler and compass method since origami can construct objects that are not possible by the ruler and compass method [6]. One of them is trisecting an angle, which we will show later.

3.1   Origami Axioms

The origami axioms consist of the following assertions. The action involved in each axiom is indicated by the words within the square brackets.

(O1) [Th] Given two points, we can make a fold along the crease passing through them.

(O2) [Br] Given two points, we can make a fold to bring one of the points onto the other.

(O3) [Br] Given two lines, we can make a fold to bring one of the lines onto the other.

(O4) [Th] Given a point P and a line m, we can make a fold along the crease that is perpendicular to m and passes through P.

(O5) [BrTh] Given two points P and Q and a line m, we can make a fold along the crease that passes through Q, such that the fold brings P onto m.

(O6) [BrBr] Given two points P and Q and two lines m and n, we can make a fold that brings P and Q onto m and n, respectively.

Algorithmically, these axioms purport to two operations: finding a crease(s) and folding the origami along the crease. Let us first focus on the issue of finding the crease and examine the implementation of these axioms.

Axiom (O1) is specified by a rewrite rule expressing an elementary formula of high-school geometry.

$$\text{Thru}[\text{Point}[a1, b1], \text{Point}[a2, b2]] \rightarrow \text{Line}[b2 - b1, a1 - a2, a2\ b1 - a1\ b2]$$

Axiom (O2) is to find the perpendicular bisector of the segment connecting the two points. Axiom (O3) is to find the bisector of the angle formed by the two lines. Axioms (O3)∼(O6) can also be concisely specified in functional logic programs, and will be the subject of fuller discussion in section 4, after we see the origami construction of trisecting an angle.

3.2   Trisecting an Angle by Origami

We explain the principles of origami construction by the example of trisecting a given angle by origami. This example makes non-trivial use of Axiom (O6) and shows the power of origami. The method is due to H. Abe as described in [7,8].

First, we define a square origami paper, whose corners are designated by the mark points "A", "B", "C" and "D". The size may be arbitrary, but for our presentation, let us fix it to 4×4. The function call

$$\text{DefOrigami}[4, 4, \text{MarkPoints} \rightarrow \{"A", "B", "C", "D"\},$$
$$\text{Context} \rightarrow "\text{TrisectAngle}\backslash"];$$

creates the desired origami. This call generates, under the context of Trisect-Angle, the variables A, B, C and D that hold the coordinates of the mark points "A", "B", "C" and "D", respectively. By this support, we can safely use wording *point* A instead of mark point "A".

Generally, the operations are performed by function calls of the form $Op[args, opt_1 \rightarrow val_1, \ldots, opt_n \rightarrow val_n]$, where *args* is a sequence of parameters, opt_1, $\ldots$, opt_n are keywords for optional parameters, and $val_1, \ldots, val_n$ are the corresponding values of these options.

We then introduce an arbitrary point, say Point[3, 4], marked by "E" by the following function call:

$$\text{PutPoint}[\{"E", \text{Point}[3, 4]\}];$$

Our problem is to trisect the angle $\angle EAB$.

We want to let F, G, H and I be the midpoints of points A and D, points B and C, points A and F, and points B and G, respectively. We mark those points by "F", "G", "H" and "I", respectively, and put them on the current origami.

$$\text{PutPoint}[\{\{"F", \text{Midpoint}[A, D]\}, \{"G", \text{Midpoint}[B, C]\},$$
$$\{"H", \text{Midpoint}[A, F]\}, \{"I", \text{Midpoint}[B, G]\}\}]$$

Note that we can obtain the midpoints by applying Axiom (O2). We skip this step, as it is straightforward.

At this point, our origami can be displayed by calling ShowOrigami[...]: (right one, left one immediately after marking E)

$$\text{ShowOrigami}[\text{More} \rightarrow \text{Graphics3D}[\{\text{Hue}[0], \text{GraphicsLine}[E, A],$$
$$\text{GraphicsLine}[H, I]\}]];$$

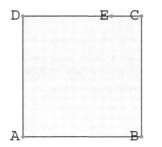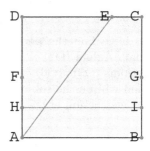

Fig. 1. Origami displays.

The keyword `More` instructs the system to display more graphical objects using the built-in *Mathematica* functions. In this case, lines in different hues are displayed.

We then make a fold along the line ensured by Axiom (O6), such that point F is brought onto line $\overline{AE}$ and point A is brought onto line $\overline{HI}$. The line is computed by $\mathtt{BrBr}[\mathtt{F}, \mathtt{Segment}[\mathtt{A}, \mathtt{E}], \mathtt{A}, \mathtt{Segment}[\mathtt{H}, \mathtt{I}]]$, where `BrBr` is the implementation of Axiom (O6). The interface to the computer origamist is $\mathtt{FoldBrBr}[\dots]$ which does folding after finding creases by $\mathtt{BrBr}[\dots]$.

$$\mathtt{FoldBrBr}[1, \mathtt{F}, \mathtt{Segment}[\mathtt{A}, \mathtt{E}], \mathtt{A}, \mathtt{Segment}[\mathtt{H}, \mathtt{I}]]$$

Which $\mathtt{line}(1, 2, 3)$?

$$\left\{ \mathtt{Line}\left[\tfrac{3}{4} + \tfrac{5}{2} \, \cos\left[\tfrac{1}{3} \, \arctan\left[\tfrac{4}{3} \right] \right], \right.$$
$$1, -\tfrac{75}{32} - \tfrac{15}{8} \, \cos\left[\tfrac{1}{3} \, \arctan\left[\tfrac{4}{3} \right] \right] - \tfrac{25}{16} \, \cos\left[\tfrac{2}{3} \, \arctan\left[\tfrac{4}{3} \right] \right]],$$
$$\mathtt{Line}\left[\tfrac{3}{4} - \tfrac{5}{4} \, \cos\left[\tfrac{1}{3} \, \arctan\left[\tfrac{4}{3} \right] \right] - \tfrac{5}{4} \, \sqrt{3} \, \sin\left[\tfrac{1}{3} \, \arctan\left[\tfrac{4}{3} \right] \right],$$
$$1, -\tfrac{75}{32} + \tfrac{15}{16} \, \cos\left[\tfrac{1}{3} \, \arctan\left[\tfrac{4}{3} \right] \right] +$$
$$\tfrac{25}{32} \, \cos\left[\tfrac{2}{3} \, \arctan\left[\tfrac{4}{3} \right] \right] + \tfrac{15}{16} \, \sqrt{3} \, \sin\left[\tfrac{1}{3} \, \arctan\left[\tfrac{4}{3} \right] \right] -$$
$$\tfrac{25}{32} \, \sqrt{3} \, \sin\left[\tfrac{2}{3} \, \arctan\left[\tfrac{4}{3} \right] \right]],$$

$$\mathtt{Line}\left[\tfrac{3}{4} - \tfrac{5}{4} \, \cos\left[\tfrac{1}{3} \, \arctan\left[\tfrac{4}{3} \right] \right] + \tfrac{5}{4} \, \sqrt{3} \, \sin\left[\tfrac{1}{3} \, \arctan\left[\tfrac{4}{3} \right] \right],$$
$$1, -\tfrac{75}{32} + \tfrac{15}{16} \, \cos\left[\tfrac{1}{3} \, \arctan\left[\tfrac{4}{3} \right] \right] +$$
$$\tfrac{25}{32} \, \cos\left[\tfrac{2}{3} \, \arctan\left[\tfrac{4}{3} \right] \right] - \tfrac{15}{16} \, \sqrt{3} \, \sin\left[\tfrac{1}{3} \, \arctan\left[\tfrac{4}{3} \right] \right] +$$
$$\left. \tfrac{25}{32} \, \sqrt{3} \, \sin\left[\tfrac{2}{3} \, \arctan\left[\tfrac{4}{3} \right] \right]] \right\}$$

In this case there are three lines that make this fold possible. The system responds by asking us along which line we want to make a fold. Let us answer to this question by giving 1 (the 6th argument of `FoldBrBr`) to the system, i.e. choosing the first line.

$$\mathtt{FoldBrBr}[1, \mathtt{F}, \mathtt{Segment}[\mathtt{A}, \mathtt{E}], \mathtt{A}, \mathtt{Segment}[\mathtt{H}, \mathtt{I}], 1, \mathtt{MarkCrease} \to \mathtt{True}];$$

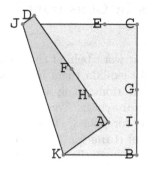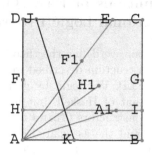

Fig. 2. Fold that trisects $\angle EAB$.

Although `FoldBrBr` is called twice with the same 5 arguments, the computation is not entirely duplicated in our system since the result of the most expensive sub-computation is memoized.

Points J and K are the end points of the crease generated by the above call since option `MarkCrease → True` is specified. Let A1, H1 and F1 be the points A, H and F after the fold. Then we revert to the origami at step 1.

$$\text{pts} = \text{PutPoint}[\{\{"A1", A\}, \{"H1", H\}, \{"F1", F\}\}];$$
$$\text{ToStep}[1, \text{pts}];$$

We now see that lines $\overline{AH1}$ and $\overline{AA1}$ trisect $\angle EAB$ in Fig. 2. The origami to the left is the one after the evaluation of `FoldBrBr[ ... ]` above, and the origami to the right is displayed by the following call:

```
ShowOrigami[More →
    Graphics3D[GraphicsLine[J, K],
        Hue[0.2], GraphicsLine[A, F1], GraphicsLine[A, H1],
        GraphicsLine[A, A1]},
        Hue[0], GraphicsLine[A, E], GraphicsLine[H, I]}]];
```

We can prove that $\overline{AH1}$ and $\overline{AA1}$ trisect $\angle EAB$ both symbolically and geometrically. A geometrical proof is more elegant and a good exercise for high school students. The proof is found in [7]. A proof based on symbolic computation is rather laborious. An easy way would be to use the trigonometric identity:

$$\tan[3\ \theta] = \frac{3\tan[\theta] - \tan[\theta]^3}{1 - 3\tan[\theta]^2}.$$

The coordinates of the points A1, F1 and H1 are obtained simply by evaluating the variables A1, F1 and H1. The rest of the work can be done symbolically. This leads to an interesting (albeit well-known) observation: `BrBr` amounts to solving a cubic equation. Indeed `BrTh` is related to solving quadratic equations, and `BrBr` to solving cubic equations. We will come to this point in section 5.

4 Definitions of Basic Operations in Constraint Functional Logic Programming

In this section we define the theories that are at work behind the scene of the origami construction described in section 3. We explain them in the language of Open CFLP. We begin by giving type declarations using a type discipline similar to that of Haskell, but in a *Mathematica* syntax. We can declare our own type constructors (TLine for lines, TPoint for points, etc.) by Instance[...] calls, and the associated data constructors (Line for TLine type, Point for TPoint type, etc.) by DataConstructors[...] calls. Eq is the class of types with equality, $\mathbb{R}$ is the built-in type of real numbers, and $\mathbb{B}$ is the built-in type boolean.

Instance[TLine : Eq]; Instance[TPoint : Eq];

Instance[TSegment : Eq]; Instance[TPolyPair : Eq];

Instance[TSPPair : Eq];
DataConstructors[{

Line : $\mathbb{R} \longrightarrow \mathbb{R} \longrightarrow \mathbb{R} \longrightarrow$ TLine,

Point : $\mathbb{R} \longrightarrow \mathbb{R} \longrightarrow$ TPoint,

SPPair : TLine $\longrightarrow$ TPoint $\longrightarrow$ TSPPair,

PolyPair : list[TPoint] $\longrightarrow$ list[TPoint] $\longrightarrow$ TPolyPair,

Segment : TPoint $\longrightarrow$ TPoint $\longrightarrow$ TSegment}];

Similarly, defined (function) symbols are declared by DefinedSymbols[...] calls. We first declare the defined symbols with types as follows.

DefinedSymbols[{

DoubleVerticalBar : TLine $\longrightarrow$ TLine $\longrightarrow$ $\mathbb{B}$,

UpTee : TLine $\longrightarrow$ TLine $\longrightarrow$ $\mathbb{B}$,

DownRightVector : TPoint $\longrightarrow$ TLine $\longrightarrow$ $\mathbb{B}$,

SegmentToLine : TSegment $\longrightarrow$ TLine,

Midpoint : TPoint $\longrightarrow$ TPoint $\longrightarrow$ TPoint,

PerBisector : TPoint $\longrightarrow$ TPoint $\longrightarrow$ TLine,

SymmetricPoint : TPoint $\longrightarrow$ TLine $\longrightarrow$ TPoint,

BrTh : TPoint $\longrightarrow$ TSegment $\longrightarrow$ TPoint $\longrightarrow$ TSPPair,

BrBr : TPoint $\longrightarrow$ TSegment $\longrightarrow$ TPoint $\longrightarrow$ TSegment $\longrightarrow$ TLine}];

Then we give theories using conditional rewrite rules associated with the defined symbols. The program Prog shown in Fig. 3 declares the basic functions for origami construction.

DoubleVerticalBar (its infix operator name is ∥) and UpTee (⊥) test whether the given lines are parallel or perpendicular respectively. Evaluation of $P{\rightarrow}m$ yields True iff point P is on the line m. Midpoint[P, Q] yields the midpoint of points P and Q, and SegmentToLine[seg] transforms segment seg to

$$\text{Prog} = \text{FLPProgram}\Big[\{$$

$\quad$ $\text{Line}[a1, b1, c1] \parallel \text{Line}[a2, b2, c2] \Leftarrow a1\ b2 - a2\ b1 \rhd 0,$

$\quad$ $\text{Line}[a1, b1, c1] \perp \text{Line}[a2, b2, c2] \Leftarrow a1\ a2 + b1\ b2 \rhd 0,$

$\quad$ $\text{Point}[x, y] \rightharpoonup \text{Line}[a, b, c] \Leftarrow a\ x + b\ y + c \approx 0,$

$\quad$ $\text{SegmentToLine}[\text{Segment}[\text{Point}[x1, y1], \text{Point}[x2, y2]]] \rightarrow$

$\qquad$ $\text{Line}[y2 - y1, x1 - x2, x2\ y1 - x1\ y2],$

$\quad$ $\text{Midpoint}[\text{Point}[x1, y1], \text{Point}[x2, y2]] \rightarrow$

$\qquad$ $\text{Point}[(x1 + x2)/2, (y1 + y2)/2],$

$\quad$ $\text{PerBisector}[\text{Point}[a1, b1], \text{Point}[a2, b2]] \rightarrow$

$\qquad$ $\text{Line}\big[2(a2 - a1), 2(b2 - b1), a1^2 - a2^2 + b1^2 - b2^2\big],$

$\quad$ $\text{SymmetricPoint}[\text{Point}[x, y], \text{Line}[a, b, c]] \rightarrow$

$\qquad$ $\text{Point}\big[((b^2 - a^2)x - 2\ a\ b\ y - 2\ a\ c)/(a^2 + b^2),$

$\qquad\quad$ $((a^2 - b^2)y - 2\ a\ b\ x - 2\ b\ c)/(a^2 + b^2)\big],$

$\quad$ $\text{BrTh}[P, \text{seg}, Q] \rightarrow \text{SPPair}[n, R] \Leftarrow$

$\qquad$ $\{\text{PerBisector}[P, R] \rhd n, Q \rightharpoonup n, R \rightharpoonup \text{SegmentToLine}[\text{seg}]\},$

$\quad$ $\text{BrBr}[P, s1, Q, s2] \rightarrow m \Leftarrow$

$\qquad$ $\{m \approx \text{Line}[a, 1, c], P2 \approx \text{SymmetricPoint}[P, m],$

$\qquad\quad$ $Q2 \approx \text{SymmetricPoint}[Q, m], \text{SegmentToLine}[s1] \rhd n1,$

$\qquad\quad$ $P2 \rightharpoonup n1, \text{SegmentToLine}[s2] \rhd n2, Q2 \rightharpoonup n2\},$

$\quad$ $\text{BrBr}[P, s1, Q, s2] \rightarrow m \Leftarrow$

$\qquad$ $\{m \approx \text{Line}[1, 0, c], P2 \approx \text{SymmetricPoint}[P, m],$

$\qquad\quad$ $Q2 \approx \text{SymmetricPoint}[Q, m], \text{SegmentToLine}[s1] \rhd n1,$

$\qquad\quad$ $P2 \rightharpoonup n1, \text{SegmentToLine}[s2] \rhd n2, Q2 \rightharpoonup n2\}\}\Big];$

Fig. 3. Basic origami theory in Open CFLP.

the line that extends the segment. Function $\texttt{Thru}$, the implementation of Axiom (O1) is omitted here since in practice $\texttt{SegmentToLine}$ can do the same job. $\texttt{PerBisector}$(perpendicular bisector) and $\texttt{SymmetricPoint}$ deserve more explanation in the context of constraint functional logic programming. We initially had a definition of $\texttt{PerBisector}$ below.

$\quad$ $\text{PerBisector}[P, Q] \rightarrow$

$\qquad$ $\text{ToLine}[x, y] \Leftarrow \{\text{Segment}[P, Q] \perp \text{Segment}[S, R],$

$\qquad\quad$ $R \approx \text{Point}[x, y], S \approx \text{Midpoint}[P, Q]\}$

This means that there exists a point $R(x, y)$ such that $\overline{PQ} \perp \overline{SR}$, where S is the midpoint of $\overline{PQ}$. This is the declarative meaning of a perpendicular bisector. A slight complication occurs in our program that a set of points has to be converted to a line by $\texttt{ToLine}[x, y]$.

It is possible, for instance, to solve the equation $\texttt{PerBisector}[\texttt{Point}[1, 0],$ $\texttt{Point}[0, 1]] \rhd x$. The solution is $x \rightarrow \text{Line}[-1, 1, 0]$, and can be solved easily by our system. However, even for symbolic values $a1, b1, a2$ and $b2$, the constraint

PerBisector[Point[a1, b1], Point[a2, b2]] ⊳ x is solvable. It will return the solution $x \rightarrow$ Line[2(a2 − a1), 2(b2 − b1), a1^2 − a2^2 + b1^2 − b2^2]. Therefore, we refine the original rewrite rule by the above result. This gives the following rewrite rule:

$$\text{PerBisector}[\text{Point}[a1, b1], \text{Point}[a2, b2]] \rightarrow$$
$$\text{Line}[2(a2 − a1), 2(b2 − b1), a1^2 − a2^2 + b1^2 − b2^2]$$

Likewise we can define Bisector, the partial implementation of Axiom (O3), starting with the definition, using the auxiliary function Distance[P, m], which computes the distance between point P and line m.

$$\text{Bisector}[m, n] \rightarrow \text{ToLine}[x, y] \Leftarrow$$
$$\{\text{Distance}[P, m] \approx \text{Distance}[P, n], P \approx \text{Point}[x, y]\}$$

As in PerBisector, Bisector[Line[a1, b1, c1], Line[a2, b2, c2]] ⊳ x is solvable symbolically. Since the solution is complicated, we did not include the definition of Bisector in Fig. 3. Our system, however, runs the more efficient code for given parameter Line[a1, b1, c1] and Line[a2, b2, c2] as shown below. The elimination of the duplicated common subexpressions by local variables (using With construct of *Mathematica*) is done manually.

$$\text{With}\Big[\Big\{u = \tfrac{\sqrt{a1^2 + b1^2}}{\sqrt{a2^2 + b2^2}}\Big\},$$
$$\quad \text{With}[\{v1 = a1 + u\ a2, w1 = b1 + u\ b2, v2 = a1 − u\ a2,$$
$$\quad\quad w2 = b1 − u\ b2\},$$
$$\quad \text{If}[(v1 == 0 \land w1 == 0),$$
$$\quad\quad \text{If}[(v2 == 0 \land w2 == 0), \{\}, \{\text{Line}[v2, w2, c1 − u\ c2]\}],$$
$$\quad\quad \text{If}[(v2 == 0 \land w2 == 0), \{\text{Line}[v1, w1, c1 + u\ c2]\},$$
$$\quad\quad \{\text{Line}[v1, w1, c1 + u\ c2], \text{Line}[v2, w2, c1 − u\ c2]\}]]]]$$

The definition of SymmetricPoint is similarly derived.

The application of the above refined rewrite rules involves no solving of equations, and hence it is more efficient. This kind of program manipulation without resort to other frame of reasoning about the program is possible in our systems.

We can further make the following more general remark on constraint (functional logic) programming. Constraint solving is in many cases slow; slower than other possible methods that do not involve solving, due to the very nature of problem solving. Namely, constraints are statements closer to problem specification rather than those for execution. However, as our examples show, when constraint solvers deliver solutions in the form of executable symbolic programs, we can partially overcome the problem of inefficiency. This is an instance of partial evaluation in the context of constraint programming.

BrTh and BrBr are the implementations of Axioms (O5) and (O6), respectively. BrTh[P, *seg*, Q] returns a pair SPPair[n, R] consisting of the crease n passing through point Q and point R, where R is the point on the line extending segment *seg*, to which point P is brought by the fold along n. BrBr[P, *s1*, Q, *s2*] returns the crease m such that the fold along m brings P onto the line extending segment *s1*, and Q onto the line extending *s2*. It is very easy to read off this declarative meaning from the rewrite rules.

5   Examples

In this section we show two examples of origami constructions: one for illustrating mathematical origami construction and the other for illustrating art origami construction. The first one is an origami construction for solving a quadratic equation. We solve this to show the functionality of Open CFLP.

Problem 1. Solve the quadratic equation $x^2 + p\,x + q = 0$ by origami.

The following method is due to [7]. We consider a sheet of paper whose corners are

$$0 = \text{Point}[0,0]; P = \text{Point}[-p,0]; X = \text{Point}[-p,q]; Q = \text{Point}[0,q];$$

To make our description concrete, we assume $p = 4$ and $q = 3$. We consider the points U = Point[0, 1], M = Midpoint[X, U] and the segment seg determined by P and O

$$p = 4; q = 3; U = \text{Point}[0,1]; M = \text{Midpoint}[X,U];$$
$$\text{seg} = \text{Segment}[P,0];$$

It can be shown that the solution X of the equation SPPair[n, Point[X, 0]] $\approx$ BrTh[U, seg, M] in variables n and X is a solution of $x^2 + p\,x + q = 0$. With Open CFLP, we pose the problem of finding X as follows:

$$\text{Prob} = \text{exists}[\{X\}, \text{SPPair}[n, \text{Point}[X,0]] \approx \text{BrTh}[U, \text{seg}, M]];$$

Finally, we inform the system of what solvers to employ and how to combine their solving capabilities. For solving Prob we need only 2 solvers: a solver which can process user defined functions, and a solver which can solve polynomial equations over $\mathbb{R}$. Open CFLP provides default implementations for both solvers: LNSolver (Lazy Narrowing Solver) for equational reasoning with user defined functions, and PolynSolver for systems of polynomial equations.

$$\text{polyn} = \text{MkLocalSolver}[\text{"PolynSolver"}];$$
$$\text{flp} = \text{MkLocalSolver}[\text{"LNSolver"}];$$

Some solvers must be configured in order to work properly. To solve the goal Prob, we configure flp so that it can reason with the theory Prog and employ the calculus LCNCd (deterministic lazy conditional narrowing calculus). We first apply flp to the goal Prob. The solver flp reduces Prob to an equivalent problem without user defined function symbols, and then the solver polyn computes

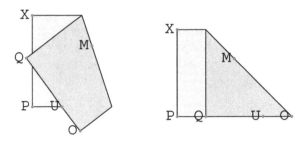

Fig. 4. Origami folds giving solutions of a quadratic equation.

the bindings for n and X by solving the intermediate problem. The sequential application of these solvers is specified by the combinator seq.

ConfigSolver[flp, {Program → Prog, Calculus → "LCNCd"}];
ApplyCollaborative[seq[{flp, polyn}], {Prob}]

yields the following solution.

$$\{\{X \rightarrow -3\}, \{X \rightarrow -1\}\}$$

Figure 4 shows the origami folds that give the solutions: the value of the x-coordinate of point U is the solution.

Problem 2. Construct an origami of a crane.

This example shows another feature of our origami environment. Here we are more interested in producing an art piece, and the system can perform approximate numeric computation for the sake of efficiency. A computer origamist can change the mode of computation by setting the global variable $exact = False.

We developed the following folding algorithm for manipulating origamis. Recall that one-step fold of an origami consists of finding a crease and making a fold along the crease. The fold obeys the following algorithm.

Given Origami[i] = Origami[i, *planes, order*], and a plane *plane* = Plane[*id, poly, neighbors, mpoints*] in *planes*, the algorithm performs the following:

1. Divide the polygon *poly* into two polygons *poly1* and *poly2,* where *poly1* is to be rotated by the fold and *poly2* is not rotated. We take *poly1* = *empty* and *poly2* = *poly* if *poly* is not divided.
2. Collect all the planes that are to be rotated together with *poly1* using the neighborhood relation *neighbors.* Let *moved* be the list of collected planes.
3. Rotate all the planes in *moved* and mark points in *mpoints* if they are on the moved planes. Let *newplanes* be the list of all the planes after the rotation.
4. Compute the overlay relation *neworder* of all the planes in *newplanes.*
5. Set Origami[$i + 1$] = Origami[$i + 1$, *newplanes, neworder*].

When we deal with 2D origamis that are performed by Origami Axioms, it suffices to consider two modes of folds, i.e. mountain fold and valley fold, which rotate the planes by angle π and $-\pi$, respectively. However, for art origami we need more sophisticated folds. We furthermore implemented inside reverse fold (which is called *naka wari ori* in Japanese, meaning "fold by splitting in the middle") and outside reverse fold (*kabuse ori* in Japanese, meaning overlay fold). The inside reverse fold is used in constructing an origami of a crane. The following sequence of calls of the fold functions will construct the crane as shown in Fig. 6.

```
SetView["3D"]; DefOrigami[4, 4];
ValleyFold[DefCrease[{4, 4}, {0, 0}], π];
InsideReverseFold[{2, 3}, DefCrease[{4, 2}, {2, 2}]];
InsideReverseFold[{4, 6}, DefCrease[{2, 2}, {2, 0}]];
InsideReverseFold[{13, 12}, DefCrease[{2, 2√2 − 2}, {4, 0}]];
InsideReverseFold[{24, 7}, DefCrease[{4, 0}, {6 − 2√2, 2}]];
InsideReverseFold[{8, 9}, DefCrease[{2, 2√2 − 2}, {4, 0}]];
InsideReverseFold[{5, 16}, DefCrease[{4, 0}, {6 − 2√2, 2}]];
ValleyFold[DefCrease[{2, 2√2 − 2}, {6 − 2√2, 2}], π];
ValleyFold[DefCrease[{2, 2√2 − 2}, {6 − 2√2, 2}], −π];
ValleyFold[DefCrease[{2, 2 − 2√2 + 2√(4 − 2√2)}, {4, 0}], π];
ValleyFold[DefCrease[{4, 0}, {2 + 2√2 − 2√(4 − 2√2), 2}], π];
ValleyFold[DefCrease[{2, 2 − 2√2 + 2√(4 − 2√2)}, {4, 0}], −π];
ValleyFold[DefCrease[{4, 0}, {2 + 2√2 − 2√(4 − 2√2), 2}], −π];
InsideReverseFold[{20, 28},
    DefCrease[{4 − √2, √2}, {2√2 + 2√(10 − 7√2), 2}]];
InsideReverseFold[{36, 52},
DefCrease[{2, 4 − 2√2 − 2√(10 − 7√2)}, {4 − √2, √2}]];
InsideReverseFold[{41, 57}, DefCrease[{3, 4}, {2, 2√2}]];
ValleyFold[DefCrease[{2 + 2√2 − 2√(4 − 2√2), 2},
    {2, 2 − 2√2 + 2√(4 − 2√2)}], π/2];
ValleyFold[C[{2 + 2√2 − 2√(4 − 2√2), 2}, {2, 2 − 2√2 + 2√(4 − 2√2)}],
```

Fig. 5. Program for constructing Origami crane.

Above, DefCrease[{*x1, y1*}, {*x2, y2*}] defines the crease from Point[*x1, y1*] to Point[*x2, y2*]. The first parameter of InsideReverseFold[...] is the pair of plane id's, which is determined interactively.

Finally, we view the crane in a different angle by evaluating the following:

```
ShowOrigami[ShowId → False, ViewPoint → {−0.723, 1.114, −3.112}];
```

The image produced by this call is shown in Fig. 7.

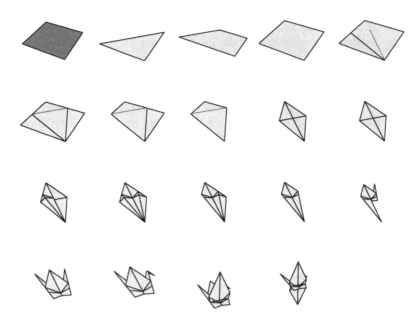

Fig. 6. Stepwise construction of Origami crane.

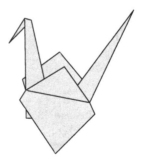

Fig. 7. Origami crane.

6 Conclusion

We have illustrated computer-supported origami construction and have shown the significant role played by the constraint functional logic programming paradigm in program development. Our examples have shown that origami construction has an aspect of geometrical problem solving, which requires constraint solving on geometrical objects. Origami bridges geometrical construction and numeric and symbolic computations. Implementing origami construction has revealed many interesting research themes: integration of constraint, functional and logic programming paradigms and combination of modes of computation such as symbolic, numeric and graphics computation. The implementation of an origami environment based on our previous work on Open CFLP and the experiences with the symbolic algebra system *Mathematica* brought insights to new programming paradigms and pedagogical implications to mathematics and computer science.

Concerning the related works, we draw ideas from the research community of constraint functional logic programming and mathematical and art origami communities. As far as we know the application of constraint functional logic programming to origami is new, although some researchers recognize the importance of integrating constraint solvers in the functional logic programming systems such as Curry [10] and Toy [11].

The research on origami has by far longer history and has enjoyed wide range of supports and enthusiasm from artists, educators, mathematicians and computer scientists. We can find many interesting web sites devoted to origami. Nevertheless, our computer origami as described in this paper is original in that we can successfully integrate geometrical constraint solving, symbolic and numeric computing and graphics processing in computerizing origami construction. We are aware of research on origami simulations, for example [9], which also has references to some earlier works. Their work focusses on simulating the operation of paper folding on the computer screen, not on the computational aspect of origami. Currently, we are working on the full integration of Open CFLP with an origami simulation engine and a web page interface to support the activities of computer origamists. By providing the internet origami construction service, we hope to open a new research area of computer origami.

References

[1] N. Kobayashi, M. Marin, and T. Ida. Collaborative Constraint Functional Logic Programming System in an Open Environment. *IEICE Transactions on Information and Systems*, E86-D(1), pp. 63–70, January 2003.

[2] M. Marin., T. Ida, and W. Schreiner. CFLP: A *Mathematica* Implementation of a Distributed Constraint Solving System. In *The Mathematica Journal,* 8(2), pp. 287–300, 2001.

[3] H. Takahashi and T. Ida. Origami Programming Environment. In *Challenging the Boundaries of Symbolic Computation, Proceedings of 5th International Mathematica Symposium (IMS'2003)*, P. Mitic, P. Ramsden, and J. Carne, editors, Imperial College Press. pp. 413–420, 2003.

[4] H. Huzita. Axiomatic Development of Origami Geometry. In *Proceedings of the First International Meeting of Origami Science and Technology*, pp. 143–158, 1989.

[5] T. Hull. Origami and Geometric Constructions.
     `http://web.merrimack.edu/~thull/geoconst.html`, 1997.

[6] Tzer-lin Chen. Proof of the impossibility of trisecting an angle with Euclidean tools, *Math. Mag. 39,* pp. 239–241, 1966.

[7]   R. Geretschläger. *Geometric Constructions in Origami* (in Japanese, translation by H. Fukagawa), Morikita Publishing Co., 2002.

[8]   K. Fushimi. *Science of Origami,* a supplement to Saiensu, p.8, Oct. 1980.

[9]   S. Miyazaki, T. Yasuda, S. Yokoi and J. Toriwaki. An Origami Playing Simulator in the Virtual Space, The Journal of Visualization and Computer Animation, Vol.7, No. 1, pp.25–42, 1996.

[10] M. Hanus (eds.) Curry: A Truly Integrated Functional Logic Language, `http://www.informatik.uni-kiel.de/~curry`, 2002.

[11] J. C. Gonzales-Moreno, T. Hortala-Gonzalez, F.J. Lopez-Fraguas, and M. Rodriguez-Artalejo, An Approach to Declarative Programming Based on a Rewrite Logic, Journal of Logic Programming, Vol. 40, No. 1, pp. 47–87, 1999.

[12] S. Wolfram, The Mathematica Book, 3rd edition, Wolfram Media and Cambridge University Press, 1996.

A Typeful and Tagless Representation for XML Documents*

Dengping Zhu and Hongwei Xi

Computer Science Department
Boston University
{zhudp, hwxi}@cs.bu.edu

Abstract. When constructing programs to process XML documents, we immediately face the question as to how XML documents should be represented internally in the programming language we use. Currently, most representations for XML documents are typeless in the sense that the type information of an XML document cannot be reflected in the type of the representation of the document (if the representation is assumed to be typed). Though convenient to construct, a typeless representation for XML documents often makes use of a large number of representation tags, which not only require some significant amount of space to store but may also incur numerous run-time tag checks when the represented documents are processed. Moreover, with a typeless representation for XML documents, it becomes difficult or even impossible to statically capture program invariants that are related to the type information of XML documents. Building upon our recent work on guarded recursive datatypes, we present an approach to representing XML documents in this paper that not only allows the type information of an XML document to be reflected in the type of the representation of the document but also significantly reduces the need for representation tags that are required in typeless representations. With this approach, we become able to process XML documents in a typeful manner, thus reaping various well-known software engineering benefits from the presence of types.

1 Introduction

XML (eXtensible Markup Language) [13] is a simple and flexible text format derived from SGML. Originally designed to support large-scale electronic publishing, XML is now also playing an increasingly important role in the exchange of a wide variety of data on the Web and elsewhere. As a markup language, XML adds structural information around the data in a document. For instance, an XML document in text format is presented in the left part of Figure 1. We use the name *start tag* (*end tag*) for what is denoted by the syntax <*tagname*> (</*tagname*>) in XML. Also, we use the name *data* loosely for the contents between tags. A tagged element, or element for short, consists of a start tag and an

---

* Partially supported by NSF grants no. CCR-0224244 and no. CCR-0229480

```
<addrbook>
  <person>                                  <!DOCTYPE addrbook [
    <name>Dengping Zhu</name>                 <!ELEMENT addrbook (person*)>
    <email>zhudp@cs.bu.edu</email>            <!ELEMENT person (name, (email)?)>
  </person>                                   <!ELEMENT name (#PCDATA)>
  <person>                                    <!ELEMENT email (#PCDATA)>
    <name>Hongwei Xi</name>                 ] >
  </person>
</addrbook>
```

Fig. 1. An XML document and a DTD

end tag, which may enclose data or any sequence of other elements. A well-formed XML document consists of a single root element that contains other properly nested elements. For instance, in the XML document in Figure 1, `<name>` is a start tag, `</name>` is an end tag, and `Dengping Zhu` is a piece of data, and the start and end tags for the root element are `<addrbook>` and `</addrbook>`, respectively.

Currently, there have been many proposed type systems for XML (e.g., XML Schema [10,14,15], RELAX NG [8], etc.), and most of these type systems extend as well as refine the notion of DTD (Document Type Definition), which itself is a simple type system designed for describing the structure of XML documents [13]. As an example, we present a DTD in the right part of Figure 1, to which the XML document in the left part conforms. Essentially, the DTD defines a document type containing a root element *addrbook* and three other elements *person, name* and *email*; an *addrbook* element contains a (possibly empty) sequence of *person* elements, and a *person* element contains a *name* element followed by an *email* element, and a *name* element contains some character data, and an *email* element contains some character data as well.

```
datatype element = E of string * content list
    and content = CE of element | CT of string

(* The following is a generic representation of the XML
   document in Figure 1 *)

E ("addrbook", [CE (E  ("person", [CE (E ("name",  CT "Denping Zhu")),
               CE (E  ("email", CT "zhudp@cs.bu.edu"))])),
               CE (E  ("person", [CE (E ("name",  CT "Hongwei Xi"))])])])
```

Fig. 2. A generic representation for XML

In order to construct programs for processing XML documents, we need to form some data structure to represent the documents internally in the program-

```
datatype addrbook = Addrbook of person list
    and person = Person of name * email option
    and name = Name of string
    and email = Email of string

(* The following is a specific representation of the XML
   document in Figure 1 *)

Addrbook [Person (Name "Dengping Zhu", SOME  (Email "zhudp@cs.bu.edu")),
         Person (Name "Hongwei Xi", NONE) ]
```

Fig. 3. A specific representation for XML

ming language we use. In Figure 2, we declare a datatype *element* in Standard
ML (SML) [6] for this purpose. Evidently, each XML document[1] can be readily represented as a value of type *element*. However, with this approach, the
type information of an XML document is completely lost in the type of its representation. In the following presentation, we refer to this representation as a
generic representation for XML documents. This is essentially the first of the
two approaches presented in [12] with which various generic combinators can
be implemented to facilitate the construction of programs for processing XML
documents. Though viable, this approach makes it impossible to verify through
static type-checking whether the representation of an XML document is valid,
that is, it is well-formed and conforms to a specified DTD. Also, a great number
of constructors (*E*, *CE* and *CT*) are often needed to represent XML documents,
potentially resulting in less efficient processing of XML documents.

We can also declare a datatype *addrbook* in Figure 3 to represent the particular XML document in Figure 1. In the following representation, we refer to
this representation as a *specific representation* for XML documents. This is essentially the second of the two approaches presented in [12], where a translation
from DTDs to types in Haskell is given. While this approach does allow us to use
types to differentiate XML documents conforming to distinct DTDs, a troubling
problem occurs: It now seems difficult or even impossible to construct programs
for processing XML documents that are polymorphic on DTDs.

Clearly, there is a serious contention between the first and the second approaches above. In [4], it is proposed that the specific representation (in the
second approach) be used to represent XML documents and generic programming as is supported in Generic Haskell [2] be adopted to implement generic
combinators to facilitate the construction of programs for processing XML documents. In particular, it is shown in [4] that a function can be constructed in
Generic Haskell to compress XML documents conforming to distinct DTDs. We,
however, take an alternative in this paper. We are to present a representation for
XML documents that not only allows the type information of an XML document
to be reflected in the type of its representation but also significantly (though,

---

[1] We ignore attribute lists in XML documents at this moment.

not completely if the document conforms to a cyclic DTD) reduces the need for numerous representation tags.[2] This representation is based upon a recently invented notion of guarded recursive datatypes [17]. General speaking, we are to introduce a type constructor *XML* that takes a type index i to form a type *XML*(i) for XML documents conforming to the DTD denoted by i; a value of type *XML*(i) consists of a *type* part and a *data* part such that the former represents the structure of an XML document while the latter represents the data of the document. In this paper we will skip the generation of this representation because it can be readily done by a validator.

We organize the rest of the paper as follows. In Section 2, we introduce a type index language $\mathcal{L}_{dtd}$ in which type index expressions can be formed to represent DTDs. We then present a typeful and tagless representation for XML documents in Section 3 and use some examples to show how such a representation can effectively support XML document processing. In Section 4, we report some measurements gathered from processing an XML document and give a brief explanation about the measurements. We mention some related work in Section 5 and then conclude.

2   The Type Index Language $\mathcal{L}_{dtd}$

In Dependent ML [18,16], a language schema is presented for extending ML with a restricted form of dependent types where type index expressions are required to be drawn from a given constraint domain or a type index language as we now call it. We use DML($\mathcal{L}$) for such an extension, where $\mathcal{L}$ denotes the given type index language.

In this section, we present a type index language $\mathcal{L}_{dtd}$ based on DTDs. To ease the presentation, we do not treat the feature of attribute lists in DTDs. However, we emphasize that there is no obstacle in theory that prevents us from handling attribute lists. The language $\mathcal{L}_{dtd}$ is typed, and we use the name *sort* for a type in $\mathcal{L}_{dtd}$ so as to avoid potential confusion. The syntax of $\mathcal{L}_{dtd}$ is given as follows.

$$
\begin{array}{ll}
\text{sorts} & \gamma ::= tag \mid doc \\
\text{index exp.} & i ::= a \mid t \mid b \mid \underline{elemdoc}(t) \mid \underline{altdoc}(i_1, i_2) \mid \\
& \quad \underline{seqdoc}(i_1, i_2) \mid \underline{stardoc}(i) \mid \underline{plusdoc}(i) \mid \underline{optdoc}(i) \\
\text{index var. ctx.} & \phi ::= \emptyset \mid \phi, a : \gamma \mid \phi, i_1 \equiv i_2 \\
\text{index subst.} & \theta ::= [] \mid \theta[a \mapsto i]
\end{array}
$$

For each tag <*tagname*> in XML, we assume there exists a corresponding type index constant t in $\mathcal{L}_{dtd}$: t is referred to as a *tag index* with the name *tagname*. We assume a base sort *tag* for tag indexes. Also, we assume a base sort *doc* and use the name *document type index* (or simply *doctype index*) for a term of the sort *doc*. Intuitively, a doctype index is used to describe the type of a content in

---

[2] We use the name *representation tag* for a tag used in the representation of an XML document, which should be distinguished from a start or end tag in the document.

an XML document. We use γ for a sort, which is either *tag* or *doc*, and a for a variable ranging over index expressions. We use b for some base doctype indexes such as *empdoc* for empty content and *strdoc* for string content. We use i for an index expression, which is either a tag index denoted by t or a doctype index denoted by d. Also, we assume the existence of a signature $\mathcal{S}$ that associates each tag index t with a doctype index $\mathcal{S}(t)$ such that $\mathcal{S}(t)$ is the doctype index for contents that can be placed between tags <*tagname*> and </*tagname*>, where *tagname* is the name of t. To facilitate presentation, we may write $\langle t \rangle$, $(d_1 \mid d_2)$, $(d_1; d_2)$, $d\star$, $d+$ and $d?$ for *elemdoc*(t), *altdoc*(d_1, d_2), *seqdoc*(d_1, d_2), *stardoc*(d), *plusdoc*(d) and *optdoc*(d), respectively. We say a content in an XML document is of doctype index d if the structure of the content is described by d. Intuitively, given doctype indexes d_1 and d_2,

- $\langle t \rangle$ is the doctype index for an element that encloses a content of doctype index $\mathcal{S}(t)$ with tags <*tagname*> and </*tagname*>, where *tagname* is the name of the tag index t.
- $(d_1 \mid d_2)$ is the doctype index for a content of doctype index d_1 or d_2, and
- $(d_1; d_2)$ is the doctype index for a content consisting of some content of doctype index d_1 followed by some other content of doctype index d_2, and
- $d\star$ is the doctype index for a possibly empty sequence of contents of doctype index d, and
- $d+$ is the doctype index for a nonempty sequence of contents of doctype index d, and
- $d?$ is the doctype index for a content that is either empty or of doctype index d.

For instance, the DTD in Figure 1 introduces four tag indexes *name*, *email*, *person* and *addrbook*, which are associated with the following doctype indexes:

$$\mathcal{S}(name) = \underline{strdoc} \qquad\qquad \mathcal{S}(email) = \underline{strdoc}$$

$$\mathcal{S}(person) = (\langle name \rangle; \langle email \rangle?) \qquad \mathcal{S}(addrbook) = \langle person \rangle\star$$

Note that recursion may be involved in the declaration of a DTD. For instance, the following DTD makes use of recursion as the content of a *folder* element may contain other *folder* elements.

```
<!DOCTYPE folder [
  <!ELEMENT folder (record, (record | folder)*)>
  <!ELEMENT record EMPTY>
]>
```

It is soon to become clear that recursion in DTD poses some serious difficulties in forming a typeful representation for XML documents. The above DTD introduces two tag indexes *folder* and *record*, which are associated with the following doctype indexes:

$$\mathcal{S}(folder) = (\langle record \rangle; (\langle record \rangle \mid \langle folder \rangle)\star) \qquad \mathcal{S}(record) = \underline{empdoc}$$

$$\frac{}{\vdash \emptyset \; [ictx]} \qquad \frac{\vdash \phi \; [ictx]}{\vdash \phi, a : \gamma \; [ictx]} \qquad \frac{\vdash \phi \; [ictx] \quad \phi \vdash i_1 : \gamma \quad \phi \vdash i_2 : \gamma}{\vdash \phi, i_1 \equiv i_2 \; [ictx]}$$

Fig. 4. The rules for forming ind. var. contexts

$$\frac{\vdash \phi \; [ictx]}{\phi \vdash b : doc} \qquad \frac{\vdash \phi \; [ictx] \quad \phi(a) = \gamma}{\phi \vdash a : \gamma} \qquad \frac{\vdash \phi \; [ictx]}{\phi \vdash t : tag}$$

$$\frac{\phi \vdash t : tag}{\phi \vdash \underline{elemdoc}(t) : doc} \qquad \frac{\phi \vdash i_1 : doc \quad \phi \vdash i_2 : doc}{\phi \vdash \underline{altdoc}(i_1, i_2) : doc} \qquad \frac{\phi \vdash i_1 : doc \quad \phi \vdash i_2 : doc}{\phi \vdash \underline{seqdoc}(i_1, i_2) : doc}$$

$$\frac{\phi \vdash i : doc}{\phi \vdash \underline{stardoc}(i) : doc} \qquad \frac{\phi \vdash i : doc}{\phi \vdash \underline{plusdoc}(i) : doc} \qquad \frac{\phi \vdash i : doc}{\phi \vdash \underline{optdoc}(i) : doc}$$

Fig. 5. Sorting Rules for $\mathcal{L}_{dtd}$

In general, it should be straightforward to turn a DTD into a list of tags and then associate with each of these tags a properly chosen doctype index, and we here omit the effort to formalize this process.

We use ϕ for index variable contexts. In addition to assigning sorts to index variables, we can also assume equalities on index expressions in an index variable context. We use θ for index substitutions: [] stands for the empty substitution, and $\theta[a \mapsto i]$ extends θ with an extra link from a to i. Given i and θ, we use $i[\theta]$ for the result of applying θ to i, which is defined in a standard manner. We use a judgment of the form $\vdash \phi \; [ictx]$ to mean that ϕ is well-formed. In addition, we use a judgment of the form $\phi \vdash i : doc$ to mean that i can be assigned the sort doc under ϕ. The rules for deriving these judgments are given in Figure 4 and Figure 5.

Given two index expressions i_1 and i_2, we write $i_1 = i_2$ to mean that i_1 and i_2 are syntactically the same. Please notice the difference between $i_1 = i_2$ and $i_1 \equiv i_2$. The following rules are for deriving judgments of the form $\vdash \theta : \phi$, which roughly means that θ matches ϕ.

$$\frac{}{\vdash [] : \cdot} \qquad \frac{\vdash \theta : \phi \quad \vdash i : \gamma}{\vdash \theta[a \mapsto i] : \phi, a : \gamma} \qquad \frac{\vdash \theta : \phi \quad i_1[\theta] = i_2[\theta]}{\vdash \theta : \Delta, i_1 \equiv i_2}$$

We use $\phi \models i_1 \equiv i_2$ for a type index constraint; this constraint is satisfied if we have $\vdash i_1[\theta] = i_2[\theta]$ for every θ such that $\vdash \theta : \phi$ is derivable. As can be expected, we have the following proposition.

Proposition 1.

- If $\phi \vdash i : \gamma$ is derivable, then $\phi \models i \equiv i$ holds.
- If $\phi \models i_1 \equiv i_2$ holds, then $\phi \models i_2 \equiv i_1$ also holds.

$$\frac{const \text{ is not } const'}{\boldsymbol{a}:\boldsymbol{\gamma}, const(i_1,\ldots,i_n) \equiv const'(i'_1,\ldots,i'_{n'}), \phi \vdash i \equiv i'} \qquad \frac{\boldsymbol{a}:\boldsymbol{\gamma} \vdash i:\gamma}{\boldsymbol{a}:\boldsymbol{\gamma} \vdash i \equiv i}$$

$$\frac{\boldsymbol{a}:\boldsymbol{\gamma}, \phi \vdash i \equiv i'}{\boldsymbol{a}:\boldsymbol{\gamma}, a \equiv a, \phi \vdash i \equiv i'} \qquad \frac{i_0 \text{ contains a free occurrence of } a \text{ but is not } a}{\boldsymbol{a}:\boldsymbol{\gamma}, a \equiv i_0, \phi \vdash i \equiv i'}$$

$$\frac{i_0 \text{ contains a free occurrence of } a \text{ but is not } a}{\boldsymbol{a}:\boldsymbol{\gamma}, i_0 \equiv a, \phi \vdash i \equiv i'}$$

$$\frac{i_0 \text{ contains no free occurrences of } a}{\boldsymbol{a}:\boldsymbol{\gamma}, \phi \vdash i[a \mapsto i_0] \equiv i'[a \mapsto i_0]}{\boldsymbol{a}:\boldsymbol{\gamma}, a \equiv i_0, \phi \vdash i \equiv i'} \qquad \frac{i_0 \text{ contains no free occurrences of } a}{\boldsymbol{a}:\boldsymbol{\gamma}, \phi \vdash i[a \mapsto i_0] \equiv i'[a \mapsto i_0]}{\boldsymbol{a}:\boldsymbol{\gamma}, i_0 \equiv a, \phi \vdash i \equiv i'}$$

$$\frac{\boldsymbol{a}:\boldsymbol{\gamma}, i_1 \equiv i'_1,\ldots,i_n \equiv i'_n, \phi \vdash i \equiv i'}{\boldsymbol{a}:\boldsymbol{\gamma}, const(i_1,\ldots,i_n) \equiv const(i'_1,\ldots,i'_n), \phi \vdash i \equiv i'}$$

Fig. 6. The rules for solving constraints

– If $\phi \models i_1 \equiv i_2$ and $\phi \models i_2 \equiv i_3$ hold, then $\phi \models i_1 \equiv i_3$ also holds.

The rules for solving type index constraints are given in Figure 6, where *const* and *const'* range over tag indexes t, *elemdoc*, *altdoc*, *seqdoc*, *stardoc*, *plusdoc* and *optdoc*. The following proposition justifies both the soundness and completeness of these rules.

Proposition 2. *A type index constraint* $\phi \models i_1 \equiv i_2$ *is satisfied if and only if we can use the rules in Figure 6 to derive* $\phi \vdash i_1 \equiv i_2$.

Proof. Assume that $\phi = (\boldsymbol{a}, \phi')$ for some ϕ' that does not begin with an index variable. The proof follows from induction on the lexicographic ordering (n_1, n_2), where n_1 is the number of free index variables in ϕ' and n_2 is the size of ϕ'.

With the type index language $\mathcal{L}_{\text{dtd}}$ being well-defined, the language $\text{DML}(\mathcal{L}_{\text{dtd}})$ is also well-defined according to the DML language schema [16,18]. In particular, type-checking in $\text{DML}(\mathcal{L}_{\text{dtd}})$ involves generating and then solving constraints of the form $\phi \vdash i_1 \equiv i_2$.

3 Representing XML Documents

In this section, we present a typeful and tagless representation for XML documents, which not only allows the type information of an XML document to be reflected in the type of the representation of the document but also makes it possible to significantly eliminate the need for representation tags in the representation of the document.

An XML document is to be represented as a pair (rep, dat) such that rep represents the structure of the document and dat represents the data in the

```
datatype ELEM (tag) = {'a,t:tag,d:doc}. ELEM (t) of 'a TAG (t,d) * 'a

and (type) REP (doc) =
(unit) REPemp (empdoc)
| (string) REPstr (strdoc)
| {'a,t:tag,d:doc}. (ELEM(t)) REPelem (elemdoc(t))
| {'a,t:tag,d:doc}. ('a) REPelem' (elemdoc(t)) of 'a TAG (t, d)
| {'a1,'a2,d1:doc,d2:doc}.
     ('a1+'a2) REPalt (altdoc(d1,d2)) of 'a1 REP (d1) * 'a2 REP (d2)
| {'a1,'a2,d1:doc,d2:doc}.
     ('a1*'a2) REPseq (seqdoc(d1,d2)) of 'a1 REP (d1) * 'a2 REP (d2)
| {'a,d:doc}. ('a list) REPstar (stardoc(d)) of 'a REP(d)
| {'a,d:doc}. ('a * 'a list) REPplus (plusdoc(d)) of 'a REP(d)
| {'a,d:doc}. ('a option) REPopt (optdoc(d)) of 'a REP(d)

datatype XML (doc) = {'a, d:doc}. XML(d) of 'a REP (d) * 'a
```

Fig. 7. Datatypes for representing XML documents

document. This representation makes use of guarded recursive (g.r.) datatypes, which, syntactically, are like dependent datatypes though types may be used as type indexes. Please find more details about g.r. datatypes in [17]. In the following presentation, we also allow type variables as well as equalities between types to be declared in an index variable context ϕ.

$$
\begin{aligned}
\mathcal{T}(\underline{empdoc}) &= \mathbf{1} \\
\mathcal{T}(\underline{strdoc}) &= string \\
\mathcal{T}(\underline{elemdoc}(t)) &= ELEM(t) \\
\mathcal{T}(\underline{altdoc}(d_1, d_2)) &= \mathcal{T}(d_1) + \mathcal{T}(d_2) \\
\mathcal{T}(\underline{seqdoc}(d_1, d_2)) &= \mathcal{T}(d_1) * \mathcal{T}(d_2) \\
\mathcal{T}(\underline{stardoc}(d)) &= (\mathcal{T}(d))\,list \\
\mathcal{T}(\underline{plusdoc}(d)) &= \mathcal{T}(d) * (\mathcal{T}(d))\,list \\
\mathcal{T}(\underline{optdoc}(d)) &= (\mathcal{T}(d))\,option
\end{aligned}
\qquad
\begin{aligned}
\mathcal{R}(\underline{empdoc}) &= REPemp \\
\mathcal{R}(\underline{strdoc}) &= REPstr \\
\mathcal{R}(\underline{elemdoc}(t)) &= REPelem \\
\mathcal{R}(\underline{altdoc}(d_1, d_2)) &= REPalt(\mathcal{R}(d_1), \mathcal{R}(d_2)) \\
\mathcal{R}(\underline{seqdoc}(d_1, d_2)) &= REPseq(\mathcal{R}(d_1), \mathcal{R}(d_2)) \\
\mathcal{R}(\underline{stardoc}(d)) &= REPstar(\mathcal{R}(d)) \\
\mathcal{R}(\underline{plusdoc}(d)) &= REPplus(\mathcal{R}(d)) \\
\mathcal{R}(\underline{optdoc}(d)) &= REPopt(\mathcal{R}(d))
\end{aligned}
$$

Fig. 8. Two functions on doctypes

We use TAG for a type constructor that takes a type τ, a tag index t and a doctype index d to form a type $(\tau)\,TAG(t, d)$. Also, we introduce a language construct **ifEqTag**. Given expressions e_1, e_2, e_3, e_4, the concrete syntax for the expression **ifEqTag**(e_1, e_2, e_3, e_4) is given as follows,

$$\textbf{ifEqTag } (\ulcorner e_1 \urcorner, \ulcorner e_2 \urcorner) \textbf{ then } \ulcorner e_3 \urcorner \textbf{ else } \ulcorner e_4 \urcorner$$

```
(REPelem,
ELEM (TAGaddrbook,
[ ELEM (TAGperson,
        (ELEM (TAGname, "Dengping Zhu"),
                SOME (ELEM (TAGemail, "zhudp@cs.bu.edu")))))
    ELEM (TAGperson, (ELEM (TAGname, "Hongwei Xi"), NONE))]))
```

Fig. 9. An example of XML representation

```
(REPelem,
ELEM (TAGfolder,
(ELEM (TAGrecord, ()),
    [ (inr (ELEM (TAGfolder, (ELEM (TAGrecord, ()), []))))]))))
```

Fig. 10. Another example of XML representation

where we assume that for each $1 \leq i \leq 4$, $\ulcorner e_i \urcorner$ is the representation of e_i in concrete syntax. Intuitively, in order to evaluate this expression, we first evaluate e_1 to a tag constant c_1 and then evaluate e_2 to another tag constant c_2; if c_1 equals c_2, we evaluate e_3; otherwise, we evaluate e_4. The rule for typing the construct **ifEqTag** is given as follows:

$$\frac{\phi; \Gamma \vdash e_1 : (\tau_1) \, TAG(t_1, d_1) \quad \phi; \Gamma \vdash e_2 : (\tau_2) \, TAG(t_2, d_2) \\ \phi, \tau_1 \equiv \tau_2, t_1 \equiv t_2, d_1 \equiv d_2; \Gamma \vdash e_3 : \tau \quad \phi; \Gamma \vdash e_4 : \tau}{\phi; \Gamma \vdash \mathbf{ifEqTag}(e_1, e_2, e_3, e_4) : \tau}$$

Note that we use $\phi; \Gamma \vdash e : \tau$ for a typing judgment, where Γ is a context for assigning types to free expression variables in e. The essential point in the above typing rules is simple: If e_1 and e_2 are of types $(\tau_1) \, TAG(t_1, d_1)$ and $(\tau_2) \, TAG(t_2, d_2)$, respectively, then we can assume $\tau_1 \equiv \tau_2$, $t_1 \equiv t_2$ and $d_1 \equiv d_2$ when typing e_3 (since e_1 and e_2 must evaluate to the same tag constant in order for e_3 to be evaluated).

As usual, we use value constructors *inl* and *inr* to form values of sum types, which are assigned the following types,

$$inl : \forall \alpha \forall \beta. \alpha \to \alpha + \beta$$
$$inr : \forall \alpha \forall \beta. \beta \to \alpha + \beta$$

and employ pattern matching to decompose values of sum types. We declare three datatype constructors *ELEM*, *REP* and *XML* in Figure 7. For instance, the syntax indicates that the value constructor *ELEM* associated with the type constructor *ELEM* is assigned the following type:

$$\Pi t : tag.\Pi d : doc.(\alpha) \, TAG(t, d) * \alpha \to ELEM(t)$$

and the value constructor *REPseq* associated with the type constructor *REP* is assigned the following type:

$$\Pi d_1 : doc.\Pi d_2 : doc.(\alpha_1) REP(d_1) * (\alpha_2) REP(d_2) \to (\alpha_1 * \alpha_2) REP(\underline{seqdoc}(d_1, d_2))$$

Intuitively, given a type τ, a tag index t and a doctype index d, $ELEM(t)$ is the type for representing a content of doctype index $\underline{elemdoc}(t)$, and $(\tau)REP(d)$ is the type for what we call a proof term that shows how a content of doctype index d can be represented as a value of type τ, and $XML(d)$ is the type for a value representing a content of doctype index d. We also assume the existence of a function $repOfTag$ of type $\forall \alpha.(\alpha)TAG(t,d) \rightarrow (\alpha)REP(d)$. For instance, such a function can be readily constructed with the following approach. We define two functions $\mathcal{T}(\cdot)$ and $\mathcal{R}(\cdot)$ on doctypes in Figure 8 such that for each doctype d, $\mathcal{T}(d)$ is a type and $\mathcal{R}(d)$ is a value of type $(\mathcal{T}(d))REP(d)$. Note that we use $\mathbf{1}$ for the unit type. For each tag index t, we assign the type $(ELEM(t))TAG(t,\mathcal{S}(t))$ to the tag constant c corresponding to t, and then define $repOfTag(c)$ to be $\mathcal{R}(\mathcal{S}(t))$. As an example, the values of the function $repOfTag$ on the tag constants $TAGaddrbook$, $TAGperson$, $TAGname$ and $TAGemail$ are given below,

$$repOfTag(TAGaddrbook) = REPstar(REPelem)$$
$$repOfTag(TAGperson) = REPseq(REPelem, REPopt(REPelem))$$
$$repOfTag(TAGname) = REPstr$$
$$repOfTag(TAGemail) = REPstr$$

and the XML document in Figure 1 is represented as a pair in Figure 9. Clearly, fewer representation tags are present at this time than before. As another example, the representation of the following XML document is given in Figure 10,

```
<folder>
  <record/><folder><record/></folder>
</folder>
```

which conforms to the DTD defined on page 5. Note that `<record/>` is a shorthand for `<record></record>`. The values of the function $repOfTag$ on tag constants $TAGfolder$ and $TAGrecord$ are given as follows:

$$repOfTag(TAGfolder) = REPseq(REPelem, REPstar(REPalt(REPelem, REPelem)))$$
$$repOfTag(TAGrecord) = REPemp$$

We next show that more representation tags can be removed. Given a tag

index t, we say $t > t'$ holds if $\underline{elemdoc}(t')$ occurs in $\mathcal{S}(t)$. For instance, both $addrbook > person$ and $person > name$ hold, and $folder > folder$ holds as well. Let $>^*$ be the transitive closure of $>$ and $\not>^*$ be the complement of $>^*$. For instance, we have $addrbook >^* name$ and $person \not>^* person$. We say that a tag index t is recursive if $t >^* t$ holds. We now define two functions $\mathcal{T}'(\cdot)$ and $\mathcal{R}'(\cdot)$ in Figure 11, where $c(t)$ stands for the tag constant corresponding to tag index t. As an example, we have

$$\mathcal{T}'(addrbook) = (string * (string)option)list$$
$$\mathcal{R}'(addrbook) = REPelem'(TAGaddrbook)$$

$$\mathcal{T}'(\underline{empdoc}) = 1$$
$$\mathcal{T}'(\underline{strdoc}) = string$$
$$\mathcal{T}'(\underline{elemdoc}(t)) = ELEM(t)$$
$$\mathcal{T}'(\underline{elemdoc}(t)) = \mathcal{T}'(\mathcal{S}(t))$$
$$\mathcal{T}'(\underline{altdoc}(d_1, d_2)) = \mathcal{T}'(d_1) + \mathcal{T}'(d_2)$$
$$\mathcal{T}'(\underline{seqdoc}(d_1, d_2)) = \mathcal{T}'(d_1) * \mathcal{T}'(d_2)$$
$$\mathcal{T}'(\underline{stardoc}(d)) = (\mathcal{T}'(d)) \, list$$
$$\mathcal{T}'(\underline{plusdoc}(d)) = \mathcal{T}'(d) * (\mathcal{T}'(d)) \, list$$
$$\mathcal{T}'(\underline{optdoc}(d)) = (\mathcal{T}'(d)) \, option$$

$$\mathcal{R}'(\underline{empdoc}) = REPemp$$
$$\mathcal{R}'(\underline{strdoc}) = REPstr$$
$$\mathcal{R}'(\underline{elemdoc}(t)) = REPelem \text{ if } t >^* t$$
$$\mathcal{R}'(\underline{elemdoc}(t)) = REPelem'(c(t)) \text{ if } t \not>^* t$$
$$\mathcal{R}'(\underline{altdoc}(d_1, d_2)) = REPalt(\mathcal{R}'(d_1), \mathcal{R}'(d_2))$$
$$\mathcal{R}'(\underline{seqdoc}(d_1, d_2)) = REPseq(\mathcal{R}'(d_1), \mathcal{R}'(d_2))$$
$$\mathcal{R}'(\underline{stardoc}(d)) = REPstar(\mathcal{R}'(d))$$
$$\mathcal{R}'(\underline{plusdoc}(d)) = REPplus(\mathcal{R}'(d))$$
$$\mathcal{R}'(\underline{optdoc}(d)) = REPopt(\mathcal{R}'(d))$$

Fig. 11. Another two functions on doctypes

For each tag index t, we assign the type $(\mathcal{T}'(t)) \, TAG(t, \mathcal{S}(t))$ to $c(t)$, which stands for the tag constant c corresponding to t, and we define $repOfTag(c(t)) = \mathcal{R}'(\mathcal{S}(t))$. For instance, we now have the following:

$$repOfTag(TAGaddrbook) = REPstar(REPelem'(TAGperson))$$
$$repOfTag(TAGperson) = REPseq(REPelem'(TAGname), REPopt(REPelem'(TAGemail)))$$
$$repOfTag(TAGname) = REPstr$$
$$repOfTag(TAGemail) = REPstr$$
$$repOfTag(TAGfolder) =$$
$$REPseq(REPelem'(TAGrecord), REPstar(REPalt(REPemp, REPelem)))$$
$$repOfTag(TAGrecord) = REPemp$$

The two XML documents represented in Figure 9 and Figure 10 can now be represented as follows,

```
(* the first example *)
(REPelem' (TAGaddrbook),
 [("Dengping Zhu", SOME "zhudp@cs.bu.edu"), ("Hongwei Xi", NONE)])
```

```
(* the second example *)
(REPelem,
 ELEM (TAGfolder, ((), [inr (ELEM (TAGfolder, ((), [])))])))
```

where far fewer representation tags are involved.

With this approach, an XML document is represented as a pair (rep, dat), and *there is no need for representation tags in dat if the XML document conforming to a DTD that involves no recursion* (i.e., there is no recursive tag indexes in the doctype corresponding to the DTD).

When processing XML documents, we often encounter situations where we need to select certain parts out of a given XML content according to some criterion. In Figure 12, we implement a function *select* in $DML(\mathcal{L}_{dtd})$ for selecting out of a given XML content the first element satisfying some chosen criterion.

```
fun select xml tag pred =
  let
      fun aux REPelem =
          (fn dat => let
                val ELEM (tag', dat') = dat
            in
                ifEqTag (tag, tag') then
                   if pred dat then SOME dat else aux (repOfTag tag') dat'
                else aux (repOfTag tag') dat'
            end)
        | aux (REPelem tag') = let
              val f = aux (repOfTag tag')
            in
              fn dat =>
                ifEqTag (tag, tag')
                  if pred (ELEM (tag, dat)) then SOME (ELEM (tag, dat) else f dat
                  else f dat
            end
        | aux (REPalt (pf1, pf2)) = let
              val f1 = aux pf1 and f2 = aux pf2
            in fn inl (dat) => f1 dat | inr (dat) => f2 dat end
        | aux (REPseq (pf1, pf2)) = let
              val f1 = aux pf1 and f2 = aux pf2
            in
              fn (dat1, dat2) =>
                case f1 dat1 of NONE => f2 dat2 | res as SOME _ => res
            end
        | aux (REPstar pf) = auxList pf
        | aux (REPplus pf) = let
              val f = auxList pf
            in fn (dat, dats) => f (dat :: dats) end
        | aux (REPopt pf) = let
              val f = aux pf
            in fn NONE => NONE | SOME (dat) => f dat end
        withtype {'a,d:doc}. 'a REP(d) -> 'a -> (ELEM(t)) option

      and auxList pf = let
          val f = aux pf
          fun fList [] = NONE
            | fList (dat :: dats) =
              (case f dat of NONE => fList dats | res as SOME _ => res)
          withtype 'a list -> (ELEM(t)) option
        in fList end
        withtype {'a,d:doc}. 'a REP(d) -> 'a list -> (ELEM(t)) option
  in
      let val XML(pf, dat) = xml in aux pf dat end
  end
withtype
  {'a,t:tag,d1:doc,d2:doc}.
    XML(d1) -> 'a TAG (t,d2) -> (ELEM(t) -> bool) -> (ELEM(t)) option
```

Fig. 12. Another selection function on XML elements

Note that the type assigned to *select* is formally written as follows,

$$\Pi d_1 : doc.\Pi t : tag.\Pi d_2 : doc.$$
$$XML(d_1) \rightarrow (\alpha)\,TAG(t, d_2) \rightarrow (ELEM(t) \rightarrow bool) \rightarrow (ELEM(t))\,option$$

which clearly implies that *select* can be applied to any pair of XML document and tag constant. Note that the auxiliary function *aux* in the implementation of *select* takes a value of type $(\tau)REP(d)$ to produce a specialized function that can only be applied to a value of type τ representing some content of doctype index d. This means that we have an opportunity to stage the function *aux* so that it can generate efficient specialized code (at run-time) to search XML contents.

4 Measurements

We report some measurements gathered from an experiment processing an XML document *mybib* containing about 800 entries in bibtex style. The main purpose of the experiment is to provide a proof of concept: The proposed typeful and tagless representation for XML documents can indeed be used to implement functions processing XML documents. However, the software engineering benefits from using a typeful representation for XML documents in implementing such functions are difficult to measure directly.

When the generic representation in Section 1 is used to represent *mybib*, we notice that about 15% of space is spent on storing the representation tags. On the other hand, when the typeful and tagless representation in Section 3 is used, only less than 0.5% of the space is spent on representing the structure of the document and there is *no* need for the representation tags required in the generic representation (as *mybib* conforms to a DTD involving no recursion)

When processing an XML document, we often want to collect all elements enclosed between tags <*tagname*> and </*tagname*> for some *tagname*. For instance, we may want to collect all the titles (of books, articles, technical reports, etc.) in *mybib*. For this purpose, we need a function *selectAll* similar to the function *select* defined previously. Instead of selecting the first of the elements satisfying a chosen criterion, the function *selectAll* selects all of them. We have implemented three versions of *selectAll*.

1. The first one is a select function based on the generic representation presented in Figure 2, and its implementation is similar to *select* in Figure 12.
2. The second one is a select function based on the the typeful and tagless representation in Section 3, and its implementation is similar to *select* in Figure 12.
3. The third one is a staged version of the second one in which we make use of run-time code generation.

The following table lists the various measurements on times spent on collecting all the title elements in *mybib*. The time unit is second.

No.	Sys. time	GC time	Real time
1	0.41	0.02	0.43
2	0.10	0.00	0.10
3	0.05	0.00	0.05

We have also measured times spent on collecting other elements and the measurements are similar in nature. Note that the second and the third implementations of *selectAll* are approximately 4 and 8 times faster than the first one, respectively. This is not surprising as these implementations can tell whether an element is potentially to occur in a content by only inspecting the structure of the content while the first implementation needs to inspect the entire content. This intuition is verified by the following expriment in which the structure of the searched XML document *mybib* is made available to the function *selectAll* while the generic representation is used to represent *mybib*. This time, the measurements are similar to those gathered using the second implementation above.

No.	Sys. time	GC time	Real time
1′	0.12	0.01	0.13

Clearly, the measurements imply that the most significant factor here is whether the structure of an XML content can be made available to a search function on the content. Regardless whether a representation for XML is typeful or typeless, we think that some information on the structure of an XML document should be made available in the representation of the document so as to facilitate efficient search on the document. Also, the measurements indicate that run-time code generation can be employed to significantly speed search on XML documents.

5   Related Work and Conclusion

There have been various attempts to construct functional programs for processing XML documents. In [12], two approaches are presented for processing XML documents in Haskell [9]. The first approach uses a generic representation for XML documents that makes no use of any type information of these documents, making it impossible to use types to differentiate XML documents conforming to distinct DTDs. With this approach, generic combinators can be implemented to facilitate the construction of programs for processing XML documents. The second approach represents each XML document as a value of a special datatype (automatically) generated according to the DTD to which the XML document conforms. With this approach, XML documents conforming to distinct DTDs can be differentiated with type, but it becomes difficult or even impossible to implement programs for processing XML documents that are polymorphic on DTDs. An approach to addressing the issue is through generic programming as is proposed in Generic Haskell [2], and an XML compressor implemented in Generic Haskell is given a detailed description in [1].

In XDuce [3], a functional language is proposed where types based on regular expressions can be formed to represent DTDs. The development of the type index langugage $\mathcal{L}_{dtd}$ in Section 2 bears some resemblance to the regular expression types. However, it is currently unclear how the type system in XDuce can be extended to effectively handle polymorphism (beyond what subtyping is able to achieve). Another typed functional language XMλ is presented in [5] to facilitate XML document processing. In XMλ, DTDs can be encoded as types and row polymorphism is used to support generic XML processing functions. We are currently working along a different research line: Instead of designing a new language to process XML documents, we are primarily interested in a typeful embedding of XML in a general purpose language (e.g., DML extended with guarded recursive datatypes in this case). A typeful representation for XML documents was proposed in [11]. There, an XML document can be represented as a program in a family of domain specific languages guaranteeing that the generated documents are well-formed and valid (to a certain extent), and each language in the family of languages is implemented as a combinator library. However, this approach seems, at least currently if not inherently, incapable of handling destruction of XML documents (in a typeful manner), which is of the concern when transformation on XML documents needs to be implemented.

There are also a number of proposed typechecking algorithms for various XML processing languages in the database community. For instance, K-pebble tree transducer [7] is a general framework for XML transformers, where the type system is based on tree automaton. These works are largely of a different nature from ours and are usually not concerned with the actual implementation of XML processing functions in a given programming language.

In this paper, we have presented an approach to representing XML documents that not only allows the type information of an XML document to be reflected in the type of the representation of the document and but also obviates the need for representation tags that are otherwise required in a typeless representation. With this approach, we become able to process XML documents in a typeful manner, thus reaping various well-known software engineering benefits from the presence of types. This work also yields evidence in support of the use of DML-style dependent types in practical programming. In future, we seek to extend our approach to capture more type information (e.g. based on XML schema) of XML documents. Also, we plan to use the presented typeful and tagless XML representation to implement languages such as XQuery and XSLT.

Acknowledgments. We thank Chiyan Chen, Sa Cui, Allyn Dimock, Joe Hallett, Assaf Kfoury, Rui Shi and Jin Ye for providing us with their valuable comments on the paper.

References

1. F. Atanassow, D. Clarke, and J. Jeuring. Scripting XML with Generic Haskell. In *Proceedings of Simposio Brasileiro de Linguagens de Programacao (SBLP '03)*, Ouro Preto, Brazil, May 2003.
2. D. Clarke, R. Hinze, J. Jeuring, A. Löh, L. Meertens, and D. Swierstra. Generic Haskell. Available at: http://www.generic-haskell.org/.
3. H. Hosoya and B. C. Pierce. "XDuce: A Typed XML Processing Language". In *Int'l Workshop on the Web and Databases (WebDB)*, Dallas, TX, 2000.
4. J. Jeuring and P. Hagg. Generic Programming for XML Tools. Technical Report UU-CS-2002-023, Utrecht University, 2002.
5. E. Meijer and M. Shields. XMLambda: A functional language for constructing and manipulating XML documents, 1999.
6. R. Milner, M. Tofte, R. W. Harper, and D. MacQueen. *The Definition of Standard ML (Revised)*. MIT Press, Cambridge, Massachusetts, 1997.
7. T. Milo, D. Suciu, and V. Vianu. Typechecking for XML Transformers. In *Proceedings of the Nineteenth ACM SIGMOD-SIGACT-SIGART Symposium on Principles of Database Systems*, pages 11–22. ACM, 2000.
8. OASIS Technical Committee. RELAX NG Specification, December 2001. Available at: http://www.oasis-open.org/committees/relax-ng/spec-20011203.html.
9. S. Peyton Jones et al. Haskell 98 – A non-strict, purely functional language. Available at: http://www.haskell.org/onlinereport/, Feb. 1999.
10. J. Siméon and P. Wadler. The Essence of XML. In *Proceedings of the 30th ACM SIGPLAN Symposium on Principles of Programming Languages*, pages 1–13, New Orleans, January 2003.
11. P. Thiemann. A typed representation for HTML and XML documents in Haskell. *Journal of functional programming*, 12((4&5)):435–468, 2002.
12. M. Wallace and C. Runciman. Haskell and XML: Generic Combinators or Type-Based Translation? In *Proceedings of the Fourth ACM SIGPLAN International Conference on Functional Programming (ICFP'99)*, volume 34-9, pages 148–159, N.Y., 27–29 1999. ACM Press.
13. World Wide Web Consortium. Extensible Markup Language (XML). Version 1.0 (Second Edition). W3C Recommendation 6 October 2002. http://www.w3.org/TR/REC-xml.
14. World Wide Web Consortium. XML Schema Part 1: Structures. W3C Recommendation 2 May 2001. Available at http://www.w3.org/TR/xmlschema-1.
15. World Wide Web Consortium. XML Schema Part 2: Datatypes. W3C Recommendation 2 May 2001. Available at http://www.w3.org/TR/xmlschema-2.
16. H. Xi. *Dependent Types in Practical Programming*. PhD thesis, Carnegie Mellon University, 1998. pp. viii+189. Available as http://www.cs.cmu.edu/~hwxi/DML/thesis.ps.
17. H. Xi, C. Chen, and G. Chen. Guarded recursive datatype constructors. In *Proceedings of the 30th ACM SIGPLAN Symposium on Principles of Programming Languages*, pages 224–235, New Orleans, January 2003.
18. H. Xi and F. Pfenning. Dependent types in practical programming. In *Proceedings of ACM SIGPLAN Symposium on Principles of Programming Languages*, pages 214–227, San Antonio, Texas, January 1999.

Dataflow Pointcut in Aspect-Oriented Programming

Hidehiko Masuhara and Kazunori Kawauchi

Graduate School of Arts and Sciences, University of Tokyo
Tokyo 153–8902 Japan
{masuhara,kazu}@graco.c.u-tokyo.ac.jp

Abstract. A dataflow-based pointcut is proposed for aspect-oriented programming (AOP) languages. The pointcut specifies where aspects should be applied based on the origins of values. It is designed to be compatible with the other kinds of pointcuts in existing AOP languages. Primary application fields of the pointcut are the aspects in which flow of information is important, such as security. This paper presents the design of the pointcut with a web-application example, and its prototype implementation.

1 Introduction

Aspect-oriented programming (AOP) languages support modularization of crosscutting concerns[6,11]. A concern crosscuts a software system when its implementation does not fit in existing modules such as procedures and classes, and causes modifications to many modules without AOP. Previous studies have shown that AOP supports modularization of such crosscutting concerns as profiling[5], persistence[16], distribution[9] and optimization[3,17].

One of the important mechanisms in AOP is called pointcut-and-advice, which is found in many AOP languages including AspectJ[10]. The mechanism allows the programmer to declare additional or alternative behaviors to program execution by writing aspects. An aspect is a module that contains a set of advice declarations. A join point is a point in execution whose behavior can be affected by advice. Each advice declaration has a pointcut that specifies a set of join points and a body that specifies behavior at the specified join points.

1.1 Pointcut-and-Advice Mechanism in AspectJ

For concreteness of the discussion, the rest of the paper assumes the AspectJ's pointcut-and-advice mechanism. However, most part of the discussion should also be applicable to the other AOP languages with similar mechanisms.

In AspectJ, the join points are operations on objects, including method calls, object constructions and accesses to instance variables. The pointcuts are written in a sub-language that has primitive predicates on the kinds of join points, binders to extract values from join points, and operators to combine pointcuts.

A. Ohori (Ed.): APLAS 2003, LNCS 2895, pp. 105–121, 2003.

An advice declaration consists of a keyword to specify the timing of execution, a pointcut to specify matching join points, and a block of Java statements to specify behavior.

The following is an example aspect, which adds a "cookie" to every generated response in Servlet[4]-based web applications:

```
aspect CookieInsertion {
  pointcut generatePage(ServletResponse r) :
    call(void Servlet+.do*(..)) && args(*,r);
  after(ServletResponse r): generatePage(r) {
    r.addCookie(new Cookie("...","..."));
  }
}
```

The second and third lines define a pointcut named generatePage, which matches method call join points with certain signatures, and extracts a value from the join point. The inside of the call pointcut specifies that the method must be defined in a subclass of Servlet (N.B. "+" means any subclass) and the name of the method begins with do (N.B. "*" means any string). The args(*,r) pointcut binds variable r to the second argument of the call so that the advice body can access to it.

The third to fifth lines are an advice declaration. The keyword after means that the execution of the advice follows the execution of a matching join point. After the keyword, there are a formal parameter to the advice (in the parentheses), a pointcut, and a body of the advice (in the curly brackets). To sum up, when doPost method (or doGet, etc.) finishes, the advice calls addCookie method on the second parameter to doPost method.

1.2   Expressiveness of Pointcuts

In pointcut-and-advice mechanisms, pointcuts serve as the interface between an aspect and a target program. In order to apply aspects to many but particular points in a program, elaborated pointcut descriptions are needed. It is sometimes difficult to write pointcuts when the pointcut language does not have appropriate predicates that distinguish the characteristics of the application points.

The claim of the paper is that a pointcut that can address the origins of data, or *dataflow* between join points, is useful to write concise aspects. This is especially so for security-related aspects, in which flow of information is primary considerations. To the best of the author's knowledge, there have been no such pointcuts in existing AOP languages.

We propose a new kind of pointcut, called dflow pointcut, that identifies join points based on the origins of data. It is designed as an extension to AspectJ's pointcut language; dflow pointcuts can be used in conjunction with the other kinds of pointcuts in AspectJ. This makes it easy for the programmers to adopt dflow with minimal efforts.

The rest of the paper is organized as follows. Section 2 gives an example problem. Section 3 presents the design of the dataflow-based pointcut, and how it

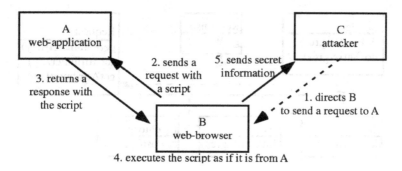

Fig. 1. An Exploit of a Cross-site Scripting Problem

can solve the problem. Section 4 presents a prototype implementation to clarify the semantics of the pointcut. Section 5 shows approaches to efficient implementations. Section 6 discusses related work. Section 7 summarizes the paper.

2 Motivating Example: Fixing a Security Problem in Web-Applications

2.1 Cross-Site Scripting Problem

Cross-site scripting is a security problem in web-applications. By exploiting a flaw of a web-application, an attacker can reveal secret information from the browser of the web-application's client[1]. The following scenario with three principals, namely (A) a web-application, (B) a web-browser of a client of A, and (C) an attacker, explains an attack (Fig. 1):

1. C directs B to send a request to A[1]. The request contains a malicious script as a parameter.
2. B sends the request to A. For example, the request may go to a login page of a shopping site, and a script is embedded as a parameter to the ID field.
3. A returns a web page as a response to B's request. A has a cross-site scripting problem when the malicious script appears as a part of the response. For example, the shopping site may return a page that indicates a failure of login with the given ID.
4. B executes the malicious script in the returned page with privileges for A.
5. The malicious script accesses secret information in B that should only be accessed by A.

The problem could have been avoided if A did not return the malicious script to B. A solution to this problem on the A's side is not to generate pages by using a string that comes from any untrusted principal. A simple implementation

---
[1] This can be accomplished by giving B a document with a link to a malicious address, or by exploiting a web-browser's bug.

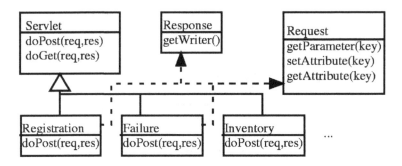

Fig. 2. Structure of a Web Application

is to remove special characters that constitute scripts from strings that come from untrusted principals, and to replace them with non-special (or quoted) characters. This solution is usually called *sanitizing*.

We here define a following sanitizing task for a web-application:

> Assume that the web-application is to generate a web page[2]. When a string that originates from anyone untrusted by the web-application appears in the generated page, it replaces special characters in the string with quoted ones.

By replacing special characters with quoted ones, the browser that receives a generated page no longer interprets the string as an executable script.

2.2 How Sanitizing Crosscuts a Web Application

In the web-applications that dynamically generates many pages, the sanitizing can be a crosscutting concern because its implementation could involve with many parts of the program. Here, we assume a web-application on Java servlets framework[4], which defines a class for each kind of pages. Fig. 2 shows a class structure of the web-application. Each `Servlet` subclass represents a particular kind of pages. When a client browser sends a request for a URL, the framework automatically creates an instance of a respective `Servlet` subclass, and then invokes `doPost` (or `doGet`, etc.) with objects representing the request and a response. The method can read values to the input fields from the request object, and generates a new page by writing into a stream in the response object. Alternatively, a method can delegate another method to generate a page after performing some process.

Fig. 3 shows definitions of some of the `Servlet` subclasses. When `doPost` method of `Registration` class is invoked, it merely checks whether the requested ID is found in the database, and transfer itself to either `Inventory`

---

[2] Another approach is to replace special characters when the web-application receives strings from browsers. It is not recommended because the replacement might affect the intermediate process unexpectedly. Also, it can not sanitize strings that come to the application via methods other than HTTP[2].

```
class Registration extends Servlet {
  void doPost(Request req, Response res) {
    String id = req.getParameter("ID");        //read input field
    if (<id is found in the database>)
      <transfer to an Inventory page>
    else {
      req.setAttribute("PREV", req.getURL()); //store current URL as an
      <transfer to a Failure page>            //originating address of the
    }                                         //transferred page
  }
}

class Failure extends Servlet {
  void doPost(Request req, Response res) {
    PrintWriter out = res.getWriter();
    out.println("<HTML>...Login failed for: ");
    out.println(req.getParameter("ID"));       //read input field & print
    out.println("...<a href=");
    out.println(req.getAttribute("PREV"));     //back to the originating page
    out.println(">go back</a>...");            //by using the stored address
  }
}
```

Fig. 3. Implementation of `Servlet` Subclasses (Type names are abbreviated due to space restrictions.)

page or `Failure` page. In `Failure` class, it displays a message of failure with the requested ID. It also places a link to the previous page by reading information in the attributes of the request.

The sanitizing task is to wrap the call to `getParameter` method in `Failure` class with a method that replaces special characters. Although the task needs to change only one place in the application, it crosscuts the application because the similar modifications need to be done in many sibling classes when those classes also use the results from `getParameter` for responding.

This paper assumes that `getParameter` is the only source of interested strings. This assumption can be easily relaxed by enumerating the other sources as well as `getParameter` in the pointcut definitions in the rest of the paper.

2.3   Usefulness of Dataflow

Since the sanitizing task crosscuts, it looks a good idea to implement it as aspects. However, it sometimes is not easy to do so with existing pointcut-and-advice mechanisms because they do not offer pointcuts to address dataflow, which is the primary factor in the sanitizing task.

The problem can be illustrated by examining the (incomplete) aspect definition in Fig. 4. The `respondClientString` pointcut is supposed to intercept any join point that prints an unauthorized string to a client. (By unauthorized, we mean that a string is created from one of client's input parameters.) With properly defined `respondClientString`, the task of sanitizing is merely to replace all

```
aspect Sanitizing {
pointcut respondClientString(String s) : ...; // incomplete

Object around(String s) : respondClientString(s) {
    return proceed(quote(s));             //continue with sanitized s
}

String quote(String s) {
    return <replace all special characters in s>;
}
}
```

Fig. 4. (Incomplete) Aspect for the Sanitizing Task

special characters in the unauthorized string, and then continue the intercepted join point with the replaced string[3].

With existing kinds of pointcuts, it is not possible to write an appropriate `respondClientString` in a declarative manner.

- First, a straightforward definition is not appropriate. For example, the following pointcut will intercept strings that are to be printed as a part of a response to a client. However, it will intercept strings including 'authorized' ones:

```
pointcut respondClientString(String s) :
 call(* PrintWriter.print*(String)) && args(s)
 && within(Servlet+);
```

- Second, even if one could write an appropriate pointcut definition, the definition is less declarative. For example, an appropriate `respondClientString` could be defined with auxiliary advice declarations that detect and trace unauthorized strings. However, those advice declarations are not declarative because they have to monitor every operations that involve with (possibly) unauthorized strings.

In order to define `respondClientString` in a declarative manner, a pointcut that can identify join points based on the origins, or *dataflow*, of values is useful. The next two reasons support this claim.

First, dataflow can use non-local information for determining the points of sanitizing. For example, the result of `getAttribute` in `Failure` class in Fig. 3 needs no sanitizing because if we trace the dataflow, it turns out to be originally obtained by `getURL` (i.e., not by `getParameter`) in `Registration` class.

Second, dataflow can capture derived values. For example, assume that a web-application takes a parameter string out from a client's request, and creates

---

[3] In AspectJ, `proceed` is a special form to do so. When the formal parameters of the advice (i.e., `s`) is bound by `args` pointcut (e.g., `args(s)`), the arguments to the `proceed` (i.e., `quote(s)`) replace the original arguments in the continued execution.

a new string by appending some prefix to the string, the new string will also be treated as well as the original parameter string.

3 Dataflow Pointcut

We propose a new kind of pointcut based on dataflow, namely dflow. This section first presents its syntax and example usage for the simplest case, and then explains additional constructs for more complicated cases.

3.1 Pointcut Definition

The following syntax defines a pointcut p:

$$p ::= \texttt{call}(s) \mid \texttt{args}(x,x,\ldots) \mid p\texttt{\&\&}p \mid p\texttt{||}p$$
$$::= \texttt{dflow}[x,x]\,(p) \mid \texttt{returns}(x)$$

where s ranges over method signature patterns and x ranges over variables.

The first line defines existing pointcuts in AspectJ[4]. call(s) matches calls to methods with matching signatures to s. args($x_1,\ldots,x_n$) matches any calls to n-arguments methods, and binds the arguments to the respective variables $x_1,\ldots,x_n$. Operators && and || combine pointcuts conjunctively and disjunctively, respectively.

The second line defines new pointcuts. dflow[x,x'] (p) matches if there is a dataflow from x' to x. Variable x should be bound to a value in the current join point. (Therefore, dflow must be used in conjunction with some other pointcut, such as args(x), that binds x to a value in the current join point.) Variable x' should be bound to a value in a past join point matching to p. (Therefore, p must have a sub-pointcut that binds a value to x'.) returns(x) is similar to args, but binds a return value from the join point to variable x. This is intended to be used only in the body of dflow, as a return value is not yet available when a current join point is created.

By using dflow, the pointcut for the sanitizing task can be defined as follows:

```
pointcut respondClientString(String o) :
  call(* PrintWriter.print*(String)) && args(o) && within(Servlet+)
  && dflow[o,i](call(String Request.getParameter(String))
                && returns(i));
```

The second line is not changed from the one in Section 2.3, which matches calls to print methods in Servlet subclasses, and binds the parameter string to variable o. The dflow pointcut restricts the join points to such ones that the parameter string originates from a return value of getParameter in a past join point.

---

[4] AspectJ has more pointcuts than the ones presented here. We omit them for simplicity.

3.2 Dataflow Relation

The condition how dflow pointcut identifies join points can be elaborated as follows: assume x is bound to a value in the current join point, $\mathtt{dflow}[x,x'](p)$ matches the join point if there exists a past join point that matches p, and the value of x originates from a value bound to x' in the past join point. By originating from a value, we mean the value is used for deriving an interested value. For example, when two strings are concatinated, the concatinated string originates from those two strings. We let the originating-from relation be transitive; e.g., the origins of the two strings are considered as the origins of the concatinated string as well.

The originating-from relation is defined as follows. Let v and w are two values. v originates from w when

- v and w are the identical value, or
- v is a result of a primitive computation using $u_1, \ldots, u_n$, and u_i originates from w for some i $(1 \leq i \leq n)$.

The above definition is sufficient for languages only with primitive values. When a language also has compound values, such as arrays and objects, we need to extend the matching condition for dflow. Although it needs further study to give a feasible condition, we tentatively extended the definition in the following ways. $\mathtt{dflow}[x,x'](p)$ matches when the value of x or a value reachable from the value of x originates from the value of x' or a value reachable from the value of x'.

3.3 Excluding Condition

We also defined an extended syntax of dflow for excluding particular dataflows. We call the mechanism bypassing.

A motivation of bypassing can be explained in terms of the sanitizing task. Assume a Servlet subclass that manually quotes the client's inputs:

```
class ShippingConfirmation extends Servlet {
  void doPost(Request request, Response response) {
    PrintWriter out = response.getWriter();
    String address = quote(request.getParameter("ADDR"));
    out.print("...Please confirm delivery address:");
    out.print(address);
    ...
  }
}
```

When an object of this class runs with Sanitizing aspect after filling its pointcut definition with the one in Section 3.1, the aspect intercepts method calls that print address in ShippingConfirmation. As address has already quoted string, it doubly applies quote to the quoted string.

The following extended dflow syntax excludes dataflows that go through certain join points:

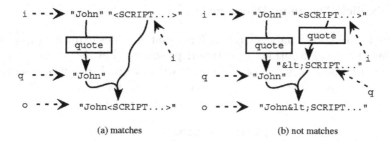

Fig. 5. How dataflow is restricted in `dflow[o,i](...) bypassing[q](...)`.

$$p ::= \text{dflow}[x,x]\,(p)\ \text{bypassing}\,[x]\,(p)$$

Intuitively, a **bypassing** clause specifies join points that should not appear along with a dataflow. By using **bypassing**, the following pointcut avoids intercepting quoted strings:

```
pointcut respondClientString(String o) :
 call(* PrintWriter.print*(String)) && args(o) && within(Servlet+)
 && dflow[o,i](call(String Request.getParameter(String))
               && returns(i))
       bypassing[q](call(String *.quote(String)) && returns(q));
```

The **bypassing** clause requires that o (an argument to print method) to originate from i (a return value from `getParameter`) but not through q (a return value from `quote`) after i.

Precisely, **bypassing** requires existence of at least one dataflow that does not go through join points matching to the pointcut in the **bypassing** clause. Fig.5 illustrates computations that generate concatenated strings from two strings. Assume that the original strings at the top of the figure are the results of `getParameter` in the above example. Then the **dflow** pointcut with **bypassing** clause matches the computation (a) because there is a dataflow to the string at the bottom of the figure without going through **quote**. On the other hand, it does not match the computation (b) because all dataflows go through **quote**; i.e., there are no dataflows bypassing **quote**.

The semantics of **bypassing** clause can be defined by slightly extending the originating-from relation. Let v and w are two values. v originates from w bypassing x in p, when:

- there have been no such a join point that matches p and the value bound to x is identical to v, and
- either of the following conditions holds:
  - v and w are the identical value, or
  - v is a result of a primitive computation using $u_1, \ldots, u_n$, and u_i originates from w bypassing x in p for some i ($1 \leq i \leq n$).

3.4   Explicit Dataflow Propagation

We provide an additional declaration form that specifies explicit propagation of dataflow through executions in external programs. This is useful in an open-ended environment, where a program runs with external code whose source programs are not available (e.g., a class library distributed in a binary format).

A declaration is written as a member of an aspect in the following form:

$$\text{declare propagate: } p \text{ from } x,x,\ldots \text{ to } x,x,\ldots;$$

where p and x range over pointcuts and variables. The form requests that, when a join point matching to p is executed, it will regard that the values of the to-variables originate from the values of the from-variables.

For example, assume that a program uses update method of Cipher class for encryption (or decryption), but the system has no access to the source code of the class. With the following declaration, the system will regard that the return value from Cipher.update originates from its argument. As a result, if a string matches dflow pointcut, the Cipher encrypted string of the string also matches to the dflow pointcut.

```
aspect PropagateOverEncryption {
  declare propagate: call(byte[] Cipher.update(byte[]))
      && args(in) && returns(out) from in to out;
}
```

The propagate declarations are designed to be reusable; i.e., once someone defined propagate declarations for a library, the users of the library merely need to import those declarations to track dataflow over the library.

The propagate declarations would be sufficient for the libraries that have only dataflows between input and output parameters. Coping with more complicated cases, such as the ones involving with structured data or the ones with conditional dataflows, is left for further study.

3.5   Notes on Scalability

The proposed pointcut has potential for more realistic and complicated situations than those in the examples presented so far. Below, we discuss two possible situations.

More Sources of Unauthorized Strings. A web-application would obtain unauthorized values by executing methods other than getParameter. For example, results of Request.getURL() might contain an arbitrary string. Or, a web-application may manually unquote strings for some purposes.

The sanitizing aspect can cope with such situations by enumerating possible sources of unauthorized values in the dflow pointcut. The following definition is a revised pointcut:

```
pointcut respondClientString(String o) :
 call(* PrintWriter.print*(String)) && args(o) && within(Servlet+)
 && dflow[o,i]((call(String Request.getParameter(String))
               || call(String Request.getURL())
               || call(String *.unquote(String)))
              && returns(i));
```

where the fourth and fifth lines are for incorporating additional sources.

External Storage. Practical web-applications often use external storage for persistently keeping information. Since `dflow` pointcuts (or any other information flow analysis techniques) only keep track of the dataflows in an program, an unauthorized value stored in external storage could be recognized as authorized after it gets retrieved.

We believe that AOP helps to solve such problems by allowing the programmer to extend the sanitizing aspect that manually traces unauthorized values.

- It has an additional advice declaration to mark unauthorized data in a database. When the web-application writes an unauthorized value into a database, the advice puts a flag into an extra attribute of the written record. Such an advice can be defined in a similar manner to the existing sanitizing advice.
- The extended `respondClientString` pointcut captures values that originate from a value in the database but only when the value has a flag. This extension can be achieved by adding a pointcut to match reads of the database with conditional expression to check the flag into the `dflow` sub-pointcut.

4   Prototype Implementation

We build a prototype implementation[5] of a language with `dflow` in order to clarify the semantics, and to establish a standpoint for optimized implementations. It is implemented as an extension to Aspect SandBox (ASB)[14], which is a modeling framework for AOP mechanisms including the pointcut-and-advice.

The prototype implementation is based on a simple, pure object-oriented language with a pointctu-and-advice mechanism simplified from the one in AspectJ. It dynamically tests and executes pointcuts and advice; i.e., when a join point is to be executed (e.g., a method is to be called), it looks for advice declarations that have pointcuts matching to the join point, and executes the advice bodies. The detailed semantics and mechanism can be found in the other literatures[14,23].

The implementation for `dflow` consists of the three parts: (1) keeping track of dataflow of values, (2) matching a join point to a `dflow` pointcut, and (3) dealing with `propagate` declaration. The following three subsections explain those in this order.

For simplicity, the language lacks the following features: primitive values, exceptions, dynamic class loading, static type system, and wildcards in pointcuts.

---
[5] Available from `http://www.graco.c.u-tokyo.ac.jp/ppp/projects/dflow/` .

4.1   Dataflow Tags

In order to track a dataflow, the system gives a unique identifier to each `dflow` pointcut. We hereafter call such an identifier a dataflow tag. The system also associates a mutable cell to each value for recording a set of dataflow tags. A notation $\text{dflow}^t\,[x,y]\,(p)$ expresses a pointcut $\text{dflow}\,[x,y]\,(p)$ with its tag t. The following three operations manipulate dataflow tags of a value v: $get(v)$ retrives a set of associated tags from v, $add(v,T)$ (where T is a set of dataflow tags) puts all tags in T to the associated tags of v, and $remove(v,T)$ takes all tags in T from the associated tags of v. We also write $get(x)$, $add(x,T)$, and $remove(x,T)$ for denoting operations on the value bound to variable x.

The dataflow tags associated with a value represent the following property: for $\text{dflow}^t\,[x,y]\,(p)$, when $t \in get(v)$, there was a join point that matches p and v originates from the value of y in p. This property is preserved in the following ways:

1. It associates an empty dataflow tags to newly created value v.
2. When a join point is created, for each pointcut

$$\text{dflow}^t\,[x,y]\,(p) \ \text{bypassing}\,[z]\,(q)$$

   in a program, it matches the join point to p and q, respectively. When the join point matches p, it performs $add(y, \{t\})$. When the join point matches q, it performs $remove(z, \{t\})$.[6] (For a pointcut without `bypassing` clause, q is regarded as a pointcut that matches no join points.)
3. When primitive operation $o(v_1, \ldots, v_n)$ yields a result value v_r, it performs $add(v_r, get(v_1) \cup \cdots \cup get(v_n))$.

4.2   Pointcut Matching

It is straightforward to match a join point to `dflow` pointcut. Pointcut $\text{dflow}^t\,[x,y]\,(p)$ matches when $t \in get(x)$.

Note that $\text{dflow}\,[x,y]\,(p)$ pointcut must be used in conjunction with another pointcut (e.g., $\text{args}\,(x)$) that binds a value to variable x. In order to match sub-pointcuts in a right order, a compound pointcut is first transformed into its disjunctive normal form. Then, for each conjunctive pointcut $p_1 \&\& \cdots \&\& p_n$, all p_is that do not have `dflow` are first matched, which bind values to variables. The remaining p_is with `dflow` test dataflow tags of the values bound to the variables. This rule is basically the same to `if` pointcut in AspectJ, which can test values of variables bound by the other pointcut.

4.3   Explicit Dataflow Propagation

A `propagate` declaration causes a propagation of dataflow tags at the matching join points. Given the following declaration:

---

[6] Note that add and $remove$ operations are side-effecting in order to cope with aliasing.

declare propagate: p from $x_1,\ldots,x_m$ to $y_1,\ldots,y_n$;

when a join point matches p, it performs $add(y_i, get(x_1) \cup \cdots \cup get(x_m))$ for all i ($1 \leq i \leq n$).

Note that the system should manipulate dataflow tags after the execution of the join point if a variable is bound by **returns** pointcut. This should not be a problem because the advice mechanism has no access during the execution of the external code.

5   Towards Efficient Implementation

A compiler-based implementation is being designed. The implementation (1) statically matches as much pointcuts as possible, and (2) eliminates unnecessary dataflow tag operations. Our approaches are to (1) use AspectJ compiler after translating **dflow** pointcuts into existing pointcuts and advice, and to (2) use static dataflow analysis.

5.1   Translating **dflow** into AspectJ

Pointcut matching, which is dynamically performed in the prototype implementation, can statically matched to the locations in the source program in most cases[15].

The first step naively translates **dflow** pointcuts into AspectJ's **pointcuts** and advice. The AspectJ compiler will then eliminates the overheads of dynamic pointcut matching for the existing kinds of pointcuts.

The implementation has to associate dataflow tags for each value. A set of dataflow tags can be represented as bit-vectors since we have fixed number of **dflow** declarations in a given program. For regular objects, the bit-vectors can be installed by using inter-type declaration mechanism in AspectJ or by extending Java virtual machine. For primitive values and arrays, we translate the given program into the one that explicitly manage such bit-vectors separately.

Management of dataflow tags can be implemented as advice declarations in AspectJ. Basically, $\mathtt{dflow}^t[x, y](p)$ pointcut is translated into **if** pointcut an advice declaration. The pointcut itself becomes the following pointcut that checks dataflow tags of the specified variable:

$$\text{if } (\langle t \text{ is in } get(x)\rangle)$$

Additionally, the pointcut generates the following advice declaration for associating a dataflow tag to a value:

$$\mathtt{before}(y) \;:\; p \;\{\; \langle \text{perform } add(y, \{t\})\rangle \;\}$$

(or it may be **after** advice when y is bound by **returns** pointcut in p). In addition, for each primitive operation, a code fragment that propagates dataflow tags will be inserted. This should be done by program transformation as primitive operations do not create join points in AspectJ[7].

AspectJ compiler statically resolves most pointcut matchings. The remaining overheads in the translated program are (1) the `if` pointcuts to test dataflow tags (but this is not significant as they appear at limited locations, and each test merely takes constant time), (2) the advice to associate dataflow tags (also, this is not significant as they merely sets a bit at limited locations), and (3) the operations to propagate dataflow tags upon primitive operations.

5.2   Eliminating Unnecessary Dataflow Tags

The second step eliminates dataflow tags that are proven to be useless. Each pointcut p has the source code locations that can create matching join points. Given a `dflow`^{t}`[x,y]` (p) pointcut, it can determine the source code locations where dataflows from y can reach. Existing information flow analysis should be able to do this job. Then, from the source code locations where no dataflows of `dflow` pointcut can reach, we can eliminate dataflow tag operations. Similary, when static analysis finds that a class involves with no dataflow, the slots for dataflow tags can be eliminated from the class.

Even at locations where some dataflow reach of, dataflow tag operations can be optimized by aggregating them per basic block (i.e., a series of operations that has no control transfers). For example, the following code, which computes the magnitude of two complex numbers, will have an dataflow tag operation for each primitive computation:

```
r0=r1*r2-i1*i2; i0=r1*i2+r2*i1; m=Math.sqrt(r0*r0+i0*i0);
```

However, those operations can be aggregated as

$$add(\texttt{m}, get(\texttt{r1}) \cup get(\texttt{i1}) \cup get(\texttt{r2}) \cup get(\texttt{i2})) \ .$$

Those optimizations will ensure that programs without `dflow` pointcut have no overheads. The authors expect that the optimizations will eliminate a large amount of overheads from programs with `dflow`, but the quantitative evaluations are yet to be done.

6   Related Work

Giving more expressiveness to pointcuts in AOP languages are studied in many ways. Some offer pointcuts that can examine calling context[10], execution history[21], and static structures of a program[7].

---

[7] In an AOP language that offers more flexible selection of join points (e.g., [20]), it would be possible to write advice declarations that propagates dataflow tags over primtive operations.

Demeter is an AOP system that can declaratively specify traversals over object graphs[12,13]. It allows to examine relation between objects, but the relation is about a structure of data in a snapshot of an execution.

There are systems that can examine dataflow in a program either in a static or dynamic manner (e.g., Confined Types[18] and taint-checks in Perl[22]). Those are useful for *checking* security enforcement. On the other hand, when a breach of the security enforcement is found by those systems, the programmer may have to fix many modules in the program without AOP support.

Information flow analyses (e.g., [19]) can detect a secret that can leak by indirect means, such as the conditional context and timing. For example, the following code does not have direct dataflow from b to x, but information about b indirectly leaks in x:

```
if (b) { x = 0; } else { x = 1; }
```

As we have shortly discussed, our dataflow definition only deals with direct information flow. It does not regard a dataflow from b to x. Extending dataflow definition to include such indirect information flow, is left for future study.

7 Conclusion

We proposed `dflow` pointcut that identifies join points based on the dataflow of values in aspect-oriented programming (AOP) languages. The pointcut allows the programmers to write more declarative aspects where the origins of data are important. The pointcut is designed to be used with the other existing kinds of pointcuts. An interpreter-based implementation is developed on top of Aspect SandBox.

The usefulness of the `dflow` pointcut is explained by an example—sanitizing web-applications. Although the paper showed only one example, we believe the notion of dataflow would be useful in many situations. Our plan is to apply the pointcut to many programs, such as design patterns[8] and the other kinds of security problems.

The design space of the `dflow` pointcut is large enough for further study. Especially, to find a right balance between the declarativness of the pointcut and the runtime efficiency is curcially important. It will also be crucially important to give a formal framework of `dflow` pointcut so that we can reason about completeness of the semantics.

Acknowledgments. The authors would like to thank Naoki Kobayashi and Atsushi Igarashi for their comments on an early draft of the paper. The authors would also like to anonymous reviewers for their comments.

References

1. CERT. Malicious HTML tags embedded in client web requests. Advisory Report CA-2000-02, CERT, February 2000.
2. CERT Coordination Center. Understanding malicious content mitigation for web developers. Tech tips, CERT, February 2000.
3. Yvonne Coady, Gregor Kiczales, Mike Feeley, and Greg Smolyn. Using AspectC to improve the modularity of path-specific customization in operating system code. In *Proceedings of the 8th European software engineering conference held jointly with 9th ACM SIGSOFT symposium on Foundations of software engineering*, pages 88–98, Vienna, Austria, 2001.
4. James Duncan Davidson and Suzanne Ahmed. Java servlet API specification: Version 2.1a. Technical Document of Sun Microsystems, November 1998. http://java.sun.com/products/servlet/.
5. Jonathan Davies, Nick Huismans, Rory Slaney, Sian Whiting, Matthew Webster, and Robert Berry. Aspect oriented profiler. a practitioner report presented at AOSD2003, March 2003.
6. Tzilla Elrad, Robert E. Filman, and Atef Bader. Aspect-oriented programming. *Comm. ACM*, 44(10):29–32, October 2001.
7. Kris Gybels and Johan Brichau. Arranging language features for more robust pattern-based crosscuts. In *Proceedings of the 2nd International Conference on Aspect-Oriented Software Development (AOSD2003)*, pages 60–69. ACM Press, 2003.
8. Jan Hannemann and Gregor Kiczales. Design pattern implementation in Java and AspectJ. In *Proceedings of the 17th Annual ACM conference on Object-Oriented Programming, Systems, Languages, and Applications (OOPSLA2002)*, pages 161–173, November 2002.
9. Mik A. Kersten and Gail C. Murphy. Atlas: A case study in building a web-based learning environment using aspect-oriented programming. In *Proc. ACM Conf. Object-oriented Programming, Systems, Languages, and Applications*, pages 340–352. ACM, 1999.
10. Gregor Kiczales, Erik Hilsdale, Jim Hugunin, Mik Kersten, Jeffrey Palm, and William G. Griswold. An overview of AspectJ. In *ECOOP 2001*, pages 327–353, 2001.
11. Gregor Kiczales, John Lamping, Anurag Menhdhekar, Chris Maeda, Cristina Lopes, Jean-Marc Loingtier, and John Irwin. Aspect-oriented programming. In Mehmet Akşit and Satoshi Matsuoka, editors, *ECOOP '97 — Object-Oriented Programming 11th European Conference*, number 1241 in Lecture Notes in Computer Science, pages 220–242, Jyväskylä, Finland, 1997. Springer-Verlag.
12. Karl Lieberherr, Doug Orleans, and Johan Ovlinger. Aspect-oriented programming with adaptive methods. *Comm. ACM*, 44(10):39–41, October 2001.
13. Karl J. Lieberherr. *Adaptive Object-Oriented Software: the Demeter Method with Propagation Patterns*. PWS Publishing Company, Boston, 1996.
14. Hidehiko Masuhara and Gregor Kiczales. Modeling crosscutting in aspect-oriented mechanisms. In Luca Cardelli, editor, *Proceedings of European Conference on Object-Oriented Programming (ECOOP2003)*, volume 2743 of *Lecture Notes in Computer Science*, pages 2–28, Darmstadt, Germany, July 2003. Springer-Verlag.
15. Hidehiko Masuhara, Gregor Kiczales, and Chris Dutchyn. A compilation and optimization model for aspect-oriented programs. In *Proceedings of 12th International Conference on Compiler Construction (CC2003)*, volume 2622 of *Lecture Notes in Computer Science*, pages 46–60, 2003.

16. Awais Rashid and Ruzanna Chitchyan. Persistence as an aspect. In *Proceedings of the 2nd International Conference on Aspect-Oriented Software Development (AOSD2003)*, pages 120–129. ACM Press, March 2003.
17. Marc Ségura-Devillechaise, Jean-Marc Menaud, Gilles Muller, and Julia L. Lawall. Web cache prefetching as an aspect: Towards a dynamic-weaving based solution. In *Proceedings of the 2nd International Conference on Aspect-Oriented Software Development (AOSD2003)*, pages 110–119. ACM Press, 2003.
18. Jan Vitek and Boris Bokowski. Confined types. In *Proceedings of the 1999 ACM SIGPLAN conference on Object-Oriented Programming, Systems, Languages, and Applications (OOPSLA99)*, pages 82–96. ACM Press, 1999.
19. D. Volpano, G. Smith, and C Irvine. A sound type system for secure flow analysis. *Journal of Computer Security*, 4(3):167–187, 1996.
20. David Walker, Steve Zdancewic, and Jay Ligatti. A theory of aspects. In *ICFP2003*, 2003.
21. Robert J. Walker and Gail C. Murphy. Implicit context: Easing software evolution and reuse. In *Proceedings of the eighth international symposium on Foundations of software engineering for twenty-first century applications (FSE-8)*, volume 25(6) of *ACM SIGSOFT Software Engineering Notes*, pages 69–78, San Diego, California, USA, November 2000.
22. Larry Wall and Randal Schwartz. *Programming Perl*. O'Reilly and Associates, 1991.
23. Mitchell Wand, Gregor Kiczales, and Chris Dutchyn. A semantics for advice and dynamic join points in aspect-oriented programming. In Ron Cytron and Gary T. Leavens, editors, *Foundations of Aspect-Oriented Langauges (FOAL2002)*, Technical Report TR#02–06, Department of Computer Science, Iowa State University, pages 1–8, Enschede, The Netherlands, April 2002.

Affine-Based Size-Change Termination

Hugh Anderson and Siau-Cheng Khoo

Department of Computer Science
School of Computing
National University of Singapore
{hugh,khoosc}@comp.nus.edu.sg

Abstract. The size-change principle devised by Lee, Jones and Ben-Amram, provides an effective method of determining program termination for recursive functions over well-founded types. Termination analysis using the principle involves the classification of functions either into size-change terminating ones, or ones which are not size-change terminating. Size-change graphs are constructed to represent the functions, and decreasing parameter sizes in those graphs that are idempotent are identified. In this paper, we propose a translation of the size-change graphs to affine-based graphs, in which affine relations among parameters are expressed by Presburger formulæ. We show the correctness of our translation by defining the size-change graph composition in terms of affine relation manipulation, and identifying the idempotent size-change graphs with transitive closures in affine relations. We then propose an affine-based termination analysis, in which more refined termination size-change information is admissible by affine relations. Specifically, our affine-related analysis improves the effectiveness of the termination analysis by capturing constant changes in parameter sizes, affine relationships of the sizes of the source parameters, and contextual information pertaining to function calls. We state and reason about the corresponding soundness and termination of this affine-related analysis. Our approach widens the set of size-change terminating functions.

1 Introduction

There are many approaches to termination analysis. For example, Colón and Sipma [4] use linear ranking functions to prove termination of program loops. Another approach could be to limit the *language* to ensure termination: if any function defined over an inductive type is restricted in the form of the definition to one using the elimination rule of the type, then the function is known to terminate [6]. An alternative method derives from the observation that, in the case of a program with well-founded data,

> "*a program terminates on all inputs if every infinite call sequence would cause an infinite descent in some program values*" [12]

In this framework, we have a finite number of functions, with the underlying data types of at least some of the parameters expected to be well-founded. In addition, the only

A. Ohori (Ed.): APLAS 2003, LNCS 2895, pp. 122–140, 2003.

technique for repetition is recursion. Given this framework, we can give the intuition behind the size-change termination method. We begin by considering the *size* of the function parameters. If the type of the parameter was a natural number, then the size of this parameter could be its value, and we cannot reduce the size of this natural number indefinitely, as eventually it will reach zero and may no longer be reduced. If the type of the parameter was an inductively defined list of items, then the size of this parameter could be its length, and again we cannot reduce the size of this list indefinitely, as eventually it will reach the empty list and (again) may no longer be reduced. Both of these parameter types are well-founded, and it is on the use of these data types that the termination method relies.

Consider a non-terminating program. This program can only be non-terminating through an infinite recursion through at least one function entry point, since the number of different functions is finite. If we consider the chain of possible function calls within each one of those functions, and determine the size-change of each of its parameters between successive calls, then if any one of those parameters reduces on each call, we have a conflict. In particular, if it reduces infinitely often, then the data is not well-founded. As a result of this, we can assert the contrapositive, an observation that may be made over a program with well-founded data types which precludes it from being non-terminating; *"if every infinite call sequence in a program would cause an infinite descent in some program values then the program terminates on all inputs"*. This gives the intuition behind the size-change termination method. Note that size-change termination is not a general termination method, but it is still useful.

In [12], Lee, Jones, and Ben-Amram present a practical technique for deriving program termination properties using the size-change termination method (hereafter called LJB-analysis), by constructing a set of size-change graphs for the program. These size-change graphs approximate, to a set of four symbolic values, the relation between the sizes of source parameters and destination arguments for each call to a function. We believe a more refined representation of size-change relation can widen the set of size-change terminating functions. In particular, Presburger formulæ, or affine relations in particular, may be a good candidate for encoding size-change graphs, for the following three reasons:

1. They allow the capturing of constant changes in parameter size. This allows the effect of constant increment and decrement to be cancelled out during the analysis.
2. They can express size change of a destination argument by a linear combination of source parameters. This enables more accurate representation of size change.
3. They can constrain the size change information with information about call context, thus naturally extending the analysis to be context-sensitive. The LJB-analysis method ignores test conditions, but these can be expressed naturally using Presburger constraints.

To illustrate that our termination analysis is strictly more powerful than the LJB-analysis, we list below three example programs in a simple first-order function definition language which can be successfully analyzed for termination by our analysis, but which are outside the scope of LJB-analysis. The first example alternately increases and reduces a parameter on successive function calls corresponding to the first reason above.

```
f(m) = if m ≤ 0 then 1 else g(m + 1);
g(n) = if n ≤ 0 then 1 else f(n - 2);
```

An example of the second reason given is the following function in which the LJB-analysis is unable to establish that the first argument must decrease:

```
k(m, n) = if m ≤ 0 then 1 else k(m - n, n + 1);
```

An example of the third reason given is the following function in which the variables are all natural numbers, and only one of the two calls can be performed, constrained by the condition $m < n$. The LJB-analysis fails to establish termination:

```
j(m, n) = if m + n = 0 then 0
          else if m < n then j(m - 1, n + 1)
               else j(m + 1, n - 1);
```

In this paper, we elaborate on the use of affine relations to capture size-change information, and show the soundness and termination of our analysis.

In Sections 2 and 3, preliminary definitions and notation used in the paper are outlined along with a brief outline of the LJB size-change termination method. In Section 4 we introduce the concept of affine-based size-change graphs, and provide a translation of LJB's size-change graphs to affine-based size-change graphs. In Section 5 we give an algorithm for building the closure of affine size-change graphs, and explore various properties of the algorithm. In Section 6 we show how this new process can establish termination properties for a wider range of functions than the original method, using a simple example. In Section 7 we outline the relation of this work to others, and conclude with some observations about the direction of our research in this area.

2   Preliminaries

In order to concentrate on the mechanism behind our termination analysis, we choose to work on a simple first-order functional language, defined in Table 1. Additional language features can be included in the subject language. As these will only complicate the generation of the initial set of size-change graphs, but not the analysis, we prefer not to include them in our discussion.

Affine relations are captured using Presburger formulæ, and each such relation has explicitly identified source and destination parameters. The syntax is defined in Table 2.

Throughout the paper, we assume the function parameters to take values of the *naturals* type $\mathbb{N}$, which is well-founded. Correspondingly, our affine relations are defined over naturals. We interpret an affine relation as a set of pairs of numbers satisfying the affine relation. For example, the following affine relation $\phi = \{[m, n] \rightarrow [p] : p = m + n + 1\}$

Table 1. The language syntax

x	$\in$ Var	$\langle$ Variables $\rangle$
op	$\in$ Prim	$\langle$ Primitive operators $\rangle$
f, g, h	$\in$ FName	$\langle$ Function names $\rangle$
c	$\in$ Const	$\langle$ Constants $\rangle$
e	$\in$ Exp	$\langle$ Expressions $\rangle$
	e ::= if e_0 then e_1 else e_2	
	$\mid x \mid c \mid e_1 \, op \, e_2 \mid f(e_1, \ldots, e_n)$	
d	$\in$ Decl	$\langle$ Definitions $\rangle$
	d ::= $f \, x_1 \, \ldots \, x_n = e$	

Table 2. Syntax of Presburger formulæ

Formulæ:	$\phi \in$ F	$\langle$ Formulæ $\rangle$	
	ϕ ::= $\psi \mid \{[v_1, \ldots, v_m] \to [w_1, \ldots, w_n] : \psi\}$		
	ψ ::= $\delta \mid \neg\psi \mid \exists v.\psi \mid \psi_1 \vee \psi_2 \mid \psi_1 \wedge \psi_2$		
Size Formulæ:	$\delta \in$ Fb	$\langle$ Boolean expressions $\rangle$	
	δ ::= True $\mid$ False $\mid a_1 = a_2 \mid a_1 \neq a_2$		
	$\mid a_1 < a_2 \mid a_1 > a_2 \mid a_1 \leq a_2 \mid a_1 \geq a_2$		
	$a \in$ Aexp	$\langle$ Arithmetic expressions $\rangle$	
	a ::= $n \mid v \mid n \star a \mid a_1 + a_2 \mid -a$		
	$n \in \mathbb{Z}$	$\langle$ Integer constants $\rangle$	

can be interpreted as a subset of $\mathbb{N}^2 \times \mathbb{N}$. Some of the pairs belonging to this set are: $([1, 0], [2])$, $([3, 4], [8])$ and so on.

This interpretation enables us to talk about subset inclusion between set solutions of affine relations. It induces a partial ordering relationship among the affine relations, and corresponds nicely to the implication relation between two affine relations, when viewed as Presburger formulæ. As a result, ϕ implies the relation

$$\phi' = \{[m, n] \to [p] : p > m + n\}$$

because the set generated by ϕ is a subset of that generated by ϕ', denoted by $\phi \subseteq \phi'$. Throughout the paper, we adopt the subset notation as relation implication.

Operations over affine relations: The first operation of interest is the composition operation for affine relations. This operation is meaningful only when we interpret an affine relation as a binary relation over two sets of parameters. The idea of composing two relations, as in $\phi_1 \circ \phi_2$, is to identify the second parameter set of ϕ_1 with the first parameter set of ϕ_2. Formally, composition is defined as follows:

$$\phi_1 \circ \phi_2 \stackrel{def}{=} \{(x, z) \mid \exists y : (x, y) \in \phi_1 \wedge (y, z) \in \phi_2\}$$

Thus, for composition over two affine relations $\phi_1 \circ \phi_2$ to be definable, we must have the number of parameters in the first set of ϕ_2 to be the same as the number of parameters in the second set of ϕ_1.

Fact 1. The composition operator over affine relations is monotone.

The second operation of interest is the union of affine relations. This is definable when all the affine relations have the same set of parameters, modulo variable renaming. Formally, union is defined as follows:

$$\phi_1 \cup \phi_2 \overset{def}{=} \{(x,y) \mid (x,y) \in \phi_1 \vee (x,y) \in \phi_2\}$$

Fact 2. The union operation over a set of affine relations is monotone. In fact, the union operation computes the least upper bound of the set of affine relations, if we consider all affine relations with the same set of parameters as a lattice partially ordered by set inclusion.

The third operation of interest is the transitive closure operation over an affine relation. It is defined for an affine relation ϕ as follows:

$$\phi^+ \overset{def}{=} \bigcup_{i \geq 0} \phi^i$$

where ϕ^i means composing ϕ with itself i times. Note that for the closure operation to work properly, ϕ must be represented as a relation over two sets of parameters, with both sets of equal size. From facts 1 and 2, we deduce that the transitive closure operation is monotone.

Fact 3. The transitive closure operation is idempotent. That is, $\phi^+ \circ \phi^+ = \phi^+$.

3 LJB Size-Change Termination

In LJB-analysis, the size-change graphs approximate the relation between the sizes of source parameters and destination arguments for each call to a function. In the size-change graph, we record only the following information about each destination argument:

- it is the same size ($=$) as some source parameter;
- it is smaller ($\downarrow$) than some source parameter;
- it is either the same size or smaller ($\overset{=}{\downarrow}$) than some source parameter;
- it is larger than some source parameter, or it has no clearly defined relation to the source parameters (unknown).

These simple relations are the only ones used to form the size-change graphs in [11,12], and we will refer to this style of size-change graph as an LJB *size-change graph*.

Definition 1. *An LJB size-change graph is a size-change graph, with each destination argument having a simple relation (=, ↓, $\overline{↓}$ or* unknown*) to each source parameter.*

We encode an LJB size-change graph by specifying a tuple relation between the source parameters and destination arguments, although the existing literature normally uses a graphical representation. Consider the following functions:

```
f(x, y) = if x ≥ 0 then y else g(x, 0, y − 1);
g(m, n, o) = if o = 0 then m + n + 1 else f(m + 1, o);
```

In Figure 1(a), we are specifying that in function $f(x, y)$, calling function $g(m, n, o)$, the first argument is the same *size* as x (=), the second has no relation to the parameters of f (unknown), and the third is always smaller than y (↓). Similarly for the other function in Figure 1(b). We do not draw the unknown relation on the diagram.

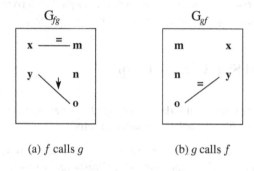

(a) f calls g (b) g calls f

Fig. 1. LJB size-change graphs

We now use the two graphs to analyze the mutually recursive functions for termination. A non-terminating sequence beginning with function f would involve an infinite succession of calls to (alternately) the functions f and g. New graphs are constructed, representing the composition of the two original graphs as shown in Figure 2.

These graphs represent the two successive calls, and demonstrate that the y parameter must reduce. We may express the infinite call sequence as the regular expression $(fg)^n$ or $f(gf)^n$. We know that the sequences $f \circ g$ and $g \circ f$ must occur infinitely often, and are the only infinite call sequences for the program. As a result, since every infinite call sequence in a program would cause an infinite descent in a program value, then the program terminates on all inputs.

The central theorem of the LJB size-change graph construction algorithm, explained and proved in [12], is:

Theorem 1. *Program P is not size-change terminating iff $\mathcal{G}$ contains $g : f \to f$ such that $g = g \circ_G g$ and g has no arc of the form $x \overset{↓}{\to} x$, where $\mathcal{G}$ is the set of possible size-change graphs, and $\circ_G$ represents the composition of two size-change graphs.*

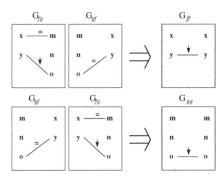

Fig. 2. LJB size-change graphs for functions $f \circ g$ and $g \circ f$

This theorem gives rise to a relatively efficient technique for deriving termination properties from a closure computation over the size-change graphs.

4   Affine-Based Size-Change Graphs

Within the general framework of LJB size-change termination analysis, we now develop concepts for the new affine-based size-change graphs.

We elect to represent size-change information using the notation and syntax of the Omega calculator and library [9], which can manipulate Presburger formulæ. We term the graphs thus represented *affine size-change graphs*.

Definition 2 (Affine graph). *An affine size-change graph is a size-change graph such that each destination argument is constrained by the source parameters arranged in an affine relation.*

Such a graph is sometimes termed an affine tuple relation, mapping n-tuples to m-tuples constrained by an affine formula. In the LJB size-change graph, the possible relations between a source parameter m and a destination argument m' are just simple ones such as $=, \downarrow, \bar{\bar{\downarrow}}$ or unknown. By contrast, in an affine size-change graph, the possible relations between a source parameter m and a destination argument m' can be any expression represented by a Presburger formula. For example, $m' \leq 2m - 4$ is a valid relation in an affine size-change graph.

4.1   Translation of Size-Change Graphs

In this section, we translate the LJB size-change graphs as described in [12] to our affine size-change graph form. We provide a definition of the LJB-graph composition in terms of operations on affine relations. Notwithstanding the fact that the correctness of the translation is important to the correctness of our latter development, the process of translation also sheds light on the correctness and termination of affine-based termination analysis.

Given two lists of source parameters and destination arguments, we consider a set $\mathcal{G}$ and a set $\mathcal{F}$ of (respectively) all possible LJB-graphs and affine graphs generated from these lists. We define a translation that maps LJB-graphs to affine graphs, as follows:

Definition 3 ($g2a$ **Translation**). *For each edge e_i in $g \in \mathcal{G}$, translation $g2a :: \mathcal{G} \to \mathcal{F}$ produces an affine relation r_i according to the following translation:*

$$
\begin{array}{ccc}
e_i & & r_i \\[2mm]
m \xrightarrow{=} n & \mapsto & n = m \\[2mm]
m \xrightarrow{\downarrow} n & \mapsto & n < m \\[2mm]
m \xrightarrow{\overset{=}{\downarrow}} n & \mapsto & n \leq m
\end{array}
$$

In addition, for each source parameter x_j and destination argument y_k, we associate the constraint $x_j \geq 0$ and $y_k \geq 0$, respectively. Finally, we have

$$
g2a(g) = \{[x_1, \ldots, x_m] \to [y_1, \ldots, y_n] : (\bigwedge_i r_i) \wedge \mathcal{D}\}
$$

$$
\mathcal{D} = (\bigwedge_j x_j \geq 0) \wedge (\bigwedge_k y_k \geq 0)
$$

Note that we do not map edges with the unknown symbol to any constraint, since the symbol implies no knowledge about how the parameter size is changed. We note that $g2a$ is an injection. The relation $\mathcal{D}$ specifies the *boundary constraints*, and asserts that all parameters take non-negative values.

In order to show the correctness of our translation, we define an *abstraction function* from affine graphs to LJB-graphs.

Definition 4 (**Abstraction** $a2g$). *The abstraction $a2g : \mathcal{F} \to \mathcal{G}$ is defined as follows:*

$$
a2g(a) = g2a^{-1}(\pi(a))
$$

where π is defined as follows:

$$
\begin{aligned}
\pi(a) &= \{[x_1, \ldots, x_m] \to [y_1, \ldots, y_n] : r \wedge \mathcal{D}\}; \\
r &= \{\bigwedge (y_j \ op \ x_i) \mid a \subseteq P(x_i, y_j, op), \ 1 \leq i \leq m, \\
&\qquad\qquad\qquad\qquad 1 \leq j \leq n, \ op \in \{=, <, \leq\}\}; \\
P(u, v, op) &= \{[x_1, \ldots, x_m] \to [y_1, \ldots, y_n] : v \ op \ u \wedge \mathcal{D}\};
\end{aligned}
$$

π is composed of projection functions that project a graph a onto a rectangular polygon enclosing a. This polygon is made up of affine relations of the following forms: y op x where y is a destination argument, x is a source parameter, and op is either $=$, $<$, or $\leq$. In addition, we have that all source parameters and destination arguments are constrained to be non-negative. It is easy to show that the function π, and consequently $a2g$, are monotone.

An example of the use of the function π is

$$\pi(\{[x,y] \rightarrow [x',y'] : x' = x+2 \wedge x' = y-1 \wedge \mathcal{D}\}) = \{[x,y] \rightarrow [x',y'] : x' < y \wedge \mathcal{D}\}$$

where it is seen that the π function retains exactly the information used in LJB-analysis.

In the following, we use $\circ_F$ to represent affine-graph composition.

Property 1. Function π enjoys the following properties:

1. $id_a \subseteq \pi$.
2. It is *idempotent*: $\pi \circ \pi = \pi$.
3. For any $a_1, a_2 \in \mathcal{F}$,
$$\pi(a_1 \circ_F a_2) \subseteq \pi(a_1) \circ_F \pi(a_2).$$

We now provide a definition of LJB-graph composition in terms of affine-graph operations, and give a characterization of the idempotent LJB-graphs using affine graphs.

Lemma 1 (LJB-graph composition $\circ_G$). *For all $g_1, g_2 \in \mathcal{G}$,*

$$g_1 \circ_G g_2 \overset{def}{=} a2g(g2a(g_1) \circ_F g2a(g_2))$$

Functions $a2g$ and $g2a$ are "tightly" related, in the following sense:

Property 2. Let id_F be the identity function on $\mathcal{F}$, and id_G that of $\mathcal{G}$. The following holds:
$$g2a \circ a2g \subseteq id_F$$
$$a2g \circ g2a = id_G$$

Now, we have the following theorem relating the idempotent LJB-graph to affine graphs:

Theorem 2 (Idempotent Graphs). *Let $g \in \mathcal{G}$ and $a = g2a(g)$.*

$$g \circ_G g = g \text{ if and only if } \pi(a) = a \text{ and } a = a^+.$$

We omit the proof due to space constraints, but it may be found in an extended technical report [2].

5   Affine-Based Termination Analysis

The affine-based termination analysis is computed in a similar fashion to the LJB-analysis. The analysis begins with the set of affine graphs representing parameter size-change for each function call in the program. Consequently, arguments' size changes are captured during the analysis for all possible call sequences. This change is computed by composing the existing affine size-change graphs in all the legitimate combinations.

The Omega library [9] can calculate the composition of affine relations efficiently, and assist in the calculation of the closure for a set of such relations. For example, consider the following program:

```
f(m) = if m ≤ 0 then 1 else g(m + 1);
g(n) = if n ≤ 0 then 1 else f(n − 2);
```

The corresponding affine size-change graphs for the call to function g in f (let's label it f_1), and the call to function f in g (label it g_1), are encoded with two affine relations using the Omega library representation as follows:

$$f_1 = \{[m] \to [m'] : m' = m + 1 \wedge \mathcal{D}\}$$
$$g_1 = \{[n] \to [n'] : n' = n - 2 \wedge \mathcal{D}\}$$

In each of these representations, the source parameters and destination arguments have one member each, constrained by a relation expressed as a Presburger formula. The first expresses that the destination m' must be one more than the source m. The second expresses that the destination n' must be two less than the source n. From this we can see that we are not only capturing the information about size reduction, but also the size of parameter changes, and perhaps other more subtle relationships. There already exist well-documented ways for extracting affine relations from a program for other purposes. For example, [10] describes a contextual analysis to retrieve such information using sized types. For lack of space, we omit the details in this paper.

5.1   Associating Affine with Abstract Graphs

A crucial administrative task in ensuring termination of our analysis is the association of each affine graph with an abstract graph. We could view this as a process of *classifying* our affine size-change graphs. The elements of the abstract size-change graphs provide the different classifications, and the affine graphs provide concrete instances of some of these classifications. An abstract graph is defined as follows:

Definition 5 (Abstract graph). *An affine size-change graph is called an abstract graph if all its parameters are non-negative, and each of its destination parameters y_i can only be related to the source parameters x_j in an affine relation y_i op x_j, where op $\in$ $=, <, >, \leq, \geq$. Moreover, there is no other affine relation among the parameters.*

We see that the set of affine graphs produced from LJB-graphs via the translation $g2a$ is a set of abstract graphs. To obtain a more accurate termination analysis, we need to extend this set of abstract graphs to include those of which the destination parameter can have size greater than some source parameters.

Given a program, we generate all its possible abstract graphs $\mathcal{A}$. Let $\mathcal{F}$ be the corresponding affine graphs that can possibly be created from the program. We then associate each affine graph with an abstract graph in $\mathcal{A}$, as follows:

$$\forall f \in \mathcal{F}, a \in \mathcal{A}, associate(f, a) \stackrel{def}{=} a = \bigcap_i \{r_i \mid f \subseteq r_i, \ r_i \in \mathcal{A}\}$$

where $\phi_1 \cap \phi_2 \stackrel{def}{=} \{(x, y) \mid (x, y) \in \phi_1 \wedge (x, y) \in \phi_2\}$.

We note that the associated abstract graph a thus obtained is minimum, in that any other abstract graph that "contains" the affine graph f will also contain a. Consequently, we call it the *minimum association*.

It is important to point out that, in actual implementation of the algorithm, we maintain not just the association of graphs, but also (approximated) information about call sequences leading to the creation of that particular graph. This call-sequence information is crucial to the accuracy of the termination analysis. However, as the inclusion of call-sequence manipulation will obscure the presentation of our algorithm, we ignore, without loss of generality, call-sequence information in our presentation.

Consider the example given earlier in this section. The minimal set of possible abstract graphs A for the program is $A = \{A_1, A_2, \ldots, A_{10}\}$, where,

For the label f_1:	For the label g_1:
$A_1 = \{[m] \to [m'] : m' < m\}$	$A_6 = \{[n] \to [n'] : n' < n\}$
$A_2 = \{[m] \to [m'] : m' \leq m\}$	$A_7 = \{[n] \to [n'] : n' \leq n\}$
$A_3 = \{[m] \to [m'] : m' = m\}$	$A_8 = \{[n] \to [n'] : n' = n\}$
$A_4 = \{[m] \to [m'] : m' > m\}$	$A_9 = \{[n] \to [n'] : n' > n\}$
$A_5 = \{[m] \to [m']\}$	$A_{10} = \{[n] \to [n']\}$

In the graphs above, and for the rest of this paper we omit the inclusion of the boundary constraints $\mathcal{D}$. Note that in these tables we only consider the operations $=, <, >, \leq$, excluding the $\geq$ operator. In this particular analysis, the $\geq$ operator does not add any information of interest. The initial set of affine graphs for the functions is $F = \{F_1, F_2\}$ where:

$$F_1 = \{[m] \to [m'] : m' = m + 1\}$$
$$F_2 = \{[n] \to [n'] : n' = n - 2\}$$

The elements F_1 and F_2 are concrete instances of the elements A_4 and A_6 of A, as

$$\{[m] \to [m'] : m' = m + 1\} \subseteq \{[m] \to [m'] : m' > m\}$$
$$\{[n] \to [n'] : n' = n - 2\} \subseteq \{[n] \to [n'] : n' < n\}$$

and we associate each affine graph with its classification using the set of pairs

$$C = \{(F_1, A_4), (F_2, A_6)\}$$

The process of *classifying* our affine size-change graphs using the abstract size-change graphs, leads to a finite number of affine size-change graphs. We use this property in the proof of termination of the termination analysis algorithm.

5.2 Affine-Based Closure Algorithm

The core of the termination analysis is the algorithm $\mathcal{T}$, which builds the closure of the new set of affine size-change graphs F uses a simple technique, constructing the compositions of the existing affine size-change graphs until no new affine graphs are created. The algorithm $\mathcal{T}$:

```
Classify initial affine graphs into C';
C := ∅;
while C' ≠ C do {
    C := C';
    F' := generate(C);
    foreach g ∈ F' {
        (r, Ag) := classify(g, C');
        if idempotent(g, Ag) then
            g := g⁺;
        g := ω(hull(r ∪ g));
        if nullgraph(r) then
            C' := C' ∪ (g, Ag)
        else
            C' := (C'\(r, Ag)) ∪ (g, Ag);
    }
}
```

The main idea of the algorithm, ignoring the termination issues, can be described using the following metaphor: recall that each affine graph can be associated with a minimum abstract graph. Imagine each abstract graph (there are a finite number of them) as a container, which will contain those affine graphs under its minimal association. The containers will have a cap labeled with the corresponding abstract graph. Thus, some containers will be considered as idempotent containers when they are labeled/capped with an idempotent abstract graph.

Initially, only the initial set of affine graphs will be kept in some of the containers. At each iteration of the algorithm, a composition operation will be performed among all legitimate pairs of affine graphs, including self-composition. The resulting set of affine graphs will again be placed in the respective containers they are (minimally) associated with. Assume that such an iteration process will eventually terminate, with no more new affine graphs created. Then we need to identify those non-empty idempotent containers, checking their cap to see if the idempotent abstract graphs labeled therein contain a decreasing edge. If all these idempotent abstract graphs have decreasing edges, we conclude that the associated program terminates. If one of these graphs does not have a decreasing edge, we shall conclude that the associated program does not belong to the size-change terminating programs.

Suppose we associate each affine size-change graph with its classification, using the set of pairs

$$C = \{(F_1, A_j), (F_2, A_k), \ldots\}$$

This set grows in size as the algorithm runs, but has a maximum size determined by the size of $\mathcal{A}$. The function classify returns a pair (r, A_k), with r a null graph if this classification has not been made before, or with the previous value for the affine size-change graph if this classification has been made before. The function generate returns a new set of affine size-change graphs constructed by composing any possible pairs of existing size-change graphs. The legitimate compositions only include those which result in a legitimate call sequence, as is the case for LJB-analysis. In the event that a graph g is idempotent, we keep the transitive closure g^+ of the graph, reflecting the idea that any idempotent graph may result in an infinite series of calls through itself. The function ω performs a widening operation to produce an affine graph that is larger than the argument graph. This is a common technique used in ensuring finite generation of abstract values [7]. The function idempotent checks if a graph g and its self composition $g \circ g$ are both minimally associated with the same abstract graph A_g.

In contrast with the metaphor described above, the algorithm maintains at most *one* affine graph in each container (classification). When a new graph is found to belong to an existing non-empty container, it is combined with the existing graph in the container, using the union, hull, and widening operations. Finally, the algorithm's main structure C is continually updated into C' until it reaches a fixed point.

A widening operator: In order to guarantee termination for our algorithm, we propose a widening operation, which retains as much information as possible from the container of affine graphs, and guarantees the stabilization of the affine graph in that container under graph composition. The idea of using a widening operator to control termination is not new, and can be found in (for example)[7,13].

To better understand how our widening function ω is defined, we first note that the affine constraints in an affine graph can be divided into three sets:

1. The boundary constraints, $\mathcal{D}$.
2. The contextual constraints, $\mathcal{K}$: for the context in which the call represented by the affine graph is called. There are no destination arguments in these constraints.
3. The output constraints $\mathcal{E}$: this constrains the destination arguments by other variables, such as source parameters.

Furthermore, an output constraint over destination argument y_j can be expressed as follows:

$$y_j \; op \; \Sigma_k a_k x_k - \Sigma_l b_l x_l' + c$$

where $op \in \{=, <, >, \leq, \geq\}$, x_k, x'_l are source parameters, $a_k, b_l \geq 0$ and c is any integer.

Definition 6. *Given that the affine relations in an affine graph a can be divided into three sets of constraints, $\mathcal{D}$, $\mathcal{K}$, and $\mathcal{E}$, as described above. The widening operator ω applying over a may now be defined as follows:*

$$\omega(a) = \{[x_1, \ldots, x_m] \rightarrow [y_1, \ldots, y_n] : (\bigwedge_i E(r_i)) \wedge \mathcal{D} \wedge (\bigwedge_j K(r'_j)) | r_i \in \mathcal{E}, r'_j \in \mathcal{K}\}$$

where $E(r_i)$ is a function defined by the following table (assume $c > 0$):

Form of r_i	Conditions	$E(r_i)$
$y \ op \ x + c$	$op \in \{=, >, \geq\}$	$y \ op \ x + c$
$y = \Sigma_k a_k x_k + c$	$a_k > 0, k > 1$	$\bigwedge_k y \geq a_k x_k + c$
$y > \Sigma_k a_k x_k + c$	$a_k > 0, k > 1$	$\bigwedge_k y > a_k x_k + c$
$y \geq \Sigma_k a_k x_k + c$	$a_k > 0, k > 1$	$\bigwedge_k y \geq a_k x_k + c$
$y \ op \ x - c$	$op \in \{=, <, \leq\}$	$y \ op \ x - c$
$y = x - (\Sigma_l b_l x_l) - c$	$b_l > 0, l > 0$	$y \leq x - c$
$y < x - (\Sigma_l b_l x_l) - c$	$b_l > 0, l > 0$	$y < x - c$
$y \leq x - (\Sigma_l b_l x_l) - c$	$b_l > 0, l > 0$	$y \leq x - c$
all other forms		true

and $K(r'_j)$ is a function defined by the following table (assuming $c > 0$, and m and n are arbitrary variables):

Form of r'_j	Conditions	$K(r'_j)$
$m \ op \ n$	$op \in \{=, <, >, \leq, \geq\}$	$m \ op \ n$
$m \ op \ c$	$op \in \{=, >, \geq\}$	$m \ op \ c$
all other forms		true

Imagine our mn-tuple relations in $m + n$-space. For example if our source tuple had two parameters (x, y) and our destination arguments just one (z) then we might imagine a 3-space, with the axes x, y and z. The widening operation projects an arbitrary affine relation onto each of the two axes x and y. A relation such as $z = x + y + 4$ would be widened to

$$z \geq x + 4 \wedge z \geq y + 4$$

Property 3. The widening operator ω defined in Definition 6 is monotone and idempotent. Furthermore, for any $a \in \mathcal{F}, \omega(a) \subseteq \pi(a)$.

In addition to being monotone, ω also ensures the generation of a finite number of affine graphs which are less precise than the initial one. For instance, if an application of ω produces an affine graph having the following constraint:

$$y \geq 5x_1 + 2x_2 + 3$$

then, there are only a finite number of constraints which are of identical form

$$y \geq \Sigma_k a_k x_k + c$$

and are less precise, namely:

$$y \geq d_1 x_1 + d_2 x_2 + d_3$$

where $0 < d_1 < 5$, $0 < d_2 < 2$ and $0 < d_3 < 3$. This finiteness in the number of less precise constraints guarantees that iterative computation of affine graphs will stabilize in a finite number of steps.

Definition 7. *An affine graph of the following form is said to be in stable form:*

$$\{[x_1, \ldots, x_m] \to [y_1, \ldots, y_n] : Er \wedge D \wedge Kr\}$$

where Er and Kr are conjunctions of constraints of the forms described by the range of functions E and K respectively.

Property 4. Given an affine graph g defined in a stable form, there are a finite number of affine graphs of identical form which are less precise than g.

5.3   Properties of Affine-Based Termination Analysis

It is easy to verify that the analysis, if it terminates, computes more accurate information than the LJB-analysis. To see that, we drop all the contextual information in the initial affine graphs collected, by making all such contextual information true. We then replace the widening operator ω in our analysis by π defined in Definition 4. This turns those affine graphs, which are associated with idempotent abstract graphs, into their respective abstract graphs during the analysis. With these changes, we obtain an analysis that mimics the computation of LJB-analysis.

Termination of the algorithm: The key components of the algorithm ensure that the algorithm terminates. In the following proof, we use the finite cardinality of the size-change graphs, and the monotonic nature of the graph operations.

Theorem 3. *The algorithm $\mathcal{T}$ terminates.*

Proof. The algorithm terminates when $\mathcal{C}'$ is no longer changing. $\mathcal{C}'$ can change in only two ways, either by

1. *creating* an association for a new abstract graph A_g, or by
2. *replacing* an existing set element (r, A_g) with a new (g', A_g).

Proof of termination is done here by showing that neither of the above actions can be done an infinite number of times. We omit the details of the proof due to space constraints, but it may be found in the extended technical report [2].

6 Example Using Affine Size-Change Graphs

In this example we demonstrate constant change cancellation. In an earlier section, we introduced the following two affine size-change graphs:

$$F_1 = \{[m] \to [m'] : m' = m + 1\}$$
$$F_2 = \{[n] \to [n'] : n' = n - 2\}$$

Our initial value for $\mathcal{C}$ is

$$c_1 = \{(F_1, A_4), (F_2, A_6)\}$$

The first call to `generate` returns the following new affine size-change graphs:

$$F_3 = \{[n] \to [n'] : n' = n - 1\} \qquad \text{(from the sequence } g_1 f_1)$$
$$F_4 = \{[m] \to [m'] : m' = m - 1\} \qquad \text{(from the sequence } f_1 g_1)$$

Since these are idempotent, we calculate the closure of F_3 and F_4:

$$F_3 = \{[n] \to [n'] : n' < n\}$$
$$F_4 = \{[m] \to [m'] : m' < m\}$$

After this first iteration, $\mathcal{C}$ has the value

$$c_2 = \{(F_1, A_4), (F_2, A_6), (F_3, A_{11}), (F_4, A_{12})\}$$

where

$$A_{11} = \{[n] \to [n'] : n' < n\}$$
$$A_{12} = \{[m] \to [m'] : m' < m\}$$

After a few more iterations we get one more graph, and $\mathcal{C}$ has a stable value. The new graph is:

$$F_5 = \{[m] \to [n'] : n' \le m\} \qquad \text{(from the sequence } f_1 g_1 f_1)$$

The idempotent functions are F_3 and F_4, which each have a reducing parameter, and so we conclude that the size-change termination property applies to this function. There are other examples showing context analysis in the extended technical report [2].

In general, using this technique we can capture termination for all the functions captured by the LJB technique, and also some others. In other words we can capture termination for a larger set of programs.

7   Related Work and Conclusion

This paper presented an approach to improve the analysis of program termination properties based on the size-change termination method. We encoded size-change graphs using Presburger formulæ representing affine relations, and explored more refined size-change graphs admissible by these affine relations. The algorithm for calculating the closure of the affine size-change graphs has been shown to terminate. Consequently, our affine-related analysis improves the effectiveness of the LJB termination analysis by capturing constant changes in parameter sizes, and affine relationships of the sizes of the source parameters. Our approach widens the set of functions that are size-change terminating.

The way in which we attempt to find closures is different from the normal approach of finding closures and fixed points. Conventionally, program analysis will attempt to find a closure for each function definition, such as those found in [3] and in the work on termination done for the Mercury system [15], and many works on program analysis, for example [1,7,8]. In our approach, we express the ultimate closure in terms of several closures called the idempotent graphs. This is similar to the idea of polyvariant program analysis [5,16], but differs in that there are also some graphs around during the analysis which cannot be made idempotent, yet are important for closure building. There are two ways to obtain polyvariant information for termination analysis: one way is to make use of the constraint enabling the call. Such constraints are commonly obtained from the conditional tests of the code leading to the call. The use of Presburger formulæ enables us to easily include such information in the analysis, resulting in a context-sensitive analysis [13,14].

Another way to capture polyvariant information is to capture the possible function call sequence, such as a function g can be called from another function f, but not from k. The LJB-analysis uses this information to achieve polyvariant analysis. While this information can be captured in our algorithm (by creating more distinct abstract graphs with call sequence information), we do not present it, due to lack of space. Nevertheless, it will be interesting to look into integrating call-sequence information into constraints, so that there is only one source for controlling polyvariance.

As it is, the termination analysis deals with a set of mutually recursive functions at a time. It would be interesting to investigate the modularity of the analysis, so that each function can be analyzed separately, and the results from various functions be composed to yield the final termination result. One such opportunity is to integrate the affine-based termination analysis with a type-based system. Currently, we have begun working towards a type-inference system which collects the relevant size-change information for performing this sort of termination analysis.

The use of constraints in expressing argument change enables us to consider termination beyond the *well-founded* method. For example, through constraints, we can express the fact that an increasing argument can be bounded above. This idea has been explored in the work on sized typing in [3]. The bounded-increment of an argument is also investigated in [4], which computes a linear ranking function for a loop-based program. In contrast, our technique deals directly with recursive function calls instead of loop-based programs. We plan to enhance the existing technique to include such techniques.

Acknowledgements. The authors would like to thank Lindsay Groves and the anonymous referees for their many insightful and helpful comments. This work has been supported by the research grant R-252-000-138-112.

References

1. A. Aiken. Introduction to Set Constraint-Based Program Analysis. *Science of Computer Programming*, 35(1999):79–111, 1999.
2. H. Anderson and S.C. Khoo. Affine-Based Size-Change Termination. Technical Report TRA9/03, National University of Singapore, September 2003.
3. W.N. Chin and S.C. Khoo. Calculating Sized Types. In *Partial Evaluation and Semantic-Based Program Manipulation*, pages 62–72, 2000.
4. M. Colón and H. Sipma. Practical Methods for Proving Program Termination. In *14th International Conference on Computer Aided Verification (CAV)*, volume 2404 of *Lecture Notes in Computer Science*, pages 442–454. Springer, 2002.
5. C. Consel. Polyvariant Binding-Time Analysis For Applicative Languages. In *Partial Evaluation and Semantic-Based Program Manipulation*, pages 66–77, 1993.
6. T. Coquand and C. Paulin. Inductively Defined Types. In P. Martin-Lof and G.Mints, editors, *Proceedings of COLOG'88*, volume 417 of *Lecture Notes in Computer Science*, pages 50–66. ACM, Springer, 1990.
7. P. Cousot and N. Halbwachs. Automatic Discovery of Linear Restraints Among Variables of a Program. In *Conference Record of the Fifth Annual ACM SIGPLAN-SIGACT Symposium on Principles of Programming Languages*, pages 84–97, Tucson, Arizona, 1978. ACMPress, New York, NY.
8. N. Heintze. *Set Based Program Analysis*. PhD thesis, CMU, 1992.
9. P. Kelly, V. Maslov, W. Pugh, E. Rosser, T. Shpeisman, and D. Wonnacott. The Omega Library Version 1.1.0 Interface Guide. Technical report, University of Maryland, College Park, November 1996.
10. S.C. Khoo and K. Shi. Output Constraint Specialization. *ACM SIGPLAN ASIA Symposium on Partial Evaluation and Semantics-Based Program Manipulation*, pages 106–116, September 2002.
11. C.S. Lee. Program Termination Analysis in Polynomial Time. In Don Batory, Charles Consel, and Walid Taha, editors, *Generative Programming and Component Engineering: ACM SIGPLAN/SIGSOFT Conference, GPCE 2002*, volume 2487 of Lecture Notes in Computer Science, pages 218–235. ACM, Springer, October 2002.

12. C.S. Lee, N.D. Jones, and A.M. Ben-Amram. The Size-Change Principle for Program Termination. In *Proceedings of the 28th Annual ACM SIGPLAN-SIGACT Symposium on Principles of Programming Languages*, volume 28, pages 81–92. ACM press, January 2001.
13. F. Nielson, H.R. Nielson, and C. Hankin. *Principles of Program Analysis.* Springer, 1999.
14. O. Shivers. Control Flow Analysis in Scheme. *ACM SIGPLAN Notices*, 7(1):164–174, 1988.
15. C. Speirs, Z. Somogyi, and H. Sondergaard. Termination Analysis for Mercury. In *Static Analysis Symposium*, pages 160–171, 1997.
16. W. Vanhoof and M. Bruynooghe. Binding-time Analysis for Mercury. In *International Conference on Logic Programming*, pages 500–514, 1999.

Using Locality of Flow in Dataflow Analyses

Ravindra D V

Computer Science and Automation, Indian Institute of Science, India,
ravindra@csa.iisc.ernet.in

Abstract. Dataflow analysis using specifications which are not expressible as uni-directional analyses have found limited use in practice inspite
of the fact that they can be shorter and more comprehensible than a corresponding decomposition. This is largely due to the fact that straightforward iterative algorithms on such analyses have non-linear time complexity in the size of the control flowgraph.
In this paper, we unify the traditional classes of uni-directional and bi-
directional analyses into a more natural class of *local flow* analyses. The
dataflow equations for this class can be compactly encoded as matrix-
vector equations on a path-algebra. We then use methods from path-
algebra to derive efficient algorithms for solving the set of equations. In
the best case, we can achieve the efficiency of uni-directional analyses.
Otherwise, we can decrease the complexity of the analysis as compared
with a generic iterative analysis.

1 Introduction

Dataflow analyses in optimizing compilers are commonly solved by finding the
least (or greatest) fixed-point of a function using a simple iterative strategy. In
order to be practicable, the number of iterations to reach the fixed-point must
be a constant at least on 'typical' programs. Essentially, the complexity of an
analysis must be linear in the size of the control flow graph (CFG).

In program analysis based on the flow graph, the 'function' is a system of
dataflow equations of the form $x_i = f_i(x_{j_1}, \ldots, x_{j_{m_i}})$ where variable x_i is associated with node i of the CFG and the function f_i denotes how the information
x_i is computed. Analyses are classified based on the variables $x_{j_1} \ldots x_{j_{m_i}}$ which
occur in the definition of x_i. If all the elements of x are dependent exclusively
on their respective predecessors or successors in the CFG, the formulation is
said to be uni-directional (forward and backward respectively). If x_i can depend
on nodes adjacent to it (predecessors or successors), then the formulation is
classified as bi-directional.

Special classes of function properties have already been studied for the complexity of iterative analysis [14]. These are restrictions on the form of the function
to satisfy properties beyond monotonicity. The most efficient (and useful) class
in this setting is the *iterative form* with a quadratic complexity (i.e. the number of iterations is linear). Conventional dataflow analyses which we consider
here are a subclass of this class. Linear complexity is achieved in uni-directional

A. Ohori (Ed.): APLAS 2003, LNCS 2895, pp. 141–158, 2003.
© Springer-Verlag Berlin Heidelberg 2003

frameworks by other means based on the control flow structure like reducibility in interval analysis [7], the language syntax in structural analysis [16] or by a proper traversal order of the flow graph in general [1]. In contrast to this, solution of bi-directional frameworks using iterative analysis is quadratic, even on flow graphs which occur in practice.

When a problem is formulated as a more complex analysis, the traditional approach is to look for a sequence of uni-directional analyses which together solve the original problem. This requires us to factor the problem in terms of a set of new analyses and also prove that the sequence correctly implements the complex analysis. A problem which was specified as one dataflow analysis now requires multiple analyses. Further, this decomposition is not possible for all analyses. We must then accept a loss of precision and settle for a weaker form of the analysis (which is safe, but less precise).

In this paper, we bridge this gap in efficiency by using the structure of the dataflow equations. Our goals are the following: we should be able to directly solve the dataflow equations without generation of intermediate frameworks or transient data. Second, if the formulation admits a decomposition into uni-directional flows, our algorithm must be as efficient as a typical uni-directional analysis. In the general case, it can be anywhere from linear to quadratic in the size of the CFG. It is however, always better than a naive iterative analysis.

We first generalize uni-directional and bi-directional to a more natural *local-flow* analysis. We then study the solution of local flow problems using path algebra [2,4]. Solution of equations over a path algebra fits in very well with the notion of locality which we wish to use in solving the local-flow analyses.

In the next section, we briefly review notions from path algebra with special emphasis on the solution of equations of the form $x = Tx + b$ where x, b are vectors and T is a square matrix. In Section 3, we map dataflow problems onto this equation. We precisely define what we mean by local-flow analysis using restrictions on T. In Section 4, we will look at methods which use the structure of T to solve local-flow problems efficiently. Finally, we will illustrate our algorithm on flows which occur in practice showing its applicability as well as its limitations. In the rest of this section, we will give a brief overview of our approach and contrast it with other methods for speeding up dataflow analysis.

Consider the system of equations $x_i = f_i(x_1, \ldots, x_n)$ representing a program analysis (solving for x). We can define a dataflow dependence graph (DFDG) which has one node for each variable and an edge from node x_n to node x_m if x_m is used in defining x_n (x_m appears in $f_n(x)$). If we use iterative methods, it can be shown that number of iterations to reach the fixed-point is upper-bounded by a parameter called the *depth* of the DFDG under some assumptions. For uni-directional analyses, the DFDG is either the CFG or its reversal. Empirical observations have shown that the depth of a CFG is bound by a small constant (around three) [1]. Hence, uni-directional analyses are efficient in practice.

We now consider analyses with more general DFDGs which are nevertheless derived from the CFG and its reversal. More precisely, if A, A' denote the adjacency matrix of the CFG and its reversal respectively, we consider DFDGs whose adjacency matrices are "polynomials" in A and A': AA', $A'A$, $A'^2A + AA'$, $AA' + A + A'$ etc. Starting with this graph, we use both the restricted structure and the properties of the lattice to identify some special subgraphs in the DFDG. These subgraphs are handled so that they effectively do not contribute to the depth of the graph. In general, the DFDG can be partitioned by simply partitioning the edge-set. But we identify two criteria to choose our sub-graphs: First, the complexity of identification of all such sub-graphs must be linear in the size of the CFG. Second, the complexity of finding fixed-points within the subgraph must be linear in the number of nodes in the subgraph. The goal of this transformation is to bound the effective depth of the final DFDG by some constant (at least in practice).

In practice, there are not many problems which are inherently bi-directional. But, one can synthesize complex flows by combining analyses. This might improve the effectiveness of each of the participating analyses. A well-known example is the elimination of partial redundancies [12] (PRE). Yet another reason is to short-circuit the explicit computation of auxiliary information. We can set up one equation for a set of analyses and solve for the 'primary' analysis. The combined analysis may not be faster or more precise, but it does decrease the size of the dataflow analyzer. The important thing here is that analyses underlying complex flows were uni-directional except that they were not of the same kind (all forward or all backward). Such compositions usually give rise to DFDGs of the kind we indicated earlier.

One early use of path-algebra has been in the work of Tarjan [17] who calls it regular-expression algebra. It is restricted to uni-directional analyses and is a divide-and-conquer style of solution of a linear equation. In our approach, we do not look for hierarchy. Instead, we look for opportunities to propagate information faster over some segments of paths which are important for the analysis. Indeed, the graph decompositions we define here cannot be easily nested into a hierarchy.

PRE has been a focus of a lot of research in designing uni-directional frameworks which are equivalent to bi-directional ones [10,15]. However, certain formulations of PRE itself are not decomposable by some means (see [9] for one such formulation). This makes more general frameworks like those presented in [8] relevant.

A parallel stream of research is in combining optimizations as studied by [18], [5] using composite lattices to propagate information or by extending the dataflow framework with local graph transformations [11]. The emphasis is on the safety of the analysis under general flow functions which nevertheless are still uni-directional in nature. That is orthogonal to the structure of flow which we are analyzing here.

A closely related approach to the one presented here is *interval analysis* or its more general counterpart, *structural analysis*[16]. In structural analysis, the dataflow solution templates are based on the syntactic structures provided by the language like while-statements or conditionals. The input flow graph is then decomposed into these structural templates and the dataflow equations are solved on this new representation. One can view the graph decompositions presented here as an extension of structural analysis to a flow-aware situation. The set of templates is no longer specified by the syntax of the language, but by the particular analysis to be solved. The efficiency of dataflow analysis on the template may depend on non-structural properties like the form of the functions f_i and the information lattice. An important difference is that structural analysis is done once before any form of dataflow analysis is done. Backward and forward analyses are mapped onto the structure so built (called the 'control tree'). In contrast, the decomposition here is tailored to the structure of the DFDG which is dependent on the analysis (at least a class of analyses). Therefore, the decomposition must be *fast* unlike structural analysis whose cost is amortized by the speed-up of the remaining analyses.

The idea of isolating the 'cross-flows' has been described in the context of code-motion algorithms [15]. Our partitioning strategy can be viewed as an approach to abstract out such idioms. In this case, we will see that a complemented lattice is required for such cross-flow isolation to work efficiently. The second difference is that we can work directly with the more concise bi-directional formulations.

2   Fixed-Point Equations on Path Algebra

The notation and theorems in this section are based on [4]. A path algebra is a set P augmented with two operators $+$ and $\cdot$ with the following properties:

1. $+$ is commutative, idempotent and associative.
2. $\cdot$ is associative and distributes over $+$.
3. There exists a zero element $\phi \in P$ such that $\phi + x = x + \phi = x$, $\phi \cdot x = x \cdot \phi = \phi$ for all x in P.
4. There exists a unit element $e \in P$ such that $e \cdot x = x \cdot e = x$ for all x in P.

For convenience, we denote the path-algebra also by P. The operator $\cdot$ is usually dropped, xy denotes $x \cdot y$. A path algebra defines a partial order with respect to $+$, viz. $x \preceq y \iff x + y = y$. For an element $x \in P$, x^n denotes the n-times repeated product with itself $(x \cdot x \cdot$ (n times) $\cdot x \cdot x)$ and x^0 is defined as e. The *closure* of an element x is defined as

$$x^* = \sum_{n \geq 0} x^n$$

where $\sum$ denotes summation using $+$.

We can construct a matrix path-algebra, M_P, over square matrices (with an implicit dimension) using elements from P. The $+$ and $\cdot$ for M_P are defined as in a normal matrix-algebra except that addition and multiplication are replaced by $+$ and $\cdot$ respectively. It can be verified that this definition does produce a path-algebra. We also construct a vector path-algebra V_P of column vectors (again with an implicit dimension). The $+$ and $\cdot$ operators are element-wise operations of the corresponding elements. We assume that the dimensions of M_P and V_P are the same. In such a case, multiplication of matrices, a matrix with a vector etc. are defined as in a normal algebra. Note that the partial order $\preceq$ can be extended as an element-wise operation to M_P and V_P since it has been defined using $+$. The zero and unit elements in V_P are ϕ (a vector with all elements ϕ), e (a vector all elements e). The zero and unit elements in M_P are Φ (a matrix with all entries ϕ) and E (a diagonal matrix with all principal diagonal elements e).

We are interested in solving some equations on the path-algebra. The following theorem captures the solution of linear fixed-point equations:

Theorem 1. *The equation* $x = tx + b$ *where* $t, b \in P$ *has* $x = t^*b$ *as the least solution in* P. *The equation* $x = Tx + b$ *where* $T \in M_P$ *and* $b \in V_P$ *has* $x = T^*b$ *as the least solution in* V_P. *The equation* $X = TX + B$ *where* $T, B \in M_P$ *has* $X = T^*B$ *as the least solution in* M_P.

To relate path-algebra to fixed-points in lattices, we note that a complete, distributive lattice with zero and unit elements satisfies the axioms of a path algebra. Both $(L, \vee, \wedge)$ and $(L, \wedge, \vee)$ are path algebras. The preceding theorem is the fixed-point computation of $f(x) = (t \wedge x) \vee b$. The assumption of distributivity is already implicit in the solution of dataflow frameworks when we approximate the meet-over-all-paths solution as a maximal fixed-point solution [6].

Note 1. An equation of the form $x = (t \wedge x) \vee b$ has a trivial solution b when the path-algebra is built from a lattice. The interesting and useful case for analyses is the matrix-vector form. Unlike L and V_L, T^* is not equal to E for all matrices in M_L. An analysis essentially involves computing the expression T^*b without finding T^* explicitly.

One additional assumption we make is that x^* exists and requires only a finite number of x^n to be accumulated, i.e. there is an $N \geq 0$ such that $x^* = x^0 + x^1 + \cdots + x^N$.

3 Mapping Dataflow Analysis to Path Algebra

All our graphs are directed graphs. The node-set, edge-set and adjacency matrix of a graph G are denoted $V(G)$, $E(G)$ and $A(G)$ respectively. The matrix M' denotes the transpose of M. Boolean matrices contain the path-algebra zero and unit element for 0 and 1 so that expressions of the form TA, TA' are admissible. For a node n, $V^-(n)$, $E^-(n)$ and $d^-(n)$ denote the set of predecessors, set of in-edges and the in-degree respectively. The corresponding "out" terms are denoted by $V^+(n)$, $E^+(n)$ and $d^+(n)$.

The *size* of a graph (denoted $|G|$) is the sum of the number of nodes (denoted $|V(G)|$) and the number of edges (denoted $|E(G)|$) in the graph.

We reserve the letter G for graphs, the letter A for adjacency matrices, D to denote diagonal matrices and T for general matrices. Vectors are denoted by b, p, q; x, y represent variables. If u is a vector, then $D(u)$ denotes a diagonal matrix with $D_{ii} = u_i$. We assume that the analysis is stated in terms of the nodes of the CFG.

The equation $x = Tx + b$ from the previous section is readily mapped onto dataflow equations of the form $x_i = \sum T_{ij}x_j + b_i$ under our assumptions about the information lattice. We now need to interpret the matrix T in terms of the adjacency matrix of the CFG, A and its transpose A'.

Mapping Uni-directional Analyses

Consider the dataflow equation for a forward-flow problem:

$$x_i = b_i + \sum_{j \in V^-(i)} T_{ij}x_j$$

In order to convert this into a matrix equation, we handle two different cases:

1. The simpler case is when T_{ij} is independent of j. Then, T can be written as $D(t)$ where t is a vector. The equation reduces to $x_i = b_i + t_i \sum_{j \in V^-(i)} x_j$ which can be written as a matrix-vector equation $x = D(t)A'x + b$. Most analyses are of this kind: reaching definitions, available expressions, copy propagation, constant propagation etc. A node does not distinguish between its DFDG predecessors in any way.
2. We can reduce the more general case to the previous case by replacing the equation for x_i by the following set of equations:

$$y_{ij} = T_{ij}x_j \text{ if } j \in V^-(i)$$
$$x_i = b_i + \sum_{j \in V^-(i)} y_{ij}$$

   Essentially, we have introduced a node along each incoming edge into the node i and accumulated that information. This new graph has a structure where all incoming edges to a node have the same label, i.e. the first case.

For backward flow, the equation in the first case changes to $x = DAx + b$. The handling of the second case does not introduce any new inefficiencies at least in this case. The complexity of uni-directional analysis depends on the size of the graph. The conventional assumption is that the CFG is sparse. We have a total of $|G|$ equations after the addition of the new nodes.

Mapping Bi-directional Analyses

Bi-directional analyses have more elaborate matrix equations. We will specify only the first one (PRE) in detail. The rest of them are simply listed out as abstract matrix-vector equations.

[PRE] As an example of a more complex flow which is decomposable into uni-directional flows, consider the formulation of PRE taken from [9]:

$$\text{PPIN}_i = \text{PAVIN}_i \cap (\text{ANTLOC}_i \cup \text{TRANSP}_i \cap \text{PPOUT}_i) \cap$$
$$\cap_{j \in V^-(i)} (\text{AVOUT}_j \cup \text{PPOUT}_j)$$
$$\text{PPOUT}_i = \cap_{k \in V^+(i)} \text{PPIN}_k$$

The exact interpretation of the vectors used here is not important. For our purpose, we want to solve for PPIN and PPOUT. If we choose simpler symbolic names for each element, we end up with:

$$x_i = p_i + (q_i(r_i + y_i)) + \sum_{j \in V^-(i)} s_j y_j$$

$$y_i = \sum_{k \in V^+(i)} x_k$$

where $\cap$ is $+$ and $\cup$ is $\cdot$. The matrix-vector form can be written as: $x = p + D(q)r + D(q)y + A'D(s)y$ and $y = Ax$. Eliminating y from the first equation and casting it in the $x = Tx + b$ form, we get an equation in x (in its abstract form): $x = b + D_1 Ax + A'D_2 Ax = (D_1 A + A'D_2 A)x + b$.

[CHSA] A more involved bi-directional analysis for which clustering only par-tially helps is the CHSA algorithm (formulation from [8]) whose dataflow equations can be abstracted out as:

$$x = D(p)y + D(q)Ay$$
$$y = r + D(t)x + D(u)A'x$$

Eliminating x from the second equation, $y = r + D(t)D(p)y + D(t)D(q)Ay + D(u)A'D(p)y + D(u)A'D(q)Ay$ which can be reduced to $y = b + D_1 y + D_2 Ay + D_3 A'D_4 y + D_5 A'D_6 Ay$. The term $D_1 y$ can be safely dropped using the fact that $a + a.b = a$ for any a, b. So, we end up with an equation of the form $y = (D_1 A + D_2 A'D_3 + D_4 A'D_5 A)y + b$.

In problems which occur in practice, we observe that the matrix T is a "polynomial" in A and A'. We call the matrix obtained from T after suppressing all terms except A and A' as the *dataflow matrix*. The dataflow matrix essentially tells us the exact dependence pattern between the variables involved in the dataflow equation. In the examples, it is A for backward analysis, A' for forward analysis, $A + A'A$ for PRE and $A + A' + A'A$ for CHSA. We define various classes of dataflow problems using the dataflow matrix.

Definition 1. *An analysis whose dataflow matrix is A or A' is said to be uni-directional. An analysis whose dataflow matrix whose product terms are of the form $A^i A'^j$ or $A'^i A^j$ where $i, j \leq 1$ are said to be bi-directional.*

The latter reflects the conventional definition that a node depends on its predecessors or successors. For example, this allows $AA' + A'A + A'$ but not $A^2A' + AA'A + A^2$.

Definition 2. *Analyses whose dataflow matrix is a polynomial in A and A' are called* local flow *analyses.*

The 'locality' emphasizes the fact that product terms composed of A^k and A'^k denote the (k-distant) neighbourhood of a node in the CFG (which are edges in the DFDG). For example, $A^2A' + AA'A + A^2$ captures direct dataflow dependence of a node on (certain) nodes which are at a distance three from it.

The dataflow matrix is a boolean matrix and is precisely the adjacency matrix of the DFDG. Each edge $e : (i, j)$ in the DFDG can be labelled with $L(e) = T_{ij}$. A DFDG may sometimes have multiple edges between two nodes. In such cases, we can accumulate them into a single label for the purpose of defining T_{ij} properly. A more common thing is that the edges correspond to different kinds of flows and this case is handled by a form of node-replication. An alternative is to use the strategy we used in the second case of uni-directional analysis to split up such edges.

Efficiency of an Iterative Algorithm

In this section, we generalize some notions from conventional analyses based on the CFG to the more general setting based on the DFDG.

For measuring the complexity of an iterative analysis, we should use the size of the CFG as the reference. Suppose G is the CFG and G_d is the DFDG for the analysis. Then, an algorithm which takes $O(|V(G)| + |E(G)|)$ or $O(|V(G_d)|)$ is considered efficient. The former is due to the sparseness of conventional CFGs. The latter is due to the fact that the DFDG does not increase the number of nodes beyond the size of the CFG. But, an algorithm which takes $O(|E(G_d)|)$ is *not* considered to be of linear complexity since the number of edges in G_d can be $O(|V(G)|^2)$.

A simple way of solving a set of dataflow equations is the two-step process: Initialize $x^{(0)} = \phi$ and iterate $x^{(n+1)} = f(x^{(n)})$ till $x^{(n+1)} = x^{(n)}$. But this does not capture the conventional iteration where we reuse the value $x_m^{(i)}$ in the evaluation of x_n which comes later. The following scheme is closer to an in-place update:

1. Choose a *node ordering* of the nodes in the DFDG, say $n_1, n_2, \ldots, n_m$ where m is the number of DFDG nodes. A node-ordering is a permutation of the nodes.
2. In each iteration, visit the dataflow equations in the order generated in the first step. Compute $x_i' = f_i(x_1', \ldots, x_{i-1}', x_i, x_{i+1}, \ldots, x_n)$ where x_i' denotes the next estimate $(x_i^{(n+1)})$ and the x_i denotes the current estimate. The variables $x_1, x_2, \ldots, x_{i-1}$ are those which occur before x_i in the node-ordering.

Since the node-order imposes a linear-order on the nodes of the DFDG, it is possible that the order is "against the flow" of some edges. Such an edge and the node-order are said to be incompatible with each other. The matrix T is a polynomial in A and A'. We already assumed that T^* is expressible as a sum of a finite sequence $T^0 + \ldots + T^N$. This implies that only a finite set of paths between the nodes of the DFDG need to be considered for the analysis. We call such paths *useful*. The relation between the incompatible edges in such paths and the number of iterations can be put into a general principle: *If information required for an analysis can be computed by considering only a finite set of paths in the DFDG, then the number of iterations for a given node-order is not more than 1 + the maximum number of incompatible edges in any path in that set.* We normally require one more iteration to detect the fixed-point.

The relation between depth and number of iterations is conventionally used in uni-directional analyses [1]. The useful paths in that case are the acyclic paths in the graph. The node-orders are *depth-first* (or reverse depth-first) orders which have been empirically shown to converge within a constant number of iterations [1]. However, no such good node-orders are available for more general analyses. The generalized theory [8] refines depth to another graph parameter called the *width*. Apart from using incompatible edges, width also incorporates subsumption of information flow between multiple parallel paths along which information propagates. Our choice of depth here is motivated by the intent of extending the simpler uni-directional analyses to directly solve certain kinds of bi-directional formulations.

The basic idea of local-flow analysis is to consider some segments of a valid path. These segments are then short-circuited so that they do not contribute to the depth of the analysis. This can change the complexity of the analysis in some cases (from quadratic to linear) or simply make the analysis faster. The basis for this is the solution of the fixed-point equation by partitioning.

4   Partitioning of Fixed-Point Equations

The base iteration scheme to solve the equation $x = Tx + b$ is to start with an initial estimate $x^{(0)} = b$ and iterate $x^{(i)} = Tx^{(i-1)} + b$ till $x^{(i)}$ stabilizes (reaches a fix-point). Other schemes for computing the fixed-point are compared against this scheme for validity. We will describe only one other scheme. But, by using it on the DFDG or on an augmented DFDG, we can get others.

Before we partition T, we make all its diagonal elements zero. This corresponds to removing self-loops from the DFDG. The following theorem tells us how to accommodate them into the solution later:

Theorem 2. *Let T be written as $D + B$ where D is a diagonal matrix and B has a zero diagonal. Then, the solution of $x = Tx + b$ and $x = D^*Bx + D^*b$ are identical.*

Proof. The solution $x = T^*b$ can be written as $x = (D + B)^*b = (D^*B)^*D^*b$ (using the identity $(x+y)^* = (x^*y)^*x^*$). This can be viewed as the least solution for $x = D^*Bx + D^*b$.

If the underlying set (from which the vectors and matrices are built) is a lattice, then $D^* = E$ since the non-zero elements along the principal diagonal will be of the form $e + d_{ii} + d_{ii}^2 \cdots$ which is always e. Therefore, the latter equation simplifies to $x = Bx + b$. Essentially, if any transformation results in self-loops in the DFDG, we can drop such edges with no effect on the final solution.

Let G be the DFDG for the equation $x = Tx + b$. Let H be a subgraph of G induced on a subset of nodes in G. Let the dimension of G and H be denoted g and h respectively. Without loss of generality, assume that the first h vertices of G are the ones chosen for inducing H, i.e., T has been partitioned into four parts at the h'th row and h'th column. We indicate these partitions by subscripted indices. i.e. $T = \begin{pmatrix} T_{11} & T_{12} \\ T_{21} & T_{22} \end{pmatrix}$ and $b = \begin{pmatrix} b_1 \\ b_2 \end{pmatrix}$ where T_{11} is a $h \times h$ matrix corresponding to H and b_1 is the local information associated with the nodes in H. The first decomposition is C-decomposition:

Theorem 3. *The iteration scheme*

$$x_1^{(i)} = T_{11}^* \left(T_{12} x_2^{(i-1)} + b_1 \right)$$
$$x_2^{(i)} = T_{21} x_1^{(i)} + b_2 + T_{22} x_2^{(i-1)}$$

converges to the least fixed-point solution of $x = Tx + b$ with the initial vector $x_1^{(0)} = \phi, x_2^{(0)} = \phi$ and $x = \begin{pmatrix} x_1 \\ x_2 \end{pmatrix}$

The iteration scheme implied by this decomposition is to consider each iteration in G as (in this order):

1. Propagate the effect of the nodes from $G \setminus H$ to H (the term $T_{12} x_2^{(i-1)} + b_1$).
2. Perform a complete fixed-point iteration in H. This is indicated by the $T_{11}^*(\ldots)$ term.
3. Propagate the effect of the nodes from H to $G \setminus H$. This simply uses the updated value of x_1 and the current x_2 and updates the nodes in $G \setminus H$ as in conventional iterative analysis.

If H can be induced to be a "good" graph, then the dataflow analysis within H becomes fast. We intend to construct H so that its fixed-point can be computed without any iteration in linear-time. More precisely, we define a *cluster* as follows:

Definition 3. *A cluster is a dataflow framework (G, f) in which the evaluation of the fix-point of f is linear in the number of nodes in G, i.e, $O(|V(G)|)$.*

The term $x_1^{(i)}$ computed at each stage is essentially the solution of the dataflow framework restricted to H. Unlike the conventional notion of efficiency which is determined by the size of G, analysis within a cluster must depend only on the number of nodes in G.

Based on this theorem, we can think of dataflow analysis in terms of clusters ("clustered dataflow analysis" or "clustered iteration scheme") instead of nodes.

The graph G can be successively partitioned into $H_1, H_2, H_3 \ldots$.. The limiting case of a cluster is a single node which is a trivial cluster.

The proof of correctness for the partitioning scheme is straightforward, based on the computation of the closure of a matrix by partitioning [4]. But, here we are interested in the effect of clustering on iterative analysis. In Theorem (3), the computation of x_i in H uses the estimates of x_i from the previous iterations (in particular, those which are in $G \setminus H$). Therefore, this partition of G using the cluster H defines a partial node-order.

Lemma 1. *Let H be an induced subgraph of G. Then, the nodes from $V(H)$ appear before the nodes from $V(G \setminus H)$ in any node-order associated with an iterative analysis using H as a cluster.*

As a consequence of this, all edges which enter a cluster are incompatible with the node-order and all edges leaving the cluster are compatible with it. This is a negative consequence of clustering. Due to the term $T_{11}^* \ldots$ in $x_1^{(i)}$, we have some positive effect on the iterative analysis:

Theorem 4. *Let H be identified as a cluster within G. Then, incompatible edges within H do not contribute to the number of iterations required by a clustered iteration scheme to reach the fixed-point.*

Proof. In order to prove this, we use a model based on the definition of an analysis: If G is a DFDG and P is the set of useful paths, consider G^* which has an edge for each path in P. If e_1-e_2-$\ldots$-e_n is a path, then let the label of the edge for this path in G^* be $L(e_1) \cdot L(e_2) \cdot \ldots \cdot L(e_n)$. By construction, dataflow analysis on G is identical to a one step computation of the form $x_i = \sum_{j \in V - (i)} T_{ij}^* x_j$ on G^* where T_{ij}^* is the sum of the labels on the edges between node i and j in G^*.

Edges in G^* can be divided into segments: $p = g_1 h_1 g_2 h_2 \ldots$ where g_i contains edges in $G \setminus H$ while h_i contains edges that are part of H.

The graph in C-decomposition can be viewed as the replacement of the graph H within G with H^*. When information along this path enters a h_i-segment, the fixed-point computation in H will propagate the information through the complete h_i-segment in T_{11}^* computation in the current iteration. This updated estimate is then propagated to the first node in g_{i+1} in the second stage of the iteration (the computation of x_2) in Theorem 3. Therefore, the depth of p is determined only by the g_i-segments of the path p. Since the number of iterations is no more than the maximum depth of any such path, it follows that only the edges in $E(G \setminus H)$ can affect the clustered iteration scheme.

Note 2. The edges entering and leaving a cluster *do* contribute to the depth of the analysis. Only the edges which are completely between the cluster nodes are no longer relevant.

Note 3. Our interpretation of a cluster in this theorem has served only one purpose: it short-circuits the in-cluster segments of useful paths. But, clustering *does not* enable any simple form of graph condensation. That depends on the edges entering and leaving the cluster, the closed-form expression of the fixed-point within the cluster and the reachability information between the entries and exits of the cluster. We use cluster analysis to sequentially decompose flow (i.e. reapply clustering within $G \setminus H$). We prove that a certain graph is a cluster independently in most cases.

C-decomposition on a DFDG corresponds to a node partition. We can define an edge partition using an extension of C-decomposition. Let E_c be a subset of edges for which we want to define a cluster. Then, we replace each node n which is incident on some edge in E_c by two nodes n and n_c. All cluster edges will be between the n_c-nodes and the non-cluster edges between the n-nodes. Finally, there are edges between (n, n_c) and (n_c, n) labelled with e (the lattice unit element). The iteration scheme in this case has four steps in each iteration:

$$x_{1c}^{(i)} = x_1^{(i-1)}$$
$$x_{1c}^{(i)} = T_{11}^* \left(T_{12} x_2^{(i-1)} + b_1 \right)$$
$$x_1^{(i-1)} = x_{1c}^{(i)}$$
$$x_2^{(i)} = T_{12} x_{1c}^{(i)} + b_2 + T_{22} x_2^{(i-1)}$$

Here, x_{1c} contains all the n_c-nodes. The vector x_2 contains the remaining nodes (include the n-nodes corresponding to n_c-nodes, written as x_1). The only change is that the propagation of x_n between the two copies is done before they are used in an iteration (the first and third step). Due to the way they are used in the scheme, the new edges do not increase the number of iterations though at least one of the edges must be incompatible with a node-order. They are solely used to synchronize the $x^{(i)}$-values of various copies of a node.

We will use the term *cluster* for the subgraph as well as the restriction of the dataflow framework to this graph. The latter is completely defined by the containing framework once we identify the subgraph.

5   Dataflow Analysis with Clusters

Dataflow analysis with clusters is a two-phase algorithm. The first phase is the decomposition of the edges of the DFDG into clusters. This phase takes the dataflow equations as input (which implicitly code the DFDG) and generates a sequence of dataflow equations on clusters $[C_1, C_2, \ldots, C_N]$ and G' which represents the residual flow. The second phase is the actual *clustered analysis* procedure which is a simple fixed-point iteration using clusters instead of nodes:

1: $x \leftarrow \mathbf{0}$
2: **repeat**
3:     $x' \leftarrow x$
4:     **for** i : 1 **to** N **do**

5:      $x'_{1i} \leftarrow T^*_{11i}(T_{12i}x'_{2i} + b_{1i})$
6:      $x'_{2i} \leftarrow x'_{2i} + T_{21i}x^{(n)}_{1i} + b_{2i}$
7:      **end for**
8:      $x'_{2N} \leftarrow x'_{2N} + T_{22N}x'_{2N}$
9:   **until** $x = x'$

For brevity, we have written the next estimate as x'. This becomes the current estimate x in the next iteration of the loop. The matrices T_{11n} denote the clusters at each stage: T_{111} is based on T, and at a stage k, T_{11k} is based on $T_{22(k-1)}$ (the non-cluster part of the remaining graph). We also reuse the estimates of elements of x as they are computed. Step 5 denotes the fix-point iteration within the cluster. Step 6 denotes the effect of the cluster on the non-cluster part of the graph. Note that one must accumulate such estimates since the edges from the cluster (T_{21i}) may not be the only DFDG edges incident on the nodes in the non-cluster part. These two steps are repeated for each cluster $C_1, C_2, \ldots C_N$. Finally, Step 7 propagates the dataflow information internally within the remaining graph after C_N. This is the term $T_{22}x_2^{(i-1)}$ in the statement of Theorem (3).

The first phase of decomposing into clusters depends on the dataflow framework. Since we restrict ourselves to local flow problems, we find that most patterns can be easily identified from the structure of the dataflow equations. In this section, we will explain the identification and use of clusters with examples.

Clustering is meant to exist with current uni-directional analysis methods. The strategy is to separate out *cross-flows* systematically such that the graph $G \setminus H$ eventually becomes a graph suitable for uni-directional analysis. The general idea is to show that a special graph (in the graph-theoretic sense) can be found as a subgraph of the DFDG. Examples which we shall encounter here are directed acyclic graphs, complete graphs, bi-directional paths and circuits (a closed path). The second step is define the labels on the edges of these subgraphs. Once we define the labels (and each such labelled edge is actually present in the DFDG), the dataflow framework on this subgraph is designated a cluster if we can prove that the fixed-point computation is linear in the number of nodes in the subgraph.

Dataflow equations of the form $x = DAx + b$ and $x = DA'x + b$ are simple. They are known to be efficient without any form of clustering. But, one cluster which is applicable in general is a directed acyclic graph. We can identify the extended basic block as a cluster. This is a purely structural pattern. Dataflow analysis on a DAG is linear-time when nodes are visited in a topological order irrespective of the labels on the edges.

The first form of interesting flow is $x = ADA'x + b$ or $x = A'DAx + b$. Flows of these kinds are called "cross-flows". Let $B = A'DA$. Then,

$$B_{ij} = \sum_k A'_{ik}(DA)_{kj} = \sum_k A_{ki}\left(\sum_l D_{kl}A_{lj}\right) = \sum_k A_{ki}D_{kk}A_{kj}$$

This term indicates that a node j which shares a common predecessor k with the node i will generate a flow whose label is D_{kk}. If we view it from the node k, all

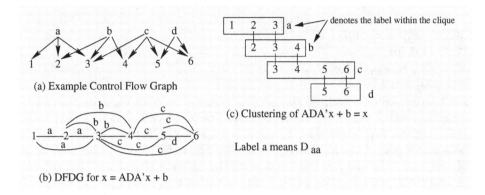

(a) Example Control Flow Graph

(b) DFDG for x = ADA'x + b

(c) Clustering of ADA'x + b = x

Label a means D_{aa}

Fig. 1. Cross Flow for A'DA

the successors of the node k induce a clique due to this flow with all the labels being identical, viz. D_{kk}. This is illustrated in Fig. 1. The CFG in Fig. 1(a) induces the shown in Fig. 1(b).

Our second cluster which captures this pattern is the *complete graph*. It is a cluster under some conditions (let K_n denote the complete graph on n vertices):

1. A node-equation is of the form $x_i = b_i + d_i \sum x_j$.
2. The information lattice is complemented. For every $a \in L$, there exists a (unique) element a' such that $a \vee a' = 1$.

The fixed-point solution of this system of equations is $x_i^* = b_i + d_i \sum_{j \neq i} b_j$. This computation is $O(n^2)$ is general since the sum-term must be evaluated for each node. However, if the lattice is complemented, we can rewrite b_i as $(d_i + d_i')b_i$. Then, $x_i^* = d_i'b_i + d_i \sum b_j$. The term $\sum b_j$ can be computed once in linear-time and the final vector x^* can be computed in linear-time. A straightforward iteration in K_n can potentially require $O(n^2)$.

Using this cluster, we now define our clusters on edges as follows: for each node n in G, collect all the edges labelled D_{nn} as one cluster. For instance, we collect the edges $(1,2), (2,3)$ and $(1,3)$ labelled a to form the first cluster (123) and so on. Replication of nodes takes place automatically. The vertical edges between the clusters in Fig. 1(c) are the synchronizing edges (between copies of 2, 3 in the first and second cluster and so on). In the figure, we have chosen to create clusters in the order a, b, c and d (Recall that clustering is defined only one cluster at a time). However, the clustering can be done in any order. We get the same structure with a possibly different ordering of the clusters. We can find the fixed-point of this chain of cliques in linear time by a three-stage algorithm (assuming that useful paths are acyclic paths):

$$F_1 = K_1^*(\mathbf{0})$$
$$F_i = K_i^*(F_{i-1})$$
$$B_n = K_n^*(\mathbf{0})$$

$$B_i = K_i^*(B_{i+1})$$
$$x_i = K_i^*(B_i + F_i)$$

Here, K_i denotes the i'th clique and $K_i^*(\perp)$ denotes the fixed-point computation within K_i regarding it as a cluster. The first two equations are the forward scan through the sequence of cliques. The next two equations are the backward scan. The final step aggregates these two flows and propagates them through the cliques again. The total time taken is linear in the number of nodes in the DFDG. This complicated structure satisfies all the restrictions of a cluster. We can therefore use this itself as a cluster.

Using this flow, we can now solve flows of the form $x = AD'Ax + DA'x + b$ or $x = AD'Ax + DAx + b$. The clustering proceeds as above. But, instead of an empty graph finally, we will end up with the residual flow corresponding to the DA or DA' term. This is handled by a conventional iterative analysis update step. This means that one can solve the bi-directional formulation of PRE directly in linear-time if the cliques due to cross-flows $(A'DA)$ are isolated from the main flow (DA). Further, the conventional structural analysis methods can be applied on this residual flow which is uni-directional in nature.

The last case of $x = D_1Ax + D_2A'x + b$ cannot be satisfactorily handled. While each of these flows is independently efficient, their combination is not decomposable easily. Intuitively, we see that when two nodes are connected by edges in both directions, at least one of them must be incompatible with any node-order. In this case, if we consider a good traversal (say, depth-first) for one of the flows, it is precisely a traversal which is bad for the other flow (which requires reverse depth-first). However, there are some patterns which we still can identify using the fact that $A + A'$ is effectively an undirected graph. We identify two clusters: a bi-directional path and a circuit for use in this context.

A *bi-directional path* can be regarded as a cluster. It is defined by a system of equations of the form $x_i = d_i + b_i x_{i+1} + f_i x_{i-1}$ with the appropriate terms dropped at the end-points. The fixed-point can be computed by a three-pass algorithm (assuming that the useful paths are the acyclic paths):

$$F_1 = \emptyset$$
$$F_i = f_i(F_{i-1} + d_{i-1})$$
$$B_n = \emptyset$$
$$B_i = b_i(B_{i+1} + d_{i+1})$$
$$x_i = B_i + F_i + d_i$$

The computation of F, B and x is linear-time. Therefore, this graph is a cluster. This is very similar to what we used in the chain of cliques case for the ADA' analysis (when there is only a single node, its fixed-point is just d_n). This is one of the few cases where clusters can be nested in the conventional sense of condensation.

A *bi-directional circuit* can be regarded as a cluster. The equations of are of the form $x_i = f_i x_{i+1} + b_i x_{i-1} + d_i$, i = 1, 2, ..., n. In this context, any symbol s_{n+1} corresponds to s_1 and s_{1-1} corresponds to s_n cyclically. One can find the fix-point in linear time using the following scheme:

1. Let $F_n = \phi$; $F_i = (F_{i+1} + d_i)f_{i-1}$, for i = $n - 1, \ldots, 1$. Define $F = F_1$.
2. Let $B_1 = \phi$; $B_i = (B_{i-1} + d_i)b_{i+1}$, for i = $2, \ldots, n$. Define $B = B_n$.
3. Let $Y_n = F$ and $Y_i = f_i(d_{i+1} + Y_{i+1})$ for $i = n - 1, \ldots 1$.
4. Let $Z_1 = B$ and $Z_i = b_i(Z_{i-1} + d_{i-1})$ for $i = 2, \ldots n$.
5. The fix-point $x_i^* = d_i + Y_i + Z_i$.

Each of these steps is linear and therefore the fix-point can be found in linear-time. The basic idea of the algorithm is that the each node in a bi-directional circuit contributes to another node through two paths: one clockwise using the b_i-edges and one anti-clockwise using the f_i-edges. We need to accumulate all such effects in linear-time.

We can now use circuits and paths to speed up the analysis of $D_1 A x + D_2 A' x = b$. It is known that the edges of an undirected graph can be partitioned into a collection of at-most $\frac{n}{2}$ edge-disjoint paths and circuits where n is the number of nodes (a constructive proof in [3]). Alternatively, a simple way is to consider a spanning tree (we already have the depth-first tree in most cases). Adding an edge to a spanning tree creates one circuit. We remove that circuit and repeat the edge-addition with the new forest of trees, thereby generating a collection of circuits and paths (but there may be more than $\frac{n}{2}$ of them). In any case, we cannot bound the depth of the resulting graph in terms of the CFG's depth. We have simply short-circuited some paths within the complete set of paths. However, we currently have not formally quantified the benefit of such a decomposition.

Higher powers of A and A' have more edges, but the structure reflects the ones we studied here. For example, a product term like $A'^m A^n$ will create an edge between two nodes u and v if there exists a node w such that there is a w-u path with m edges and w-v path with n edges. This again induces cliques. But, all such flow can be handled with the linear-time clustering we described for the $A'A$ case, both within the cliques as well as the chain of cliques.

6   Conclusion and Future Work

Path-algebra forms a useful basis for reasoning with dataflow analyses which occur in practice. We have mainly concentrated on presenting the framework and showing how decomposable problems are handled. The advantage of this approach is that each problem can tailor the clusters to their flow pattern. In this paper, we were concerned with efficiency. But, a cluster can be any collection of edges which are "interesting". Since most dataflow analyses generate similar patterns, extending the structural analysis to incorporate patterns like circuits, cliques and so on helps in decomposing complex flows generated by local-flow problems. In the cases where they fail to speed up analysis in terms of the order complexity, clusters do decrease the amount of iterative analysis which must be done.

The presence of flows like $A + A'$ has not yet been considered more rigorously. We are investigating the use of edge flow with node flow to accommodate such flows. The goal would be a system of mixed node-edge equations where cluster analysis creates a sequence like node-listing in uni-directional analysis.

While our definition of a cluster does not depend on the form of the function, we have restricted ourselves to first-order analyses. One can translate these ideas to a more abstract domain: evaluation of the fix-point within a subgraph corresponds to a partial evaluation of the function; terms like A^k and A'^k can be mapped onto computing the fix-point of f^k instead of f (which will be the same. The former will require lesser number of iterations, but might be more expensive to evaluate than the latter). It is difficult to quantify the efficiency of clustering in an abstract domain. One of the advantages of a path-algebra is that it is general enough to contain both uni-directional and bi-directional analysis while allowing us to reason with the structure of the flow.

References

1. Alfred V. Aho, Ravi Sethi, and Jeffrey D. Ullman. *Compilers - Principles, Tools and Techniques*. Addison Wesley, Reading, Mass., 1986.
2. Roland Backhouse and Bernard Carré. Regular algebra applied to path-finding problems. *Journal of Institute of Mathematics and its Applications*, 15:161–186, 1975.
3. Claude Berge. *Graphs*. North Holland, 2nd edition, 1985.
4. Bernard Carré. *Graphs and Networks*. Oxford Applied Mathematics and Computing Science Series. Clarendon Press, Oxford, 1979.
5. Cliff Click and Keith Cooper. Combining analyses, combining optimizations. *ACM Transactions on Programming Languages and Systems*, 17(2):181–196, 1995.
6. John B. Kam and Jeffrey D. Ullman. Monotone dataflow analysis frameworks. *Acta Informatica*, 7(3):305–318, 1977.
7. Ken Kennedy. *A survey of data flow analysis techniques*, pages 5–54. In Muchnick and Jones [13], 1981.
8. Uday Khedkar and Dhananjay M Dhamdhere. A generalized theory of bit-vector dataflow analysis. *ACM Transactions on Programming Languages and Systems*, 16(5):1472–1511, 1994.
9. Uday Khedkhar and Dhananjay M Dhamdhere. Bidirectional analysis: Myths and reality. *ACM SIGPLAN Notices*, 34(6):47–57, 1999.
10. J Knoop, O Rüthing, and B Steffen. Optimal code motion. *ACM Transactions on Programming Languages and Systems*, 16(4):1117–1155, 1994.
11. Sorin Lerner, David Grove, and Craig Chambers. Composing dataflow analyses and transformations. In *29st Annual ACM Symposium on Principles of Programming Languages*, pages 270–282, 2002.
12. E. Morel and C. Renvoise. Global optimization by supression of partial redundancies. *Communications of the ACM*, 22(2):96–103, 1979.
13. Steve S. Muchnick and Neil D. Jones, editors. *Program Flow Analysis: Theory and Applications*. Prentice Hall, Englewood Cliffs, NJ, 1981.

14. Hanne Riis Neilson and Flemming Nielson. Bounded fixed point iteration. In *19th Annual ACM Symposium on Principles of Programming Languages*, pages 71–82, 1992.
15. O Rüthing. Code motion in the presence of critical edges without bidirectional data flow analysis. *Science of Computer Programming*, 39:2–29, 2001.
16. Micha Sharir. Structural analysis: A new approach to flow analysis in optimizing compilers. *Computer Languages*, 5(3):141–153, 1980.
17. Robert E. Tarjan. Fast algorithms for solving path problems. *Journal of ACM*, 28(3):594–614, 1981.
18. M N Wegman and F K Zadeck. Constant propagation with conditional branches. *ACM Transactions on Programming Languages and Systems*, 13(2):181–210, 1991.

A Differential Fixpoint Evaluation Framework for Non-distributive Systems*

Joonseon Ahn and Yong Jin Kwon

Hankuk Aviation University, Hwajundong, Koyang, Kyungkido 412-791, Korea
jsahn@mail.hangkong.ac.kr,
yjkwon@tikwon.hangkong.ac.kr

Abstract. We devise a differential fixpoint computation method and develop a new worklist algorithm based on it. Differential methods avoid redundant computation by calculating only the increment of repeated computations. Compared with other differential methods, our method deals with non-distributive functions which often occur in practical program analyses. Also, our worklist algorithm can adopt any worklist scheduling policy satisfying restrictions imposed by differential evaluation. As a practical application, we present an abstract interpretation framework and implement constant and alias analysis and memory lifetime analysis based on it. Our experiment shows that our method can save computation and worklist scheduling is important also in differential evaluations.

Keywords: fixpoint computation, worklist algorithm, differential evaluation, static analysis, abstract interpretation

1 Introduction

In many static analysis frameworks such as conventional data flow analysis [6] and abstract interpretation [2,3,8], an analysis of a program is expressed using simultaneous equations which express relations among program points. The solution of the equations is usually given by fixpoints of a monotonic increasing function and most analysis time is consumed to compute such fixpoints.

In this paper, we propose a differential fixpoint computation algorithm. In naive methods, the unknowns are initialized with the least element of the value domains and the function is applied iteratively until the results become stable. In such iterations, because new intermediate results include their former results, each function application performs much redundant computation and gets more expensive by the iteration. We try to avoid such redundancy by computing only the increment of each intermediate result.

---

* This research was supported by IRC (Internet Information Retrieval Research Center) in Hankuk Aviation University. IRC is a Kyounggi-Province Regional Research Center designed by Korea Science and Engineering Foundation and Ministry of Science & Technology.

A. Ohori (Ed.): APLAS 2003, LNCS 2895, pp. 159–175, 2003.

Compared with other differential methods, our framework has the following good points. First, our method deals with non-distributive systems using differential evaluation rules. This is necessary because functions obtained from many practical applications are often non-distributive, Also, our differential worklist algorithm can adopt any worklist scheduling policy. Many previous works and our experiment in this paper show that appropriate worklist scheduling is essential for good performance [12,14].

Differential computation is usually proposed in situations where computation with larger value is more expensive. It has been originally proposed for program optimization. Fong and Ullman devised an optimization technique of "reduction in strength" and used it to optimize set-theoretic language programs [9,1]. Paige and Schwartz generalized it with "finite differencing" [4]. Liu presented a general framework "incrementalization" for differential program optimization [15]. However, they can still be applied to limited operations on limited data structures.

Our method is not a program optimization technique and can be used to develop differential fixpoint evaluators. For fixpoint computations, a technique called "semi-naive evaluation" was proposed for differential evaluation of queries in deductive databases [7]. Also, Fecht et al. proposed a differential fixpoint computation method for distributive constraint systems [13,14]. However, all of them deal with distributive systems only. For non-distributive systems, our previous work[17] and Eo and Yi's work [19] presented differential fixpoint evaluation algorithms for abstract interpretation. However, they force FIFO(first-in first out) worklist scheduling.

This paper is organized as follows. Section 2 defines the form of equational systems to be solved and explains the idea of differential evaluation. In Section 3, we present a new differential worklist algorithm. In Section 4, as an application of our method, we present an abstract interpretation framework. In Section 5, a constant and alias analysis based on the abstract interpretation framework is presented. Section 6 describes our implementation and presents experimental results. Section 7 concludes this paper.

2   Differential Evaluation of Fixpoints

Equational systems to be solved are simultaneous equations of the form $x_1 = e_1, x_2 = e_2, \ldots, x_n = e_n$. We assume that

1. Variables x_i's store value of complete lattice domains D. ($x_i \in Var$)
2. $e_i \in Exp$ are expressions which include the variables. We have a rule $Eval : Env \times Exp \to D$ which evaluates expressions into an element of D in finite time given an environment $E \in Env : Var \to D$.
3. The evaluation of e_i's are monotonic increasing with respect to environments, that is $\forall E_1, E_2 \in Env$ satisfying $E_1 \sqsubset E_2$, $Eval(E_1, e_i) \sqsubset Eval(E_2, e_i)$, where $E_1 \sqsubset E_2$ means $\forall x \in Domain(E_1)$, $E_1(x) \sqsubset E_2(x)$.

The solution of such equations can be given with a least fixpoint of the function $F(\overline{x}) = (e_1, \ldots, e_n)$ where $\overline{x} = (x_1, \ldots, x_n)$. We can compute the least fixpoint of F using the following algorithm. In the algorithm, $F(\overline{v})$ can be evaluated using $(Eval(E, e_1), \ldots, Eval(E, e_n))$ where $E = \{x_1 \to v_1, \ldots, x_n \to v_n\}$.

$$
\begin{aligned}
&\overline{v} \leftarrow \overline{\perp} \quad / * \ \overline{v} = (v_1, \ldots, v_n), \ \overline{\perp} = (\perp, \ldots, \perp) \ * / \\
&\text{do} \ \{ \\
&\quad \overline{v} \leftarrow F(\overline{v}) \\
&\} \ \text{until} \ (\overline{v} \ \text{does not change})
\end{aligned}
\tag{1}
$$

However, this naive algorithm does much redundant computation. F is applied iteratively and the new results always include the former results. Therefore, once an element is included in $\overline{v}$, $F(\overline{v})$ is computed using the element repeatedly until the result of $F(\overline{v})$ becomes stable.

If we have an efficient F^δ which satisfies the following equation, we can avoid such redundant computation, where $\sqcup$ is the join operator for lattice domains.

$$
F(\overline{v} \sqcup \overline{v}^\delta) = F(\overline{v}) \sqcup F^\delta(\overline{v}, \overline{v}^\delta)
\tag{2}
$$

$F^\delta(\overline{v}, \overline{v}^\delta)$ includes the difference between $F(\overline{v})$ and $F(\overline{v} \sqcup \overline{v}^\delta)$ caused by the increase of its parameter from $\overline{v}$ to $\overline{v} \sqcup \overline{v}^\delta$. In the best case where F is distributive with respect to $\sqcup$, $F^\delta(\overline{v}, \overline{v}^\delta)$ can be given by $F(\overline{v}^\delta)$. If we can evaluate $F^\delta(\overline{v}, \overline{v}^\delta)$ efficiently given large $\overline{v}$ and small $\overline{v}^\delta$, we can compute $F(\overline{v} \sqcup \overline{v}^\delta)$ from $F(\overline{v})$ avoiding much redundant computation.

Having such F^δ, we can compute the least fixpoint of F as follows.

$$
\begin{aligned}
&\overline{pv} \leftarrow \overline{\perp} \quad\quad\quad\ / * \ \overline{pv} = (pv_1, \ldots, pv_n) \ * / \\
&\overline{v} \leftarrow F(\overline{\perp}) \quad\quad\ / * \ \overline{v} = (v_1, \ldots, v_n) \quad\ * / \\
&\overline{v}^\delta \leftarrow F(\overline{\perp}) \quad\quad\ / * \ \overline{v}^\delta = (v_1^\delta, \ldots, v_n^\delta) \quad * / \\
&\text{while} \ (\overline{v} \neq \overline{pv}) \ \{ \\
&\quad \overline{v}^\delta \leftarrow F^\delta(\overline{pv}, \overline{v}^\delta) \\
&\quad \overline{pv} \leftarrow \overline{v} \\
&\quad \overline{v} \leftarrow \overline{pv} \sqcup \overline{v}^\delta \\
&\}
\end{aligned}
\tag{3}
$$

This algorithm computes $F(\overline{v})$ by computing the increment from $\overline{v}$ to $F(\overline{v})$ using F^δ. Let $\overline{v}_{i+1} = F(\overline{v}_i)$. Starting from $\overline{v}_0 = \overline{\perp}$ and $\overline{v}_1 = \overline{v}_1^\delta = F(\overline{\perp})$, $\overline{v}_i$'s are computed until they become stable. At the start of an i-th iteration, the value of $\overline{v}$, $\overline{pv}$ and $\overline{v}^\delta$ can be regarded as $\overline{v}_i$, $\overline{v}_{i-1}$ and $\overline{v}_i^\delta$, respectively, and we compute $\overline{v}_{i+1}^\delta$ and $\overline{v}_{i+1}$ using $\overline{v}_{i+1}^\delta \leftarrow F^\delta(\overline{v}_{i-1}, \overline{v}_i^\delta)$ and $\overline{v}_{i+1} \leftarrow \overline{v}_i \sqcup \overline{v}_{i+1}^\delta$.

We can prove $\overline{v}_{i+1} = \overline{v}_i \sqcup \overline{v}_{i+1}^\delta$ using an induction. For $i = 0$, $\overline{v}_1 = F(\overline{v}_0) = \overline{\perp} \sqcup F(\overline{v}_0) = \overline{v}_0 \sqcup \overline{v}_1^\delta$. For $i > 0$, $\overline{v}_{i+1} = F(\overline{v}_i) = F(\overline{v}_{i-1} \sqcup \overline{v}_i^\delta) = F(\overline{v}_{i-1}) \sqcup F^\delta(\overline{v}_{i-1}, \overline{v}_i^\delta) = \overline{v}_i \sqcup \overline{v}_{i+1}^\delta$ by the induction hypothesis and the definition of F^δ.

The differential algorithm can be more efficient in that computing the increment $F^\delta(\overline{v}_{i-1}, \overline{v}_i^\delta)$ can be cheaper than $F(\overline{v}_i)$. On the other hand, the differential algorithm has an additional overhead of the join operation $\overline{v}_{i+1} = \overline{v}_i \sqcup \overline{v}_{i+1}^\delta$. If computing only increments can save more computation than the join operation, the differential method can reduce overall computation.

For the differential fixpoint computation, we need the following additional assumption about our simultaneous equations.

```
/ *   X[]  : the variable environment which stores the value of x_i's     */
/ *   use[]  : the set of expression indexes which use x_i                 */
/ *   worklist : the set of expressions which must be reevaluated          */
worklist ← {1, 2, ..., n}      / * initialized with all expression indexes */
while (worklist ≠ φ) {
    i ← Extract(worklist)              / * i is extracted from worklist */
    x ← Eval(X, e_i)     / * if Eval(X, e_i) uses X[j], i is added to use[j] */
    if (x ≠ X[i]) {                    / * The new value is greater than X[i] */
        X[i] ← x
        worklist ← worklist ∪ use[i]
    }
}
```

Fig. 1. A naive worklist algorithm

2'. For $e_i \in Exp$, we have a differential evaluation rule $Eval^\Delta : Env \times Env \times Exp \to D$ which satisfies the following where $(E \sqcup E^\delta)(x) = E(x) \sqcup E^\delta(x)$.

$$Eval(E \sqcup E^\delta, e) = Eval(E, e) \sqcup Eval^\Delta(E, E^\delta, e) \tag{4}$$

Using $Eval^\Delta$, we can compute the value of $F^\delta(\overline{v}, \overline{v}^\delta)$ as follows.

$$F^\delta(\overline{v}, \overline{v}^\delta) = (Eval^\Delta(E, E^\delta, e_1), \ldots, Eval^\Delta(E, E^\delta, e_n))$$
$$\text{where } E = \{x_1 \to v_1, \ldots, x_n \to v_n\} \text{ and } E^\delta = \{x_1 \to v_1^\delta, \ldots, x_n \to v_n^\delta\} \tag{5}$$

3 Worklist Algorithm for Differential Evaluation

The fixpoint algorithms shown in the previous section is not practical because it evaluates all the e_i's given an increase of any v_j. Therefore, most practical implementations [5,12,13,14] use worklist algorithms.

Fig. 1 is a worklist algorithm based on the non-differential algorithm of (1). In the worklist algorithm, $Eval(X, e_i)$ evaluates a value of e_i given an variable environment which is stored in an array X where the value of x_i is given with $X[i]$. Although environments are defined to be elements of a function domain in the former definitions, we use arrays instead in worklist algorithms for brevity. worklist stores indexes of expressions which must be reevaluated and use[i] stores indexes of expressions which use the value of x_i for evaluation. If x_i increases, use[i] is added to worklist for reevaluation. In this way, we can compute fixpoints by evaluating only those e_i's which can increase by reevaluation.

For the differential evaluation, we also need a differential worklist algorithm. A differential worklist algorithm can be given by adding statements for initialization and replacing $X[i] \leftarrow Eval(X, e_i)$ with $dX[i] \leftarrow Eval^\Delta(X, dX, e_i)$; $V[i] = X[i] \sqcup dX[i]$ where X, V and dX stores the former value, the current value and the recent increment of expressions, respectively.

```
/ *  V[i]  :  the current value of x_i = e_i                          */
/ *  X[i]  :  the former value of x_i (initialized with ⊥)            */
/ *  dX[i]  :  recent increment of x_i                                */
/ *  timestamp[i]  :  time of the last evaluation of each expression */
worklist ← {1, 2, ..., n}
eval_count ← 0
for (i = 1 to n){
    V[i] ← Eval(X, e_i)    / * If Eval(X, e_i) uses X[j], i is added to use[j] * /
    dX[i] ← V[i]
}
while (worklist ≠ φ) {
    i ← Extract(worklist)
    foreach (w ∈ use[i])
        if (timestamp[i] > timestamp[w]) {
            timestamp[w] ← eval_count ++
            dV ← Eval^Δ(X, dX, e_w)
            / * If Eval^Δ(X, dX, e_w) uses X[j] or dX[j], w is added to use[j] * /
            New_V ← V[w] ⊔ dV
            if (New_V ≠ V[w]) {
                worklist ← worklist ∪ {w}
                dX[w] ← dX[w] ⊔ dV
                V[w] ← New_V
            }
        }
    X[i] ← V[i]
    dX[i] ← ⊥
}
```

Fig. 2. A differential worklist algorithm for arbitrary worklist scheduling

However, the differential evaluation needs additional considerations. We must be careful so that the evaluations use appropriate increments of variables. For example, assume that the value of e_3 increases by dv and e_1 and e_2 in $use[3]$ are added to the worklist. Then, there can be the following cases.

- If e_1 and e_2 are evaluated before a reevaluation of e_3, $X[3]$ and $dX[3]$ are assigned with $V[3]$ and $\bot$, respectively, to prevent redundant use of dv.
- If e_3 is reevaluated and increases by dv' again before the evaluation of e_1 and e_2, we must store $dv \sqcup dv'$ and $dv' \sqcup V[3]$ in $dX[3]$ and $V[3]$, respectively.
- If e_3 is reevaluated and increases by dv' after only e_1 is reevaluated, the appropriate increments of e_3 to be used for the next evaluation of e_1 and e_2 become dv' and $dv \sqcup dv'$, respectively.

The problem of using appropriate increments can be solved as follows.

- We can use a FIFO scheduling for the worklist. Then, if expressions in $use[i]$ are added to the worklist from the increase of e_i, they are always evaluated before the reevaluation of e_i, which results in only the first case. [17,19].

– Otherwise, we can maintain environments of used variables separately for each expression in the worklist [13].

The first method loses the chance of optimization using worklist scheduling. The second was used in distributive systems [13] where only the increment is needed for evaluating new increment. In non-distributive systems, this method incurs much overhead because we must allocate or update the environment of all the used variables for each expression in $use[i]$ separately given an increase of e_i.

We devise a new approach for maintaining worklists. Given an increase of e_i, our method adds its index i to the worklist instead of the indexes in $use[i]$. Then, extracting i from the worklist later, we evaluate expressions in $use[i]$. In this way, we can guarantee that all the expressions in $use[i]$ are evaluated using the same increment of e_i without any restriction against worklist scheduling.

Fig. 2 shows our new algorithm. $worklist$ stores expressions whose value have increased. Extracting i from $worklist$, for each w in $use[i]$, new increment of e_w is computed using $Eval^\Delta(X, dX, e_w)$. If $V[w] \sqcup Eval^\Delta(X, dX, e_w)$ is larger than $V[w]$, $V[w]$ and $dX[w]$ are updated and w is added to $worklist$. After all the expressions in $use[i]$ are evaluated, $X[i]$ and $dX[i]$ becomes $V[i]$ and $\perp$.

$timestamp[]$ stores the last evaluation time of each expression and is used to prevent redundant evaluations. For example, assume that e_1 and e_2 are in the worklist, where $use[1]$ and $use[2]$ include e_3, and we extract e_1 and e_2 from the worklist where e_1 is selected first. In this case, e_3 can be evaluated twice although the first evaluation of e_3 already reflected the increase of e_2. By examining the last evaluation time of expressions, we can avoid the second evaluation of e_3 noticing that the evaluation of e_3 is more recent than e_2.

4   An Application: Abstract Interpretation

Abstract interpretation is a semantic-based program analysis framework, where an analysis is associated with an abstract interpreter and abstract domains which approximate concrete semantics. It executes a program using an abstract interpreter and gives sound information about the runtime behavior of the program.

An abstract interpreter $\overline{I}$ is recursively defined for each input language construct and maps evaluation environments to evaluation results. We call the environments and results prestates and poststates, respectively. Prestates usually approximate memory states before the evaluation of each expression in a given program and poststates approximate concrete evaluation results which are usually resulting value or memory states following the evaluation. Given a program, the interpreter is recursively instantiated and relates poststates and prestates of expressions composing the program. The relations form simultaneous equations, whose solution is a sound analysis result.

In this section, we present a language for defining various analyses based on abstract interpretation and its differential and non-differential evaluation rules. Then, in the following section, we explain an equational view of program analyses and where our method can save computation using an example of constant and alias analysis.

$$e \in Exp ::= \quad c \mid x \mid op\ e \mid e_1 \sqcup e_2 \mid (e_1, \ldots, e_n) \mid e.i \mid \{e\} \mid \texttt{mapjoin}\ (\lambda x.e')\ e$$
$$\mid e_1[e_3/e_2] \mid \texttt{ap}\ e_1\ e_2 \mid \texttt{if}\ (e_0 \sqsubset e_1)\ e_2\ e_3 \mid \texttt{let}\ x = e_1\ \texttt{in}\ e_2\ \texttt{end}$$

Fig. 3. Abstract expressions

$S_\bot^\top$	a lifted domain of a set S (a flat domain)
$D_1 \times \cdots \times D_n$	a product domain
2^S	a powerset domain of a set S
$S \to D$	a function domain

Fig. 4. Domains for our abstract expressions : *Lattice*

$$Eval(E, c) = \mathbf{c} \qquad Eval(E,\ x)\ =\ E(x)$$

$$\frac{Eval(E, e) = v}{Eval(E, op\ e) = \mathbf{op}\ v} \qquad \frac{Eval(E, e_i) = v_i \quad (i = 1, 2)}{Eval(E, e_1 \sqcup e_2) = v_1 \sqcup v_2}$$

$$\frac{Eval(E, e) = v \quad (v \in (S_\bot^\top - \{\bot, \top\}))}{Eval(E, \{e\}) = \{v\}}$$

$$\frac{Eval(E, e') = \{v_1, \ldots, v_n\},\ Eval(E + \{x \to v_i\}, e) = \{v_1', \ldots, v_n'\}}{Eval(E, \texttt{mapjoin}\ \lambda x.e\ e') = v_1' \sqcup \ldots \sqcup v_n'}$$

$$\frac{Eval(E, e_i) = v_i \quad (1 \le i \le n)}{Eval(E, (e_1, \ldots, e_n)) = (v_1, \ldots, v_n)} \qquad \frac{Eval(E, e) = (v_1, \ldots, v_n)}{Eval(E, e.i) = v_i \quad (1 \le i \le n)}$$

$$\frac{Eval(E, e_i) = v_i \quad (i = 1, 2,\quad v_2 \in (S_\bot^\top - \{\bot, \top\}))}{Eval(E, \texttt{ap}\ e_1\ e_2) = @\ v_1\ v_2,\ \text{where}\ @\ \bot_{S \to D}\ v\ = \bot_D}$$
$$@\ v_0[v_1/v_2]\ v = v_1 \qquad \text{if } v = v_2$$
$$= @\ v_0\ v \quad \text{otherwise}$$

$$\frac{Eval(E, e_i) = v_i \quad (i = 1, 2, 3,\quad v_3 \in (S_\bot^\top - \{\bot, \top\}))}{Eval(E, e_1[e_2/e_3]) = v_1[v_2/v_3]}$$

$$\frac{Eval(E, e_i) = v_i \quad (1 \le i \le 4)}{Eval(E, \texttt{if}\ (e_0 \sqsubset e_1)\ e_2\ e_3) = v_2 \quad \text{if } v_0 \sqcup v_1 = v_1}$$
$$= v_3 \quad \text{otherwise}$$

$$\frac{Eval(E, e) = v,\quad Eval(E + \{x \to v\}, e') = v'}{Eval(E, \texttt{let}\ x = e\ \texttt{in}\ e'\ \texttt{end}) = v',}$$
$$\text{where}\ (E_1 + E_2)(x) = E_2(x) \quad \text{if } x \in dom(E_2)$$
$$= E_1(x) \quad \text{otherwise}$$

Fig. 5. The evaluation rule *Eval: Env $\times$ Exp $\to$ Lattice*

4.1   Abstract Expressions Language

Fig. 3 shows the syntax of our abstract expression language which is used to define abstract semantics and forms simultaneous equations. Expressions are evaluated to elements of semantic domains shown in Fig. 4.

Fig. 5 presents the evaluation rule *Eval*. A constant c is evaluated to its semantic value $\mathbf{c}$. The value of a variable is given by the environment. In the rule for *op e*, **op** represents the semantic meaning of a primitive operator *op*. $e_1 \sqcup e_2$ joins lattice values resulting from e_1 and e_2. The result of $(e_1, \ldots, e_n)$ is constructed from its partial results and *e.i* returns i-th element of the product lattice value. $\{e\}$ generates an element of a powerset domain, where e results in a non-bottom and non-top element of a flat lattice domain, which must be guaranteed by the analysis designer. `mapjoin` applies a lambda expression to each element of a set and joins all the results.

During evaluation, we assume the subtype relation between S and $S_\perp^\top$. A set element $v \in S$ is casted to an element of $S_\perp^\top$ when it becomes an evaluation result. Also, a flat domain element $v \in (S_\perp^\top - \{\perp, \top\})$ is casted to an element of S when v is used to construct an element of a powerset domain 2^S or v is applied to a function value $f \in S \to D$.

$e_1[e_2/e_3]$ updates the function value from e_1 so that it maps the value resulted from e_3 to the value of e_2. `ap` e_1 e_2 applies the function value resulting from e_1 to the value of e_2. `if` $(e_0 \sqsubseteq e_1)$ e_2 e_3 evaluates one of the alternatives comparing the value of e_0 and e_1. `let` expressions are used to bind variables locally.

4.2   Differential Evaluation Rule

For differential fixpoint computation, we need a differential evaluation rule $Eval^\Delta$ which satisfies Equation (4). Fig. 6 shows our differential evaluation rule.

Constant expressions are evaluated to $\perp$ because their results are always same. The increments of variable expressions are obtained from the increment of their environments. The increment of a join expression is obtained by joining the increments of its operands. The increments of tuple expressions and tuple element selections are also obtained from the increments of their elements.

A set expressions $\{e\}$ is computed to an element of a powerset domain 2^S. Therefore, e must be evaluated to an element of $S_\perp^\top - \{\perp, \top\}$. Then, because $Eval(E, e) \sqsubseteq Eval(E \sqcup E^\delta, e)$, it is always true that $Eval(E, e) = Eval(E \sqcup E^\delta, e)$. Therefore, the increment becomes $\{\}$.

For `mapjoin` , we evaluate $v_i^\delta = Eval^\Delta(E + \{x \to v_i\}, E^\delta + \{x \to v_i\}, e)$ for each element v_i which was also included in $Eval(E, e')$ to reflect E^δ to the evaluation of e with the same binding of x as the former evaluation. For v_i''s which are newly included in $Eval(E \sqcup E^\delta, e')$, we evaluate $Eval((E \sqcup E^\delta) + \{x \to v_i'\}, e)$. Then, we join all those results.

$e_1[e_2/e_3]$ updates the increment of e_1 so that the value of e_3 is mapped to the increment of e_2. e_3 is evaluated to the same value as the former evaluation because the value of e_3 is a non-top and non-bottom element of a flat lattice. For the same reason, the former value of e_2 is used in the rule for $Eval^\Delta(E, E^\delta, \text{ap } e_1 \, e_2)$.

$$Eval^{\Delta}(E, E^{\delta}, c) = \bot \qquad\qquad Eval^{\Delta}(E, E^{\delta}, x) = E^{\delta}(x)$$

$$\frac{Eval(E, e) = v, \quad Eval^{\Delta}(E, E^{\delta}, e) = v'}{Eval^{\Delta}(E, E^{\delta}, op\ e) = \begin{array}{ll} \mathbf{op}\ v' & \text{if } \mathbf{op} \text{ is distributive w.r.t. } \sqcup \\ \mathbf{op}\ (v \sqcup v') & \text{otherwise} \end{array}}$$

$$\frac{Eval^{\Delta}(E, E^{\delta}, e_i) = v_i\ (i = 1,2)}{Eval^{\Delta}(E, E^{\delta}, e_1 \sqcup e_2) = v_1 \sqcup v_2} \qquad \frac{Eval^{\Delta}(E, E^{\delta}, e) = (v_1, \ldots, v_n)}{Eval^{\Delta}(E, E^{\delta}, e.i) = v_i\ (1 \le i \le n)}$$

$$\frac{Eval^{\Delta}(E, E^{\delta}, e_i) = v_i\ (1 \le i \le n)}{Eval^{\Delta}(E, E^{\delta}, (e_1, \ldots, e_n)) = (v_1, \ldots, v_n)} \qquad Eval^{\Delta}(E, E^{\delta}, \{e\}) = \{\}$$

$$\frac{\begin{array}{l} Eval(E, e') = \{v_1, \ldots, v_n\}, \quad Eval^{\Delta}(E, E^{\delta}, e') = \{v'_1, \ldots, v'_m\}, \\ Eval^{\Delta}(E + \{x \to v_i\}, E^{\delta} + \{x \to v_i\}, e) = v_i^{\delta}\ (1 \le i \le n), \\ Eval((E \sqcup E^{\delta}) + \{x \to v'_i\}, e) = v''_i\ (1 \le i \le m) \end{array}}{Eval^{\Delta}(E, E^{\delta}, \mathtt{mapjoin}\ (\lambda x.e)\ e') = v_1^{\delta} \sqcup \ldots \sqcup v_n^{\delta} \sqcup v''_1 \sqcup \ldots \sqcup v''_n}$$

$$\frac{Eval^{\Delta}(E, E^{\delta}, e_i) = v_i\ (i = 1,2), \quad Eval(E, e_3) = v_3}{Eval^{\Delta}(E, E^{\delta}, e_1[e_2/e_3]) = v_1[v_2/v_3]}$$

$$\frac{Eval^{\Delta}(E, E^{\delta}, e_1) = v_1, \quad Eval(E, e_2) = v_2}{Eval^{\Delta}(E, E^{\delta}, \mathtt{ap}\ e_1\ e_2) = (@\ v_1\ v_2)}$$

$$\frac{Eval(E, e_i) = v_i, \quad Eval^{\Delta}(E, E^{\delta}, e_1) = v_i^{\delta}, \quad (1 \le i \le 4)}{\begin{array}{l} Eval^{\Delta}(E, E^{\delta}, \mathtt{if}\ (e_0 \sqsubseteq e_1)\ e_2\ e_3) \\ \quad = v_2^{\delta} \quad \text{if } (v_0 \sqcup v_1) = v_1 \text{ and } (v_0 \sqcup v_0^{\delta}) \sqcup (v_1 \sqcup v_1^{\delta}) = (v_1 \sqcup v_1^{\delta}) \\ \quad = v_3^{\delta} \quad \text{if } (v_0 \sqcup v_1) \neq v_1 \text{ and } (v_0 \sqcup v_0^{\delta}) \sqcup (v_1 \sqcup v_1^{\delta}) \neq (v_1 \sqcup v_1^{\delta}) \\ \quad = Eval((E \sqcup E^{\delta}), \mathtt{if}\ (e_0 \sqsubseteq e_1)\ e_2\ e_3) \quad \text{otherwise} \end{array}}$$

$$\frac{\begin{array}{l} Eval(E, e) = v, \quad Eval^{\Delta}(E, E^{\delta}, e) = v', \\ Eval^{\Delta}(E + \{x \to v\}, E^{\delta} + \{x \to v'\}, e') = v'' \end{array}}{Eval^{\Delta}(E, E^{\delta}, \mathtt{let}\ x = e\ \mathtt{in}\ e'\ \mathtt{end}) = v''}$$

Fig. 6. The differential evaluation rule : $Env \times Env \times Exp \to Lattice$

For $\mathtt{if}$ expressions, differential evaluation is possible only when the control flow is the same as the former evaluation. For $\mathtt{let}\ x = e\ \mathtt{in}\ e'\ \mathtt{end}$, e' is evaluated under two environments, where the former environment binds x with the former value of e and the second environment binds x with the increment of e.

Before stating the correctness of the differential evaluation rule, we define a restriction of expressions. We say an expression e is *entirely monotonic* if and only if for any subexpression e' of e and $\forall E_1, E_2 \in Env$ which satisfy $E_1 \sqsubseteq E_2$, it is always true that $Eval(E_1, e') \sqsubseteq Eval(E_2, e')$. The following theorem states the correctness of our differential evaluation rule.

Theorem 1. $\forall E, E^{\delta} \in Env$ *and an entirely monotonic expression* $e \in Exp$, *if* $Eval(E, e) = v$ *and* $Eval(E \sqcup E^{\delta}, e) = v'$, *then* $v' = v \sqcup Eval^{\Delta}(E, E^{\delta}, e)$.

The proof of this theorem is given using a structural induction in Appendix.

$$
\begin{aligned}
e \in Mil ::=\ &\texttt{const}\ c \mid +\ e_1\ e_2 \mid id \mid \texttt{create}\ e_1\ id \mid \texttt{read}\ e_1 \mid \texttt{write}\ e_1\ e_2 \\
&\mid\ \texttt{procedure}\ (x_1\ \ldots\ x_n)\ e_1 \mid \texttt{call}\ e_1\ e_2\ \ldots e_n \\
&\mid\ \texttt{begin}\ e_1 \ldots e_n \mid \texttt{if}\ e_1\ e_2\ e_3
\end{aligned}
$$

Fig. 7. The input language : MIL

$$
\begin{aligned}
X_i^+ &\in Prestate &&:= Memory \\
X_i^- &\in Poststate &&:= Memory \times Value \\
&Memory &&:= SetId \to Value \\
&Value &&:= Loc \times Clo \times Int \\
&Loc &&:= 2^{SetId} \\
&Clo &&:= 2^{SetProc} \\
&Int &&:= 2^{SetInt}
\end{aligned}
$$

Fig. 8. Abstract domains for constant and alias analysis

5 An Example: Constant and Alias Analysis

As a concrete example we present a constant and alias analysis based on the abstract interpretation framework given in the previous section. The analysis answers the following questions.

1. Does a variable always have the same value at a program point ?
2. Which variables refer the same memory location at a program point ?

The abstract semantics of the analysis was presented in [11] and we demonstrate an equational view of the analysis by presenting a rule for generating simultaneous equations given a program. By examining the form of equations generated from the rule, we also explain why our differential method can optimize practical analyses.

5.1 The Input Language

The language for input programs is MIL(MIPRAC Interprocedural Language [10]). It is an intermediate language for implementing practical languages and there exist front-ends for ANSI-C, Fortran and Scheme.

The syntax of MIL is given in Fig. 7. c represents integer constants and + stands for primitive operators on integers. id represents a memory location, which can store a integer, a function closure or a memory location. **create** expressions allocate any size of memory for id. **read** and **write** expressions are used to access memory locations. **procedure** expressions create function closures and **call** expressions are function applications. A **begin** expression evaluates subexpressions one by one and the value of the last expression becomes the result. In MIL, iterations are expressed using tail-recursive procedure calls.

$$
\begin{aligned}
&e_i = \text{const } c \;\;\Rightarrow\;\; X_i^- = (X_i^+, (\bot_L, \bot_C, \{c\})) \\
&e_i = id \;\;\Rightarrow\;\; X_i^- = (X_i^+, (\{Loc(id)\}, \bot_C, \bot_Z)) \\
&e_i = +\ e_{i_1}\ e_{i_2} \\
&\quad \Rightarrow X_{i_1}^+ = X_i^+; \;\; X_{i_2}^+ = X_{i_1}^-.1; \\
&\quad\quad X_i^- = (X_{i_2}^-.1, \\
&\quad\quad\quad (\bot_L, \bot_C, \text{mapjoin }(\lambda x.(\text{mapjoin }(\lambda y.\{x+y\})\ X_{i_2}^-.2.3))\ X_{i_1}^-.2.3)) \\
&e_i = \text{create } e_{i_1}\ id \;\Rightarrow\; X_{i_1}^+ = X_i^+; \; X_i^- = (X_{i_1}^-.1, (\{NewLoc(id)\}, \bot_C, \bot_Z)) \\
&e_i = \text{read } e_{i_1} \\
&\quad \Rightarrow X_{i_1}^+ = X_i^+; \;\; X_i^- = (X_{i_1}^-.1, \text{ mapjoin }(\lambda x.(\text{ap }(X_{i_1}^-.1)\ x))\ X_{i_1}^-.2.1) \\
&e_i = \text{write } e_{i_1}\ e_{i_2} \\
&\quad \Rightarrow X_{i_1}^+ = X_i^+; \;\; X_{i_2}^+ = X_{i_1}^-.1; \\
&\quad\quad X_i^- = (\text{mapjoin }(\lambda x. X_{i_2}^-.1[(\text{ap } X_{i_2}^-.1\ x)/x])\ X_{i_1}^-.2.1,\ X_{i_2}^-.2) \\
&e_i = \text{procedure } (x_1\ \dots\ x_n)\ e_{i_1} \\
&\quad \Rightarrow X_{i_1}^+ = \text{mapjoin} \\
&\quad\quad (\lambda j.(X_{lastsub(j)}^-.1)[X_{sub(j,2)}^-.2/Loc(x_1)]\dots[X_{sub(j,n+1)}^-.2/Loc(x_n)]) \\
&\quad\quad (\text{mapjoin }(\lambda j.\text{if }(\{p\} \sqsubset X_{subexp(j,1)}^-.2.2)\ \{j\}\ \{\ \})\ Calls^n); \\
&\quad\quad \text{where } Calls^n = \{j \mid e_j = \text{call } e_{j_0}\dots e_{j_m} \text{ and } n \le m\} \\
&\quad\quad X_i^- = (X_i^+.1, (\bot_L, \{ProcId(i)\}, \bot_Z)) \\
&e_i = \text{call } e_{i_0}\ e_{i_1}\ \dots e_{i_n}\ (n \ge 0) \\
&\quad \Rightarrow X_{i_0}^+ = X_i^+; \;\; X_{i_j}^+ = X_{i_{j-1}}^-.1\ (1 \le j \le n); \\
&\quad\quad X_i^- = \text{mapjoin }(\lambda x.\text{if }(\{NumOfParam(x)\} \sqsubset \{1,\dots,n\})\ X_{body(x)}^-\ \bot) \\
&\quad\quad X_{i_0}^-.2.2 \\
&e_i = \text{begin } e_{i_1}\dots e_{i_n} \;\Rightarrow\; X_{i_1}^+ = X_i^+; \; X_i^- = X_{i_n}^-; \; X_{i_j}^+ = X_{i_{j-1}}^-.1\ (2 \le j \le n) \\
&e_i = \text{if } e_{i_1}\ e_{i_2}\ e_{i_3} \\
&\quad \Rightarrow X_{i_1}^+ = X_i^+; \;\; X_{i_2}^+ = X_{i_1}^-.1; \;\; X_{i_3}^+ = X_{i_1}^-.1; \;\; X_i^- = X_{i_2}^- \sqcup X_{i_3}^-
\end{aligned}
$$

Fig. 9. Generating equations for constant and alias analysis

5.2   Abstract Domains for Constant and Alias Analysis

Fig. 8 shows the domains for the analysis. X_i^+ and X_i^- represent the prestate and the poststate of e_i, respectively. $X_i^-.1$ is the memory state following the evaluation of e_i and $X_i^-.2$ is the resulting value. *Memory* abstracts memory states and maps an element of *SetId* to an element of *Value*, where *SetId* is the set of all the memory locations. Because a memory location can store pointers, closures or integers, *Value* is the product lattice of *Loc*, *Clo* and *Int*, which are powerset domains of *SetId*, *SetProc* and *SetInt*, respectively. *SetProc* and *SetInt* are sets of all the procedure indexes and integer values, respectively. Using powerset domains, we can store all the possible value a memory location can have.

5.3   Rules for Generating Simultaneous Equations

Using the abstract domains of Fig. 8, we can construct an abstract semantics of MIL for constant and alias analysis. Here, we omit the abstract semantics and present only the rule for constructing equations because the rule directly reflects the abstract semantics.

Fig. 9 shows the rule for generating equations. It is applied to all the subexpressions of an input program and constructs simultaneous equations which relate all the prestates and poststates. All the expressions composing the equations are entirely monotonic increasing and have the form of our abstract expression given in Fig. 3. The solution of the equation is a sound analysis result.

For const expressions, the memory state remains the same and the result value includes only its integer value. id does not change memory state either and its result includes the memory location for the identifier.

+ e_{i_1} e_{i_2} evaluates e_{i_1} and e_{i_2} and applies primitive operator +. From the evaluation order, $X_{i_1}^+$ is the same as X_i^+ and $X_{i_1}^-.1$ becomes $X_{i_2}^+$. Because primitive operations have no side-effects, $X_i^-.1$ is the same as $X_{i_2}^-.1$. To get all the possible results, we apply the operator to all the possible pairs.

create e_{i_1} id allocates a new memory location for id, where e_{i_1} is the size of the memory location. Our abstract semantics abstracts the memory cell size.

read e_{i_1} reads the memory location e_{i_1} points to. Because the Loc value of e_{i_1} includes all the possible locations, we join all the value stored in those locations.

write e_{i_1} e_{i_2} updates the memory location to which e_{i_1} points with the value of e_{i_2}. Because $X_{i_1}^-.2.1$ includes all the possible locations, the sound result is obtained by joining all the memory states each of which is obtained by selecting a location $l \in X_{i_1}^-.2.1$ and updating the location l of $X_{i_2}^-.1$ with the value of e_{i_2}.

For begin $e_{i_1} \ldots e_{i_n}$, the memory state following the evaluation of e_{i_j} becomes the prestate of $e_{i_{(j+1)}}$. And, the poststate of e_{i_n} becomes overall result.

For if e_{i_1} e_{i_2} e_{i_3}, because the boolean part is evaluated first, the memory state following e_{i_1} becomes the prestate of e_{i_2} and e_{i_3}. Our abstract semantics abstracts the selection of the alternatives. Therefore, the poststate of the if expression is obtained by joining the poststates of e_{i_2} and e_{i_3}.

call $e_{i_0} \ldots e_{i_n}$ applies the function closure value from e_{i_0} to the following actual parameters. Because the Clo value from e_{i_0} includes all the possible function closures, the poststate is obtained by joining the poststates of bodies of those functions for which the call statement has sufficient actual parameters. $NumOfParam(x)$ is the number of formal parameters of a function closure x.

$e_i = $ procedure $(x_1 \ldots x_n)$ e_{i_1} creates a function closure, where $ProcId(i)$ gives a procedure name for it. To evaluate the prestate of the procedure body we must first find all the possible call sites. $Calls^n$ is the set of call sites which has at least n actual parameters. It can be obtained statically given a program. Then, (mapjoin $(\lambda j.$if $(\{ProcId(i)\} \sqsubseteq X_{subexp(j,1)}^-.2.2)$ $\{j\}$ $\{$ $\})$ $Calls^n$) selects the call sites that may call the procedure, where $subexp(j,1)$ is the index of the first subexpression of e_j. Then, $\lambda j.(X_{lastsub(j)}^-.1)[X_{sub(j,2)}^-.2/x_1] \ldots [X_{sub(j,n+1)}^-.2/x_n]$ evaluates the prestate of the function body given a procedure call e_j by updating the poststate of the last subexpression of e_j using call-by-value bindings. We compute this for all the call sites and join the resulting memory states.

Investigating the equations, we can find room for our differential method to save computation. Most optimization occurs in mapjoin operations.

In the rule for **read** expressions, we compute **mapjoin** $(\lambda x.(\text{ap } (X_{i_1}^-.1) \; x))$ $((X_{i_1}^-.2).1)$. Let us assume that we are evaluating the expression under the environment $E \sqcup E^\delta$, where E^δ is the increment of the environment since the previous evaluation under E. In the differential evaluation, we apply the current memory state $Eval(E \sqcup E^\delta, X_{i_1}^-.1)$ to only new memory locations in $Eval^\Delta(E, E^\delta, X_{i_1}^-.2.1)$. For the locations in $Eval(E, X_{i_1}^-.2.1)$, we apply $Eval^\Delta(E, E^\delta, X_{i_1}^-.1)$ to read only the increment of their value. Join operations with smaller value are usually cheaper than larger values. Also, if the value of the memory location $l \in Eval(E, X_{i_1}^-.2.1)$ has not increased since the previous evaluation, their increment becomes $\bot$ which can be omitted from the overall join operation.

For **write** expressions, our differential rule evaluates the increment of memory states by considering the increment of written value and the newly introduced memory locations for updating. If the written value has not increased, we can save computation by joining only those memory states resulting from the update of newly introduced locations,

In the evaluation of prestates of procedure bodies, the differential evaluation computes the increment of the prestate of the function body considering newly introduced call sites, increase of calling environments and increase of actual parameters. For those call sites e_j which were considered in the previous evaluation and whose prestates and actual parameters are the same as before, the value of $(X_{lastsub(j)}^-.1)[X_{sub(j,2)}^-.2/x_1] \ldots [X_{sub(j,n+1)}^-.2/x_n]$ becomes $\bot$ and we can save join of memory states which is very expensive in practice.

For the poststate of a **call** expression, the differential method joins the poststate of a function body only when the function closure is newly introduced to the call site or the poststate of the function body has increased.

For primitive operations, we can also save computations by considering newly introduced integer pairs only.

6   Implementation and Experiments

We have applied our differential evaluation method to Z1 [11], an static analysis system based on abstract interpretation. To compare the performance, we have also implemented the non-differential worklist algorithm.

In our implementation, an aimed analysis is described by specifying abstract lattice domains and abstract semantics using the specification language Z1 which is almost similar to the abstract expression of Fig. 3. Then, an abstract domain library and an abstract equation generator are generated from the specification. The domain library is a C program which includes functions for the lattice domains. Generating the equation generator is not automated yet. The equation generator produces simultaneous equations given an input program. Then, the least fixpoint is computed using the differential or the naive worklist algorithm.

We implemented the constant and alias analysis of Sec. 5 and a memory lifetime analysis[11]. The memory life time analysis estimates, for each memory location, the intervals from its creation to its last access times. It also estimates,

Table 1. Fixpoint computation time for program analysis

analysis	Constant and Alias Analysis				Memory Lifetime Analysis			
worklist scheduling	FIFO		LIFO		FIFO		LIFO	
used algorithm program	Naive	Diff	Naive	Diff	Naive	Diff	Naive	Diff
amoeba(36^1,6062^2)	44.15^3	16.11	74.14	3.39	2892.3	2966.1	2816.1	1860.5
simplex(448,8739)	120.14	49.13	296.12	7.41	5596.1	6009.5	7444.5	4219.6
gauss(54,4710)	34.43	20.14	34.51	1.51	2364.1	2575.1	2503.4	1465.3
TIS(102,6028)	12.48	10.08	4.00	1.43	4093.1	4455.4	369.5	348.39
gauss1(34,1863)	9.25	11.57	0.24	0.26	170.0	209.6	1.39	2.13
wator(45,3467)	59.20	95.04	4.21	2.06	1920.2	2146.3	650.3	692.5

1:number of procedures, 2:number of expressions, 3:cpu execution time(sec.)

for each program point, the interval that the control reaches to the program point after the creation of each memory location.

For experiments, a linux server with Pentium-3 700MHz processor and 256 MB main memory is used. We used two worklist scheduling policies of FIFO and LIFO(last-in first-out). The programs "amoeba", which optimizes a non-linear function of multiple variables, "simplex", which optimizes a system of linear constraints, and "gauss", which is a Gaussian elimination program are numerical programs written in Fortran. "TIS" is a program from Perfect Benchmarks. "wator" is written in C and simulates an ecological system of fish&shark [12]. The results are run-times for analyzing each program using the differential and the naive non-differential worklist algorithm. The correctness of our differential algorithm is assured by comparing the analysis results and number of evaluations. To this end, we made the evaluation order of the two algorithms be exactly the same by adding the statement "for $(i=1$ to $n)$ $\{X[i] \leftarrow Eval(X, e_i)\}$" before the start of the naive algorithm of Fig. 1. This modification consumes little additional execution time and has no affect on the correctness of the algorithm.

The experimental result is shown in Table 1. In constant and alias analysis, our method shows acceptable speed up for four and five programs in FIFO and LIFO scheduling, respectively. Especially with amoeba, simplex and gauss programs, in case of LIFO scheduling, the differential method was more than twenty times faster than the naive method. With "gauss1" and "wator", the naive method was faster than our method. This occurs because our differential method imposes additional computation for joining increments with the former intermediate results. In memory lifetime analysis using LIFO scheduling, the differential method shows acceptable speed up for five programs. However, with FIFO scheduling, the naive method was a little faster although the difference is not so large. In most cases, LIFO scheduling is more efficient than FIFO, which shows the importance of worklist scheduling. Also, for all cases of the analyses and input programs with the exception of gauss1 and wator, the differential evaluation using LIFO scheduling is most fast.

7   Conclusion

This paper provides a differential framework for computing fixpoints of non-distributive systems. Also, we have developed a new differential worklist algorithm which can adopt any worklist scheduling policy.

Using the worklist algorithm, we have implemented two practical program analyses of constant and alias analysis and memory lifetime analysis. Although the overhead of joining partial results is revealed with a few cases, the experiment shows promising speed up for many practical programs. Also, two worklist scheduling of FIFO and LIFO are tested and LIFO scheduling is more efficient in most cases, which shows the importance of worklist scheduling.

There can be the following future research directions. First, we must identify the overhead of the differential method more clearly and find a method to avoid it. If the overhead is indispensable, we need to find static or dynamic criteria to decide weather our differential algorithm should be used. Also, it is necessary to find a worklist scheduling method suitable for the differential evaluation.

References

1. A. C. Fong and J. D. Ullman, "Induction variables in very high-level languages", In *6th ACM Symp. on Principles of Programming Languages*, (1976) 104–112
2. Patrick Cousot and Radhia Cousot, "Abstract interpretation : a unified lattice model for static analysis of program by construction of approximation of fixpoints", In *4th ACM Symp. on Principles of Programming Languages*, (1977), 238–252
3. Patric Cousot and Radhia Cousot, "Systematic design of program analysis frameworks", In *6th ACM Symp. on Principles of Programming Languages*, (1979) 269–282
4. Robert Paige and Shaye Koenig, "Finite differencing of computable expressions", *ACM Trans. on Programming Languages and Systems*, Vol. 4 No. 3 (1982) 402–454
5. Neil Jones and Alan Mycroft, "Data flow analysis of applicative programs using minimal function graphs", In *13th ACM Symp. on Principles of Programming Languages*, (1986) 296–306
6. Barbara G. Ryder and Marvin C. Paull, "Elimination algorithms for data flow analysis", *ACM Computing Surveys*, Vol. 18 No. 3 (1986) 277–316
7. Francois Bancilhon and Raghu Ramakrishnan, "An amateur's introduction to recursive query processing strategies", In *ACM SIGMOD Conference on Management of Data*, (1986) 16–52
8. Samson Abramsky and Chris Hankin (ed.) , *Abstract Interpretation of Declarative Languages. Computers and Their Applications*, Ellis Horwood (1987)
9. Alfred V. Aho, Ravi Sethi and Jeffrey D. Ullman, *Compilers, principles, techniques, and tools*, Addison Wesley (1988)
10. Williams Ludwell Harrison III and Zahira Ammarguellat, "A program's eye view of MIPRAC", In D. Gelernter, A. Nicolau and D. Padua (ed.), *Languages and Compilers for Parallel Computing*, MIT Press (1992)
11. Kwangkeun Yi, *Automatic Generation and Management of Program Analyses*, Ph.D. Thesis, CSRD, University of Illinois at Urbana-Champaign (1993)
12. Li-ling Chen, Luddy Harrison and Kwangkeun Yi, "Efficient computation of fixpoints that arise in complex program analysis", *Journal of Programming Languages*, Vol. 3 No. 1 (1995) 31–68

13. Christian Fecht and Helmut Seidl, "Propagating differences: an efficient new fixpoint algorithm for distributive constraint systems", In *Proc. of European Symp. on Programming (ESOP)*, LNCS Vol. 1381, Springer Verlag (1998) 90–104
14. Christian Fecht and Helmut Seidl, "A faster solver for general systems of equations", *Science of Computer Programming*, Vol. 35 No. 2 (1999) 137–161
15. Yanhong A. Liu, "Efficiency by incrementalization : an introduction. *Higher-Order and Symbolic Computation*", Vol.13, No.4 (2000) 289–313
16. Kwangkeun Yi, "Yet another ensemble of abstract interpreter, higher-order dataflow equations, and model checking", Technical Memorandum ROPAS-2001-10, Research On Program Analysis System, KAIST (2001)
17. Joonseon Ahn, "A Differential Evaluation of Fixpoint Iterations", *Proc. of The Second Asian Workshop on Programming Language and Systems*, Taejon (2001) 171–182
18. Andrzej Murawski and Kwangkeun Yi, "Static Monotonicity Analysis for Lambda-definable Functions over Lattices", *Proc. of Third International Workshop on Verification, Model Checking and Abstract Interpretation*, Venice, LNCS Vol. 2294, Sprinter Verlag (2002) 139–153
19. Hyunjun Eo, Kwangkeun Yi, "An Improved Differential Fixpoint Iteration Method for Program Analysis", *Proc. of The Third Asian Workshop on Programming Language and Systems*, Shanghai, China, (2002)

A   Proof of Theorem 1

Theorem 1. $\forall E, E^\delta \in Env$ *and an entirely monotonic expression* $e \in Exp$, *if* $Eval(E, e) = v$ *and* $Eval(E \sqcup E^\delta, e) = v'$, *then* $v' = v \sqcup Eval^\Delta(E, E^\delta, e)$.

We can prove this theorem using an structural induction. For this, we must show that this theorem is true for each expression construct. For brevity, only two cases of function update and `mapjoin` expressions are shown here.

(i) $e = e_1[e_2/e_3]$
If $Eval(E, e) = v$ and $Eval(E \sqcup E^\delta, e) = v'$, there exist v_1, v_2, v_3, v_1', v_2' and v_3' which are obtained as follows.

$$Eval(E, e_i) = v_i$$
$$Eval(E \sqcup E^\delta, e_i) = v_i' \ (1 \le i \le 3)$$
$$v = v_1[v_2/v_3]$$
$$v' = v_1'[v_2'/v_3']$$

Then, $v_3 = v_3'$ because v_3 and v_3' are non-bottom and non-top values of a flat domain and $v_3 \sqcup v_3' = v_3'$. Also, from the induction hypothesis, there exist v_i^δ's which satisfy

$$v_i^\delta = Eval^\Delta(E, E^\delta, e_i), \quad v_i' = v_i \sqcup v_i^\delta \ (i = 1, 2)$$

Therefore, we can evaluate $v^\delta = Eval^\Delta(E, E^\delta, e) = v_1^\delta[v_2^\delta/v_3]$.
Now, we only have to show that $v' = v \sqcup v^\delta$. We prove this by showing $\forall s, (@ \ v' \ s) = (@ \ (v \sqcup v^\delta) \ s)$ as follows. If $s = v_3$,

$@ \ (v \sqcup v^{\delta}) \ s \ = \ (@ \ v \ s) \sqcup (@ \ v^{\delta} \ s) \ = \ v_2 \sqcup v_2^{\delta} \ = \ v_2' \ = \ @ \ v' \ s$. Otherwise, if $s \neq v_3$, $@ \ (v \sqcup v^{\delta}) \ s \ = \ (@ \ v \ s) \sqcup (@ \ v^{\delta} \ s) \ = \ (@ \ v_1 \ s) \sqcup (@ \ v_1^{\delta} \ s) \ = \ @ \ (v_1 \sqcup v_1^{\delta}) \ s \ = \ @ \ v_1' \ s \ = \ @ \ v' \ s$ by the induction hypothesis. Therefore, the theorem is true in the case $e = e_1[e_2/e_3]$.

(ii) $e = \texttt{mapjoin} \ (\lambda x.e_1) \ e_2$

If $Eval(E, e) = v$ and $Eval(E \sqcup E^{\delta}, e) = v'$, there exist v_2 and v_2' which satisfy the following,

$$
\begin{aligned}
v_2 &= Eval(E, e_2) = \{s_1, s_2, \ldots, s_m\}, \\
v &= Eval(E + \{x \to s_1\}, e) \sqcup \ldots \sqcup Eval(E + \{x \to s_m\}, e_1), \\
v_2' &= Eval(E \sqcup E^{\delta}, e_2) = \{s_1, s_2, \ldots, s_m, s_{m+1} \ldots, s_n\}, \\
v' &= Eval((E \sqcup E^{\delta}) + \{x \to s_1\}, e_1) \sqcup \ldots \\
&\quad \sqcup Eval((E \sqcup E^{\delta}) + \{x \to s_m\}, e_1) \sqcup \\
&\quad \sqcup Eval((E \sqcup E^{\delta}) + \{x \to s_{m+1}\}, e_1) \sqcup \ldots \\
&\quad \sqcup Eval((E \sqcup E^{\delta}) + \{x \to s_n\}, e_1).
\end{aligned}
$$

Also, from the induction hypothesis, there exist v_2^{δ} which satisfies

$$
\begin{aligned}
v_2^{\delta} &= Eval^{\Delta}(E, E^{\delta}, e_2) = \{s_1^{\delta}, s_2^{\delta}, \ldots, s_l^{\delta}\}, \\
v_2 \sqcup v_2^{\delta} &= v_2 \cup v_2^{\delta} = v_2'.
\end{aligned}
$$

First, we must prove that we can evaluate $v^{\delta} = Eval^{\Delta}(E, E^{\delta}, e)$. For each $s_i \in v_2$, because $(E + \{x \to s_i\}) \sqcup (E^{\delta} + \{x \to s_i\}) = (E \sqcup E^{\delta}) + \{x \to s_i\}$ and we have evaluated v and v', we can evaluate $v_i^{\delta} = Eval^{\Delta}(E + \{x \to s_i\}, E^{\delta} + \{x \to s_i\}, e_1)$ from the induction hypothesis. Also, for each $s_i \in v_2^{\delta}$, we can evaluate $v_i'' = Eval((E \sqcup E^{\delta}) + \{x \to s_i^{\delta}\}, e_1)$ because $s_i^{\delta} \in v_2$ and we have already evaluated it to get v'. Therefore, we can evaluate $Eval^{\Delta}(E, E^{\delta}, e)$.

Now, we prove that $v' = v \sqcup v^{\delta}$.

$$
\begin{aligned}
&v \sqcup v^{\delta} \\
&= Eval(E + \{x \to s_1\}, e_1) \sqcup \ldots \sqcup Eval(E + \{x \to s_m\}, e_1) \\
&\quad \sqcup Eval^{\Delta}(E + \{x \to s_1\}, E^{\delta} + \{x \to s_1\}, e_1) \sqcup \ldots \\
&\quad \sqcup Eval^{\Delta}(E + \{x \to s_m\}, E^{\delta} + \{x \to s_m\}, e_1) \\
&\quad \sqcup Eval((E \sqcup E^{\delta}) + \{x \to s_1^{\delta}\}, e_1) \sqcup \ldots \sqcup Eval((E \sqcup E^{\delta}) + \{x \to s_l^{\delta}\}, e_1) \\
&= Eval(E + \{x \to s_1\}, e_1) \sqcup Eval^{\Delta}(E + \{x \to s_1\}, E^{\delta} + \{x \to s_1\}, e_1) \sqcup \ldots \\
&\quad \sqcup Eval(E + \{x \to s_m\}, e_1) \sqcup Eval^{\Delta}(E + \{x \to s_m\}, E^{\delta} + \{x \to s_m\}, e_1) \\
&\quad \sqcup Eval((E \sqcup E^{\delta}) + \{x \to s_1^{\delta}\}, e_1) \sqcup \ldots \sqcup Eval((E \sqcup E^{\delta}) + \{x \to s_l^{\delta}\}, e_1) \\
&= Eval((E \sqcup E^{\delta}) + \{x \to s_1\}, e_1) \sqcup \ldots \sqcup Eval((E \sqcup E^{\delta}) + \{x \to s_m\}, e_1) \\
&\quad \sqcup Eval((E \sqcup E^{\delta}) + \{x \to s_1^{\delta}\}, e_1) \sqcup \ldots \sqcup Eval((E \sqcup E^{\delta}) + \{x \to s_l^{\delta}\}, e_1) \\
&= Eval((E \sqcup E^{\delta}) + \{x \to s_1\}, e_1) \sqcup \ldots \sqcup Eval((E \sqcup E^{\delta}) + \{x \to s_n\}, e_1) \\
&= v'
\end{aligned}
$$

The last equality is valid because $\forall 1 \leq j \leq l$, $s_j^{\delta} \in \{s_1, \ldots, s_n\}$ and $(m + 1) \leq \forall i \leq n$, $s_i \in \{s_1^{\delta}, \ldots, s_l^{\delta}\}$. Therefore, the theorem is true in the case $e = \texttt{mapjoin} \ (\lambda x.e_1) \ e_2$.

Other expression constructs can also be proved in the same way. $\square$

Model Checking: From Hardware to Software

Thomas A. Henzinger

University of California, Berkeley

While model checking has influenced industrial practice in sequential circuit verification for some time now, the use of model checking for program verification has proved elusive until recently. One of the main reasons is that boolean finite-state abstractions are readily available for circuits, but not for programs. A central problem in software model checking, therefore, is to find an abstraction of the input program which is sufficiently fine to prove or disprove the desired property, and yet sufficiently coarse to allow the exhaustive exploration of the abstract state space by a model checker. For this purpose, it is often useful to abstract the values of program variables by recording, instead, at each program location the truth values of critical predicates. A key insight is that the critical predicates can be discovered automatically using counterexample-guided abstraction refinement, which starts with a coarse abstraction of the program and iteratively refines the abstraction until either a bug is found or the property is proved. Furthermore, if the abstraction is refined lazily, then a critical predicate is evaluated only at those program locations where its value is relevant.

The lazy-abstraction mechanism forms the foundation of the Berkeley BLAST project. BLAST is a model checker for C programs with respect to properties that are specified as temporal safety monitors. Given a program and a property, BLAST provides either an error trace, which exhibits a violation of the property, or a succinct proof certificate in the form of an abstract reachability tree. To verify real-world programs, the lazy-abstraction mechanism of BLAST is integrated with methods that handle data manipulation (through theorem proving), function calls (through context-free reachability analysis), pointers (through alias analysis), and threads. In particular, for multi-threaded programs, an algorithm called thread-modular abstraction refinement (TAR) is used to automatically generate for each thread an abstraction that summarizes the interference of the thread with other threads. This allows the compositional analysis of concurrent software. BLAST has been applied successfully, without user intervention, to Linux and Windows device drivers with tens of thousands of lines of C code.

The work reported here is joint with Ranjit Jhala, Rupak Majumdar, Shaz Qadeer, and Gregoire Sutre [1,2]. BLAST was originally inspired by the Microsoft SLAM project [3].

References

1. T.A. Henzinger, R. Jhala, R. Majumdar, and G. Sutre. Lazy abstraction. In *Proc. Principles of Programming Languages* (POPL), pp. 58–70. ACM Press, 2002.

A. Ohori (Ed.): APLAS 2003, LNCS 2895, pp. 176–177, 2003.
© Springer-Verlag Berlin Heidelberg 2003

2. T.A. Henzinger, R. Jhala, R. Majumdar, and S. Qadeer. Thread-modular abstraction refinement. In *Proc. Computer-Aided Verification* (CAV), Lecture Notes in Computer Science 2725, pp. 262–274. Springer-Verlag, 2003.

3. T. Ball and S.K. Rajamani. The SLAM project: Debugging system software via static analysis. In *Proc. Principles of Programming Languages* (POPL), pp. 1–3. ACM Press, 2002.

Executing Verified Compiler Specification

Koji Okuma[1] and Yasuhiko Minamide[2]

[1] Doctoral Program in Engineering
University of Tsukuba
[2] Institute of Information Sciences and Electronics
University of Tsukuba
{okuma,minamide}@score.is.tsukuba.ac.jp

Abstract. Much work has been done in verifying a compiler specification, both in hand-written and mechanical proofs. However, there is still a gap between a correct compiler specification and a correct compiler implementation. To fill this gap and obtain a correct compiler implementation, we take the approach of generating a compiler from its specification. We verified the correctness of a compiler specification with the theorem prover Isabelle/HOL, and generated a Standard ML code corresponding to the specification with Isabelle's code generation facility. The generated compiler can be executed with some hand-written codes, and it compiles a small functional programming language into the Java virtual machine with several program transformations.

1   Introduction

Correctness of a compiler can be achieved by a correct specification and implementation. A specification of a compiler is formalized with a mapping between source and target languages. This mapping is required to be proved that it preserves a meaning between the two languages. An implementation of a compiler need to be proved correct in terms of this compiler specification. Our approach here, is to prove correctness of compiler specification and derive an implementation from it.

Our compiler takes a small functional programming language as input and compiles it to the Java virtual machine. The syntax of the source language is based on Scheme and it has the basic features of Lisp, such as lists and higher-order functions. We verified the correctness of its compiler specification with the theorem prover Isabelle/HOL [13] and generated a Standard ML code corresponding to the specification with Isabelle's code generation facility [2].

We specified the compiler with a subset of Isabelle/HOL including datatypes and primitive recursive functions that directly correspond to the functional language Standard ML. Although Isabelle/HOL can translate some other features, this restriction makes the translation more trustworthy and easier to coordinate with the hand-written parser and output routine. The other part of the specification including the semantics of the languages need not be executed. Therefore, it can be written with the full expressive power of Isabelle/HOL without this restriction.

A. Ohori (Ed.): APLAS 2003, LNCS 2895, pp. 178–194, 2003.

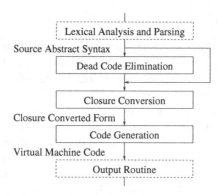

Fig. 1. The structure of our compiler

The structure of our compiler is shown in Figure 1. The closure conversion phase translates a program with lexically nested functions into a program with only top-level functions. The code generation phase translates a closure-converted program into a Java virtual machine code. Operational semantics of these three languages are formalized as inductively defined relations. We verified that all translations in the compiler preserve the meaning of a program. As an example of an optimization, we also formalized simple dead code elimination for the source language. The verification of this optimization was relatively easy compared to the other part of our verification.

To make our compiler executable, we wrote a parser and an output routine by hand in ML. In the figure, the code generated by Isabelle/HOL is shown in solid boxes, and the code written by hand is shown in dashed boxes. In addition to these routines, we supplied a small library routine written in Java to implement some primitives. However, these library routines are not verified in this paper. The resulting compiler successfully compiled several Scheme programs of 200–550 lines. The specification of our compiler can be obtained from http://www.score.is.tsukuba.ac.jp/~okuma/vc/.

This paper is organized as follows. In Section 2, we explain the notation used in this paper, and describe the code generation facility provided by Isabelle/HOL. In Sections 3 and 4, we describe the formalization of our compiler along its organization. In Section 5, we describe integration of the generated code and hand-written programs, and describe some experimental results. Finally, we review related work and present some conclusions.

2   Isabelle/HOL

In this section, we describe the basic features of Isabelle/HOL. In particular, we explain Isabelle/HOL's code generation facility, which is used to generate our executable compiler.

2.1   Isabelle/HOL

Isabelle is a generic, interactive theorem prover that can be instantiated with several object logics. Isabelle/HOL is an instantiation of Isabelle to Church's higher-order logic [13]. We wrote our proofs in Isabelle's new syntax Isar[18], which enabled us to write human-readable and structured proofs. We refer to Isabelle/HOL as HOL in the remainder of this paper.

HOL is equipped with the usual logical connectives, such as $\vee$, $\wedge$, $\rightarrow$, $\forall$, $\exists$. Types follow the syntax of ML, except the function arrow is $\Rightarrow$. HOL supports inductive datatypes similar to those of functional programming languages, and both primitive and well-founded recursive functions. In HOL, we can define a set inductively that we will use to formalize operational semantics.

2.2   Executable Specification in HOL

HOL has a facility to generate a code from a specification [2]. It translates several HOL elements into an executable Standard ML code. Elements that can be code-generated are: datatypes, recursive functions (both primitive recursive and well-founded recursive functions), and inductive definitions. The translation of datatypes and recursive functions is straightforward. However, the translation of an inductive definition is more complicated. HOL applies a mode analysis and generates a program that simulates a logic programming language.

Of the executable features of HOL, we only use features that directly correspond to those of ML, such as datatype definitions and primitive recursive functions. We do this because we think it would be easier to interact and the translation can be trusted. Note that these restrictions are only applied to the specification of the compiler. Semantics and other relations that are defined to prove correctness need not be executed. Specifications of a compiler can be written easily in functional style, and proofs can be written with HOL's full expressive power.

Consider the following specification in HOL. This example specifies the datatype for natural numbers and the primitive recursive function for the addition of natural numbers.

```
datatype
  nat = 0 | Suc nat

primrec
  "add 0 y = y"
  "add (Suc x) y = Suc (add x y)"
```

This program is translated into the following program in Standard ML by the code generation facility. Except for some renaming, this translation is straightforward and, therefore, we think that this translation can be trusted.

```
datatype Code_nat = nat_0 | nat_Suc of Code_nat
```

```
fun add nat_0 y = y
  | add (nat_Suc x) y = nat_Suc (add x y)
```

However, the translation described above has a problem. Types defined in HOL are translated into new types in Standard ML, and there is no way to obtain interoperability with existing datatypes in ML. We used HOL's method, which translates types in HOL to those of ML directly, to overcome this problem. In the following specification, the type *nat*, and the constants *0* and *Suc* are translated into *int* and corresponding operations in Standard ML. This translation is done literally; underscore '_' in the description is substituted by the arguments of the original terms. There is no check in this translation with respect to either syntax or semantics of ML. Therefore, care must be taken when specifying this correspondence.

types_code
   "nat"   (*"int"*)

consts_code
   "0"   (*"0"*)
   "Suc"   (*"(_ + 1)"*)

This form of translation is essential to obtain interoperability with the parser and the output routine as well as reasonable performance of the generated code.

3   Source Language and Closure Conversion

The specification of our compiler consists of an abstract syntax and compilation functions. To verify correctness of the specified compiler, the semantics of each language must also be specified. We proved that each translation preserves a meaning with respect to their semantics. We now describe the specification of the source language and closure conversion.

3.1   Source Language

Our source language is a pure subset of Scheme, which has the following features: lexical scoping, higher-order functions and list manipulation. As basic data types, we include boolean values, integers and symbols. Features currently not supported include: mutually recursive functions, imperative features and continuation.

We represented our source language as an abstract syntax defined by the following datatype declaration in HOL:

```
datatype exp = NumExp int
             | BoolExp bool
             | SymExp symbol
             | NullExp
             | VarExp variable
```

```
| UniExp uop exp
| BinExp bop exp exp
| IfExp exp exp exp
| LetExp variable exp exp
| FunExp variable "variable list" exp exp
| AppExp exp "exp list"
```

The type `variable` is a synonym of `nat`, which is the built-in datatype to express natural numbers. To represent base types, such as symbols and integers, we introduced new types `symbol` and `int`. Primitive operators are either unary or binary, and expressed by datatypes `uop` and `bop`. Note that, `FunExp` in datatype specifies not only a function definition but also a main expression to be evaluated. The expression below defines a function that adds two arguments, and evaluates its application with arguments 1 and 2.

```
constdefs
  addprog :: exp
  "addprog == FunExp 0 [1, 2]
                (BinExp PlusOp (VarExp 1) (VarExp 2))
                (AppExp (VarExp 0) [(NumExp 1), (NumExp 2)])"
```

The semantics of the source language is specified as big-step natural semantics. We define this as a relation on a value environment, a source expression and a value. We defined datatypes `value` and `env`, to represent values and environments as follows:

```
types   'a env = "(variable * 'a) list"
```

```
datatype value = IntVal int
              | BoolVal bool
              | SymVal symbol
              | NullVal
              | ConsVal value value
              | ClsVal variable "value env" "variable list" exp
```

An environment is represented as an association list. A value `ClsVal f env xs exp` represents the closure of a recursive function where `f` is the name of the function, `env` is the environment mapping each free variable to a value and `xs` is the list of formal parameters.

Finally, we define the semantics of this language as an inductively defined relation `eval` as:

```
consts   eval  :: "(value env * exp * value) set"
```

```
inductive eval
  intros
  var : "⟦lookup E n  = Some v⟧ ⟹ (E, VarExp n, v) ∈ eval"
  lete : "⟦(E, e1, v1) ∈ eval;
          ((x, v1)#E, e2, v) ∈ eval⟧
              ⟹ (E, LetExp x e1 e2, v) ∈ eval"
  ...
```

The definition above shows the case of a variable and a `let`-expression. The definition of the semantics is standard. Please refer to the proof scripts for details.

3.2 Closure Conversion

The first phase of our compiler is closure conversion, which achieves a separation between code and data. This translates a lexically nested function to a code abstracted with an extra environment that contains the free variables occurring in the original function. After this translation, the code becomes closed, and separated from the data. This enables nested functions to be defined at the top level and shared by all closures that are instances of these functions. Consider the following program written in Scheme.

```
(define (f x y) (let ((g (lambda (z) (+ x y z)))) g))
```

The function g contains free variables x and y. Closure conversion eliminates direct references to these variables by replacing them with references to an explicit environment. The above program is translated to the following program.

```
(define (g env z) (let ((x (car env))
                        (y (cdr env)))
                   (+ x y z)))

(define (f x y) (cons g (cons x y)))
```

In this example, the closure and the environment are implemented with cons cells.

Conceptually, closure conversion divides into two phases.

1. The first phase makes all functions closed by abstracting them with an environment.
2. The second phase lifts all functions to the top level.

Most of the previous formal accounts of closure conversion formalize only the first phase [7,11], but compilers usually perform these two phases as one transformation. Because we need to extract an executable compiler from the specification, we formalized closure conversion as a transformation that performs these two phases simultaneously.

The target language of closure conversion differs from the source language in that: it does not include a function definition, but an operation for creating a closure explicitly. A program in the target language is represented as a pair of declaration of top level functions and an expression evaluated under the declaration. The following are datatypes to represent the target language.

```
types   decl  = "variable list * variable list * cexp"
        decls = "decl env"

datatype cexp = ⋯
              | MkCls variable "variable list"
```

primrec
```
"clsconv (VarExp x)          = (VarExp x, [])"
"clsconv (FunExp f as e1 e2) = let (e1', ds1) = clsconv e1 in
                               let (e2', ds2) = clsconv e2 in
                               let xs = diff (fv e1) (f#as) in
                               (LetExp f (MkCls f xs) e2',
                                ins (f, xs, as, e1')
                                    (union ds1 ds2))"
"clsconv (AppExp f es)       = let (f',  ds1) = clsconv f in
                               let (es', ds2) = clsconv_list es in
                               (AppExp f' es', union ds1 ds2)"
...
```

Fig. 2. Closure conversion

The type `decls` represents a declaration of top level functions and is a mapping from variables to definitions of functions. The definition of a function consists of the list of free variables, the list of formal parameters and its body. The expression of the target language, `cexp`, includes the operation `MkCls f xs` that creates a closure of the function `f` with the environment containing values of `xs`.

We formalized closure conversion as a primitive recursive function with the following type.

consts
```
clsconv :: "exp ⇒ cexp * decls"
```

As we described above, the conversion function translates an expression in the source language into a pair of an expression in the target language and a declaration of top level functions. The main part of the translation is shown in Figure 2. To transform a function definition, `e1` and `e2` are translated into `e1'` and `e2'`, respectively. It also produces declarations `ds1` and `ds2`. To construct the closure of the function, we need to compute the set of free variables that occur in the function body by `diff (fv e1) (f#as)`. Finally, the declaration corresponding to the function `f` is inserted into the union of `ds1` and `ds2`.

In this definition, we represented sets by lists and used the following manipulation functions:

consts
```
fv :: "exp ⇒ variable list"
diff    :: "['a list, 'a list] ⇒ 'a list"
union   :: "['a list, 'a list] ⇒ 'a list"
```

where `fv exp` computes the set of free variables of `exp`. These functions are easily defined as primitive recursive functions. HOL has the built-in type constructor `set` to represent possibly infinite sets, and automated theorem-proving methods work very well for operations on `set`. However, we could not use them for closure conversion because an executable code cannot be extracted for the operations on `set`. Many lemmas on our set operations are required in proving correctness of the translation. To eliminate unnecessary proof work, we showed that each set operation we defined is compatible with the corresponding built-in set operation. For example, the following lemma shows that the union of two lists is equivalent to the union of two sets. The function *set* used in this example is a conversion function from lists to sets.

    lemma `union_set: "set (union A B) = set A ∪ set B"`

With these lemmas, most lemmas on our set operations are proved automatically.

3.3   Verification of Closure Conversion

We proved correctness of closure conversion in HOL. To formalize correctness of the transformation, we first introduce the following datatype representing observable values.

    datatype `ovalue = IntVal int`
                      `| BoolVal bool`
                      `| SymVal symbol`
                      `| NullVal`
                      `| ConsVal`
                      `| ClsVal`

We consider integers, boolean values, symbols and null as observable values, but the detailed structures of cons cells and closures are ignored. Values of the source and target languages are coerced into observable values by the following functions.

    consts
      `value2obs :: "value ⇒ ovalue"`
      `cvalue2obs :: "cvalue ⇒ ovalue"`

The following is the correctness theorem verified in HOL. The theorem says that if M is evaluated to v under the empty environment *[]*, the translated expression M' is evaluated to v' under the empty environment *[]* and the declaration D generated by closure conversion. Furthermore, the values v and v' correspond to the same observable value.

    theorem assumes `"([], M, v) ∈ Lang.eval "   "fv M = []"`
        shows `"let (M',D) = clsconv M in func D ⟶`
              `(∃v'. (D, [], M', v') ∈ CLang.eval ∧`
                  `value2obs v = cvalue2obs v')"`

Note an extra condition *func D* in the theorem. This condition is necessary to lift function definitions to the top level.

    constdefs
      `func :: "('a, 'b) list ⇒ bool"`
      `"func D == (∀f x y. elem (f, x) D ⟶ elem (f, y) D ⟶ x = y)"`

The function *elem* is the membership predicate on a list. This condition is satisfied if function names are distinct. In our hand-written parser, each variable is renamed to a fresh integer value to satisfy this condition.

To prove the theorem above, we needed to prove a generalized statement, which was proved by induction on the derivation of $(E, M, v) \in eval$. The proof consists of approximately 750 lines.

4   Code Generation

The code generation phase of our compiler translates a closure-converted program into a Java virtual machine code. We chose the Java virtual machine (JVM) as the target of our compiler for the following reasons. First, it is easier to translate our source language into JVM than a conventional machine language, because its instructions are stack-based and we can assume memory management of JVM. Secondly, a formalization of JVM has been studied extensively in several works for type soundness of JVM and there are several works that have already formalized it using theorem provers [8,9].

For the verification of our compiler, we formalized JVM from the beginning because existing formalizations do not include sufficient instructions to generate an executable code for our compiler and we can also simplify our verification by restricting features of the virtual machine.

The first step of our verification is to clarify what should be verified. Our compiler consists of the code generated from the verified specification and the small quantity of hand-written code. The hand-written code contains a small library written in Java to implement some primitives of the source language. In our verification, we focused on the verification of the core of the compiler and did not verify correctness of the library. For real programming languages, implementation of some primitives are complicated and their correctness proofs will be non-trivial. We think that a verification of the library is a different issue.

The rest of our verification is similar to the verification of closure conversion, but it was much more difficult than that of closure conversion. The specification of code generation and its verification is approximately 2400 lines.

4.1   Formalization of a Virtual Machine

We formalized a small subset of the Java virtual machine, so that it is sufficient to generate the code of the source language. The instruction set is restricted to a small subset and the form of an object is also restricted. The following summarizes the restrictions of our virtual machine.

- classes have only one method
- branching instructions do not jump backward
- no interface, no exception, no thread and no inheritance

Our compiler translates a closure into an object with one method and each function is translated into a class. To simplify the virtual machine, we did not introduce a class with multiple methods. Branch instructions only jump forward because our source language does not have a loop construct.

Instructions of our virtual machine are formalized by the following datatype:

```
datatype
  'a instr = ALoad nat
           | IAdd
           ...
           | Dup
           | New cname
           | Invoke nat
           | PrimCall 'a
```

where the type variable 'a is used to parameterize the set of instructions with primitives provided by the library. We briefly describe the instructions defined above. ALoad instruction loads an object reference from local variables. New f makes a new instance of class f. Invoke instruction invokes a method of the class corresponding to closures. It only takes a number of arguments, since an object can be determined from the operand stack and each object has only one method. PrimCall instruction is a pseudo instruction introduced to call primitives.

The following is a part of the primitives implemented in the library.

```
datatype
  prim = PrimMkCons
       | PrimCar
       | PrimCdr
       ...
```

We split the specification of semantics of these primitives from the specification of the virtual machine. The semantics of each of these primitives is specified as a relation describing their effects on a state of the virtual machine. The specification below, defines the semantics of the primitives.

```
consts
  prim_spec :: "(prim heap * vmVal list * prim * prim heap *
  vmVal) set"

inductive prim_spec
intros
  mkcons : "l ∉ dom H ⟹
      (H, [v2,v1], PrimMkCons,
        H(l ↦ PrimObj PrimMkCons [v1, v2]), VmAddr l) ∈ prim_spec"
  car : "H(l) = Some (PrimObj PrimMkCons [v,v'])
      ⟹ (H, [VmAddr l], PrimCar, H, v) ∈ prim_spec"
  ...
```

For example, the primitive PrimMkCons creates a fresh cons cell PrimObj PrimMkCons [v1, v2] on the heap for the arguments v1 and v2. The heap of the virtual machine is also abstracted with primitives to represent abstract objects with PrimObj. We assume that the primitives implemented in the library satisfy the above specification.

```
consts
  cgExp :: "variable list ⇒ cexp ⇒ prim instr list"
primrec
  "cgExp E (NumExp n) = [Ldc n, PrimCall PrimMkInt]"
  "cgExp E (VarExp x) = [ALoad (the (assign E x))]"
  "cgExp E (MkCls f xs) = (New f) # cgCls E f xs"
  "cgExp E (AppExp f es) = (cgExp E f) @ [CheckCls] @
                           (cgExps E es) @ [Invoke (length es)]"
  ...
```

Fig. 3. Code generation function

The semantics of the virtual machine is based on the semantics of primitives, and specified as small-step natural semantics. The semantics is defined as an inductively defined relation with the following type:

```
consts
  exec :: "(class * prim heap * frame * prim codes *
           prim heap * frame) set"
```

Type *frame* used above, is a record of an operand stack and a local variable environment. $(D * H * F * C * H' * F') \in exec$ means, the heap H and the frame F are transformed to H' and F' respectively by the code C under the class declaration D. We write $D \vdash < H, F, C > \leadsto < H', F' >$ to describe this relation.

4.2   Code Generation

The code generation of our compiler is similar to that of other compilers from functional languages into JVM [3,1]. We explain the major section of the code generation phase and the main theorem we verified. The main part of the code generator is the function that translates an expression into a list of instructions as shown in Figure 3. In the definition, integer expression *NumExp n* is translated into the instruction sequence: *Ldc n* instruction puts an integer constant *n* on the operand stack, and *PrimMkInt* primitive creates a new integer object from it.

A variable is translated to the load instruction of the local variable obtained by an assignment function. The assignment function translates a variable into a local variable according to a list of variables *E*. It assigns the n-th variable from the tail of the list to the n-th local variable. This assignment is specified by the following primitive recursive function.

```
consts
  assign :: "'a list ⇒ 'a ⇒ nat option"
primrec
  "assign [] n     = None"
  "assign (x#xs) n = (if n = x then Some (length xs)
                               else assign xs n)"
```

This translation of a variable is correct only if the list of variables used in the translation satisfies some condition: intuitively, variables in the list must be distinct, but a weaker condition is sufficient. This is guaranteed by the well-formedness of the declaration we discuss later in this section.

A function application is translated to a sequence of: a code for the function part, codes for arguments and method invocation. `CheckCls` pseudo instruction interleaved in this sequence checks that the function translated is an instance of a closure class. This check is required so that a generated code is type-checked by the bytecode verifier of JVM and translated into `checkcast` instruction of JVM.

The most complicated part of the code generation phase is the handling of closures. A function is represented by a class with one "apply" method. This class may contain instance variables to keep values for the free variables. When compiling a function, instructions to create a new instance of the corresponding class and to store all free variables into the closure is inserted. Storing all free variables into the closure is accomplished by the following function.

```
consts
   cgCls :: "variable list ⇒ cname ⇒ variable list ⇒ prim
codes"
primrec
   "cgCls E f [] = []"
   "cgCls E f (x#xs) = (cgCls E f xs) @
                       [Dup,ALoad (the (assign E x)),PutField f x]"
```

It can be seen that each value is loaded from the corresponding local variable and stored to a class instance by `PutField`.

The following is the correctness theorem we verified in HOL.

```
theorem assumes "(D, [], e, v) ∈ eval" "wf_decls D"
   shows "∃H' F'.cgDecls D⊢<newheap,newframe,cgExp[]e>⤳< H',F' >
                    ∧ (D, H', v, hd (opstack F')) ∈ valeq"
```

The generated code `cgExp [] e` is executed under the empty heap `newheap` and empty frame `newframe`. The theorem says, if expression e is evaluated to a value v under a declaration D, the execution of the generated code transforms the empty heap and frame into heap H' and frame F'. Furthermore, the value that is on the top of operand stack F' corresponds to the value v under the class declaration D and the obtained heap H'.

In this correctness theorem, well-formedness of the declaration D is essential. To satisfy this condition, we defined a well-formedness predicate on the source language as:

- all function names must be distinct.
- the variable names of the arguments of a function must be distinct.
- a function name and the variable names of its arguments must be different.

If a source program is well-formed, we can show that the closure conversion produces a well-formed declaration. In addition, we can show the condition of

closure conversion shown in Section 3.3 can be satisfied by this predicate. Therefore, the entire compilation process is correct assuming that the source program
is well-formed.

Note that our verification of the code generator has several limitations. Our
specification of the compiler does not calculate the size of the operand stack and
the number of local variables used in each method. It is not verified that the
compiler produces a code that is compliant with the bytecode verifier of JVM.

5   The Generated Compiler and Its Evaluation

The specification and correctness proof of the compiler is approximately 5000
lines of HOL proof scripts. From this specification, 300 lines of an executable
Standard ML code is generated. To make the compiler executable, we provided
a parser and an output routine written in ML and some library code written in
Java. Codes written in ML and Java are approximately 700 lines and 120 lines
respectively. In this section, we describe integration with hand-written codes and
then present some preliminary experiments with the resulting compiler.

5.1   Integration with Hand-Written Codes

From the specification, we obtain the abstract syntax of the source language.
Types that appears in the abstract syntax are translated to types of ML, according to the following declaration:

```
types_code
  "variable"    ("int")
  "int"         ("int")
  "symbol"      ("string")
```

Among these declarations, translations of int and symbol are essential to coordinate with the parser. The type variable, which is a type synonym of nat,
can be used in our compiler. However, it is obviously inefficient to take nat as a
datatype for the variables and compilation time became from two times to eight
times more inefficient in our experiment. Therefore, we applied this translation.
In the parser, each identifier that occurs in source code is replaced by a fresh
integer value, so that the well-formedness condition required by the correctness
proof is satisfied.

The output routine produces an assembly code in the syntax of the Jasmin
bytecode assembler [10] and this assembler is used to generate a Java bytecode.
Because the instructions of our virtual machine almost directly correspond to
those of the Java virtual machine, writing the output routine for the compiler is
straightforward. One twist was needed in the output routine because a branch
instruction of our virtual machine takes a relative address and Jasmin uses a
label to specify the target address of a branch instruction.

We also formalized a simple dead code elimination. This eliminates a function definition that is not used in the main expression. The verification of this

Table 1. Compilation time (in seconds)

program	#lines	vc total	vc w/o jasmin	bigloo	kawa
symbdiff	376	1.87	0.08	0.46	2.90
boyer	552	2.13	0.11	0.32	2.82
sets	349	1.74	0.04	0.55	2.62
sk	181	1.59	0.05	0.25	2.34
art	3008	54.44	51.56	4.22	3.82

optimization was relatively simple compared to the remainder of our verification and completed in approximately one day. This optimization works in combination with the other part of our compiler and eliminates unused primitives and library procedures.

5.2   Experimental Results

We tested the generated compiler on several programs: a symbolic differentiation program (symbdiff), a tautology checker (boyer), a set module implemented with a balanced binary tree (sets) and a translator from the lambda calculus to combinatory logic (sk). These examples were selected from the Scheme repository and successfully compiled/executed with few modifications.

We compared compilation times of these programs with the existing Scheme to Java compilers Bigloo and Kawa[1]. A 650MHz Ultra SPARC IIi processor with 256MB of memory, using: Poly ML 4.1.3, Sun J2SDK 1.4.1, Bigloo 2.6a and Kawa 1.7 was used for the experiment. Through this comparison, we refer our compiler as vc (verified compiler). Table 1 shows compilation times. The column "vc total" shows the compilation time including the time spent by Jasmin, and the column "vc w/o jasmin" shows the compilation time without Jasmin. The program "art" is an artificial large example with a large number of variable definitions. Compilation time of this program is more than ten times slower than the time for the other two compilers. We consider this problem is caused by the naive implementation of various data structures: we represented sets by lists and used association lists to handle identifiers. We think refining the implementation of data structures used in the compiler is one of the first tasks to make the compiler realistic.

We also conducted preliminary experiments regarding execution times. we chose the programs: Fibonnatti function, Takeuchi's function, eight queen program and tautology checker. Results are shown in Table 2. The column "bigloo opt" shows the execution time of the code generated by Bigloo with optimization. Note that the comparison is disadvantageous to Bigloo and Kawa because our compiler supports only a small subset of Scheme and that simplifies a compilation. Regardless of that, execution times for Bigloo with optimization are much

---

[1] Bigloo is written in C, and Kawa is written in Java. Both compilers were tested without any command line options

Table 2. Execution time (in seconds)

program	vc	bigloo	bigloo opt	kawa
fib	32.12	33.14	1.31	42.72
tak	0.48	0.74	0.62	1.58
queens	2.14	2.13	0.98	12.47
boyer	69.37	6.33	3.62	262.52

faster than those of our compiler. To generate more efficient code, we need to improve the translations in our compiler and incorporate standard optimizations such as inlining and constant folding.

6   Related Work

Various system components including language implementations were verified using the Boyer-Moore theorem prover [4,12,19]. The Boyer-Moore theorem prover is first-order and its specification language is Lisp based. Therefore, their specification of the language implementations can be executed. Although it is possible to verify compilers in theorem provers based on a first-order logic as their works demonstrated, expressiveness of a higher-order logic was of considerable assistance in verifying the correctness of our compiler.

Oliva, Ramsdell and Wand verified a specification of the VLISP compiler [14]. VLISP compiles a dialect of Scheme designed for system programming. The semantics of the language is described in denotational semantics. They wrote a correctness proof of the compiler specification by hand. The compiler is written based on this specification, but there is no verification of the implementation.

Stepney wrote a specification of a compiler in the Z specification language and proved correctness of the compiler specification by hand [16]. The specification was translated into an executable Prolog program by a syntax-based hand-translation. Stringer-Calvert translated the specification of this compiler into PVS [15] and verified its correctness [17]. The approach of this work is closely related to ours in sense that the executable compiler is obtained from the specification. However, we believe that the code generation of HOL is more trustworthy and we obtain a more realistic compiler because the translation is more direct.

The same approach of generating a compiler from the specification was taken by Curzon [5]. He verified the correctness of an assembler for the high-level assembly language Vista with the HOL theorem prover [6] and generated an executable assembler in ML with an automated tool. However, issues concerning the resulting compiler and its evaluation are not described in detail.

7   Conclusions and Future Work

We have verified a specification of a compiler from a functional language to the Java virtual machine in Isabelle/HOL. An executable compiler was derived from the specification with the code generation facility of Isabelle/HOL. In our development, most time was spent in proving correctness of the compiler. We think recent progress in theorem proving have made verification of compilers more feasible. Especially, the human-readable structured proof language of Isabelle[18] made our verification easier.

The compiler was tested for several Scheme programs and the compile times were acceptable. However, the compilation of an artificial large program revealed inefficiency in the compiler.

We are planning to refine and extend our compiler in various respects to make it more realistic. To compile large examples, we will need to extend the features supported by the source language and improve data structures used in the compiler. With respect to performance of code generated by the compiler, first we wish to refine the algorithms used in the current specification. Second, we intend to introduce several basic optimizations into our compiler specification, such as inlining.

References

1. N. Benton, A. Kennedy, and G. Russell. Compiling Standard ML to Java byte-codes. In *Proceedings of the ACM SIGPLAN International Conference on Functional Programming (ICFP '98)*, volume 34(1), pages 129–140, 1999.
2. S. Berghofer and T. Nipkow. Executing higher order logic. In *Proceedings of International Workshop on Types for Proofs and Programs*, volume 2277 of *Lecture Notes in Computer Science*, pages 24–40. Springer-Verlag, 2002.
3. P. Bothner. Kawa—compiling dynamic languages to the Java VM. In *Proceedings of the USENIX 1998 Technical Conference, FREENIX Track*, New Orleans, LA, 1998. USENIX Association.
4. R. S. Boyer and J. S. Moore. *A Computational Logic Handbook*. Academic Press, 1988.
5. P. Curzon. A verified Vista implementation final report. Technical Report 311, University of Cambridge Computer Laboratory, 1993.
6. M. J. C. Gordon and T. F. Melham. *Introduction to HOL : A Theorem Proving Environment for Higher Order Logic*. Cambridge University Press, Cambridge, 1993.
7. J. Hannan. A type system for closure conversion. In *Proceedings of the Workshop on Types for Program Analysis*, pages 48–62, 1995.
8. G. Klein and T. Nipkow. Verified lightweight bytecode verification. *Concurrency and Computation: Practice and Experience*, 13:1133–1151, 2001.
9. G. Klein and T. Nipkow. Verified bytecode verifiers. *Theoretical Computer Science*, 298:583–626, 2003.
10. J. Meyer. Jasmin home page. http://mrl.nyu.edu/~meyer/jasmin/.
11. Y. Minamide, J. G. Morrisett, and R. Harper. Typed closure conversion. In *Proceedings of Symposium on Principles of Programming Languages*, pages 271–283, 1996.

12. J. S. Moore. A mechanically verified language implementation. Technical Report 30, Computational Logic Inc., 1988.
13. T. Nipkow, L. C. Paulson, and M. Wenzel. *Isabelle/HOL : A Proof Assistant for Higher-Order Logic*, volume 2283 of *Lecture Notes in Computer Science*. Springer-Verlag, 2002.
14. D. P. Oliva, J. D. Ramsdell, and M. Wand. The VLISP verified PreScheme compiler. *Lisp and Symbolic Computation*, 8(1/2):111–182, 1995.
15. S. Owre, N. Shankar, J. M. Rushby, and D. W. J. Stringer-Calvert. *PVS Language Reference*. Computer Science Laboratory, SRI International, Menlo Park, CA, Sept. 1999.
16. S. Stepney. *High Integrity Compilation : a case study*. Prentice-Hall, 1993.
17. D. W. Stringer-Calvert. *Mechanical Verification of Compiler Correctness*. PhD thesis, Department of Computer Science, University of York, Mar. 1998.
18. M. Wenzel. Isar - a generic interpretative approach to readable formal proof documents. In *Proceedings of International Conference on Theorem Proving in Higher Order Logics*, pages 167–184, 1999.
19. W. D. Young. A verified code generator for a subset of Gypsy. Technical Report 33, Computational Logic Inc., 1988.

Controlling and Optimizing the Usage of One Resource

Antoine Galland[1,3] and Mathieu Baudet[2]

[1] Gemplus Research Labs,
La Vigie, avenue du Jujubier,
ZI Athelia IV, 13705 La Ciotat Cedex, France
antoine.galland@research.gemplus.com
[2] LSV/CNRS UMR 8643 & INRIA Futurs Projet SECSI & ENS Cachan,
61, avenue du Président Wilson, 94235 Cachan Cedex, France
mathieu.baudet@lsv.ens-cachan.fr
[3] Pierre & Marie Curie University, LIP6 Laboratory,
8, rue du Capitaine Scott, 75015 Paris, France

Abstract. This paper studies the problem of resource availability in the context of mobile code for embedded systems such as smart cards. It presents an architecture dedicated to controlling the usage of a single resource in a multi-process operating system. Its specificity lies in its ability to improve the task scheduling in order to spare resources. Our architecture comprises two parts. The first statically computes the resource needs using a dedicated lattice. The second guarantees at runtime that there will always be enough resources for every application to terminate, thanks to an efficient deadlock-avoidance algorithm. The example studied here is an implementation on a JVM (Java Virtual Machine) for smart cards, dealing with a realistic subset of the Java bytecode.

1 Introduction

A smart card is a device with stringent hardware constraints: low-power CPU, low throughput serial I/O, little memory (typically 1−4 kb RAM, 32−128 kb ROM and 16−64 kb Flash RAM). But its tamper resistance [19] makes it one of the mobile computing devices of choice. From the emergence of smart cards [26] to the present, integrating a high level of safety with so few resources has always been the main challenge of smart card manufacturers. Hence, one has to keep in mind that optimizing physical and logic resources usage is of prime importance in such a constrained system.

Modern smart card platforms offer the opportunity to download code into the card while it is in the user's possession—this is called *post issuance*. This new functionality raises new problems as far as the security of mobile code for smart cards is concerned, since hostile applets can be developed and downloaded into the card. In Java Card [4], various solutions have been studied to integrate a Java bytecode verifier into a smart card in order to make sure that programs are well-typed [2,11,23]. After type-safe verification, resource control is the logical

A. Ohori (Ed.): APLAS 2003, LNCS 2895, pp. 195–211, 2003.

next step to ensure reliability [10]. Indeed application providers would like guarantees that their applets will have all the required resources for safe execution throughout their lifespan.

The aim of this paper is to propose an architecture that solves these two problems, i.e., optimizing resource usage and guaranteeing availability in a multi-application environment. Section 2 studies different models of resource control and introduces the problem of deadlock avoidance. Section 3 presents our framework of code analysis and deadlock avoidance on a single resource. Then Section 4 details its implementation on an architecture for smart cards. Finally, Section 5 provides some benchmarks and Section 6 is the conclusion.

2   Related Literature

2.1   Resource Control

When mobile code is uploaded to a new host—in our study a smart card—there is no guarantee that there will be enough resources to complete its execution. The most commonly adopted solution is to use a contract-based approach of resource management [22]. In this approach, each applet must declare its resource requirements in a contract. Once the smart card accepts a contract, it must meet its requirements during the applet's lifespan. Since the uploaded applet is not considered as trustworthy, safeguards must be established. Runtime techniques are generally used to control allocations, which implies costly monitoring. Moreover, when the contract is canceled, it is often too late to recover applet execution even if a call-back mechanism can be used [8].

To reduce runtime extra-costs, it may be preferable to check once and for all whether an applet respects its own contract. This generally implies bounding its resource consumptions by means of static control-flow analysis or type systems [7,16]. These approaches are complex, as a consequence, it is difficult to incorporate them directly into a smart card. In this case, some techniques inspired of "Proof-Carrying Code" from Lee and Necula [25] can be used to check on line the resource bounds computed off line [24].

Once a smart card commits itself to respecting specific resource requirements, the simplest solution to ensure availability is to reserve and lock all the required resources at start-up. This is the solution used in Java Card 2.1 [4] for heap memory allocation. Smart card developers gather all necessary memory initializations[1] needed at start-up to avoid running out of memory later. This implies that additional memory allocations cannot be ensured.

The drawback of this solution is the waste of resources when multiple applets are used. Indeed applets will seldom use all their reserved quotas simultaneously. On the contrary it is more likely that peaks of resource usage will occur at different times. Moreover, if this is not the case, we might consider delaying one or more tasks to avoid this situation. In short, resource usage is currently far from being optimized.

---

[1] in the `javacard.framework.Applet.install()` method.

Our objective is to guarantee resource availability to every applet, while minimizing the global needs of the system. Most approaches described above do not solve these two problems simultaneously. Thus we are looking for a framework that is more economical than one that blocks all resources at start-up, while offering the same level of dependability.

2.2 Relation to Deadlock Avoidance

In most systems, when a program requests more resources than the amount available, an error is reported and the task terminated. For our purpose, however, a thriftier solution would be to suspend the requesting task temporarily, in the hope that some resource might be released later. In this case, allocation and deallocation methods are equivalent to the P (locking) and V (unlocking) synchronizing primitives [12].

This approach leads to two well-known problems of concurrency theory: starvation and deadlocks. Starvation only occurs in the presence of non-terminating programs, and therefore is usually not a problem on smart cards. Concerning the problem of deadlock prevention, it was first studied by Dijkstra [12]. A convenient geometrical representation exists and it is called *progress graphs* (see Figure 1). The axes represent the progress rate of each task through the time.

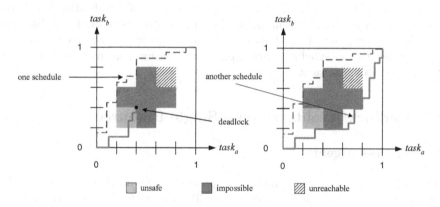

Fig. 1. Progress graph and deadlock avoidance

Impossible areas are those for which the sum of the instantaneous consumptions is greater than the amount of resource available. A *valid schedule* is a path which avoids impossible areas. A state is considered *safe* if there exists a schedule starting from this thread that ends every task. On the contrary, *unsafe states* lead to deadlock. Deadlock-avoidance algorithms generally consist in detecting unsafe states (deadlock *prediction*) and avoiding them at runtime.

The first deadlock-avoidance algorithm, *the banker's algorithm*, was introduced by Dijkstra [12]. In the case of reusable resources without partial requests, Habermann [15] solved the deadlock-prediction problem in polynomial time. Later, Gold [14] proved that deadlock prediction is NP-complete in general and is polynomial for several sub-problems including the case of one resource. Deadlock avoidance has since been studied and used in many resource allocation systems, such as the flexible manufacturing systems (FMS) [21,13].

In the rest of this paper we first present a generalization of Gold's safety criterion for a single resource [14]. Gold reasons directly on lists of partial requests, not processes. Accordingly it is unclear from Gold's paper how to compile processes into partial requests (or "blocks" in the present study). Furthermore, Gold's method only applies to processes where parallel composition is not nested. Our algorithm can handle a more general class of systems, modeled by a simple process algebra. It relies on a dedicated data-structure called "normalized lists" which allows for very fast computations and thus is perfectly suitable for dynamic scheduling. Thanks to the lattice structure of normalized lists, the framework of abstract interpretation applies; this allows us to design a static analysis of the program requirements in most programming languages, provided allocations and deallocations are explicit. Once the programs have been annotated with the results of the analysis, they can be safely executed under the control of a deadlock-avoidance unit. This unit works by reading the static information at runtime and by applying the safety criterion to the term which models the overall state of the system. Finally, as an application of our deadlock-avoidance framework, an implementation for the Java bytecode is presented and discussed. A noticeable property of this implementation is that it is an ordinary Java package. Thanks to the synchronization primitives of Java, no modification of any specific JVM is necessary.

3   Deadlock Avoidance on a Single Resource

3.1   Process Algebra

We first consider a simple language of processes, intended to model a pool of threads accessing a single resource. This will prove useful later on. Terms of our language, called *processes* or *programs*, are defined by the following grammar:

$$p ::= \epsilon \mid x \mid (p\,p) \mid (p \parallel p)$$

where x denotes an integer, positive or negative. Intuitively, the meaning of this syntax can be described as follows:

- ϵ represents the empty program (thus already terminated),
- x stands for an instruction that allocates an amount x of the resource (which means deallocating some of it when x is negative),
- $(p_1\,p_2)$ denotes a sequence of processes: p_1 then p_2,
- $(p_1 \parallel p_2)$ is the program that executes p_1 and p_2 concurrently.

Table 1. Small-step semantics

$$\frac{}{(\epsilon\, p)\xrightarrow{\epsilon} p} \qquad \frac{}{(\epsilon\|p)\xrightarrow{\epsilon} p} \qquad \frac{}{(p\|\epsilon)\xrightarrow{\epsilon} p} \qquad \text{(structural rules)}$$

$$\frac{}{x\xrightarrow{x}\epsilon} \qquad \frac{p\xrightarrow{\epsilon*}\xrightarrow{x}\xrightarrow{\epsilon*}p'}{p\xrightarrow{x}p'} \qquad \text{(evaluation rules)}$$

$$\frac{p_1\xrightarrow{x}p_1'}{(p_1\,p_2)\xrightarrow{x}(p_1'\,p_2)} \quad \frac{p_1\xrightarrow{x}p_1'}{(p_1\|p_2)\xrightarrow{x}(p_1'\|p_2)} \quad \frac{p_2\xrightarrow{x}p_2'}{(p_1\|p_2)\xrightarrow{x}(p_1\|p_2')} \quad \text{(context rules)}$$

To formalize our language's semantics, we choose a system of labelled transitions described in Table 1. ϵ-transitions do nothing but simplify terms, whereas normal transitions *emit* an allocation x.

Following the usual conventions of automata, sequences of transitions emit a list of integers: $p \xrightarrow{x_1 x_2 \ldots x_n} p'$ if $p \xrightarrow{x_1}\xrightarrow{x_2}\cdots\xrightarrow{x_n} p'$. It is easy to prove, using these semantics, that every program eventually terminates—after emitting all its allocations. Thus we can define the execution traces of program p as the set of every list $l = x_1 x_2 \ldots x_n$ such that $p \xrightarrow{l} \epsilon$. For instance, the traces of $((1\,2)\|-3)$ are: $1\,2\,(-3)$, $1\,(-3)\,2$ and $(-3)\,1\,2$.

Given an execution trace, we can easily define the amount of resource that is needed, which we call *cost* of the trace:

$$\mathcal{C}(x_1 x_2 \ldots x_n) \stackrel{def}{=} \max_{0\leq i\leq n}\left(\sum_{1\leq j\leq i} x_j\right) \quad \text{thus } \mathcal{C}(l)\geq 0 \text{ and } \mathcal{C}(\epsilon) \stackrel{def}{=} 0.$$

Using this, we are now able to formulate a simple criterion of safety. Assuming that a state is described by term p of the process algebra, and given a certain amount M of available resource, the state p will be safe if and only if there exists a trace l such that: $p \xrightarrow{l} \epsilon$ and $\mathcal{C}(l) \leq M$. Thus a criterion for the safety of state p is simply: $\min\{\mathcal{C}(l), p \xrightarrow{l} \epsilon\} \leq M$.

What we need now is an efficient way to compute this minimum, which we call the *cost of process p*:

$$\mathcal{C}(p) \stackrel{def}{=} \min\{\mathcal{C}(l), p \xrightarrow{l} \epsilon\}$$

3.2 Computing Process Costs with Normalized Lists

A first class of algorithms which can be thought of to compute $\mathcal{C}(p)$ consists in exploring the transition system between p and ϵ. With dynamic-programming techniques, such algorithms would require linear time dependent on the size of the transition system. Unfortunately this size grows exponentially with the number of threads (state-explosion phenomenon), so these algorithms are not suited to our purpose.

Table 2. A first algorithm with blocks

$B(\epsilon)$	$= (0, 0)$
$B(x)$	$= (\max(x, 0), x)$
$B(p_1\, p_2)$	$= B(p_1) \cdot B(p_2)$
$B(p_1 \,\|\, p_2)$	$= B(p_1) \times B(p_2)$
where:	
$(c_1, \delta_1) \cdot (c_2, \delta_2)$	$= (\max(c_1, \delta_1 + c_2),\ \delta_1 + \delta_2)$
$(c_1, \delta_1) \times (c_2, \delta_2)$	$= (\min(\max(c_1, \delta_1 + c_2), \max(c_2, \delta_2 + c_1)),\ \delta_1 + \delta_2)$

Instead, we shall rely upon the fact that only one resource is considered and investigate a more semantical approach, where $\mathcal{C}(p)$ is computed recursively over p.

As a first attempt in this direction, the algorithm presented in Table 2 recursively computes a pair of integer $B(p)$.

It can be shown that, for each p, the first coordinate of $B(p)$ is an upper-approximation of $\mathcal{C}(p)$, whereas the second one computes the sum of all the allocations. For instance, a run on the previous example: $B((1\,2)\|{-}3) = B(1\,2) \times (0, -3) = (3, 3) \times (0, -3) = (0, 0)$ gives here the exact answer $\mathcal{C}((1\,2)\|{-}3) = 0$.

Pairs of integers computed by the function $B(\_)$ are of the form (c, δ) where $c \geq \max(0, \delta)$. As they take a natural place in our problem, we shall henceforth call such pairs *blocks*. These are equivalent to Gold's *partial requests* [14] which are actually the pairs $(c, c - \delta)$. Figure 2 illustrates the intuition behind blocks and the $\cdot$-operator.

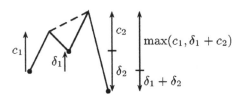

Fig. 2. Merging blocks with $\cdot$

Although fast and simple, the algorithm in Table 2, that uses blocks, unfortunately gives very poor results on more complicated entries. Two reasons may be put advanced to account for this fact:

- First, the $\times$-operator does not reflect the associativity of parallel composition. For instance, $((2, 0) \times (1, 1)) \times (0, -1) = (2, 1) \times (0, -1) = (1, 0)$ whereas $(2, 0) \times ((1, 1) \times (0, -1)) = (2, 0) \times (0, 0) = (2, 0)$.
- Second, the $\cdot$-operator causes a significant loss of information, by merging the internal steps of a sequence together. For example, although the cost of $(-1\,1)\|(2\,{-}1)$ is **1**, the algorithm fails to find the optimal trace $(-1\,2\,{-}1\,1)$: $B((-1\,1)\|(2\,{-}1)) = B((-1\,1)) \times B((2\,{-}1)) = (0, 0) \times (2, 1) = (\mathbf{2}, 1)$.

To solve the first problem, one possibility would be to generalize the $\times$-operator so as to deal with a pool of blocks. A natural way to do this is to define:

$$(c_1, \delta_1) \times \ldots \times (c_n, \delta_n) \stackrel{def}{=} \prod_{\sigma \in \Sigma_n} (c_{\sigma 1}, \delta_{\sigma 1}) \cdot \ldots \cdot (c_{\sigma n}, \delta_{\sigma n})$$

$$= \left(\min_{\sigma \in \Sigma_n} \max_{1 \le i \le n} \left(c_{\sigma i} + \sum_{1 \le j < i} \delta_{\sigma j} \right), \sum_{1 \le i \le n} \delta_i \right)$$

where Σ_n stands for the set of all permutations on $\{1 \ldots n\}$ and $\sqcap$ is the greatest lower bound on pairs of integers. After doing this, we face a non-trivial minimization problem—which can be seen as a scheduling problem. Fortunately it can be solved in polynomial time, one of the optimal permutations being obtained by sorting the set of blocks according to the following total quasi-ordering (total, reflexive, transitive relation):

$$(c_1, \delta_1) \preceq (c_2, \delta_2) \text{ iff:} \quad \begin{array}{ll} \delta_1 \le 0 \text{ and } \delta_2 \ge 0 & (1) \\ \text{or } \delta_1 < 0, \delta_2 < 0 \text{ and } c_1 \le c_2 & (2) \\ \text{or } \delta_1 > 0, \delta_2 > 0 \text{ and } \delta_1 - c_1 \le \delta_2 - c_2 & (3) \end{array}$$

Thus the previous quantity can be computed in $O(n \log(n))$ (i.e., the cost of sorting), which gives us the generalization of $\times$ we were looking for. The definition of $\preceq$ relies basically on the same ideas as Gold's generalized banker's algorithm [14]: for instance rule (1) means "producers before consumers," rule (2) means "better producers first" and rule (3) can be seen as the time-reversed image of (2).

We now address the second issue: to reduce the loss of information caused by the $\cdot$-operator. What the previous example $(-1\,1)\|(2\,-1)$ suggests, is that merging blocks implies losing many valid schedules. Actually the traces that are lost are those that interleave the processes together.

For this reason we work with *lists of blocks* instead of blocks so as to keep more information about code behavior. In this way, the $\cdot$-operator will not always *merge* blocks as it did previously. For instance, we decide that $(0, -2) \cdot (2, 2) = (0, -2)(2, 2)$, which is more precise than $(0, 0)$. Indeed $(0, -2)(2, 2)$ in parallel with $(2, 0)$ can be scheduled $(0, -2)(2, 0)(2, 2)$ which costs 0, whereas $(0, 0)$ in parallel with $(2, 0)$ costs 2. By cost of a list of blocks, we mean the quantity defined by: $\mathcal{C}((c_1, \delta_1) \ldots (c_n, \delta_n)) \stackrel{def}{=} \max_{1 \le i \le n} \left(c_i + \sum_{1 \le j < i} \delta_j \right)$ and $\mathcal{C}(\epsilon) \stackrel{def}{=} 0$ where ϵ stands for the empty list.

Defining $\cdot$ as the usual concatenation of lists (working in the free monoid on blocks) would lead to structures with nearly the same size as the program, so we need a way to simplify the data. Thus, we introduce a procedure of *normalization* of lists. To this end we define a relation S between blocks called the *simplification relation*, which determines which blocks can be soundly merged. Intuitively two blocks can be merged if every schedule that separates them can be rewritten in an equivalent or possibly less expensive schedule that leaves them adjacent. This idea is expressed by the following definition:

$$(c_1, \delta_1)\mathcal{S}(c_2, \delta_2) \text{ iff: } \forall l, \quad \begin{vmatrix} \mathcal{C}((c_1, \delta_1)l(c_2, \delta_2)) \geq \mathcal{C}((c_1, \delta_1)(c_2, \delta_2)l) \\ \text{or } \mathcal{C}((c_1, \delta_1)l(c_2, \delta_2)) \geq \mathcal{C}(l(c_1, \delta_1)(c_2, \delta_2)) \end{vmatrix}$$

which can be written in a more convenient way:

$$(c_1, \delta_1)\mathcal{S}(c_2, \delta_2) \text{ iff: } \begin{vmatrix} \delta_2 \leq 0 \text{ and } c_1 \geq c_2 + \delta_1 \\ \text{or } \delta_1 \geq 0 \text{ and } c_1 \leq c_2 + \delta_1 \end{vmatrix}$$

We then consider the following rewriting rules on lists of blocks:

$$(c_1, \delta_1)(c_2, \delta_2) \rightarrow (\max(c_1, \delta_1 + c_2), \delta_1 + \delta_2) \text{ whenever } (c_1, \delta_1)\mathcal{S}(c_2, \delta_2)$$
$$(0, 0) \rightarrow \epsilon$$

It is an easy check that these rules are both confluent and strongly normalizing; therefore $\rightarrow$ terminates for every list, on a unique *normal form*. From now on, lists in normal form will be called *normalized lists*. Figure 3 illustrates the strong constraints imposed by the normalization.

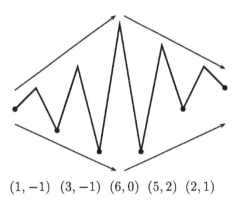

$$(1, -1) \quad (3, -1) \quad (6, 0) \quad (5, 2) \quad (2, 1)$$

Fig. 3. General aspect of normalized lists

A key property of normalized lists is that they are sorted for $\preceq$, the previously mentioned quasi-ordering. Thanks to this property and to the normalization rules, we are able to generalize the $\times$-operator to any set of lists, so that it still corresponds to optimal schedules of blocks. Instead of sorting the blocks, we shall simply *merge* the normalized lists—in the sense of the merge sort for $\preceq$ (see e.g., [18]).

Finally Table 3 describes an algorithm that computes recursively a list of blocks $L(p)$ that is "equivalent" to p. It can be shown that for each p, $\mathcal{C}(p) = \mathcal{C}(L(p))$. The fact that the algorithm is sound *and* complete results from the careful choice of the simplification relation $\mathcal{S}$ and from the existence of an exact scheduling algorithm given by the total quasi-ordering $\preceq$.

Table 3. Final algorithm with lists of blocks

$$
\begin{array}{ll}
L(\epsilon) & = \epsilon \\
L(x) & = (\max(x,0),\ x) \text{ if } x \neq 0,\ \epsilon \text{ otherwise} \\
L(p_1\,p_2) & = L(p_1) \cdot L(p_2) \\
L(p_1 \,\|\, p_2) & = L(p_1) \times L(p_2) \\
\text{where:} & \\
l_1 \cdot l_2 & = normalize(l_1 l_2) \\
l_1 \times l_2 & = normalize(merge(l_1, l_2))
\end{array}
$$

Given the linear complexity of the *normalize-* and *merge-*operations, our algorithm finally computes $\mathcal{C}(p)$ in time $O(m\,n)$, where n is the size of p and m its depth (as a binary tree). In practice, moreover, we noticed that the size of normalized lists seldom exceeds ten blocks (see our experimental study in section 5.1). Hence process costs are computed in practically linear time.

3.3   Static Analysis

So far we have explained how to quickly compute the cost of a system—and thus whether it is safe or not—provided that it is modeled by a term of our process algebra. We now need a way to represent systems that execute real programs. This is done by analyzing the programs statically, and by annotating them with the extracted information. In this way, the deadlock-avoidance unit will be able to track the system state at runtime, and to detect unsafe areas before they occur.

Given the previous algorithm for computing process costs, normalized lists appear as a natural data-structure to represent information on resource demands during the analysis. However, branching instructions (if, while...) are not handled directly by the previous algorithm. A general framework for analyzing programs is abstract interpretation [6]. This usually requires a lattice structure.

Fortunately, it turns out that normalized lists can be equipped with a lattice structure, where the ordering $\sqsubseteq$ (reflexive, transitive, antisymmetric) represents loss of information in a natural way. For instance $l_1 \sqsubseteq l_2$ iff $\forall l, \mathcal{C}(l_1 \times l) \leq \mathcal{C}(l_2 \times l)$. $\sqsubseteq$ is also stable by any context: $l_1 \sqsubseteq l_2$ implies $\forall l, (l_1 \times l) \sqsubseteq (l_2 \times l), (l_1\,l) \sqsubseteq (l_2\,l)$ and $(l\,l_1) \sqsubseteq (l\,l_2)$.

Thanks to this structure we are able to apply the theory of abstract interpretation to analyze general programming languages, provided allocations and deallocations are explicit. Otherwise another preliminary static analysis may be required so as to infer upper bounds to the allocations (and lower bounds to the deallocations); this falls outside the scope of this paper.

We describe the lattice operations on normalized lists in Table 4. The least upper bound $\sqcup$ requires an auxiliary function *join*, described in Table 5, whose first argument x is seen intuitively as an offset between the beginning of the two lists. The opposite operator $-$ is meant to reverse the signs of the variations of a list. Arithmetic operations on $\mathbb{Z}$ are extended to $\mathbb{Z} \cup \{\pm\infty\}$ in the usual way with

Table 4. The lattice of normalized lists

Ordering	$: l_1 \sqsubseteq l_2$ iff $\mathcal{C}(l_1 \times -l_2) = 0$
Least upper bound	$: l_1 \sqcup l_2 = normalize(join(0, l_1, l_2))$
Greatest lower bound	$: l_1 \sqcap l_2 = -((-l_1) \sqcup (-l_2))$
Least element	$: \perp = (0, -\infty)$
Greatest element	$: \top = (+\infty, +\infty)$
Opposite	$: -((c_1, \delta_1) \ldots (c_n, \delta_n)) =$
	$normalize((0, -c_1)(\max(-\delta_1, 0), -\delta_1) \ldots (0, -c_n)(\max(-\delta_n, 0), -\delta_n))$

Table 5. Computing the least upper bound

$$join(x, \epsilon, \epsilon) = \epsilon$$
$$join(x, (c_1, \delta_1)q_1, \epsilon) = shift(x, c_1, \delta_1) join(x + \delta_1, q_1, \epsilon)$$
$$join(x, \epsilon, (c_2, \delta_2)q_2) = shift(-x, c_2, \delta_2) join(x - \delta_2, \epsilon, q_2)$$
$$join(x, (c_1, \delta_1)q_1, (c_2, \delta_2)q_2)) = shift(x, c_1, \delta_1) join(x + \delta_1, q_1, l_2) \text{ when } (c_1, \delta_1) \preceq (c_2, \delta_2)$$
$$join(x, (c_1, \delta_1)q_1, (c_2, \delta_2)q_2)) = shift(-x, c_2, \delta_2) join(x - \delta_2, l_1, q_2) \text{ otherwise}$$

$$shift(x, c, \delta) = (\max(c, x) - \max(0, x), \max(\delta, x) - \max(0, x))$$

the convention $(+\infty) + (-\infty) = +\infty$. Proving these algorithms would require more involved tools than we intend discuss here (see [1]).

In the following section, we shall see more closely how to apply these ideas in practice, through the implementation of a framework to analyze and execute Java class files for smart cards.

4   Application to Java on Smart Cards

We now describe an architecture dedicated to smart cards, which can analyze Java class files and control their access to one resource. Due to the limited computing power of smart cards (memory and CPU), not all operations can be done on card. Therefore, we use a split architecture (off card/on card) to delegate complex computations off the card. The off-card part is in charge of resource prediction on Java applications while the on-card part prevents resource deadlock through a resource server. The following sections explain in more detail the role of each part.

4.1   Static Analysis of Java Programs (off Card)

The analysis algorithm, programmed in Java, comprises three parts. First, we summarize the control-flow graph of each application. Then we extract and summarize information about resource requirements using normalized lists. Finally, this information is used to annotate the Java class files.

Control-Flow Graph. The aim of this part is to build the most precise representation of the application's control-flow graph. This stage constructs the method call graph (inter-method analysis) and a control-flow graph for each method (intra-method analysis).

Runtime method dispatch, exception handling and dynamic thread creation make Java control-flow hard to compute statically. Control flow estimation for object-oriented languages is usually called "class analysis" [9]. In our case, virtual methods can be handled in a conservative way by computing for each object variable a super-set of the parent classes. As for the exceptions, one possibility is to over-approximate the set of exception handlers associated with each program point [3]. Both solutions require there be fixed a pool of Java classes to analyze (Java API plus smart card applications). It means that our approach would not work in an environment with dynamic class loading. Concerning Java thread creation and destruction (`thread.start()` and `thread.join()`), at this point our analysis requires that when a thread is *joined*, its creation point can be determined statically.

To speed up the next stages of the analysis, the control-flow graph of each method is stored as a directed graph where only control instructions (branch, fork, join, call) and allocation/deallocation operations are kept.

Abstract Interpretation Using Normalized-List Lattice. This stage analyzes the resource allocations of each method and determines the annotations that will be added to the bytecode. Annotations consist basically in normalized lists that represent the future allocations of the thread. These are computed by a backward abstract interpretation [6] using lattice operations from Table 4. The least upper bound operation $\sqcup$ is used for branches and loops. For loops, the convergence of the computation is ensured by the fact that: for each normalized list $l = (x_1, \delta_1)\ldots(x_n, \delta_n)$, if $\sum_i \delta_i \leq 0$ (no leak of resource) then $l \cdot l \sqsubseteq l$; in other words, only one iteration over the loop is needed. Otherwise, when a resource leak is detected, we put directly $\top$ as a result of the analysis for this portion of code. Due to the fact that each method is analyzed independently, i.e., ignoring call contexts, the deadlock-avoidance algorithm has to track and restore the real call contexts at runtime. Hence, annotations are added when we enter and return from a method (the same applies for threads). Figure 4 gives an illustration—translated into Java for convenience—of the annotations added to the Java bytecode. The "global contract" for instance, corresponds to:

$$(5,2)(2,1) = \underbrace{L(1)}_{\texttt{alloc(1)}} \cdot (\underbrace{(L(4) \cdot L(-3))}_{\texttt{thread.start()}} \times (\underbrace{(L(-2) \sqcup L(2))}_{\texttt{foo(args)}} \cdot \underbrace{L(-1)}_{\texttt{alloc(-1)}}))$$

Optimizations can be carried out to reduce unnecessary calls to the server. For example, when a method does not handle a resource, it not necessary to enclose calls to it in a `Server.call(..)`–`Server.discard()` pair. During the final stage, the parameters for the server calls (normalized lists) are stored in the corresponding Java classes. Once the Java classes have been annotated, they can be used by the on-card resource server.

Before

```
1  class SimpleExample implements Executable {
2
3    int [] getGlobalAnnotation() {
4      return null;
5    }
6
7    void run(String[] args){
8      Server.alloc(1)
9      SimpleThread thread = new SimpleThread();
10
11     thread.start();
12
13     foo(args);
14
15     Server.alloc(-1);
16
17   }
18
19   void foo(Object obj) {
20     if (obj == null) {
21       Server.alloc(-2);
22     } else {
23       Server.alloc(2);
24     }
25
26   }
27
28   static class SimpleThread extends Thread {
29     public void run() {
30       Server.alloc(4);
31       Server.alloc(-3);
32
33   }
34 }
```

After

```
1  class SimpleExample implements Executable {
2
3    int [] getGlobalAnnotation() {
4      return [(5,2),(2,1)]; // global contract
5    }
6
7    void run(String[] args){
8      Server.alloc(1,[(4,1)(2,1)]);
9      SimpleThread thread = new SimpleThread();
10     Server.fork([(2,1)], thread, [(4,1)]);
11     thread.start();
12     Server.call([(2,2)], [0,-1]);
13     foo(args);
14     Server.discard();
15     Server.alloc(-1,[]);
16     Server.end();
17   }
18
19   void foo(Object obj) {
20     if (obj == null) {
21       Server.alloc(-2,[]);
22     } else {
23       Server.alloc(2,[]);
24     }
25     Server.end();
26   }
27
28   static class SimpleThread extends Thread {
29     public void run() {
30       Server.alloc(4, [(0,-3)]);
31       Server.alloc(-3,  []);
32       Server.end();
33   }
34 }
```

Fig. 4. Example of annotations using the resource server API

4.2 Dynamic Resource Avoidance (on Card)

We have designed our resource server completely in Java over a Java Virtual Machine (JVM) dedicated to low-end embedded systems and next generation smart cards [20]. This experimental JVM is more similar to J2ME [17] than to a standard Java Card [4]. It supports, for example, Java threads which are necessary for our resource server.

The resource server is informed of any context change through annotations (resource allocation, deallocation, thread creation, application start ...) which we call *requests*. For each request, our deadlock-avoidance algorithm simulates the transaction, that is: the state of the server is updated and our safety algorithm is applied to compute an estimated cost C, to be compared with the amount of resource still available M. If it leads to a safe state ($C \leq M$), the transaction is made. If not (unsafe state detected), the thread of the requesting application is suspended and the server state restored. The thread will be woken up when the server state has changed. The Java thread API is used (`wait()` and `notifyAll()`) to suspend and wake up threads. The chosen implementation for the server state is a tree similar to the syntax trees of our previous process algebra, and having each thread mapped to one of its leaves.

The scheduling algorithm is distributed between the internal JVM scheduler and the resource server. The former is in charge of equity access to the CPU among threads (using a round-robin algorithm for example), and the latter ensures deadlock avoidance over the JVM scheduler. The advantage of this design is that the JVM and its internal scheduler do not need to be modified. Thanks to the Java Thread API, the resource server is implemented completely in Java. The next section presents experimental results of this architecture.

5   Experimental Results

5.1   Experimental Study of List Normalization

To have an idea of the statistical behavior of normalization, we studied the length after normalization of random lists of length n. One drawing of lots consisted in generating a vector $(a_0, \ldots , a_n)$ whose elements were uniformly selected between $-m$ and $+m$. This vector was then translated into a list of n elementary blocks $(\max(x_1, 0), x_1) \ldots (\max(x_n, 0), x_n)$ where $x_k = a_k - a_{k-1}$ represents the variation of resource between states a_{k-1} and a_k. The next table shows the length after normalization of samples of 1000 random lists for $m = 100$:

initial length	minimum	average	maximum
10	1	2.47	5
100	1	4.21	9
1000	1	4.43	9
10000	1	4.41	9

As n tends to infinity with m fixed, the average size of normalized lists tends to an extremely low limit. This observation was done for other models of randomization as well. In practice the size of normalized lists seldom exceeds ten blocks.

5.2   Experimental Validation

We have tested our resource server on a generic resource (a simple resource counter). The goal was to evaluate the cost and benefit of this architecture before adapting it to a real resource. Results are given for three test programs ($\texttt{Test}_i$). Each test is made of several threads that model a group of concurrent applications. It performs no operations but allocations and deallocations on the resource. Table 6 compares the resource necessary according to three models of resource control and discusses equity (i.e., CPU time-sharing) between applications:

- The first model reserves all resources needed for applications at start-up. The reserved resource represents the *worst case* consumption for the entire test. There is no resource optimization, but each application can run at anytime so the equity between applications is full.

- The second model runs an approximated deadlock-avoidance algorithm based on blocks. Although interleaved schedules are possible, these are not considered while detecting unsafe states. Hence the deadlock prediction is over-conservative and the equity between applications is weak.
- The third model is the one presented in this paper, where deadlock avoidance is based on normalized lists. Threads are suspended only when a deadlock may occur—although one cannot be sure it will, because of the branching instructions. In practice equity is strong because applications are seldom suspended for a long time.

Table 6. Resource needs and equity for each model.

	Resource needs per model		
	No optimization	Blocks	Norm. Lists
Test1 (2 threads)	18	16	16
Test2 (4 threads)	12	6	2
Test3 (2 threads)	7	4	4
Equity (in practice)	full	weak	strong

These tests demonstrate that large gains can be obtained (e.g., Table 6, Test2 and Test3). Sometimes, there is less incentive for using our deadlock-avoidance scheme (e.g., Test1). In these cases, it is important to notice that gains (or not) can be computed in advance, and a card loader may therefore decide whether to apply our techniques prior to launching an application, depending on the estimated gains and the available resources.

As for the cost of code annotation, the Java binary file (.class) of an annotated application is 47% larger than the original code. That represents worst cases possible increase, as the test programs *only* perform allocations and deallocations and no other computation. Moreover the increase is due more to the inserted code (server calls) than to the data (normalized lists); hence, appropriate coding of the server calls would allow large savings.

Concerning the dynamic on-card behavior of the resource server, CPU time-sharing measurements confirm that mixed scheduling between the resource server and the internal Java scheduler is suitable for CPU equity and deadlock avoidance. Moreover, the dynamic deadlock avoidance caused no noticeable slowing down in practice thanks mainly to the small size of normalized lists (see section 5.1).

6   Conclusion

Reserving all the required resources at start-up is a simple and efficient way to guarantee resource availability. The drawback of this solution is the waste of resources as it is scaled up. We have proposed an architecture that can both guarantee the availability of one resource and optimize its usage with a deadlock-avoidance algorithm. Our contribution is first a generalization of Gold's results for a single resource to a more expressive class of systems, modeled by a simple process algebra. Our algorithm, based on a dedicated data-structure called "normalized lists," takes linear time in practice and thus, is perfectly suitable for dynamic scheduling. Thanks to the lattice structure of normalized lists, abstract interpretation techniques can be applied and yield to an efficient deadlock-avoidance algorithm for real programming languages. We successfully applied our architecture to a realistic subset of Java bytecode. We should stress that no modification of the JVM is needed and that our annotated class files remain Java compliant.

The model of resource control discussed is this paper has been designed to optimize resource saving. Even though this resource gain has a price (our algorithms are non-trivial), we believe our model is appropriate for many heavily constrained systems.

In a theoretical way, several improvements can be considered in the future. First, we may want to handle possibly non-terminating idioms (I/O functions, endless loops). Second, it would be interesting to extend this framework to deal with several resources. However, solving this difficult problem (NP-complete in general) would certainly involve drastic over-approximations. Lastly, we have not yet considered checking the consistency of program annotations. This is actually a concern since static analysis is done off card and thus is untrusted. As with Java Card type verification, three approaches may be thought of: certification by a third party, on-card static verification and on-card runtime verification.

In a practical way, several studies are currently investigated. The main one is to apply our model to a real resource, among the choices : memory, files, buffers of communication. The main problem is to find where allocations/deallocations are implied in a program and to determine the amount of resource needed. Memory is the most critical resource for smart card manufacturers. But controlling memory usage becomes especially difficult in garbage-collected languages. We are currently adapting *escape analysis* [5] techniques in order to statically predict the releases of memory of a Java application. The objective is to determine the relevant conditions of using this model of resource.

References

1. M. Baudet. Contrôle de ressource et évitement des interblocages sur la mémoire. Master's thesis, DEA Programmation (Paris), Gemplus Research Labs, September 2002.
2. L. Casset, L. Burdy, and A. Requet. Formal Development of an embedded verifier for Java Card Byte Code. In *the IEEE International Conference on Dependable Systems & Networks (DSN)*, pages 51–58, Washington, D.C., USA, June 2002.
3. B.-M. Chang, J.-W. Jo, K. Yi, and K.-M. Choe. Interprocedural Exception Analysis for Java. In *16th ACM Symposium on Applied Computing (SAC)*, LasVegas, USA, March 2001.

4. Z. Chen. *Java Card^{TM} Technology for Smart Cards : Architecture and Programmer's Guide*. The Java^{TM} Series. Addison Wesley, 2000.
5. J.-D. Choi, M. Gupta, M. Serrano, V. C. Sreedhar, and S. Midkiff. Escape Analysis for Java^{TM}. In *ACM conference on Object-Oriented Programming, Systems, Languages and Applications (OOPSLA'99)*, pages 2–19, Denver USA, 1999.
6. P. Cousot and R. Cousot. Abstract interpretation: a unified lattice model for static analysis of programs by construction or approximation of fixpoints. In *the 4th Annual ACM SIGPLAN-SIGACT*, pages 238–252, Los Angeles, California, 1977.
7. K. Crary and S. Weirich. Resource Bound Certification. In *Proceedings of the 27th ACM SIGPLAN-SIGACT Symposium on Principles of Programming Languages (POPL)*, pages 184–198, Boston, MA, January 2000.
8. G. Czajkowski and T. von Eicken. JRes: A Resource Accounting Interface for Java. In *Annual ACM SIGPLAN Conference on Object-Oriented Programming, Systems, Languages, and Applications (OOPSLA)*, pages 21–35, Canada, 1998.
9. G. DeFouw, D. Grove, and C. Chambers. Fast Interprocedural Class Analysis. In *Proceedings of the 25th ACM SIGPLAN-SIGACT Symposium on Principles of Programming Languages (POPL)*, pages 222–236, San Diego, CA, USA, 1998.
10. D. Deville, A. Galland, G. Grimaud, and S. Jean. Assessing the future of Smart Card Operating Systems. In *4th e-Smart Conference*, Sophia Antipolis, France, September 17–19 2003.
11. D. Deville and G. Grimaud. Building an "impossible" verifier on a Java Card. In *2nd USENIX Workshop on Industrial Experiences with Systems Software (WIESS)*, Boston, USA, December 2002.
12. E. W. Dijkstra. Cooperating sequential processes. In F. Genuys, editor, *Programming Languages: NATO Advanced Study Institute*, pages 43–112. Academic Press, 1968.
13. J. Ezpeleta, F. Tricas, F. Garcia-Valles, and J. Colom. A banker's solution for deadlock avoidance in FMS with flexible routing and multiresource states. *IEEE Transactions on Robotics & Automation*, 18(4):621–625, August 2002.
14. E. M. Gold. Deadlock prediction: Easy and difficult cases. *SIAM Journal on Computing*, 7(3):320–336, August 1978.
15. A. N. Habermann. Prevention of system deadlocks. *Communications of the ACM*, 12(7):373–377, 1969.
16. M. Hofmann and S. Jost. Static prediction of heap space usage for first-order functional programs. In *Proceedings of the 30th ACM SIGPLAN-SIGACT Symposium on Principles of Programming Languages (POPL)*, New Orleans, 2003.
17. Java^{TM} 2 Platform Micro Edition (J2ME^{TM}). Connected Limited Device Configuration (CLDC) Specification Version 1.0. http://java.sun.com/j2me/.
18. D. E. Knuth. *The Art of Computer Programming, volume 3: (2nd ed.) sorting and searching*. Addison Wesley Longman Publishing Co., Inc., 1998.
19. O. Kömmerling and M. G. Kuhn. Design Principles for Tamper-Resistant Smartcard Processors. In *USENIX Workshop on Smartcard Technology (Smartcard'99)*, pages 9–20, Chicago, Illinois, USA, May 10–11 1999.
20. L. Lagosanto. Next-Generation Embedded Java Operating System for Smart Cards. In *Gemplus Developer Conference*, Singapore, November 2002.
21. M. Lawley and S. Reveliotis. Deadlock Avoidance for Sequential Resource Allocation Systems: Hard and Easy Cases. *The Journal of FMS*, 13(4):385–404, 2001.
22. N. le Sommer and F. Guidec. A Contract-Based Approach of Resource-Constrained Software Deployment. In *the 1st IFIP/ACM Working Conference on Component Deployment*, volume 2370 of *LNCS*, pages 15–30, Berlin, Germany, June 2002.

23. X. Leroy. Bytecode Verification for Java smart card. *Software Practice & Experience*, 32:319–340, 2002.
24. Mobile Resource Guarantees (MRG). European Project IST-2001-33149, 2002. `http://www.dcs.ed.ac.uk/home/mrg/`.
25. G. C. Necula. Proof–Carrying Code. In *the 24th ACM SIGPLAN-SIGACT symposium on principles of programming Languages*, Paris, France, January 1997.
26. J.-J. Quisquater. The adolescence of smart cards. *Future Generation Computer Systems*, 13:3–7, 1997.

Resource Usage Verification

Kim Marriott[1], Peter J. Stuckey[2], and Martin Sulzmann[3]

[1] School of Computer Science and Software Engineering
Monash University, Vic. 3800, Australia
marriott@mail.csse.monash.edu.au
[2] Department of Computer Science and Software Engineering
The University of Melbourne, Vic. 3010, Australia
pjs@cs.mu.oz.au
[3] School of Computing, National University of Singapore
S16 Level 5, 3 Science Drive 2, Singapore 117543
sulzmann@comp.nus.edu.sg

Abstract. We investigate how to automatically verify that resources such as files are not used improperly or unsafely by a program. We employ a mixture of compile-time analysis and run-time testing to verify that a program conforms to a resource usage policy specified by a deterministic finite state automata (DFA) which details allowed sequences of operations on resources. Our approach has four main phases. The first is to generate a context-free grammar which safely approximates the resource usage behaviour of the program. This, rather than the original program, is analysed in subsequent phases. The second phase checks whether the grammar satisfies the resource usage policy and, if not, where the problems arise. The third phase determines where to place a minimal set of run-time tests and the fourth determines how to instrument the program to compute the state information required for the tests.

1 Introduction

The difficulty of developing and then maintaining large, complex but still reliable software systems is well known, and in spite of many efforts to improve reliability over the last few decades, the problems have not been solved. This issue has been compounded by the rise of the world-wide web, applets and e-commerce, since people are now using more software from sources they have no good reason to trust. It is thus vital that we develop better techniques for building reliable, trustworthy software systems. One promising approach is to develop better tools for automatically analyzing the integrity (reliability, security, etc) of software systems.

Here we focus on automatically verifying that "resources" such as files or global variables are not used improperly or unsafely by a program. For instance checking that all files are opened before reading or writing and finally closed. More exactly, we wish to verify that a program conforms to a resource usage policy which details allowed sequences of operations on resources such as reading, writing, or closing. This is assumed to be a regular language specified by a

A. Ohori (Ed.): APLAS 2003, LNCS 2895, pp. 212–229, 2003.

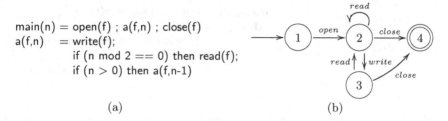

main(n) = open(f) ; a(f,n) ; close(f)
a(f,n)   = write(f);
          if (n mod 2 == 0) then read(f);
          if (n > 0) then a(f,n-1)

(a)   (b)

Fig. 1. (a) A program fragment and (b) a DFA for a simple file resource policy.

deterministic finite state automata (DFA). We verify that a program does not violate such a policy by employing a mixture of compile-time analysis and run-time testing.

Consider the program fragment shown in Figure 1(a). Our running example will be to verify that this program satisfies the resource policy specified by the DFA given in Figure 1(b). Note that in order to simplify the figure the DFA is incomplete: there is an implicit error state e which is reached whenever the DFA sees an invalid token.

Our conceptual starting point is the *instrumented program* which threads a (mutable) variable s through the program to track the current state of the DFA during execution and has run-time checks on s to ensure that the resource policy is not violated:

Example 1. The instrumented version of the program of Figure 1(a) is

main(n) = s := 1; $test_{open}$(s); open(f); $track_{open}$(s);
          a(f,n); $test_{close}$(s); close(f); $track_{close}$(s); $test_{final}$(s)
a(f,n)   = $test_{write}$(s); write(f); $track_{write}$(s);
          if (n mod2 == 0) then ($test_{read}$(s); read(f); $track_{read}$(s))
          if (n > 0) then a(f,n-1);

where $test_{usage}$ checks that the current state allows that usage of the resource or else aborts, e.g. $test_{read}(s)$ checks that s is either 2 or 3 while $test_{final}$ checks that the current state is a final state, and $track_{usage}$, updates the state given that this usage has just been performed, i.e. $track_{read}$ maps states 2 and 3 to 2.

However, naively instrumenting programs in this way may introduce substantial run-time overhead. Ideally we wish to verify conformance at compile-time, but if this is not possible, then we wish to insert a minimal number of run-time tests into the program and to reduce the overhead of state tracking.

Our approach has four main phases, all of which rely on sophisticated compile-time analysis. The first phase is to generate a context-free grammar whose terminals symbols correspond to resource usages and which safely approximates the resource usage behaviour of the program. For brevity we omit this step. The basic idea is to employ a type and effect system [1] to abstract

$M \rightarrow open \ A \ close$
$A \rightarrow write \ B \ C$
$B \rightarrow \epsilon$
$B \rightarrow read$
$C \rightarrow \epsilon$
$C \rightarrow A$

(a)

```
main(n) = open(f); a(f,n); close(f)
a(f,n)   = write(f);
           if (n mod2 == 0) then (read(f); s := 2)
           else s := 3;
           if (n > 0) then (test_{2}(s); a(f,n-1))
```

(b)

Fig. 2. Corresponding grammar and modified code for the program of Figure 1(a)

the resource usage behaviour of a simply-typed ML-like language. Details can be found in an accompanying technical report [2]. For the purposes of this paper, we restrict ourselves to a first-order language.

Example 2. The grammar corresponding to the program in Figure 1(a) is shown in Figure 2(a). Note how each if-then construct is converted to non-deterministic grammar rules, one for each case.

This grammar, rather than the original program, is analysed in subsequent phases. Importantly, the analyses employed in the subsequent three phases are exact, i.e. they give the perfect result. Thus it is only in this first phase that true approximation takes place.

Every sequence of resource operations that can occur when executing the original program is required to be a sentence in the language, $L(G)$, of the approximating grammar G. Thus the program satisfies the resource policy specified by the DFA, M, if $L(G) \subseteq L(M)$ where $L(M)$ is the language of M. The second phase of our approach (detailed in Section 2) is to check whether this is true or not, and if not, to determine at which points in the grammar strings not in $L(M)$ may be generated. For our running example our analysis shows that the program does not necessarily respect the resource usage policy, since the error state can be reached. If instead the line if (n mod 2 == 0) then read(f); was simply read(f) then our analysis would show that the program will never violate the protocol.

The next two phases are used if the grammar cannot be proven to satisfy the resource policy. In the third phase (described in Section 3) we determine where to place the run-time tests. The final phase (described in Section 4) determines how to add state computation to the code. The resulting program is guaranteed to respect the resource usage policy or abort before it actually violates the policy. It also performs substantially fewer tests and less state computation than the first naive instrumented version of the program. For instance, the code for the program of Figure 1(a) generated by our approach is shown in Figure 2(b). Note that $test_{\{2\}}(s)$ checks that state s is in the set $\{2\}$, i.e. it is 2, aborting execution if it is not.

Our main technical contributions are:

- A generic four phase methodology based on approximating the resource usage behaviour of a program by a grammar G for verifying that a program meets a resource usage policy.

- A polynomial time analysis and algorithm to annotate G, and hence P, with a minimal set of run-time tests to ensure that it satisfies the resource usage policy specified by M.
- A polynomial time analysis and algorithm to annotate G, and hence P, with minimal instrumentation needed to track state needed for run-time tests to ensure that it satisfies the resource usage policy specified by M.

2   Checking a Resource Usage Policy

We assume some fixed set of resource usage primitives such as open, read, write and close which are applied to a particular resource r. A resource is specified by its type and abstract location. For simplicity we ignore the aliasing problem between resources. That is, resources are assumed to be explicitely annotated with must-alias information. The resource usage behaviour of a program P is captured by its *resource usage traces*. These are sequences of the calls to the resource usage primitives that can be made in some execution of the program. We distinguish between *complete* traces which follow the behaviour until the program terminates and *partial* traces. For instance, for our example program from Figure 1 (a),

$$open(f), write(f), read(f), write(f), close(f)$$

is a complete trace while $open(f), write(f), read(f)$ is a partial trace.

The first step in our approach is to approximate the resource usage behaviour of a program P by a *context-free grammar* G. This consists of a set Σ of terminal symbols where each symbol corresponds to the application of a particular resource usage primitive to a particular resource (this is called a primitive resource effect), a set N_G of non-terminal symbols, a start symbol $S_G \in N_G$ and a set of production rules R_G. We require:

(a) for each complete resource usage trace w for P, $w \in L(G)$, and
(b) for each partial resource usage trace w for P, $ww' \in L(G)$, for some w'.

For instance, the grammar in Figure 2 (a) approximates Figure 1 (a). The details of the approximation process can be found in [2]. For our simply-typed ML-like language the approximation grammar is linear in the size of the input program.

We assume that a *resource usage policy* is a regular language specified by an DFA, M. For example, the policy "we must open the resource before reading and writing an arbitrary number of times, with no two consecutive writes, before closing" is specified by the DFA in Figure 1. A resource usage policy can refer to more than one resource, thus one might have a policy stating that a program has no more than two files open. Of course more than one resource usage policy may apply to a program: For simplicity we check and instrument for each policy independently.

One complication is that a particular resource usage policy M does not necessarily refer to all of the primitive resources in G. Therefore, we need to project away all of the uses of "irrelevant" resources. For each terminal symbol X in G which corresponds to the use of an irrelevant resource, we introduce a new production rule $X \to \epsilon$ where X is now considered a non-terminal symbol. We usually leave the above transformation implicit.

We assume that M, the DFA detailing the resource usage policy, is a quadruple (Σ, Q, T, q_0) where Σ is the alphabet of symbols, i.e. the set of primitive resource usage effects, for the resources in the policy, Q is a set of states containing a single distinguished error state e, $T : \Sigma \times Q \to Q$ is a deterministic complete transition function with $T(x, e) = e$ for all $x \in \Sigma$ and $q_0 \in Q$ is the start state. We define $T^\star$ the extended transition function to be

$$T^\star(\epsilon, q) = q$$
$$T^\star(x\alpha, q) = T^\star(\alpha, T(x, q))$$

For simplicity we assume that all states are final states except for e. This is allowable since acceptance by final state in machine M' can be simulated by building a new machine M for M' such that $\alpha \in L(M')$ iff $\alpha\$ \in L(M)$. M is constructed by adding an extra symbol $\$$ into Σ and a new state f, and setting $T(\$, q) = f$ when q is a final state, and otherwise e the error state. We add an action $\$$ to the end of the main routine of the code we are checking. (Note *close* plays a similar role to that of $\$$ in the running example).

The form of the DFA we use (acceptance by non-error) is important because it allows us to restrict attention to resource traces that are prefixes of correct resource behaviour. Any prefix of a correct resource behaviour avoids the error state.

It is straightforward to use our approximating grammar G to check whether the original program satisfies a resource policy specified by the DFA M. Since, any possible resource behaviour of the program will be described by G, we know that the program satisfies the resource policy specified by M if $L(G) \subseteq L(M)$.

The problem of determining whether a regular language $L(M)$ contains a context-free language $L(G)$ is well-known to be decidable (e.g. [3]). We simply construct a push down automata for the language $L(G) \cap \overline{L(M)}$ (the intersection of a context-free grammar and a finite automata) and check whether it is empty.

However this indirect approach is not well-suited to our purposes since it does not indicate which parts of the grammar violate the policy (which is important for providing feedback to the programmer and for introducing run-time tests). For these reasons we now give a more constructive process for determining whether a regular language contains a context-free language.

Our decision procedure is based on a simple abstract interpretation of the grammar G which details which states in the DFA M can be reached when generating sentences in the language of G.

The main step of the analysis is to compute for each symbol X in G and state q in M the set of states that can be reached from q when accepting all sentences that can be generated from X. I.e. we compute $\{T^\star(w, q) \mid X \Rightarrow^\star_G w$ and $w \in \Sigma^\star\}$. This is the least fixpoint of the equations

$$reach(X, q) = \{T(X, q)\} \text{ if } X \in \Sigma$$
$$reach(X, q) = \bigcup\{reach_{seq}(\gamma, q) | (X \to \gamma) \in G\} \text{ if } X \in N_G$$

$$reach_{seq}(\epsilon, q) = \{q\}$$

$$reach_{seq}(X\gamma, q) = \bigcup\{reach_{seq}(\gamma, q')|q' \in reach(X, q)\}.$$

It is straightforward to show by induction that

Theorem 1. $reach(X, q) = \{T^\star(w, q) \mid X \Rightarrow_G^\star w \ and \ w \in \Sigma^\star\}$

Thus we have a decision procedure for the problem of interest

Corollary 1. $L(G) \subseteq L(M)$ iff $e \notin reach(S_G, q_0)$.

Example 3. The interesting calculations of reachability for the grammar of Example 2 are: $reach(M, 1) = \{4, e\}$, $reach(B, 3) = \{2, 3\}$, $reach(A, 2) = \{2, 3, e\}$, $reach(A, 3) = \{e\}$, $reach(C, 2) = \{2, 3, e\}$, and $reach(C, 3) = \{3, e\}$. We use e to indicate the implicit error state of Figure 1(b). Note that by definition $reach(X, e) = e$ for all $X \in N_G$.

Importantly, $reach(S_G, q_0)$ can be computed in polynomial time. This is because we can compute $reach(S_G, q_0)$ by computing the Kleene-sequence for $reach$. This can be done in polynomial time since the Kleene sequence is at most $|Q| \cdot |N_G| \cdot |Q|$ long and each element in the sequence can be computed in $|Q| \cdot |N_G| \cdot |R_G|$, where $|\cdot|$ denotes set cardinality and $|R_G|$ is the total number of symbols in the productions.

We can also use this information to annotate the grammar and so indicate where the policy is violated. The idea is that we annotate the grammar G with states which the DFA M could be in if M was recognising the string in parallel with G.

The first step is to compute the *call patterns*, $cp(V)$, for each $V \in N_G$, i.e. the set $\{T^\star(w, q_0)|S_G \Rightarrow_G^\star wV\gamma \ and \ w \in \Sigma^\star\}$. This is the least fixpoint of

$$cp(S_G) \supseteq \{q_0\}$$

$$cp(V) \supseteq Reach_{seq}(\gamma_1, cp(X)) \text{ for each } X \to \gamma_1 V \gamma_2 \in R_G$$

where $Reach_{seq}(\gamma, Q) = \bigcup\{reach_{seq}(\gamma, q)|q \in Q\}$.

Theorem 2. *For all $V \in N_G$, $cp(V) = \{T^\star(w, q_0)|S_G \Rightarrow_G^\star wV\gamma \ and \ w \in \Sigma^\star\}$*

We can now annotate each production $X \to X_1 \cdots X_n$ in the grammar with *program points* $X \to {}^{pp_1}X_1{}^{pp_2} \ldots {}^{pp_n}X_n{}^{pp_{n+1}}$. The program point pp_k is the set of possible states M is in before the sentence generated from X_k is accepted by M. The annotation is simply given by

$$pp_1 = cp(X)$$

$$pp_{k+1} = Reach_{seq}(X_k, pp_k), \text{ for } k = 1, ..n$$

Example 4. The calling patterns calculated for the grammar of Example 2 are $cp(M) = \{1\}$, $cp(B) = \{3, e\}$, $cp(A) = \{2, 3, e\}$ and $cp(C) = \{2, 3, e\}$. The annotations are as follows:

$$M \rightarrow {}^{\{1\}}open^{\{2\}}A^{\{2,3,e\}}close^{\{4,e\}}$$
$$A \rightarrow {}^{\{2,3,e\}}write^{\{3,e\}}B^{\{2,3,e\}}C^{\{2,3,e\}}$$
$$B \rightarrow {}^{\{3,e\}}$$
$$B \rightarrow {}^{\{3,e\}}read^{\{2,e\}}$$
$$C \rightarrow {}^{\{2,3,e\}}$$
$$C \rightarrow {}^{\{2,3,e\}}A^{\{2,3,e\}}$$

Consider a production $R \equiv X \rightarrow X_1 \cdots X_n$ and let $S_G \Rightarrow_G^{\star} \gamma_1 X \gamma_2 \Rightarrow_R \gamma_1 X_1' \cdots X_n' \gamma_2$. We say that X_k' is an *instance* of X_k since it was generated by the rule R and corresponds to X_k.

Theorem 3. *For each annotated production* $X \rightarrow {}^{pp_1}X_1{}^{pp_2} \ldots {}^{pp_n}X_n{}^{pp_{n+1}}$ *and* $k \in \{1, \ldots, n\}$,

$$pp_k = \{T^{\star}(w, q_0) | w \in \Sigma^{\star} \text{ s.t. } S_G \Rightarrow_G^{\star} wV\gamma \text{ and } V \text{ is an instance of } X_k\}$$

Computing the call patterns and annotations can again be done in polynomial time. The important point is that for an annotated production $X \rightarrow {}^{pp_1}X_1{}^{pp_2} \ldots {}^{pp_n}X_n{}^{pp_{n+1}}$ we know that a terminal symbol X_k can cause an error if for some $q \in pp_k \setminus \{e\}$, $T(X_k, q) = e$. This indicates that the grammar (and hence maybe the program) can be in non-error state q just before resource usage X_k is performed, and that performing X_k in this state will violate the policy. This can be used to provide feedback to the programmer about where the original program may violate the protocol.

Example 5. The only terminal symbol which can cause an error in Example 4 is the *write* symbol in the rule for A, since $T(write, 3) = e$.

As we shall now see this information can also be used to add run-time tests to the program.

3   Adding Run-Time Tests

Of course we cannot always prove that a program satisfies a resource usage policy: this may be because of inaccuracy introduced by approximating the program by a grammar, or because the program when executed with some input does not satisfy the policy. In such cases we can add run-time checks to ensure that the program aborts before the policy is violated.

As we saw in Example 1 the simplest approach is to instrument the program so as to explicitly keep track of which state in M it is in and whenever a resource usage primitive is applied to the resource first checking that this usage is valid for that state, aborting if not, and then appropriately updating the state. This is not a new idea, see for instance [4]. However, naively instrumenting programs in this way may introduce substantial run-time overhead. In this and the following section we show how simple analyses of the grammar approximating the program allow us to instrument the program with substantially less run-time overhead. In particular we use analyses to determine which tests are really needed and where they can be best placed. We also use analyses to reduce the amount of instrumentation required.

In order to bridge the gap between an instrumented program and the grammar G approximating the program we introduce the *instrumented grammar*, G_{inst}, which is an attribute grammar with essentially the same structure as G but which has attributes to model the instrumentation of the instrumented program.

The instrumented grammar G_{inst} corresponding to G has a non-terminal symbol X' for each $X \in N_G \cup \Sigma$. Each such non-terminal symbol has two attributes, *in* and *out*, ranging over Q where *in* is inherited and *out* is synthesized. For simplicity and without loss of generality we assume that G only has a single instance of its start symbol S_G. The start symbol for G_{inst} is S'_G and we set $S'_G.in$ to q_0. For each production $V \rightarrow X_1 \cdots X_n \in R_G$, there is a corresponding production $V' \rightarrow X'_1 \cdots X'_n$ in the instrumented grammar with attribute rules[1]

$$\$1.in := \$\$.in \qquad \$(k+1).in := \$k.out \text{ for } k = 1, \dots, n-1 \qquad \$\$.out := \$n.out$$

For each production $V \rightarrow \epsilon$ there is a corresponding production $V' \rightarrow \epsilon$ with attribute rule $\$\$.out := \$\$.in$. And for each terminal $X \in \Sigma$ there is a production $X' \rightarrow X$ with attribute rules $\$\$.out := T(X, \$\$.in)$. It is straightforward to prove the following results.

Lemma 1. $S_G \Rightarrow^*_G X_1 \dots X_m$ iff $S'_G \Rightarrow^*_{G_{inst}} X'_1 \dots X'_m$

Lemma 2. $L(G) = L(G_{inst})$

Lemma 3. If $S'_G \Rightarrow^*_{G_{inst}} wX'\gamma$ for $w \in \Sigma^*$ then $X'.in = T^*(w, q_0)$.

Example 6. The instrumented grammar corresponding to the grammar G of Example 2 is

$M' \rightarrow open'\ A'\ close'$	$\{\$1.in := \$\$.in; \$2.in := \$1.out; \$3.in := \$2.out; \$\$.out := \$3.out\}$	
$A' \rightarrow write'\ B'\ C'$	$\{\$1.in := \$\$.in; \$2.in := \$1.out; \$3.in := \$2.out; \$\$.out := \$3.out\}$	
$B' \rightarrow \epsilon$	$\{\$\$.out := \$\$.in\}$	
$B' \rightarrow read'$	$\{\$1.in := \$\$.in; \$\$.out := \$1.out\}$	
$C' \rightarrow \epsilon$	$\{\$\$.out := \$\$.in\}$	
$C' \rightarrow A'$	$\{\$1.in := \$\$.in; \$\$.out := \$1.out\}$	
$open' \rightarrow open$	$\{\$\$.out := T(open, \$\$.in)\}$	
$close' \rightarrow close$	$\{\$\$.out := T(close, \$\$.in)\}$	
$read' \rightarrow read$	$\{\$\$.out := T(read, \$\$.in)\}$	
$write' \rightarrow write$	$\{\$\$.out := T(write, \$\$.in)\}$	

We will analyse and annotate instrumented grammars in the obvious way: by simply ignoring the attributes and treating them as a context free grammar.

---

[1] We use YACC-like notation: $\$\$.a$ refers to attribute a of the LHS symbol and $\$k.a$ refers to attribute a of the kth RHS symbol.

Thus we can actually analyse G and use this to annotate G_{inst}. Interestingly, we can understand the analyses as simple abstract interpretations [5] of the instrumented grammar. For instance, the information at program point pp_k is the set of values that $X'_k.in$ can take.

Of course the whole point of this exercise is to allow us to add run-time tests to the right-hand side of the instrumented grammar. We introduce as needed non-terminal symbols $test_S$ for $S \subseteq Q$ with a single inherited attribute in and the defining production $test_S \to \epsilon$ with the attribute test $\$\$.in \in S$. Note that we assume that if an attribute test fails for some sentence then that sentence is not in the language of the attribute grammar.

We extend our analyses to handle these symbols in the obvious way by defining $reach(test_S, q) = \{q\} \cap S$.

At first glance it might seem that the only place to consider adding tests is immediately before those terminal symbols which can cause an error. However, it is often possible to place tests earlier than this. Our basic idea for adding run-time tests is to take an annotated instrumented grammar and use an analysis to determine at which program points it is possible to identify states which must inevitably lead to failure. This identifies all of the places one could usefully consider adding tests.

The first thing we need to do is to determine for each $V \in N_G$, the *definite failure states* $fs(V)$. This is the set of states q such that $T^*(w, q) = e$ for all $w \in \Sigma^*$ s.t. $S_G \Rightarrow^*_G \gamma V w$. This is essentially the dual problem to working out the calling patterns for each symbol. It is the greatest fixpoint of

$$fs(S_G) = \{e\}$$
$$fs(X) \subseteq \bigcap_{V \to \gamma_1 X \gamma_2 \in R_G} \{q \in Q | reach_{seq}(\gamma_2, q) \subseteq fs(V)\}$$

Note that for all V, $e \in fs(V)$.

Theorem 4. $fs(V) = \{q \in Q | T^*(w, q) = \{e\} \ \forall \ w \in \Sigma^* \ s.t. \ S_G \Rightarrow^*_G \gamma V w\}$.

We can use this analysis to add information to an annotated grammar. At each program point we record the subset of states at that point that definitely lead to failure. Consider the annotated production $X \to {}^{pp_1} X_1 {}^{pp_2} \ldots {}^{pp_n} X_n {}^{pp_{n+1}}$. We add for each program point pp_k, the set fpp_k which is the subset of pp_k which will definitely lead to an error. This additional annotation is simply given by $fpp_k = \{q \in pp_k | reach_{seq}(X_k \ldots X_n, q) \subseteq fs(X)\}$, for $k = 1, \ldots, n+1$.

Example 7. For grammar G of Example 2 we have $fs(M) = \{e\}$, $fs(B) = \{1, e\}$, $fs(A) = \{1, e\}$, and $fs(C) = \{1, e\}$. The annotations where pp_k is split into $pp_k \setminus fpp_k$ and fpp_k are as follows:

$$M \to {}^{\{1\},\{\}} open {}^{\{2\},\{\}} A {}^{\{2,3\},\{e\}} close {}^{\{4\},\{e\}}$$
$$A \to {}^{\{2\},\{3,e\}} write {}^{\{3\},\{e\}} B {}^{\{2,3\},\{e\}} C {}^{\{2,3\},\{e\}}$$
$$B \to {}^{\{3\},\{e\}}$$
$$B \to {}^{\{3\},\{e\}} read {}^{\{2\},\{e\}}$$
$$C \to {}^{\{2,3\},\{e\}}$$
$$C \to {}^{\{2\},\{3,e\}} A {}^{\{2,3\},\{e\}}$$

For instance the annotation $^{\{2\},\{3,e\}}$ before A in the last rule indicates that being in state 3 at this point definitely leads to error while being in state 2 may not.

Computing the definite failure states and this additional annotation can again be done in polynomial time.

Theorem 5. *For each annotated production* $X \to {}^{fpp_1}X_1{}^{fpp_2}\ldots{}^{fpp_n}X_n{}^{fpp_{n+1}}$ *we have*

$$fpp_1 = \{q \in Q | T^\star(w,q) = e \ \forall w \in \Sigma^\star \ s.t. \ S_G \Rightarrow^\star_G \gamma X w\}$$

and for $k \in \{1,\ldots,n\}$,

$$\begin{aligned} fpp_{k+1} = \{q \in Q | \ T^\star(w,q) = e \ \forall w \in \Sigma^\star \ s.t. \ S_G \Rightarrow^\star_G \gamma V w \\ and \ V \ is \ an \ instance \ of \ X_k\} \end{aligned}$$

The motivation for adding this extra information is that it tells us where it is useful to add tests to the instrumented grammar and so to the original program. It is sensible to consider adding a test at any program point for which $fpp_k \setminus \{e\} \neq \emptyset$ since a test at this point can distinguish between the states in fpp_k which can never lead to success and those in $pp_k \setminus fpp_k$ which may not lead to failure.

Thus the basic step in adding run-time tests to the instrumented grammar G_{inst} is the following. Let $X' \to X'_1 \ldots X'_n$ be a production in G_{inst}, such that $fpp_k \setminus \{e\} \neq \emptyset$ for some $k \in \{1,\ldots,n+1\}$. Let $S = pp_k \setminus fpp_k$. The *refinement* of G_{inst} for this production and program point is the grammar G'_{inst} obtained by replacing this production by the production $X' \to X'_1 \ldots X'_{k-1} \ tests \ X'_k \ldots X'_n$ with essentially the same attribute rules (more precisely, each $\$j$ must be replaced by $\$(j+1)$ for $j \geq k$) and an attribute rule to copy the state after X'_{k-1} to the inherited attribute for $test_S$, $\$k.in := \$(k-1).out$. If $k = 1$ then this action is $\$1.in := \$\$.in$.

Example 8. Consider the instrumented production rule $C \to A$ before and after the addition of the $test_{\{2\}}$ non-terminal before A to obtain the rule $C \to test_{\{2\}} \ A$. The instrumented production rules are

$$C \to A \qquad \{\$1.in := \$\$.in; \$\$.out := \$1.out\}$$

$$\begin{aligned} test_{\{2\}} \to \epsilon \qquad &\{\$\$.in \in \{2\}\} \\ C \to test_{\{2\}} \ A \qquad &\{\$1.in := \$\$.in; \$2.in := \$\$.in; \$\$.out := \$2.out\} \end{aligned}$$

Lemma 4. *Let* G'_{inst} *be a refinement of* G_{inst}. *Then*
(a) $L(G_{inst}) \cap L(M) = L(G'_{inst}) \cap L(M)$, *and*
(b) $L(G'_{inst}) \subset L(G_{inst})$.

The algorithm for adding run-time tests to an instrumented grammar G_{inst} to ensure conformance with the protocol given by an DFA M is therefore

1. Annotate G_{inst} with program point and definite failure state information.
2. Stop if for all program points $fpp_k = \emptyset$ and return G_{inst}.
3. Choose some production R in G_{inst} and program point k in R, such that $fpp_k \setminus \{e\} \neq \emptyset$.
4. Refine G_{inst} using R and program point k.
5. Goto Step 1.

It follows from Lemma 4 that

Theorem 6. *Let G_{inst} be the instrumented grammar input to the above algorithm and G'_{inst} the output grammar. Then $L(G'_{inst}) = L(G_{inst}) \cap L(M)$.*

Furthermore, the above algorithm always terminates and has time complexity which is polynomial in the size of G_{inst} and M. This is because we can add at most one test for each program point in the original G_{inst}. Thus the main iteration loop can only occur G_{inst} times and the final and all intermediate programs are $O(G_{inst})$. The result follows since annotation and refinement of each intermediate program takes polynomial time in the size of the intermediate program and M.

Of course the algorithm for adding run-time tests is non-deterministic in the choice of which program points and production are used for each refinement step. One possible strategy is to perform tests as early as possible so as to detect failure as early as possible. Thus in this case we always choose the first program point and production found in a depth first traversal of the productions in G_{inst} from the start symbol.

Example 9. For our running example, we can add a test at the program point in C before A since the state 3 definitely leads to a resource usage error. The revised grammar, with the run-time test $test_S$ indicating that the program should abort if the DFA is not in a state in set S, and with updated program point information is as follows:

$$M \to {}^{\{1\},\{\}}open^{\{2\},\{\}}A^{\{2,3\}\{\}}close^{\{4\},\{\}}$$
$$A \to {}^{\{2\},\{\}}write^{\{3\},\{\}}B^{\{2,3\},\{\}}C^{\{2,3\},\{\}}$$
$$B \to {}^{\{3\},\{\}}$$
$$B \to {}^{\{3\},\{\}}read^{\{2\},\{\}}$$
$$C \to {}^{\{2,3\},\{\}}$$
$$C \to {}^{\{2,3\},\{\}}test_{\{2\}}{}^{\{2\},\{\}}A^{\{2,3\},\{\}}$$

Note how the error state no longer occurs at any program point indicating that with this revised grammar $L(G) \subseteq L(M)$.

Another strategy would be to annotate each program point with a cost of putting a test there which is proportional to the number of times we expect the corresponding point in the underlying program to be reached. In this case we might choose the program point with least cost for refinement.

Regardless, the important point is that our analysis tells us precisely at which program points in the instrumented grammar and hence the original program it is useful to consider adding a run-time test.

4   Tracking State

Once we have determined where to add run-time tests to our instrumented grammar and hence to the original program we need to determine where we need to track state. At an extreme position, if we have not needed to add any run-time tests then clearly there is little point in instrumenting the grammar or program. And, in general we do not need to instrument the program beyond the point tests will be performed. However there is actually considerably more scope for reducing instrumentation. The idea is that we first identify at each program point which states behave equivalently in the sense that they will succeed or fail in exactly the same way.

We let $equiv(Q)$ denote the set of all equivalence relations of the set of states Q. $equiv(Q)$ forms a complete lattice ordered by logical implication, i.e. for $\equiv_1, \equiv_2 \in equiv(Q)$, $\equiv_1 \leq \equiv_2$ iff $\equiv_2 \rightarrow \equiv_1$, where the least element is the equivalence relation in which all elements are equivalent. For convenience we treat an equivalence relation as both a binary infix predicate and as the set of pairs (q, q') for which equivalence holds.

Our first analysis is $eq(X, \equiv)$. This computes the new equivalence $\equiv'$ such that $q \equiv' q'$ iff $T^\star(w, q) \equiv T^\star(w, q')$ for all $w \in \Sigma^\star$ such that $X \Rightarrow_G^\star w$.

This is the least fixpoint of the equations

$$eq(test_S, \equiv) = \{(q, q') \in \equiv \mid \{q, q'\} \subseteq S \vee \{q, q'\} \subseteq Q \setminus S\}$$
$$eq(X, \equiv) = \{(q, q') \mid q, q' \in Q, T(X, q) \equiv T(X, q')\} \text{ if } X \in \Sigma$$
$$eq(X, \equiv) = \bigcap\{eq_{seq}(\gamma, \equiv) \mid X \rightarrow \gamma \in R_{G_{inst}}\} \text{ if } X \in N_G$$
$$eq_{seq}(\epsilon, \equiv) = \equiv$$
$$eq_{seq}(X\gamma, \equiv) = eq(X, eq_{seq}(\gamma, \equiv)).$$

The effect of the first equation for eq is to split the partitions in $\equiv$ so that equivalent states behave equivalently in the test. The remaining equations state that for a terminal symbol X two states are equivalent if T maps them to equivalent states, while for a non-terminal symbol X, two states are equivalent if they are equivalent for all rules defining X.

Theorem 7. $eq(X, \equiv) = \{(q, q') \mid T^\star(w, q) \equiv T^\star(w, q') \; \forall w \in \Sigma^\star s.t. \; X \Rightarrow_G^\star w\}$

We can use this as the basis for further annotating an annotated instrumented grammar G (which may contain tests). We first compute the *post state equivalence*, $pse(V)$, for each non-terminal symbol V, that is the states that for all possible future sequence of resource usages w act equivalently.

This is the least fixpoint of

$$pse(S_G) = \{(q, q') \mid q, q' \in Q \setminus \{e\}\} \cup \{(e, e)\}$$
$$pse(X) = \bigcap\{eq_{seq}(\gamma_2, pse(V)) \mid (V \rightarrow \gamma_1 X \gamma_2) \in R_{G_{inst}}\}$$

Theorem 8. *For all non-terminal symbols V,*

$$pse(V) = \{(q, q') \mid (T^\star(w, q) = e) \leftrightarrow (T^\star(w, q') = e) \forall w \in \Sigma^\star \; s.t. \; S_G \Rightarrow_G^\star \gamma V w\}$$

We can use this analysis to add information to an annotated grammar. At each program point we can also record the equivalence relation of states at that point.

Consider the annotated production $X \rightarrow {}^{pp_1}X_1{}^{pp_2}\ldots{}^{pp_n}X_n{}^{pp_{n+1}}$. We add for each program point pp_k, the equivalence relationship epp_k between the states in pp_k. This additional annotation is simply given by

$$epp_k = \{(q,q')|q,q' \in pp_k, q \equiv q'\}$$

where $\equiv$ is $eq_{seq}(X_k \ldots X_n, pse(X))$ for $k = 1, \ldots, n+1$.

This also allows us to compute the *call pattern equivalence*, $cpe(V)$, for each non-terminal symbol V, which is $\bigcap\{epp_1|V \rightarrow {}^{epp_1}\alpha{}^{epp_{n+1}} \in R_{G_{inst}}\}$. Computing the equivalence relation and annotation again takes polynomial time because the height of $equiv(Q)$ is $|Q|$.

Example 10. The equivalence annotations, post state equivalences and call pattern equivalences for the instrumented grammar of Example 9 are as follows:

$$\begin{aligned}
{}^{\{1\}}M^{\{4\}} &\rightarrow {}^{\{1\}}open^{\{2\}}A^{\{2,3\}}close^{\{4\}}\\
{}^{\{2\}}A^{\{2,3\}} &\rightarrow {}^{\{2\}}write^{\{3\}}B^{\{2\},\{3\}}C^{\{2,3\}}\\
{}^{\{3\}}B^{\{2\},\{3\}} &\rightarrow {}^{\{3\}}\\
{}^{\{3\}}B^{\{2\},\{3\}} &\rightarrow {}^{\{3\}}read^{\{2\}}\\
{}^{\{2\},\{3\}}C^{\{2,3\}} &\rightarrow {}^{\{2,3\}}\\
{}^{\{2\},\{3\}}C^{\{2,3\}} &\rightarrow {}^{\{2\},\{3\}}test_{\{2\}}{}^{\{2\}}A^{\{2,3\}}
\end{aligned}$$

If all states are equivalent at a particular point then we do not need to track state at that point. Hence, in our example we only need to track the state in B before it is tested in C. Thus, the final instrumented program is that shown in Figure 2 (b).

The first step in determining the necessary instrumentation is to choose a name r for each equivalence class at each program point pp_k. We define function $can_k(q)$ to return the name of the equivalence class of $q \in pp_k$ and $rep_k(r)$ to return some representative state $q \in pp_k$ in the equivalence class called r. Similarly, we choose names for the equivalence classes in $cpe(V)$ and $pse(V)$ for each non-terminal V and define $can_{cpe(V)}, can_{pse(V)}, rep_{cpe(V)},$ and $rep_{pse(V)}$ in the analogous way. The choice of names is important to reduce the amount of computation required in the instrumentation. We will return to this issue.

We now try and minimize the amount of state computation performed. One important case is when an equivalence relation at a program point or for a symbol's call patterns is *uniform* in the sense that all states belong to the same equivalence class. Clearly, at such points we do not need to track state.

Another case when we can reduce instrumentation is when a non-terminal symbol X is deterministic in the sense that for all relevant q, $|reach(X,q)| = 1$. In this case we do not need to track state when executing the code corresponding to X since we know that the state reached after X will be q' where $\{q'\} = reach(X,q)$.

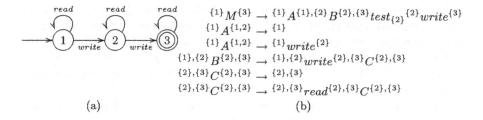

$$^{\{1\}}M^{\{3\}} \rightarrow {}^{\{1\}}A^{\{1\},\{2\}}B^{\{2\},\{3\}}test_{\{2\}}{}^{\{2\}}write^{\{3\}}$$
$$^{\{1\}}A^{\{1,2\}} \rightarrow {}^{\{1\}}$$
$$^{\{1\}}A^{\{1,2\}} \rightarrow {}^{\{1\}}write^{\{2\}}$$
$$^{\{1\},\{2\}}B^{\{2\},\{3\}} \rightarrow {}^{\{1\},\{2\}}write^{\{2\},\{3\}}C^{\{2\},\{3\}}$$
$$^{\{2\},\{3\}}C^{\{2\},\{3\}} \rightarrow {}^{\{2\},\{3\}}$$
$$^{\{2\},\{3\}}C^{\{2\},\{3\}} \rightarrow {}^{\{2\},\{3\}}read^{\{2\},\{3\}}C^{\{2\},\{3\}}$$

(a)   (b)

Fig. 3. A DFA and grammar illustrating determinism

Example 11. To illustrate why determinism is useful consider a policy defined by the DFA in Figure 3(a) and the annotated and partitioned grammar shown in Figure 3(b) Even though the state is important throughout B and C, B is deterministic since $reach(B,1) = \{2\}$ and $reach(B,2) = \{3\}$. Hence we do not need to track state inside B or C: we can simply determine the state after B from the state before.

We can weaken this notion of determinism to take into account state equivalence. We say symbol V is *deterministic (modulo equivalence)* if it is either a terminal symbol, corresponds to a terminal symbol, is a test or if for all $q \in cp(V)$, $q_1, q_2 \in reach(V,q)$ implies $q_1 \equiv_{ps} q_2$ where $\equiv_{ps}$ is $pse(V)$.

We can now determine for each symbol V whether it needs an input state or needs to compute an output state. More exactly, V *requires an input state* if $cpe(V)$ is not uniform and either V is not deterministic or the definition of V contains a test (in particular if V is a test itself). V *requires an output state* if $pse(V)$ is not uniform and V is not deterministic.

Example 12. Given the annotated program in Example 10 we find C requires an input state and B requires an output state.

Given an instrumented grammar with tests G_{inst} we create a new minimally instrumented grammar G_{min} as follows. For each non-terminal symbol not corresponding to a terminal symbol V', we have a non-terminal symbol V'' which has an inherited attribute $in : Q$ if V' requires an input state and a synthesized attribute $out : Q$ if V' requires an output state. S_G'' is the start state of G_{min}. Now consider a (non-test) annotated production in G_{inst} , $X' \rightarrow {}^{pp_1}X_1'{}^{pp_2}\ldots{}^{pp_n}X_n'{}^{pp_{n+1}}$. We first identify at which program points state is required:

- pp_{n+1} *needs state* if X' requires an output state,
- pp_k *needs state* if X_k' requires an input state or pp_{k+1} needs state and epp_k is not uniform, for $k = n, .., 1$.

We construct the corresponding production in G_{min} as follows. We replace all symbols V' in the production by V''.

Now we insert non-terminal symbols to perform the appropriate state equivalence class tracking and creation. We make use of the non-terminal symbols

$create\_state_r$ with a single synthesized attribute out defined by $create\_state_r \rightarrow$ ϵ with attribute rule $\$\$.out = r$ where r is the name of an equivalence class of states, and the non-terminal symbols $track\_state_F$ with inherited attribute in and synthesized attribute out defined by $track\_state_F \rightarrow \epsilon$ with attribute rule $\$\$.out = F(\$\$.in)$ where F is a function from equivalence classes of states to equivalence classes of states.

We do this as follows. If pp_k needs state, but epp_k is uniform, then insert a $create\_state_r$ at the program point where $r = can_k(q)$ for some $q \in pp_k$. If X_k'' requires an input state, then add a $track\_state_F$ immediately before X_k'' where $F = can_{cpe(X_k'')} \circ rep_k$ to convert from the names for the equivalence states at that program point to those used for the calling patterns for X_k''. If pp_k needs state and X_{k-1}'' requires an output state, then add a $track\_state_F$ immediately after X_{k-1}'' where $F = can_k \circ rep_{pse(X_{k-1}'')}$ to convert from the names for the equivalence states returned from X_{k-1}'' to those used at that program point. Add similar conversion symbols at the start of the production if X' requires an input state, and at the end if X' requires an output state. If pp_k needs state and X_{k-1}'' does not require an output state, then add a $track\_state_F$ immediately after X_{k-1}'' where F is $\lambda r.can_k(q)$ where $q \in reach(X_{k-1}'', can_{k-1}(r))$ to track the state change in the deterministic (modulo equivalence) symbol X_{k-1}''. We then perform further optimisation by removing calls to $track\_state_F$ when F is the identity and composing adjacent calls to $track\_state_F$ if the intermediate state is not used. Finally we add appropriate attribute rules to link the out attribute of the preceding symbol with the in attribute of the following.

When choosing the names for equivalence states we try to ensure that the state transformer function associated with a deterministic function is the identity function and that those on call entry and exit are identity. A similar idea was previously suggested in [6].

Theorem 9. *Let G_{inst} be the instrumented grammar input to the above algorithm and G_{min} the output grammar. Then $L(G_{inst}) = L(G_{min})$.*

5   Related Work

Approaches to verification of resource usage can be categorised as either static, dynamic or mixed. Static approaches attempt to determine at compile time that a program satisfies the resource usage protocol, dynamic approaches instrument the program so as to abort at runtime before a violation occurs, while mixed approaches like ours use static analysis to minimize the runtime instrumentation.

Most attention has been paid to static approaches. Vault [7] and Cyclone [8] are both safe variants of C which employ type-checking methods to statically enforce correct resource management behaviour of programs. However, in both languages, the programmer is required to provide a significant number of declarations since the system does not perform inference.

Resource usage verification in the context of an object-oriented language has been studied by Tan, Ou and Walker [9]. They extend Java with "scoped methods". Conditions on the usage of such methods can be imposed via explicit program annotations which can be specified by regular expressions.

Igarashi and Kobayashi [10] also propose a powerful static approach for reasoning about resource usages. However, they do not fix how to specify the valid traces of resource usages. Hence, decidability and complexity of resource verification depends on the underlying policy specification language. Another difference is that resource usages are recorded in the environment whereas we use a type and effect system. This makes it difficult in their approach to determine precisely when a certain resource is used. They solve the problem by introducing boxing and unboxing operators which can however easily lead to imprecise analysis results.

Other recent static approaches are described in Foster, Terauchi and Aiken [11], Hallem, Chelf, Xie and Dengler [12], Das, Lerner and Seigle [13], and Chen and Wagner [14]. The approach by Foster et. al. enforces correct resource usage behaviour via flow sensitive qualifiers which are attached to resources. Qualifiers are taken from a lattice which seem to be less powerful than the DFAs we consider (we believe they cannot specify the policy in Figure 1). The system by Hallem et. al. provides a specification language based on state machines to enforce correct resource usage behaviour. Their main motivation is to find as many serious bugs as possible. The system has been implemented and seems to scale well to large programs. However, soundness has been traded in for efficiency, i. e. some incorrect resource usages might remain undetected. The work by Das et. al. appears to be very similiar to [12]. One of the main differences seems that [13] provides sound analyses. The work of Chen and Wagner uses a DFA M to describe security properties and tests whether CFG G approximating the program is such that $L(G) \subseteq L(M)$ similar to the work herein. Since all of the above works are static approaches, they do not consider how to insert run-time tests into a program when the program cannot be proven to satisfy a particular resource usage policy.

Schneider [4] considers security properties specifiable by DFA's, and uses a dynamic approach that threads the security computation through the code. In [15], Erlingsson and Schneider consider how to specialize a security automaton to a program. Similiar ideas are discussed by Walker [16] and Thiemann [17] in a type-theoretic setting. However, since none of these approaches uses sophisticated static analysis the resulting instrumented program may perform unnecessary tests and state tracking when compared with our mixed approach.

The approach most similar to ours is that of Colcombet and Fradet [6] who also use a mixed approach. They propose instrumenting a program with a sufficient (minimal) number of run-time checks to enforce a certain resource usage policy and use an analysis to determine state equivalences to reduce tracking. Our approach is inherently more accurate and so leads to less instrumentation and run-time checks. This is for two main reasons. First, their approach maps

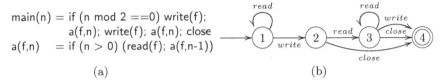

```
main(n) = if (n mod 2 ==0) write(f);
          a(f,n); write(f); a(f,n); close
a(f,n)  = if (n > 0) (read(f); a(f,n-1))
```

(a)   (b)

Fig. 4. (a) A program fragment and (b) a DFA for a file resource policy.

the program to a finite automata rather than a context-free grammar.[2] This
makes the analyses much simpler, in particular determining equivalence classes
of states, and extraction of the finite automata from the original program but
means they lose accuracy and may introduce unnecessary tests and instrumentation. The second reason is that they do not consider moving tests earlier in the
computation and perform the placement of tests and state tracking in the same
phase. This may lead to more complicated state tracking since they sometimes
track error states and the need to track state for a longer period. On the other
hand they focus much more on how to maximize the number of state transformations which are the identity (an NP-complete problem) in the instrumented
program.

To illustrate the relative benefits of our approach consider the program and
the policy specified in Figure 4. The approach of Colcombet and Fradet gives

```
main(n) = s := 1; if (n mod 2 == 0) (write(f); s := 2);
          a(f,n); if (s == 1) then s := 2 else if (s == 3) then s := 4;
          write(f); a(f,n); if (s != 2 && s != 3) then abort;
          close
a(f,n)  = if (n > 0) (read(f); if (s == 2) then s := 3; a(f,n-1))
```

while our approach places the test earlier and realises there is no need to track
state at all

```
main(n) = if (n mod 2 ==0) (abort; write(f)); a(f,n); write(f); a(f,n); close
a(f,n)  = if (n > 0) (read(f); a(f,n-1))
```

6   Conclusion

We have described a powerful and theoretically well-founded process for performing compile-time and run-time verification that a program satisfies a particular
resource usage policy specified by a DFA. At the heart of our approach is the
approximation of a program's resource usage behaviour by a grammar. Various
sophisticated analyses working on this grammar allow us to determine whether
the original program satisfies the policy, or if it does not, where run-time tests

---

[2] Colcombet and Fradet do sketch how to extend their approach to treat the program
as a context-free grammar, but this is not formalised and essentially collapses back
to the treatment as a finite automata in order to perform state minimization.

and state tracking code need to be inserted into the original program. We believe our work provides a strong theoretical basis for automatic verification of resource usage policies.

References

1. Talpin, J., Jouvelot, P.: The type and effect discipline. In: Proc. of LICS'92, IEEE (1992) 162–173
2. Marriott, K., Stuckey, P., Sulzmann, M.: Resource usage verification. Technical report, University of Melbourne (2003) www.cs.mu.oz.au/~pjs/ruv.ps.gz.
3. Sudkamp, T.: Languages and Machines. Addison-Wesley (1988)
4. Schneider, F.B.: Enforceable security policies. Information and System Security **3** (2000) 30–50
5. Cousot, P., Cousot, R.: Abstract interpretation: A unified lattice model for static analysis of programs by construction or approximation of fixpoints. In: Proc. of POPL'77, ACM (1977) 238–252
6. Colcombet, T., Fradet, P.: Enforcing trace properties by program transformation. In: Proc. of POPL'00, ACM (2000) 54–66
7. DeLine, R., Fähndrich, M.: Enforcing high-level protocols in low-level software. In: Proc. of PLDI'01, ACM (2001) 59–69
8. Grossman, D., Morrisett, G., T. Jim, M.H., Wang, Y., Cheney, J.: Region-based memory management in cyclone. In: Proc. of PLDI'01, ACM (2001) 282–293
9. G. Tan, X.O., Walker, D.: Resource usage analysis via scoped methods. In: Foundations of Object-Oriented Languages (FOOL'10). (2003)
10. Igarashi, A., Kobayashi, N.: Resource usage analysis. In: Proc. of POPL'02, ACM (2002) 331–342
11. J. S. Foster, T.T., Aiken, A.: Flow-sensitive type qualifiers. In: Proc. of PLDI'02, ACM (2002) 1–12
12. Hallem, S., Chelf, B., Xie, Y., Engler, D.: A system and language for building system-specific, static analyses. In: Proc. of PLDI'02, ACM (2002) 69–82
13. Das, M., Lerner, S., Seigle, M.: ESP: path-sensitive program verification in polynomial time. In: Proc. of PLDI'02, ACM (2002) 57–68
14. Chen, H., Wagner, D.: Mops: an infrastructure for examining security properties of software. In: Proc. of CCS'02. (2002) 235–244
15. Erlingsson, U., Schneider, F.B.: SASI enforcement of security policies: A retrospective. In: Proc. of the 1999 New Security Paradigm Workshop. (1999)
16. Walker, D.: A type system for expressive security policies. In: Proc. of POPL'00, ACM (2000) 254–267
17. Thiemann, P.: Enforcing safety properties using type specialization. In: Proc. of ESOP'01. Volume 2028 of LNCS., Springer (2001)

Automatic Construction of Hoare Proofs from Abstract Interpretation Results

Sunae Seo[1], Hongseok Yang[2], and Kwangkeun Yi[3]

[1] Department of Computer Science,
Korea Advanced Institute of Science and Technology
`saseo@ropas.kaist.ac.kr`
[2] MICROS Research Center,
Korea Advanced Institute of Science and Technology
`hyang@kaist.ac.kr`
[3] School of Computer Science and Engineering,
Seoul National University
`kwang@ropas.snu.ac.kr`

Abstract. By combining program logic and static analysis, we present an automatic approach to construct program proofs to be used in Proof-Carrying Code. We use Hoare logic in representing the proofs of program properties, and the abstract interpretation in computing the program properties. This combination automatizes proof construction; an abstract interpretation automatically estimates program properties (approximate invariants) of our interest, and our proof-construction method constructs a Hoare-proof for those approximate invariants. The proof-checking side (code consumer's side) is insensitive to a specific static analysis; the assertions in the Hoare proofs are always first-order logic formulas for integers, into which we first compile the abstract interpreters' results. Both the property-compilation and the proof construction refer to the standard safety conditions that are prescribed in the abstract interpretation framework. We demonstrate this approach for a simple imperative language with an example property being the integer ranges of program variables. We prove the correctness of our approach, and analyze the size complexity of the generated proofs.

1 Introduction

Necula and Lee's seminal work [11,12] on Proof-Carrying Code(PCC) and its subsequent developments [14,13,1,7] have been a convincing technology for certifying the safety of mobile code, yet how to achieve the code's safety proofs is still open for alternatives. The existing proof construction process either assumes that the programmer provides the program invariants [11,12,13], thus being not fully automatic, or is limited to a class of properties that are automatically inferable by the current type system technologies [7,2,10].

In this paper we present a method for automatically constructing the program proofs, to be used in the PCC framework. We use a combination of static analysis and program logic. We use the abstract interpretation [4,3] for the static analysis

A. Ohori (Ed.): APLAS 2003, LNCS 2895, pp. 230–245, 2003.

and Hoare logic [9] for the program logic. An abstract interpreter first estimates program invariants. For the computed invariants, we construct Hoare proofs using the standard Hoare logic rules. For example, suppose that the program property that we have to establish is the range of integer values of program variables. We employ an abstract interpreter that estimates the range by an integer interval. The estimated integer-interval for every variable at each program point is an invariant for which we will construct Hoare proofs. Since the invariants from abstract interpretations are approximate in general, they sometimes do not exactly fit with the Hoare logic rules. This gap is filled by the safety proofs of the used abstract interpreter. These safety proofs are for the standard safety conditions prescribed in the abstract interpretation framework.

In order to make the proof-checking side (code consumer's side) insensitive to a specific static analysis, we fix the assertion language in Hoare logic to first-order logic for integers,[1] into which we have to translate abstract interpretation results. This translation procedure is nicely defined by referencing the concretization formulas of the used abstract interpreter.

Note that our method still requires the code producer to design an abstract interpreter that estimates the desired properties (program invariants) in a right cost-accuracy balance. Although designing such an abstract interpreter is generally demanding, our method is still appealing because the once-designed abstract interpreter can be used repeatedly for all programs of the same language, as long as their properties to verify and check remain the same.

The code consumer's side remains simple. Checking the Hoare proofs is simply by pattern-matching the proof tree nodes against the corresponding Hoare logic rules. Checking if the proofs are about the accompanied code is straightforward, because the program texts are embedded in the Hoare proofs.

Because the trusted computing base(TCB) is the standard Hoare logic rules with first-order logic for integers, the TCB size amounts to the number of proof rules in Hoare logic and first-order logic for integers. The number of Hoare logic rule is linear to the number of syntactic constructs of the source programming language. The size of first-order logic rules for integers can vary depending on where we strike the balance between the number of rules and proof size. We can reduce this part of the TCB by using the foundational PCC [1,2,7] approach.

Our work is based on Cousot and Cousot's insight for the connection between program logic and static analysis [5,6]. They showed that the set of assertions can be considered as an abstract domain; thus, an abstract interpretation can be used to find assertions that denote approximate invariants, and these assertions can be used to verify a program. Recently, Heintze et al. [8] further developed Cousot and Cousot's insight so that both program logic and static analysis can get benefits from each other. Our work strenghens this connection bewteen program logic and static analysis. We use a static analysis not just to find approximate invariant assertions but also to obtain machine-checkable proofs, which show that those assertions indeed approximate program invariants.

---

[1] Our method is not necessarily limited to first-order logic. It only requires that the assertion language have first-order quantifiers.

In this paper we demonstrate our method for a simple imperative language with integer variables. In Section 2, we explain the generic abstract interpreter, which can be instantiated to an analysis for a specific program property. In Section 3, we present an algorithm that gets a program annotated with the abstract interpretation results, and gives a Hoare proof for the program. In Section 4, we conclude.

2   Generic Abstract Interpretation

We consider abstract interpretations that are instances of Cousot's generic abstract interpretation [3]. The generic abstract interpretation (Figure 2) is about a simple imperative programming language (Figure 1).

$Commands$ $C ::= x := E \mid C; C \mid \text{if } B \text{ then } C \text{ else } C \text{ fi} \mid \text{while } B \text{ do } C \text{ od}$
$Expressions$ $E ::= n \mid x \mid E + E$
$Boolean\ Expressions\ B ::= \text{tt} \mid \text{ff} \mid E = E \mid E < E \mid B \wedge B \mid B \vee B$

Fig. 1. Syntax of a Simple Imperative Language

The abstract interpretation is generic because it is parameterized by an abstract domain $\mathcal{A}$ with a lattice structure $(\sqsubseteq, \bot, \sqcup, \sqcap, \top)$, an abstraction function $\alpha: \mathcal{P}(\text{Ints}) \to \mathcal{A}$, a concretization function $\gamma: \mathcal{A} \to \mathcal{P}(\text{Ints})$, and the following abstract operators:

$$\hat{+} : \mathcal{A} \times \mathcal{A} \to \mathcal{A}$$
$$\hat{+}^{\triangleleft} : (\mathcal{A} \times \mathcal{A} \times \mathcal{A}) \to \mathcal{A} \times \mathcal{A}$$
$$\hat{=}^{\triangleleft} : \mathcal{A} \times \mathcal{A} \to \mathcal{A} \times \mathcal{A}$$
$$\hat{<}^{\triangleleft} : \mathcal{A} \times \mathcal{A} \to \mathcal{A} \times \mathcal{A}$$

The operator $\hat{+}$ abstracts the addition of integers. The other operators make an abstract interpretation more precise by employing the notion of "backward abstract interpretation" [6,3]. When $\hat{+}^{\triangleleft}(a, b, c)$ gives the pair (a', b'), the set $\gamma(a')$ of integers contains integers in $\gamma(a)$ excluding some integers n such that "$n + b \neq c$." Similarly, the other operators $\hat{=}^{\triangleleft}$ and $\hat{<}^{\triangleleft}$ exclude integers based on $=$ or $<$: when $\hat{=}^{\triangleleft}(a, b)$ is (a', b'), the set $\gamma(a')$ contains integers in $\gamma(a)$ excluding some integers n that are not equal to any n' in $\gamma(b)$; and when $\hat{<}^{\triangleleft}(a, b) = (a', b')$, the set $\gamma(a')$ excludes some integers n such that "$n \not< b$." For these operators $\hat{+}^{\triangleleft}, \hat{=}^{\triangleleft}, \hat{<}^{\triangleleft}$, we use subscripts $-_0$ and $-_1$ to denote the first and second of the result, respectively.

Given a program, the abstract interpreter associates an *abstract* state with each program point. An abstract state $\hat{s}$ is a map from a finite set Vars of variables to $\mathcal{A}$, and means a set of concrete states, denoted $\gamma(\hat{s})$:

$$s \in \gamma(\hat{s}) \iff \forall x \in \mathsf{Vars}: \; s(x) \in \gamma(\hat{s}(x))$$

When the abstract interpreter associates $\hat{s}$ with a program point, $\gamma(\hat{s})$ contains all the states that are possible at the point during execution.

The interpretation of commands and expressions is standard except the cases of a conditional statement and a loop. In those cases, we use backward semantics $[\![-]\!]_b$ for accurate analysis of branches. Let $\hat{s}$ be an abstract state, and let a be an abstract value. The backward semantics $[\![B]\!]_b\hat{s}$ for boolean expression B makes $\hat{s}$ smaller by excluding some concrete states in $\gamma(\hat{s})$ that violate the condition B. The abstract state $[\![E]\!]_b\hat{s}\,a$ excludes some concrete states s in $\gamma(\hat{s})$ where the concrete value of E is not approximated by a.

In the interpreter definition, we use macro $\neg B$ which expands to a boolean expression without negation. We move $\neg$ inside $\vee$ or $\wedge$ by de-Morgan's laws[2], and then transform the negation of atomic boolean expressions by the usual equivalence: $\neg(E{=}E') \iff E{<}E' \vee E{>}E'$ and $\neg(E{<}E') \iff E{=}E' \vee E{>}E'$.

The generic abstract interpretation in Figure 2 can be instantiated to various program analyses. For instance, when we want to design an analysis (called interval analysis) that estimates program variables' values by integer intervals, we can use, for $\mathcal{A}$, an interval domain

$$\{\bot\} \cup \{[n,m] \mid (n,m \in \mathsf{Ints} \cup \{-\infty,\infty\}) \wedge n \le m\},$$

and the abstract operators defined as in Figure 3.

The instantiated abstract interpretation is sound when the abstract domain and operators are chosen appropriately. The abstract domain $\mathcal{A}$ should be a complete lattice, Galois-connected by abstraction $\alpha\colon \mathcal{P}(\mathsf{Ints}) \to \mathcal{A}$ and concretization $\gamma\colon \mathcal{A} \to \mathcal{P}(\mathsf{Ints})$. The abstract operators should satisfy the requirements in Figure 4. The Galois connection means that the order in abstract domain $\mathcal{A}$ corresponds to the approximation order among the concrete correspondents. The abstract operators' safety arguments dictate that their abstract results must subsume their concrete correspondents.

3   Construction of Hoare Proofs

The main result of this paper is an algorithm that constructs proofs in Hoare logic from abstract interpretation results. In this section, we will explain this construction algorithm.

3.1   Translation Function

Our algorithm is parameterized by a *translation* function, which compiles abstract interpretation results into formulas in first-order logic. Let tr be a translation function that takes a pair of an abstract value a and an expression E, and

---

[2] $\neg(B \wedge B') \Leftrightarrow \neg B \vee \neg B'$ and $\neg(B \vee B') \Leftrightarrow \neg B \wedge \neg B'$

$$\hat{s} \in \mathsf{AbsStates} \stackrel{\Delta}{=} \mathsf{Vars} \to \mathcal{A}$$

Commands

$$[C] \ : \ \mathsf{AbsStates} \to \mathsf{AbsStates}$$
$$[x{:=}E]\hat{s} = \hat{s}[x \mapsto ([E]\,\hat{s})]$$
$$[\texttt{if } B \texttt{ then } C_0 \texttt{ else } C_1 \texttt{ fi}]\hat{s} = [C_0]([B]_b\hat{s}) \sqcup [C_1]([\neg B]_b\hat{s})$$
$$[\texttt{while } B \texttt{ do } C \texttt{ od}]\hat{s} = [\neg B]_b\big(\mathit{lfp}\ \lambda\hat{s}'.\ \hat{s} \sqcup [C]([B]_b\hat{s}')\big)$$
$$[C_0;C_1]\hat{s} = [C_1]([C_0]\hat{s})$$

Integer Expressions

$$[E] \ : \ \mathsf{AbsStates} \to \mathcal{A}$$
$$[n]\hat{s} = \alpha(\{n\})$$
$$[x]\hat{s} = \hat{s}(x)$$
$$[E_0{+}E_1]\hat{s} = [E_0]\hat{s} \mathbin{\hat{+}} [E_1]\hat{s}$$

Backward Abstract Semantics of Boolean Expressions

$$[B]_b \ : \ \mathsf{AbsStates} \to \mathsf{AbsStates}$$
$$[\texttt{tt}]_b\hat{s} = \hat{s}$$
$$[\texttt{ff}]_b\hat{s} = \lambda x \in \mathsf{Vars}.\ \bot$$
$$[E_0{=}E_1]_b\hat{s} = \big([E_0]_b\hat{s}\,(\hat{=}_0^{\triangleleft}([E_0]\hat{s},[E_1]\hat{s}))\big) \ \sqcap\ \big([E_1]_b\hat{s}\,(\hat{=}_1^{\triangleleft}([E_0]\hat{s},[E_1]\hat{s}))\big)$$
$$[E_0{<}E_1]_b\hat{s} = \big([E_0]_b\hat{s}\,(\hat{<}_0^{\triangleleft}([E_0]\hat{s},[E_1]\hat{s}))\big) \ \sqcap\ \big([E_1]_b\hat{s}\,(\hat{<}_1^{\triangleleft}([E_0]\hat{s},[E_1]\hat{s}))\big)$$
$$[B_0{\wedge}B_1]_b\hat{s} = [B_0]_b\hat{s} \ \sqcap\ [B_1]_b\hat{s}$$
$$[B_0{\vee}B_1]_b\hat{s} = [B_0]_b\hat{s} \ \sqcup\ [B_1]_b\hat{s}$$

Backward Abstract Semantics of Integer Expressions

$$[E]_b \ : \ \mathsf{AbsStates} \to \mathcal{A} \to \mathsf{AbsStates}$$
$$[n]_b\hat{s}\,a = \begin{cases} \hat{s} & \text{if } \alpha(\{n\}) \sqsubseteq a \\ \lambda x \in \mathsf{Vars}.\ \bot & \text{otherwise} \end{cases}$$
$$[x]_b\hat{s}\,a = \hat{s}[x \mapsto (\hat{s}(x) \sqcap a)]$$
$$[E_0{+}E_1]_b\hat{s}\,a = \big([E_0]_b\hat{s}\,(\hat{+}_0^{\triangleleft}([E_0]\hat{s},[E_1]\hat{s},a))\big) \ \sqcap\ \big([E_1]_b\hat{s}\,(\hat{+}_1^{\triangleleft}([E_0]\hat{s},[E_1]\hat{s},a))\big)$$

Fig. 2. Generic Abstract Interpretation

gives a first-order logic formula φ about E. Formula $\mathsf{tr}(a,E)$ intuitively means "$E \in \gamma(a)$": $\mathsf{tr}(a,E)$ holds in a concrete state s precisely when the value of E at s belongs to $\gamma(a)$. The formal definition of a translation requires that the function tr satisfy the following conditions:

- Monotonicity: for all a, a', and E, if $a \sqsubseteq a'$, then $\mathsf{tr}(a,E)$ implies $\mathsf{tr}(a',E)$;
- Meet Preservation: for all a, a', and E, the formula $\mathsf{tr}(a \sqcap a',E)$ is equivalent to $\mathsf{tr}(a,E) \wedge \mathsf{tr}(a',E)$;
- Strictness: for all E, the formula $\mathsf{tr}(\bot,E)$ is $\texttt{ff}$;
- Constants Preservation: for all integers n, the formula $\mathsf{tr}(\alpha(\{n\}),n)$ holds;
- Closedness: $\mathsf{Free}(\mathsf{tr}(a,E)) = \mathsf{Free}(E)$ for all a and E; and
- Commutativity: $\mathsf{tr}(a,E)[E'/x] = \mathsf{tr}(a,E[E'/x])$ for all a, E, E', and x.

$$[n_0, m_0] \hat{+} [n_1, m_1] \triangleq [n_0 + n_1, m_0 + m_1]$$
$$\hat{+}_i^{\triangleleft}([n_0, m_0], [n_1, m_1], [n_2, m_2]) \triangleq [n_i, m_i] \sqcap [n_2 - m_{1-i}, m_2 - n_{1-i}]$$
$$\hat{=}_i^{\triangleleft}([n_0, m_0], [n_1, m_1]) \triangleq [n_0, m_0] \sqcap [n_1, m_1]$$
$$\hat{<}^{\triangleleft}([n_0, m_0], [n_1, m_1]) \triangleq \begin{cases} (\bot, \bot) & \text{if } m_1 \leq n_0 \\ ([n_0, \min X_0], [\max X_1, m_1]) & \text{otherwise} \end{cases}$$
$$(\text{where } X_0 = \{m_0, m_1 - 1\}, \ X_1 = \{n_0 + 1, n_1\})$$

Fig. 3. Abstract Operators for an Interval Analysis

$$a_0 \hat{+} a_1 \sqsupseteq \alpha(\{n_0 + n_1 \mid n_i \in \gamma(a_i)\})$$
$$\hat{+}_i^{\triangleleft}(a_0, a_1, a_2) \sqsupseteq \alpha(\{n_i \in \gamma(a_i) \mid \exists n_{i-1} \in \gamma(a_{i-1}), \ n_2 \in \gamma(a_2) : \ n_0 + n_1 = n_2\})$$
$$\hat{=}_i^{\triangleleft}(a_0, a_1) \sqsupseteq \alpha(\{n_i \in \gamma(a_i) \mid \exists n_{1-i} \in \gamma(a_{1-i}) : \ n_i = n_{i-1}\})$$
$$\hat{<}_i^{\triangleleft}(a_0, a_1) \sqsupseteq \alpha(\{n_i \in \gamma(a_i) \mid \exists n_{1-i} \in \gamma(a_{1-i}) : \ n_0 < n_1\})$$

Fig. 4. Safety of Abstract Operators

The first four conditions are from the corresponding properties of the concretiza-tion γ: the concretization γ is monotone, preserves $\sqcap$ and $\bot$, and maps $\alpha(\{n\})$ to a set containing n. The other two conditions say that $\mathsf{tr}(a, E)$ expresses $\gamma(a)$ by a formula with holes, and then fills the hole with E.

For the interval analysis, we can use the translation tr defined as follows:

$$\mathsf{tr}([n, m], E) \triangleq (n \leq E) \wedge (E \leq m) \qquad \mathsf{tr}(\bot, E) \triangleq \mathtt{ff}$$

Note that tr for the interval analysis is monotone and preserves $\sqcap$ and $\bot$, and that $\mathsf{tr}([n, m], -)$ is a formula $(n < -) \wedge (- < m)$ with two holes, which are filled by the second argument; thus, tr satisfies the other two conditions for a translation.

Map trst is a natural extension of tr for abstract states:

$$\mathsf{trst}(\hat{s}) \triangleq \bigwedge_{x \in \mathsf{Vars}} \mathsf{tr}(\hat{s}(x), x)$$

Formula $\mathsf{trst}(\hat{s})$ means the concretization of $\hat{s}$: $\mathsf{trst}(\hat{s})$ holds for a concrete state s precisely when s is in $\gamma(\hat{s})$. For instance, the abstract state $[x \mapsto [2, 3], y \mapsto [1, 5]]$ from the interval analysis gets translated into a formula as follows:

$$\begin{aligned} \mathsf{trst}([x \mapsto [2, 3], y \mapsto [1, 5]]) &= \mathsf{tr}([2, 3], x) \wedge \mathsf{tr}([1, 5], y) \\ &= 2 \leq x \wedge x \leq 3 \wedge 1 \leq y \wedge y \leq 5 \end{aligned}$$

3.2   Algorithm

Our algorithm is parameterized by abstract domain and operators, and their soundness proofs. Suppose that we have obtained a program analysis by instantiating the generic abstract interpretation with an abstract domain $\mathcal{A}$ with a lattice structure $(\sqsubseteq, \bot, \sqcup, \sqcap, \top)$, and abstract operators $\hat{+}, \hat{+}^{\triangleleft}, \hat{=}^{\triangleleft}, \hat{<}^{\triangleleft}$. We can specialize our algorithm for this analysis by providing a translation function tr for the domain $\mathcal{A}$, and procedures that prove in first-order logic the soundness of tr and the abstract operators. These procedures must satisfy the specifications in Figure 5. Note that the procedures monTr, meetTr, conTr imply that tr is monotone, preserves $\sqcap$ and maps each $\alpha(\{n\})$ to a set containing n; and that the remaining procedures fAdd, bAdd_i, bEql_i, bInEql_i manifest that the abstract operators $\hat{+}, \hat{+}^{\triangleleft}, \hat{=}^{\triangleleft}, \hat{<}^{\triangleleft}$ satisfy the requirements in Figure 4.

The input of our algorithm is a command in the simple imperative language (Figure 1) annotated with the results of an abstract interpretation. Let $\mathcal{I}$ be an instance of the generic abstract interpretation, and C a command. The analysis $\mathcal{I}$ annotates each point of C with an abstract state $\hat{s}$, so that the output is a term A in the following grammar:

$$A ::= [\hat{s}] R [\hat{s}]$$
$$R ::= x{:=}E \mid A;A \mid \texttt{if } B \texttt{ then } A \texttt{ else } A \texttt{ fi} \mid [\texttt{inv } \hat{s}] \texttt{while } B \texttt{ do } A \texttt{ od}$$

Note that the annotation specifies the pre- and post-conditions for each subcommand of C, and also provides loop invariants $[\texttt{inv } \hat{s}]$. For each annotated command of the form A or R, we denote the corresponding command without annotation using $\overline{A}$ or $\overline{R}$.

Given an annotated program A, our algorithm gives a proof in Hoare logic. This Hoare proof shows that each annotation $\hat{s}$ in A holds: the formula $\mathsf{trst}(\hat{s})$ holds at the annotated place in the command $\overline{A}$. For example, from an annotated assignment $[\hat{s}]x := y[\hat{s}']$, the algorithm gives the following proof tree:

$$\cfrac{\cfrac{\mathsf{tr}(\hat{s}(y), y) \Rightarrow \mathsf{tr}(\hat{s}'(x), y)}{\mathsf{trst}(\hat{s}) \Rightarrow \mathsf{trst}(\hat{s}')[y/x]} \qquad \{\mathsf{trst}(\hat{s}')[y/x]\}\, x := y\, \{\mathsf{trst}(\hat{s}')\}}{\{\mathsf{trst}(\hat{s})\}\, x := y\, \{\mathsf{trst}(\hat{s}')\}}$$

Note that this tree is derivable because $\hat{s}(y) = \hat{s}'(x) = \hat{s}'(y)$: the generic abstract interpretation requires that $\hat{s}'$ be the abstract state $\hat{s}[x \mapsto \hat{s}(y)]$.

Our algorithm, denoted $\mathcal{T}$, calls three subroutines $\mathcal{E}$, $\mathcal{E}_b$, and $\mathcal{B}_b$. Subroutine $\mathcal{E}$ constructs proofs that show that the forward abstract interpretation of expressions is correct. Given an abstract state $\hat{s}$ and an expression E, subroutine $\mathcal{E}$ produces a proof of the form:

$$\cfrac{\vdots}{\mathsf{trst}(\hat{s}) \Rightarrow \mathsf{tr}(\llbracket E \rrbracket \hat{s}, E)}$$

The proved implication says that the abstract value $\llbracket E \rrbracket \hat{s}$ "contains" all the possible values of E at some state s in $\gamma(\hat{s})$.

For all expressions E, E_0, E_1, abstract values a, a_0, a_1, b, and integers n

- $\mathsf{monTr}(a, b, E)$ for $a \sqsubseteq b$ is a proof tree for

$$\mathsf{tr}(a, E) \Rightarrow \mathsf{tr}(b, E);$$

- $\mathsf{meetTr}(a, b, E)$ is a proof tree for

$$\bigl(\mathsf{tr}(a, E) \wedge \mathsf{tr}(b, E)\bigr) \Rightarrow \mathsf{tr}(a \sqcap b, E);$$

- $\mathsf{conTr}(n)$ is a proof tree for

$$\mathsf{tr}(\alpha(\{n\}), n)$$

- $\mathsf{fAdd}(a_0, a_1, E_0, E_1)$ is a proof tree for

$$\bigl(\mathsf{tr}(a_0, E_0) \wedge \mathsf{tr}(a_1, E_1)\bigr) \Rightarrow \mathsf{tr}(a_0 \hat{+} a_1, E_0 + E_1);$$

- $\mathsf{bEql}_i(a_0, a_1, E)$ is a proof tree for

$$\Bigl(\exists x.\, \mathsf{tr}(a_i, E) \wedge \mathsf{tr}(a_{1-i}, x) \wedge E = x\Bigr) \Rightarrow \mathsf{tr}(\hat{=}_i^{\sphericalangle}(a_0, a_1), E);$$

- $\mathsf{bInEql}_0(a_0, a_1, E)$ is a proof tree for

$$\Bigl(\exists x.\, \mathsf{tr}(a_0, E) \wedge \mathsf{tr}(a_1, x) \wedge E_0 < x\Bigr) \Rightarrow \mathsf{tr}(\hat{<}_0^{\sphericalangle}(a_0, a_1), E);$$

- $\mathsf{bInEql}_1(a_0, a_1, E)$ is a proof tree for

$$\Bigl(\exists x.\, \mathsf{tr}(a_0, x) \wedge \mathsf{tr}(a_1, E) \wedge x < E_1\Bigr) \Rightarrow \mathsf{tr}(\hat{<}_1^{\sphericalangle}(a_0, a_1), E);$$

- $\mathsf{bAdd}_i(a_0, a_1, b, E)$ is a proof tree for

$$\Bigl(\exists x.\, \mathsf{tr}(a_i, E) \wedge \mathsf{tr}(a_{1-i}, x) \wedge \mathsf{tr}(b, E + x)\Bigr) \Rightarrow \mathsf{tr}(\hat{+}_i^{\sphericalangle}(a_0, a_1, b), E).$$

Fig. 5. Safety Proofs Generated by Analysis-Specific Procedures

Other subroutines $\mathcal{E}_b$ and $\mathcal{B}_b$ are about backward abstract interpretations. Given an abstract state $\hat{s}$, an expression E and an abstract value a, the subroutine $\mathcal{E}_b$ produces the following proof:

$$\frac{\vdots}{\mathsf{trst}(\hat{s}) \wedge \mathsf{tr}(a, E) \Rightarrow \mathsf{trst}(\llbracket E \rrbracket_b \hat{s}\, a)}$$

This proof shows that the backward interpretation $\llbracket E \rrbracket_b$ of expression E is correct; the set $\gamma(\llbracket E \rrbracket_b \hat{s}\, a)$ of states can exclude a state s in $\gamma(\hat{s})$ only when the value of E at s is not in $\gamma(a)$. Subroutine $\mathcal{B}_b$ outputs, for an abstract state $\hat{s}$ and a boolean expression B, the following proof:

$$\frac{\vdots}{\mathsf{trst}(\hat{s}) \wedge B \Rightarrow \mathsf{trst}(\llbracket B \rrbracket_b \hat{s})}$$

The proved implication says that a state s in $\gamma(\hat{s})$ can be pruned in $\gamma(\llbracket B \rrbracket_b \hat{s})$ only when the boolean expression B is false at the state s. Thus, it implies that the backward abstract interpretation of boolean expressions is correct.

Case $A \equiv [\hat{s}]x := E[\hat{s}']$

$$\frac{\mathsf{trst}(\hat{s}) \Rightarrow \left(\wedge_{y \in \mathsf{Vars} - \{x\}} \mathsf{tr}(\hat{s}'(y), y) \right) \quad \mathcal{E}(\hat{s}, E)}{\mathsf{trst}(\hat{s}) \Rightarrow \mathsf{trst}(\hat{s}')[E/x]} \qquad \frac{}{\{\mathsf{trst}(\hat{s}')[E/x]\}\, x := E\,\{\mathsf{trst}(\hat{s}')\}}$$
$$\frac{}{\{\mathsf{trst}(\hat{s})\}\, x := E\,\{\mathsf{trst}(\hat{s}')\}}$$

Case $A \equiv [\hat{s}]\mathtt{if}\ B\ \mathtt{then}\ [\hat{s}_1]R_1[\hat{s}_1']\ \mathtt{else}\ [\hat{s}_2]R_2[\hat{s}_2']\ \mathtt{fi}[\hat{s}']$

$$\frac{\mathcal{B}_b(\hat{s}, B) \quad \mathcal{T}([\hat{s}_1]R_1[\hat{s}_1']) \quad \mathsf{monSt}(\hat{s}_1', \hat{s}_1' \sqcup \hat{s}_2')}{\{\mathsf{trst}(\hat{s}) \wedge B\}\, \overline{R_1}\, \{\mathsf{trst}(\hat{s}')\}} \qquad \frac{\mathcal{B}_b(\hat{s}, \neg B) \quad \mathcal{T}([\hat{s}_2]R_2[\hat{s}_2']) \quad \mathsf{monSt}(\hat{s}_2', \hat{s}_1' \sqcup \hat{s}_2')}{\{\mathsf{trst}(\hat{s}) \wedge \neg B\}\, \overline{R_2}\, \{\mathsf{trst}(\hat{s}')\}}$$
$$\frac{}{\{\mathsf{trst}(\hat{s})\}\, \mathtt{if}\ B\ \mathtt{then}\ \overline{R_1}\ \mathtt{else}\ \overline{R_2}\ \mathtt{fi}\, \{\mathsf{trst}(\hat{s}')\}}$$

Case $A \equiv [\hat{s}]([\mathsf{inv}\ \hat{s}_0]\mathtt{while}\ B\ \mathtt{do}\ [\hat{s}_1]R_1[\hat{s}_1']\ \mathtt{od})[\hat{s}']$

$$\frac{\mathcal{B}_b(\hat{s}_0, B) \quad \mathcal{T}([\hat{s}_1]R_1[\hat{s}_1']) \quad \mathsf{monSt}(\hat{s}_1', \hat{s}_0)}{\{\mathsf{trst}(\hat{s}_0) \wedge B\}\, \overline{R_1}\, \{\mathsf{trst}(\hat{s}_0)\}}$$
$$\frac{\mathsf{monSt}(\hat{s}, \hat{s}_0) \quad \{\mathsf{trst}(\hat{s}_0)\}\, \mathtt{while}\ B\ \mathtt{do}\ \overline{R_1}\ \mathtt{od}\, \{\mathsf{trst}(\hat{s}_0) \wedge \neg B\} \quad \mathcal{B}_b(\hat{s}_0, \neg B)}{\{\mathsf{trst}(\hat{s})\}\, \mathtt{while}\ B\ \mathtt{do}\ \overline{R_1}\ \mathtt{od}\, \{\mathsf{trst}(\hat{s}')\}}$$

Case $A \equiv [\hat{s}]A_1; A_2[\hat{s}']$

$$\frac{\mathcal{T}(A_1) \quad \mathcal{T}(A_2)}{\{\mathsf{trst}(\hat{s})\}\, \overline{A_1; A_2}\, \{\mathsf{trst}(\hat{s}')\}}$$

Fig. 6. Proof Construction $\mathcal{T}(A)$ for an Annotated Program A

The main algorithm $\mathcal{T}$ is shown in Figure 6, and three subroutines $\mathcal{E}$, $\mathcal{E}_b$, and $\mathcal{B}_b$ are, respectively, in Figure 7, 8, and 9. In the algorithms, we use macros monSt and meetSt, which, respectively, extend monTr and meetTr (Figure 5) to abstract states. Let $x_0, \ldots, x_n$ be the enumeration of all variables in Vars, and let $\hat{s}$ and $\hat{s}'$ be abstract states. The macro $\mathsf{monSt}(\hat{s}, \hat{s}')$ expands to the following tree:

$$\frac{\mathsf{monTr}(\hat{s}(x_0), \hat{s}'(x_0), x_0) \quad \cdots \quad \mathsf{monTr}(\hat{s}(x_n), \hat{s}'(x_n), x_n)}{\mathsf{trst}(\hat{s}) \Rightarrow \mathsf{trst}(\hat{s}')}$$

Note that this tree becomes a proof tree when $\hat{s} \sqsubseteq \hat{s}'$; it is because, if $\hat{s}(x_i) \sqsubseteq \hat{s}'(x_i)$, $\mathsf{monTr}(\hat{s}(x_i), \hat{s}'(x_i), x_i)$ is a proof tree. On the other hand, the macro $\mathsf{meetSt}(\hat{s}, \hat{s}')$ always expands to the proof tree:

$$\frac{\mathsf{meetTr}(\hat{s}(x_0), \hat{s}'(x_0), x_0) \quad \cdots \quad \mathsf{meetTr}(\hat{s}(x_n), \hat{s}'(x_n), x_n)}{\mathsf{trst}(\hat{s}) \wedge \mathsf{trst}(\hat{s}') \Rightarrow \mathsf{trst}(\hat{s} \sqcap \hat{s}')}$$

Case $E \equiv n$

$$\frac{}{\mathsf{trst}(\hat{s}) \Rightarrow \mathsf{tr}(\llbracket n \rrbracket \hat{s}, n)} \mathsf{conTr}(n)$$

Case $E \equiv x$

$$\frac{}{\mathsf{trst}(\hat{s}) \Rightarrow \mathsf{tr}(\llbracket x \rrbracket \hat{s}, x)}$$

Case $E \equiv E_0 + E_1$

$$\frac{\dfrac{\mathcal{E}(\hat{s}, E_0) \quad \mathcal{E}(\hat{s}, E_1)}{\mathsf{trst}(\hat{s}) \Rightarrow \mathsf{tr}(\llbracket E_0 \rrbracket \hat{s}, E_0) \wedge \mathsf{tr}(\llbracket E_1 \rrbracket \hat{s}, E_1)} \quad \mathsf{fAdd}(\llbracket E_0 \rrbracket \hat{s}, \llbracket E_1 \rrbracket \hat{s}, E_0, E_1)}{\mathsf{trst}(\hat{s}) \Rightarrow \mathsf{tr}(\llbracket E_0 + E_1 \rrbracket \hat{s}, E_0 + E_1)}$$

Fig. 7. Proof Construction $\mathcal{E}(\hat{s}, E)$

Case $E \equiv n$
if $(\alpha(\{n\}) \sqsubseteq a)$ then

$$\frac{\mathsf{trst}(\hat{s}) \Rightarrow \mathsf{trst}(\llbracket n \rrbracket_b \hat{s} \; a)}{\mathsf{trst}(\hat{s}) \wedge \mathsf{tr}(a, n) \Rightarrow \mathsf{trst}(\llbracket n \rrbracket_b \hat{s} \; a)}$$

else

$$\frac{\mathsf{tr}(a, n) \Rightarrow \mathsf{trst}(\llbracket n \rrbracket_b \hat{s} \; a)}{\mathsf{trst}(\hat{s}) \wedge \mathsf{tr}(a, n) \Rightarrow \mathsf{trst}(\llbracket n \rrbracket_b \hat{s} \; a)}$$

Case $E \equiv x$

$$\frac{\mathsf{meetTr}(\hat{s}(x), a, x)}{\mathsf{trst}(\hat{s}) \wedge \mathsf{tr}(a, x) \Rightarrow \mathsf{trst}(\llbracket x \rrbracket_b \hat{s} \; a)}$$

Case $E \equiv E_0 + E_1$
let $(b_0, b_1) \stackrel{\Delta}{=} \hat{+}^{\triangleleft}(\llbracket E_0 \rrbracket \hat{s}, \llbracket E_1 \rrbracket \hat{s}, a)$ and $(\hat{s}_0, \hat{s}_1) \stackrel{\Delta}{=} (\llbracket E_0 \rrbracket_b \hat{s} \; b_0, \llbracket E_1 \rrbracket_b \hat{s} \; b_1)$

$$\frac{\dfrac{\dfrac{\tau_0 \quad \mathcal{E}_b(\hat{s}, b_0, E_0)}{\mathsf{trst}(\hat{s}) \wedge \mathsf{tr}(a, E_0 + E_1) \Rightarrow \mathsf{trst}(\hat{s}_0)} \quad \dfrac{\tau_1 \quad \mathcal{E}_b(\hat{s}, b_1, E_1)}{\mathsf{trst}(\hat{s}) \wedge \mathsf{tr}(a, E_0 + E_1) \Rightarrow \mathsf{trst}(\hat{s}_1)}}{\mathsf{trst}(\hat{s}) \wedge \mathsf{tr}(a, E_0 + E_1) \Rightarrow \mathsf{trst}(\hat{s}_0) \wedge \mathsf{trst}(\hat{s}_1)} \quad \mathsf{meetSt}(\hat{s}_0, \hat{s}_1)}{\mathsf{trst}(\hat{s}) \wedge \mathsf{tr}(a, E_0 + E_1) \Rightarrow \mathsf{trst}(\llbracket E_0 + E_1 \rrbracket_b \hat{s} \; a)}$$

where τ_i is:

$$\psi_i \stackrel{\Delta}{=} \exists x.\, \mathsf{tr}(\llbracket E_i \rrbracket \hat{s}, E_i) \wedge \mathsf{tr}(\llbracket E_{1-i} \rrbracket \hat{s}, x) \wedge \mathsf{tr}(a, E_i + x)$$

$$\frac{\dfrac{\dfrac{\dfrac{\mathcal{E}(\hat{s}, E_0) \quad \mathcal{E}(\hat{s}, E_1)}{\mathsf{trst}(\hat{s}) \Rightarrow \mathsf{tr}(\llbracket E_0 \rrbracket \hat{s}, E_0) \wedge \mathsf{tr}(\llbracket E_1 \rrbracket \hat{s}, E_1)}}{\mathsf{trst}(\hat{s}) \wedge \mathsf{tr}(a, E_0 + E_1) \Rightarrow \mathsf{tr}(\llbracket E_0 \rrbracket \hat{s}, E_0) \wedge \mathsf{tr}(\llbracket E_1 \rrbracket \hat{s}, E_1) \wedge \mathsf{tr}(a, E_0 + E_1)}}{\mathsf{trst}(\hat{s}) \wedge \mathsf{tr}(a, E_0 + E_1) \Rightarrow \psi_i}}{\mathsf{trst}(\hat{s}) \wedge \mathsf{tr}(a, E_0 + E_1) \Rightarrow \mathsf{trst}(\hat{s}) \wedge \psi_i} \quad \dfrac{\mathsf{bAdd}_i(\llbracket E_0 \rrbracket \hat{s}, \llbracket E_1 \rrbracket \hat{s}, a, E_i)}{\mathsf{trst}(\hat{s}) \wedge \psi_i \Rightarrow \mathsf{trst}(\hat{s}) \wedge \mathsf{tr}(b_i, E_i)}}{\mathsf{trst}(\hat{s}) \wedge \mathsf{tr}(a, E_0 + E_1) \Rightarrow \mathsf{trst}(\hat{s}) \wedge \mathsf{tr}(b_i, E_i)}$$

Fig. 8. Proof Construction $\mathcal{E}_b(\hat{s}, a, E)$

Case $B \equiv \mathtt{tt}$

$$\frac{\mathsf{trst}(\hat{s}) \Rightarrow \mathsf{trst}(\llbracket \mathtt{tt} \rrbracket_b \hat{s})}{\mathsf{trst}(\hat{s}) \wedge \mathtt{tt} \Rightarrow \mathsf{trst}(\llbracket \mathtt{tt} \rrbracket_b \hat{s})}$$

Case $B \equiv \mathtt{ff}$

$$\frac{\mathtt{ff} \Rightarrow \mathsf{trst}(\llbracket \mathtt{ff} \rrbracket_b \hat{s})}{\mathsf{trst}(\hat{s}) \wedge \mathtt{ff} \Rightarrow \mathsf{trst}(\llbracket \mathtt{ff} \rrbracket_b \hat{s})}$$

Case $B \equiv E_0 = E_1$

let $(b_0, b_1) \stackrel{\Delta}{=} \stackrel{\triangleleft}{=}(\llbracket E_0 \rrbracket \hat{s}, \llbracket E_1 \rrbracket \hat{s})$ and $(\hat{s}_0, \hat{s}_1) \stackrel{\Delta}{=} (\llbracket E_0 \rrbracket_b \hat{s}\, b_0, \llbracket E_1 \rrbracket_b \hat{s}\, b_1)$

$$\frac{\dfrac{\tau_0 \quad \mathcal{E}_b(\hat{s}, b_0, E_0)}{\mathsf{trst}(\hat{s}) \wedge E_0 = E_1 \Rightarrow \mathsf{trst}(\hat{s}_0)} \quad \dfrac{\tau_1 \quad \mathcal{E}_b(\hat{s}, b_1, E_1)}{\mathsf{trst}(\hat{s}) \wedge E_0 = E_1 \Rightarrow \mathsf{trst}(\hat{s}_1)}}{\dfrac{\mathsf{trst}(\hat{s}) \wedge E_0 = E_1 \Rightarrow \mathsf{trst}(\hat{s}_0) \wedge \mathsf{trst}(\hat{s}_1) \qquad \mathsf{meetSt}(\hat{s}_0, \hat{s}_1)}{\mathsf{trst}(\hat{s}) \wedge E_0 = E_1 \Rightarrow \mathsf{trst}(\llbracket E_0 = E_1 \rrbracket_b \hat{s})}}$$

where τ_i is:

$$\psi_i \stackrel{\Delta}{=} \exists x.\, \mathsf{tr}(\llbracket E_i \rrbracket \hat{s}, E_i) \wedge \mathsf{tr}(\llbracket E_{1-i} \rrbracket \hat{s}, x) \wedge E_i = x$$

$$\frac{\dfrac{\dfrac{\mathcal{E}(\hat{s}, E_0) \quad \mathcal{E}(\hat{s}, E_1)}{\mathsf{trst}(\hat{s}) \Rightarrow \mathsf{tr}(\llbracket E_0 \rrbracket \hat{s}, E_0) \wedge \mathsf{tr}(\llbracket E_1 \rrbracket \hat{s}, E_1)}}{\dfrac{\mathsf{trst}(\hat{s}) \wedge E_0 = E_1 \Rightarrow \mathsf{tr}(\llbracket E_0 \rrbracket \hat{s}, E_0) \wedge \mathsf{tr}(\llbracket E_1 \rrbracket \hat{s}, E_1) \wedge E_0 = E_1}{\mathsf{trst}(\hat{s}) \wedge E_0 = E_1 \Rightarrow \mathsf{trst}(\hat{s}) \wedge \psi_i}} \quad \dfrac{\mathsf{bEql}_i(\llbracket E_0 \rrbracket \hat{s}, \llbracket E_1 \rrbracket \hat{s}, E_i)}{\mathsf{trst}(\hat{s}) \wedge \psi_i \Rightarrow \mathsf{trst}(\hat{s}) \wedge \mathsf{tr}(b_i, E_i)}}{\mathsf{trst}(\hat{s}) \wedge E_0 = E_1 \Rightarrow \mathsf{trst}(\hat{s}) \wedge \mathsf{tr}(b_i, E_i)}$$

Case $B \equiv E_0 < E_1$

let $(b_0, b_1) \stackrel{\Delta}{=} \stackrel{\triangleleft}{<}(\llbracket E_0 \rrbracket \hat{s}, \llbracket E_1 \rrbracket \hat{s})$ and $(\hat{s}_0, \hat{s}_1) \stackrel{\Delta}{=} (\llbracket E_0 \rrbracket_b \hat{s}\, b_0, \llbracket E_1 \rrbracket_b \hat{s}\, b_1)$

$$\frac{\dfrac{\tau_0 \quad \mathcal{E}_b(\hat{s}, b_0, E_0)}{\mathsf{trst}(\hat{s}) \wedge E_0 < E_1 \Rightarrow \mathsf{trst}(\hat{s}_0)} \quad \dfrac{\tau_1 \quad \mathcal{E}_b(\hat{s}, b_1, E_1)}{\mathsf{trst}(\hat{s}) \wedge E_0 < E_1 \Rightarrow \mathsf{trst}(\hat{s}_1)}}{\dfrac{\mathsf{trst}(\hat{s}) \wedge E_0 < E_1 \Rightarrow \mathsf{trst}(\hat{s}_0) \wedge \mathsf{trst}(\hat{s}_1) \qquad \mathsf{meetSt}(\hat{s}_0, \hat{s}_1)}{\mathsf{trst}(\hat{s}) \wedge E_0 < E_1 \Rightarrow \mathsf{trst}(\llbracket E_0 < E_1 \rrbracket_b \hat{s})}}$$

where τ_i is:

$$\psi_0 \stackrel{\Delta}{=} \exists x.\, \mathsf{tr}(\llbracket E_0 \rrbracket \hat{s}, E_0) \wedge \mathsf{tr}(\llbracket E_1 \rrbracket \hat{s}, x) \wedge E_0 < x \qquad \psi_1 \stackrel{\Delta}{=} \exists x.\, \mathsf{tr}(\llbracket E_0 \rrbracket \hat{s}, x) \wedge \mathsf{tr}(\llbracket E_1 \rrbracket \hat{s}, E_1) \wedge x < E_1$$

$$\frac{\dfrac{\dfrac{\mathcal{E}(\hat{s}, E_0) \quad \mathcal{E}(\hat{s}, E_1)}{\mathsf{trst}(\hat{s}) \Rightarrow \mathsf{tr}(\llbracket E_0 \rrbracket \hat{s}, E_0) \wedge \mathsf{tr}(\llbracket E_1 \rrbracket \hat{s}, E_1)}}{\dfrac{\mathsf{trst}(\hat{s}) \wedge E_0 < E_1 \Rightarrow \mathsf{tr}(\llbracket E_0 \rrbracket \hat{s}, E_0) \wedge \mathsf{tr}(\llbracket E_1 \rrbracket \hat{s}, E_1) \wedge E_0 < E_1}{\mathsf{trst}(\hat{s}) \wedge E_0 < E_1 \Rightarrow \mathsf{trst}(\hat{s}) \wedge \psi_i}} \quad \dfrac{\mathsf{bInEql}_i(\llbracket E_0 \rrbracket \hat{s}, \llbracket E_1 \rrbracket \hat{s}, E_i)}{\mathsf{trst}(\hat{s}) \wedge \psi_i \Rightarrow \mathsf{trst}(\hat{s}) \wedge \mathsf{tr}(b_i, E_i)}}{\mathsf{trst}(\hat{s}) \wedge E_0 < E_1 \Rightarrow \mathsf{trst}(\hat{s}) \wedge \mathsf{tr}(b_i, E_i)}$$

Case $B \equiv B_0 \wedge B_1$

$$\frac{\dfrac{\mathcal{B}_b(\hat{s}, B_0) \quad \mathcal{B}_b(\hat{s}, B_1)}{\mathsf{trst}(\hat{s}) \wedge (B_0 \wedge B_1) \Rightarrow \mathsf{trst}(\llbracket B_0 \rrbracket_b \hat{s}) \wedge \mathsf{trst}(\llbracket B_1 \rrbracket_b \hat{s}) \quad \mathsf{meetSt}(\llbracket B_0 \rrbracket_b \hat{s}, \llbracket B_1 \rrbracket_b \hat{s})}}{\mathsf{trst}(\hat{s}) \wedge (B_0 \wedge B_1) \Rightarrow \mathsf{trst}(\llbracket B_0 \wedge B_1 \rrbracket_b \hat{s})}$$

Case $B \equiv B_0 \vee B_1$

$$\frac{\dfrac{\dfrac{\mathcal{B}_b(\hat{s}, B_0) \quad \mathsf{monSt}(\llbracket B_0 \rrbracket_b \hat{s}, \llbracket B_0 \vee B_1 \rrbracket_b \hat{s})}{\mathsf{trst}(\hat{s}) \wedge B_0 \Rightarrow \mathsf{trst}(\llbracket B_0 \vee B_1 \rrbracket_b \hat{s})} \quad \dfrac{\mathcal{B}_b(\hat{s}, B_1) \quad \mathsf{monSt}(\llbracket B_1 \rrbracket_b \hat{s}, \llbracket B_0 \vee B_1 \rrbracket_b \hat{s})}{\mathsf{trst}(\hat{s}) \wedge B_1 \Rightarrow \mathsf{trst}(\llbracket B_0 \vee B_1 \rrbracket_b \hat{s})}}{(\mathsf{trst}(\hat{s}) \wedge B_0) \vee (\mathsf{trst}(\hat{s}) \wedge B_1) \Rightarrow \mathsf{trst}(\llbracket B_0 \vee B_1 \rrbracket_b \hat{s})}}{\mathsf{trst}(\hat{s}) \wedge (B_0 \vee B_1) \Rightarrow \mathsf{trst}(\llbracket B_0 \vee B_1 \rrbracket_b \hat{s})}$$

Fig. 9. Proof Construction $\mathcal{B}_b(\hat{s}, B)$

Lemma 1. *The subroutines $\mathcal{E}$, $\mathcal{E}_b$, and $\mathcal{B}_b$ output proof trees. That is, the output trees are derivable in first-order logic.*

Proof. The lemma can be shown by induction on the structure of the input boolean or integer expression. Each induction step can be shown by the definition of the generic abstraction interpretation, and the specification (Figure 5) for the provided procedures. □

Theorem 1. *If an annotated command A is the result of an abstract interpretation, the tree $\mathcal{T}(A)$ is a proof tree in Hoare logic.*

Proof. We prove by induction on the structure of A.

- A is $[\hat{s}]x\!:=\!E[\hat{s}']$: In this case, we need to show that the subtree τ of $\mathcal{T}(A)$ for $\mathrm{trst}(\hat{s}) \Rightarrow \mathrm{trst}(\hat{s}')[E/x]$ is derivable in first-order logic. From the generic abstract interpretation of $x := E$, we have

$$\hat{s}' = \hat{s}[x \mapsto [\![E]\!]\hat{s}].$$

  Thus, $\hat{s}'(y) = \hat{s}(y)$ for all y in $\mathsf{Vars} - \{x\}$. And $\mathrm{tr}([\![E]\!]\hat{s}, E) = \mathrm{tr}([\![x]\!]\hat{s}', E)$, which implies that the tree $\mathcal{E}(\hat{s}, E)$ is for the formula

$$\mathrm{trst}(\hat{s}) \Rightarrow \mathrm{tr}([\![x]\!]\hat{s}', E).$$

  Since $\mathcal{E}(\hat{s}, E)$ is a proof tree (Lemma 1), the tree τ is derivable.
- A is $[\hat{s}]\mathtt{if}\ B\ \mathtt{then}\ [\hat{s}_1]R_1[\hat{s}_1']\ \mathtt{else}\ [\hat{s}_2]R_2[\hat{s}_2']\ \mathtt{fi}[\hat{s}']$: From the generic abstraction interpretation, we have

$$\hat{s}_1' \sqcup \hat{s}_2' = \hat{s}',\quad \hat{s}_1 = [\![B]\!]_b\hat{s},\quad \text{and}\quad \hat{s}_2 = [\![\neg B]\!]_b\hat{s}.$$

  Note that $\mathcal{B}_b(\hat{s}, B)$ and $\mathcal{B}_b(\hat{s}, \neg B)$ are both derivable (Lemma 1), and that for $i = 0, 1$, the tree $\mathsf{monSt}(\hat{s}_i', \hat{s}_1' \sqcup \hat{s}_2')$ is derivable because $\hat{s}_i' \sqsubseteq \hat{s}_1' \sqcup \hat{s}_2'$. Therefore, the induction hypothesis implies that the tree is derivable.
- A is $[\hat{s}]([\mathsf{inv}\ \hat{s}_0]\mathtt{while}\ B\ \mathtt{do}\ [\hat{s}_1]R_1[\hat{s}_1']\ \mathtt{od})[\hat{s}']$: From the generic abstraction interpretation, we have

$$\hat{s} \sqsubseteq \hat{s}_0,\quad \hat{s}_1' \sqsubseteq \hat{s}_0,\quad \hat{s}_1 = [\![B]\!]_b\hat{s}_0,\quad \text{and}\quad \hat{s}' = [\![\neg B]\!]_b\hat{s}_0.$$

  The correctness of $\mathcal{B}_b$, the assumption for monSt, and the induction hypothesis imply that the tree $\mathcal{T}(A)$ is derivable.
- A is $[\hat{s}]A_1;A_2[\hat{s}']$: Let $[\hat{s}_1]R_1[\hat{s}_1']$ be A_1, and let $[\hat{s}_2]R_2[\hat{s}_2']$ be A_2. From the generic abstract interpretation, we have

$$\hat{s} = \hat{s}_1,\quad \hat{s}_1' = \hat{s}_2,\quad \text{and}\quad \hat{s}_2' = \hat{s}'.$$

  Therefore, the induction hypothesis shows that $\mathcal{T}(A)$ is a proof tree. □

We illustrate algorithm $\mathcal{T}$ with an example from the interval analysis. Consider the following program A annotated with the analysis results, integer intervals of program variables.

$$[x \mapsto [1,4], y \mapsto [2,5]]$$
$$\text{if } (x = y + 1) \text{ then } [x \mapsto [3,4], y \mapsto [2,3]]$$
$$x := x + y$$
$$[x \mapsto [5,7], y \mapsto [2,3]]$$
$$\text{else } [x \mapsto [1,4], y \mapsto [2,5]]$$
$$x := x + 1$$
$$[x \mapsto [2,5], y \mapsto [2,5]]$$
$$\text{fi}$$
$$[x \mapsto [2,7], y \mapsto [2,5]]$$

When algorithm $\mathcal{T}$ gets the input A, it first recurses for sub-command $x := x+y$, and for $x := x + 1$, and obtains Hoare proofs, one for the Hoare triple H_0

$$\{3 \leq x \leq 4 \wedge 2 \leq y \leq 3\} \, x := x + y \, \{5 \leq x \leq 7 \wedge 2 \leq y \leq 3\}$$

and the other for the Hoare triple H_1

$$\{1 \leq x \leq 4 \wedge 2 \leq y \leq 5\} \, x := x + 1 \, \{2 \leq x \leq 5 \wedge 2 \leq y \leq 5\}.$$

Note that there is a "gap" between these triples and what's needed to complete a proof for the input A. That is, the pre- and post-conditions of triples H_0 and H_1 do not match with those of the required triples in the following Hoare proof:

$$
\cfrac{
\left\{\begin{array}{l} 1 \leq x \leq 4 \\ \wedge\, 2 \leq y \leq 5 \\ \wedge\, x = y + 1 \end{array}\right\} x := x + y \left\{\begin{array}{l} 2 \leq x \leq 7 \\ \wedge\, 2 \leq y \leq 5 \end{array}\right\}
\quad
\left\{\begin{array}{l} 1 \leq x \leq 4 \\ \wedge\, 2 \leq y \leq 5 \\ \wedge\, x \neq y + 1 \end{array}\right\} x := x + 1 \left\{\begin{array}{l} 2 \leq x \leq 7 \\ \wedge\, 2 \leq y \leq 5 \end{array}\right\}
}{
\left\{\begin{array}{l} 1 \leq x \leq 4 \\ \wedge\, 2 \leq y \leq 5 \end{array}\right\} \text{if } x = y + 1 \text{ then } x := x + y \text{ else } x := x + 1 \text{ fi} \left\{\begin{array}{l} 2 \leq x \leq 7 \\ \wedge\, 2 \leq y \leq 5 \end{array}\right\}
}
$$

Algorithm $\mathcal{T}$ fills this gap by calling $\mathcal{B}_b$ and monTr. The calls to $\mathcal{B}_b$ give proofs for implications between pre-conditions:

$$1 \leq x \leq 4 \wedge 2 \leq y \leq 5 \wedge x = y + 1 \quad \Rightarrow \quad 3 \leq x \leq 4 \wedge 2 \leq y \leq 3$$
$$1 \leq x \leq 4 \wedge 2 \leq y \leq 5 \wedge x \neq y + 1 \quad \Rightarrow \quad 1 \leq x \leq 4 \wedge 2 \leq y \leq 5$$

and the calls to monTr give proofs for implications between post-conditions:

$$5 \leq x \leq 7 \wedge 2 \leq y \leq 3 \quad \Rightarrow \quad 2 \leq x \leq 7 \wedge 2 \leq y \leq 5$$
$$2 \leq x \leq 5 \wedge 2 \leq y \leq 5 \quad \Rightarrow \quad 2 \leq x \leq 7 \wedge 2 \leq y \leq 5.$$

3.3 Size of Generated Proof Trees

We measure the size of an output tree from $\mathcal{T}$ by counting the nodes in the tree. While counting these nodes, we will assume that each call to the provided procedures, such as monTr, meetTr and fAdd, returns a proof tree with a single node. Note that the size k of a tree τ, computed under this assumption, still gives an upper bound for the number of nodes in τ; when each call to the provided procedures gives a proof tree with at most k' nodes, the tree τ can have at most $k \times k'$ nodes. Let |Vars| be the cardinality of Vars. Since we always use for Vars the set of variables in the input program, |Vars| denotes the number of variables in the input program. Let the size of an expression or a command be the number of its tokens. For instance, the size of the expression $y + z + 1$ is 5, and the size of the command $x := y + z + 1; x := 2$ is 11.

Lemma 2. *For an expression E of size n and an abstract state $\hat{s}$, the tree $\mathcal{E}(\hat{s}, E)$ has $O(n)$ nodes.*

Proof. Subroutine $\mathcal{E}$ recurses only when $E = E_0 + E_1$. In that case, it calls itself for disjoint subparts E_0 and E_1 of E. Thus, there can be only $O(n)$-many recursive calls to $\mathcal{E}$. This number of recursive calls limits the size of the tree $\mathcal{E}(\hat{s}, E)$ to $O(n)$. $\square$

Lemma 3. *For an expression E of size n, an abstract state $\hat{s}$, and an abstract value a, the tree $\mathcal{E}_b(\hat{s}, a, E)$ has $O(n^2 + n \times$ |Vars|$)$ nodes.*

Proof. Subroutine $\mathcal{E}_b$ can recurse only $O(n)$ times, because of the same reason as in the proof of Lemma 2. Thus, $\mathcal{E}$ is called $O(n)$-times in $\mathcal{E}_b$, and the macro meetSt is expanded $O(n)$ times giving $O(n \times$ |Vars|$)$-many calls to meetTr. Since each call to $\mathcal{E}$ can add $O(n)$ nodes, the tree $\mathcal{E}_b(\hat{s}, s, E)$ has $O(n) + O(n^2) + O(n \times$ |Vars|$) = O(n^2 + n \times$ |Vars|$)$ nodes. $\square$

Lemma 4. *For a boolean expression B of size n and an abstract state $\hat{s}$, the tree $\mathcal{B}_b(\hat{s}, B)$ has $O(n^2 + n \times$ |Vars|$)$ nodes.*

Proof. Subroutine $\mathcal{B}_b$ recurses only when $B = B_1 \vee B_2$ or $B = B_1 \wedge B_2$. In both cases, the recursive calls are for disjoint subparts of B. So, $\mathcal{B}_b(E)$ recurses only $O(n)$ times. This number of recursive calls bounds the number of macro expansions of meetSt and monSt, so that meetTr and monTr can be called $O(n \times$ |Vars|$)$ times. As of the calls to $\mathcal{E}$ and $\mathcal{E}_b$ in $\mathcal{B}_b$, we observe that both $\mathcal{E}$ and $\mathcal{E}_b$ are called in $\mathcal{B}_b$ only when $\mathcal{B}_b$ does not recurse; moreover, when $n_0, n_1, \ldots, n_k$ are the size of inputs to all these calls to $\mathcal{E}$ and $\mathcal{E}_b$, the sum $\Sigma_{i=0}^{k} n_i$ is $O(n)$. Therefore, although $\mathcal{E}$ and $\mathcal{E}_b$ are called $O(n)$ times, only $O(n)$ nodes are constructed from all the calls to $\mathcal{E}$, and $O(n^2 + n \times$ |Vars|$)$ nodes from all the calls to $\mathcal{E}_b$; when $O(n) = \Sigma_{i=0}^{k} n_i$, we have $O(n^l) = \Sigma_{i=0}^{k} (n_i)^l$ for all natural numbers l. Therefore, the tree $\mathcal{B}_b(\hat{s}, B)$ can have $O(n) + O(n \times$ |Vars|$) + O(n) + O(n^2 + n \times$ |Vars|$) = O(n^2 + n \times$ |Vars|$)$ nodes. $\square$

Proposition 1. *For a command $\overline{A}$ of size n, the tree $\mathcal{T}(A)$ has $O(n^2 + n \times$ |Vars|$)$ nodes.*

Proof. Algorithm $\mathcal{T}$ calls itself $O(n)$ times. Thus, the macro monSt is expanded $O(n)$ times, giving $O(n \times |\mathsf{Vars}|)$ calls to monTr. For the calls to $\mathcal{B}_b$ and $\mathcal{E}$, we note that when $n_0, \ldots, n_k$ are the sizes of inputs to all the calls to $\mathcal{B}_b$ and $\mathcal{E}$, the sum $\Sigma_{i=0}^{k} n_i$ is $O(n)$. We can use the argument in the proof of Lemma 4 to prove that all the calls to $\mathcal{B}_b$ can construct $O(n^2 + n \times |\mathsf{Vars}|)$ nodes, and all the calls to $\mathcal{E}$ $O(n)$ nodes. The tree $\mathcal{T}(A)$, therefore, has $O(n) + O(n \times |\mathsf{Vars}|) + O(n^2 + n \times |\mathsf{Vars}|) + O(n) = O(n^2 + n \times |\mathsf{Vars}|)$ nodes. $\qquad\square$

We expect that in practice, the sizes of generated proofs are significantly smaller than the worst case $O(n^2 + n \times |\mathsf{Vars}|)$, because boolean or integer expressions in programs are usually short: their sizes are practically constant compared to the size of a program.

4   Conclusion

We have presented an algorithm that automatically constructs Hoare proofs for program's approximate invariants annotated by abstract interpreters. The gap between the approximate invariants and the Hoare-logic rules is filled by the safety proofs of the used abstract interpreter. Although our algorithm still requires a well-designed abstract interpreter and its safety proofs, it reduces the complexity of proof construction, because 1) the same abstract interpreter can be used repeatedly for multiple programs; 2) the needed safety proofs of the used abstract interpreter are standard ones prescribed by the abstract interpretation framework.

The method reported in this paper suggests a yet another framework of PCC, where the proof construction process is fully automatic, and the code properties it can verify and check are more general than types. We will employ this method in our planned PCC compiler system. The compiler uses abstract interpretations and our method to construct safety proofs of the input programs. The compiler then compiles the obtained proofs for the source code into proofs for the compiled target code. This compiled proof and code pairs are to be checked by the code consumer. Developing such a "proof compiler" technology is our next goal.

Currently we are implementing our algorithm for a simple imperative language extended with arrays and procedures. An abstract interpreter verifies that all array references are within bounds. Through this implementation, we expect to use similar ideas as [13] in engineering the proof sizes.

Acknowledgements. Seo and Yang were supported by grant No. R08-2003-000-10370-0 from the Basic Research Program of the Korea Science & Engineering Foundation. Yi was supported by Creative Research Initiatives of the Korean Ministry of Science and Technology.

References

1. A. W. Appel. Foundational proof-carrying code. In *Proceedings of the 16th Annual IEEE Symposium on Logic in Computer Science*, pages 247–258, June 2001.
2. A. W. Appel and A. P. Felty. A semantic model of types and machine instructions for proof-carrying code. In *Proceedings of the ACM SIGPLAN-SIGACT Symposium on Principles of Programming Languages*, pages 243–253, January 2000.
3. P. Cousot. The calculational design of a generic abstract interpreter. In M. Broy and R. Steinbrüggen, editors, *Calculational System Design*. NATO ASI Series F. IOS Press, Amsterdam, 1999.
4. P. Cousot and R. Cousot. Abstract interpretation: a unified lattice model for static analysis of programs by construction or approximation of fixpoints. In *Proceedings of the ACM SIGPLAN-SIGACT Symposium on Principles of Programming Languages*, pages 238–252, January 1977.
5. P. Cousot and R. Cousot. Automatic synthesis of optimal invariant assertions: mathematical foundations. In *ACM Symposium on Artificial Intelligence and Programming Languages*, volume 12, pages 1–12, Rochester, NY, ACM SIGPLAN Notices, August 1977.
6. P. Cousot and R. Cousot. Systematic design of program analysis frameworks. In *Conference Record of the Sixth Annual ACM SIGPLAN-SIGACT Symposium on Principles of Programming Languages*, pages 269–282, San Antonio, Texas, 1979. ACM Press, New York, NY.
7. N. Hamid, Z. Shao, V. Trifonov, S. Monnier, and Z. Ni. A syntactic approach to foundational proof-carrying code. In *Proceedings of the 17th Annual IEEE Symposium on Logic in Computer Science*, pages 89–100, June 2002.
8. Nevin Heintze, Joxan Jaffar, and Razvan Voicu. A framework for combining analysis and verification. In *Proceedings of the ACM SIGPLAN-SIGACT Symposium on Principles of Programming Languages*, pages 26–39, Boston, MA, USA, January 2000.
9. C. A. R. Hoare. An axiomatic basis for computer programming. *Communications of the ACM*, 12(10):576–580, 1969.
10. G. Morrisett, D. Walker, K. Crary, and N. Glew. From System F to typed assembly language. In *Proceedings of the ACM SIGPLAN-SIGACT Symposium on Principles of Programming Languages*, pages 85–97, January 1998.
11. G. C. Necula. Proof-carrying code. In *Proceedings of the ACM SIGPLAN-SIGACT Symposium on Principles of Programming Languages*, pages 106–119, January 1997.
12. G. C. Necula and P. Lee. Safe, untrusted agents using proof-carrying code. In *Special Issue on Mobile Agent Security*, volume 1419 of *Lecture Notes in Computer Science*, pages 61–91. Springer-Verlag, 1997.
13. G. C. Necula and S. P. Rahul. Oracle-based checking of untrusted software. In *Proceedings of the ACM SIGPLAN-SIGACT Symposium on Principles of Programming Languages*, pages 142–154, January 2001.
14. G. C. Necula and R. Schneck. Proof-carrying code with untrusted proof rules. In *Software Security – Theories and Systems*, volume 2609 of *Lecture Notes in Computer Science*, pages 283–298. Springer-Verlag, November 2002.

A Program Inverter for a Functional Language with Equality and Constructors

Robert Glück[1]* and Masahiko Kawabe[2]

[1] PRESTO, JST & Institute for Software Production Technology
Waseda University, School of Science and Engineering
Tokyo 169-8555, Japan, glueck@acm.org
[2] Waseda University, Graduate School of Science and Engineering
Tokyo 169-8555, Japan,
kawabe@futamura.info.waseda.ac.jp

Abstract. We present a method for automatic program inversion in a
first-order functional programming language. We formalize the transformation and illustrate it with several examples including the automatic
derivation of a program for run-length decoding from a program for run-
length encoding. This derivation is not possible with other automatic
program inversion methods. One of our key observations is that the duplication of values and testing of their equality are two sides of the same
coin in program inversion. This leads us to the design of a new self-inverse
primitive function that considerably simplifies the automatic inversion of
programs.

1 Introduction

Many problems in computation can be specified in terms of computing the inverse of an easily constructed function [3]. We regard program inversion, beside
program specialization and program composition, as one of the three fundamental operations of metacomputation [10]. The idea of program inversion can be
traced back to reference [7]. Recent work [16] has focused on the converse of a
function theorem [3], inverse computation of functional programs [2], and the
transformation of interpreters into inverse interpreters by partial evaluation [9].
Despite the fundamental importance of program inversion as tool for program
transformation, relatively few papers have been devoted to this topic.

Program inversion has been studied in the context of Undo facilities for editors, transaction systems, and so on (*e.g.*, [4,5,15]). These facilities usually rely
on cumulative methods that record parts of the forward computation. The size of
such a trace depends on the number of computation steps (examples are editors,
debuggers, image processors). In contrast to these methods, we do not require
several forward computation steps before reversing the last computation steps.
We are interested in generating 'stand-alone' inverse programs from a given program. Examples are programs for encoding and decoding data when files are sent

---

* On leave from DIKU, Department of Computer Science, University of Copenhagen.

A. Ohori (Ed.): APLAS 2003, LNCS 2895, pp. 246–264, 2003.

via networks. We consider one-to-one functions and not relations with multiple solutions. Logic programming is suited to find multiple solutions and can be regarded as inverse interpretation, but we are interested in program inversion. Our goal is to generate inverse programs. For a more detailed description of these notions, see reference [1].

The first method developed for automatic program inversion of first-order functional programs appears to be the program inverter by Korf and Eppstein [14,8] (we call it KEinv for short). It is one of only two general-purpose automatic program inverters that have been built (the other one is InvX [13]). The key feature is the inversion of multiple functions with multiple parameters which together form an injective system of functions. KEinv uses postcondition inference heuristics as the basis for the transformation. Global inversion is based on the local invertibility of program constructs.

The contribution of this paper is an *automatic method for program inversion* of first-order function programs with constructors and equality test. One of our key observations is that the *duplication of values* and *testing of equality* are two sides of the same coin in program inversion. Based on this observation, we designed a self-inverse primitive function that considerably simplifies the inversion of programs.

Another important ingredient is the representation of a program as a logical formula in a disjunctive normal form representing atomic operations in the source program and dissolving the nesting of case-expressions. Inversion is then performed on this representation and reduces to a straightforward backward reading of the atomic formulas. As a result our method can automatically invert programs that are beyond the capability of KEinv, such as the automatic generation of a program for run-length decoding from a program for run-length encoding. However, KEinv also includes numbers and arithmetic; our capabilities in that area are less. They also use postcondition heuristics, which we have not added to our system.

These insights are an important step towards our research goals because, beside InvX, KEinv appears to be the only existing general-purpose automatic program inverter. Manual methods [7,12,3,16] and semi-automatic methods [6] exist, but require ingenuity and human insight. Our goal is to achieve further automation of general-purpose program inversion.

This paper is organized as follows. First, we introduce the inversion of functions (Sect. 2) and define the source language (Sect. 3). Then we discuss our solution of the main challenges of program inversion (Sect. 4) and present our inversion method (Sect. 5). We discuss limitations and extensions (Sect. 6) and related work (Sect. 7), and then give a conclusion (Sect. 8).

2   Program Inversion

The goal of program inversion is to find an *inverse program* $q^{-1} : B \to A$ of a program $q : A \to B$ such that for all values $x \in A$ and $y \in B$ we have

$$q(x) = y \iff q^{-1}(y) = x .\tag{1}$$

Here, equality means strong equivalence (either both sides of an equation are defined and equal, or both sides are undefined). Observe that the definition of an inverse program does not state the properties of the inverse in isolation. The definition tells us that, if a program q terminates on input x and returns output y, then the inverse program q^{-1} terminates on y and returns x, and vice versa. This implies that both programs are *injective* (they need not be surjective or total). The definition is symmetric with respect to q and q^{-1}, which means that it is arbitrary which of the two programs we call the 'source program' and which we call the 'inverse program'. The equation does not assert properties for programs q and q^{-1} outside the domains A and B.

A program *inv* is a *program inverter* if, for all injective programs q, the result of applying *inv* to q yields an inverse program q^{-1} of q: $inv(q) = q^{-1}$. In practice, even when it is certain that an efficient inverse program q^{-1} exists, the automatic derivation of such a procedure from q by a program inverter may be difficult or impossible.[1] This paper presents a method for automatic program inversion that can automatically convert a large class of injective programs into their inverse. For instance, we will see that we can automatically obtain a program for run-length decoding from a program for run-length encoding.

3   Source Language

We are concerned with a first-order functional language. A program q is a sequence of function definitions d where the body of each definition is a term t constructed from variables, constructors, function calls and case-expressions (Fig. 1 where $m > 0$, $n \geq 0$). For simplicity, we assume that all functions are unary. The language has a call-by-value semantics.

An example is the program for run-length encoding (Fig. 3): function *pack* encodes a list of symbols as a list of symbol-number pairs, where the number specifies how many copies of a symbol have to be generated upon decoding. For instance, $pack([AABCCC]) = [\langle A\ 2\rangle\langle B\ 1\rangle\langle C\ 3\rangle]$.[2] Function *pack* maximizes the counter in each symbol-number pair: we never have an encoding like $\langle C\ 2\rangle\langle C\ 1\rangle$, but rather, always $\langle C\ 3\rangle$. This implies that the symbols in two adjacent symbol-number pairs are never equal. Fig. 4 shows the inverse function $pack^{-1}$. In the implementation, we use unary numbers. The primitive function $\lfloor\cdot\rfloor$ checks the equality of two values: $\lfloor\langle v\ v'\rangle\rfloor = \langle v\rangle$ if $v = v'$. In the absence of equality, the values are returned unchanged: $\lfloor\langle v\ v'\rangle\rfloor = \langle v\ v'\rangle$ if $v \neq v'$. This will be defined below. We assume that $\lfloor\cdot\rfloor \in$ Functions, but write $\lfloor...\rfloor$ instead of $\lfloor\rfloor(...)$.

We consider only *well-formed* programs. We require that each variable occurring in a term be defined. As usual, we require that no two patterns p_i and p_j in a case-expression contain the same constructor (patterns are orthogonal) and

---

[1] There exists a program inverter that returns, for every q, a *trivial inverse* q^{-1} [1].

[2] We use the shorthand notation $x : xs$ and $[\ ]$ for the constructors $Cons(x\ xs)$ and Nil. For $x_1 : x_2 : ... : x_n : [\ ]$ we write $[x_1 x_2 ... x_n]$, or sometimes $x_1 x_2 ... x_n$. A tuple $\langle x_1 ... x_n\rangle$ is a shorthand notation for an n-ary constructor $C_n(x_1 ... x_n)$.

Grammar

$$q ::= d_1 \ldots d_m \qquad\qquad\qquad\text{(program)}$$
$$d ::= f(x) \triangleq t \qquad\qquad\qquad\text{(definition)}$$
$$t ::= x \qquad\qquad\qquad\qquad\text{(variable)}$$
$$\mid\ c(t_1 \ldots t_n) \qquad\qquad\quad\text{(constructor)}$$
$$\mid\ f(t) \qquad\qquad\qquad\quad\text{(function call)}$$
$$\mid\ \textbf{case } t \textbf{ of } p_1 \to t_1 \ \ldots\ p_m \to t_m \qquad\text{(case-expression)}$$
$$p ::= c(x_1 \ldots x_n) \qquad\qquad\quad\text{(flat pattern)}$$

Syntax domains

$q \in$ Programs	$t \in$ Terms	$x \in$ Variables	$f \in$ Functions
$d \in$ Definitions	$p \in$ Patterns	$c \in$ Constructors	

Fig. 1. Abstract syntax of the source language

$$v ::= c(v_1 \ldots v_n) \qquad\qquad\text{(value)}$$
$$r ::= f(x) \qquad\qquad\qquad\text{(redex)}$$
$$\mid\ c(x_1 \ldots x_n)$$
$$\mid\ \textbf{case } x \textbf{ of } p_1 \to t_1 \ \ldots\ p_m \to t_m$$
$$e ::= [\_] \qquad\qquad\qquad\text{(evaluation context)}$$
$$\mid\ f(e)$$
$$\mid\ c(x_1 \ldots x_{i-1}\ e\ t_{i+1} \ldots t_n)$$
$$\mid\ \textbf{case } e \textbf{ of } p_1 \to t_1 \ \ldots\ p_m \to t_m$$

Fig. 2. Value, redex and evaluation context

that all patterns are linear (no variable occurs more than once in a pattern). For simplicity, we also require that no defined variable be redefined by a pattern.

During evaluation, a term can be decomposed into redex and evaluation context (Fig. 2). A value v is a constructor c with arguments $v_1, ..., v_n$. A redex r is a term in which the outermost construction (function call, constructor or case-expression) can be reduced without reducing subterms first. An evaluation context e is a term with a 'hole' $[\_]$.

Design Choice. We assume a primitive function $\lfloor \cdot \rfloor$ defined as follows:

$$\lfloor \langle v \rangle \rfloor \overset{\text{def}}{=} \langle v\ v \rangle \qquad\qquad\text{(duplication)}$$

$$\lfloor \langle v\ v' \rangle \rfloor \overset{\text{def}}{=} \begin{cases} \langle v \rangle & \text{if } v = v' \\ \langle v\ v' \rangle & \text{if } v \neq v' \end{cases} \qquad\text{(equality test)}$$

The function duplicates a value or performs an equality test. In the former case, given a single value, a pair with identical values is returned; in the latter case, given a pair of identical values, a single value is returned; otherwise the pair is returned unchanged. There are mainly two ways of using this function.

(1) *Duplication.* A value can be duplicated by a case-expression with $\lfloor\langle t\rangle\rfloor$ as argument: the resulting value of t is bound to x_1 and x_2. These two variables can then be used in t'. This construction makes the duplication of values explicit.

$$\textbf{case } \lfloor\langle t\rangle\rfloor \textbf{ of } \langle x_1\ x_2\rangle \to t'$$

(2) *Equality test.* The equality of two values can be tested by a case-expression with $\lfloor\langle t\ t'\rangle\rfloor$ as argument: if the resulting values of t and t' are identical then t_1 is evaluated with x bound to the identical value; otherwise, x and y are bound to the values of t and t', respectively.

$$\textbf{case } \lfloor\langle t\ t'\rangle\rfloor \textbf{ of } \langle x\rangle \to t_1;\ \langle x\ y\rangle \to t_2$$

The function has the following important properties:

$$\lfloor\langle v\rangle\rfloor = \langle v_1'\ v_2'\rangle \iff \langle v\rangle = \lfloor\langle v_1'\ v_2'\rangle\rfloor$$
$$\lfloor\langle v_1\ v_2\rangle\rfloor = \langle v'\rangle \iff \langle v_1\ v_2\rangle = \lfloor\langle v'\rangle\rfloor$$
$$\lfloor\langle v_1\ v_2\rangle\rfloor = \langle v_1'\ v_2'\rangle \iff \langle v_1\ v_2\rangle = \lfloor\langle v_1'\ v_2'\rangle\rfloor$$

Thus, the function has the property $\lfloor\bullet\rfloor = \circ \iff \bullet = \lfloor\circ\rfloor$. It is its own inverse:

$$\lfloor\cdot\rfloor^{-1} = \lfloor\cdot\rfloor$$

The advantage of this unusual function definition for program inversion is that it makes it easier to deal with two sides of the same coin: the duplication of a value and the equality test. *This is one of our key observations*: the duplication of a value in a source program becomes an equality test in the inverse program, and vice versa. Also, we can deal with a call to this primitive function during inversion in exactly the same way as with a call to a user-defined function. From a programming perspective, multiple occurrences of a variable in a term or non-linear patterns can be implemented by this function (recall function *pack* in Fig. 3). The functionality provided by $\lfloor\cdot\rfloor$ can also be realized by traditional constructions (*e.g.*, a conditional with an equality [19]), but we found that this complicates the inversion rules and made this design choice.

The following diagram illustrates the duality of duplication and equality testing in forward and backward computation. Duplication implies that two variables have identical values; an equality test checks whether the values of two variables are identical and we can use a single variable instead.

$$\lfloor\langle x\rangle\rfloor = \langle x_1\ x_2\rangle \qquad\qquad \langle x\rangle = \lfloor\langle x_1\ x_2\rangle\rfloor$$

$$pack(s) \triangleq \textbf{case } s \textbf{ of}$$
$$[\,] \to [\,]$$
$$c_1 : r \to \textbf{case } pack(r) \textbf{ of}$$
$$[\,] \to \langle c_1\ 1 \rangle : [\,]$$
$$h : t \to \textbf{case } h \textbf{ of}$$
$$\langle c_2\ n \rangle \to \textbf{case } \lfloor \langle c_1\ c_2 \rangle \rfloor \textbf{ of}$$
$$\langle c \rangle \to \langle c\ S(n) \rangle : t$$
$$\langle c_1'\ c_2' \rangle \to \langle c_1'\ 1 \rangle : (\langle c_2'\ n \rangle : t)$$

Fig. 3. Program $pack$

$$pack^{-1}(w) \triangleq$$
$$\textbf{case } w \textbf{ of}$$
$$[\,] \to [\,]$$
$$x : y \to \textbf{case } x \textbf{ of}$$
$$\langle x_1\ x_2 \rangle \to \textbf{case } x_2 \textbf{ of}$$
$$1 \to \textbf{case } y \textbf{ of}$$
$$[\,] \to x_1 : pack^{-1}([\,])$$
$$o : t \to \textbf{case } o \textbf{ of}$$
$$\langle c_2'\ n \rangle \to \textbf{case } \lfloor \langle x_1\ c_2' \rangle \rfloor \textbf{ of}$$
$$\langle c_1\ c_2 \rangle \to c_1 : pack^{-1}(\langle c_2\ n \rangle : t)$$
$$S(n) \to \textbf{case } \lfloor \langle x_1 \rangle \rfloor \textbf{ of } \langle c_1\ c_2 \rangle \to c_1 : pack^{-1}(\langle c_2\ n \rangle : y)$$

Fig. 4. Program $pack^{-1}$

For example, in function $pack$ (Fig. 3) the equality of two adjacent symbols, c_1 and c_2, is tested in the innermost case-expression. In the last line of inverse function $pack^{-1}$ (Fig. 4), symbol x_1 is duplicated. The case of non-equality of two adjacent symbols in $pack$ corresponds to the case of non-equality in $pack^{-1}$. The assertion that those symbols are not equal is checked in forward and backward computation.

4   Challenges to Program Inversion

We now investigate two main challenges to automatic program inversion. Programs that satisfy the following two conditions are *well-formed for inversion* and our inversion method will always produce an inverse program.

The Inverse of a Conditional. The most challenging point in program inversion is the inversion of conditionals (here, case-expressions). To calculate the input from a given output, we must know which of the m branches in a case-expression the source program took to produce that output, since *only one* of the branches was executed in the forward calculation (our language is deterministic). To make this choice in an inverse program, we must know m postconditions, R_i, one for each branch, such that for each pair of postconditions, we have: $R_i \wedge R_j = false$ $(1 \leq i < j \leq m)$. This divides the set of output values into m disjoint sets, and we can choose the correct branch by testing the given output value using the postconditions.

Postconditions that are suitable for program inversion can be derived by hand (*e.g.*, [7,12]). In automatic program inversion they must be inferred from a source program. The program inverter KEinv [8] uses a heuristic method, and the language in which its postconditions are expressed consists of the primitive predicates available for the source language's value domain consisting of lists and integers. In general, there is no automatic method that would always find mutually exclusive postconditions, even if they exist.

Our value domain consists of constructors, and thus we decided to take a simpler approach. We formulate a criterion which can be checked locally for each function definition. We view the body of a function definition as a tree where the function head is the root, each case-expression corresponds to a node with branches, and the leaves of the tree are terms, l, consisting only of variables, constructors, and function calls. For example, in function *pack*, we have four leaves with the terms:

(a) $[\,]$ (c) $\langle c\ S(n)\rangle\!:\!t$

(b) $\langle c_1\ 1\rangle\!:\![\,]$ (d) $\langle c_1'\ 1\rangle\!:\!(\langle c_2'\ n\rangle\!:\!t)$

where (a) returns an empty list; (b) returns a non-empty list containing a single pair that has constructor 1 as its second component; (c) returns a non-empty list with a pair containing constructor $S(\_)$ as its second component, and (d) produces a list that is different from the values returned in (a–c). In short, all four branches in function *pack* return values that are pairwise disjoint. By performing pattern matching on an output value, we can decide from which of the four branches that value must have originated.

In addition to constructors and variables, a leaf term can contain function calls. For example, two leaf terms may be $A(f(B(x)))$ and $A(f(C(x)))$. Since we assume that all functions are injective, these two terms represent two different sets of values (an injective function f applied to two different input values returns two different output values). On the other hand, for leaf terms $A(f(B(x)))$ and $A(g(C(x)))$, we have not enough knowledge about f and g to decide whether their output values are different. We formalize the orthogonality test for the leaf terms of a function definition as follows:

(1) We require that, for each pair l and l' of leaf terms from different branches in a function, we have $\mathcal{P}[\![\,l,\ l'\,]\!] = \bot$. The test is defined as follows (ϵ denotes the identity substitution and for any substitution θ we have $\bot \circ \theta = \theta \circ \bot = \bot$):

$$\begin{aligned}
\mathcal{P}[\![\, x,\, x'\,]\!] &= \{x \mapsto x'\} \\
\mathcal{P}[\![\, f(l),\, f(l')\,]\!] &= \mathcal{P}[\![\, l,\, l'\,]\!] \\
\mathcal{P}[\![\, c(l_1 \dots l_n),\, c(l'_1 \dots l'_n)\,]\!] &= \mathcal{P}[\![\, l_1,\, l'_1\,]\!] \circ \cdots \circ \mathcal{P}[\![\, l_n,\, l'_n\,]\!] \\
\mathcal{P}[\![\, c(l_1 \dots l_n),\, c'(l'_1 \dots l'_m)\,]\!] &= \bot \quad \text{if } c \neq c' \\
\text{otherwise: } \mathcal{P}[\![\, l,\, l'\,]\!] &= \epsilon
\end{aligned}$$

Criterion (1) is a sufficient condition for a program to be injective if it applies to all functions defined in that program. If the postconditions of two branches are mutually exclusive, $\mathcal{P}[\![\, l,\, l'\,]\!] = \bot$, then the sets of values they return are disjoint. Otherwise, we cannot be sure. To be more discriminating when this test is not decisive, we examine terms at nodes closer to the root. This test is more involved. Criterion (1) is sufficient for all programs in this paper except for inverting the inverse function $pack^{-1}$, which requires a refinement of the criterion (to show that the last two branches of that function have mutually exclusive postconditions).

As motivating example, consider the case where the leaf terms of two branches 'unify' (here $\mathcal{P}[\![\, y,\, y'\,]\!] = \{y \mapsto y'\}$):

$$
\begin{aligned}
\text{(a)} \ \dots &\to \mathbf{case}\ f(\mathrm{A}(x))\ \mathbf{of}\ \mathrm{C}(y) \to y \\
\text{(b)} \ \dots &\to \mathbf{case}\ f(\mathrm{B}(x'))\ \mathbf{of}\ \mathrm{C}(y') \to y'
\end{aligned}
$$

We find that (a) and (b) have mutually exclusive postconditions (the values y and y' are different because f is assumed to be injective). To summarize, when criteria (1) fails, we also check terms computing values in corresponding positions. This test is a more involved due to nested case-expressions.

(1') Given the ith branch, let l_i be its leaf term and let S_i be the set of all pattern-argument pairs of case-expressions. Given the ith and jth branch, if $\mathcal{P}[\![\, l_i,\, l_j\,]\!] \neq \bot$, then perform the following check. The two branches have mutually exclusive postconditions if

$$\langle S_i, S_j, l_i, l_j, \mathcal{P}[\![\, l_i,\, l_j\,]\!] \rangle \overset{*}{\hookrightarrow} \langle S'_i, S'_j, l'_i, l'_j, \bot \rangle$$

where $\langle S_i, S_j, l_i, l_j, \theta \rangle \hookrightarrow \langle S_i \setminus \{\langle p\ l'_i \rangle\},\, S_j \setminus \{\langle p\theta\ l'_j \rangle\},\, l'_i, l'_j, \theta \circ \mathcal{P}[\![\, l'_i,\, l'_j\,]\!] \rangle$

if there exists p such that $\langle p\ l'_i \rangle \in S$ and $\langle p\theta\ l'_j \rangle \in S'$

For example, the 3rd and 4th branch in function $pack^{-1}$ have mutually exclusive postconditions because in one step with $\hookrightarrow$ we have $\mathcal{P}[\![\, \lfloor \langle x_1\ c'_2 \rangle \rfloor,\, \lfloor \langle x_1 \rangle \rfloor\,]\!] = \bot$:

$$\left\langle
\begin{array}{c}
\{ \dots, \langle \langle c_1\ c_2 \rangle\ \lfloor \langle x_1\ c'_2 \rangle \rfloor \rangle \},\ \{ \dots, \langle \langle c_1\ c_2 \rangle\ \lfloor \langle x_1 \rangle \rfloor \rangle \} \\
c_1 : pack^{-1}(\langle c_2\ n \rangle {:} t),\ c_1 : pack^{-1}(\langle c_2\ n \rangle {:} y) \\
\{ c_1 \mapsto c_1, c_2 \mapsto c_2, \dots \}
\end{array}
\right\rangle
\hookrightarrow
\left\langle
\begin{array}{c}
\{ \dots \},\ \{ \dots \} \\
\lfloor \langle x_1\ c'_2 \rangle \rfloor,\ \lfloor \langle x_1 \rangle \rfloor \\
\bot
\end{array}
\right\rangle$$

Dead Variables. Another challenging point in program inversion is when input values are discarded. Consider the selection function *first* defined by

$$first(x) \triangleq \textbf{case } x \textbf{ of } h{:}t \rightarrow h$$

Besides the fact that the function is not injective, the value of variable t is lost. When we invert such a program, we have to guess 'lost values'. In general, there are infinitely many possible guesses. The function may be invertible with respect to a precondition that ensures a constant value for t. Detecting suitable preconditions when values are lost is beyond the scope of our method. We adopted a straightforward solution which we call the "preservation of values" requirement.

(2) We require that each defined variable be used once in each branch.

Thus, a variable's value is always part of the output, and the only way to "diminish the amount of the output" is to reduce pairs into singletons by $\lfloor \langle t \; t' \rangle \rfloor$. But, in this case, no information is lost because both values need to be identical.

5   A Method for Program Inversion

We now present a method for the automatic inversion of programs that are well-formed for inversion. Our method uses logical formulas as internal representation. It consists of a frontend $\mathcal{A}[\![\, \cdot \,]\!]$ and a backend $\mathcal{Z}[\![\, \cdot \,]\!]$ that translate from a function to a formula and vice versa. Inversion $\mathcal{I}_0[\![\, \cdot \,]\!]$ itself is then performed on the formula by backward reading. To simplify inversion of a program, inversion is carried out on a formula, rather than on the source program. The structure of the program inverter is shown in Fig. 5. We now give its definition and explain each of its components in the remainder of this section.

Definition 1 (program inverter). *Let q be a program well-formed for inversion. Then* program inverter $[\![\cdot]\!]^{-1}_{pgm}$ *is defined by*

$$[\![q]\!]^{-1}_{pgm} \stackrel{\text{def}}{=} \{ [\![d]\!]^{-1} \mid d \in q \} \quad \textit{where} \quad [\![d]\!]^{-1} \stackrel{\text{def}}{=} \mathcal{Z}[\![\, \mathcal{I}_0[\![\, \mathcal{A}[\![\, d \,]\!] \,]\!] \,]\!]$$

5.1   Translating between Function and Formula

The translation of a function to a logical formula makes it easier to invert the function (other representations are possible). During the translation, each construction is decomposed into a formula. A formula ϕ is constructed from atomic formulas, conjunctions and disjunctions. An atomic formula a is either a predicate that marks a variable x as input $in(x)$ or as output $out(y)$, an equality representing a function call $f(x)=y$, a constructor application $c(x_1 \ldots x_n)=y$, or a pattern matching $x=c(y_1 \ldots y_n)$.

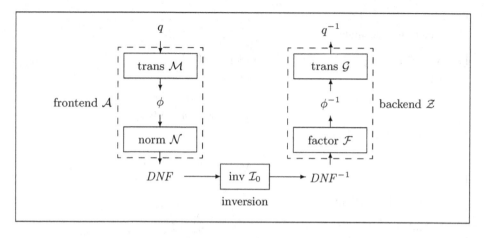

Fig. 5. Structure of the program inverter

$$\phi ::= \ a \ | \ \phi_1 \wedge \phi_2 \ | \ \phi_1 \vee \phi_2$$
$$a ::= \ \text{in}(x) \ | \ \text{out}(y) \ | \ f(x){=}y \ | \ c(x_1 \ldots x_n){=}y \ | \ x{=}c(y_1 \ldots y_n)$$

An atomic formula can be thought of as representing an 'atomic operation' (function call, constructor application, pattern matching). As a convention, the left-hand side of an equation is defined only in terms of input variables (here x) and the right-hand side is defined only in terms of output variables (here y). The intended forward reading of the equalities is from left to right. Atomic formulas are connected by conjunctions (representing a sequence of atomic operations), disjunctions (representing branches of a case-expression).

Definition 2 (frontend, backend). *Let d be a definition in a program well-formed for inversion. Then,* frontend $\mathcal{A}[\![\,\cdot\,]\!]$ *and* backend $\mathcal{Z}[\![\,\cdot\,]\!]$ *are defined by*

$$\mathcal{A}[\![\,d\,]\!] \stackrel{\text{def}}{=} \mathcal{N}_0[\![\,\mathcal{M}_0[\![\,d\,]\!]\,]\!]$$
$$\mathcal{Z}[\![\,d\,]\!] \stackrel{\text{def}}{=} \mathcal{G}_0[\![\,\mathcal{F}_0[\![\,d\,]\!]\,]\!]$$

Composition $\mathcal{Z}[\![\,\mathcal{A}[\![\,d\,]\!]\,]\!]$ returns the same definition modulo renaming of variables and reordering of nested case-expressions that do not depend on each other. The composition of the translations is a semantics-preserving transformation. The frontend and backend are conventional translators from functions to formulas, and vice versa.

For instance, the two steps of converting function *pack* to a formula are shown in Fig. 8 (to save space, commas (,) denote conjunctions). First, *pack* is converted into a nested formula by $\mathcal{M}_0[\![\,\cdot\,]\!]$. The formal parameter s is marked as input, $\text{in}(s)$, and the outermost case-expression is decomposed into a conjunction containing $s{=}[\,]$ and another containing $s{=}c_1 : r$. Further study of the formula

Function-to-formula:

$$\mathcal{M}_0[\![\, f(x) \triangleq t \,]\!] \qquad\qquad = \mathrm{in}(x) \wedge \mathcal{M}[\![\, t \,]\!]$$

$$\mathcal{M}[\![\, y \,]\!] \qquad\qquad\qquad = \mathrm{out}(y)$$

$$\mathcal{M}[\![\, e[\, f(x) \,] \,]\!] \qquad\qquad = f(x){=}\hat{y} \wedge \mathcal{M}[\![\, e[\, \hat{y} \,] \,]\!]$$

$$\mathcal{M}[\![\, e[\, c(x_1 \ldots x_n) \,] \,]\!] \qquad = c(x_1 \ldots x_n){=}\hat{y} \wedge \mathcal{M}[\![\, e[\, \hat{y} \,] \,]\!]$$

$$\mathcal{M}[\![\, e[\, \mathbf{case}\ x\ \mathbf{of}\ \{c_j(y_{j1} \ldots y_{jn_j}) \to t_j\}_{j=1}^m \,] \,]\!]$$

$$= \bigvee_{j=1}^m x{=}c_j(y_{j1} \ldots y_{jn_j}) \wedge \mathcal{M}[\![\, e[\, t_j \,] \,]\!]$$

Formula-to-function:

$$\mathcal{G}_0[\![\, \mathrm{in}(x) \wedge \phi \,]\!] \qquad\quad = f^{-1}(x) \triangleq \mathcal{G}[\![\, \phi \,]\!]$$

$$\mathcal{G}[\![\, \mathrm{out}(y) \,]\!] \qquad\qquad = y$$

$$\mathcal{G}[\![\, f(x){=}y \wedge \phi \,]\!] \qquad = \mathcal{G}[\![\, \phi \,]\!]\{y \mapsto f(x)\}$$

$$\mathcal{G}[\![\, c(x_1 \ldots x_n){=}y \wedge \phi \,]\!] = \mathcal{G}[\![\, \phi \,]\!]\{y \mapsto c(x_1 \ldots x_n)\}$$

$$\mathcal{G}[\![\, \bigvee_{j=1}^m x{=}c_j(x_{j1} \ldots x_{jn_j}) \wedge \phi_j \,]\!] = \mathbf{case}\ x\ \mathbf{of}\ \{c_j(x_{j1} \ldots x_{jn_j}) \to \mathcal{G}[\![\, \phi_j \,]\!]\}_{j=1}^m$$

Fig. 6. Translation from function to formula, and vice versa

reveals how other constructions in the program are represented by atomic formulas. Second, the formula is normalized into a disjunctive normal form by $\mathcal{N}_0[\![\, \cdot \,]\!]$. The original nesting is dissolved and all branches are 'parallel', separated only by a disjunction at the top level. Now each branch contains the entire path from the root $(\mathrm{in}(s))$ to the leaf (e.g., $\mathrm{out}(q)$). Note that several auxiliary variables had to be introduced because each construct was represented by several atomic formulas, e.g., variable b to connect the call $pack(r){=}b$ with the use of its result.

Translations. The two translations, $\mathcal{M}_0[\![\, \cdot \,]\!]$ and $\mathcal{G}_0[\![\, \cdot \,]\!]$, between a function and a formula are shown in Fig. 6. $\mathcal{M}_0[\![\, \cdot \,]\!]$ converts a function to a formula (using redex and evaluation context to decompose a term in accordance with its operational semantics; see Fig. 2) and $\mathcal{G}_0[\![\, \cdot \,]\!]$ translates a formula to a function. Nested constructor applications are decomposed into single constructor applications when they are converted into a formula (recall the definition of redex and evaluation context in Fig. 2). When converting a formula to a function, single constructor applications are nested. We use the notation $\hat{x}$ to denote a fresh variable; expression $t_1\{y \mapsto t_2\}$ denotes the result of replacing all occurrences of variable y in term t_1 by term t_2. Note that there is exactly one occurrence of variable y in term t_1 due to the fact that the source program is well-formed.

$$\mathcal{F}_0[\![\ \bigvee_{j=1}^{m} \mathrm{in}(x_j) \wedge \phi_j\ ]\!] \qquad = \mathrm{in}(\hat{x}) \wedge \mathcal{F}[\![\ \bigvee_{j=1}^{m} \phi_j\{x_j \mapsto \hat{x}\}\ ]\!]$$

$$\mathcal{F}[\![\ \mathrm{out}(y)\ ]\!] \qquad\qquad = \mathrm{out}(y)$$

$$\mathcal{F}[\![\ \bigvee_{j=1}^{m} f(x){=}y_j \wedge \phi_j\ ]\!] \qquad = f(x){=}\hat{y} \wedge \mathcal{F}[\![\ \bigvee_{j=1}^{m} \phi_j\{y_j \mapsto \hat{y}\}\ ]\!]$$

$$\mathcal{F}[\![\ \bigvee_{j=1}^{m} c(x_1 \dots x_n){=}y_j \wedge \phi_j\ ]\!] \quad = c(x_1 \dots x_n){=}\hat{y} \wedge \mathcal{F}[\![\ \bigvee_{j=1}^{m} \phi_j\{y_j \mapsto \hat{y}\}\ ]\!]$$

$$\mathcal{F}[\![\ \bigvee_{j=1}^{m} x{=}c_j(y_{j1} \dots y_{jn_j}) \wedge \phi_j\ ]\!] = \bigvee_{j=1}^{m'} x{=}c'_j(y'_{j1} \dots y'_{jn'_j}) \wedge \mathcal{F}[\![\ \phi'_j\ ]\!]$$

$$\text{where} \quad \bigvee_{j=1}^{m} x{=}c_j(y_{j1} \dots y_{jn_j}) \wedge \phi_j \stackrel{*}{\rightsquigarrow} \bigvee_{j=1}^{m'} x{=}c'_j(y'_{j1} \dots y'_{jn'_j}) \wedge \phi'_j$$

with $\rightsquigarrow$ to search for mutually exclusive postconditions:

$$(x{=}c(y_1 \dots y_n) \wedge \phi_1) \vee (x{=}c(y'_1 \dots y'_n) \wedge \phi_2) \vee \phi$$
$$\rightsquigarrow x{=}c(\hat{y}_1 \dots \hat{y}_n) \wedge (\phi_1\{y_i \mapsto \hat{y}_i\}_{i=1}^{n} \vee \phi_2\{y_i \mapsto \hat{y}_i\}_{i=1}^{n}) \vee \phi$$

Note: Left-side variables $(x, x_1, ...)$ must not occur in ϕ_j. Some of the c_j can be identical, but all c'_j are different. The order of atomic formulas in conjunctions is ignored.

Fig. 7. Factorization

Normalization. After translating a function to a formula, we convert the formula into its *disjunctive normal form* (DNF) by normalization $\mathcal{N}_0[\![\ \cdot\ ]\!]$. We can think of this as 'flattening' all nested case-expressions. This normalization of a logical formula is standard and not shown here. Recall that in the disjunctive normal form, all disjunctions are at the top level, connecting formulas consisting of conjunctions of atomic formulas. An example is shown in Fig. 8, where the formula obtained by translating function *pack* to a formula is converted to its disjunctive normal form.

Factorization. Before translating a formula to a function definition, we need to factor out common atomic formulas from disjunctions. This is necessary because patterns in case-expressions cannot be nested in our language. This reintroduces nested case-expressions in a program. The factorization $\mathcal{F}[\![\ \cdot\ ]\!]$ is shown in Fig. 7.

If all m disjunctions in a DNF contain a call to the same function $f(x){=}y_j$ using the same argument x, then we factor this call out of all m branches and replace all output variables y_j by the same fresh variable $\hat{y}$. Similarly, if all m disjunctions contain the constructor application $c(x_1 \dots x_n){=}y_j$. The most involved part is when we meet pattern matchings $x{=}c_j(y_{j1} \dots y_{jn_j})$. Here, some of the constructors c_j may be identical, and we only want to factor those common patterns out of the disjunctions. In Fig. 7, this is achieved by an auxiliary func-

1) Function-to-formula translation:

$$\mathrm{in}(s), \left(\begin{array}{l} s=[\,], \ [\,]=a, \ \mathrm{out}(a) \\ \vee \ s=c_1\!:\!r, \ pack(r)=b, \\ \qquad \left(\begin{array}{l} b=[\,], \ 1=e, \ \langle c_1\ e\rangle=f, \ [\,]=z, \ f\!:\!z=g, \ \mathrm{out}(g) \\ \vee \ b=h\!:\!t, \ h=\langle c_2\ n\rangle, \ \langle c_1\ c_2\rangle=u, \ \lfloor u\rfloor=v, \\ \qquad \left(\begin{array}{l} v=\langle c\rangle, \ \mathrm{S}(n)=i, \ \langle c\ i\rangle=j, \ j\!:\!t=k, \ \mathrm{out}(k) \\ \vee \ v=\langle c'_1\ c'_2\rangle, \ 1=l, \ \langle c'_1\ l\rangle=m, \ \langle c'_2\ n\rangle=o, \\ \qquad o\!:\!t=p, \ m\!:\!p=q, \ \mathrm{out}(q) \end{array}\right) \end{array}\right) \end{array}\right)$$

2) Disjunctive normal form:

$\mathrm{in}(s), \ s=[\,], \ [\,]=a, \ \mathrm{out}(a)$
$\vee \ \mathrm{in}(s), \ s=c_1\!:\!r, \ pack(r)=b, \ b=[\,], \ 1=e, \ \langle c_1\ e\rangle=f, \ [\,]=z, \ f\!:\!z=g, \ \mathrm{out}(g)$
$\vee \ \mathrm{in}(s), \ s=c_1\!:\!r, \ pack(r)=b, \ b=h\!:\!t, \ h=\langle c_2\ n\rangle, \ \langle c_1\ c_2\rangle=u, \ \lfloor u\rfloor=v, \ v=\langle c\rangle,$
$\quad \mathrm{S}(n)=i, \ \langle c\ i\rangle=j, \ j\!:\!t=k, \ \mathrm{out}(k)$
$\vee \ \mathrm{in}(s), \ s=c_1\!:\!r, \ pack(r)=b, \ b=h\!:\!t, \ h=\langle c_2\ n\rangle, \ \langle c_1\ c_2\rangle=u, \ \lfloor u\rfloor=v, \ v=\langle c'_1\ c'_2\rangle,$
$\quad 1=l, \ \langle c'_1\ l\rangle=m, \ \langle c'_2\ n\rangle=o, \ o\!:\!t=p, \ m\!:\!p=q, \ \mathrm{out}(q)$

3) Inversion:

$\mathrm{out}(s), \ [\,]=s, \ a=[\,], \ \mathrm{in}(a)$
$\vee \ \mathrm{out}(s), \ c_1\!:\!r=s, \ pack^{-1}(b)=r, \ [\,]=b, \ e=1, \ f=\langle c_1\ e\rangle, \ z=[\,], \ g=f\!:\!z, \ \mathrm{in}(g)$
$\vee \ \mathrm{out}(s), \ c_1\!:\!r=s, \ pack^{-1}(b)=r, \ h\!:\!t=b, \ \langle c_2\ n\rangle=h, \ u=\langle c_1\ c_2\rangle, \ \lfloor v\rfloor=u,$
$\quad \langle c\rangle=v, \ i=\mathrm{S}(n), \ j=\langle c\ i\rangle, \ k=j\!:\!t, \ \mathrm{in}(k)$
$\vee \ \mathrm{out}(s), \ c_1\!:\!r=s, \ pack^{-1}(b)=r, \ h\!:\!t=b, \ \langle c_2\ n\rangle=h, \ u=\langle c_1\ c_2\rangle, \ \lfloor v\rfloor=u,$
$\quad \langle c'_1\ c'_2\rangle=v, \ l=1, \ m=\langle c'_1\ l\rangle, \ o=\langle c'_2\ n\rangle, \ p=o\!:\!t, \ q=m\!:\!p, \ \mathrm{in}(q)$

4) Factorization:

$$\mathrm{in}(w), \left(\begin{array}{l} w=[\,], \ [\,]=s, \ \mathrm{out}(s) \\ \vee \ w=x\!:\!y, \ x=\langle x_1\ x_2\rangle, \\ \qquad \left(\begin{array}{l} x_2=1, \ \left(\begin{array}{l} y=[\,], \ [\,]=b, \ pack^{-1}(b)=r, \ x_1\!:\!r=s, \ \mathrm{out}(s) \\ \vee \ y=o\!:\!t, \ o=\langle c'_2\ n\rangle, \ \langle x_1\ c'_2\rangle=v, \ \lfloor v\rfloor=u, \\ \quad u=\langle c_1\ c_2\rangle, \ \langle c_2\ n\rangle=h, \ h\!:\!t=b, \\ \quad pack^{-1}(b)=r, \ c_1\!:\!r=s, \ \mathrm{out}(s) \end{array}\right) \\ \vee \ x_2=\mathrm{S}(n), \ \langle x_1\rangle=v, \ \lfloor v\rfloor=u, \ u=\langle c_1\ c_2\rangle, \ \langle c_2\ n\rangle=h, \\ \quad h\!:\!y=b, \ pack^{-1}(b)=r, \ c_1\!:\!r=s, \ \mathrm{out}(s) \end{array}\right) \end{array}\right)$$

Fig. 8. Translation, normalization, backward reading, and factorization of *pack*

$$
\begin{array}{ll}
\mathcal{I}_0[\![\ \bigvee_{j=1}^{m} \phi_j\ ]\!] \;=\; \bigvee_{j=1}^{m} \mathcal{I}_1[\![\ \phi_j\ ]\!] &
\begin{aligned}
\mathcal{I}[\![\ \mathrm{in}(x)\ ]\!] &= \mathrm{out}(x)\\
\mathcal{I}[\![\ \mathrm{out}(y)\ ]\!] &= \mathrm{in}(y)\\
\mathcal{I}[\![\ f(x){=}y\ ]\!] &= f^{-1}(y){=}x\\
\end{aligned}\\[6pt]
\mathcal{I}_1[\![\ \bigwedge_{j=1}^{m} \phi_j\ ]\!] \;=\; \bigwedge_{j=1}^{m} \mathcal{I}[\![\ \phi_j\ ]\!] &
\begin{aligned}
\mathcal{I}[\![\ c(x_1\ldots x_n){=}y\ ]\!] &= y{=}c(x_1\ldots x_n)\\
\mathcal{I}[\![\ x{=}c(y_1\ldots y_n)\ ]\!] &= c(y_1\ldots y_n){=}x
\end{aligned}
\end{array}
$$

Fig. 9. Inversion: backward reading

tion. These steps are repeated until all common atomic formulas are factored out of the disjunctions. This prepares for the construction of the inverse program. An example of factorization can be seen in Fig. 8. For instance, the matchings $l{=}1$ and $e{=}1$ contained in the second and fourth conjunctions, respectively, could be factored out into $x_2{=}1$. In the inverse program $pack^{-1}$, this becomes one of the patterns in a case-expression (Fig. 4). An inspection of the example reveals similar correspondences and factorizations.

5.2   Inversion by Backward Reading

Atomic formulas are easily inverted by reading the intended meaning backwards. The idea of 'backward reading' programs can be found in [7,12]. We follow this method for atomic formulas. The rules for our formula representation are shown in Fig. 9. The inverse of $\mathrm{in}(x)$ is $\mathrm{out}(x)$ and vice versa; the inverse of function call $f(x){=}y$ is $f^{-1}(y){=}x$; the inverse of constructor application $c(x_1\ldots x_n){=}y$ is pattern matching $y{=}c(x_1\ldots x_n)$ and vice versa. As we recall from Sect. 2, a convenient detail is that primitive function $\lfloor\cdot\rfloor$ is its own inverse: $\lfloor\cdot\rfloor^{-1} = \lfloor\cdot\rfloor$. Thus, we can write the inverse of $\lfloor x\rfloor{=}y$ immediately as $\lfloor y\rfloor{=}x$. Observe that the inversion performs no unfold/fold on functions. It terminates on all formulas. We see that global inversion of a program is based on the local invertibility of atomic formulas (also called 'compositional program inversion').

The result of backward reading the normal form is shown in Fig. 8. Compare the disjunctive normal form of function $pack$ before and after the transformation. The order of atomic formulas is unchanged, their order does not matter in a conjunction, but each atomic formula is inverted according to the rules in Fig. 9. For instance, $pack(r){=}b$ becomes $pack^{-1}(b){=}r$. According to our convention, input and output variables switched sides. The treatment of calls to recursive functions is surprisingly easy.

After the backward reading, the formula is converted into a program by $\mathcal{Z}[\![\ \cdot\ ]\!]$. Inversion was successful; the inverse program $pack^{-1}$ is shown in Fig. 4. We have automatically produced an unpack function from a pack function. For instance, to unpack a packed symbol list: $pack^{-1}([\langle A\ 2\rangle\langle B\ 1\rangle\langle C\ 3\rangle]) = [AABCCC]$.

5.3   Termination, Correctness, and Non-degradation

Program inverter $[\![q]\!]^{-1}_{pgm}$ terminates on every program q that is well-formed for inversion. It is easy to see by structural induction that each of the transformations terminates (frontend, inversion, backend) for all its respective inputs (function, formula). The correctness of the transformation follows from the correctness of the frontend and backend, and the correctness of the backward reading.

Due to our particular method of inverting programs, inverse programs have the following property: if the program takes n steps to compute an output value y from an input value x, then the inverse program takes n steps to compute x from y. The downside of this property is that our inverse programs are never faster; the upside is that the efficiency is never degraded. This is only the case for our inversion method because we perform no unfold/fold steps (it does not hold for program inversion in general).

To see this, we examine the inversion of formulas. We assume that the computation of each atomic formula requires one unit of time. The inversion rules only redirect the intended computation; they neither add nor omit atomic operations. All source programs are injective, which means that the backward computation has to follow the reversed path of the forward computation to produce the input from the output. There is no unfold/fold or generalization that could shorten or extend a computation path. The translation in the frontend and in the backend does not add or omit operations. Thus, the computation path of forward and backward computation are identical.

6   More Examples

This section shows more examples of automatic program inversion using our method. Consider the following three examples.

(1) The first example is the inversion of a program containing two function definitions (Fig. 10). Function *fib* computes two neighboring Fibonacci numbers. For example, $\mathit{fib}(0) = \langle 1\ 1\rangle$, $\mathit{fib}(1) = \langle 1\ 2\rangle$, $\mathit{fib}(2) = \langle 2\ 3\rangle$, and so on. The definition of *fib* is injective. Function *plus* is defined by $\mathit{plus}(\langle x\ y\rangle) = \langle x\ x + y\rangle$. Duplication and equality tests are realized by $\lfloor \cdot \rfloor$. As usual, integers are represented by unary numbers. Automatic inversion of both functions is successful and produces the two inverse functions fib^{-1} and plus^{-1} (Fig. 10). For instance, we can now compute $\mathit{fib}^{-1}(\langle 34\ 55\rangle) = 8$ and $\mathit{plus}^{-1}(\langle 3\ 5\rangle) = \langle 3\ 2\rangle$.

(2) The second example is the inversion of function *mir* which appends to an input list the reversed input list (Fig. 11). For instance, $\mathit{mir}(\mathrm{ABC}) = \mathrm{ABCCBA}$. The auxiliary function *tailcons* appends a value at the end of a list. If we assume that the inverse of *tailcons*, $\mathit{tailcons}^{-1}$, is given, automatic inversion is successful. It produces function mir^{-1} (Fig. 11). Therefore, to undo the mirroring operation, we can use $\mathit{mir}^{-1}(\mathrm{ABCCBA}) = \mathrm{ABC}$. The function is undefined when applied to an incorrect input, *e.g.*, $\mathit{mir}^{-1}(\mathrm{ACBA})$.

(3) Finally, all four inverse programs (pack^{-1}, fib^{-1}, plus^{-1}, mir^{-1}) can be inverted again and we get their original definitions back (modulo renaming of

$$\begin{aligned}
fib(x) \quad &\triangleq \textbf{case } x \textbf{ of } 0 \to \lfloor \langle 1 \rangle \rfloor \\
&\qquad\qquad S(y) \to \textbf{case } fib(y) \textbf{ of} \\
&\qquad\qquad\qquad\qquad \langle u\ v \rangle \to \textbf{case } plus(\langle v\ u \rangle) \textbf{ of } \langle w\ z \rangle \to \lfloor \langle w\ z \rangle \rfloor \\[4pt]
fib^{-1}(a) \quad &\triangleq \textbf{case } \lfloor a \rfloor \textbf{ of} \\
&\qquad \langle b \rangle \to \textbf{case } b \textbf{ of } 1 \to 0 \\
&\qquad \langle w\ z \rangle \to \textbf{case } plus^{-1}(\langle w\ z \rangle) \textbf{ of } \langle v\ u \rangle \to S(fib^{-1}(\langle u\ v \rangle)) \\[4pt]
plus(z) \quad &\triangleq \textbf{case } z \textbf{ of} \\
&\qquad \langle x\ y \rangle \to \textbf{case } y \textbf{ of } 0 \to \lfloor \langle x \rangle \rfloor \\
&\qquad\qquad\qquad\qquad S(w) \to \textbf{case } plus(\langle x\ w \rangle) \textbf{ of } \langle u\ v \rangle \to \lfloor \langle u\ S(v) \rangle \rfloor \\[4pt]
plus^{-1}(h) \quad &\triangleq \textbf{case } \lfloor h \rfloor \textbf{ of } \langle x \rangle \to \langle x\ 0 \rangle \\
&\qquad\qquad\qquad\qquad \langle u\ e \rangle \to \textbf{case } e \textbf{ of} \\
&\qquad\qquad\qquad\qquad\qquad S(v) \to \textbf{case } plus^{-1}(\langle u\ v \rangle) \textbf{ of } \langle x\ w \rangle \to \langle x\ S(w) \rangle
\end{aligned}$$

Fig. 10. Functions fib and $plus$ and their inverse functions

$$\begin{aligned}
mir(x) \quad &\triangleq \textbf{case } x \textbf{ of } [\,] \to [\,] \\
&\qquad\qquad h{:}t \to \textbf{case } \lfloor \langle h \rangle \rfloor \textbf{ of } \langle h_1\ h_2 \rangle \to h_1{:}tailcons(\langle mir(t), h_2 \rangle) \\[4pt]
mir^{-1}(g) \quad &\triangleq \textbf{case } g \textbf{ of } [\,] \to [\,] \\
&\qquad\qquad h_1{:}e \to \textbf{case } tailcons^{-1}(e) \textbf{ of} \\
&\qquad\qquad\qquad \langle c, h_2 \rangle \to \textbf{case } \lfloor \langle h_1\ h_2 \rangle \rfloor \textbf{ of } \langle h \rangle \to h{:}mir^{-1}(c)
\end{aligned}$$

Fig. 11. Function mir and its inverse function

variables and reordering of nested case-expressions).

A limitation of the present method is the lack of postcondition heuristics that can use global information about the output of a function. For example, using the well-formed criteria from Sect. 4, function $tailcons$ is not well-formed for inversion because criterion (1) is not enough to show that the output sets are different (the first branch is a singleton list; the second branch returns a list with at least two elements since $tailcons$ always returns a non-empty list). Owing to the postcondition heuristics in KEinv, $tailcons$ can be inverted with KEinv, while we cannot perform this inversion. This leaves room for future work.

$$\begin{aligned}
tailcons(a) \quad &\triangleq \textbf{case } a \textbf{ of} \\
&\qquad \langle x\ y \rangle \to \textbf{case } x \textbf{ of } [\,] \to y{:}[\,] \\
&\qquad\qquad\qquad\qquad u{:}v \to u{:}tailcons(\langle v\ y \rangle)
\end{aligned}$$

Similarly, tail-recursive functions are not well-formed according to criterion (1) in Sect. 4 because one of the branches contains only a function call, while other branches will contain variables or constructors. For example, the tail-recursive version of function *reverse* can not be inverted with the present method. This requires a non-local criterion for testing invertibility.

7 Related Work

The method presented in this paper is based on the principle of global inversion based on local invertibility [7,12]. The work was inspired by KEinv [14,8]. In contrast to KEinv, our method can successfully deal with equality and duplication of variables. Most studies on functional languages and program inversion have involved program inversion by hand (*e.g.*, [16]). They may be more powerful at the price of automation. This is the usual trade-off. Inversion based on Refal graphs [18,11,20,17] is related to the present method in that both use atomic operations for inversion; a more detailed comparison will be a topic of future work. An algorithm for inverse computation can be found in [1,2]. It performs inverse computation also on programs that are not injective.

8 Conclusion

We presented a method suited for automatic program inversion in a functional language with constructors and equality. A key observation was that value duplication and equality are two sides of the same coin in program inversion. Based on this observation, we introduced a self-inverse primitive function that simplifies the inversion considerably. We introduced well-formedness for inversion based on orthogonal output domains. To simplify inversion of a program, inversion is carried out on the disjunctive normal form of a logical formula representing atomic operations in our languages, rather than on the source language. The inversion method is split into a frontend and backend and inversion proper. This clean and modular structure of the inversion makes it easy to verify the correctness of our method.

Tasks for future work include the refinement of our well-formedness criteria. We have seen two examples where it excluded a program that could be inverted by other methods. We have presented our method using a small functional language and based on several simplifying assumptions, but we believe that our results can be ported to other functional languages, such as Lisp, at the price of somewhat more involved inversion rules. We have not included integer arithmetic and have represented integers by unary numbers. This worked surprisingly well, for example, for inverting a version of Fibonacci numbers. However, adding arithmetic will make our method more practical. A possible extension might involve constraint systems for which well-established theories exist.

Acknowledgements. We are grateful to Alberto Pettorossi and Maurizio Proietti for valuable comments on an earlier version of our inversion method. The example of Fibonacci inversion and other technical improvements are a result of these discussions. Thanks to the anonymous reviewers for their feedback.

References

1. S. M. Abramov, R. Glück. Principles of inverse computation and the universal resolving algorithm. In T. Æ. Mogensen, D. Schmidt, I. H. Sudborough (eds.), *The Essence of Computation: Complexity, Analysis, Transformation*, LNCS 2566, 269–295. Springer-Verlag, 2002.
2. S. M. Abramov, R. Glück. The universal resolving algorithm and its correctness: inverse computation in a functional language. *Science of Computer Programming*, 43(2-3):193–229, 2002.
3. R. Bird, O. de Moor. *Algebra of Programming*. Prentice Hall International Series in Computer Science. Prentice Hall, 1997.
4. J. S. Briggs. Generating reversible programs. *Software Practice and Experience*, 17:439–453, 1987.
5. C. D. Carothers, K. S. Perumalla, R. M. Fujimoto. Efficient optimistic parallel simulations using reverse computation. *ACM TOMACS*, 9(3):224–253, 1999.
6. J. Darlington. An experimental program transformation and synthesis system. *Artificial Intelligence*, 16(1):1–46, 1981.
7. E. W. Dijkstra. Program inversion. In F. L. Bauer, M. Broy (eds.), *Program Construction: International Summer School*, LNCS 69, 54–57. Springer-Verlag, 1978.
8. D. Eppstein. A heuristic approach to program inversion. In *Int. Joint Conference on Artificial Intelligence (IJCAI-85)*, 219–221. Morgan Kaufmann, Inc., 1985.
9. R. Glück, Y. Kawada, T. Hashimoto. Transforming interpreters into inverse interpreters by partial evaluation. In *Proceedings of the ACM Workshop on Partial Evaluation and Semantics-Based Program Manipulation*, 10–19. ACM Press, 2003.
10. R. Glück, A. V. Klimov. Metacomputation as a tool for formal linguistic modeling. In R. Trappl (ed.), *Cybernetics and Systems '94*, Vol. 2, 1563–1570. World Scientific, 1994.
11. R. Glück, V. F. Turchin. Application of metasystem transition to function inversion and transformation. In *Proceedings of the Int. Symposium on Symbolic and Algebraic Computation (ISSAC'90)*, 286–287. ACM Press, 1990.
12. D. Gries. *The Science of Programming*, chapter 21 Inverting Programs, 265–274. Texts and Monographs in Computer Science. Springer-Verlag, 1981.
13. H. Khoshnevisan, K. M. Sephton. InvX: An automatic function inverter. In N. Dershowitz (ed.), *Rewriting Techniques and Applications. Proceedings*, LNCS 355, 564–568. Springer-Verlag, 1989.
14. R. E. Korf. Inversion of applicative programs. In *Int. Joint Conference on Artificial Intelligence (IJCAI-81)*, 1007–1009. William Kaufmann, Inc., 1981.
15. G. B. Leeman. A formal approach to undo operations in programming languages. *ACM TOPLAS*, 8(1):50–97, 1986.
16. S.-C. Mu, R. Bird. Inverting functions as folds. In E. A. Boiten, B. Möller (eds.), *Mathematics of Program Construction. Proceedings*, LNCS 2386, 209–232. Springer-Verlag, 2002.
17. A. P. Nemytykh, V. A. Pinchuk. Program transformation with metasystem transitions: experiments with a supercompiler. In D. Bjørner, M. Broy, I. V. Pottosin (eds.), *Perspectives of System Informatics. Proceedings*, LNCS 1181, 249–260. Springer-Verlag, 1996.

18. A. Y. Romanenko. Inversion and metacomputation. In *Proceedings of the ACM Symposium on Partial Evaluation and Semantics-Based Program Manipulation*, 12–22. ACM Press, 1991.
19. M. H. Sørensen, R. Glück, N. D. Jones. A positive supercompiler. *Journal of Functional Programming*, 6(6):811–838, 1996.
20. V. F. Turchin. Program transformation with metasystem transitions. *Journal of Functional Programming*, 3(3):283–313, 1993.

Rebuilding a Tree from Its Traversals:
A Case Study of Program Inversion

Shin-Cheng Mu[1] and Richard Bird[2]

[1] Information Processing Lab, Dep. of Math. Informatics, University of Tokyo, 7-3-1
Hongo, Bunkyo-ku, Tokyo 113-8656, Japan
[2] Programming Research Group, University of Oxford, Wolfson Building, Parks
Road, Oxford OX1 3QD, UK

Abstract. Given the inorder and preorder traversal of a binary tree
whose labels are all distinct, one can reconstruct the tree. This article
examines two existing algorithms for rebuilding the tree in a functional
framework, using existing theory on function inversion. We also present
a new, although complicated, algorithm by trying another possibility not
explored before.

1 Introduction

It is well known that, given the inorder and preorder traversal of a binary tree
whose labels are all distinct, one can reconstruct the tree uniquely. The problem
has been recorded in [10, Sect. 2.3.1, Exercise 7] as an exercise; Knuth briefly
described why it can be done and commented that it "would be an interesting
exercise" to write a program for the task. Indeed, it has become a classic problem
to tackle for those who study program inversion. For example, see [5,15].

All of the above work on the problem is based on program inversion in an
imperative style. As van de Snepscheut noted in [15], one class of solutions attempts to invert an iterative algorithm, while the other class delivers a recursive
algorithm. In this article we will look at the problem in a functional style, and
attempt to derive these algorithms using existing theory on function inversion.

2 Problem Specification

To formalise the problem, consider internally labelled binary trees defined by
the following datatype:

data $Tree\ \alpha = Null\ |\ Node\ (\alpha,\ Tree\ \alpha,\ Tree\ \alpha)$

Inorder and preorder traversal on the trees can then be defined as:

$$
\begin{aligned}
&preorder, inorder &&:: Tree\ \alpha \to [\alpha] \\
&preorder\ Null &&= [\,] \\
&preorder\ (Node\ (a, u, v)) &&= [a] \mathbin{+\!\!+} preorder\ u \mathbin{+\!\!+} preorder\ v \\
&inorder\ Null &&= [\,] \\
&inorder\ (Node\ (a, u, v)) &&= inorder\ u \mathbin{+\!\!+} [a] \mathbin{+\!\!+} inorder\ v
\end{aligned}
$$

A. Ohori (Ed.): APLAS 2003, LNCS 2895, pp. 265–282, 2003.
© Springer-Verlag Berlin Heidelberg 2003

Define *pinorder* to be the function returning both the preorder and inorder of a tree:

$$pinorder :: Tree\,\alpha \rightarrow ([\alpha], [\alpha])$$
$$pinorder = fork\,(preorder, inorder)$$

where $fork\,(f, g)\,a = (f\,a, g\,a)$. The task involves constructing the inverse of *pinorder*. But what exactly does *the inverse* mean?

A function $f :: \alpha \rightarrow \beta$ has inverse $f^{-1} :: \beta \rightarrow \alpha$ if for all $a :: \alpha$ and $b :: \beta$ we have[1]:

$$f\,a = b \equiv f^{-1}\,b = a$$

This definition implies that f^{-1} is also a (possibly partial) function, a restriction which we will relax in Sect. 4.1. This function f^{-1} exists if and only if f is an injection – that is, for all b there exists at most one a such that $f\,a = b$. For instance, id, the identity function, is inverse to itself. In the case of *pinorder*, its inverse exists only when we restrict the domain of input trees to those containing no duplicated labels. To be more formal, we should have included this constraint as a predicate in the definition of *pinorder*. To reduce the amount of details, however, we will allow a bit of hands waving and assume that *pinorder* is a partial function taking only trees with labels all distinct.

3   The Compositional Approach

Most published work on program inversion is based on what we call the *compositional approach*, be it procedural [6,7,5,16,15,14] or functional [8]. The basic strategy, from a functional perspective, is to exploit various distributivity laws. In particular, provided that f^{-1} and g^{-1} both exist, we have that

$$(f \cdot g)^{-1} = g^{-1} \cdot f^{-1} \tag{1}$$

and that

$$(f \cup g)^{-1} = f^{-1} \cup g^{-1} \tag{2}$$

if f and g have disjoint ranges. Here the $\cup$ operator denotes set union, if we see a function as a set of pairs of input and output. A function defined in many clauses can be seen as the union of the separate clauses. Defining the product operator on pairs of functions to be:

$$(f \times g)\,(a, b) = (f\,a, g\,b)$$

(which generalises to triples in the obvious way), we also have that inverses distribute into products:

$$(f \times g)^{-1} = (f^{-1} \times g^{-1}) \tag{3}$$

---

[1] The symbol $\equiv$ is read "if and only if".

Finally, we have $(f^{-1})^{-1} = f$ and $id^{-1} = id$. In order to compute f^{-1}, the compositional approach to function inversion starts with expanding the definition of f and try to push the inverse operator to the leaves of the expression. The process continues until we reach some primitive whose inverse is either predefined or trivial. With this approach, a sequentially composed program is "run backwards". The challenging part is when we encounter conditionals, in such cases we have somehow to decide which branch the result was from. This is the approach we will try in this section.

3.1   Unfolding a Tree

Standard transformations yield the following recursive definition of *pinorder*:

$$pinorder\ Null \qquad\qquad = ([\,],[\,])$$
$$pinorder\ (Node(a,x,y)) = pi\,(a,pinorder\ x,pinorder\ y)$$
$$\textbf{where}\ \ pi\ ::\ (\alpha,([\alpha],[\alpha]),([\alpha],[\alpha])) \rightarrow ([\alpha],[\alpha])$$
$$pi\,(a,(x_1,y_1),(x_2,y_2))\ =\ ([a] \mathbin{+\!\!+} x_1 \mathbin{+\!\!+} x_2, y_1 \mathbin{+\!\!+} [a] \mathbin{+\!\!+} y_2)$$

Notice first that the two clauses of *pinorder* have disjoint ranges – the second clause always generates pairs of non-empty lists. According to (2), to construct the inverse of *pinorder* we can invert the two clauses separately and join them together. The first clause can simply be inverted to a partial function taking $([\,],[\,])$ to *Null*. The second clause of *pinorder* can also be written in point-free style as

$$pi \cdot (a \times pinorder \times pinorder) \cdot Node^{-1}$$

where $Node^{-1}$ corresponds to pattern matching. Its inverse, according to (1) and (3), is

$$Node \cdot (a \times pinorder^{-1} \times pinorder^{-1}) \cdot pi^{-1}$$

We can invert *pinorder* if we can invert *pi*. In summary, define:

$$rebuild\,([\,],[\,]) = Null$$
$$rebuild\,(x,y)\ = (Node \cdot (id \times rebuild \times rebuild) \cdot pi^{-1})\,(x,y)$$

The function *rebuild* is the inverse of *pinorder* if pi^{-1} exists.

Note that the wish that pi^{-1} exists is a rather strong one. Every injective function f has a functional inverse f^{-1}. As we shall see in Sect. 4.1, however, it is possible that a non-injective function f does not have a functional inverse, but its *converse*, the notion of inverse generalised to relations, reduces to a function after being composed with something else. In the particular case here, however, *pi* does have a functional inverse if its domain is restricted to triples $(a,(x_1,y_1),(x_2,y_2))$ where a does not present in either y_1 or y_2, and that the length of x_i equals y_i for $i \in \{1,2\}$ (it can be proved inductively that it is indeed the case in the usage of *pi* in *pinorder* if the input tree has distinct labels). Such a partial function *pi* has as its inverse:

$$pi^{-1}\,(a:x,y) = (a,(x_1,y_1),(x_2,y_2))$$
$$\textbf{where}\ \ y_1 \mathbin{+\!\!+} [a] \mathbin{+\!\!+} y_2 = y$$
$$x_1 \mathbin{+\!\!+}_{(len\ y_1)} x_2 = x$$

where the pattern $x_1 \mathbin{+\!\!+}_n x_2 = x$ splits into two such that x_1 has length n. Haskell programmers would have written $(x_1, x_2) = \textit{splitAt } n\, x$.

This is how in [10] Knuth explained why indeed the tree can be uniquely constructed. However, a naive implementation would result in a cubic time algorithm, because searching for an a in y and splitting x are both linear-time operations. In the next sections we will remove this linear-time overhead by a common functional program derviation technique.

3.2   Eliminating Repeated Traversals

Directly implementing *rebuild* as defined in the last section results in a slow algorithm because the input lists are repeatedly traversed. For example, the list x is split into x_1 and x_2. This requires traversing x from the front. In the next level of recursion, however, x_1 will also be split into two, and the prefix of x is thus traversed again.

It is a common technique in functional program derivation to reorder the splitting of lists such that the repeated traversal can be avoided by introducing extra outputs and exploiting the associativity of $\mathbin{+\!\!+}$. Define *reb* as a partial function on non-empty x and y as:

$$\textit{reb } a\, (x, y) = (\textit{rebuild } (x_1, y_1), x_2, y_2)$$
$$\textbf{where } y_1 \mathbin{+\!\!+} [a] \mathbin{+\!\!+} y_2 = y$$
$$x_1 \mathbin{+\!\!+}_{(\textit{len } y_1)} x_2 = x$$

The aim now is to derive a recursive definition for *reb*. The case when y starts with a is relatively simple:

$$\textit{reb } a\, (x, a : y)$$
$$= \quad \{\text{by definition, since } [] \mathbin{+\!\!+} [a] \mathbin{+\!\!+} y = a : y\}$$
$$(\textit{rebuild } ([], []), x, y)$$
$$= \quad \{\text{by definition of } \textit{rebuild}\}$$
$$(\textit{Null}, x, y)$$

For the general case, we derive:

$$\textit{reb } a\, (b : x, y)$$
$$= \quad \{\text{by definition, let } y_1 \mathbin{+\!\!+} [a] \mathbin{+\!\!+} y_2 = y$$
$$\text{and } x_1 \mathbin{+\!\!+}_{(\textit{len } y_1)} x_2 = x\}$$
$$(\textit{rebuild } (b : x_1, y_1), x_2, y_2)$$
$$= \quad \{\text{by definition of } \textit{rebuild}, \text{ let } y_3 \mathbin{+\!\!+} [b] \mathbin{+\!\!+} y_4 = y_1$$
$$\text{and } x_3 \mathbin{+\!\!+}_{(\textit{len } y_3)} x_4 = x_1\}$$
$$(\textit{Node } (b, \textit{rebuild } (x_3, y_3), \textit{rebuild } (x_4, y_4)), x_2, y_2)$$
$$= \quad \{\text{since } y_3 \mathbin{+\!\!+} [b] \mathbin{+\!\!+} (y_4 \mathbin{+\!\!+} [a] \mathbin{+\!\!+} y_2) = y$$
$$\text{and } x_3 \mathbin{+\!\!+}_{(\textit{len } y_3)} (x_4 \mathbin{+\!\!+} x_2) = x; \text{ we have}$$
$$(t_3, x_4 \mathbin{+\!\!+} x_2, y_4 \mathbin{+\!\!+} [a] \mathbin{+\!\!+} y_2) = \textit{reb } b\, (x, y) \text{ for some } t_3\}$$

$$(Node\ (b, t_3, rebuild\ (x_4, y_4)), x_2, y_2)$$
$$=\quad \{\text{let}\ (t_4, x_2, y_2) = reb\ a\ (x_4 + \!\!\!+ x_2, y_4 + \!\!\!+ [a] + \!\!\!+ y_2)\}$$
$$(Node\ (b, t_3, t_4), x_2, y_2)$$

Denoting $x_4 + \!\!\!+ x_2$ by x_5 and $y_4 + \!\!\!+ [a] + \!\!\!+ y_2$ by y_5, we have just derived the following recursive definition of reb:

$$reb\ a\ (x, a : y) = (Null, x, y)$$
$$reb\ a\ (b : x, y) = \textbf{let}\ (t_3, x_5, y_5) = reb\ b\ (x, y)$$
$$(t_4, x_2, y_2) = reb\ a\ (x_5, y_5)$$
$$\textbf{in}\ \ (Node\ (b, t_3, t_4), x_2, y_2)$$

The use of duplicated as in the first pattern is non-standard. In Haskell we would need an explicit equality test.

To be complete, we still need to work out a definition of *rebuild* in term of *reb*. Since *reb* is defined on non-empty input only, we deal with the empty case separately:

$$rebuild\ ([], []) = Null$$

For the non-empty case, the following equivalence is trivial to verify:

$$rebuild\ (a : x, y) = \textbf{let}\ (t_1, x', y') = reb\ a\ (x, y)$$
$$t_2 = rebuild\ (x', y')$$
$$\textbf{in}\ \ Node\ (a, t_1, t_2)$$

A Haskell implementation of the algorithm is given in Fig. 1. We have actually reinvented the recursive algorithm in [15] in a functional style. In the next section, we will continue to see how the other, iterative, class of algorithms can be derived functionally.

```
data Tree a = Null | Node a (Tree a) (Tree a) deriving Show

rebuild :: Eq a => ([a],[a]) -> Tree a
rebuild ([],[]) = Null
rebuild (a:x, y) = let (t, x', y')   = reb a (x,y)
                   in Node a t (rebuild (x',y'))

reb :: Eq a => a -> ([a],[a]) -> (Tree a,[a],[a])
reb a (x@(~(b:x1)),y)
 | head y == a  =  (Null, x, tail y)
 | otherwise    =  let (t1, x', y')   = reb b (x1, y)
                       (t2, x'', y'') = reb a (x', y')
                   in (Node b t1 t2, x'', y'')
```

Fig. 1. Haskell code implementing $pinorder^{-1}$.

4   Two Folding Algorithms

In Sect. 3, we started from the original program, and constructed a program in one go that builds a tree having both the specified inorder and preorder traversal. The expressiveness of relations, on the other hand, allows us to deal with the problem in a more modular way. In this section we will try a different approach, by first constructing a non-deterministic program that builds a tree with the specified inorder traversal, and then refine the program such that it generates only the tree with the required preorder traversal.

To talk about a program that *non-deterministically* generates a possible result, we will introduce relations in Sect. 4.1. The development of the algorithm will be presented in Sect. 4.2 and Sect. 4.3. The derived algorithm, expressed as a fold on in the input list, turns out to be the functional counterpart of Chen and Udding's algorithm in [5]. Finally in Sect. 4.4, we will briefly discuss an alternative algorithm dual to the on in Sect. 4.3.

4.1   From Functions to Relations

A relation of type $\alpha \rightarrow \beta$ is a set of pairs (a, b), where $a :: \alpha$ is drawn from the domain and $b :: \beta$ from the range. A function is a relation that is *simple* (a value in the domain is mapped to no more than one value in the range) and *entire* (every value in the domain is mapped to something). Composition of relations is defined by:

$$(a, c) \in R \cdot S \equiv \exists b :: (a, b) \in S \wedge (b, c) \in R$$

If we relax the entireness condition, we get partial functions. A useful class of partial functions is given by the *coreflexsives*. A coreflexive is a sub-relation of *id*. It serves as a filter, letting through only those values satisfying certain constraints. We denote the conversion from predicates (boolean-valued functions) to coreflexives by the operator ?. For a predicate p, we have

$$(a, a) \in p? \equiv p \, a$$

Given a relation $R :: \alpha \rightarrow \beta$, its *converse*, denoted by $R° :: \beta \rightarrow \alpha$, is obtained by swapping the pairs in R:

$$(b, a) \in R° \equiv (a, b) \in R$$

It is the generalisation of inverse to relations.

Real programs are deterministic. Therefore the result of a derivation has to be a function in order to be mapped to a program. Being able to have relations as intermediate results, however, allows the derivation to proceed in a more flexible way, as we will see in the incoming sections.

4.2   Unflattening an Internally Labelled Binary Tree

Back to the problem of building trees from its traversals. Or aim was to construct $pinorder° = (fork \, (preorder, inorder))°$, which takes a pair of traversals and yields a tree. The familiar Haskell function *curry* converts a function on pairs to a higher-order function, defined below[2]:

$$curry \quad :: ((\alpha, \beta) \to \gamma) \to \alpha \to \beta \to \gamma$$
$$curry \, f \, a \, b = f \, (a, b)$$

When the function is the converse of a fork, we have the following property:

$$curry \, (fork \, (R, f))^{\circ} \, a = ((a \text{ ==}) \cdot R)? \cdot f^{\circ} \tag{4}$$

To get an intuition of (4), let R, f and a have types $\gamma \to \alpha$, $\gamma \to \beta$, and α, respectively. The term $(fork \, (R, f))^{\circ}$ thus has type $(\alpha, \beta) \to \gamma$. The left-hand side of (4) takes a value $b :: \beta$, passes the pair (a, b) to $(fork \, (R, f))^{\circ}$, and returns $c :: \gamma$ such that c is mapped to a by R and $f \, c = b$. The right-hand side does the same by mapping b to an arbitrary c using f°, and taking only those cs mapped to a by R. The proof of (4) relies on expressing forks as *intersections* of relations and applying more primitive algebraic relational calculus. Interested readers are referred to [12].

Define *rebuild* = *curry pinorder*. By (4), we have

$$rebuild \, x = ((x \text{ ==}) \cdot preorder)? \cdot inorder^{\circ}$$

The converse of *inorder* takes a list as the input, and maps it to an arbitrary tree whose inorder traversal is the given list. The coreflexive $((x \text{ ==}) \cdot preorder)?$ then acts as a filter, picking the tree whose preorder traversal is the list x. Our aim is to construct *rebuild x*, assuming that x does not contain duplicated elements. Writing *rebuild* this way is possible only with the expressiveness of relations.

The aim of this section is to invert *inorder*. In [13], the same approach was applied to solve similar problems, building trees under some optimal or validity constraints. They all use the same core algorithm developed in this section but differ in the refinement step to be described in the next section.

How does one build a tree with a given inorder traversal? In the compositional approach, since *inorder* is defined as a fold, its inverse would be constructed as an unfold, like what we did in Sect. 3.1.

Alternatively, one can build such a tree as a fold over the given list. So, given a tree whose inorder traversal is x, how does one add another node to the tree, such that the inorder traversal of the new tree is $a : x$? One way to do it is illustrated in Fig. 2: we divide the left spine of the tree in two parts, move down the lower part for one level, and attach a to the end. If we call this operation *add*, the relational fold *foldr add Null* constructs a tree whose inorder traversal is the given list, i.e., *foldr add Null* is a sub-relation of $inorder^{\circ}$. But can we construct *all* the legal trees this way? In other words, does $inorder^{\circ}$ equal *foldr add Null*?

The *converse-of-a-function theorem* [4,11,13] gives conditions under which the converse of a function equals a fold. What matters is whether the function satisfies certain properties, rather than its particular definition. Its specialised version for lists reads:

---

[2] Cautious readers would notice that f here is a function while *curry* in (4) takes relational arguments. Factoring out the variable b and substitute f for R, we get $curry \, R \, a = R \cdot fork \, (const \, a, id)$, which can be taken as its generalisation to relations.

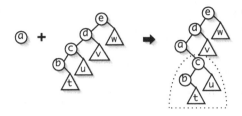

Fig. 2. Spine representation for internally labelled trees.

Theorem 1. Given a function $f :: \beta \to [\alpha]$, if we can find a relation $step :: \alpha \to \beta \to \beta$ and a value $base :: \beta$ that are jointly surjective and :

$$f\ base = [\ ]$$
$$f\ (step\ a\ x) = a : f\ x$$

then we have:

$$f^\circ = foldr\ step\ base$$

By *jointly surjectiveness* we mean that *base* and the range of *step* covers all the values in β.

Returning to *add*, we could have start with deriving *inorder*° directly using Theorem 1. To allow an efficient implementation of *add*, however, it turns out that it is preferable to introduce another representation for trees. The following type *Spine a* represents the spine of an internally labelled binary tree:

type $Spine\ \alpha = [(\alpha,\ Tree\ \alpha)]$

For example, the tree on the left-hand side of Fig. 2 is represented by the list

$$[(b, t), (c, u), (d, v), (e, w)]$$

The conversion from a spine tree to the ordinary representation can be performed by the function *roll* defined below:

$$roll :: Spine\ \alpha \to Tree\ \alpha$$
$$roll = foldl\ join\ Null$$
$$\textbf{where }\ join\ u\ (a, v) = Node\ (a, u, v)$$

The reader is reminded that the introduction of *Spine* is merely for the sake of efficiency. As we will see later, with *Spine* it is easier to attach leaves as shown in Fig. 2. Without *Spine*, we still get the same algorithm, but on a different datatype.

Our aim now is to find a relation *add* and a value *zero* such that

$$(inorder \cdot roll)^\circ = foldr\ add\ zero$$

According to the converse-of-a-function theorem, the above equality holds if

$$inorder\,(roll\ zero) = [\,] \tag{5}$$
$$inorder\,(roll\,(add\ a\ us)) = a : inorder\,(roll\ us) \tag{6}$$

To satisfy (5), we can choose $zero = Null$. To derive an add satisfying (6), we will need a property distributing $inorder$ into the subtrees on the spine:

$$inorder \cdot roll = concat \cdot map\,(cons \cdot (id \times inorder)) \tag{7}$$

where the functor $\times$ is define by $(f \times g)\,(x, y) = (f\,x, g\,y)$. Starting from the left-hand side of (6) and assume $us = vs \mathbin{+\!\!+} ws$, we derive:

$$a : inorder\,(roll\,(vs \mathbin{+\!\!+} ws))$$
$$= \quad \{(7)\}$$
$$a : concat\,(map\,(cons \cdot (id \times inorder))\,(vs \mathbin{+\!\!+} ws))$$
$$= \quad \{\text{since } concat \text{ and } map \text{ distributes over } \mathbin{+\!\!+}\}$$
$$a : concat\,(map\,(cons \cdot (id \times inorder))\,vs) \mathbin{+\!\!+}$$
$$\quad concat\,(map\,(cons \cdot (id \times inorder))\,ws)$$
$$= \quad \{(7)\}$$
$$a : inorder\,(roll\ vs) \mathbin{+\!\!+}$$
$$\quad concat\,(map\,(cons \cdot (id \times inorder))\,ws)$$
$$= \quad \{\text{definition of } concat \text{ and } map\}$$
$$concat\,(map\,(cons \cdot (id \times inorder))\,((a, roll\ vs) : ws))$$
$$= \quad \{(7)\}$$
$$inorder\,(roll\,((a, roll\ vs) : ws))$$

We therefore have $add\ a\,(vs \mathbin{+\!\!+} ws) = (a, roll\ vs) : ws$. The cases for $add\ a\,[\,]$ and $add\ a\,[u]$ turn out to be absorbed by the above case, and the derivations are left as exercises for the reader. Thus we choose:

$$add \qquad\qquad :: \alpha \rightarrow Spine\ \alpha \rightarrow Spine\ \alpha$$
$$add\ a\,(us \mathbin{+\!\!+} vs) = (a, roll\ us) : vs$$

It is not a function because of the non-deterministic pattern $us \mathbin{+\!\!+} vs$.

It is also not difficult to see that $Null$ and add are jointly surjective, since if a tree is not $Null$, it must be a result of adding its leftmost element on the spine to some tree. We therefore conclude that

$$(inorder \cdot roll)^{\circ} = foldr\ add\ Null$$

Since $roll$ is an isomorphism, we have $inorder^{\circ} = roll \cdot foldr\ add\ Null$.

For some intuition what add does, consider Fig. 2 again. As mentioned before, the tree on the left-hand side is represented in the spine representation as $[(b, t), (c, u), (d, v), (e, w)]$. The one on the right-hand side, on the other hand, is represented by $[(a, roll\,[(b, t), (c, u)]), (d, v), (e, w)]$ and results from splitting the former list, one of the five ways to split it into two.

4.3   Enforcing a Preorder

Now recall our the specification of *rebuild*

$$rebuild\ x = ((x\ ==) \cdot preorder)? \cdot inorder°$$

In the last section we have inverted *inorder* as a relational fold and switched to a spine representation, yielding:

$$
\begin{aligned}
&rebuild\ x \\
&= ((x\ ==) \cdot preorder)? \cdot roll \cdot foldr\ add\ Null \\
&= roll \cdot (hasPreorder\ x)? \cdot foldr\ add\ Null
\end{aligned}
$$

where *hasPreorder* $x = (x\ ==) \cdot preorder \cdot roll$. We now want to fuse (*hasPreorder* x)? into the fold to efficiently generate the one tree which has the correct preorder traversal. The *fold-fusion* theorem for lists says:

Theorem 2.

$$R \cdot foldr\ S\ e = foldr\ T\ d \Leftarrow R \cdot S\ a = T\ a \cdot R \wedge ((e, d') \in R \equiv d' = d)$$

However, *hasPreorder* x is too strong an invariant to enforce within the fold: it is impossible to make the constructed tree to have the same preorder traversal in each iteration.

Instead, we will try to find a weaker constraint to fuse into the fold. Define *preorderF* to be the preorder traversal of forests:

$$preorderF = concat \cdot map\ preorder$$

Look at Fig. 2 again. The preorder traversal of the tree on the left-hand side is

$$[e, d, c, b] \mathbin{+\!\!+} preorderF\ [t, u, v, w]$$

that is, to go down along the left spine, then traverse through the subtrees upwards. In general, given a spine tree *us*, its preorder traversal is

$$reverse\ (map\ fst\ us) \mathbin{+\!\!+} preorderF\ (map\ snd\ us)$$

We will call the part before $+\!\!+$ the *prefix* and that after $+\!\!+$ the *suffix* of the traversal. Now look at the tree on the right-hand side. Its preorder traversal is

$$[e, d, a, c, b] \mathbin{+\!\!+} preorderF\ [t, u, v, w]$$

It is not difficult to see that when we add a node a to a spine tree *us*, the suffix of its preorder traversal does not change. The new node a is always inserted to the prefix.

With this insight, we split *hasPreorder* into two parts:

$$
\begin{aligned}
&hasPreorder && :: Eq\ \alpha \Rightarrow [\alpha] \rightarrow Spine\ \alpha \rightarrow Bool \\
&hasPreorder\ x\ us &&= prefixOk\ x\ us \wedge suffixOk\ x\ us \\
&suffixOk\ x\ us &&= preorderF\ (map\ snd\ us)\ \textbf{isSuffixOf}\ x \\
&prefixOk\ x\ us &&= reverse\ (map\ fst\ us) == (x \ominus preorderF\ (map\ snd\ us))
\end{aligned}
$$

where $x \ominus y$ removes y from the tail of x and is defined by:

$x \ominus y = z$ **where** $z + \!\!\!+\, y = x$

The expression x **isSuffixOf** y yields true if x is a suffix of y. The use of boldface font here indicates that it is an infix operator (and binds looser than function applications). The plan is to fuse only *suffixOk x* into the fold while leaving *prefixOk x* outside.

There is a slight problem, however. The invariant *suffixOk x* does not prevent the fold from generating, say, a leftist tree with all *null* along the spine, since the empty list is indeed a suffix of any list. Such a tree may be bound to be rejected later. Look again at the right-hand side of Fig. 2. Assume we know that the preorder traversal of the tree we want is $x = [.. d, c, b] + \!\!\!+\, preorderF [t, u, v, w]$. The tree in the right-hand side of Fig. 2, although satisfying *suffixOk x*, is bound to be wrong because d is the next immediate symbol but a now stands in the way between d and c, and there is no way to change the order afterwards. Thus when we find a proper location to insert a new node, we shall be more aggressive and consume as much suffix of x as possible. The following predicate *lookahead x* ensures that in the constructed tree, the next immediate symbol in x will be consumed:

$lookahead \quad :: Eq\, \alpha \Rightarrow [\alpha] \to Spine\, \alpha \to Bool$
$lookahead\, x\, us = length\, us \leq 1 \,\vee$
$\qquad\qquad\qquad (map\, fst\, us)\, !!\, 1 \neq last\, x'$
$\quad$ **where** $x' = x \ominus preorderF\, (map\, snd\, us)$

Apparently *lookahead x* is weaker than *hasPreorder x*. Define

$ok\, x\, us = suffixOk\, x\, us \wedge lookhead\, x\, us$

which will be our invariant in the fold, we have

$hasPreorder\, x\, us = prefixOk\, x\, us \wedge ok\, x\, us$ \hfill (8)

The derivation goes:

$\quad rebuild$
$= \quad \{\text{definition}\}$
$\quad ((x ==) \cdot preorder)? \cdot inorder^{\circ}$
$= \quad \{\text{inverting } inorder, \text{ moving } roll \text{ to the left}\}$
$\quad roll \cdot (hasPreorder\, x)? \cdot foldr\, add\, null$
$= \quad \{\text{by (8)}\}$
$\quad roll \cdot (prefixOk\, x)? \cdot (ok\, x)? \cdot foldr\, add\, null$
$= \quad \{\text{fold fusion, assume } nodup\, x\}$
$\quad roll \cdot (prefixOk\, x)? \cdot foldr\, (add'\, x)\, null$

To justify the fusion step, it can be shown that if x contains no duplicated elements, the following fusion condition holds:

$(ok\, x)? \cdot add\, a = add'\, x\, a \cdot (ok\, x)?$

where add' is defined by:

$$add' :: Eq\,\alpha \Rightarrow [\alpha] \rightarrow (\alpha, Spine\,\alpha) \rightarrow Spine\,\alpha$$
$$add'\,x\,(a, us) = up\,a\,null\,(us, x \ominus preorderF\,(map\,snd\,us))$$

$$up :: Eq\,\alpha \Rightarrow \alpha \rightarrow Tree\,\alpha \rightarrow (Spine\,\alpha, [\alpha]) \rightarrow Spine\,\alpha$$
$$up\,a\,v\,([], x) = [(a, v)]$$
$$up\,a\,v\,((b, u) : us, x \mathbin{+\!\!+} [b'])$$
$$\quad |\ b == b' \quad = \quad up\,a\,(node\,(b, (v, u)))\,(us, x)$$
$$\quad |\ otherwise = \quad (a, v) : (b, u) : us$$

In words, the function up traces the left spine upwards and consume the values on the spine if they match the tail of x. It tries to roll as much as possible before adding a to the end of the spine.

As a final optimisation, we can avoid re-computing $x \ominus$ $preorderF\,(map\,snd\,us)$ from scratch by applying a tupling transformation, having the fold returning a pair. The Haskell implementation is shown in Fig. 3. The fold in $rebuild$ returns a pair of a tree and a list representing $x \ominus preorderF\,(map\,snd\,us)$. Since the list is consumed from the end, we represent it in reverse. The function $rollpf$ implements $roll \cdot (prefixOk\,x)?$.

```
data Tree a = Null | Node a (Tree a) (Tree a)
              deriving (Show,Eq)

rebuild :: Eq a => [a] -> [a] -> Tree a
rebuild x = rollpf . foldr add' ([],reverse x)
      where add' a (us,x) = up a Null (us,x)
            up a v ([],x) = ([(a,v)],x)
            up a v ((b,u):us, b':x)
                | b == b' = up a (Node b v u) (us, x)
                | otherwise = ((a,v):(b,u):us, b':x)

rollpf :: Eq a => ([(a,Tree a)],[a]) -> Tree a
rollpf (us,x) = rp Null (us,x)
where     rp v ([],[]) = v
          rp v ((b,u):us, b':x)
              | b == b' = rp (Node b v u) (us,x)
```

Fig. 3. Rebuilding a tree from its traversals via a fold.

Figure 4 shows an example of this algorithm in action. The part in boldface font indicates $preorderF\,(map\,snd\,us)$. Notice how the preorder traversals on of the trees under the spine always form a suffix of the given list $[a, b, c, d, e, f]$. We have actually reinvented the algorithm proposed in [5], but in a functional style.

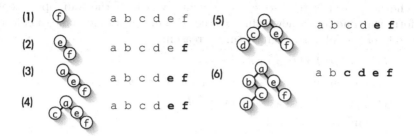

Fig. 4. Building a tree from preorder **abcdef** and inorder **bdcaef**. The preorder traversals of the trees under the spine is written in boldface font.

4.4 Building a Tree with a Given Preorder

The reader might justifiably complain that the derivation works because, by luck, we choose to invert *inorder* first. Had we started with defining *pinorder* = *fork* (*inorder*, *preorder*), we would have come up with

$$((x ==) \cdot inorder)? \cdot preorder^\circ$$

We would then have to invert *preorder*, and then enforce, on the resulting fold, the constraint that the tree built must have a given inorder traversal. Does the alternative still work? In fact, it does, and the result is a new, though more complicated, algorithm. We sketch an outline of its development in this section.

We first seek to invert *preorder*. For this problem it turns out that it makes more sense to work on forests rather than trees. Recall *preorderF* :: [*Tree* α] → [α] defined by *preorderF* = *concat* · *map preorder*. The reader can easily verify, with the converse-of-a-function theorem, that *preorderF* can be inverted as below:

$$
\begin{aligned}
preorderF^\circ &= foldr\ step\ [\,] \\
step\ a\ us &= tip\ a : us \\
&\quad \square\ lbr\ (a, head\ us) : tail\ us\ \square\ rbr\ (a, head\ us) : tail\ us \\
&\quad \square\ node(a, (us!!0, us!!1)) : tail\ (tail\ us)
\end{aligned}
$$

where the $\square$ operator denotes non-deterministic choice. The helper functions *tip*, *lbr* and *rbr* respectively creates a tip tree, a tree with only the left branch, and a tree with only the right branch. They are defined by:

$$
\begin{aligned}
tip\ a &= Node\ (a, Null, Null) \\
lbr\ (a, t) &= Node\ (a, t, Null) \\
rbr\ (a, t) &= Node\ (a, Null, t)
\end{aligned}
$$

In words, the relation *step* extends a forest in one of the four possible ways: adding a new tip tree, extending the leftmost tree in the forest by making it a left-subtree or a right-subtree, or combining the two leftmost trees, if they exist.

The next step is to discover a guideline which of the four operations to perform when adding a new value. We need to invent an invariant to enforce in the body of the fold. To begin with, we reason:

$$((x \mathrel{==}) \cdot inorder)? \cdot preorder^{\circ}$$

$$= \quad \{\text{since } preorder = preorderF \cdot wrap, \text{ where } wrap\, a = [a]\}$$

$$((x \mathrel{==}) \cdot inorder)? \cdot wrap^{\circ} \cdot preorderF^{\circ}$$

$$= \quad \{\text{some trivial manipulation}\}$$

$$wrap^{\circ} \cdot ((x \mathrel{==}) \cdot concat \cdot map\, inorder)? \cdot preorderF^{\circ}$$

Again, the condition $(x \mathrel{==}) \cdot concat \cdot map\, inorder$ is too strong to maintain. Luckily, it turns out that the weaker constraint

$$(\textbf{isSubSeqOf } x) \cdot concat \cdot map\, inorder$$

will do, where $(\textbf{isSubSeqOf } x)\, y = y\ \textbf{isSubSeqOf } x$ yields true if y is a subsequence of x. That is, we require that during the construction of the forest, the inorder traversal of each tree shall always form segments of x, in correct order. Figure 5 demonstrates the process of constructing the same tree as that in Fig. 4. This time notice how the inorder traversal of the constructed forest always forms a subsequence of the given list $[b, d, c, a, e, f]$.

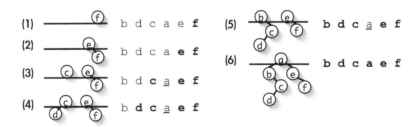

Fig. 5. Yet another way to build a tree from preorder `abcdef` and inorder `bdcaef`.

After some pencil-and-paper work, one will realise that to decide how to extend the forest while maintaining the invariant above, it is necessary to take into consideration two more entities in the given inorder traversal: the skipped segments between the trees in the current forest (the underlined parts in Fig. 5), and the element immediately next to the first tree (e.g., a in (2) and d in (3) of Fig. 5).

The algorithm is implemented in Fig. 6, where the functions *add* and *join* reflect the rules. In each step of the fold in *rebuild*, the variable x represents the reversed prefix of the given inorder traversal to the left of the first tree, i.e., the "unprocessed" prefix. The function *isNext x a* tests whether a is the next element. The skipped segments, on the other hand, is paired with each tree in the forest. The fold thus yields the type $([\alpha], [(\mathit{Tree}\ \alpha, [\alpha])])$.

Let a be the new node to add to the forest. When the forest is empty, the function *newtree* is called to create a new singleton tree. Otherwise denote by t the leftmost tree in the forest. If a is the next element in x, the function *rbr* is called to make t a right branch of a. If a equals the first element in the skipped segment next to t, on the other hand, the function *join* is called to decide whether to attach t as a left subtree or to attach two subtrees to a. When none of the cases hold, we make a a separate singleton tree by *newtree*, which also computes the new x and the new skipped segment.

```
type AForest a = [(Tree a, [a])]

rebuild :: Eq a => [a] -> [a] -> Tree a
rebuild x = fst . unwrap . snd . foldr add (reverse x, [])
  where add :: Eq a => a -> ([a],AForest a) -> ([a],AForest a)
        add a xu@(x, [])     = newtree a xu
        add a xu@(x, (t,[]):us)
          | isNext x a = (tail x, (rbr a t, []):us)
          | otherwise = newtree a xu
        add a xu@(x,(t,b:bs):us)
          | a == b = (x, join a (t,bs) us)
          | isNext x a = (tail x, (rbr a t, b:bs):us)
          | otherwise = newtree a xu

        join a (t,[]) [] = [(lbr a t,[])]
        join a (t,[]) ((u,y):us) = (Node a t u, y) : us
        join a (t,bs) us = (lbr a t, bs):us

        newtree a (x,us) = (x', (tip a, y):us)
        where (x',y) = skip x a

        isNext [] a = False
        isNext (b:bs) a = a == b

    skip x a = locate a [] x
      where locate a y [] = ([],y)
            locate a y (b:x) | a == b = (x,y)
                             | otherwise = locate a (b:y) x
```

Fig. 6. An implementation of the second folding algorithm.

All functions called by *add*, apart from *skip*, are constant-time operations, and each element in x is skipped only once. Therefore, the program runs in linear time, but with a bigger constant overhead than that in Sect. 4.3. To the best of our knowledge, this algorithm is new. However, the rules consists of totally eight cases and are relatively complicated comparing to other algorithms in this article. It is due to that we have four possible operations to choose from, while in Sect. 4.3 there are only two – either to walk upward along the spine or to stop and attach a new node. For that reason we will not go into more detail but just present the result.

5 Conclusion and Related Work

We have looked at two classes of algorithms for the problem of building a binary tree from its traversals. The recursive algorithm turns out to be a result of the compositional approach to function inversion and a technique to eliminate repeated traversals. In [15], similar transform was presented in a procedural style.

The iterative algorithm, on the other hand, is related to the converse-of-a-function theorem. It allows us to consider inorder and preorder traversals separately. The first step in [5] was to transform the recursive definition of *pinorder* into an iteration by introducing a stack. The same effect we achieved by introducing the spine representation. By exploiting symmetricity, we also discovered a new, but complicated, linear-time algorithm. In both cases, the actions we perform on the spine or the forest resemble a shift-reduce parser. In fact, the one of the early motivating example of the converse-of-a-function theorem was precedence parsing [11]. It is certainly possible to derive a full shift-reduce parser using the theorem, although it will be a laborious exercise.

The reader might complain that introducing a spine representation is too inventive a step, if not itself the answer to the problem. Our defence is that the spine representation is there to enable traversing the tree upwards from the left-most tip, which is more a concern of efficiency than an algorithmic one. In fact, for some applications in [12], where the converse-of-a-function theorem is also applied, we actually prefer not to use *Spine*. Some earlier algorithms solve problems similar to that addressed in this paper without the use of the spine representation, at least not explicitly. The derivation of [5] introduced a stack represented by a list, which served the same purpose of the spine we use. In [9] another similar problem was considered. The resulting algorithm does not use the spine explicitly. Instead, the author introduced pairs using a tupling transform. One might see it as implicitly storing the spine in the machine stack.

One of the purposes of this article is to advocate relational program derivation. So far, its most successful application area is probably in dealing with optimisation problems [3,4]. Program inversion may be another application where a relational approach is useful [12]. An alternative way to talk about inverses is by set-valued functions[8]. At least within the two application fields, the relations provide a natural and concise framework, avoiding having to take care of the bookkeeping details of maintaining a set of results. The algebra of relations, however, is notorious for having too many rules, and it remains to see whether the complexity can be kept within a manageable scale. See [2,4] for a fuller introduction to the relational theory of program derivation.

This article concerns only manual program derivation, where the algorithm is the delivered result. Complementarily, [1] introduced their *universal resolving algorithm* to construct an inverse interpreter that actually compute the values delivered by the inversed function. Furthermore, the inverse interpreter can be partially evaluated to produce a *program* that performs the inverted task.

Acknowledgement The converse-of-a-function theorem was first proposed by Oege de Moor [4,11]. He also significantly simplified the derivation in Sect. 3 after reading an earlier draft of the first author's thesis. The authors would also like to thank the members of the Algebra of Programming group in Oxford University Computing Laboratory for valuable discussions, Robert Glück for encouraging research on this topic, and Zhenjiang Hu for his edits and comments.

References

1. S. M. Abramov and R. Glück. The universal resolving algorithm: inverse computation in a functional language. *Science of Computer Programming*, 43:193–299, 2002.
2. R. C. Backhouse and P. F. Hoogendijk. Elements of a relational theory of datatypes. In B. Möller, H. A. Partsch, and S. A. Schuman, editors, *Formal Program Development. Proc. IFIP TC2/WG 2.1 State of the Art Seminar.*, number 755 in Lecture Notes in Computer Science, pages 7–42. Springer-Verlag, January 1992.
3. R. S. Bird and O. de Moor. From dynamic programming to greedy algorithms. In B. Möller, editor, *Procs. State-of-the-Art Seminar on Formal Program Development*, number 755 in Lecture Notes in Computer Science. Springer-Verlag, 1993.
4. R. S. Bird and O. de Moor. *Algebra of Programming*. International Series in Computer Science. Prentice Hall, 1997.
5. W. Chen and J. T. Udding. Program inversion: more than fun! *Science of Computer Programming*, 15:1–13, 1990.
6. E. W. Dijkstra. Program inversion. Technical Report EWD671, Eindhoven University of Technology, 1978.
7. D. Gries and J. L. van de Snepscheut. Inorder traversal of a binary tree and its inversion. In E. W. Dijkstra, editor, *Formal Development of Programs and Proofs*, pages 37–42. Addison Wesley, 1990.
8. P. G. Harrison and H. Khoshnevisan. On the synthesis of function inverses. *Acta Informatica*, 29:211–239, 1992.
9. R. Hinze. Constructing tournament representations: An exercise in pointwise relational programming. In E. Boiten and B. Möller, editors, *Sixth International Conference on Mathematics of Program Construction*, number 2386 in Lecture Notes in Computer Science, Dagstuhl, Germany, July 2002. Springer-Verlag.
10. D. E. Knuth. *The Art of Computer Programming Volume 1: Fundamental Algorithms, 3rd Edition*. Addison Wesley, 1997.
11. O. de Moor and J. Gibbons. Pointwise relational programming. In *Proceedings of Algebraic Methodology and Software Technology 2000*, number 1816 in Lecture Notes in Computer Science, pages 371–390. Springer-Verlag, May 2000.
12. S.-C. Mu. *A Calculational Approach to Program Inversion*. PhD thesis, Oxford University Computing Laboratory, 2003.
13. S.-C. Mu and R. S. Bird. Inverting functions as folds. In E. Boiten and B. Möller, editors, *Sixth International Conference on Mathematics of Program Construction*, number 2386 in Lecture Notes in Computer Science, pages 209–232. Springer-Verlag, July 2002.

14. B. Schoenmakers. Inorder traversal of a binary heap and its inversion in optimal time and space. In *Mathematics of Program Construction 1992*, number 669 in Lecture Notes in Computer Science, pages 291–301. Springer-Verlag, 1993.
15. J. L. van de Snepscheut. Inversion of a recursive tree traversal. Technical Report JAN 171a, California Institute of Technology, May 1991. Available online at `ftp://ftp.cs.caltech.edu/tr/cs-tr-91-07.ps.Z` .
16. J. von Wright. Program inversion in the refinement calculus. *Information Processing Letters*, 37:95–100, 1991.

Type Inference with Structural Subtyping: A Faithful Formalization of an Efficient Constraint Solver

Vincent Simonet

INRIA Rocquencourt
Vincent.Simonet@inria.fr

Abstract. We are interested in type inference in the presence of *structural* subtyping from a pragmatic perspective. This work combines theoretical and practical contributions: first, it provides a faithful description of an efficient algorithm for solving and simplifying constraints; whose correctness is formally proved. Besides, the framework has been implemented in Objective Caml, yielding a generic type inference engine. Its efficiency is assessed by a complexity result and a series of experiments in realistic cases.

1 Introduction

1.1 Subtyping

Subtyping is a key feature of many type systems for programming languages. Previous works have shown how to integrate it into languages such as the simply typed λ-calculus, ML or Haskell. It appears as the basis of many object-oriented languages, e.g. [1]; and it allows designing fine-grained type systems for advanced programming constructs, e.g. [2]. It is also well suited for extending standard type systems in order to perform some static analysis, such as detection of uncaught exceptions [3], data [4] or information [5] flow analyses.

In all cases, subtyping consists of a partial order $\leq$ on types and a subsumption rule that allows every expression which has some type to be used with any greater type, as proposed by Mitchell [6] and Cardelli [7]. The subtyping order may reflect a variety of concepts: inclusion of mathematical domains, class hierarchy in object oriented languages, principals in security analyses, for instance.

As a consequence, the definition of the subtyping order itself varies. In this paper, we are interested in the case of *structural* subtyping, where comparable types must have the same shape and can only differ by their *atomic leaves*. (This contrasts with *non-structural* subtyping where different type constructors may be comparable; in particular, a least type $\perp$ and a greatest type $\top$ may be supplied. This also differs from *atomic* subtyping where there is no type constructor but only *atoms* belonging to some poset.) Structural subtyping is of particular interest when one intends to enrich a unification-based type system, such as ML's, with annotations belonging to a poset of *atoms*. In this case, the subtyping order may be simply defined by lifting the poset order along the

A. Ohori (Ed.): APLAS 2003, LNCS 2895, pp. 283–302, 2003.

existing type structure. Following the complexity study of Tiuryn [8] and Hoang and Mitchell [9], we will assume the atomic poset to be a lattice.

1.2   Type Inference

Type inference consists in automatically determining the possible types of a piece of code. First, it allows type errors to be detected at compile time, without forcing programmers to include type annotations in programs. Second, a variety of program analyzes may be described as type inference processes.

The first algorithm for type inference with atomic subtyping was proposed by Mitchell [6,10] and improved for handling structural subtyping by Fuh and Mishra [11,12]. However, quoting Hoang and Mitchell [9], *"it has seen little if any practical use"*, mostly because *"it is inefficient and the output, even for relatively simple input expressions, appears excessively long and cumbersome to read"*. The theoretical complexity of the problem has been largely studied. Tiuryn [8] showed that deciding satisfiability of subtyping constraints between atoms is *PSPACE-hard* in the general case; and in the common case where the atomic poset is a disjoint union of lattices, it is solvable in linear time. Hoang and Mitchell [9] proved the equivalence of constraint resolution with typability (in the simply typed λ-calculus with subtyping). Frey [13] settled completely the complexity of the general case, showing it is *PSPACE-complete*. Lastly, Kuncak and Rinard [14] recently showed the first order theory of structural subtyping of non-recursive types to be decidable. Besides, in an attempt to overcome the practical limitation of the first algorithms, several researchers have investigated simplification heuristics in a variety of settings [15,16,17,18]. Rehof [19] also studies this question from a theoretical viewpoint, proving the existence of *minimal* typings in atomic subtyping and setting an exponential lower bound on their size. Simplification is useful because it may speed up type inference and make type information more readable for the user. However, to the best of our knowledge, only a small number of realistic type inference systems with *let*-polymorphism and (a flavor of) subtyping have been published [20,21,22,23,24].

Structural subtyping has also been studied throughout a series of specific applications. Among them, one may mention Foster's work about type qualifiers [25,26] and the introduction of boolean constraints for binding-time analysis [27]. Both involve a type system with structural subtyping; however their type inference algorithm consists, in short, in expanding type structure and decomposing constraints without performing simplifications until obtaining a problem which involves only atoms and can be handled by an external solver. This contrasts with our approach which emphasizes the interlacing of resolution and simplification.

Type systems with subtyping associate not only a type to an expression but also a set of *constraints*, stating assumptions about the subtype order under which the typing is valid. Its presence is required by the desire to obtain most general (i.e. principal) statements which summarize all possible typings for a given expression, with a type compatibility notion which is not restricted to type instantiation, but includes all the coercions allowed by the subtyping order.

It is wise to decompose the design of a type synthesizer for a given language in two steps, whose implementation is in principle independent (although their execution is interlaced for efficiency). The first step consists in traversing the abstract syntax tree and generating types and constraints; this is in general straightforward but specific to the analysis at hand. The second step requires deciding the satisfiability of the generated constraints, and possibly rewriting them into a better but equivalent form. This remains independent from the language or even the type system itself, and relies only on the *constraint logic*. Hence, it may be delegated to a generic library taking care of constraint management.

2   Overview

In this paper, we address this question from a pragmatic perspective, our main objective resides in providing a generic, practical and scalable type inference engine featuring structural subtyping and polymorphism. Firstly, we give a faithful description of the algorithm and explain the main design choices, motivated by efficiency. Secondly, because previous works have proved this a delicate task and correctness of type inference is crucial, we provide a complete, formal proof of the framework. Lastly, we believe that experience is necessary for designing efficient techniques and advocating their scalability; so a complete implementation of the algorithms presented in this paper has been carried out in Objective Caml [28] and experienced on realistic cases. On our tests, it has shown to be slower only by a factor of 2 to 3 in comparison with standard unification (see Section 7 for details). Despite the large amount of work about structural subtyping in the literature, the faithful description of a complete type inference engine—which aims at efficiency, has been proved correct and also implemented apart from any particular application—forms an original contribution of the current work. We hope this will help such system to be widely used.

Our solving strategy sharply contrasts with some previous works about solving of subtyping constraints, e.g. [22], where a transitive closure of subtyping constraints is intertwined with decomposition. This yields a cubic-time algorithm, which cannot be improved because it performs a sort of dynamic transitive closure. It is interesting to draw a parallel with Heintze and McAllester's algorithm for control flow analysis (CFA) [29]. Whereas, in the standard approach for CFA, a transitive closure is dynamically interlaced with constraint generation, they propose a framework which first builds a certain graph and then performs a (demand-driven) closure. This gives a linear-time algorithm under the hypothesis of bounded-types. Similarly, our strategy for structural subtyping consists in postponing closure by first expanding the term structure and decomposing constraints until obtaining an atomic problem, as described in [11,8]. Although expansion may theoretically introduce a number of variables exponential in the size of the input constraint, this behavior is rare and, under the hypothesis of bounded terms, this strategy remains *quasi-linear* under the hypothesis of bounded-terms (see section 5.5). This hypothesis may be discussed [30], but we believe it to be a good approximation for the practical examples: it captures the intuition that functions generally have limited number of arguments and order.

However, a simple algorithm performing expansion and decomposition on inequalities does not scale to the type-checking of real programs: despite the linear bound, expansion may in practice severely increase the size of the problem, affecting too much the overhead of the algorithm. To avoid this, we refine the strategy in several ways. Firstly, in order to deal with expansion and decomposition in an efficient manner, we enrich the original constraint language, which basically allows expressing a conjunction of inequalities, with new constructions, named *multi-skeletons*, that allow taking advantage of the structurality of subtyping by re-using techniques found in standard constraint-based unification frameworks [31]. Roughly speaking, multi-skeletons simultaneously express standard equalities between terms (written $=$) as well as equalities between term *structures* or *shapes* (written $\approx$); hence they allow performing *unification* on both. Secondly, in order to reduce as much as possible the number of variables to be expanded, we introduce several simplifications which must be performed *throughout the expansion process*. Lastly, we provide another set of simplifications which can be realized only at the end of solving. They allow the output of concise and readable typing information, and are most beneficial in the presence of *let*-polymorphism: generalization and instantiation require duplicating constraints, hence they must be made as compact as possible beforehand.

In addition to standard structural subtyping, our system is also equipped with less common features. First, it provides rows, which increase the expressiveness of the language and are useful for type-and-effect systems, see [3,32]. Second, we deal with an original form of constraints, referred to as *weak inequalities*, which allow handling constraints such as *guards* [5] (see Section 3.3).

The remainder of the article is organized as follows. We begin by introducing the ground model of terms (Section 3) and, then, the first order logic in which constraints are expressed (Section 4). Section 5 describes the heart of the constraint resolution algorithm, and, in Section 6, we incorporate into this process simplification techniques, as discussed above. The implementation and experimental measures are presented in Section 7. The paper ends with some discussion about possible extensions. By lack of space, proofs of theorems are omitted, they can be found in the full version of the paper [33].

3   The Ground Algebra

The ground algebra is a logical model for interpreting constraints and type schemes. It consists in a set of *ground terms* and two binary relations: a subtyping order, $\leq$, and a "weak inequality", $\sqsubseteq$.

3.1   Ground Terms

Let $(\mathcal{A}, \leq_{\mathcal{A}})$ be a lattice whose elements, denoted by a, are the *atoms*. Let $\mathcal{C}$ and $\mathcal{L}$ be two denumerable sets of *type constructors* c and *row labels* ℓ, respectively.

$$\frac{a \leq_{\mathcal{A}} a'}{a \leq a'} \qquad \frac{\forall i \ v_i(c) \in \{\oplus, \odot\} \Rightarrow \tau_i \leq \tau_i' \quad \forall i \ v_i(c) \in \{\ominus, \odot\} \Rightarrow \tau_i \geq \tau_i'}{c(\tau_1, \ldots, \tau_n) \leq c(\tau_1', \ldots, \tau_n')} \qquad \frac{\forall \ell \in L \ t_\ell \leq t_\ell'}{\{\ell \mapsto t_\ell\}_{\ell \in L} \leq \{\ell \mapsto t_\ell'\}_{\ell \in L}}$$

Fig. 1. Subtyping over ground terms

Ground terms and *kinds* are defined as follows:

$$t ::= a \qquad\qquad\qquad \kappa ::= \mathsf{Atom}$$
$$\mid\ c(t, \ldots, t) \qquad\qquad \mid\ \mathsf{Type}$$
$$\mid\ \{\ell \mapsto t\}_{\ell \in L} \qquad\qquad \mid\ \mathsf{Row}_L\ \kappa$$

Ground terms include atomic constants a, which have kind Atom. Every type constructor c has a fixed arity n and a signature $\kappa_1, \ldots, \kappa_n$ which gives the expected kinds of its arguments. A *row* of kind $\mathsf{Row}_L\ \kappa$ is a mapping from labels in L to terms of kind κ, which is constant but on a finite subset of L.

3.2 Strong Subtyping

The set of ground terms is equipped with the partial order $\leq$ defined in Figure 1, called *subtyping*, which relates terms of the same kind. On atoms, it is the order $\leq_{\mathcal{A}}$. Two comparable types must have the same head constructor c; moreover, their sub-terms must be related according to the *variances* of c: for i ranging from 1 to c's arity, $v_i(c)$ is one of $\oplus$ (*covariant*), $\ominus$ (*contravariant*) or $\odot$ (*invariant*).

This subtyping relation is *structural*: two comparable terms must share the same structure or *skeleton* and only their atomic annotations may differ. This leads us to introduce an equivalence relation $\approx$ on ground terms, which is nothing but the symmetric, transitive closure of $\leq$: $t_1 \approx t_2$ (read: t_1 *has the same skeleton as* t_2) if and only if $t_1 (\leq \cup \geq)^* t_2$. Equivalence classes are referred to as *ground skeletons*. Roughly speaking, two terms have the same skeleton if they are equal, except within some non-invariant atomic annotations. In the absence of invariant arguments, skeletons would be identical to Tiuryn's shapes [8].

3.3 Weak Inequalities

Type systems with structural subtyping may require constraints relating an arbitrary term to an atom, such as *"protected types"* [34] or *"guards"* ($\lhd$ or $\blacktriangleleft$) [5]. For instance, in [5], a constraint of the form $a \lhd t$ requires the constant a to be less than or equal to one or several atoms appearing in t, whose "positions" depend on the particular structure of t: $a \lhd \mathsf{int}^{a_1}$ and $a \lhd (t_1 + t_2)^{a_1}$ are equivalent to $a \leq a_1$ while $a \lhd \mathsf{int}^{a_1} \times \mathsf{int}^{a_2}$ holds if and only if $a \leq a_1$ and $a \leq a_2$, i.e. $a \leq a_1 \sqcap a_2$.

Our framework handles such constraints in an abstract and (as far as possible) general manner by the *weak inequality* $\sqsubseteq$ defined in figure 2. $\sqsubseteq$ relates ground terms of arbitrary kind by decomposing them until atoms are obtained, which are dealt with by rule ATOM. The other rules govern decomposition of the left-hand-side (TYPE-LEFT and ROW-LEFT) and the right-hand-side (TYPE-RIGHT and ROW-RIGHT) of a weak inequality. On a type constructor c, decomposition

ATOM	TYPE-LEFT	TYPE-RIGHT	ROW-LEFT	ROW-RIGHT
$a_1 \leq_A a_2$	$\forall i \in l(c)\ t_i \sqsubset t'$	$\forall i \in r(c)\ t' \sqsubset t_i$	$\forall \ell \in L\ t_\ell \sqsubset t'$	$\forall \ell \in L\ t' \sqsubset t_\ell$
$a_1 \sqsubset a_2$	$c(\bar{t}) \sqsubset t'$	$t' \sqsubset c(\bar{t})$	$\{\ell \mapsto t_\ell\}_L \sqsubset t'$	$t' \sqsubset \{\ell \mapsto t_\ell\}_L$

Fig. 2. Weak inequalities

occurs on some of the sub-terms: we assume to non-disjoint subsets of $\{i \mid v_i(c) = \oplus\}$, $l(c)$ and $r(c)$. In short, a constraint $\tau_1 \sqsubset \tau_2$ is decomposable in a set of inequalities between some of the atoms appearing in τ_1 and some of τ_2 which are given by the respective structure of the two terms.

Although the rules defining $\sqsubset$ are not syntax-directed, they are however equivalences. In other words, all strategies for decomposing a weak inequality produce the same set of atomic inequalities. Moreover, it is worth noting that, because $l(c)$ and $r(c)$ are non-disjoint and $\sqsubset$ matches only covariant sub-terms, it is transitive and $t_1 \sqsubset t_2 \leq t_3$ or $t_1 \leq t_2 \sqsubset t_3$ imply $t_1 \sqsubset t_3$.

4   The Syntactic Algebra

4.1   The First Order Logic

Terms and constraints are part of a first order logic interpreted in the ground algebra of Section 3. For every kind κ, we assume given a distinct denumerable set of *variables* denoted by α or β. On top of variables, we build two syntactic classes, *terms* and *hand-sides*:

$$\tau ::= \alpha \mid c(\tau, \ldots, \tau) \mid (\ell : \tau, \tau) \qquad \phi ::= \alpha \mid a$$

Terms include variables, type terms made up of a type constructor and a list of sub-terms, and row terms. For the latter, Rémy's [31] syntax is adopted: the term $(\ell : \tau, \tau')$ represents the row whose entry at index ℓ is τ and whose other entries are given by τ'. Hand-sides, which are either a variable (of arbitrary kind) or an atomic constant, shall appear in weak inequalities. Variables are interpreted in the model by *assignments* ρ that are total kind-preserving mappings from variables into ground terms; they are straightforwardly extended to terms and hand-sides.

Because constructed types and row terms are handled similarly in most of our development, it is convenient to introduce a common notation for them. (Indeed, only the unification algorithm described in Section 5.1, through the rule MUTATE, requires distinguishing them.) For this purpose, we let a *symbol* f be either a type constructor or a row label. If $f = c$ then $f(\tau_1, \ldots, \tau_n)$ stands for the type $c(\tau_1, \ldots, \tau_n)$ and, if $f = \ell$, then $f(\tau_1, \tau_2)$ stands for the row $(\ell : \tau_1, \tau_2)$. The notations for variance and weak inequality propagation introduced in Section 3 are extended to symbols accordingly. A *small term* is a term of height 0 or 1, i.e. either a variable α or a symbol with variable arguments $f(\alpha_1, \ldots, \alpha_n)$.

The formulas of the first order logic are *constraints* Γ:

$$\Gamma ::= \langle \tau = \cdots = \tau \rangle^\iota \approx \cdots \approx \langle \tau = \cdots = \tau \rangle^\iota$$
$$\mid\ \alpha \leq^\iota \alpha \mid \phi \sqsubset \phi \mid \mathbf{true} \mid \mathbf{false} \mid \Gamma \wedge \Gamma \mid \exists \alpha . \Gamma$$

Constraints are interpreted in the ground algebra by a two place predicate $\cdot \vdash \cdot$ whose first argument is an assignment and whose second argument is a constraint. Its formal description can be found in the full version of the paper [33]; here, we prefer to explain their semantics in words.

First, $\langle \bar{\bar{\tau}}_1 \rangle^{\iota_1} \approx \cdots \approx \langle \bar{\bar{\tau}}_n \rangle^{\iota_n}$ is a *multi-skeleton*. It is a multi-set of *multi-equations* $\bar{\bar{\tau}}_1, \ldots, \bar{\bar{\tau}}_n$ each of which is decorated with a boolean flag $\iota_1, \ldots, \iota_n$. A multi-equation $\bar{\bar{\tau}}_i$ is a multi-set of terms written $\tau_{i,1} = \cdots = \tau_{i,n_i}$. All terms appearing in a multi-skeleton must have the same kind. The flags carried by multi-equations have no logical meaning; they are just needed by one step of constraint solving to store some termination-related data. Such a multi-skeleton is interpreted as follows: it requires that all the terms appearing in the multi-skeleton belong to a single ground skeleton and, moreover, that all terms of each multi-equation have the same interpretation. In this paper, a multi-skeleton is denoted by the meta-variable $\bar{\bar{\tau}}$, or $\bar{\bar{\alpha}}$ when it is known to contain only variables. If $\bar{\bar{\tau}}$ is $\langle \bar{\bar{\tau}}_1 \rangle^{\iota_1} \approx \cdots \approx \langle \bar{\bar{\tau}}_n \rangle^{\iota_n}$ then $\langle \bar{\bar{\tau}} \rangle^{\iota} \approx \bar{\bar{\tau}}$ stands for the multi-skeleton $\langle \bar{\bar{\tau}} \rangle^{\iota} \approx \langle \bar{\bar{\tau}}_1 \rangle^{\iota_1} \approx \cdots \approx \langle \bar{\bar{\tau}}_n \rangle^{\iota_n}$. We adopt similar notations for multi-equations and we write $\tau_1 \approx \tau_2$ and $\tau_1 = \tau_2$ for $\langle \tau_1 \rangle^0 \approx \langle \tau_2 \rangle^0$ and $\langle \tau_1 = \tau_2 \rangle^0$, respectively.

A *strong inequality* $\alpha_1 \leq^{\iota} \alpha_2$ involves a pair of variables of the same kind and a boolean flag (which has the same use as those carried by multi-equations) interpreted in the ground algebra by the subtyping order $\leq$. A weak inequality $\phi_1 \sqsubset \phi_2$ consists of a pair of hand-sides. Atomic constants, which are not part of the terms grammar, can be encoded by these constraints: the atom a may be represented in the syntactic algebra by a "fresh" variable α of kind Atom and the pair of constraints $a \sqsubset \alpha$ and $\alpha \sqsubset a$.

Other constructs allow conjunction and existential quantification of constraints. The latter allows the introduction of intermediate variables, by the type checker during the constraint generation or by the solver itself for the purpose of resolution.

One may argue that the constraint language is not minimal. Indeed, multi-equations and multi-skeletons may be encoded using strong inequalities: on may prove that $\tau_1 \approx \tau_2$ and $\tau_1 = \tau_2$ are respectively equivalent to $\exists \beta.[\beta \leq \tau_1 \wedge \beta \leq \tau_2]$ and $\tau_1 \leq \tau_2 \wedge \tau_2 \leq \tau_1$. However, such an encoding is not practical, because multi-skeletons and multi-equations allow much more efficient representation and manipulation of constraints: they allow to benefit of the efficiency of unification-based algorithms, throughout the solving process. Indeed, in most applications, the client of the solver generates inequalities, while multi-skeletons belong only to the solver's internal representation of constraints and are introduced throughout the solving process. There is another slight redundancy in the logic: if α_1 and α_2 are two variables of kind Atom, the constraints $\alpha_1 \leq \alpha_2$ and $\alpha_1 \sqsubset \alpha_2$ are equivalent. By convention, in the remainder of the paper, any occurrence of the former must be read as an instance of the latter.

We omit the sorting rules necessary to ensure that terms and constraints are well-formed, which are standard. Moreover, we consider constraints modulo the commutativity and associativity of $\wedge$; and α-conversion and scope-extrusion of existential quantifications. (A complete specification of constraint kinding and equivalence is given in [33].) A constraint is ∃-*free* if it is a conjunction of multi-skeletons and inequalities. In the following, we write $\Gamma \doteq \exists \boldsymbol{\alpha}.\Gamma'$ if and only if $\exists \boldsymbol{\alpha}.\Gamma'$ is a representative of Γ such that Γ' is ∃-free. Every constraint admits such a representation.

Given an ∃-free constraint Γ, we let the predicate $\tau \approx \tau' \in \Gamma$ (resp. $\tau = \tau' \in \Gamma$) hold if and only if τ and τ' appear in the same multi-skeleton (resp. multi-equation) in Γ. Similarly, we write $\alpha_1 \leq \alpha_2 \in \Gamma$ if a constraint $\alpha_1 \leq^\iota \alpha_2$ appears within Γ, and $\bar{\alpha}_1 \leq \bar{\alpha}_2 \in \Gamma$ if $\alpha_1 \leq \alpha_2 \in \Gamma$ for some α_1 in $\bar{\alpha}_1$ and α_2 in $\bar{\alpha}_2$. The corresponding notations are also adopted for $\sqsubseteq$.

Let Γ_1 and Γ_2 be two constraints. Γ_1 *implies* Γ_2 (we write: $\Gamma_1 \models \Gamma_2$) if and only if every assignment which satisfies Γ_1 also satisfies Γ_2. Γ_1 and Γ_2 are *equivalent* ($\Gamma_1 \simeq \Gamma_2$) if $\Gamma_1 \models \Gamma_2$ and $\Gamma_2 \models \Gamma_1$.

4.2 Schemes

A (type) *scheme* σ is a triple of a set of quantifiers $\boldsymbol{\alpha}$, a constraint Γ and a body τ, written $\forall \boldsymbol{\alpha}[\Gamma].\tau$. Given an assignment ρ setting the interpretation of free variables, a scheme denotes a set of ground terms, which is obtained by applying all solutions of the constraint to the body:

$$\llbracket \sigma \rrbracket_\rho = \uparrow\{\rho'(\tau) \mid \rho' \vdash \Gamma \text{ and } \forall \beta \notin \boldsymbol{\alpha} \ \rho'(\beta) = \rho(\beta)\}$$

The upward-closure operator (written $\uparrow$) reflects the subsumption rule equipping systems with subtyping: any program of type t may be given a super-type t'.

A scheme σ_1 is more general than σ_2 if and only if it represents a larger set of ground terms under any context: $\sigma_1 \preccurlyeq \sigma_2$ holds if and only if for every assignment ρ, $\llbracket \sigma_2 \rrbracket_\rho \subseteq \llbracket \sigma_1 \rrbracket_\rho$. We write $\sigma_1 \simeq \sigma_2$ if σ_1 and σ_2 are *equivalent*, i.e. $\sigma_2 \preccurlyeq \sigma_1$ and $\sigma_1 \preccurlyeq \sigma_2$. In particular, if Γ_1 and Γ_2 are equivalent constraints then the schemes $\forall \boldsymbol{\alpha}[\Gamma_1].\tau$ and $\forall \boldsymbol{\alpha}[\Gamma_2].\tau$ are equivalent as well.

5 Solving Constraints

We are done introducing terms and constraints. We do not present an instance of this logic dedicated to a particular program analysis, or specify how schemes are associated to programs: this is merely out of the topic of this paper, several examples can be found in the literature, e.g. [5].

We now describe an algorithm to decide whether a scheme has an instance, and so determine whether a program is well-typed. For efficiency, the algorithm must also simplify the scheme at hand, by reducing the size of the constraint. Naturally, solving must be interlaced with simplifications, so that the former benefits from the latter. However, for the sake of clarity, we divide our presentation in two parts. The first one handles a single constraint which is rewritten into an equivalent one whose satisfiability can be immediately decided. The second part consists in a series of simplification techniques which consider the constraint in its context, i.e. a scheme. They are described in Section 6 and intended to be integrated throughout the solving process, as we will explain.

GENERATE$^{\leq}$

$$\frac{\alpha \leq^1 \beta}{\alpha \leq^0 \beta \wedge \alpha \approx \beta}\rightsquigarrow$$

FUSE$^{\approx}$

$$\frac{\langle \alpha = \bar{\bar{\tau}}\rangle^\iota \approx \bar{\bar{\tau}} \wedge \langle \alpha = \bar{\bar{\tau}}'\rangle^{\iota'} \approx \bar{\bar{\tau}}'}{\langle \alpha = \bar{\bar{\tau}} = \bar{\bar{\tau}}'\rangle^{\iota \vee \iota'} \approx \bar{\bar{\tau}} \approx \bar{\bar{\tau}}'}\rightsquigarrow$$

FUSE$^{=}$

$$\frac{\langle \alpha = \bar{\tau}\rangle^\iota \approx \langle \alpha = \bar{\tau}'\rangle^{\iota'} \approx \bar{\bar{\tau}}}{\langle \alpha = \bar{\tau} = \bar{\tau}'\rangle^{\iota \vee \iota'} \approx \bar{\bar{\tau}}}\rightsquigarrow$$

DECOMPOSE$^{\approx}$

$$\frac{\langle \bar{\bar{\tau}} = f(\boldsymbol{\alpha})\rangle^1 \approx \langle \bar{\bar{\tau}}' = f(\boldsymbol{\beta})\rangle^1 \approx \bar{\bar{\tau}}}{\langle \bar{\bar{\tau}} = f(\boldsymbol{\alpha})\rangle^1 \approx \langle \bar{\bar{\tau}}' = f(\boldsymbol{\beta})\rangle^0 \approx \bar{\bar{\tau}} \wedge_i \alpha_i \approx^{v_i(f)} \beta_i}\rightsquigarrow$$

DECOMPOSE$^{=}$

$$\frac{\langle \bar{\bar{\tau}} = f(\boldsymbol{\alpha}) = f(\boldsymbol{\beta})\rangle^\iota \approx \bar{\bar{\tau}}}{\langle \bar{\bar{\tau}} = f(\boldsymbol{\alpha})\rangle^\iota \approx \bar{\bar{\tau}} \wedge_i \alpha_i = \beta_i}\rightsquigarrow$$

MUTATE

$$\frac{\bar{\bar{\tau}} \approx \langle \bar{\bar{\tau}} = \ell_b : \tau_b, \tau'\rangle^\iota}{\exists \alpha \alpha'.[\bar{\bar{\tau}} \approx \langle \bar{\bar{\tau}} = \ell_a : \tau_a, \alpha'\rangle^1 \wedge \langle \alpha' = \ell_b : \tau_b, \alpha\rangle^1 \wedge \langle \tau' = \ell_a : \tau_a, \alpha\rangle^1]}\rightsquigarrow \quad \begin{array}{l}(\text{if } \ell_a \in \mathsf{Roots}(\bar{\bar{\tau}}, \bar{\bar{\tau}}) \\ \text{and } \ell_a <_{\mathcal{L}} \ell_b)\end{array}$$

GENERALIZE

$$\frac{\bar{\bar{\tau}}[\tau/\alpha]}{\exists \alpha.[\bar{\bar{\tau}} \wedge \langle \alpha = \tau\rangle^1]}\rightsquigarrow \quad \begin{array}{l}(\text{if } \tau \text{ is not a variable and} \\ \alpha \text{ occurs in a non-variable term of } \bar{\bar{\tau}} \text{ but not in } \tau)\end{array}$$

Fig. 3. Unification (rewriting system Ω_u)

The algorithm for solving constraints is made of several steps; some of them are formalized as *rewriting systems*. A rewriting system Ω consists in a reduction relation, $-\Omega\rightarrow$, defined by a set of rules of the form

$$\Gamma_i^o \vdash \frac{\Gamma_i}{\Gamma_i'}\rightsquigarrow$$

Then $-\Omega\rightarrow$ is the smallest congruence (w.r.t. $\wedge$ and $\exists$) such that, for all i, $\Gamma_i^o \wedge \Gamma_i -\Omega\rightarrow \Gamma_i^o \wedge \Gamma_i'$. Ω is *sound* if it preserves the semantics of constraints, i.e. $\Gamma -\Omega\rightarrow \Gamma'$ implies $\Gamma \simeq \Gamma'$. It *terminates* on Γ if it has no infinite derivation whose origin is Γ. We write $\Gamma -\Omega\rightarrow \Gamma'$ if and only if $\Gamma -\Omega\rightarrow^* \Gamma'$ and Γ' is an normal form for $-\Omega\rightarrow$.

Rewriting systems are convenient to describe algorithms in a concise and precise manner, and to reason about them. Moreover, they allow abstracting away from some details of an implementation, such as an evaluation strategy specifying the order in which rules have to be applied.

5.1 Unification

The first step of the solving algorithm is made of two interlaced unification processes: one for skeletons (multi-skeletons) and the other for terms (multi-equations). Each of them is to some extent similar to unification in equational theories [31]. They are described by the rewriting system of figure 3, that intends to rewrite the input constraint into an equivalent one $\Gamma \doteq \exists \boldsymbol{\alpha}.\Gamma'$ which is *unified*. We now explain the properties which define unified constraints and how the rules make the constraint at hand satisfying them.

First and foremost, reflecting the inclusion of $\leq$ in $\approx$, **(1)** *strong inequalities must be propagated to skeletons*: if $\alpha \leq \beta \in \Gamma'$ then α and β must have the same skeleton, and $\alpha \approx \beta \in \Gamma'$ must hold. This is realized by GENERATE$^{\leq}$, which generates a multi-skeleton from every strong inequality. As a side-effect, the flag carried by the inequality decreases from 1 to 0 preventing multiple applications

EXPAND

$$\frac{\langle\bar{\bar{\alpha}}\rangle \approx \langle\bar{\bar{\tau}} = f(\boldsymbol{\beta})\rangle \approx \bar{\bar{\tau}}'}{\exists\boldsymbol{\alpha}.[\langle\bar{\bar{\alpha}} = f(\boldsymbol{\alpha})\rangle \approx \langle\bar{\bar{\tau}} = f(\boldsymbol{\beta})\rangle \approx \bar{\bar{\tau}}' \wedge_i \beta_i \approx^{v_i(f)} \alpha_i]}\rightsquigarrow$$

EXP-FUSE$^{\approx}$

$$\frac{\langle\alpha = \bar{\bar{\tau}}\rangle \approx \bar{\bar{\tau}} \wedge \langle\alpha = \bar{\bar{\alpha}}\rangle \approx \bar{\bar{\alpha}}}{\langle\alpha = \bar{\bar{\tau}} = \bar{\bar{\alpha}}\rangle \approx \bar{\bar{\tau}} \approx \bar{\bar{\alpha}}}\rightsquigarrow$$

EXP-FUSE$^{=}$

$$\frac{\langle\alpha = \bar{\bar{\tau}}\rangle \approx \langle\alpha = \bar{\bar{\alpha}}\rangle \approx \bar{\bar{\tau}}}{\langle\alpha = \bar{\bar{\tau}} = \bar{\bar{\alpha}}\rangle \approx \bar{\bar{\tau}}}\rightsquigarrow$$

DECOMPOSE$^{\leq}$

$$\begin{array}{l}\alpha = f(\boldsymbol{\alpha}) \\ \beta = f(\boldsymbol{\beta})\end{array} \vdash \frac{\alpha \leq \beta}{\wedge_i \alpha_i \leq^{v_i(f)} \beta_i}\rightsquigarrow$$

DECOMPOSE^{l}

$$\alpha = f(\boldsymbol{\alpha}) \vdash \frac{\alpha \sqsubseteq \phi}{\wedge_{i \in l(f)} \alpha_i \sqsubseteq \phi}\rightsquigarrow$$

DECOMPOSE^{r}

$$\alpha = f(\boldsymbol{\alpha}) \vdash \frac{\phi \sqsubseteq \alpha}{\wedge_{i \in r(f)} \phi \sqsubseteq \alpha_i}\rightsquigarrow$$

Fig. 4. Expansion and decomposition (rewriting system Ω_{ed})

of the rule on the same constraint. Then, **(2)** *the multi-equations of a unified constraint must be fused*, i.e. every variable can appear at most in one of them. This is made possible by the transitivity of $\approx$ and $=$: rule FUSE$^{\approx}$ merges two multi-skeletons which have a common variable and then FUSE$^{=}$ operates on pairs of multi-equations within a multi-skeleton.

Furthermore, constraints involving non-variable terms must be propagated to sub-terms. This concerns **(3)** *multi-skeletons that must be decomposed*: two non-variable terms in the same multi-skeleton must have the same root symbol and if $f(\boldsymbol{\alpha}) \approx f(\boldsymbol{\beta}) \in \Gamma'$ then, for all i, $\alpha_i \approx^{v_i(f)} \beta_i \in \Gamma'$. An application of DECOMPOSE$^{\approx}$ propagates *same-skeleton* constraints between two non-variable terms with the same head symbol to their sub-terms. This is recorded by changing the flag of one of the two multi-equations from 1 to 0: once again, this prevents successive applications of the rule on the same pair of terms. (In this rule, $\alpha_i \approx^{v_i(f)} \beta_i$ stands for $\alpha_i = \beta_i$ if $v_i(f) = \odot$ and $\alpha_i \approx \beta_i$ otherwise. Furthermore, $\Gamma \wedge_i \alpha_i \approx^{v_i(f)} \beta_i$ where i ranges from 1 to n is a shorthand for $\Gamma \wedge \alpha_1 \approx^{v_1(f)} \beta_1 \wedge \cdots \wedge \alpha_n \approx^{v_n(f)} \beta_n$.) Decomposition also occurs for multi-equations: in a unified constraint, **(4)** *every multi-equation must involve at most one non-variable term*. This is enforced thanks to DECOMPOSE$^{=}$, which is similar DECOMPOSE$^{\approx}$; however, one of the two terms may be removed here, which is sufficient to ensure termination. Besides, when a multi-equation contains two row terms with different labels, it is necessary to permute one of them by a *mutation* (rule MUTATE) in order to be able to apply DECOMPOSE$^{\approx}$ or DECOMPOSE$^{=}$. (Roots($\bar{\bar{\tau}}$) stands for the set of symbols f such that $f(\boldsymbol{\tau}) \in \bar{\bar{\tau}}$ for some $\boldsymbol{\tau}$.) In the purpose of orienting the permutation of labels, MUTATE assumes an arbitrary well-founded order $\leq_{\mathcal{L}}$ on labels. Lastly, **(5)** *a unified constraint can involve only small terms*. Thus, GENERALIZE replaces a deep occurrence of a non-variable term τ in a multi-skeleton by a fresh variable α and adds the constraint $\alpha = \tau$. This allows in particular decomposition to apply to small terms only and prevents duplicating structure.

Unification may fail if rewriting produces a constraint where two different type constructors appear as roots in the same multi-skeleton. Such a constraint is said to be a *unification error* and is not satisfiable. A constraint which satisfies the conditions (1) to (5) above and is not a unification error is *unified*.

Theorem 1 (Unification). *Assume every flag in Γ is 1. Then Ω_u terminates on Γ. If $\Gamma -_{\Omega_u} \twoheadrightarrow \Gamma'$ then Γ' is equivalent to Γ and either unified or erroneous.*

This theorem states the soundness and the completeness of the unification algorithm. Because flags carried by multi-equations are no longer used by the following steps of the algorithm, we omit them in the remainder of the paper.

In our implementation [28], unification is performed during constraint construction by the type checker. This allows unification errors to be detected immediately; thus they may be reported by the same techniques than those used in unification-based systems. What is more, only unified constraints may be stored in the solver: indeed, every multi-skeleton or multi-equation is represented by a single node. Multi-equations carry a pointer to the multi-skeleton they belong to, so that fusing can be performed efficiently by union-find. Moreover, every node has pointers to its "sub-nodes", if any; which allow decomposition. Lastly, inequalities are stored as the edges of a graph between nodes.

5.2 Occur-Check

Because recursive terms are not valid solutions for constraints in the model, one must ensure that the multi-skeletons of a constraint do not require cyclic term structures. This verification is commonly referred to as the *occur-check*. By lack of space, we omit its formal description, which is standard and can be found in [33], and just introduce notions that are useful for the following. In short, considering a constraint Γ, it requires to compute a topological ordering $\prec_\Gamma$ of variables according to the term structure imposed by Γ's multi-skeletons. Roughly speaking $\beta \prec_\Gamma \alpha$ means that β appears in a *sub-skeleton* of α. Variables which are minimal for $\prec_\Gamma$ are *terminal*. These are variables about whose structure Γ tells nothing.

It is worth noting that, because unification terminates even in the presence of cyclic structures, it is not necessary to perform an occur-check every time two terms are unified; a single invocation at the end is sufficient and more efficient.

5.3 Expansion and Decomposition

Let us first illustrate this step by an example: consider the multi-skeleton $\langle\alpha\rangle \approx \langle\beta = c(\beta_1, \ldots, \beta_n)\rangle$. Every solution of this constraint maps α to a c type; hence we can *expand* α and rewrite the constraint as $\exists\alpha.[\langle\alpha = c(\alpha_1, \ldots, \alpha_n)\rangle \approx \langle\beta = c(\beta_1, \ldots, \beta_n)\rangle]$. Besides, taking advantage of the previous expansion, it is possible to *decompose* the inequality $\alpha \leq \beta$ as a series of inequalities relating the sub-variables according to c's variances, i.e. $\alpha_1 \leq^{v_1(c)} \beta_1 \wedge \cdots \wedge \alpha_n \leq^{v_n(c)} \beta_n$.

Formally, a variable α is *expanded* in an $\exists$-free constraint Γ if there exists a non-variable term τ such that $\alpha = \tau \in \Gamma$ holds. It is *decomposed* if it does not appear in any of Γ's inequalities. We say Γ is *expanded down to* α if and only if every variable β such that $\alpha \prec_\Gamma^+ \beta$ is expanded. A constraint $\Gamma \doteq \exists \boldsymbol{\alpha}.\Gamma'$ is expanded if and only if Γ' is expanded down to all its terminal variables. We adopt the same terminology for decomposition. A unified, expanded and decomposed constraint which satisfies the occur-check is *reduced*.

The rewriting system Ω_{ed} (Figure 4) rewrites a unified constraint which satisfies the occur-check into an equivalent reduced one. Rule EXPAND performs the expansion of a non-terminal variable. Fresh variables are introduced as arguments of the symbol, with the appropriate $\approx$ and $=$ constraints. These are merged with existing multi-skeletons by rules EXP-FUSE$^\approx$ and EXP-FUSE$^=$, respectively (which are particular cases of FUSE$^\approx$ and FUSE$^=$), allowing the constraint to remain unified. Strong inequalities are decomposed by DECOMPOSE$^\leq$. In this rule, $\alpha_i \leq^{v_i(f)} \beta_i$ stands for $\alpha_i \leq \beta_i$ (resp. $\beta_i \leq \alpha_i$) if $v_i(c) = \oplus$ (resp. $\ominus$). In the case where $v_i(c) = \odot$, it must be read as the constraint **true**, which is sufficient because the equation $\alpha_i = \beta_i$ has already been generated during unification by GENERATE$^\leq$ and DECOMPOSE$^\approx$. Weak inequalities are decomposed by DECOMPOSE^l and DECOMPOSE^r.

Termination of expansion and decomposition relies on the the occur-check; that is the reason why we did not allow recursive types in the model. As an implementation strategy, it is wise to expand and decompose multi-skeletons by considering them in the topological order exposed by the occur-check; so that fresh variables and inequalities are generated only within skeletons that have not yet been dealt with.

Theorem 2 (Expansion and decomposition). *Let Γ be a unified constraint which satisfies the occur-check. Ω_{ed} terminates on Γ. If $\Gamma -_{\Omega_{ed}} \twoheadrightarrow \Gamma'$ then Γ' is equivalent to Γ and reduced.*

A constraint is *atomic* if and only if all its terms are terminal. Given a reduced constraint Γ we define its *atomic part* as the constraint $\lfloor \Gamma \rfloor$ obtained from Γ by removing all multi-skeletons which contain non-variable terms.

Theorem 3. *If Γ is reduced, then the satisfiability of Γ and $\lfloor \Gamma \rfloor$ are equivalent.*

This theorem shows that the satisfiability of a reduced constraint is equivalent to that of its atomic part. As a consequence, it is now sufficient to provide an algorithm for solving atomic constraints, which we do in the following subsection.

5.4   Solving Atomic Constraints

The algorithm for solving a $\exists$-free atomic constraint Γ consists in checking that, in the graph defined by Γ's inequalities, there is no path between two constants a_1 and a_2 such that $a_1 \not\leq_\mathcal{A} a_2$. Paths are formally defined by the predicates $\Gamma \mathrel{\approx\!\!\!\!/} \cdot \sqsubset \cdot$ and $\Gamma \mathrel{\approx\!\!\!\!/} \cdot \leq \cdot$ introduced in Figure 5 and may be checked in linear time. The following theorem states the criterion of satisfiability of atomic constraints involved by our algorithm.

Theorem 4. *Let $\Gamma \doteq \exists \boldsymbol{\alpha}.\Gamma'$ be an atomic constraint. Γ is satisfiable if and only if for all atoms a_1 and a_2, $\Gamma' \mathrel{\approx\!\!\!\!/} a_1 \sqsubset a_2$ implies $a_1 \leq_\mathcal{A} a_2$.*

$$\frac{\alpha_1 = \alpha_2 \in \Gamma \text{ or } \alpha_1 \leq \alpha_2 \in \Gamma}{\Gamma \not\approx \alpha_1 \leq \alpha_2} \qquad \frac{\phi_1 \sqsubset \phi_2 \in \Gamma}{\Gamma \not\approx \phi_1 \sqsubset \phi_2}$$

$$\frac{\Gamma \not\approx \alpha_1 \leq \alpha_2 \quad \Gamma \not\approx \alpha_2 \leq \alpha_3}{\Gamma \not\approx \alpha_1 \leq \alpha_3} \qquad \frac{\Gamma \not\approx \phi_1 \sqsubset \phi_2 \quad \Gamma \not\approx \phi_2 \sqsubset \phi_3}{\Gamma \not\approx \phi_1 \sqsubset \phi_3} \qquad \frac{\Gamma \not\approx \phi_1 \sqsubset \alpha_2 \quad \Gamma \not\approx \alpha_2 \leq \alpha_3}{\Gamma \not\approx \phi_1 \sqsubset \beta_3} \qquad \frac{\Gamma \not\approx \alpha_1 \leq \alpha_2 \quad \Gamma \not\approx \alpha_2 \sqsubset \phi_3}{\Gamma \not\approx \alpha_1 \sqsubset \phi_3}$$

Fig. 5. Syntactic implication

5.5 Complexity Analysis

We now informally discuss the theoretical complexity of the solving algorithm, i.e. the four steps described in Section 5.1 to 5.4. The input of the algorithm, a constraint Γ, is measured as its size n which is the sum of the sizes of all the involved terms, which is generally proportional to the size of the studied program. As we have explained, we make the hypothesis that the height of terms is bounded: we let h be the length of the longest chain (w.r.t. $\prec_\Gamma$) found by occur-check and a the maximal arity of constructors. For the sake of simplicity, we exclude rows of our study, whose analysis is more delicate [35].

The first step of the algorithm is the combination of two unification algorithms, one applying on multi-skeletons and the other on multi-equations, which may be—in the absence of row terms—performed separately. Hence, using a union-find algorithm, it requires time $O(n\alpha(n))$ (where α is related to an inverse of Ackermann's function) [36]. Occur-check is equivalent to a topological ordering of the graph of multi-skeletons, so it is linear in their number, which is $O(n)$. Then, under the hypothesis of bounded-terms, expansion generates at most a^h new variables for each variable in the input problem, and, the decomposition of an inequality is similarly bounded. So, these two steps cost $O(a^h n)$. Lastly, checking paths in the atomic graph can be done in linear time by a topological walk, provided that lattice operations on atoms (i.e. $\leq$, $\sqcup$ and $\sqcap$) can be computed in constant time.

6 Simplifying Constraints and Type Schemes

We are done in describing the corpus of the solving algorithm. We now have to introduce throughout this process a series of heuristics whose purpose is to reduce the size of the problem at hand, and hence improve the efficiency of solving. Simplification is a subtle problem: it must be correct (i.e. the result must be equivalent to the input) as well as efficient in computation time and effective in constraint size reduction. Following our pragmatic motivation, we do not address here the question of optimality or completeness of simplification. Instead, we present a series of techniques which we have experienced to be effective: finely combined into the solving algorithm, they allow to notably improve its efficiency.

The most critical part of solving is expansion, which is likely to introduce a lot of new variables. As we have explained, expansion is performed one multi-skeleton at a time, in the order found by the occur-check. So, in attempt to minimize its possible impact, we will apply those of our techniques that are *local* to a multi-skeleton (Section 6.1 and 6.3) just before its variables are expanded, in order to reduce the number of variables to be introduced. A second group of simplifications (Section 6.4 and 6.5) needs to consider the whole graph of atomic constraints. As a result, they are performed only once, at the end of solving. Their purpose is to overcome another costly part of type inference in presence of *let*-polymorphism: generalization and instantiation require duplicating schemes, hence they must be made as compact as possible. They also allow obtaining human-readable typing information.

Basically, there are two ways to reduce the size of schemes. The first one (featured in Sections 6.1, 6.3 and 6.5) consists in identifying variables. Formally, this consists in replacing inequalities by multi-equations, which is effective since dealing with the latter is much more efficient than with the former. The second one (Section 6.4) removes intermediate variables which are no longer useful for the final result (e.g. because they are unreachable).

In this section, we restrict our attention to schemes whose constraint is $\exists$-free. (This is not restrictive because $\forall \alpha [\exists \beta . \Gamma] . \tau$ can be rewritten into $\forall \alpha \beta [\Gamma] . \tau$.)

6.1   Collapsing Cycles

Cycle detection allows replacing a cycle of inequalities by a multi-equation in a constraint. A cycle consists in a list of multi-equations $\bar{\bar{\alpha}}_0, \ldots, \bar{\bar{\alpha}}_n$ such that $\bar{\bar{\alpha}}_1 \leq \bar{\bar{\alpha}}_2 \in \Gamma, \ldots, \bar{\bar{\alpha}}_n \leq \bar{\bar{\alpha}}_1 \in \Gamma$. Clearly, any solution ρ for Γ satisfies $\rho(\bar{\bar{\alpha}}_1) = \cdots = \rho(\bar{\bar{\alpha}}_n)$. Thus, the multi-equations $\bar{\bar{\alpha}}_0, \ldots, \bar{\bar{\alpha}}_n$ can be fused

In [37], Fähndrich *et al.* proposed a partial on-line cycle detection algorithm, which permits to collapse cycles incrementally at the same time as inequalities are generated by some closure algorithm. However, in the current paper, all the variables in a cycle of a unified constraint must belong to the same multi-skeleton. This allows considering each multi-skeleton separately—before its expansion— and thus using a standard graph algorithm for detecting cycles in linear time, which is more efficient.

6.2   Polarities

The remaining simplification techniques need to consider the constraint at hand in its context, i.e. a whole scheme describing a (piece of) program. Indeed, this allows distinguishing the type variables which represent an "input" of the program from those which stand for an "output": the former are referred to as *negative* while the latter are *positive*. Because we remain abstract from the programming language and the type system itself, these notions are only given by the variances of type constructors: roughly speaking, one may say that a covariant argument describes an output while a contravariant one stands for an input. (This is reflected by the variances commonly attributed to the $\rightarrow$ type constructor in λ-calculus or ML.) Because non-positive variables are not related to the *output* produced by the program, we are not interested with their lower bounds. Similarly, the upper bounds of non-negative variables do not matter.

For this purpose, we assign polarities [12,16,18] to variables in a scheme $\sigma = \forall \boldsymbol{\alpha}[\Gamma].\tau$: we write $\sigma \vdash \alpha : +$ (resp. $\sigma \vdash \alpha : -$) if α is *positive* (resp. *negative*) in σ. (The same variable can simultaneously be both.) Regarding variances of symbols, polarities are extended to terms by the following rule

$$\frac{\forall i \ v_i(f) \in \{\oplus, \odot\} \Rightarrow \sigma \vdash \tau_i : + \qquad \forall i \ v_i(f) \in \{\ominus, \odot\} \Rightarrow \sigma \vdash \tau_i : -}{\sigma \vdash f(\tau_1, \ldots, \tau_n) : +}$$

and its symmetric counterpart for proving $\sigma \vdash f(\tau_1, \ldots, \tau_n) : -$. Then, $\sigma \vdash \cdot : +$ and $\sigma \vdash \cdot : -$ are defined as the smallest predicates such that:

$$\sigma \vdash \tau : + \qquad \frac{\alpha \notin \alpha}{\sigma \vdash \alpha : \pm} \qquad \frac{\sigma \vdash \alpha : + \qquad \alpha = \tau' \in \Gamma}{\sigma \vdash \tau' : +} \qquad \frac{\sigma \vdash \alpha : - \qquad \alpha = \tau' \in \Gamma}{\sigma \vdash \tau' : -}$$

The first rule reflects the fact that the body describes the result produced by the associated piece of code, hence it is positive. The second rule makes every free variable bipolar, because it is likely to be related to any other piece of code. The last two rules propagate polarities throughout the structure of terms. Polarities can be computed by a simple propagation during expansion.

6.3 Reducing Chains

Constraint generation yields a large number of chains of inequalities: because subsumption is allowed at any point in a program, the type synthesizer usually generates inequalities for all of them; but many are not really used by the program at hand. Chains reduction intends to detect and remove these intermediate variables and constraints, as proposed by Eifrig *et al* [38] and, by Aiken and Fähndrich [15] in the setting of set constraints. Here, we adapt their proposal to the case of structural subtyping.

We say that $\bar{\bar{\tau}}$ is the unique predecessor of $\bar{\bar{\alpha}}$ in $\forall \boldsymbol{\alpha}[\Gamma].\tau$ if and only if $\bar{\bar{\tau}} \leq \bar{\bar{\alpha}} \in \Gamma$ and it is the only inequality involving $\bar{\bar{\alpha}}$ as right-hand-side. Symmetrically, we define unique successors. The following theorem states that a non-positive (resp. non-negative) multi-equation may be fused with its unique successor (resp. predecessor).

Theorem 5 (Chains). *Let $\sigma = \forall \boldsymbol{\alpha}[\Gamma \wedge \langle \bar{\bar{\alpha}} \rangle \approx \langle \bar{\bar{\tau}} \rangle \approx \bar{\bar{\tau}}].\tau$ be a unified scheme, satisfying the occur-check, expanded and decomposed down to $\bar{\bar{\alpha}}$. If $\bar{\bar{\alpha}}$ is non-positive (resp. non-negative) and $\bar{\bar{\tau}}$ is its unique successor (resp. predecessor) then σ is equivalent to $\forall \boldsymbol{\alpha}[\Gamma \wedge \langle \bar{\bar{\alpha}} = \bar{\bar{\tau}} \rangle \approx \bar{\bar{\tau}}].\tau$.*

6.4 Polarized Garbage Collection

Computing the scheme which describes a piece of code typically yields a large number of variables. Many of them are useful only during intermediate steps of the type generation, but are no longer essential once it is over. Garbage collection is designed to keep only polar variables in the scheme at hand, and paths from variables which are related to some input of the program (i.e. negative ones) to those which are related to some output (i.e. positive ones). Indeed, it rewrites the input constraint into a *closed* one such that: (1) every variable appearing in a multi-skeleton is polar, (2) for every inequality $\alpha_1 \leq \alpha_2$ or $\alpha_1 \sqsubseteq \alpha_2$, α_1 is negative and α_2 is positive, (3) only positive (resp. negative) variables may have a constant lower (resp. upper) bound, which—if it exists—is unique. This idea has been introduced by Trifonov and Smith [16] in the case of non-structural subtyping.

Let $\sigma = \forall \boldsymbol{\alpha}[\Gamma].\tau$ be a scheme with Γ reduced and satisfiable. We define the lower and upper bounds of α in Γ by: $\mathrm{lb}_\Gamma(\alpha) = \sqcup\{a \mid \Gamma \not\approx a \sqsubseteq \alpha\}$ and $\mathrm{ub}_\Gamma(\alpha) = \sqcap\{a \mid \Gamma \not\approx \alpha \sqsubseteq a\}$. A multi-equation is said to be polar if it contains a variable which is negative or positive. Then, $GC(\sigma)$ is $\forall \boldsymbol{\alpha}[\Gamma'].\tau$ where Γ' is the conjunction of the following constraints:

- $\langle \bar{\bar{\tau}}_1 \rangle \approx \cdots \approx \langle \bar{\bar{\tau}}_n \rangle$, for all $\bar{\bar{\tau}}_1, \ldots, \bar{\bar{\tau}}_n$ which are the polar multi-equations of one of Γ's multi-skeletons,
- $\alpha \leq \beta$, for all α and β such that $\Gamma \not\approx \alpha \leq \beta$ and $\sigma \vdash \alpha : -$ and $\sigma \vdash \beta : +$,
- $\alpha \sqsubseteq \beta$, for all α and β such that $\Gamma \not\approx \alpha \sqsubseteq \beta$ and $\sigma \vdash \alpha : -$ and $\sigma \vdash \beta : +$,
- $\mathrm{lb}_\Gamma \alpha \sqsubseteq \alpha$, for all α such that $\sigma \vdash \alpha : +$ and $\mathrm{lb}_\Gamma \alpha \neq \perp$
- $\alpha \sqsubseteq \mathrm{ub}_\Gamma \alpha$, for all α such that $\sigma \vdash \alpha : -$ and $\mathrm{ub}_\Gamma \alpha \neq \top$

It is worth noting that, once garbage collection is performed, a scheme involves only polar variables. Hence, using a suitable substitution, it may be rewritten in a body giving the whole term structure, and a constraint (consisting in a conjunction of $\approx$, $\leq$ and $\sqsubseteq$) relating variables of the body, without any intermediate one. This form is most suitable for giving human-readable type information.

6.5   Minimization

This simplification intends to reduce the number of distinct variables or terms in a constraint by detecting some equivalences. It is called *minimization* because it is similar to that of an automaton (which detects equivalent states).

Let $\sigma = \forall \boldsymbol{\alpha}[\Gamma].\tau$ be a unified scheme. Two terminal multi-equations $\bar{\alpha}_1$ and $\bar{\alpha}_2$ of the same multi-skeleton are equivalent in σ (we write $\bar{\alpha}_1 \sim_\sigma \bar{\alpha}_2$) if

- either they are non-positive and have the same successors (i.e. $\{\beta \mid \bar{\alpha}_1 \leq \beta \in \Gamma\} = \{\beta \mid \bar{\alpha}_2 \leq \beta \in \Gamma\}$ and $\{\phi \mid \bar{\alpha}_1 \sqsubseteq \phi \in \Gamma\} = \{\phi \mid \bar{\alpha}_2 \sqsubseteq \phi \in \Gamma\}$),
- or they are non-negative and have the same predecessors (i.e. $\{\beta \mid \beta \leq \bar{\alpha}_1 \in \Gamma\} = \{\beta \mid \beta \leq \bar{\alpha}_2 \in \Gamma\}$ and $\{\phi \mid \phi \sqsubseteq \bar{\alpha}_1 \in \Gamma\} = \{\phi \mid \phi \sqsubseteq \bar{\alpha}_2 \in \Gamma\}$).

Minimization consists in fusing every pair of equivalent multi-equations. So, we define $M(\sigma) = \forall \boldsymbol{\alpha}[\Gamma \wedge \{\bar{\alpha}_1 = \bar{\alpha}_2 \mid \bar{\alpha}_1 \sim_\sigma \bar{\alpha}_2\}].\tau$.

Theorem 6 (Minimization). *Let σ be a reduced and closed scheme. $M(\sigma)$ is equivalent to σ.*

Once minimization has been performed, the equivalences found between the terminal variables can be propagated throughout the term structure thanks to *hash-consing*. This is described in the full version of the paper [33]. However, this does not improve readability of the terms printed by the solver (because they are generally displayed without exhibiting sharing between internal nodes) and, according to our experiments (see Section 7), it has only a little impact on the practical efficiency.

Table 1. Experimental measures

	Caml Light		Flow Caml
	library	compiler	library
A.s.t. nodes	14002	22996	13123
1. Type inference[1]			
Unification	0.346 s	0.954 s	
Structural subtyping (Dalton)	0.966 s	2.213 s	n.a.
ratio	2.79	2.31	
2. Statistics about Dalton[2]			
Multi-equations	30345	65946	73328
Collapsing cycles	501 (2%)	1381 (2%)	1764 (2%)
Chain reduction	9135 (30%)	15967 (24%)	17239 (24%)
Garbage collection	15288 (50%)	31215 (47%)	18460 (25%)
Minimization	424 (1%)	644 (1%)	815 (1%)
Expanded variables[3]	948 (3%)	1424 (2%)	1840 (3%)
	(9% of n.t.)	(8% of n.t.)	(14% of n.t.)

[1] Benchmarks realized on a Pentium III 1 GHz (average of 100 runs)
[2] Percentages relative to the total number of multi-equations

[3] The 2nd percentage is relative to the number of non-terminal multi-eq. considered by expansion

7 Implementation and Experiments

The Dalton library [28] is a real-size implementation in Objective Caml of the algorithms described in the current paper. In this library, the constraint solver comes as a *functor* parametrized by a series of modules describing the client's type system. Hence, we hope it will be a suitable type inference engine for a variety of applications.

We have experimented with this toolkit in two prototypes. First, we designed an implementation of the Caml Light compiler that is modular w.r.t. the type system and the constraints solver used for type inference. We equipped this prototype with two engines:

- A standard unification-based solver, which implements the same type system as Caml Light,
- An instance of the Dalton library, which features an extension of the previous type system with structural subtyping, where each type constructor carry an extra atomic annotation belonging to some arbitrary lattice.

This second type system has no interest for itself, but is a good representative— in terms of constraints resolution—of real ones featuring structural subtyping in the purpose of performing some static analysis on programs, such as a data or information flow analysis. We ran them on several sets of source code files, including the Caml Light compiler and its standard library; the resulting measures appear in the first two columns of Table 1. To compare our framework with standard unification, we measure the computation time of the typing phase of compilation: on our tests, Dalton appears to be slower than unification only by a factor comprised between 2 to 3. Such measures must be interpreted carefully. However, unification is recognized to be efficient and is widely used; so we believe them to be a point assessing the practicality and the scalability of our framework. Besides, we used our solver as the type inference engine of `Flow Caml` [39], an information flow analyzer for the Caml language. The measures obtained during the analysis of its library appear in the last column of Table 1.

These experiments also provide information about the behavior of the solving algorithm and the efficiency of simplification techniques. We measured the total number of multi-equations generated throughout type generation and constraints solving, and of those which are collected by one of the simplification techniques. Chain reduction appears as a key optimization, since it approximatively eliminates one quarter of multi-equations—that are variables—*before* expansion. The direct contribution of collapsing cycles is ten times less; however, we observed that skipping this simplification affects chain reduction. Hence, expansion becomes marginal: the number of variables that are expanded represents only a few percents of the total number of multi-equations, and about a tenth of the non-terminal multi-equations considered by expansion. Simplifying before expansion is crucial: if we modify our implementation by postponing chain reduction after expansion, the number of expanded variables grow by a factor around 20. Lastly, our measures show that the contribution of garbage collection is comparable to that of chain reduction; minimization has less impact on the size of the constraints but appears crucial for readability.

8   Discussion

Our implementation handles polymorphism in a manner inspired by Trifonov and Smith [16], where all type schemes are *closed*, i.e. have no free type variables, but contain a local environment. The interest lies in the fact that generalization and instantiation simply consist in making fresh copies of schemes. This approach turns out to be reasonable in practice, mostly because, thanks to simplification, the size of copied structures is limited. However, it should also be possible to deal with polymorphism in a more standard way, by using numeric *ranks* for distinguishing generalizable variables [31]. This would require making copies of constraints *fragments*, which yields more complicated machinery. However, in both approaches, we are still faced with the problem of constraints duplication. This is largely similar to the difficulty encountered in ML, whose practical impact is limited. Furthermore, this question has been studied for the setting of a flow analysis in [40].

Several possible extensions of the system may be mentioned. An interesting question lies in the introduction of recursive terms. This should mostly require to adapt expansion which relies on the finiteness of the term structure. Besides, in this paper, $\sqsubseteq$ is only allowed to consider *covariant* arguments of type constructors. However, in [5], the combination of polymorphic equality and mutable cells requires weak inequalities to be decomposed on *invariant* arguments too. Such an extension requires introducing weak inequalities on *skeletons*. This is experimentally handled by our implementation.

References

1. Bourdoncle, F., Merz, S.: Type checking higher-order polymorphic multi-methods. In: 24th Principles of Programming Languages. (1997)
2. Pottier, F.: A versatile constraint-based type inference system. Nordic Journal of Computing **7** (2000)
3. Aiken, A.S., Fähndrich, M.: Program analysis using mixed term and set constraints. In: 4th Static Analysis Symposium. (1997)
4. Palsberg, J., O'Keefe, P.M.: A type system equivalent to flow analysis. In: 22nd Principles of Programming Languages. (1995)
5. Pottier, F., Simonet, V.: Information flow inference for ML. In: 29th Principles of Programming Languages. (2002)
6. Mitchell, J.C.: Coercion and type inference. In: 11th Principles of Programming Languages. (1984)
7. Cardelli, L.: A semantics of multiple inheritance. Information and Computation **76** (1988)
8. Tiuryn, J.: Subtype inequalities. In: 7th IEEE Symposium on Logic in Computer Science. (1992)
9. Hoang, M., Mitchell, J.C.: Lower bounds on type inference with subtypes. In: 22nd Principles of Programming Languages. (1995)
10. Mitchell, J.C.: Type inference with simple subtypes. Journal of Functional Programming **1** (1991)
11. Fuh, Y.C., Mishra, P.: Type inference with subtypes. In: European Symposium on Programming. Volume 300. (1988)
12. Fuh, Y.C., Mishra, P.: Polymorphic subtype inference: Closing the theory-practice gap. In: European Joint Conference on Theory and Practice of Software Development. Volume 352. (1989)
13. Frey, A.: Satisfying subtype inequalities in polynomial space. In: 4th Static Analysis Symposium. Number 1302 (1997)
14. Kuncak, V., Rinard, M.: Structural subtyping of non-recursive types is decidable. In: 18th IEEE Symposium on Logic in Computer Science. (2003)
15. Aiken, A.S., Fähndrich, M.: Making set-constraint based program analyses scale. Technical Report CSD-96-917, University of California, Berkeley (1996)
16. Trifonov, V., Smith, S.: Subtyping constrained types. In: 3rd Static Analysis Symposium. Volume 1145. (1996)
17. Flanagan, C., Felleisen, M.: Componential set-based analysis. In: Programming Language Design and Implementation. (1997)
18. Pottier, F.: Simplifying subtyping constraints: a theory. Information and Computation **170** (2001)
19. Rehof, J.: Minimal typings in atomic subtyping. In: 24th Principles of Programming Languages. (1997)
20. Marlow, S., Wadler, P.: A practical subtyping system for Erlang. In: International Conference on Functional Programming. (1997)
21. F hndrich, M.: *Bane*, A Library for Scalable Constraint-Based Program Analysis. PhD thesis (1999)
22. Pottier, F.: *Wallace*, an efficient implementation of type inference with subtyping. URL: http://pauillac.inria.fr/~fpottier/wallace/ (2000)
23. Frey, A.: *Jazz*. URL: http://www.exalead.com/jazz/ (1998)
24. Kodumal, J.: *Banshee*, a toolkit for building constraint-based analyses. PhD thesis (2002)

25. Foster, J.S., Fähndrich, M., Aiken, A.: A Theory of Type Qualifiers. In: Programming Language Design and Implementation. (1999)
26. Foster, J.S., Terauchi, T., Aiken, A.: Flow-sensitive type qualifiers. In: Programming Language Design and Implementation. (2002)
27. Glynn, K., Stuckey, P.J., Sulzmann, M., Søndergaard, H.: Boolean constraints for binding-time analysis. In: Programs as Data Objects. Volume 2053. (2001)
28. Simonet, V.: *Dalton*, an efficient implementation of type inference with structural subtyping. URL: `http://cristal.inria.fr/~simonet/soft/dalton/` (2002)
29. Heintze, N., McAllester, D.: Linear-time subtransitive control flow analysis. In: Programming Language Design and Implementation. (1997)
30. Saha, B., Heintze, N., Oliva, D.: Subtransitive CFA using types. Technical report, Yale University (1998)
31. Rémy, D.: Extending ML type system with a sorted equational theory. Research Report 1766, Institut de Recherche en Informatique et en Automatique (1992)
32. Pessaux, F., Leroy, X.: Type-based analysis of uncaught exceptions. ACM Transactions on Programming Languages and Systems **22** (2000)
33. Simonet, V.: Type inference with structural subtyping: A precise formalization of an efficient constraint solver. Full version.
    `http://cristal.inria.fr/ simonet/publis/simonet-structural-subtyping-full.ps.gz` (2003)
34. Abadi, M., Banerjee, A., Heintze, N., Riecke, J.G.: A core calculus of dependency. In: 26th Principles of Programming Languages. (1999)
35. Pottier, F.: A constraint-based presentation and generalization of rows. In: 18th IEEE Symposium on Logic in Computer Science. (2003)
36. Tarjan, R.E.: Efficiency of a good but not linear set union algorithm. Journal of the ACM **22** (1975)
37. F hndrich, M., Foster, J.S., Su, Z., Aiken, A.S.: Partial online cycle elimination in inclusion constraint graphs. In: Programming Language Design and Implementation. (1998)
38. Eifrig, J., Smith, S., Trifonov, V.: Sound polymorphic type inference for objects. ACM SIGPLAN Notices **30** (1995)
39. Simonet, V.: *Flow Caml*, information flow inference in Objective Caml. URL: `http://cristal.inria.fr/~simonet/soft/flowcaml/` (2002)
40. F hndrich, M., Rehof, J., Das, M.: Scalable context-sensitive flow analysis using instantiation constraints. In: Programming Language Design and Implementation. (2000)

Continuation Semantics for Parallel Haskell Dialects

Mercedes Hidalgo-Herrero[1] and Yolanda Ortega-Mallén[2]

[1] Dept. Didáctica de las Matemáticas
Facultad de Educación, Universidad Complutense de Madrid, Spain
mhidalgo@edu.ucm.es
[2] Dept. Sistemas Informáticos y Programación
Facultad CC.Matemáticas, Universidad Complutense de Madrid, Spain
yolanda@sip.ucm.es

Abstract. The aim of the present work is to compare, from a formal semantic basis, the different approaches to the parallelization of functional programming languages. For this purpose, we define a continuation semantics model which allows us to deal with side-effects and parallelism. To verify the suitability of our model we have applied it to three programming languages that introduce parallelism in very different ways, but whose common functional kernel is the lazy functional language Haskell.

1 Introduction

It is well-known that declarative programming offers good opportunities for parallel evaluation. More precisely, the different ways for exploiting the parallelism inherent in functional programs can be classified in three tendencies:

Implicit Parallelism. The parallelism inherent in the reduction semantics —independent redexes can be reduced in an arbitrary order or even in parallel— is the basis for *automatic* parallelization of functional programs.

Semi-explicit Parallelism. The programmer indicates where a parallel evaluation is desired. Either annotations for the compiler are added to the program, or parallel higher-level constructs, like skeletons or evaluation strategies, are used to express algorithms. Although the programmer controls the parallelism to some extent, the details are still implementation dependent.

Explicit Parallelism. Functional programming languages are extended with constructs for explicit process creation, communication and synchronization, so that general concurrent systems can be modelled.

R.Loogen gives in [Loo99] a similar classification, and provides a complete overview and a detailed discussion on these approaches. It is stated in that work that, when there is no explicit notion of parallel process —that is, in implicit and semi-explicit parallelism—, the denotational semantics remains unchanged. We admit that this is true if a "standard" denotational semantics is considered, where only the functional input-output relationship is considered; but the quality of a denotational semantics resides in the level of abstraction that it discloses,

A. Ohori (Ed.): APLAS 2003, LNCS 2895, pp. 303–321, 2003.

i.e. how many execution details are incorporated in the program denotation, and the utmost abstraction is to keep only the final value. One may argue that other aspects to be observed from a parallel execution, like runtimes, resource consumption, communications, etc. are implementation dependent and, thus, they should be not considered as semantical issues; at most they should be described through abstract machines.

It is our purpose to reach an intermediate level of abstraction, so that we can compare programs in terms of the amount of work, i.e. calculation, that must be done to obtain the same output from the same input. This is particularly interesting in the case of functional languages with demand-driven evaluation, which is inherently sequential and, therefore, parallelization introduces speculative parallelism —some expressions may get evaluated, whose results are never used— that should be detected and avoided. The degree of work duplication and speculation can be then semantically observed, as well as other properties concerning communications between processes. To this extent, we are interested in three different aspects:

- Functionality: the final value computed.
- Parallelism: the system topology (existing processes and connections among them) and its corresponding interactions generated by the computation.
- Distribution: the degree of work duplication and speculation.

Few research has been carried out in these directions for parallel and/or concurrent functional languages. There has been some work addressing the first two aspects, for instance, in [DB97,FH99] two denotational semantics for the strict language Concurrent ML (CML) [Rep92] are presented. Both are based on the Acceptance Trees model [Hen88], originally defined for the analysis of reactive systems. In each paper, the model is extended with value production, in order to express the overall input-output relation of functional programs. The semantic model for strict evaluation is much simpler than one for lazy evaluation, and in a concurrent setting there is no need to bother about the distribution aspects mentioned above.

1.1 Haskell Parallel Dialects

The *lazy* functional programming language Haskell [Pey03] is a wide-spectrum language widely known and used by the functional programming community. Haskell, like many other functional programming languages, has succumbed to the greediness of the parallel programming community, and different varieties of parallel or concurrent Haskell have emerged in the 90's.

The three parallel dialects of Haskell chosen for the present work, represent excellent examples of each kind of parallelism that we have explained above.

- The language pH (parallel Haskell) [NA01] adopts a parallel evaluation order (implicit parallelism), concretely in the case of data constructors with many arguments, and local definitions in program blocks. Moreover, pH adds special data structures that allow synchronization among parallel tasks, but introduce side-effects and non-determinism.

- Glasgow parallel Haskell (GPH) [THM⁺96] just introduces two special combinators

$$\mathtt{seq, par :: a \rightarrow b \rightarrow b}$$

  The former corresponds to sequential composition, while the latter indicates
  potential parallelism. These combinators are used to define *evaluation strategies* that allow the programmer to overrule laziness in favor of parallelism
  and to specify the degree of evaluation.
- The language Eden [BLOMP96] extends Haskell by a *coordination* language
  with explicit parallel process creation and streams, i.e. lazy lists, as communication channels [KM77]. Eden incorporates also a restricted form of
  non-determinism by means of a predefined non-deterministic process `merge`
  used to model many-to-one communication.

The following example illustrates the main difference between the three approaches. If we want to obtain the product of the total sum of the elements of
two given lists of integers, it can be expressed in Haskell as follows:

```
let s1 = sum l1, s2 = sum l2 in s1 * s2
```

where `sum` is a standard function that sums up all the elements in a list. Sup-
posing that lists `l1` and `l2` have been constructed already, the evaluation of this
expression sums up first the elements of `l1` and then those of `l2`. But if we
consider this same expression in pH and we have available two processors, then
the sum for each list will be done in parallel. Laziness is abandoned in favor of
parallelism; `s1` and `s2` are evaluated, eagerly, even if their result would never be
demanded by the "main" computation.

The same idea is expressed in GPH with the following expression:

```
let s1 = sum l1, s2 = sum l2 in s2 'par' (s1 * s2)
```

where e_1`'par'`e_2 requires the parallel evaluation of e_1 and e_2, and returns the
value obtained for e_2.

Finally, in the case of Eden, we write:

```
let p = process list -> sum list, s1 = p # l1, s2 = p # l2
in s1 * s2
```

where a process abstraction `p` is defined with `sum` as its body, and is instantiated
twice —by using the special infix operator `#`— thus creating two processes that
will execute `sum` in parallel with the process that is evaluating the let-expression
and is considered the *parent* of the other two processes. The parent process has to
communicate the corresponding list to each *child*, and each child communicates
the result of the sum to the parent.

1.2 A Continuation Semantics

The difficulties for parallelizing Haskell lie in laziness, a identity-sign of Haskell.
As we have mentioned above, parallelization requires some changes in the rules
for evaluation. The combination of laziness with eager evaluation is a very interesting point to be studied through a formal semantics. In general, the evaluation
of a program of this kind may give rise to different computations, where the
amount of speculative parallelism depends on the number of available processors, the scheduler decisions and the speed of basic instructions. Hence, when

defining a formal semantics for these languages one can model that speculation ranges from a *minimum*, i.e. only what it is effectively demanded is computed, to a *maximum*, i.e. every speculative computation is carried out.

Formal operational semantics have already been given for each of the three parallel languages that we are considering (or more exactly, for simplified kernels of these languages):

- For pH an operational semantics described in terms of a parallel abstract machine, in the spirit of the G-machine [Pey87], is given in [AAA+95].
- The operational semantics given in [BFKT00] for GpH is small-step for process local reduction, and big-step for the scheduling and parallelization.
- Similarly, a two-level operational semantics is given in [HOM02] for Eden: a local level for process evaluation, and a global level for the system evolution.

We intend to define a general framework where we can express the semantics of each language, in order to be able to compare the differences between the three approaches. For this purpose, the actual operational semantics are unsuitable, because they include too much detail concerning computations and the order of evaluation, and the overall meaning of programs gets lost.

Detecting work duplication and speculation requires to express somehow in the semantics the sharing/copying of closures. In order to achieve this, we depart from a *standard* denotational semantics [Sto77] just expressing the input-output relationship of functional programs, and we extend it with a notion of *process system generation*. Maintaining the process system as part of the denotation of a program means that the evaluation of an expression may produce some side-effects which must be treated with care in a lazy context. For instance, in the case of evaluating an application such as $(\backslash x.3)y$ in a process p, the evaluation of the variable y may imply the corresponding evaluation of other bindings. Whereas this is not relevant in the case of a denotational semantics which is only interested in the final value, in our approach the modifications in the process system should not be carried out, because the λ-abstraction is not strict in its argument and, therefore, the evaluation of y is not going to be demanded. Hence, process creation and value communication are side-effects which must take place only under demand. Moreover, we recall that laziness implies that arguments to function calls are evaluated at most once. Therefore, we must be careful to produce the corresponding side-effects only the first time a value is demanded.

Continuations resolve elegantly the problem of dealing with command sequencing in denotational semantics. The meaning of each command is a function returning the final result of the entire program. The command meaning receives as an extra argument a function from states to final results. This extra argument —the *continuation*— describes the "rest of the computation", that will take place if the command ever ends its execution [Rey98].

In the case of functional languages, a continuation is a function from values to final results. The semantic function for the evaluation of an expression depends on an environment and a continuation, so that the result of the entire program is obtained by applying the continuation to the value obtained for the expression.

In order to deal with side-effects in functional programming, Josephs [Jos86] combines the two views of continuations to obtain a *expression continuation*, which is a function that receives a value and produces a "command continuation" or state transformer. In [Jos89] it is described how to use these expression continuations to model accurately the order of evaluation in a denotational semantics for a lazy λ-calculus. We use these ideas to define a continuation-based denotational semantics for parallel lazy functional languages, where process creation and interprocess communication and synchronization are considered as side-effects produced during the evaluation of expressions.

In [EM02] a mixed lazy/strict semantics is presented. Apart from the fact that it does not consider any form of parallelism, the strict semantics just tests whether an expression would evaluate to a normal form, but the actual evaluation will only take place when the value is needed. This is not adequate for our case, where evaluation of an expression may produce the side-effects explained above.

As far as we know, ours is the first denotational semantics which considers this problem and expresses not only the final result, but also the interaction between processes in a lazy context.

It is not our objective to give a complete denotational semantics for each language. For our purposes, it is sufficient to concentrate on a very simple functional kernel —a lazy λ-calculus— extended with the parallel features particular to each approach. To facilitate the comparison, a uniform syntax is adopted.

The paper is structured as follows: We devote the next three sections to the parallel Haskell dialects Eden, GpH and pH. For each language we explain its main characteristics, we give its kernel syntax, and define its denotational semantics, i.e. semantic domains and semantic functions. In the last section we draw some conclusions and comment on future work.

2   Eden

Eden extends the lazy functional language Haskell with a set of *coordination* features that are based on two principal concepts: *explicit management of processes* and *implicit communication*. Functional languages distinguish between function definitions and function applications. Similarly, Eden offers *process abstractions*, i.e. abstract schemes for process behavior, and *process instantiations* for the actual creation of processes and of the corresponding communication channels.

Communication in Eden is unidirectional, from one producer to exactly one consumer. Arbitrary communication topologies can be created by means of *dynamic reply channels*. In order to provide control over where expressions are evaluated, only fully evaluated data objects are communicated; this also facilitates a distributed implementation of Eden. However, Eden retains the lazy nature of the underlying computational functional language, and lists are transmitted in a *stream*-like fashion, i.e. element by element. Concurrent threads trying to access not yet available input will be suspended. This is the only way of synchronizing Eden processes.

In Eden, *nondeterminism* is gently introduced by means of a predefined process abstraction which is used to instantiate nondeterministic processes, that fairly merge a list of input channels into a single list.

For details on the Eden language design, the interested reader is referred to [BLOMP96]. Here we just concentrate on Eden's essentials which are captured by the untyped λ-calculus whose (abstract) syntax, with two syntactic categories: identifiers ($x \in$ **Ide**) and expressions ($E \in$ **Exp**), is given in Figure 1.

$E ::=$ x	identifier
$\mid$ $\backslash x.E$	λ-abstraction
$\mid$ $x_1 \$ x_2$	lazy application
$\mid$ $x_1 \$\# x_2$	parallel application
$\mid$ $\texttt{let}\ \{x_i = E_i\}_{i=1}^{n}\ \texttt{in}\ x$	local declaration
$\mid$ $x_1 \| x_2$	choice

Fig. 1. Eden-core syntax

The calculus mixes laziness and eagerness, using two kinds of application: lazy ($\$$), and parallel ($\$\#$). The evaluation of $x_1 \$ x_2$ generates demand on the value for x_1, but the expression corresponding to x_2 is only evaluated if needed. By contrast, the evaluation of $x_1 \$\# x_2$ implies the creation of a new parallel process for evaluating $x_1 x_2$. Two channels are established between the new process and its creator: one for communicating the value of x_2 from the parent to the child, and a second one for communicating from the child to the parent the result value of $x_1 x_2$. Eden-core includes also an operator that carries out a non-deterministic choice between its two arguments.

Following [Lau93], the calculi presented in this paper have been normalized to a restricted syntax where all the subexpressions, but for the body of λ-abstractions, have been associated to variables. We have several reasons for doing this: (1) In this way all the subexpressions of any expression are shared. This maximizes the degree of sharing within a computation and guarantees that every subexpression of a program is evaluated at most once. (2) The semantic definition of lazy application is clearer, because with the normalization it is unnecessary to introduce fresh variables for the argument of the application.

2.1 Semantic Domains for Eden

The semantic domains that are needed for defining the continuation semantics for Eden are listed in Figure 2.

As it was motivated in the introduction, the meaning of a program is a continuation, or a state transformer. To deal with the non-determinism present in Eden, we consider sets of states (for a given set S, $\mathcal{P}_f(S)$ is the set of all the finite parts of S), so that a continuation transforms an initial state into a set of possible final states. In the present case a state ($s \in$ **State**) will consist of two items:

- An *environment* ($\rho \in$ **Env**) mapping identifiers to values. Environments here are analogous to stores when dealing with imperative variables. Following [Sto77], we do not consider the option of separating the environment from the state, because no evaluation in Eden produces irreversible changes

Cont	= State → SState	continuations
$\kappa \in$ **ECont**	= **EVal** → **Cont**	expression continuations
$s \in$ **State**	= **Env** × **SChan**	states
$S \in$ **SState**	= $\mathcal{P}_f(\textbf{State})$	set of states
$\rho \in$ **Env**	= **Ide** → (**Val** + {undefined})	environments
$Ch \in$ **SChan**	= $\mathcal{P}_f(\textbf{Chan})$	set of channels
Chan	= **IdProc** × **CVal** × **IdProc**	channels
CVal	= **EVal** + {unsent}	communication values
$\upsilon \in$ **Val**	= **EVal** + (**IdProc** × **Clo**) + {not_ready}	values
$\varepsilon \in$ **EVal**	= **Abs** × **Ides**	expressed values
$\alpha \in$ **Abs**	= **Ide** → **Clo**	abstraction values
$\nu \in$ **Clo**	= **IdProc** → **ECont** → **Cont**	closures
$I \in$ **Ides**	= $\mathcal{P}_f(\textbf{Ide})$	set of identifiers
$p, q \in$ **IdProc**		process identifiers

Fig. 2. Semantic domains for Eden-core

in the state, so that the preservation and restoration of the environment is easily practicable.

- A *set of channels* ($Ch \in$ **SChan**). Processes in Eden-core are not isolated entities, but they communicate through unidirectional, one-value channels. Each channel is represented by a triple ⟨producer,value,consumer⟩. The value can be either the expressed value that has been communicated, or unsent if there has been no communication through the channel.

The domain **Val** of values includes final denotational values (or *expressed values* $\varepsilon \in$ **EVal**), and closures ($\nu \in$ **Clo**), i.e. "semi"-evaluated expressions. The evaluation of a closure may imply the creation of new processes. In order to build the process system topology it is necessary to know which is the father of each newly created process. This is the reason for associating a process identifier to the closure. The special value not_ready indicates that the corresponding closure is currently being evaluated, and it is used to detect self-references.

Abstractions values ($\alpha \in$ **Abs**) are the only type of expressed values in this calculus. Each abstraction is represented by a function from identifiers to closures, together with the list of its free variables, that have to be evaluated before communicating the abstraction value through some channel.

A closure is a function that depends on (1) the process where the closure will be evaluated, and (2) the expression continuation denoting the rest of the program.

2.2 Evaluation Function for Eden

Distributing the computation in parallel processes requires indicating the process where an expression is to be evaluated. Notice that the process identifier is not necessary to distinguish its variables from those of other processes —each process owns different identifiers—, but to be able to determine the parent in possible process creations. The semantic function for evaluating expressions has the following signature:

$$\mathcal{E} : \mathbf{Exp} \rightarrow \mathbf{IdProc} \rightarrow \mathbf{ECont} \rightarrow \mathbf{Cont}.$$

After evaluating the expression, the continuation obtained by instantiating the expression continuation with the value produced for the expression carries on with the computation.

The definition of the evaluation function for Eden-core is detailed in Figure 3. We use the operator $\oplus$ to express the extension/update of environments, like for instance in $\rho \oplus \{x \mapsto \nu\}$, and $\oplus_{ch}$ in the case of the set of channels of a state:

$\mathcal{E}[\![x]\!]p\,\kappa = \mathsf{force}\,x\,\kappa$

$\mathcal{E}[\![\backslash x.E]\!]p\,\kappa = \kappa\langle\lambda x.\mathcal{E}[\![E]\!],\mathsf{fv}(\backslash x.E)\rangle$

$\mathcal{E}[\![x_1\,\$\,x_2]\!]p\,\kappa = \mathcal{E}[\![x_1]\!]p\,\kappa'$
   where $\kappa' = \lambda\langle\alpha,I\rangle.\lambda s.(\alpha\,x_2)\,p\,\kappa\,s$

$\mathcal{E}[\![x_1\,\$\#\,x_2]\!]p\,\kappa = \mathsf{forceFV}\,x_1\,\kappa'$
   where $\kappa' = \lambda\langle\alpha,I\rangle.\lambda s.(\alpha\,x_2)\,q\,\kappa''\,s$
      $q = \mathsf{newIdProc}\,s$

> $\kappa''_{min} = \lambda\langle\alpha',I'\rangle.\lambda s'.\mathsf{case}\,(\rho'\,x_2)\,\mathsf{of}$
> $\langle\alpha'',I''\rangle \in \mathbf{EVal} \longrightarrow S_d \oplus_{ch} \{\langle q,\langle\alpha,I\rangle,p\rangle\,,\langle p,\langle\alpha'',I''\rangle,q\rangle\}$
> $\mathsf{otherwise} \longrightarrow S_c \oplus_{ch} \{\langle q,\langle\alpha,I\rangle,p\rangle\,,\langle p,\mathsf{unsent},q\rangle\}$
> $\mathsf{endcase}$
> $\mathsf{where}\,(\rho',Ch') = s'$
> $S_c = \mathsf{mforceFV}\,I'\,s'$
> $S_d = \bigcup_{s_c \in S_c} \mathsf{mforceFV}\,I''\,s_c$
>
> ---
> $\kappa''_{max} = \lambda\langle\alpha',I'\rangle.\lambda s'.\bigcup_{s_c \in S_c}\mathsf{forceFV}\,x_2\,\kappa_c\,s_c$
> $\mathsf{where}\,S_c = \mathsf{mforceFV}\,I'\,s'$
> $\kappa_c = \lambda\varepsilon''.\lambda s''.\{s'' \oplus_{ch} \{\langle q,\langle\alpha,I\rangle,p\rangle,\langle p,\varepsilon'',q\rangle\}\}$

$\mathcal{E}[\![\mathsf{let}\,\{x_i = E_i\}_n\,\mathsf{in}\,x]\!]p\,\kappa = \lambda\langle\rho,Ch\rangle.\mathcal{E}[\![x]\!]p\,\kappa'\,\langle\rho',Ch\rangle$
   where $\{y_1,\ldots,y_n\} = \mathsf{newIde}\,n\,\rho$
      $\rho' = \rho \oplus \{y_i \mapsto \langle\mathcal{E}[\![E_i[y_1/x_1,\ldots,y_n/x_n]]\!],p\rangle \mid 1 \le i \le n\}$

> $\kappa'_{min} = \kappa$
>
> ---
> $\kappa'_{max} = \lambda\varepsilon.\lambda s.\mathsf{mforce}\,I\,s$
> $\mathsf{where}\,I = \{y_i \mid E_i \equiv x_1^i\,\$\#\,x_2^i \wedge 1 \le i \le n\}$

$\mathcal{E}[\![x_1|x_2]\!]p\,\kappa = \lambda s.(\mathcal{E}[\![x_1]\!]p\,\kappa\,s) \cup (\mathcal{E}[\![x_2]\!]p\,\kappa\,s)$

Fig. 3. Evaluation function for Eden-core

The evaluation of an identifier "forces" the evaluation of the value bound to that identifier in the given environment. The function force is defined in Figure 4 and is explained later.

The evaluation of a λ-abstraction produces the corresponding expressed value, that is a pair formed by a function which given an identifier returns a closure, and the set of free variables of the syntactic construction.

In the case of *lazy application*, the evaluation of the argument, x_2, is delayed until it is effectively demanded; the expression continuation, κ, given for the evaluation of the application is modified, κ' to reflect this circumstance. This κ' is the one supplied for the evaluation of the variable corresponding to the application abstraction, x_1. Therefore, once the abstraction value is obtained, it is applied to the argument variable, x_2, and the corresponding closure is evaluated.

The evaluation of a *parallel application* $x_1 \,\$\# \, x_2$ produces the creation of a new process, q. The following actions take place:

- Creation of a new process q (where q is a fresh process identifier).
- Creation of two new channels, $\langle q,\_,p \rangle, \langle p,\_,q \rangle$, between parent p and child q.
- Evaluation of x_1, to obtain the abstraction value, together with its free variables, $\langle \alpha, I \rangle$. The function forceFV, given in Figure 4, is used for this purpose. In Eden, processes do not share memory. Therefore, the heap where the new process is going to be evaluated must contain every binding related to the free variables of the value abstraction corresponding to the process body. All this information is evaluated in the parent and then "copied" to the child.
- Evaluation of x_2. As we have explained in the introduction, speculative parallelism ranges from a minimum to a maximum. In the case of Eden, we can define a *minimal semantics* where argument x_2 is evaluated only if needed, while in a *maximal semantics* this evaluation always takes place. The value for x_2 has to be communicated (from the parent to the child) together with all the information concerning its free variables. The function forceFV, given in Figure 4, is used again for evaluating x_2 and its free variables.
- Communication (of the value for x_2) from parent p to child q. Under a minimal semantics it may not occur this communication.
- Evaluation of the application $x_1 \, x_2$ in the new process q.
- Communication (of the value for $x_1 \, x_2$) from child q to parent p . Before communication, the free variables have to be evaluated too; the auxiliary function mforceFV (see Figure 4) is invoked.

Before evaluating the body of a local declaration, all the local variables, x_i, (with fresh identifiers, y_i, to avoid name clashes) are to be incorporated in the environment. Each new local variable, y_i, is bound to the proper closure, $E_i[y_j/x_j]$, which is obtained from the corresponding expression in the declaration. Closures are paired with the process identifier, p, where the declaration is being evaluated. When a local variable is defined as a parallel application, this must be evaluated too (in the case of a maximal semantics).

Finally, the *choice operator* comprises the possibility of evaluating either of its two subexpressions, x_1 and x_2.

The auxiliary functions for "forcing" the evaluation are defined in Figure 4. The action of force depends on the value bound to the identifier that is to be

$$\text{force} :: \textbf{Ide} \rightarrow \textbf{ECont} \rightarrow \textbf{Cont}$$

$$\text{force}\,x\,\kappa = \lambda\langle\rho,\text{Ch}\rangle.\textbf{case}\ (\rho\,x)\ \textbf{of}$$

$$\varepsilon \in \textbf{EVal} \longrightarrow \kappa\,\varepsilon\,\langle\rho,\text{Ch}\rangle$$

$$\langle p,\nu\rangle \in (\textbf{IdProc} \times \textbf{Clo}) \longrightarrow \nu\,p\,\kappa'\,s'$$

$$\textbf{where}\ \kappa' = \lambda\varepsilon'.\lambda\langle\rho',\text{Ch}'\rangle.\kappa\,\varepsilon'\,\langle\rho'\oplus\{x\mapsto\varepsilon'\},\text{Ch}'\rangle$$

$$s' = \langle\rho\oplus\{x\mapsto\text{not\_ready}\},\text{Ch}\rangle$$

$$\textbf{otherwise} \longrightarrow \text{wrong}$$

$$\text{forceFV} :: \textbf{Ide} \rightarrow \textbf{ECont} \rightarrow \textbf{Cont} \qquad\qquad \text{mforceFV} :: \textbf{Ides} \rightarrow \textbf{Cont}$$

$$\text{forceFV}\,x\,\kappa = \text{force}\,x\,\kappa' \qquad\qquad\qquad \text{mforceFV}\,\emptyset = \lambda s.\{s\}$$

$$\textbf{where}\ \kappa' = \lambda\langle\alpha,I\rangle.\lambda s'.\bigcup_{s''\in S''}\kappa\,\langle\alpha,I\rangle\,s'' \qquad \text{mforceFV}\,(\{x\}\cup I) = \lambda s.\bigcup_{s'\in S'}\text{mforceFV}\,I\,s'$$

$$S'' = \text{mforceFV}\,I\,s' \qquad\qquad\qquad\qquad \textbf{where}\ S' = \text{forceFV}\,x\,id_\kappa\,s$$

Fig. 4. Auxiliary semantic functions for Eden-core

"forced". In the case of an expressed value, the given expression continuation is applied to it in order to continue with the computation. In the case of a closure, this has to be evaluated and the result is bound in the environment to the identifier. During the evaluation of the closure, the identifier is bound to not_ready; if an identifier bound to not_ready is ever forced, this indicates the presence of a self-reference. After the evaluation of the closure, the expression continuation is applied to the obtained expressed value and the modified state. Of course, forcing an "undefined" location or a "not_ready" variable is a mistake.

The difference between force and forceFV lies in the scope of evaluation. The former only evaluates the closure associated to the variable, while the latter propagates the evaluation to the free variables of that closure, and to the ones corresponding to the closures of these free variables, and so on. The multiple demand for a set of identifiers is carried out by mforceFV.

In the definition of mforceFV, id_κ represents the identity for expression continuations, defined as $id_\kappa = \lambda\varepsilon.\lambda s.\{s\}$.

3   GpH

GpH (Glasgow Parallel Haskell) introduces parallelism via the annotation 'par' ; the expression e_1'par'e_2 indicates that e_1 and e_2 may be evaluated in parallel, returning the value obtained for e_2. Sequential composition is possible in GpH using 'seq' ; so that e_1'seq'e_2 evaluates e_1 and, only after obtaining the corresponding value, if any, the evaluation proceeds with e_2. In Figure 5 the syntax for GpH-core is given, which includes identifiers, λ-abstractions, lazy functional application, local declaration of variables, and both sequential and parallel composition.

$E ::= x$	identifier
$\mid \; \backslash x.E$	λ-abstraction
$\mid \; x_1 \,\$\, x_2$	lazy application
$\mid \; \texttt{let } \{x_i = E_i\}_{i=1}^n \texttt{ in } x$	local declaration
$\mid \; x_1 \,\texttt{'seq'}\, x_2$	sequential composition
$\mid \; x_1 \,\texttt{'par'}\, x_2$	parallel composition

Fig. 5. GPH-core syntax

3.1 Semantic Domains for GpH

The semantic domains that we need for GPH-core are given in Figure 6. As GPH has neither notion of process nor of communication, the program state consists only of the environment, and the rest of semantic domains are simplified; for instance, expressed values are just abstraction values, without the set of free variables.

Moreover, GPH does not introduce non-determinism. Consequently, a continuation is a state transformer which takes an environment as its argument and yields another environment.

$\mathbf{Cont}$	$= \mathbf{Env} \to \mathbf{Env}$	continuations
$\kappa \in \mathbf{ECont}$	$= \mathbf{EVal} \to \mathbf{Cont}$	expression continuations
$\rho \in \mathbf{Env}$	$= \mathbf{Ide} \to (\mathbf{Val} + \{\text{undefined}\})$	environments
$\upsilon \in \mathbf{Val}$	$= \mathbf{EVal} + \mathbf{Clo} + \{\text{not\_ready}\}$	values
$\varepsilon \in \mathbf{EVal}$	$= \mathbf{Abs}$	expressed values
$\alpha \in \mathbf{Abs}$	$= \mathbf{Ide} \to \mathbf{Clo}$	abstraction values
$\nu \in \mathbf{Clo}$	$= \mathbf{ECont} \to \mathbf{Cont}$	closures

Fig. 6. Semantic domains for GPH-core

3.2 Evaluation Function for GpH

The signature for the evaluation function $\mathcal{E}$ for GPH-core is similar to the one given for Eden-core, but without process identifiers:

$$\mathcal{E} : \mathbf{Exp} \to \mathbf{ECont} \to \mathbf{Cont}$$

whose definition is detailed in Figure 7.

The definition of the evaluation function for identifiers, λ-abstractions, and lazy applications, as well as the auxiliary function force (in Figure 8) is similar to the definition given for Eden-core, but much simpler because process identifiers, channel sets and free variables are removed.

As local declaration does not introduce parallelism, its evaluation just extends the environment with the new variables bound to the corresponding closures.

$$\mathcal{E}[\![x]\!]\kappa = \text{force}\, x\, \kappa$$

$$\mathcal{E}[\![\backslash x.E]\!]\kappa = \kappa(\lambda x.\mathcal{E}[\![E]\!])$$

$$\mathcal{E}[\![x_1 \,\$\, x_2]\!]\kappa = \mathcal{E}[\![x_1]\!]\kappa'$$
$$\text{where } \kappa' = \lambda\varepsilon.\lambda\rho.\varepsilon\, x_2\, \kappa\, \rho$$

$$\mathcal{E}[\![\texttt{let } \{x_i = E_i\}_n \texttt{ in } x]\!]\kappa = \lambda\rho.\mathcal{E}[\![x]\!]\kappa\, \rho'$$
$$\text{where } \{y_1, \ldots, y_n\} = \text{newIde}\, n\, \rho$$
$$\rho' = \rho \oplus \{y_i \mapsto \mathcal{E}[\![E_i[y_1/x_1, \ldots, y_n/x_n]]\!] \mid 1 \le i \le n\}$$

$$\mathcal{E}[\![x_1 \,\texttt{'seq'}\, x_2]\!]\kappa = \mathcal{E}[\![x_1]\!]\kappa'$$
$$\text{where } \kappa' = \lambda\varepsilon.\lambda\rho.\mathcal{E}[\![x_2]\!]\kappa\, \rho$$

$$\mathcal{E}[\![x_1 \,\texttt{'par'}\, x_2]\!]\kappa = \mathcal{E}[\![x_2]\!]\kappa'$$
$$\text{where } \kappa' = \lambda\varepsilon.\lambda\rho.\kappa\, \varepsilon\, \rho_{par}$$
$$\rho_{par} = \text{par}\, x_1\, \rho$$

Fig. 7. Evaluation function for GPH-core

In a *sequential* composition $x_1 \,\texttt{'seq'}\, x_2$ we have to respect the order of evaluation: firstly, x_1 is evaluated, and then its expression continuation evaluates x_2 only if the evaluation of x_1 has given rise to an expressed value.

In a *parallel* composition $x_1 \,\texttt{'par'}\, x_2$, x_2 is always evaluated, but the evaluation of x_1 takes place only if there are enough resources. Therefore, in a minimal semantics x_1 is not evaluated, while in a maximal semantics x_1 is evaluated in parallel. This is expressed by using the function par (see Figure 8).

force :: $\mathbf{Ide} \rightarrow \mathbf{ECont} \rightarrow \mathbf{Cont}$

force $x\, \kappa = \lambda\rho.\texttt{case }(\rho\, x)\texttt{ of}$
  $\varepsilon \in \mathbf{EVal} \longrightarrow \kappa\, \varepsilon\, \rho$
  $\nu \in \mathbf{Clo} \longrightarrow \nu\, \kappa'\, \rho'$
    where $\kappa' = \lambda\varepsilon''.\lambda\rho''.\kappa\, \varepsilon''\, \rho'' \oplus \{x \mapsto \varepsilon''\}$
      $\rho' = \rho \oplus \{x \mapsto \text{not\_ready}\}$
  not_ready $\longrightarrow$ wrong
endcase

par :: $\mathbf{Ide} \rightarrow \mathbf{Cont}$

$\text{par}_{\min}\, x = \lambda\rho.\rho$

$\text{par}_{\max}\, x = \lambda\rho.\mathcal{E}[\![x]\!]id_\kappa\, \rho$

Fig. 8. Auxiliary semantic functions for GPH-core

4 pH

This section is devoted to pH (parallel Haskell), a successor of the Id dataflow language [Nik91], adopting the notation and type system of Haskell. pH is characterized by its implicit parallelism, the mixture of strictness and laziness, and the existence of updatable cells conveying *implicit synchronization*: I-structures are *single-assigment* data structures that help producer-consumer synchronization, while M-structures are *multiple-assigment* data structures that allow mutual exclusion synchronization, introducing side-effects and non-determinism.

Figure 9 shows the syntax for the pH-core, which includes identifiers, λ-abstractions, application —strict and non-strict—, local declaration of variables, and primitive operations to create, read from, and write to updatable cells.

$E ::= x$	identifier
$\mid \backslash x.E$	λ-abstraction
$\mid x_1 \mathbin{\$} x_2$	lazy application
$\mid x_1 \mathbin{\$!} x_2$	strict application
$\mid \mathtt{let}\ \{x_i = E_i\}_{i=1}^n\ \mathtt{in}\ x$	local declaration
$\mid \mathtt{iCell}\,x \mid \mathtt{mCell}\,x$	cell creation
$\mid \mathtt{Fetch}\,x \mid \mathtt{Store}\,(x_1, x_2)$	cell operations

Fig. 9. pH-core syntax

I-cells dissociate the creation of a variable from the definition of its value, so that attempts to use the value of an I-cell are delayed until it is defined; but once an I-cell has been "filled" with a value, it can be neither emptied nor changed. On the other hand, a fetch over a M-cell empties the contents of that cell, so that any later query over it must wait until it is filled again. The behavior of both kinds of cells is summarized in Table 1.

Table 1. I-cells and M-cells behavior

	I-cell	**M-cell**
`cell`	empty I-cell creation	empty M-cell creation
`fetch`	I-cell reading error if empty	M-cell reading error if empty empty after reading
`store`	I-cell filling error if full	M-cell filling error if full

Let us explain in more detail how updatable cells introduce side-effects and non-determinism:

- A `Fetch` operation gives back the value stored in a M-cell, as a side-effect it empties the corresponding cell.
- Due to race-conditions, the evaluation of an expression may yield different values in different occasions. For an expression like

$$\mathtt{let}\ t = \mathtt{mCell}\ m\,,\ x = \mathtt{Store}\ m\,v_1,\ y = \mathtt{Store}\ m\,v_2,\ z = \mathtt{Fetch}\ m\ \mathtt{in}\ z$$

either the value of v_1 or the value of v_2 may be assigned to z.

4.1 Semantic Domains for pH

Figure 10 shows the semantic domains that we need for formalizing the semantics of pH-core. Similarly to GpH and unlike Eden, pH does not have processes or communication channels; but, in order to model the separation of creation from value definition for updatable cells, a double binding-mechanism is needed:

environments and *stores*. The *locations* of a store either contain some value or are undefined, while environments map identifiers to locations in the corresponding store.

Therefore, in the present case, the state of a program is represented by the global store ($\sigma \in$ **Store**). We have explained above how M-cells may introduce non-determinism; thus, continuations will transform a given store into a set of stores.

Similarly to the two previous approaches, the domain of values includes expressed values, closures and the special value not_ready. A new kind of values is included: (updatable) cells, that are distinguished by labels I and M. Each cell is either empty or it contains an expressed value.

Besides abstraction values —that in this case are mappings from locations to closures— the domain of expressed values includes the special value unit for expressions whose effect is not the production of a value, but the modification of the state (side-effects), like creating a cell, or storing a value in a cell.

Cont $= $ **Store** $\to$ **SStore**		continuations
$\kappa \in$ **ECont** $=$ **EVal** $\to$ **Cont**		expression continuations
$\sigma \in$ **Store** $=$ **Loc** $\to$ (**Val** $+$ {undefined})		stores
$\Sigma \in$ **SStore** $= \mathcal{P}_f($**Store**$)$		set of stores
$\rho \in$ **Env** $=$ **Ide** $\to$ **Loc**		environments
$\upsilon \in$ **Val** $=$ **EVal** $+$ **Clo** $+$ **Cell** $+$ {not_ready}		values
$\varepsilon \in$ **EVal** $=$ **Abs** $+$ {unit}		expressed values
$\alpha \in$ **Abs** $=$ **Loc** $\to$ **Clo**		abstraction values
$\nu \in$ **Clo** $=$ **ECont** $\to$ **Cont**		closures
Cell $= \{I, M\} \times ($**EVal** $+$ {empty}$)$		updatable cells
$l \in$ **Loc**		locations

Fig. 10. Semantic domains for pH-core

4.2 Evaluation Function for pH

In addition to the expression continuation, the evaluation function $\mathcal{E}$ for pH-core needs an environment for determining the locations for the free variables in the expression. Its definition is shown in Figure 11 and its signature is:

$$\mathcal{E} : \textbf{Exp} \to \textbf{Env} \to \textbf{ECont} \to \textbf{Cont}$$

The evaluation of an identifier forces the evaluation of the value stored in the corresponding location. The auxiliary function force (given in Figure 12) is very similar to those defined previously for Eden-core and GpH-core.

In the case of a λ-abstraction, the corresponding abstraction value is created and the expression continuation is applied to it.

$\mathcal{E}[\![x]\!]\rho\,\kappa = \text{force}\,(\rho\,x)\,\kappa$

$\mathcal{E}[\![\backslash x.E]\!]\rho\,\kappa = \kappa(\lambda l.\mathcal{E}[\![E]\!](\rho \oplus \{x \mapsto l\}))$

$\mathcal{E}[\![x_1\,\$\,x_2]\!]\rho\,\kappa = \mathcal{E}[\![x_1]\!]\rho\,\kappa'$
  where $\kappa' = \lambda\varepsilon.\lambda\sigma.\text{case }\varepsilon\text{ of}$
    $\varepsilon \in \mathbf{Abs} \longrightarrow \varepsilon\,l\,\kappa\,\sigma'$
      where $l = \text{freeloc}\,\sigma$
        $\sigma' = \sigma \oplus \{l \mapsto \mathcal{E}[\![x_2]\!]\rho\}$
    $\text{otherwise} \longrightarrow \text{wrong}$
  endcase

$\mathcal{E}[\![x_1\,\$!\,x_2]\!]\rho\,\kappa = \lambda\sigma.\ \bigcup_{\sigma_2 \in \Sigma_2}\ \kappa'\,(\sigma_2\,(\rho\,x_1))\,\sigma_2$
  where $\Sigma_1 = \text{force}\,(\rho\,x_1)\,id_\kappa\,\sigma$
    $\Sigma_2 = \bigcup_{\sigma_1 \in \Sigma_1}\ \text{force}\,(\rho\,x_2)\,id_\kappa\,\sigma_1$
    $\kappa' = \lambda\varepsilon.\lambda\sigma'.\text{case }\varepsilon\text{ of}$
      $\varepsilon \in \mathbf{Abs} \longrightarrow \varepsilon\,(\rho\,x_2)\,\kappa\,\sigma'$
      $\text{otherwise} \longrightarrow \text{wrong}$
    endcase

$\mathcal{E}[\![\text{let }\{x_i = E_i\}_n \text{ in } x]\!]\rho\,\kappa = \lambda\sigma.\mathcal{E}[\![x]\!]\rho'\,\kappa'\,\sigma'$
  where $\{l_1,\ldots,l_n\} = \text{freeloc}\,n\,\sigma$
    $\rho' = \rho \oplus \{x_1 \mapsto l_1,\ldots,x_n \mapsto l_n\}$
    $\sigma' = \sigma \oplus \{l_1 \mapsto \mathcal{E}[\![E_1]\!]\rho',\ldots,l_n \mapsto \mathcal{E}[\![E_n]\!]\rho'\}$
    $\kappa' = \lambda\varepsilon.\lambda\sigma''.\ \bigcup_{\sigma_d \in \Sigma_d}\ \kappa\,\varepsilon\,\sigma_d$
      where $\Sigma_d = \text{decls}\,\{x_1,\ldots,x_n\}\,\rho'\,\sigma''$

$\mathcal{E}[\![\text{iCell }x]\!]\rho\,\kappa = \lambda\sigma.\kappa\,\text{unit}\,(\sigma \oplus \{(\rho\,x) \mapsto \langle\text{I},\text{empty}\rangle\})$

$\mathcal{E}[\![\text{mCell }x]\!]\rho\,\kappa = \lambda\sigma.\kappa\,\text{unit}\,(\sigma \oplus \{(\rho\,x) \mapsto \langle\text{M},\text{empty}\rangle\})$

$\mathcal{E}[\![\text{Fetch }x]\!]\rho\,\kappa = in_{\mathbf{Cont}}(x,\lambda\varepsilon.\lambda\sigma.\kappa\,\varepsilon\,\sigma')$
  where $\sigma' = \text{case }\sigma(\rho\,x)\text{ of}$
    $\langle\text{I},\varepsilon'\rangle \longrightarrow \sigma$
    $\langle\text{M},\varepsilon'\rangle \longrightarrow \sigma \oplus \{(\rho\,x) \mapsto \langle\text{M},\text{empty}\rangle\}$
    $\text{otherwise} \longrightarrow \text{wrong}$
  endcase

$\mathcal{E}[\![\text{Store }(x_1,x_2)]\!]\rho\,\kappa = \mathcal{E}[\![x_2]\!]\rho\,\kappa'$
  where $\kappa' = \lambda\varepsilon.\lambda\sigma.(out_{\mathbf{Cont}}(x_1,\varepsilon,\kappa\,\text{unit})\,\sigma')$
    $\sigma' = \text{case }\sigma(\rho\,x_1)\text{ of}$
    $\langle\text{I},\text{empty}\rangle \longrightarrow \sigma \oplus \{(\rho\,x_1) \mapsto \langle\text{I},\varepsilon\rangle\}$
    $\langle\text{M},\text{empty}\rangle \longrightarrow \sigma \oplus \{(\rho\,x_1) \mapsto \langle\text{M},\varepsilon\rangle\}$
    $\text{otherwise} \longrightarrow \text{wrong}$
  endcase

Fig. 11. Evaluation function for pH-core

Both, *lazy* and *strict* applications, force the evaluation of the expression which will yield the abstraction. The difference is that in lazy applications the argument is stored as a closure in a new location, to be evaluated only under demand; while in strict applications the evaluation of the argument is forced before the evaluation of the application.

We have three different actions concerning updatable cells:

Creation: An empty cell is stored in the location associated to the variable. The type of the cell is reflected in the cell label.

Query: If the corresponding cell is empty an error is raised. In the case of an M-cell, the cell is emptied after consulting its content.

Store: the value is obtained and placed in the corresponding cell. If the cell is already full an error is raised.

There is a clear similitude between cells and channels: the filling of a cell resembles the action of communicating a value. On the other hand, the value of a cell can only be consulted if it is full. In a similar way, the reception of a value can only take place if the value has been sent. This point of view is denotationally expressed using the usual functions $out_{\mathbf{Cont}}$ and $in_{\mathbf{Cont}}$ (see [HI93]).

The evaluation of a local declaration is done in two phases: firstly, the environment and the store are widened with the information from the new local variables, and secondly, parallel threads are created to evaluate each variable. This is done by means of the auxiliary function decls, given in Figure 12.

In pH a program computation finishes only when every created thread has been completely evaluated. Therefore, we do not differentiate between minimal and maximal semantics (in fact, the definition given here corresponds to the maximal semantics).

---

force :: $\mathbf{Loc} \rightarrow \mathbf{ECont} \rightarrow \mathbf{Cont}$

force $\alpha\,\kappa = \lambda\sigma.$case $(\sigma\,\alpha)$ of
   $\varepsilon \in \mathbf{Abs} \longrightarrow \kappa\,\varepsilon\,\sigma$
   $\nu \in \mathbf{Clo} \longrightarrow \nu\,\kappa'\,\sigma'$
   where $\kappa' = \lambda\varepsilon''.\lambda\sigma''.\kappa\,\varepsilon''\,\sigma'' \oplus \{l \mapsto \varepsilon''\}$
          $\sigma' = \sigma \oplus \{l \mapsto$ not_ready$\}$
   otherwise $\longrightarrow$ wrong
endcase

decls :: $\mathcal{P}_f(\mathbf{Ide}) \rightarrow \mathbf{Env} \rightarrow \mathbf{Cont}$

decls $\emptyset\,\rho = \lambda\sigma.\{\sigma\}$
decls $I\,\rho =$
  $= \lambda\sigma.\bigcup_{x \in I} (\ \bigcup_{\sigma_x \in \Sigma_x}$ decls $(I \setminus \{x\})\,\rho\,\sigma_x)$
  where $\Sigma_x = \mathcal{E}[\![x]\!]\rho\,id_\kappa\,\sigma$

Fig. 12. Auxiliary semantic functions for pH-core

---

5   Conclusions and Future Work

We have used continuations to model laziness, parallelism, non-determinism and side-effects in a denotational semantics.

The differences between the three approaches —explicit, semi-explicit and implicit parallelism— are reflected in the semantic domains, where only in the first case (explicit parallelism) some notion of process is needed. Moreover, the distributed (not shared memory) nature of Eden, complicates quite a lot the semantics, because bindings have to be copied from one process to the others, while in the other two cases there are no restrictions in sharing memory.

The explicit parallelism of Eden requires special domains for representing processes: process identifiers, **IdProc**, and sets of channels, **SChan**. By contrast, GpH and pH do not need these particular domains. However, not only the domains do vary, but also the definition of the semantic function differs. The explicit parallelism of Eden resides in the evaluation of $#, where the structure of a new process is created, i.e. the corresponding channels. A point where the differences clearly arise is in theletevaluation: GPH does nothing special because these new variables are evaluated only if they are demanded, consequently they are just added to the environment; pH evaluates in parallel all the local variables and simultaneously to the main expression; thanks to the expression continuation all these variables are evaluated. Eden only evaluates –if it is not the minimal case– the variables associated to processes creation; once again this task is developed by means of the expression continuation.

Obviously, GPH with no processes, no communications, no non-determinism, and no side-effects has the simplest semantics. However simple, this semantics can help to detect speculative parallelism by comparing the final environments under the minimal and under the maximal semantics. Even though, this probably can also be done without continuations.

The semantics presented in this paper allows to extract the degree of parallelism and the amount of speculative computation. For instance, in the case of Eden, a set of channels defines an oriented graph whose nodes correspond to process identifiers and edges are labelled with the communicated values. Therefore the number of nodes of this graph coincides with the number of processes in the corresponding system. By modifying the definition of the expression continuation for the parallel application, other approaches between the minimal and the maximal semantics are possible in this framework. The speculation degree can therefore be obtained as the difference between the number of nodes in a non-minimal graph and the number of nodes in the minimal one.

Concerning pH programs, a speculative location is one that has not been needed for obtaining the final result. We could define an alternative "minimal" expression continuation for theletexpression that only introduces the closures in the store, but it does not evaluate it. Comparing the final store in the semantics given en Section 4 with the one derived from this new expression continuation we observe that the locations that do not longer appear in the new minimal version are speculative. Moreover, for a location that appears in both stores if it is bound to an expressed value or a cell in the non-minimal semantics but it is bound to a closure in the minimal, then this location is also speculative.

The analysis of the speculation in GPH follows the same ideas that we have outlined above for pH, but changing locations in the store by variables in the environment.

On the other hand, the abstraction level of the present denotational model does not permit to observe work duplication because this has to do with the copy of variables from one process to another.

One of our future tasks is to use the denotational semantics presented here to relate formally some notions concerning these languages. For instance, we intend to compare the behaviour of the communication channels of Eden with the cells of pH: an I-cell is like a channel where a thread writes some value that other threads can later read, but once this value has been set, the I-cell cannot be filled again; similarly, a channel is a one-use-only entity, although the reader of the value is unique in this case.

Acknowledgements. This work has been partially supported by the Spanish project CICYT-TIC2000-0738. We are very grateful to David de Frutos for his comments on earlier versions of Eden's semantics and to the APLAS'03 anonymous reviewers for their helpful criticisms.

References

[AAA+95]   S. Aditya, Arvind, L. Augustsson, J. Maessen, and R. S. Nikhil. Semantics of pH: A parallel dialect of Haskell. In P. Hudak, editor, *Haskell Workshop*, pages 35–49, La Jolla, Cambridge, MA, USA, YALEU/DCS/RR-1075, June 1995.

[BFKT00]   C. Baker-Finch, D. King, and P. Trinder. An operational semantics for parallel lazy evaluation. In *ACM-SIGPLAN International Conference on Functional Programming (ICFP'00)*, pages 162–173, Montreal, Canada, September 2000.

[BLOMP96]   S. Breitinger, R. Loogen, Y. Ortega-Mallén, and R. Peña. Eden – the paradise of functional-concurrent programming. In *EUROPAR'96: European Conference on Parallel Processing*, pages 710–713. LNCS 1123, Springer, 1996.

[DB97]   M. Debbabi and D. Bolignano. *ML with Concurrency: Design, Analysis, Implementation, and Application*, chapter 6: A semantic theory for ML higher-order concurrency primitives, pages 145–184. Monographs in Computer Science. Ed. F. Nielson. Springer, 1997.

[EM02]   M. van Ekelen and M. de Mol. Reasoning about explicit strictness in a lazy language using mixed lazy/strict semantics. In *Draft Proceedings of the 14th International Workshop on Implementation of Functional Languages, IFL'02*, pages 357–373. Dept. Sistemas Informáticos y Programación, Universidad Complutense de Madrid, 2002.

[FH99]   W. Ferreira and M. Hennessy. A behavioural theory of first-order CML. *Theoretical Computer Science*, 216:55–107, 1999.

[Hen88]   M. Hennessy. *Algebraic Theory of Processes*. MIT Press, 1988.

[HI93]   M. Hennessy and A. Ingólfsdóttir. A theory of communicating processes with value passing. *Information and Computation*, 107:202–236, 1993.

[HOM02]   M. Hidalgo-Herrero and Y. Ortega-Mallén. An operational semantics for the parallel language Eden. *Parallel Processing Letters. World Scientific Publishing Company*, 12(2):211–228, 2002.

[Jos86]   M. B. Josephs. *Functional programming with side-effects*. PhD thesis, Oxford University, 1986.

[Jos89]   M. B. Josephs. The semantics of lazy functional languages. *Theoretical Computer Science*, 68:105–111, 1989.

[KM77]   G. Kahn and D. MacQueen. Coroutines and networks of parallel processes. In *IFIP'77*, pages 993–998. Eds. B. Gilchrist. North-Holland, 1977.

[Lau93]   J. Launchbury. A natural semantics for lazy evaluation. In *POPL'93*, Charleston, 1993.

[Loo99]   R. Loogen. *Research Directions in Parallel Functional Programming*, chapter 3: Programming Language Constructs. Eds. K. Hammond and G. Michaelson. Springer, 1999.

[NA01]   R. S. Nikhil and Arvind. *Implicit Parallel Programing in pH*. Academic Press, 2001.

[Nik91]   R. S. Nikhil. Id (version 90.1) language reference manual. Technical Report CSG Memo 284–2, Laboratory for Computer Science, MIT, Cambridge, MA, USA, 1991.

[Pey87]   S. Peyton Jones. *Implementation of Functional Programming Languages*. Prentice Hall, 1987.

[Pey03]   S. Peyton Jones. *Haskell 98 language and libraries: the Revised Report*. Cambridge University Press, 2003.

[Rep92]   J. H. Reppy. *Higher-Order Concurrency*. PhD thesis, Cornell University (Deparyment of Computer Scienqe), 1992.

[Rey98]   J. C. Reynolds. *Theories of Programming Languages*. Cambridge University Press, 1998.

[Sto77]   J.E. Stoy. *Denotational Semantics: The Scott-Strachey Approach to Programming Language Theory*. MIT Press, Cambridge, MA, 1977.

[THM+96]   P. Trinder, K. Hammond, J. Mattson Jr., A. Partridge, and S. Peyton Jones. GUM: a portable implementation of Haskell. In *Proceedings of Programming Language Design and Implementation*, Philadephia, USA, May 1996.

Translating a Continuous-Time Temporal Logic into Timed Automata⋆

Guangyuan Li and Zhisong Tang

Key Laboratory of Computer Science, Institute of Software,
The Chinese Academy of Sciences, Beijing, 100080, P.R. of China
{ligy,cst}@ios.ac.cn

Abstract. LTLC is a continuous-time linear temporal logic for the specification of real-time systems. It can express both real-time systems and their properties. With LTLC, real-time systems can be described at different levels of abstraction, from high-level requirement specifications to low-level implementation models, and the conformance between different descriptions can be expressed by logical implication. The full logic of LTLC is undecidable. This paper will show that the existentially quantified fragment of LTLC is decidable. We achieve this goal by showing that the fragment can be translated into timed automata. Because the emptiness problem for timed automata is decidable, we then get a decision procedure for satisfiability for this fragment. This decidable part of LTLC is quite expressive. Many important real-time properties, such as bounded-response and bounded-invariance properties, can be expressed in it. The translation also enables us to develop a decision procedure for model checking real-time systems with quantifier-free LTLC specifications.

1 Introduction

In order to specify real-time systems, many temporal logics, such as Timed Computation Tree Logic [1], Metric Interval Temporal Logic[3], and Quantitative Temporal Logic[7], have been proposed. Though these logics are good at specifying properties of real-time systems, they are not suitable for describing the dynamic behavior of such systems. For the lack of the ability to describe the dynamic evolution in the state of real-time systems, they are unable to represent real-time computational models, such as Timed Automata[2] and Clocked Transition Systems[12]. So real-time systems and their properties are generally expressed with different languages: systems are described with automaton-based or transition-based abstract models, for example, Timed Automata and Clocked Transition Systems; properties are described with various modal/temporal logics.

⋆ Supported by the National High Technology Development 863 Program of China under Grant No.2001AA113200; the National Natural Science Foundation of China under Grant No.60273025; and the National Grand Fundamental Research 973 Program of China under Grant No. 2002cb312200.

A. Ohori (Ed.): APLAS 2003, LNCS 2895, pp. 322–338, 2003.

To express real-time systems and their properties uniformly, a new temporal logic, named LTLC (a Linear Temporal Logic with Continuous semantics) is proposed in [9,10]. LTLC is a combination of linear temporal logic and Clocked Transition Systems[12]. It provides a unified logical framework for expressing and reasoning about real-time systems. With LTLC, real-time systems can be described at different levels of abstraction, from high-level requirement specifications to low-level implementation models, and the conformance between different descriptions can be expressed by logical implication.

The full logic of LTLC is undecidable. This paper will show that the existentially quantified fragment of LTLC, denoted EQF(see Section 2 for formal definition), is decidable. We achieve this goal by showing that EQF can be translated into timed automata. Because the emptiness problem for timed automata is decidable, we then get a decision procedure for satisfiability for EQF. This decidable fragment of LTLC is not trivial. It is quite expressive and many important properties for real-time systems, such as reachability, fairness, bounded-response[4], bounded-invariance[4], etc., can be expressed and verified in it.

The rest of this paper is organized as follows. Section 2 gives a brief introduction to LTLC. Section 3 shows that a real-time modelling language, Timed Transition Modules, can be translated into EQF. Section 4 shows the translation from EQF into timed automata. Section 5 is a short conclusion.

2   Syntax and Semantics for LTLC

2.1   Preliminaries

Definition 1. *Let $f : \mathcal{R}^{\geq 0} \mapsto \{0,1\}$ be a boolean-valued function defined on the nonnegative reals $\mathcal{R}^{\geq 0}$, f is said to be a boolean-valued step function if there exists an unbounded increasing sequence $a_0 = 0 < a_1 < a_2 < \ldots$ of reals such that f is constant on every interval $(a_i, a_{i+1}]$.*

Definition 2. *$f : \mathcal{R}^{\geq 0} \mapsto \mathcal{R}^{\geq 0}$ is said to be a clock function if*

- *there exists a bounded increasing sequence $a_0 = 0 < a_1 < a_2 < \cdots < a_n$ of reals such that*

$$f(t) = \begin{cases} 0 & \text{if } t = 0; \\ t - a_i & \text{if } t \in (a_i, a_{i+1}]; \\ t - a_n & \text{if } t > a_n. \end{cases}$$

- *or there exists an unbounded increasing sequence $a_0 = 0 < a_1 < a_2 < \ldots$ of reals such that*

$$f(t) = \begin{cases} 0 & \text{if } t = 0; \\ t - a_i & \text{if } t \in (a_i, a_{i+1}]. \end{cases}$$

From Definition 1 and 2, boolean-valued step functions and clock functions are left continuous at every positive point.

Definition 3. *Let f be a boolean-valued step function or a clock function, a new function f' associated with f is defined by $f'(t) ::= \lim_{t_1 \to t+} f(t_1)$, where $t \in \mathcal{R}^{\geq 0}$, and $\lim_{t_1 \to t+} f(t_1)$ denotes the right-limit of f at the point t.*

2.2 Syntax of LTLC

The alphabet of LTLC consists of the following symbols.

1. A set of boolean variables: $p, q, p_1, p_2, \ldots$
2. A set of clock variables: $c, c_1, c_2, \ldots$
3. A set of constants: $0, 1, 2, 3, \ldots$
4. Relation symbols: $=, \leq$.
5. Connectives: $\neg, \wedge$.
6. Quantifier: $\exists$.
7. Temporal operators: $\prime$ (prime, newvalue), $\mathcal{U}$(until), $\diamondsuit_{(0,1)}$(occur within one unit of time).

Formulae of LTLC are defined inductively as follows.

$$\varphi ::= p \mid p' \mid (c = m) \mid (c \leq m) \mid (c' = 0) \mid (c' = c) \mid (\neg\varphi) \mid (\varphi_1 \wedge \varphi_2) \mid (\varphi_1 \mathcal{U} \varphi_2) \mid (\diamondsuit_{(0,1)}\varphi) \mid (\exists p.\varphi) \mid (\exists c.\varphi)$$

where p is a boolean variable, c a clock variable, and m a constant.

Let V be a set of variables. φ is said to be a formula over V if every variable occurring in φ is also in V.

2.3 A Continuous Semantics for LTLC

In LTLC, time is modelled by $\mathcal{R}^{\geq 0}$ and variables are interpreted by functions defined on $\mathcal{R}^{\geq 0}$. Boolean variables are interpreted by boolean-valued step functions, and clock variables by clock functions.

Definition 4. *Let V be a finite set of variables, an LTLC-interpretation (model) over V is a mapping $\mathcal{J}$ defined on V, satisfying the following conditions.*
   1. For every boolean variable $p \in V$, $\mathcal{J}$ assigns a boolean-valued step function f_p to p.
   2. For every clock variable $c \in V$, $\mathcal{J}$ assigns a clock function f_c to c.

Definition 5. *Let $\mathcal{J}$ be an LTLC-interpretation over V and φ be a formula over V. For every $t_0 \in \mathcal{R}^{\geq 0}$, the value of φ at t_0 under the interpretation $\mathcal{J}$, denoted by $\mathcal{J}(\varphi, t_0)$, is defined as follows.*

1. $\mathcal{J}(p, t_0) ::= f_p(t_0)$
2. $\mathcal{J}(p', t_0) ::= f'_p(t_0)$
3. $\mathcal{J}(c = m, t_0) ::= \begin{cases} 1 & \text{if } f_c(t_0) = m; \\ 0 & \text{otherwise.} \end{cases}$

4. $\mathcal{J}(c \leq m, t_0) ::= \begin{cases} 1 & \text{if } f_c(t_0) \leq m; \\ 0 & \text{otherwise.} \end{cases}$

5. $\mathcal{J}(c' = 0, t_0) ::= \begin{cases} 1 & \text{if } f_c'(t_0) = 0; \\ 0 & \text{otherwise.} \end{cases}$

6. $\mathcal{J}(c' = c, t_0) ::= \begin{cases} 1 & \text{if } f_c'(t_0) = f_c(t_0); \\ 0 & \text{otherwise.} \end{cases}$

7. $\mathcal{J}(\neg\varphi, t_0) ::= 1 - \mathcal{J}(\varphi, t_0).$

8. $\mathcal{J}(\varphi_1 \wedge \varphi_2, t_0) ::= \mathcal{J}(\varphi_1, t_0) \cdot \mathcal{J}(\varphi_2, t_0).$

9. $\mathcal{J}(\varphi_1 \mathcal{U} \varphi_2, t_0) ::= \begin{cases} 1 & \text{if there exists a } t_1 > t_0 \text{ such that } \mathcal{J}(\varphi_2, t_1) = 1 \\ & \text{and } \mathcal{J}(\varphi_1, t_2) = 1 \text{ holds for every } t_2 \in (t_0, t_1); \\ 0 & \text{otherwise.} \end{cases}$

10. $\mathcal{J}(\Diamond_{(0,1)}\varphi, t_0) ::= \begin{cases} 1 & \text{if there exists a } t_1 \in (t_0, t_0+1) \text{ such that } \\ & \mathcal{J}(\varphi, t_1) = 1; \\ 0 & \text{otherwise.} \end{cases}$

11. $\mathcal{J}(\exists p.\varphi, t_0) ::= \begin{cases} 1 & \text{if there exists a boolean-valued step function } g \\ & \text{such that } \mathcal{J}[g/p](\varphi, t_0) = 1; \\ 0 & \text{otherwise.} \end{cases}$

12. $\mathcal{J}(\exists c.\varphi, t_0) ::= \begin{cases} 1 & \text{if there exists a clock function } h \text{ such that } \\ & \mathcal{J}[h/c](\varphi, t_0) = 1; \\ 0 & \text{otherwise.} \end{cases}$

where f_p' is the function associated with f_p, and $\mathcal{J}[g/p]$ is an LTLC-interpretation which maps p to g and agrees with $\mathcal{J}$ on all variables distinct from p.

If $\mathcal{J}(\varphi, 0) = 1$, we say $\mathcal{J}$ is an LTLC model of φ. For a formula φ over V, we define $Mod_V(\varphi)$ to be the set of all LTLC models of φ. If $Mod_V(\varphi) \neq \emptyset$, we say φ is satisfiable.

Definition 6. *Let φ and ψ be two formulae over V. If every model of φ is also a model of ψ, then ψ is said to be a logical consequence of φ, denoted by $\varphi \models \psi$.*

Some abbreviations:

1. $false := p \wedge \neg p$ $\qquad\qquad\qquad\qquad true := \neg false$
2. $\varphi \vee \phi := \neg(\neg\varphi \wedge \neg\phi)$ $\qquad\qquad\quad \varphi \Rightarrow \phi := \neg\varphi \vee \phi$
3. $\varphi \Leftrightarrow \phi := (\varphi \Rightarrow \phi) \wedge (\phi \Rightarrow \varphi)$
4. $\Diamond\varphi := \varphi \vee (true\,\mathcal{U}\,\varphi)$ $\qquad\qquad\quad \Box\varphi := \neg\Diamond\neg\varphi$
5. $\Diamond_{[0,1)}\varphi := \varphi \vee \Diamond_{(0,1)}\varphi$ $\qquad\qquad \Box_{(0,1)}\varphi := \neg\Diamond_{(0,1)}\neg\varphi$
6. $\Diamond_{(0,1]}\varphi := \Diamond_{(0,1)}\varphi \vee ((\neg\varphi\mathcal{U}\varphi) \wedge \Box_{(0,1)}\Diamond_{(0,1)}\varphi)$
7. $\Box_{(0,1]}\varphi := \neg\Diamond_{(0,1]}\neg\varphi$
8. $\Box_{(n,n+1]}\varphi := \Box_{(n-1,n]}\Diamond_{[0,1)}\Box_{(0,1]}\varphi$
9. $\Box_{(n,m]}\varphi := \Box_{(n,n+1]}\varphi \wedge \ldots \wedge \Box_{(m-1,m]}\varphi$
10. $\Diamond_{(n,m]}\varphi := \neg\Box_{(n,m]}\neg\varphi$ $\qquad\qquad \Diamond_{(0,\infty)}\varphi := true\,\mathcal{U}\,\varphi$

11. $\Diamond_{(n,\infty)}\varphi := \Box_{(0,n]}\Diamond_{(0,\infty)}\varphi$

12. $\Diamond_{=n}\varphi := \exists c.(c' = 0 \wedge \Diamond_{(0,n]}((c=n) \wedge \varphi))$ (φ is true precisely n time units later)

Theorem 1. *The satisfiability problem for LTLC is undecidable.*

Proof. LTLC is a continuous-time temporal logic and is capable of expressing punctuality properties of the form $\Box(p \Rightarrow \Diamond_{=n} q)$. So from the conclusion in [4] we know that LTLC is undecidable.   □

An LTLC formula is called quantifier-free if it does not contain any quantifier. Many properties, such as safety ($\Box p$), reachability ($\Diamond p$), fairness ($\Box\Diamond p \Rightarrow \Box\Diamond q$), bounded-response ($\Box(p \Rightarrow \Diamond_{(0,n]}q)$) and bounded-invariance ($\Box(p \Rightarrow \Box_{(0,n]}\neg q)$), can be expressed by quantifier-free formulae.

Lemma 1. *The satisfiability problem for quantifier-free fragment of LTLC is decidable.*

Proof. Every quantifier-free LTLC formula can be translated into a timed automaton that accepts precisely all the models of the formula. We will illustrate the translation procedure in Section 4 by translating a sublanguage of LTLC into timed automata. The full translation procedure is omitted. Because the emptiness problem for timed automata is decidable, we then get the fact that the satisfiability problem for quantifier-free part of LTLC is decidable.   □

An existentially quantified formula is a formula of the form $\exists v_0 \exists v_1 \ldots \exists v_{m-1}\phi$, where $v_0, v_1, \ldots, v_{m-1}(m \geq 0)$ are variables, and ϕ is a quantifier-free formula. We use EQF to denote the set of all existentially quantified formulae of LTLC. Because $\exists v_0 \exists v_1 \ldots \exists v_{m-1}\phi$ is satisfiable if and only if ϕ is satisfiable, from Lemma 1 we get the following result.

Theorem 2. *The satisfiability problem for EQF is decidable.*

Notation 1. A state formula is an LTLC formula defined by the grammar $\varphi ::= p \,|\, (c \leq m) \,|\, (c = m) \,|\, (\neg\varphi) \,|\, (\varphi_1 \wedge \varphi_2)$. A transition formula is an LTLC formula defined by the grammar $\varphi ::= p' \,|\, (\neg p') \,|\, (c' = 0) \,|\, (c' = c) \,|\, (\varphi_1 \wedge \varphi_2)$.

3   Modelling Real-Time Systems with LTLC

Real-time systems are modelled by *timed transition modules* in this paper. The model of timed transition module is a slight variation on the model of clocked transition module[6]. A TTM (timed transition module) represents a real-time system(process) that interacts with an environment. The variables of a TTM M can be divided into three pairwise disjoint sets: the set $priv(M)$ of *private variables*, the set $read(M)$ of read variables and the set $write(M)$ of *write variables*. We refer to $ctr(M) = priv(M) \cup write(M)$ as the controlled variables, to

$obs(M) = write(M) \cup read(M)$ as the observable variables. Each *private variable* can be read and modified by the module, and neither read nor modified by the environment. Each *write variable* can be read by both the module and the environment, and modified by the module only. Each *read variable* can be read by both the module and the environment, and modified by the environment only. Every variable in timed transition modules has a type. *boolean, clock* and finite enumerating sets are frequently used types in timed transition modules. As an enumerated variable can be encoded by several boolean variables, it suffices to consider only boolean variables and clock variables in our definitions for timed transition modules.

A TTM has a finite set of locations. The module can either delay in a location for some time or jump from one location to another. Controlled boolean variables are used to encode the location information and read boolean variables represent outside signals for communication. Clock variables are used to express the timing constraints.

A TTM has a finite set of transitions. They can be divided into two kinds: jump transitions and delay transitions. A jump transition is instantaneous, it switches the module from one location to another, in zero time. A delay transition has a positive duration. During the period, the values of all controlled boolean variables remain unchanged, and the values of all controlled clock variables increase continuously at the rate 1.

Each jump transition can be written as a guarded command '$guard \longrightarrow assign$', where '$guard$' is a state formula and '$assign$' is a transition formula(see Notation 1). '$guard$' expresses the enabling condition of the transition and '$assign$' updates the values of all controlled variables. Each delay transition can be written in the form '$location \longrightarrow invariant$', where '$invariant$' is a state formula, and '$location$' is a state formula containing no clock variables.

In summary, a TTM has the form

> **module** *module_name*
> **read**   {*variable_name*: *variable_type*}*
> **write**   {*variable_name*: *variable_type*}*
> **private** {*variable_name*: *variable_type*}*
> **init**   *init_cond*
> **jump**   {*guard* $\longrightarrow$ *assign*}*
> **delay**   {*location* $\longrightarrow$ *invariant*}*

where *init_cond* is the initial condition. It is a state formula characterizing the initial states. If $\{loc_i \to inv_i\}_{i<n}$ are all delay transitions occurring in a TTM M, then $\bigvee_{i<n} loc_i$ contains each location of M, and $(loc_i \wedge loc_j)$ is a contradiction provided $i \neq j$.

Notation 2. For a boolean variable p, we write $(p' = p)$ for the formula $(p' \Leftrightarrow p)$. For a set V of variables, we write $(V' = V)$ for the formula $\bigwedge_{v \in V}(v' = v)$. Let $\alpha := guard \longrightarrow assign$ be a jump transition, and $\beta := loc \longrightarrow invar$ be a delay transition, we use TLF(α) to denote the formula '*guard∧assign*' and use TLF(β) to denote the formula '*loc ∧ invar*'.

Definition 7. *Let M be a TTM. Suppose $< v_0, v_1, v_2, \ldots, v_{m-1} >$ is an enumeration of all variables in $priv(M)$, $< \alpha_0, \alpha_1, a_2, \ldots, \alpha_{n-1} >$ all jump transitions of M, and $< \beta_0, \beta_1, \beta_2, \ldots, \beta_{l-1} >$ all delay transitions of M. Define the formula*

$$\exists v_0 \exists v_1 \ldots \exists v_{m-1}(init \wedge (\Box((V_c' = V_c) \vee \bigvee_{j<n} TLF(\alpha_j))) \wedge \Box \bigvee_{k<l} TLF(\beta_k)),$$

to be the temporal formula associated with M (denoted by $TLF(M)$), where 'init' is the initial condition of M, and V_c is the set of $ctr(M)$.

Definition 8. *We define the semantics of a TTM M by that of the temporal formula $TLF(M)$, and regard the models of $TLF(M)$ as the models of M. If $TLF(M) \models \varphi$ holds for a formula φ, we say φ is a property of M, denoted by $M \models \varphi$.*

Theorem 3. *For each TTM M and each quantifier-free formula φ which does not contain private variables of M, the problem of deciding whether φ is a property of M is decidable.*

Proof. Assume $TLF(M)$ is $\exists v_0 \exists v_1 \ldots \exists v_{m-1}\psi$, where ψ is a quantifier-free formula. Since φ is a quantifier-free formula containing no variables in $\{ v_0, v_1, \ldots, v_{m-1}\}$, then $(\exists v_0 \exists v_1 \ldots \exists v_{m-1}\psi) \wedge \neg\varphi$ is equivalent to $\exists v_0 \exists v_1 \ldots \exists v_{m-1}(\psi \wedge \neg\varphi)$. So, $M \models \varphi$ iff the formula $\exists v_0 \exists v_1 \ldots \exists v_{m-1}(\psi \wedge \neg\varphi)$ is unsatisfiable. The later is in EQF and its satisfiability is decidable. Thus we get the desired conclusion that whether $M \models \varphi$ holds is decidable.

$\Box$

Definition 9. *Two modules M_1 and M_2 are said to be compatible if $write(M_1) \cap write(M_2) = \emptyset$ and for every $v \in obs(M_1) \cap obs(M_2)$, v has the same type in M_1 and M_2. Modules $M_1, M_2, \ldots, M_n$ are said to be compatible if they are pairwise compatible.*

Definition 10 (Parallel composition). *If timed transition modules M_1, M_2, $\ldots$, M_n are compatible, we use $[M_1 \parallel M_2 \parallel \cdots \parallel M_n]$ to denote their parallel composition. Its semantics is defined by the temporal formula $TLF(M_1) \wedge TLF(M_2) \wedge \cdots \wedge TLF(M_n)$. If $TLF(M_1) \wedge TLF(M_2) \wedge \cdots \wedge TLF(M_n) \models \varphi$ for a formula φ, we say φ is a property of $[M_1 \parallel M_2 \parallel \cdots \parallel M_n]$.*

Definition 11 (Refinement and equivalence). *Let M_1 and M_2 be two timed transition modules with $write(M_1) = write(M_2)$ and $read(M_1) = read(M_2)$. If $TLF(M_1) \models TLF(M_2)$, we say that M_1 refines M_2, denoted by $M_1 \preccurlyeq M_2$. M_1 and M_2 are said to be equivalent if each of them refines the other.*

```
module       P₁
read         k : {0, 1, 2}
write        pc₁ : {0, 1, 2}
private      c : clock
init         pc₁ = 0 ∧ c = 0
jump
    pc₁ = 0 ∧ k = 0 ⟶ pc₁' = 1 ∧ c' = 0;
    pc₁ = 1 ∧ k = 1 ⟶ pc₁' = 2 ∧ c' = 0;
    pc₁ = 1 ∧ c = 3 ∧ k ≠ 1 ⟶ pc₁' = 0 ∧ c' = c;
    pc₁ = 2 ∧ c ≥ 3 ⟶ pc₁' = 0 ∧ c' = c
delay
    pc₁ = 0 ⟶ true;
    pc₁ = 1 ⟶ c ≤ 3;
    pc₁ = 2 ⟶ c ≤ 5
```

Fig. 1. Process P_1

```
module       P₂
read         k : {0, 1, 2}
write        pc₂ : {0, 1, 2}
private      c : clock
init         pc₂ = 0 ∧ c = 0
jump
    pc₂ = 0 ∧ k = 0 ⟶ pc₂' = 1 ∧ c' = 0;
    pc₂ = 1 ∧ k = 2 ⟶ pc₂' = 2 ∧ c' = 0;
    pc₂ = 1 ∧ c = 3 ∧ k ≠ 2 ⟶ pc₂' = 0 ∧ c' = c;
    pc₂ = 2 ∧ c ≥ 3 ⟶ pc₂' = 0 ∧ c' = c
delay
    pc₂ = 0 ⟶ true;
    pc₂ = 1 ⟶ c ≤ 3;
    pc₂ = 2 ⟶ c ≤ 5
```

Fig. 2. Process P_2

Example 1(the mutual exclusion problem). The timed transition module P_1 of Fig. 1 and the timed transition module P_2 of Fig. 2 model two processes that share a common resource. Each process has a critical section which contains all accesses to the common resource. At any time instant, at most one of the two processes is allowed to be in its critical section. For each $i \in \{1, 2\}$, P_i has three locations: in location ℓ_0, the process is outside the critical section; in location ℓ_1, the process is requesting to enter the critical section; in location ℓ_2, the process is inside the critical section. The timed module A in Fig. 3 is a special process introduced to arbitrate between processes P_1 and P_2. A has two locations: in location ℓ_0, the common resource is free and neither P_1 nor P_2 is in its critical section; in location ℓ_1, the common resource has been assigned to one of the two processes. k is an observable variable controlled by process A. It indicates if the common resource is unoccupied ($k = 0$), assigned to P_1 ($k = 1$), or to P_2 ($k = 2$). The initial value of k is 0. k may be set a value $i \in \{1, 2\}$ by process A

module A
read $pc_1, pc_2 : \{0, 1, 2\}$
write $k : \{0, 1, 2\}$
private $pc : \{0, 1\}; c : clock$
init $pc = 0 \wedge k = 0 \wedge c = 0$
jump
$\quad pc=0 \wedge pc_1 = 1 \longrightarrow pc' = 1 \wedge k' = 1 \wedge c' = c;$
$\quad pc=0 \wedge pc_2 = 1 \longrightarrow pc' = 1 \wedge k' = 2 \wedge c' = c;$
$\quad pc=0 \wedge pc_1 \neq 1 \wedge pc_2 \neq 1 \wedge c = 2 \longrightarrow pc' = pc \wedge k' = k \wedge c' = 0;$
$\quad pc=1 \wedge k = 1 \wedge pc_1 = 0 \longrightarrow pc' = 0 \wedge k' = 0 \wedge c' = 0;$
$\quad pc=1 \wedge k = 2 \wedge pc_2 = 0 \longrightarrow pc' = 0 \wedge k' = 0 \wedge c' = 0$
delay
$\quad pc=0 \longrightarrow c \leq 2;$
$\quad pc=1 \longrightarrow true$

Fig. 3. Process A

when P_i is requesting to enter its critical section ($pc_i = 1$). If k gets the value i, P_i will switch from location ℓ_1 to location ℓ_2 before P_i has stayed in location ℓ_1 for 3 time units. If k is still unequal to i until P_i has stayed in location ℓ_1 for 3 time units, P_i will switch to the location ℓ_0. To make them easier to understand, we re-express these processes graphically in Fig. 4 and Fig. 5.

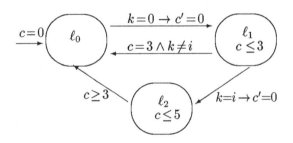

Fig. 4. Process P_i

The temporal formulae associated with P_1, P_2 and A are

$\mathrm{TLF}(P_1) = \exists c.((pc_1 = 0 \wedge c = 0) \wedge (\Box((pc_1' = pc_1 \wedge c' = c) \vee (pc_1 = 0 \wedge k = 0 \wedge pc_1' = 1 \wedge c' = 0) \vee (pc_1 = 1 \wedge k = 1 \wedge pc_1' = 2 \wedge c' = 0) \vee (pc_1 = 1 \wedge c = 3 \wedge k \neq 1 \wedge pc_1' = 0 \wedge c' = c) \vee (pc_1 = 2 \wedge c \geq 3 \wedge pc_1' = 0 \wedge c' = c))) \wedge \Box(pc_1 = 0 \vee (pc_1 = 1 \wedge c \leq 3) \vee (pc_1 = 2 \wedge c \leq 5)))$

$\mathrm{TLF}(P_2) = \exists c.((pc_2 = 0 \wedge c = 0) \wedge (\Box((pc_2' = pc_2 \wedge c' = c) \vee (pc_2 = 0 \wedge k = 0 \wedge pc_2' = 1 \wedge c' = 0) \vee (pc_2 = 1 \wedge k = 2 \wedge pc_2' = 2 \wedge c' = 0) \vee (pc_2 = 1 \wedge c = 3 \wedge k \neq 2 \wedge pc_2' = 0 \wedge c' = c) \vee (pc_2 = 2 \wedge c \geq 3 \wedge pc_2' = 0 \wedge c' = c))) \wedge \Box(pc_2 = 0 \vee (pc_2 = 1 \wedge c \leq 3) \vee (pc_2 = 2 \wedge c \leq 5)))$

$\mathrm{TLF}(A) = \exists pc.\exists c.((pc = 0 \wedge k = 0 \wedge c = 0) \wedge (\Box((pc' = pc \wedge k' = k \wedge c' = c) \vee (pc = 0 \wedge pc_1 = 1 \wedge pc' = 1 \wedge k' = 1 \wedge c' = c) \vee (pc = 0 \wedge pc_2 = 1 \wedge pc' = 1 \wedge k' = 2 \wedge c' = c) \vee (pc = 1 \wedge pc_1 \neq 1 \wedge pc_2 \neq 1 \wedge c = 2 \wedge pc' = pc \wedge k' = k \wedge c' = 0) \vee (pc = 1 \wedge k =$

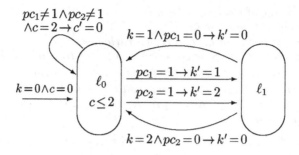

Fig. 5. Process A

$1 \wedge pc_1 = 0 \wedge pc' = 0 \wedge k' = 0 \wedge c' = 0) \vee (pc = 1 \wedge k = 2 \wedge pc_2 = 0 \wedge pc' = 0 \wedge k' = 0 \wedge c' = 0))) \wedge \Box((pc = 0 \wedge c \le 2) \vee pc = 1))$

The temporal formula associated with the composition module $[P_1 \parallel P_2 \parallel A]$ is $\text{TLF}(P_1) \wedge \text{TLF}(P_2) \wedge \text{TLF}(A)$. From Definition 5 and Definition 6 we can get $\text{TLF}(P_1) \wedge \text{TLF}(P_2) \wedge \text{TLF}(A) \models \Box((pc_1 = 2 \Rightarrow k = 1) \wedge (pc_2 = 2 \Rightarrow k = 2))$. Thus, $\Box\neg(pc_1 = 2 \wedge pc_2 = 2))$ is a property of the composition module $[P_1 \parallel P_2 \parallel A]$.

4 Constructing Timed Automata for LTLC Formulae

4.1 Timed Automata

Definition 12. *Let $\mathcal{C}$ be a finite set of clock variables, the set $\Phi(\mathcal{C})$ of clock constraints δ is defined by the grammar*

$$\delta ::= (c = m) \mid (c < m) \mid (c > m) \mid (\delta_1 \wedge \delta_2) \mid (\delta_1 \vee \delta_2),$$

where c is a clock variable in $\mathcal{C}$ and m is a nonnegative integer.

A clock interpretation σ over $\mathcal{C}$ is a mapping from $\mathcal{C}$ to the set $\mathcal{R}^{\ge 0}$ of non-negative reals. A clock interpretation σ satisfies a clock constraint δ over $\mathcal{C}$ iff δ evaluates to true according to the values given by σ. For $t \in \mathcal{R}^{\ge 0}$, we write $\sigma + t$ for the clock interpretation that assigns to each clock $c \in \mathcal{C}$ the value $\sigma(c) + t$. For $\gamma \subseteq \mathcal{C}$, we use $\sigma[\gamma := 0]$ to denote the clock interpretation that for each $c \in \gamma$ gives 0 and for each $c \in \mathcal{C} - \gamma$ gives the value $\sigma(c)$.

Definition 13. *A timed automaton M is a tuple $< \mathcal{S}_0, \mathcal{S}_1, \mathcal{S}_2, \mathcal{B}, \alpha, \mathcal{C}, \beta, \mathcal{O}, \mathcal{T}, \mathcal{F} >$, where*

- *$\mathcal{S} := \mathcal{S}_1 \cup \mathcal{S}_2$ is a finite set of locations. The elements of $\mathcal{S}_1$ are called singular locations, and the elements of $\mathcal{S}_2$ open locations.*
- *$\mathcal{S}_0 \subseteq \mathcal{S}_1$ is the set of initial locations.*
- *$\mathcal{B}$ is a finite set of boolean variables.*
- *α is a mapping from $\mathcal{S}$ to $2^{\mathcal{B}}$.*

- $\mathcal{C}$ *is a finite set of clock variables.*
- β *is a mapping from* $\mathcal{S}$ *to* $\Phi(\mathcal{C})$.
- $\mathcal{O} \subseteq \mathcal{B} \cup \mathcal{C}$ *is the set of all observable variables.*
- $\mathcal{T} \subseteq (\mathcal{S}_1 \times \mathcal{S}_2 \times 2^{\mathcal{C}}) \cup (\mathcal{S}_2 \times \mathcal{S}_1 \times 2^{\mathcal{C}})$ *is a set of transitions. Each transition* (v_1, v_2, γ) *represents a switch from location* v_1 *to location* v_2. *The set* $\gamma \subseteq \mathcal{C}$ *gives the clock variables to be reset with this switch.*
- $\mathcal{F} \subseteq 2^{\mathcal{S}}$ *is a finite set of fairness requirements. Each fairness requirement* F *is a set of locations.*

A state of M is a pair (v, σ) where $v \in \mathcal{S}$ and σ is a clock interpretation over $\mathcal{C}$. An initial state is a pair (v_0, σ_0) where $v_0 \in \mathcal{S}_0$ and $\sigma_0(c) = 0$ for all $c \in \mathcal{C}$.

Definition 14. *A run ρ of the timed automaton M is an infinite sequence*

$$(v_0, \sigma_0, t_0) \xrightarrow{\gamma_0} (v_1, \sigma_1, t_0) \xrightarrow{\gamma_1} (v_2, \sigma_2, t_1) \xrightarrow{\gamma_2} (v_3, \sigma_3, t_1) \xrightarrow{\gamma_3} (v_4, \sigma_4, t_2) \xrightarrow{\gamma_4}$$
$$(v_5, \sigma_5, t_2) \xrightarrow{\gamma_5} (v_6, \sigma_6, t_3) \xrightarrow{\gamma_6} \cdots$$

satisfying the following conditions:

1. $t_0 = 0 < t_1 < t_2 < t_3 < \ldots$ *is an unbounded increasing sequence of reals.*
2. (v_0, σ_0) *is an initial state, and for all* $i \geq 0$,
    - $v_{2i} \in \mathcal{S}_1$ *and* $v_{2i+1} \in \mathcal{S}_2$.
    - σ_i *is a clock interpretation over* $\mathcal{C}$, *and* γ_i *is subset of* $\mathcal{C}$.
    - $(v_i, v_{i+1}, \gamma_i) \in \mathcal{T}$.
    - $\sigma_{2i+1} = \sigma_{2i}[\gamma_{2i} := 0]$, *and* $\sigma_{2i+2} = (\sigma_{2i+1} + (t_{i+1} - t_i))[\gamma_{2i+1} := 0]$.
3. *For all* $t \in \mathcal{R}^{\geq 0}$,
    - *the location* $v_\rho(t)$ *at time* t *is defined by*
    $$v_\rho(t) = \begin{cases} v_{2i} & \text{if } t = t_i \\ v_{2i+1} & \text{if } t \in (t_i, t_{i+1}) \end{cases}$$
    - *the clock interpretation* $\sigma_\rho(t)$ *at time* t *is defined by*
    $$\sigma_\rho(t) = \begin{cases} \sigma_{2i} & \text{if } t = t_i \\ \sigma_{2i+1} + (t - t_i) & \text{if } t \in (t_i, t_{i+1}) \end{cases}$$
    - $\sigma_\rho(t)$ *satisfies* $\beta(v_\rho(t))$.
4. *For each fairness requirement* $F \in \mathcal{F}$ *there are infinitely many* $i \geq 0$ *with* $v_i \in F$.

Let ρ be a run of the timed automaton M. For each $p \in \mathcal{B}$, we use ρ_p to denote the *projection* of p under the run ρ, it is a function from $\mathcal{R}^{\geq 0}$ to $\{0, 1\}$ defined by

$$\rho_p(t) := \begin{cases} 1 & \text{if } p \in \alpha(v_\rho(t)) \\ 0 & \text{otherwise.} \end{cases}$$

Similarly, for each variable $c \in \mathcal{C}$, the *projection* ρ_c is a function from $\mathcal{R}^{\geq 0}$ to $\mathcal{R}^{\geq 0}$ defined by $\rho_c(t) := (\sigma_\rho(t))(c)$, for every $t \in \mathcal{R}^{\geq 0}$.

Let M be a timed automaton, and $\mathcal{O}$ be the set of all observable variables in M. Because the variables outside $\mathcal{O}$ are considered to be unimportant, we only consider the projection of observable variables when defining models for M. We use $\rho \Downarrow_{\mathcal{O}}$ to denote the *projection* of ρ onto the set $\mathcal{O}$ and define the set $Mod(M)$ of all models for timed automaton M to be the set $\{ \rho \Downarrow_{\mathcal{O}} \mid \rho \text{ is a run of M } \}$.

Theorem 4. *[2] The emptiness problem for timed automata is decidable, that is, whether a timed automaton has a model is decidable.*

4.2   Constructing Timed Automaton M_φ

In this section we use $\mathcal{L}$ to denote the set of formulae defined by the grammar

$$\varphi \ ::= \ p \,|\, p' \,|\, (c \ = \ m) \,|\, (c \ < \ m) \,|\, (c' \ = \ 0) \,|\, (c' \ = \ c) \,|\, (\neg\varphi) \,|\, (\varphi_1 \wedge \varphi_2) \,|\, (\Box\varphi) \,|\, (\Diamond_{(0,1)}\varphi)$$

Definition 15. *A formula in $\mathcal{L}$ is said to be in normalized form if it can be generated by the grammar*

$$\varphi \ ::= \ p \,|\, p' \,|\, \neg p \,|\, \neg p' \,|\, (c = m) \,|\, (c < m) \,|\, (c > m) \,|\, (c' = 0) \,|\, (c' = c) \,|\, (\varphi_1 \wedge \varphi_2) \,|\, (\varphi_1 \vee \varphi_2) \,|\, (\Box\varphi) \,|\, (\Diamond\varphi) \,|\, (\Box_{(0,1)}\varphi) \,|\, (\Diamond_{(0,1)}\varphi)$$

Lemma 2. *Every formula in $\mathcal{L}$ is equivalent to a formula in normalized form.*

Proof. Immediately from the following facts.

- $\neg(c < m) \Leftrightarrow (c = m) \vee (c > m)$
- $\neg(c = m) \Leftrightarrow (c < m) \vee (c > m)$
- $\neg(c' = 0) \Leftrightarrow (c > 0) \wedge (c' = c)$
- $\neg(c' = c) \Leftrightarrow (c > 0) \wedge (c' = 0)$

$\square$

Let $\varphi \in \mathcal{L}$ be a given formula in normalized form, we write $\mathcal{B}$ for the set of all boolean variables occurring in φ, $\mathcal{C}_1$ the set of all clock variables occurring in φ, and define the closure of φ, $cl(\varphi)$, to be the smallest set satisfying the following conditions.

1. $sing \in cl(\varphi)$ (Remark: $sing$ is a tag for labelling singular locations)
2. All subformulae of φ are in $cl(\varphi)$.
3. If $p \in \mathcal{B}$, then p and $\neg p$ are in $cl(\varphi)$.
4. If $c \in \mathcal{C}_1$, then $(c = 0)$ is in $cl(\varphi)$.
5. For each $\Box_{(0,1)}\phi$ in $cl(\varphi)$, a clock x_ϕ is in $cl(\varphi)$, and two clock constraints $(x_\phi < 1)$ and $(x_\phi \geq 1)$ are in $cl(\varphi)$.
6. For each $\Diamond_{(0,1)}\phi$ in $cl(\varphi)$, two clocks y_ϕ and z_ϕ are in $cl(\varphi)$, and two clock constraints $(y_\phi < 1)$ and $(z_\phi \leq 1)$ are in $cl(\varphi)$.

Remark. We use the clock x_ϕ to represent a proof obligation that ϕ holds as long as the clock constraint $x_\phi < 1$ holds, and y_ϕ (respectively, z_ϕ) represents a proof obligation that ϕ holds at some later time with the clock constraint $y_\phi < 1$ ($z_\phi \leq 1$). The idea of introducing auxiliary clocks to represent proof obligations comes from [3]. Some background for using these clocks can be seen in [3].

Definition 16. *A φ-atom A is a subset of $cl(\varphi)$ satisfying:*

1. *For each $p \in \mathcal{B}$,*
   - $p \in A$ iff $\neg p \notin A$.
   - *if $p' \in A$, then $\neg p' \notin A$.*
2. *For each $(\psi_1 \wedge \psi_2) \in cl(\varphi)$, $(\psi_1 \wedge \psi_2) \in A$ iff ($\psi_1 \in A$ and $\psi_2 \in A$).*

3. For each $(\psi_1 \vee \psi_2) \in cl(\varphi)$, $(\psi_1 \vee \psi_2) \in A$ iff $(\psi_1 \in A$ or $\psi_2 \in A)$.
4. If $\Box\psi \in A$, then $\psi \in A$.
5. For each $\Diamond\psi \in cl(\varphi)$, if $\psi \in A$, then $\Diamond\psi \in A$.
6. For each $c \in \mathcal{C}_1$, if A contains $(c'=0)$ and $(c'=c)$, then A contains $(c=0)$ also.
7. If there exists some $c \in \mathcal{C}_1$ such that $(c=0) \in A$, then $sing \in A$ and for all $c \in \mathcal{C}_1$, $(c=0) \in A$.
8. If $sing \notin A$, then A satisfies
   - $p' \in A$ implies $p \in A$.
   - $\neg p' \in A$ implies $\neg p \in A$.
   - for each $c \in \mathcal{C}_1$, $(c'=0) \notin A$.
   - $\Box_{(0,1)}\phi \in A$ implies $\phi \in A$.
   - for each $\Diamond_{(0,1)}\phi$ in $cl(\varphi)$, $\phi \in A$ implies $\Diamond_{(0,1)}\phi \in A$.
9. For each x_ϕ in $cl(\varphi)$, A contains precisely one of the clock constraints $(x_\phi < 1)$ and $(x_\phi \geq 1)$.

We write $Atom(\varphi)$ for the set of all φ-atoms.

Definition 17. *Given a formula $\varphi \in \mathcal{L}$ in normalized form, we define a timed automaton $M_\varphi := < S_0, S_1, S_2, \mathcal{B}, \alpha, \mathcal{C}, \beta, \mathcal{O}, \mathcal{T}, \mathcal{F} >$ as follows.*

1. $S_1 := \{ A \mid A \in Atom(\varphi)$ and $sing \in A \}$.
2. $S_2 := \{ A \mid A \in Atom(\varphi)$ and $sing \notin A \}$.
3. $S_0 := \{ A \mid A \in S_1, \varphi \in A$ and for all $c \in \mathcal{C}_1, (c=0) \in A \}$.
4. $\mathcal{B}$ is the set of all boolean variables occurring in φ.
5. For every $A \in Atom(\varphi)$, $\alpha(A) := \mathcal{B} \cap A$.
6. $\mathcal{C} := \mathcal{C}_1 \cup \mathcal{C}_2$, where $\mathcal{C}_1$ is the set of all clock variables occurring in φ, $\mathcal{C}_2 := \{ x_\phi \mid \Box_{(0,1)}\phi$ is a subformula of $\varphi \} \cup \{ y_\phi \mid \Diamond_{(0,1)}\phi$ is a subformula of $\varphi \} \cup \{ z_\phi \mid \Diamond_{(0,1)}\phi$ is a subformula of $\varphi \}$.
7. For every $A \in Atom(\varphi)$, $\beta(A)$ is the conjunction of all clock constraints occurring in A.
8. $\mathcal{O} := \mathcal{B} \cup \mathcal{C}_1$.
9. $(v_0, v_1, \lambda) \in \mathcal{T}$ if the following conditions hold.
   - Either $(v_0 \in S_1$ and $v_1 \in S_2)$ or $(v_0 \in S_2$ and $v_1 \in S_1)$.
   - If $v_0 \in S_1$ and $v_1 \in S_2$, then the following four conditions will be satisfied.
     - For every $p \in \mathcal{B}$, if $p' \in v_0$, then $p \in v_1$; and if $\neg p' \in v_0$, then $\neg p \in v_1$.
     - For every $c \in \mathcal{C}_1$, if $(c=0) \in v_0$ or $(c'=c) \in v_0$, then $c \notin \lambda$; if $(c'=0) \in v_0$ and $(c=0) \notin v_0$, then $c \in \lambda$.
     - If $\Box_{(0,1)}\phi \in v_0$, then $x_\phi \in v_1$ and $x_\phi \in \lambda$.
     - If $\Diamond_{(0,1)}\phi \in v_0$, then $y_\phi \in v_1$.
   - If $v_0 \in S_2$ and $v_1 \in S_1$, then the following four conditions will be satisfied.
     - For every $c \in \mathcal{C}$, $c \notin \lambda$, that is, $\lambda = \emptyset$.
     - $p \in v_0$ iff $p \in v_1$; $\neg p \in v_0$ iff $\neg p \in v_1$.
     - If $\Box_{(0,1)}\phi \in v_0$, then $\phi \in v_0$, $\phi \in v_1$, and $\Box_{(0,1)}\phi \in v_1$.
     - If $\Diamond_{(0,1)}\phi \in v_0$, then $z_\phi \in v_0$.

- If $\Box\varphi \in v_0$, then $\Box\varphi \in v_1$.
- If $\Diamond\varphi \in v_0$ and $\varphi \notin v_0$, then $\Diamond\varphi \in v_1$.
- If $x_\phi \in v_0$, then
  - $\phi \in v_0$, and
  - either x_ϕ or $(x_\phi \geq 1)$ is in v_1.
- If $y_\phi \in v_0$, then
  - $(y_\phi < 1)$ is in v_0, and
  - either $\phi \in v_0$, or $(y_\phi \in v_1$ and $y_\phi \notin \lambda)$.
- If $z_\phi \in v_0$, then
  - $(z_\phi \leq 1)$ is in v_0, and
  - $\phi \in v_0$, or $\phi \in v_1$, or $(z_\phi \in v_1$ and $z_\phi \notin \lambda)$.

10. $\mathcal{F} := \{ F_{(\Diamond\phi)} \mid \Diamond\phi$ is a subformula of $\varphi \}$, where $F_{(\Diamond\phi)}$ is the set $\{ v \mid v \in S_1 \cup S_2$, and $\phi \in v$ or $\Diamond\phi \notin v \}$.

Theorem 5. *For every $\varphi \in \mathcal{L}$ in normalized form, $Mod(M_\varphi) = Mod_{\mathcal{B} \cup \mathcal{C}_1}(\varphi)$.*

Proof. Let ρ be a run of M_φ. For every $p \in \mathcal{B}$, ρ_p is a boolean-valued step function and for every $c \in \mathcal{C}_1$, ρ_c is a clock function. So we can define an LTLC-interpretation J_ρ over $\mathcal{B} \cup \mathcal{C}_1$ by assigning ρ_x to x for all $x \in \mathcal{B} \cup \mathcal{C}_1$. Because $\mathcal{O} = \mathcal{B} \cup \mathcal{C}_1$, we have $J_\rho \in Mod(M_\varphi)$.

To prove $Mod(M_\varphi) \subseteq Mod_{\mathcal{B} \cup \mathcal{C}_1}(\varphi)$, we only need to show that $J_\rho \in Mod_{\mathcal{B} \cup \mathcal{C}_1}(\varphi)$. It suffices to prove the following conclusion.

(i) For each subformula ψ of φ and each $t \in \mathcal{R}^{\geq 0}$, if $\psi \in v_\rho(t)$, then $J_\rho(\psi, t) = 1$.

We prove (i) by induction on ψ.

1. ψ is p. From $p \in v_\rho(t)$, we get $p \in \alpha(v_\rho(t))$ and $\rho_p(t) = 1$. Thus we get the conclusion that $J_\rho(p, t) = 1$.
2. ψ is p'.
   - If $v_\rho(t) \in S_1$, then there exists a $v_1 \in S_2$ and a $t_1 > t$ such that $p \in v_1$ and for all $t_2 \in (t, t_1)$, $v_\rho(t) = v_1$. So we get that $\rho_p(t_2) = 1$ holds for all $t_2 \in (t, t_1)$. That is, the conclusion $J_\rho(p', t) = 1$ holds.
   - If $v_\rho(t) \in S_2$, then $p \in v_\rho(t)$ and there exists a $t_1 > t$ such that $v_\rho(t_2) = v_\rho(t)$ holds for all $t_2 \in (t, t_1)$. Then we get $\rho_p(t_2) = 1$ holds for all $t_2 \in (t, t_1)$. that is, $J_\rho(p', t) = 1$ holds.
3. ψ is $\Box\phi$. If $\Box\phi \in v_\rho(t)$, then for all $t_1 \geq t$, $\Box\phi \in v_\rho(t_1)$. Thus $\phi \in v_\rho(t_1)$ holds for all $t_1 \geq t$. By induction assumption for ϕ, we have $J_\rho(\phi, t_1) = 1$ holds for all $t_1 \geq t$. That is, $J_\rho(\Box\phi, t) = 1$ holds.
4. ψ is $\Box_{(0,1)}\phi$.
   - If $v_\rho(t) \in S_1$, then from Definition 17, we can get that $\rho_{x_\phi}(t) \leq t_1 - t$ holds for all $t_1 \in (t, t+1)$. Thus $x_\phi \in v_\rho(t_1)$ and $\phi \in v_\rho(t_1)$ will hold for all $t_1 \in (t, t+1)$. By induction assumption for ϕ, we have $J_\rho(\phi, t_1) = 1$ holds for all $t_1 \in (t, t+1)$. That is, $J_\rho(\Box_{(0,1)}\phi, t) = 1$ holds.

– If $v_\rho(t) \in S_2$, then there exists a $t_1 > t$ such that $v_\rho(t) \neq v_\rho(t_1)$ and for all $t_2 \in (t, t_1), v_\rho(t_2) = v_\rho(t)$. From Definition 17, $\phi \in v_\rho(t)$, $\phi \in v_\rho(t_1)$, $\Box_{(0,1)}\phi \in v_\rho(t_1)$ and $\rho_{x_\phi}(t_1) = 0$. Thus $x_\phi \in v_\rho(t_2)$ will hold for all $t_2 \in (t_1, t_1+1)$. So $\phi \in v_\rho(t_2)$ will hold for all $t_2 \in [t, t_1+1)$. By induction assumption for ϕ, we have $J_\rho(\phi, t_1) = 1$ holds for all $t_1 \in [t, t_1+1)$. Thus we get the conclusion that $J_\rho(\Box_{(0,1)}\phi, t) = 1$ holds.

5. The proofs for other cases of ψ are omitted here.

Because $\varphi \in v_\rho(0)$, from (i) we can get $J_\rho(\varphi, 0) = 1$. That is, $J_\rho \in Mod_{\mathcal{B} \cup \mathcal{C}_1}(\varphi)$. Thus we have got the conclusion that $Mod(M_\varphi) \subseteq Mod_{\mathcal{B} \cup \mathcal{C}_1}(\varphi)$.

Conversely, for any $J \in Mod_{\mathcal{B} \cup \mathcal{C}_1}(\varphi)$, we will construct a run ρ such that $J = \rho \Downarrow_{\mathcal{O}}$, where $\mathcal{O} = \mathcal{B} \cup \mathcal{C}_1$ is the set of all observable variables.

By Definition 4 and Definition 5, there exists an unbounded increasing sequence $a_0 = 0 < a_1 < a_2 < \cdots < a_n < \ldots$ such that: (1). for each $x \in \mathcal{B} \cup \mathcal{C}_1$, $J(x)$ is continuous in the open interval (a_i, a_{i+1}); (2). for each subformula ψ of φ, $J(\psi, t)$ is constant in the open interval (a_i, a_{i+1}); (3). for each $i \geq 0$, $a_{i+1} - a_i < 1$; (4). for each $i \geq 0$, there exists a $j > i$ such that $a_j = a_i + 1$.

Using the sequence $a_0 = 0 < a_1 < a_2 < \cdots < a_n < \ldots$, we can define a run ρ as follows.

$$\rho: (v_0, \sigma_0, a_0) \xrightarrow{\gamma_0} (v_1, \sigma_1, a_0) \xrightarrow{\emptyset} (v_2, \sigma_2, a_1) \xrightarrow{\gamma_1} (v_3, \sigma_3, a_1) \xrightarrow{\emptyset} (v_4, \sigma_4, a_2) \xrightarrow{\gamma_2} \cdots$$

1. a) $\gamma_0 := \emptyset$.
   b) For each $i > 0$,
   $\gamma_i := \{ c \mid c \in \mathcal{C}_1, f'_c(a_i) = 0 \} \cup \{ x_\phi \mid \Box_{(0,1)}\phi$ is true at $a_i \} \cup \{ y_\phi \mid \phi$ is true at a_i, or ϕ is true on (a_{i-1}, a_i), or ($\Diamond_{(0,1)}\phi$ is false at a_{i-1} and $\Diamond_{(0,1)}\phi$ is true at a_i) $\} \cup \{ z_\phi \mid \phi$ is true at a_i, or ϕ is true on (a_{i-1}, a_i), or ϕ is false on (a_i, a_{i+1}), or $\Diamond_{(0,1)}\phi$ is false at $a_i \}$
   where f_c denotes the interpretation of c under the model J (Definition 5), and f'_c is the function associated with f_c.

2. a) For each $c \in \mathcal{C}$, $\sigma_0(c) := 0$.
   b) $\sigma_{2i+1} = \sigma_{2i}[\gamma_i := 0]$, and $\sigma_{2i+2} = \sigma_{2i+1} + (a_{i+1} - a_i)$.

3. a) $v_{2i} := \{ sing \} \cup \{ \phi \mid \phi$ is a formula in $cl(\varphi)$ and is true at $a_i \} \cup \{ x_\phi \mid x_\phi \in cl(\varphi)$, and there exists a j such that $(a_j < a_i < a_j + 1)$ and $\Box_{(0,1)}\phi$ is true at $a_j \} \cup \{ y_\phi \mid y_\phi \in cl(\varphi), i > 0, \Diamond_{(0,1)}\phi$ is true at a_{i-1} and ϕ is false on $(a_{i-1}, a_i) \} \cup \{ z_\phi \mid z_\phi \in cl(\varphi), i > 0, \Diamond_{(0,1)}\phi$ is true on (a_{i-1}, a_i) and ϕ is false on $(a_{i-1}, a_i] \}$
   b) $v_{2i+1} := \{ \phi \mid \phi$ is a formula in $cl(\varphi)$ and is true on $(a_i, a_{i+1}) \} \cup \{ x_\phi \mid x_\phi \in cl(\varphi)$, and there exists a j such that $(a_j \leq a_i < a_j + 1)$ and $\Box_{(0,1)}\phi$ is true at $a_j \} \cup \{ y_\phi \mid y_\phi \in cl(\varphi)$, and $\Diamond_{(0,1)}\phi$ is true at $a_i \} \cup \{ z_\phi \mid z_\phi \in cl(\varphi)$, and $\Diamond_{(0,1)}\phi$ is true on $(a_i, a_{i+1}) \}$.

From the construction of M_φ we can verify that the above ρ is a run of M_φ and $J = \rho \Downarrow_{\mathcal{O}}$. Thus we have obtained the desired conclusion $J \in Mod(M_\varphi)$ and $Mod_{\mathcal{B} \cup \mathcal{C}_1}(\varphi) \subseteq Mod(M_\varphi)$.

□

Let $\exists v_0 \exists v_1 \ldots \exists v_{m-1} \phi$ be a formula in EQF and ϕ be a quantifier-free formula. If $M_\phi := < S_0, S_1, S_2, \mathcal{B}, \alpha, \mathcal{C}, \beta, \mathcal{O}, \mathcal{T}, \mathcal{F} >$ is the timed automaton constructed from ϕ, then $M_1 := < S_0, S_1, S_2, \mathcal{B}, \alpha, \mathcal{C}, \beta, \mathcal{O}_1, \mathcal{T}, \mathcal{F} >$ is a timed automaton corresponding to $\exists v_0 \exists v_1 \ldots \exists v_{m-1} \phi$, where $\mathcal{O}_1 := \mathcal{O} - \{v_0, v_1, \ldots, v_{m-1}\}$.

Corollary 1. *Every formula in EQF can be translated into a timed automaton.*

Combining the construction procedure in Definition 17 and the emptiness checking procedure for timed automata, we then get an algorithm for checking the satisfiability of quantifier-free fragment of LTLC.

5   Conclusion

Unlike the most existing real-time logics, LTLC can express real-time systems as well as their properties. It provides a unified logical framework for expressing and reasoning about real-time systems. This paper has shown that a meaningful fragment of LTLC is decidable and has revealed some connection between LTLC and timed automata. This connection may be of some help in our effort to find more efficient model checking algorithms for real-time systems.

As future work, we plan to focus on the algorithmic verification of real-time systems with LTLC, using the connection between LTLC and automata. We also plan to given a further examination on the expressiveness of LTLC, compared with timed automata and clocked transition systems.

Acknowledgment. We would like to thank the anonymous reviewers for their valuable comments and suggestions.

References

1. R. Alur, C. Courcoubetis, and D.L. Dill. Model-checking in dense real-time. Information and Computation, 104:2–34, 1993.
2. R. Alur and D.L. Dill. A theory of timed automata. Theoretical Computer Science, 126(2): 183–235, 1994.
3. R. Alur, T. Feder, T.A. Henzinger. The benefits of relaxing punctuality. Journal of the ACM 43:116–146, 1996.
4. R. Alur and T.A. Henzinger. Logics and models of real time: a survey. In: Real-Time: Theory in Practice [de Bakker et al. ed.], LNCS 600, Springer-Verlag, 1991.
5. R. Alur and T.A. Henzinger. A really temporal logic. Journal of the ACM 41:181–204, 1994.
6. N. Bjørner, Z. Manna, H. Sipma and T. Uribe. Deductive Verification of Real-time Systems using STeP. Theoretical Computer Science, Vol. 253, pp 27–60, 2001.
7. Y. Hirshfeld and A. Rabinovich. Quantitative Temporal Logic. In Computer Science Logic 1999, LNCS 1683, pp172–187, Springer Verlag, 1999.
8. F. Laroussinie, K. Larsen, and C. Weise. From timed automata to logic -and back, in Proceedings of the 20 th Symposium on Mathematical Foundations of Computer Science, LNCS 969, pp. 529–540, Springer-Verlag, 1995.
9. G. Li , LTLC: A Continuous-time Temporal Logic for Real-time and Hybrid Systems, PhD Thesis, Institute of Software, Chinese Academy of Sciences, March, 2001.

10. G. Li and Z. Tang, Modeling Real-Time Systems with Continuous-Time Temporal Logic, Proceedings of the 4th International Conference on Formal Engineering Methods (ICFEM 2002), Lecture Notes in Computer Science 2495, pp231–236, Springer-Verlag, 2002.
11. Z. Manna and A. Pnueli. The temporal logic of reactive and concurrent systems: Specification. Springer-verlag, New York, 1992.
12. Z. Manna and A. Pnueli. Clocked transition systems. In: Logic and Software Workshop, Beijing, China, 1995.

The Semantic Layers of Timber

Magnus Carlsson[1], Johan Nordlander[2], and Dick Kieburtz[1]

[1] Oregon Health & Science University,
{magnus,dick}@cse.ogi.edu
[2] Luleå University of Technology,
nordland@sm.luth.se

Abstract. We present a three-layered semantics of *Timber*, a language designed for programming real-time systems in a reactive, object-oriented style. The innermost layer amounts to a traditional deterministic, pure, functional language, around which we formulate a middle layer of concurrent objects, in terms of a monadic transition semantics. The outermost layer, where the language is married to deadline-driven scheduling theory, is where we define message ordering and CPU allocation to actions. Our main contributions are a formalized notion of a *time-constrained reaction*, and a demonstration of how scheduling theory, process calculii, and the lambda calculus can be jointly applied to obtain a direct and succinct semantics of a complex, real-world programming language with well-defined real-time behavior.

1 Introduction

Timber is a new programming language being developed jointly at the Oregon Health & Science University, Chalmers University of Technology, and Luleå University of Technology. The scope of Timber is wide, ranging from low-level device interfaces, over time-constrained embedded systems or interactive applications in general, to very high-level symbolic manipulation and modeling applications. In the context of this text, the distinguishing attributes of the Timber language can be summarized as follows:

- It is based on a programming model of *reactive objects*, that abandons the traditional active request for input in favor of a purely event-driven program structure [15].
- It fully integrates *concurrency* into its semantic foundation, making each object an encapsulated process whose state integrity is automatically preserved.
- It enables *real-time constraints* to be directly expressed in the source code, and opens up the possibility of doing off-line deadline-based schedulability analysis on real code.
- It is a full-fledged pure functional language that achieves referential transparency in the presence of mutable data and non-determinism by means of a monad.
- It upholds *strong static type safety* throughout, even for its message-based, tag-free interprocess communication mechanism.

A. Ohori (Ed.): APLAS 2003, LNCS 2895, pp. 339–356, 2003.

In this paper we provide a formal semantic definition of Timber. The combination of object-based concurrency, asynchronous reactivity, and purely functional declarativeness is challenging in itself, but we believe it is the existence of a real-time dimension that makes the question of a formal semantics for Timber particularly interesting. The core of our approach is the definition of a *layered* semantics, that separates the semantic concerns in such a way that each layer is meaningful and can be fully understood by referring to just the layer before it. The semantic layers of Timber can be summarized as follows:

- *The functional layer.* This layer amounts to a traditional pure functional language, similar to Haskell [17] or the pure subset of ML [10]. By pure, we mean that computations in this layer do not cause any effects related to state or input/output. We will not discuss this layer very much in this paper, but instead make sure that the other layers do not interfere with it.
- *The reactive layer* is a system of concurrent *objects* with internal state that *react* to messages passed from the environment (input), and in turn send synchronous or asynchronous *messages* to each other, and back to the environment (output). This layer constitutes a form of process calculus that embeds a purely functional sub-language. Although it abstracts away from the flow of real time, the calculus does associate with each message precise, but uninterpreted time constraints.
- *The scheduling layer.* The reactive layer leaves us with a set of messages and objects with time constraints. Some of the messages may compete for the same objects, which in turn are competing for computing resources. The scheduling layer makes precise what the constraints are for the resulting scheduling problem.

The semantic definition has been used to implement an interpreter for Timber, by which we have been able to conduct serious practical evaluations of the language (spanning such diverse areas as GUI toolkit implementation [13] and embedded robot control [7]). A compiler aimed at stand-alone embedded systems is also being developed in tandem with the language specification. We consider the main contributions of this paper to be: (1) a formal definition of the *time-constrained reactions* that give Timber its distinct flavor, and (2) a demonstration of how scheduling theory, process calculii, and the lambda calculus can be jointly applied to obtain a direct and succinct semantics of a complex, real-world programming language with well-defined real-time behavior.

The rest of the paper is organized as follows: Section 2 introduces Timber with an example of an embedded controller. Section 3 constitutes the core of the paper, as it defines the semantics of Timber in three separate subsections corresponding to each semantic layer. Related work is then discussed in Section 4, before we conclude in Section 5.

2   An Embedded Timber System

Although Timber is a general-purpose programming language, it has been designed to target *embedded systems* in particular. The software of such a system, when written in Timber, consists of a number of *objects* which mostly sit and wait for incoming *events* from the physical environment of the embedded system. On the lowest level, events are picked up by peripheral devices, and are transformed into interrupts injected into the CPU. Each interrupt is converted into an *asynchronous message* that has one particular object in the Timber program as its destination. Each message is associated with a *time constraint* in the form of a *baseline* and a *deadline*, both of which are absolute times. The baseline constrains the starting point of a reaction and also functions as a reference point to which time expressions might subsequently relate; it is normally set to the absolute time of the interrupt. The deadline is the time by which the system must have *reacted* to the event for the system to behave correctly. In the tradition of declarative programming , this parameter thus acts as a specification for a correct Timber implementation, ultimately derived from the time constants of the physical environment with which the system interacts.

Once an interrupt has injected a message into a Timber program, the system is no longer in an idle state. The message has *excited* the system, and the destination object starts reacting to the message so that a response can be delivered. As a result, the object may alter its state, and send secondary messages to other objects in the system, some of which may be *synchronous*. Synchronous communication means that the object will rendezvous with the destination object, facilitating two-way communication. Some of the secondary messages generated during the excited state can have baselines and deadlines that are larger than the original, interrupt-triggered message. For example, a car alarm system may react immediately to an event from a motion sensor by turning on the alarm, but also schedule a secondary, delayed reaction that turns off the alarm after a minute.[1] However, eventually the chain reaction caused by an external event will cling out, and the system goes back to an idle state.

Because a Timber system is concurrent, multiple reactions caused by independent external events may be in effect at the same time. It is the job of the presented semantics to specify how the interactions within such a system are supposed to behave.

2.1   Templates, Actions, and Requests

The syntax of Timber is strongly influenced by Haskell [17]. In fact, it stems directly from the object-oriented Haskell extension *O'Haskell*, and can be seen as a successor of that language [12].

To describe Timber more concretely, we present a complete Timber program that implements the car alarm refereed to above in Figure 1. This program is supposed to run on a naked machine, with no other software than the Timber program itself. On such a machine, the environment provides merely two operations, as the definition of the record type `Environment` indicates: one for writing a byte to an I/O port, and one for reading. These methods are synchronous, as indicated by the monadic type constructor `Request`. On the other

---

[1] A delay perceived as much longer than a minute, though!

hand, the interface a naked program presents to its environment will merely consist of handlers for (a subset of) the interrupts supported by the hardware. This is expressed as a list of asynchronous methods (actions) paired with interrupt numbers, as the type `Program` prescribes.

A Timber program is a function from the program environment to a *template* that returns an interface to an object. At boot time, the template `alarm` will be executed, thereby creating one instance of an alarm handling object, whose interface is the desired interrupt vector.

```
record Environment where
    write      :: Port -> Byte -> Request ()
    read       :: Port -> Request Byte

record Program where
    irqvector  :: [(Irq,Action)]

alarm :: Environment -> Template Program
alarm env =
  template
      trigged := True
  in let
      moved = before (100*milliseconds) action
          if trigged then
              env.write siren 1
              trigged := False
              after (1*minutes) turnoff
              after (10*minutes) enable
      turnoff = action
          env.write siren 0
      enable = action
          trigged := True
  in record
      irqvector = [(motionsensor,moved)]
```

Fig. 1. The car alarm program.

We assume that there is a particular I/O port `siren`, whose least significant bit controls the car siren, and that the interrupt number `motionsensor` is associated with the event generated by a motion sensor on the car.

The definition of `alarm` reveals a template for an object with one internal state variable `trigged`, initialized to `True`. The purpose of `trigged`, as we will see, is to ensure that once the alarm goes off, there will be a grace period until it is possible to trigger the alarm again.

The returned interrupt vector associates the action `moved` with the motion sensor interrupt. When `moved` is invoked, and if the alarm is trigged, it will turn on the siren, and set `trigger` to false. It will also invoke two local asynchronous methods, each one with a lower time bound on the actual message reception. The first message, which is scheduled to be handled one minute after the motion sensor event, simply turns off the siren. The second message, which will arrive after ten minutes, re-enables the alarm so that it may go off again.

By means of the keyword **before**, action `moved` is declared to have a deadline of one tenth of a second. This means that a correct implementation of the program is required to turn on the alarm within 100 milliseconds after the motion sensor event. This deadline also carries over to the secondary actions, which for example means that the alarm will shut off no later than one minute and 0.1 seconds after the motion sensor event (and no earlier than one minute after the event, by the lower time bound).

The handling of delays in our example captures a characterizing aspect of the reactive semantics of Timber. Instead of temporarily halting execution at some traditional "sleep" statement, our method moved will terminate as quickly as the CPU allows, leaving the alarm object free to react to any pending or subsequent calls to moved, even while the 1 and 10 minute delay phases are active. A degraded motion sensor generating bursts of interrupts will thus be handled gracefully by our program; something that would require considerably more work in a language where events are queued and event-handling can be arbitrarily delayed.

```
alarm env = do
  self <- new True
  let moved = act self ⟨0,100*milliseconds⟩
                  (do trigged <- get
                      if trigged then do
                          env.write sirenport 1
                          set False
                          aft (1*minutes) turnoff
                          aft (10*minutes) enable
                      else return () )
      turnoff = act self ⟨0,0⟩
                  (env.write sirenport 0)
      enable = act self ⟨0,0⟩
                  (set True)
  return ( record irqs = [(motionsensor,moved)] )
```

Fig. 2. The car alarm program, desugared.

2.2 The O Monad

```
return:: a -> O s a
(>>=) :: O s a -> (a -> O s b) -> O s b
handle:: O s a -> (Error -> O s a) -> O s a
raise :: Error -> O s a
bef   :: Time -> O s a -> O s a
aft   :: Time -> O s a -> O s a
set   :: s -> O s ()
get   :: O s s
new   :: s -> O s' (Ref s)
act   :: Ref s -> (Time,Time) -> O s a -> O s' Msg
abort :: Msg -> O s ()
req   :: Ref s -> O s a -> O s' a
```

Fig. 3. The constants in the O monad.

The Timber constructs **template**, **action**, and **request** are nothing but syntactic sugar for monadic computations that take place in the O monad, as described in [14,12]. The type O s a stands for a computation that can be executed inside an object whose local state has type s, resulting in a value of type a. In the full Timber language, *polymorphic subtyping* is applied to give constants that are independent of the local state a more flexible type (see for example the types Action and Request mentioned above) [13]. However, we will ignore this issue in the following presentation, as it has no operational implications.

A desugared version of the alarm program is given in Figure 2. Strictly speaking, the program is not a literate result of the desugaring rules—for readability, we introduced the do-notation and performed some cosmetic simplifications.

The desugared program refers to a number of primitive operations in the O monad, whose type signature are given in Figure 3. An informal meaning of these constants can be obtained by comparing the desugared program in Figure 2 with the original. Their precise formal meaning will be the subject of the next section. The actual desugaring rules are given in Appendix A.

3   The Semantic Layers

3.1   The Functional Layer

We will not specify very much of the functional layer in this presentation; instead we will view it as a strength of our layered approach that so much of the first layer can be left unspecified. One of the benefits with a monadic marriage of effects and evaluation is that it is independent of the evaluation semantics— this property has even been proposed as the definition of what *purely functional* means in the presence of effects [19].

$$\text{return } e_1 \text{ >>= } e_2 \mapsto e_2\, e_1$$
$$\text{raise } e_1 \text{ >>= } e_2 \mapsto \text{raise } e_1$$
$$\text{return } e_1 \text{ `handle` } e_2 \mapsto \text{return } e_1$$
$$\text{raise } e_1 \text{ `handle` } e_2 \mapsto e_2\, e_1$$
$$\text{bef } d'\ (\text{act } n\ \langle b, d\rangle\ e) \mapsto \text{act } n\ \langle b, d'\rangle\ e$$
$$\text{aft } b'\ (\text{act } n\ \langle b, d\rangle\ e) \mapsto \text{act } n\ \langle b', d\rangle\ e$$

Fig. 4. Functional layer: reduction rules.

That said, it is also the case that a lazy semantics in the style of Haskell adds extra difficulties to the time and space analysis of programs, something which is of increased importance in the construction of real-time and embedded software. For this reason, we are actually shifting to a strict semantics for Timber, which is a clear breach with the tradition of its predecessors. Still, strictness should not be confused with impurity, and to underline this distinction, we will assume a very general semantics that is open to both both lazy and strict interpretation in this paper. We hope to be able to report on the specifics of strictness in Timber in later work, especially concerning the treatment of recursive values and imprecise exceptions [4,11,8].

We assume that there is a language $\mathcal{E}$ of expressions that includes the pure lambda calculus, and whose semantics is given in terms of a small-step evaluation relation $\mapsto$. Let e range over such expressions. Moreover, we assume that the expressions of $\mathcal{E}$ can be assigned types by means of judgments of the form $\Gamma \vdash e : \tau$, where τ ranges over the types of $\mathcal{E}$, and Γ stands for typing assumptions.

A concrete example of what $\mathcal{E}$ and $\mapsto$ might look like can be found in [12]. There a semantics is described that allows concurrent reduction of all redeces in an expression, even under a lambda. We will neither assume nor preclude such a general semantics here, but for the purpose of proving type soundness of the reaction layer, we require at least the following property:

Theorem 1 (Subject reduction). *If* $\Gamma \vdash e : \tau$ *and* $e \mapsto e'$, *then* $\Gamma \vdash e' : \tau$.

In order to connect this language with the reactive semantics of the next section, we extend $\mathcal{E}$ with the constants of Figure 3, and the extra evaluation rules of Figure 4.

The first four constants listed in Figure 3 constitute a standard exception-handling monad, for which meaning is given by the first four rules of Figure 4. Likewise, the constants **bef** and **aft** merely serve to modify the time constraint argument of the **act** constant, so their full meaning is also defined in the functional layer.

The remaining constants, however, are treated as *uninterpreted constructors* by the functional semantics—it is giving meaning to those constants that is the purpose of the reactive semantic layer. Similarly, concrete realization of the type constructors O, **Ref** and **Msg** is postponed until the reactive layer is defined; as far as the functional layer is concerned, O, **Ref** and **Msg** are just opaque, abstract types.

3.2 The Reactive Layer

To give semantics to the reactive layer, we regard a running Timber program as a system of concurrent processes, defined by the grammar in Figure 5. A primitive process is either

- an *empty message*, tagged with the name m. This is the remnant of a message that is either delivered or aborted;
- a *message* tagged with m, carrying the code e, to be executed by an object with name n, obeying the time constraint c. In the case of a synchronous message, it also carries a *continuation* K, which amounts to a suspended requesting object (see below);
- an *idle object* with identity n, which maintains its state s awaiting activation by messages;
- an *active object* with identity n, state s, executing the code e with the time constraint c. In case the object is servicing a synchronous request, the continuation K amounts to the suspended requesting object.

$$P ::= \langle\rangle_m \quad \text{Empty message}$$
$$| \quad \langle n, e, K\rangle_m^c \quad \text{Pending message}$$
$$| \quad (\!|s|\!)_n \quad \text{Idle object}$$
$$| \quad (\!|s, e, K|\!)_n^c \quad \text{Active object}$$
$$| \quad P \parallel P \quad \text{Parallel composition}$$
$$| \quad \nu n. P \quad \text{Restriction}$$

Fig. 5. The process grammar.

Finally, processes can be composed in parallel, and the scope of names used for object identities and message tags can be restricted. We will assume that parallel composition has precedence over the restriction operator, which therefore always extend as far to the right as possible.

Continuations are requesting objects that are waiting for a request (synchronous message) to finish. Since a requesting object can in turn be servicing requests from other objects, continuations are defined recursively, according to the following grammar that denotes a *requesting object* or an *empty continuation*:

$$K ::= (\!|s, \mathcal{M}, K|\!)_n \mid 0$$

A requesting object with identity n contains the state s, and a *reaction context* $\mathcal{M}$, which is an expression with a hole, waiting to be filled by the result of the request. Just as for normal objects, there is a continuation K as well, in case the requesting object is servicing a request from another object. For asynchronous messages, and objects that are not servicing requests, the continuation is empty.

Reaction contexts are used in two ways in the reactive layer. As we have already seen, they are used in an unsaturated way to denote expressions with holes in requesting objects. They are also used in the following section to pinpoint where in an expression the reaction rules operate. Reaction contexts are given by the grammar

$$\mathcal{M} ::= \mathcal{M} \text{ >>= } e \mid \mathcal{M} \text{ `handle' } e \mid [] \ .$$

The structural congruence relation. In order for the relation to bring relevant process terms together for the reaction rules given in the next section, we assume that processes can be rearranged by the *structural congruence* $\equiv$, induced by the elements in Figure 6. These allow for the process terms to be rearranged and renamed, so that *e.g.* a message and its destination object can be juxtaposed for the relevant rule to apply. The last two elements of the equivalence allow us to garbage collect inert objects or messages that cannot possibly interact

ASSOCIATIVITY	$P_1 \parallel (P_2 \parallel P_3) \equiv (P_1 \parallel P_2) \parallel P_3$
SYMMETRY	$P_1 \parallel P_2 \equiv P_2 \parallel P_1$
SCOPE EXTENSION	$P_1 \parallel \nu n. P_2 \equiv \nu n. P_1 \parallel P_2$
	if $n \notin fv(P_1)$
SCOPE COMMUTATIVITY	$\nu n. \nu m. P \equiv \nu m. \nu n. P$
RENAMING	$\nu n. P \equiv \nu m. [^m/_n]P$
	if $m \notin fv(P_1)$
INERT MESSAGE	$P \parallel \nu m. \langle\rangle_m \equiv P$
INERT OBJECT	$P \parallel \nu n. (\!|s|\!)_n \equiv P$

Fig. 6. The structural congruence.

with any other process in the system. More specifically, an idle object whose identity is unknown to the rest of the system cannot possibly receive any message. Similarly, an empty message whose tag is "forgotten" can be eliminated.

The reactive relation. The reactive layer of our semantics consists of a *reaction relation* $\longrightarrow$, that defines how objects interact with messages and alter internal state. The reaction relation is characterized by the axioms shown in Figure 7, which together with the structural rules in Figure 8 define $\longrightarrow$ for general process terms. Most of the axioms use a reduction context to pinpoint the next relevant O monad constant inside an active object.

Rules SET and GET allows for the local state of an object to be written or read. The next three rules introduce a fresh name on the right-hand side by using restriction, and we tacitly assume here that the names m, n' do not occur free in the process term on the left-hand side.

Rule NEW defines creation a new, idle object whose identity is returned to the creator, and with an initial state as specified by the argument to the constant **new**.

$$\text{SET} \qquad (\!\!|s, \mathcal{M}[\mathtt{set}\ e], K|\!\!)_n^c \longrightarrow (\!\!|e, \mathcal{M}[\mathtt{return}\ ()], K|\!\!)_n^c$$

$$\text{GET} \qquad (\!\!|s, \mathcal{M}[\mathtt{get}], K|\!\!)_n^c \longrightarrow (\!\!|s, \mathcal{M}[\mathtt{return}\ s], K|\!\!)_n^c$$

$$\text{NEW} \qquad (\!\!|s, \mathcal{M}[\mathtt{new}\ e], K|\!\!)_n^c \longrightarrow \nu n'.\,(\!\!|s, \mathcal{M}[\mathtt{return}\ n'], K|\!\!)_n^c \parallel (\!\!|e|\!\!)_{n'}$$

$$\text{ACT} \qquad (\!\!|s, \mathcal{M}[\mathtt{act}\ n'\ d\ e], K|\!\!)_n^c \longrightarrow \nu m.\,(\!\!|s, \mathcal{M}[\mathtt{return}\ m], K|\!\!)_n^c \parallel \langle n', e, 0\rangle_m^{c+d}$$

$$\text{REQ} \qquad (\!\!|s, \mathcal{M}[\mathtt{req}\ n'\ e], K|\!\!)_n^c \longrightarrow \nu m.\,\langle n', e, (\!\!|s, \mathcal{M}, K|\!\!)_n\rangle_m^c$$

$$\text{RUN} \qquad (\!\!|s|\!\!)_n \parallel \langle n, e, K\rangle_m^c \longrightarrow (\!\!|s, e, K|\!\!)_n^c \parallel \langle\rangle_m$$

$$\text{DONE} \qquad (\!\!|s, r\ e, 0|\!\!)_n^c \longrightarrow (\!\!|s|\!\!)_n \qquad \textit{where}\ r \in \{\mathtt{raise}, \mathtt{return}\}$$

$$\text{REP} \qquad (\!\!|s, r\ e, (\!\!|s', \mathcal{M}, K|\!\!)_m|\!\!)_n^c \longrightarrow (\!\!|s|\!\!)_n \parallel (\!\!|s', \mathcal{M}[r\ e], K|\!\!)_m^c$$
$$\textit{where}\ r \in \{\mathtt{raise}, \mathtt{return}\}$$

$$\text{ABORT}\ (\!\!|s, \mathcal{M}[\mathtt{abort}\ m], K|\!\!)_n^c \parallel P \longrightarrow (\!\!|s, \mathcal{M}[\mathtt{return}\ ()], K|\!\!)_n^c \parallel \langle\rangle_m$$
$$\textit{where}\ P \in \{\langle n', e, 0\rangle_m^{c'}, \langle\rangle_m\}$$

Fig. 7. Reactive layer: axioms.

In rule ACT, an object is sending an asynchronous message with code e to a destination object n'. The time constraint, or *timeline*, of a message is computed by adding the *relative* time constraint d to the constraint of the sending object. The addition of time constraints is described in more detail in the section 3.2. Note that, as a consequence of the substitution-based evaluation semantics we have assumed, messages contain the actual code to be run by destination objects, instead of just method names. This should not be confused with breaking the abstraction barrier of objects, since object interfaces normally expose only action and request values, not the object identifiers themselves. Without knowledge of an object's identity, it is impossible to send arbitrary code to it.

Rule REQ forms a synchronous message, by suspending the requesting object and embedding it as a continuation within the message. Here the unsaturated context $\mathcal{M}$ of the caller is saved, so that it can eventually be filled with the result of the request. The time constraint of a synchronous message is the same as that of the requesting object—the intuition here is that a request is analogous to a function call, and that servicing such a call can be neither more nor less urgent than the computation of the caller.

$$\frac{P \equiv P' \qquad P' \longrightarrow Q' \qquad Q' \equiv Q}{P \longrightarrow Q}\ \text{EQUIV}$$

$$\frac{P \longrightarrow P'}{P \parallel Q \longrightarrow P' \parallel Q}\ \text{PAR}$$

$$\frac{P \longrightarrow P'}{\nu n.\,P \longrightarrow \nu n.\,P'}\ \text{RES}$$

Fig. 8. Reactive layer: structural rules.

In rule RUN, an idle object is juxtaposed to a message with matching destination. The "payload" of the message (the code, continuation and time constraint) is extracted from the message, which is left empty. This rule forms the essence of what constitutes a reaction in Timber.

When an active object eventually reaches a terminating state (as represented by a code expression of the form return e or raise e), the action taken depends on its continuation. Rule DONE specifies that an object executing an asynchronous message just silently enters the idle state, where it will be ready to accept new messages. An object occupied by a request, on the other hand, also needs to reply to the requesting object. This is handled in the rule REP, in which the waiting caller context $\mathcal{M}$ is applied to the reply (which may be an exception), and the continuation is released as an active object again. At the same time, the servicing object turns idle, ready for new messages.

The ABORT rule shows how a pending message can be turned into an empty one before delivery, thus effectively removing it from the system. If the destination object has already started executing the message, or if the message was previously aborted, the rule will match against an empty message instead, leaving it unaffected.

Finally, there is a rule EVAL that connects the functional and reactive layers, by promoting evaluation to reaction:

$$\frac{s \mapsto s' \quad e \mapsto e'}{(\!|s, \mathcal{M}[e], K|\!)_n^c \longrightarrow (\!|s', \mathcal{M}[e'], K|\!)_n^c} \ \text{EVAL}$$

Note that we allow for the concurrent evaluation both the state and code components of an object here, although with a strict functional layer, the state component will of course already be a value.

Timeline arithmetic. The time constraint, or *timeline*, of an asynchronous message is obtained by adding the time constraint $\langle b, d \rangle$ of the sending object to the *relative* timeline $\langle \beta, \delta \rangle$ supplied to the constructor act. This operation is defined as follows:

$$\langle b, d \rangle + \langle \beta, \delta \rangle = \langle max(b, b + \beta), max(d, b + \beta + \delta) \rangle \ \text{if } \delta > 0$$
$$= \langle max(b, b + \beta), max(d, d + \beta) \rangle \qquad \text{if } \delta \leq 0$$

The maximum functions used here serve to ensure that the timeline of a message cannot be tighter than the timeline of the sending object; *i.e.*, both the baseline and the deadline of a message must be at least as large as those of the sender. This prevents the introduction of paradoxical situations where servicing a secondary reaction would be more urgent than executing the code that caused it.

As can be seen, a special case occurs when the relative deadline of a message is zero or below; then the deadline of the sender is kept but interpreted relative to the new baseline. This is how the two delayed messages sent in the moved method in Figure 2 are assigned their deadlines of 1 minute + 100 milliseconds, and 10 minutes + 100 milliseconds, respectively.

Note that this exception is added purely for the convenience of the programmer, who would otherwise always have to specify an explicit deadline whenever a new baseline is given. Note also that a relative deadline of zero amounts to a timeline that cannot be satisfied by any kind of finite computing resource, so an exception for this value does not really limit the expressiveness for the programmer.

Deadlock. A Timber program that only uses asynchronous communication is guaranteed to be free from deadlock; however, since the sender of a synchronous message is unresponsive while it waits for a reply, the potential of deadlock arises. On the other hand, unlike many other languages and interprocess communication mechanisms, Timber allows for really cheap detection of deadlock. What is required is that each object keeps a pointer to the servicing object as long as it is blocked in a request, and that that the req operation starts by checking that setting up such a pointer will not result in cycle. If this is indeed the case, req results in an exception.

Preferably, our reaction semantics should formalize this behavior, as it is of utmost importance for the correctness of systems in which deadlock can occur. Unfortunately, our recursive definition of continuations actually denotes a linked structure that points in the other direction; from a server to its current client, if any. Duplicating this structure with links going in the forward direction makes the reaction axioms look extremely clumsy, and we have not found the formal definition of deadlock detection valuable enough to outweigh its cost. Instead we supplement the reaction axioms of Figure 7 with an informal rule that reads

$$(\!(s, \mathcal{M}[\texttt{req } n'\ e], K)\!)_n^c \longrightarrow (\!(s, \mathcal{M}[\texttt{raise Deadlock}], K)\!)_n^c$$

if the sending object n is found by following the forward pointers starting at n'. It is our hope that a neater way of specifying this behavior can eventually be developed.

Properties of the reactive layer. Analogous to the subject reduction property that we assume for the functional layer, we establish what we may call a *subject reaction* property for our process calculus; *i.e.*, the property that all reaction rules preserve well typedness of processes. Well-typedness is defined by the straightforward typing judgments of Appendix B, and the subject reaction theorem looks as follows:

Theorem 2 (Subject Reaction). *If $\Gamma \vdash P$ well-typed and $P \longrightarrow Q$, then $\Gamma \vdash Q$ well-typed.*

An attractive property of our layered semantics is that reduction and reaction live in independent worlds. There are no side effects in the functional layer, its only role is to enable rules in the deterministic layer, and further reduction cannot retract any choices already enabled. This can be captured in a diamond property that we call *functional soundness*, which says that the $\mapsto$ and $\longrightarrow$ relations commute.

Let $\underset{\text{EVAL}}{\longrightarrow}$ be the relation formed by the structural rules in Figure 8 and rule EVAL, but none of the axioms in Figure 7. Let $\underset{\neg\text{EVAL}}{\longrightarrow}$ be the reaction relation formed by including the structural rules and the axioms, but not rule EVAL.

Theorem 3 (Functional soundness). *If $P \underset{\neg\text{EVAL}}{\longrightarrow} Q$ and $P \underset{\text{EVAL}}{\longrightarrow} P'$, then there is a Q' such that $P' \underset{\neg\text{EVAL}}{\longrightarrow} Q'$ and $Q \underset{\text{EVAL}}{\longrightarrow} Q'$.*

The reader is referred to [12] for more elaboration and proofs of the above properties.

3.3   The Scheduling Layer

The reactive layer leaves us with a system that is highly non-deterministic—it says nothing about in which order objects should run messages, or in which order concurrently active objects may progress. The scheduling layer puts some extra constraints on the system, by consulting the hitherto uninterpreted time constraints attached to messages and objects. The requirements on the scheduler are formulated in terms of a *real-time trace*.

Definition 1 (Real-time trace). *A real-time transition is a transition $P \longrightarrow Q$ associated with a value t of some totally ordered time domain, written $P \xrightarrow{t} Q$. A real-time trace $\mathcal{T}$ is a possibly infinite sequence of real-time transitions $P_i \xrightarrow{t_i} P_{i+1}$ such that $t_i < t_{i+1}$. We call each P_i in a real-time trace a* trace state.

A real-time trace thus represents the execution of a Timber program on some specific machine, with machine-specific real-time behavior embedded in the t_i. Our first goal is to define which real-time behaviors are acceptable with respect to the time-constraints of a program.

Definition 2 (Transition timeline). *Let the timeline of a reaction axiom be the pair c as it occurs in the reaction rules of Figure 7, and let the timeline of a structural reaction rule be the timeline of its single reaction premise. We now define the timeline of a transition $P \xrightarrow{t} Q$ as the timeline of the rule used to derive $P \longrightarrow Q$.*

This definition leads to the notion of *timeliness*:

Definition 3 (Timeliness). *A real-time transition $P \xrightarrow{t} Q$ with timeline $\langle b, d \rangle$ is timely iff $b \le t \le d$. A real-time trace $\mathcal{T}$ is timely iff every transition in $\mathcal{T}$ is timely.*

Our second goal is to constrain the dispatching of messages to occur in priority order. First we need to formalize the notion of a dispatch:

Definition 4 (Dispatch). *A dispatch from $\mathcal{T}$ is a real-time transition $P \xrightarrow{t} P'$ derived from rule RUN, such that P is the final trace state of $\mathcal{T}$. An (n, Q)-dispatch from $\mathcal{T}$ is a dispatch from $\mathcal{T}$ where n is the name of the activated object, and Q is the dispatched message.*

The intention is that whenever there are several possible dispatches from some $\mathcal{T}$, the semantics should prescribe which one is chosen. To this end we will need to define an ordering relation between messages.

First, we let timelines be sorted primarily according to their deadlines.

Definition 5 (Timeline ordering). $\langle b, d \rangle < \langle b, d \rangle$ *iff* $d < d'$, *or* $d = d'$ *and* $b < b'$.

Second, we want to induce an ordering on messages whose timelines are identical. We will assume, without loss of generality, that ν-bound names are chosen to be unique in a trace state, and that the renaming congruence rule is never applied in an EQUIV transition. This makes it possible to uniquely determine the time when a bound name appears in a trace.

Definition 6 (Binding times). *The* binding time $bt(n, \mathcal{T})$ *of a name* n *in a real-time trace* $\mathcal{T}$ *is the largest time* t_i *associated with a real-time transition* $P_i \xrightarrow{t_i} P_{i+1}$ *in* $\mathcal{T}$, *such that* P_{i+1} *contains a* ν-*binder for* n *but* P_i *does not.*

From the previous two definitions we can construct a partial order on pending messages.

Definition 7 (Message ordering). $\langle n, e, K \rangle_m^c <_{\mathcal{T}} \langle n, e', K' \rangle_{m'}^{c'}$ *iff* $c < c'$, *or* $c = c'$ *and* $bt(m, \mathcal{T}) < bt(m', \mathcal{T})$

Note that this definition only relates messages aimed for some particular object, and that these messages are actually totally ordered.

From the ordering of messages follows the notion of a *minimal* dispatch.

Definition 8 (Minimal dispatch). *An* (n, Q)-*dispatch from* $\mathcal{T}$ *is minimal iff, for all possible* (n, Q')-*dispatches from* $\mathcal{T}$, $Q <_{\mathcal{T}} Q'$. *A dispatch from* $\mathcal{T}$ *is minimal if it is a minimal* (n, Q)-*dispatch from* $\mathcal{T}$ *for some* n *and* Q.

Finally, the timeliness and minimality constraints can be applied to real-time traces in order to identify the *valid* ones.

Definition 9 (Valid trace). *A real-time trace* $\mathcal{T}$ *is valid iff* $\mathcal{T}$ *is timely and every dispatch from a prefix* $\mathcal{T}'$ *of* $\mathcal{T}$ *is minimal.*

The real-time semantics of a Timber program is thus the set of valid traces it generates.

Some notes regarding these definitions:

1. The notion of minimality makes message dispatching fully deterministic. What the semantics prescribes is actually a *priority queue* of messages for each object, that resorts to FIFO order when priorities (timelines) are identical. This is also how our Timber compiler implements the semantics. Our reasons for defining message queuing here and not in the reactive layer are twofold: First, the complexity that arises from maintaining explicit queues in the process calculus is daunting. Second, leaving out ordering concerns is more in line with the process calculus tradition, and allows for easier comparison between Timber and other languages based on similar formalisms, like Concurrent Haskell.

2. All scheduling flexibility is captured in the selection of which object to run—because message order is fixed, the reaction axioms of Figure 7 do not offer any flexibility in choosing the next transition for a particular object. On the other hand, whenever there are several objects capable of making a timely transition, the semantics allows any one of them to be chosen. This opens up for pre-emptive scheduling, and coincides with our intuition that objects execute in parallel, but are internally sequential.

3. It follows from the monotonicity of real time that if a dispatch meets the baseline constraint of its timeliness requirement, all transitions involving the same object up to its next idle state will also meet the baseline constraint. Likewise, if an object becomes idle by means of a DONE or REP transition that meets its deadline, all transitions involving this object since it was last idle must also have met this deadline.

4. Meeting the baseline constraint of a dispatch is always feasible; it just amounts to refraining from making a certain transition. This can easily be implemented by putting messages on hold in a system-wide timer queue until their baselines have passed. On the other hand, meeting a deadline constraint is always going to be a fight against time and finite resources. Statically determining whether the execution of a Timber program will give rise to a valid trace in this respect is in general infeasible; however, we note that scheduling theory and feasibility analysis is available for attacking this problem, at least for a restricted set of Timber programs.

5. It can be argued that a Timber implementation should be able to continue execution, even if the deadline constraint of the timeliness requirement cannot be met for some part of its trace. Indeed, this is also what our Timber compiler currently does. However, it is not clear what the best way of achieving deadline fault tolerance would be, so we take the conservative route and let the Timber semantics specify only the desired program behavior at this stage.

On a uni-processor system, the scheduling problems generated by our semantics bear an attractively close resemblance to the problems addressed by deadline-based scheduling theory [21]. In fact, the well-known optimality result for fully preemptive Earliest-Deadline-First scheduling [3] can be directly recast to the Timber setting as follows:

Theorem 4 (Optimality of EDF). *For a given real-time trace, let the execution time attributed to a transition only depend on the reaction axiom from which the transition is derived. Moreover, let a re-ordering of the trace be the result of repeatedly applying the equivalence* $P \parallel Q \longrightarrow P' \parallel Q \longrightarrow P' \parallel Q' \equiv P \parallel Q \longrightarrow P \parallel Q' \longrightarrow P' \parallel Q'$ *(structurally lifted to transitions).*

Then, if there exists a re-ordering of transitions that results in a timely trace, re-ordering the transitions according to the principle of EDF will also result in a timely trace.

It is our intention to study this correspondence in considerable more detail, especially how the presence of baseline constraints affects existing feasibility theory. However, it should also be noted that the scheduling layer semantics does not *prescribe* EDF scheduling. In particular, static schedules produced by off-line simulations of a program is an interesting alternative we are also looking into [9].

4   Related Work

The actions in Timber resemble the *tasks* in the E machine [5], where the programmer can specify that a reaction to an event should be delivered precisely at a certain point in time. Consequently, the output of a task will be queued until it is time to react, and the E machine becomes a deterministic system, in sharp contrast to Timber. Similarly, the language H [22] is a Haskell-like language where functions over *timestamped messages* are interconnected through ports. For an input message, a timestamp indicates the time of an event, and for output, it specifies exactly when the message should be output from the system.

In the *synchronous* programming school (Esterel, Signal, Lustre), programs are usually conducted by one or more periodic clocks, and computations are assumed to terminate within a clock period [2]. In contrast, Timber does not make any assumptions about periodic behavior, even though it shares the concept of reactivity with the synchronous languages.

The UDP Calculus [20,25] provides a formalism for expressing detailed behavior of distributed systems that communicate via the UDP protocol. Part of the structure of our process calculus can be found in the UDP Calculus as well; for example the representation of hosts (objects) as process terms tagged with unique names, and the modelling of messages as free-floating terms in their own right. The UDP Calculus has a basic notion of time constraints in the shape of terms annotated with timers, although at present this facility is only meant to model message propagation delays and timeout options. Moreover, the focus on actual UDP implementations in existing operating systems makes the UDP Calculus more narrow in scope than Timber, but also significantly more complex: the number of transition axioms in the UDP Calculus is 78, for example, where we get away with about 10.

The language Hume [18] has similar design motives as Timber: it has asynchronous, concurrent processes, is based on a pure functional core, and targets embedded, time-critical systems. However, Hume is an example of languages that identify the concept of *real time* with bounds on resources, not with means for specifying time constraints for the delivery of reactions to events. Apart from Hume, this group of languages also include Real-Time FRP and Embedded ML [24,6].

On a historical note, Embedded Gofer [23] is an extension to a Haskell precursor Haskell aimed at supporting embedded systems. It has an incremental garbage collector, and direct access to interrupts and I/O ports, but lacks any internal notion of time. The same can also be said for Erlang [1]. Although it has been successfully applied in large real-time telecom switching systems, it only provides best-effort, fixed-priority scheduling, and lacks a static type-safety property.

The technique of separating a semantics into a purely functional layer and an effectful process calculus layer has been used in the definition of Concurrent Haskell [16] and O'Haskell [14]. Although it is well known that a functional language can be encoded in process calculii, such an encoding would obscure the semantic stratification we wish to emphasize.

5   Conclusions and Future Work

We have given a semantics for Timber, stratified into independent layers for functional evaluation, object and message reactions, and time-sensitive scheduling. The language is implemented in terms of an full-featured interpreter, and we are currently developing a compiler that generates C code for targeting embedded systems. In the near future, we plan to apply and implement deadline-based scheduling analysis techniques for Timber, and nail down the specifics of shifting to a strict semantics in the functional layer.

Acknowledgments. The design of the Timber language has been influenced by contributions by many people within the Timber group at OHSU; Iavor Diatchki and Mark Jones in particular have been active in the development of Timber's time-constrained reactions. We would also like to thank members of the PacSoft research group at OHSU for valuable feedback, notably Thomas Hallgren.

References

1. J. Armstrong, R. Virding, C. Wikström, and M. Williams. *Concurrent Programming in Erlang*. Prentice Hall, 1996.
2. A. Benveniste, P. Caspi, S. A. Edwards, N. Halbwachs, P. Le Guernic, and R. de Simone. The synchronous languages 12 years later. *Proceedings of the IEEE*, 91(1), January 2003.
3. M. Dertouzos. Control Robotics: the Procedural Control of Physical Processes. *Information Processing*, 74, 1974.
4. L. Erkök and J. Launchbury. Recursive monadic bindings. In *Proceedings of the Fifth ACM SIGPLAN International Conference on Functional Programming, ICFP'00*, pages 174–185. ACM Press, September 2000.
5. T. A. Henzinger and C. M. Kirsch. The embedded machine: Predictable, portable real-time code. In *Proceedings of the ACM SIGPLAN Conference on Programming Language Design and Implementation (PLDI)*, 2002.
6. J. Hughes and L. Pareto. Recursion and dynamic data-structures in bounded space: Towards embedded ML programming. In *International Conference on Functional Programming*, pages 70–81, 1999.
7. M. P. Jones, M. Carlsson, and J. Nordlander. Composed, and in control: Programming the Timber robot.
   http://www.cse.ogi.edu/~mpj/timbot/ComposedAndInControl.pdf, 2002.

8. S. L. P. Jones, A. Reid, F. Henderson, C. A. R. Hoare, and S. Marlow. A semantics for imprecise exceptions. In *SIGPLAN Conference on Programming Language Design and Implementation*, pages 25–36, 1999.
9. R. Kieburtz. Real-time reactive programming for embedded controllers. ftp://cse.ogi.edu/pub/pacsoft/papers/timed.ps, 2001.
10. R. Milner, M. Tofte, and R. Harper. *The Definition of Standard ML*. MIT Press, 1990.
11. E. Moggi and A. Sabry. An abstract monadic semantics for value recursion. In *Workshop on Fixed Points in Computer Science*, 2003.
12. J. Nordlander. *Reactive Objects and Functional Programming*. Phd thesis, Department of Computer Science, Chalmers University of Technology, Gothenburg, 1999.
13. J. Nordlander. Polymorphic subtyping in O'Haskell. *Science of Computer Programming*, 43(2–3), 2002.
14. J. Nordlander and M. Carlsson. Reactive Objects in a Functional Language – An escape from the evil "I". In *Proceedings of the Haskell Workshop*, Amsterdam, Holland, 1997.
15. J. Nordlander, M. Jones, M. Carlsson, D. Kieburtz, and A. Black. Reactive objects. In *The Fifth IEEE International Symposium on Object-Oriented Real-Time Distributed Computing (ISORC 2002)*, 2002.
16. S. Peyton Jones, A. Gordon, and S. Finne. Concurrent Haskell. In *ACM Principles of Programming Languages*, pages 295–308, St Petersburg, FL, Jan. 1996. ACM Press.
17. S. Peyton Jones et al. Report on the programming language Haskell 98, a nonstrict, purely functional language. http://haskell.org, February 1999.
18. A. Reb n Portillo, K. Hammond, H.-W. Loidl, and P. Vasconcelos. Granularity analysis using automatic size and time cost inference. In *Proceedings of IFL '02– Implementation of Functional Languages*. Springer Verlag, September 2002.
19. A. Sabry. What is a Purely Functional Language? *Journal of Functional Programming*, 8(1):1–22, 1998.
20. A. Serjantov, P. Sewell, and K. Wansbrough. The UDP Calculus: Rigorous Semantics for Real Networking. In *Theoretical Aspects of Computer Software, 4th International Symposium, TACS 2001*, Sendai, Japan, Oct 2001.
21. J. Stankovich, editor. *Deadline Scheduling for Real-time Systems, EDF and Related Algorithms*. Kluwer, 1998.
22. S. Truv . A new H for real-time programming. http://www.cs.chalmers.se/~truve/NewH.ps.
23. M. Wallace and C. Runciman. Lambdas in the liftshaft - functional programming and an embedded architecture. In *Functional Programming Languages and Computer Architecture*, pages 249–258, 1995.
24. Z. Wan, W. Taha, and P. Hudak. Real-time FRP. In *International Conference on Functional Programming (ICFP '01)*, Florence, Italy, September 2001.
25. K. Wansbrough, M. Norrish, P. Sewell, and A. Serjantov. Timing UDP: mechanized semantics for sockets, threads and failures. In *11th European Symposium on Programming, ESOP 2002*, Grenoble, France, April 2002.

A Desugaring

$$[\![\mathbf{do}\ c]\!]_v = [\![c]\!]_v$$
$$[\![\mathbf{do}\ p\ \texttt{<-}\ e;\ cs]\!]_v = [\![e]\!]_v\ \texttt{>>=}\ \backslash\ p\ \texttt{->}\ [\![\mathbf{do}\ cs]\!]_v$$
$$[\![\mathbf{do}\ c;\ cs]\!]_v = [\![c]\!]_v\ \texttt{>>}\ [\![\mathbf{do}\ cs]\!]_v$$
$$[\![\mathbf{do\ let}\ ds;\ cs]\!]_v = [\![\mathbf{let}\ ds\ \mathbf{in\ do}\ cs]\!]_v$$
$$[\![\mathbf{template}\ as\ \mathbf{in}\ e]\!]_v = \left[\!\!\left[\begin{array}{l}\mathbf{do\ self\ \texttt{<-}\ new}\ es\\ \mathbf{return}\ e\end{array}\right]\!\!\right]_{v'}$$
$$\text{where}\ \begin{cases} v' = [\ x\ |\ x := e \leftarrow as\ ] \\ es = [\ e\ |\ x := e \leftarrow as\ ]\end{cases}$$
$$[\![\mathbf{action}\ cs]\!]_v = \mathbf{act\ self}\ \langle 0,0\rangle\ [\![\mathbf{do}\ cs]\!]_v$$
$$[\![\mathbf{request}\ cs]\!]_v = \mathbf{req\ self}\ [\![\mathbf{do}\ cs]\!]_v$$
$$[\![\mathbf{before}]\!]_v = \mathbf{bef}$$
$$[\![\mathbf{after}]\!]_v = \mathbf{aft}$$

$$[\![p := e]\!]_v = [\![\mathbf{set}\ ((\backslash\ p\ \texttt{->}\ v)\ e)]\!]_v$$
$$\text{if}\ fv(p) \subseteq v$$
$$[\![e]\!]_v = \mathbf{get}\ \texttt{>>=}\ \backslash\ v\ \texttt{->}\ [\![e]\!]_v$$
$$\text{if}\ fv(e) \cap v \neq \emptyset$$
$$[\![e]\!]_v = [\![e]\!]_v$$
$$\text{otherwise}$$

B Well-Typed Processes

Typing judgments for processes and continuations are given below. $\tau \rightsquigarrow$ is the type of a continuation waiting for a reply of type τ. Reduction contexts are given function types, treating their hole as a normal, abstracted variable.

$$\frac{\Gamma \vdash n : \mathtt{Ref}\ \rho \qquad \Gamma \vdash e : \mathbf{0}\ \rho\ \tau}{\Gamma \vdash K : \tau \rightsquigarrow \qquad \Gamma \vdash c : (\mathtt{Time},\mathtt{Time}) \qquad \Gamma \vdash m : \mathtt{Msg}}{\Gamma \vdash \langle n, e, K\rangle_m^c\ \text{well-typed}}\ \text{PENDING}$$

$$\frac{\Gamma \vdash s : \rho \qquad \Gamma \vdash e : \mathbf{0}\ \rho\ \tau}{\Gamma \vdash K : \tau \rightsquigarrow \qquad \Gamma \vdash c : (\mathtt{Time},\mathtt{Time}) \qquad \Gamma \vdash n : \mathtt{Ref}\ \rho}{\Gamma \vdash (\!|s, e, K|\!)_n^c\ \text{well-typed}}\ \text{ACTIVE}$$

$$\frac{\Gamma \vdash m : \mathtt{Msg}}{\Gamma \vdash \langle\rangle_m\ \text{well-typed}}\ \text{EMPTY} \qquad \frac{\Gamma \vdash s : \rho \qquad \Gamma \vdash n : \mathtt{Ref}\ \rho}{\Gamma \vdash (\!|s|\!)_n\ \text{well-typed}}\ \text{IDLE}$$

$$\frac{\Gamma \vdash P\ \text{well-typed} \qquad \Gamma \vdash P'\ \text{well-typed}}{\Gamma \vdash P \parallel P'\ \text{well-typed}}\ \text{PARALLEL}$$

$$\frac{\Gamma, n : \tau \vdash P\ \text{well-typed}}{\Gamma \vdash \nu n.\,P\ \text{well-typed}}\ \text{RESTRICTION}$$

$$\frac{\Gamma \vdash s : \rho \qquad \Gamma \vdash \mathcal{M} : \tau \to \mathbf{0}\ \rho\ \sigma \qquad \Gamma \vdash K : \sigma \rightsquigarrow \qquad \Gamma \vdash n : \mathtt{Ref}\ \rho}{\Gamma \vdash (\!|s, \mathcal{M}, K|\!)_n : \tau \rightsquigarrow}\ \text{CONT}$$

$$\frac{}{\Gamma \vdash 0 : \tau \rightsquigarrow}\ \text{EMPTYCONT} \qquad \frac{\Gamma, [\,] : \tau \vdash \mathcal{M}[\,] : \mathbf{0}\ \sigma\ \rho}{\Gamma \vdash \mathcal{M} : \tau \to \mathbf{0}\ \sigma\ \rho}\ \text{CONTEXT}$$

Scrap Your Boilerplate
Invited Talk

Simon Peyton Jones[1] and Ralf Lämmel[2]

[1] Microsoft Research, Cambridge
[2] Vrije University, Amsterdam

Many programs traverse data structures built from rich mutually-recursive data types. Such programs often have a great deal of "boilerplate" code that simply walks the structure, hiding a small amount of "real" code that constitutes the reason for the traversal. "Generic programming" is the umbrella term to describe a wide variety of programming technology directed at this problem. All these techniques aim to provide mechanical support for the "boilerplate" part, leaving the programmer free to concentrate on the important part of the algorithm. Such generic programs are much more robust to data structure evolution because they contain many fewer lines of type-specific code.

The trouble is that most generic programming techniques either require significant support from the programming language itself, or are inconvenient for the programmer. In this talk I will describe a new approach to generic programming based on the functional language Haskell, which combines programming convenience with very modest demands on the language. Our approach is simple to understand, elegant, reasonably efficient, and handles all the data types found in conventional functional programming languages. It makes essential use of rank-2 polymorphism, an extension found in some implementations of Haskell.

The talk is a development of work first reported in "Scrap your boilerplate", Laemmel & Peyton Jones, Proc ACM SIGPLAN Workshop on Types in Language Design and Implementation (TLDI 2003), New Orleans, Jan 2003.

A. Ohori (Ed.): APLAS 2003, LNCS 2895, p. 357, 2003.

Correctness of a Higher-Order Removal Transformation through a Relational Reasoning*

Susumu Nishimura

Department of Mathematics, Faculty of Science, Kyoto University
susumu@math.kyoto-u.ac.jp

Abstract. The syntactic logical relations developed by Pitts are applied to show the correctness of a higher-order removal program transformation algorithm. The convenient proof method that resorts to the induction on the structure of programs does not apply because of the circular references to be introduced by the transformation. Using a variant of the syntactic logical relations, in which every pair of the transformation source and target are related, one can break the circularity and make an inductive proof go through. This demonstrates that the syntactic logical relations provide a basis of another general proof method for showing the correctness of program transformations.

1 Introduction

The aim of program transformation is to improve the run-time efficiency, keeping the semantics of the source program. The correctness proof on a program transformation algorithm is usually done by an inductive argument on the program structure, where each induction step is proved by an equational reasoning on the general syntactic pattern of the corresponding local transformation site. This inductive proof principle applies to a large class of program transformation algorithms, but there are certain ones that require a stronger one.

In this paper, we demonstrate that the *syntactic logical relations* developed by Pitts [14] can serve as another powerful device for proving the correctness of program transformations. The logical relations are a type-indexed family of relations $\{\Delta_\tau\}_\tau$ between program expressions, where each Δ_τ is inductively defined on the structure of type τ [9]. Pitts developed an operational technique to construct logical relations over a syntactic domain and called them 'syntactic' logical relations. He also showed that the syntactic logical relations coincide with the observational equivalence relation, i. e., $(M, M') \in \Delta_\tau$ for some τ iff M and M' show the same evaluation behavior when they are embedded in any context of a larger program.

The syntactic logical relations provide a firm basis for arguing the observational equivalence between the transformation source and target. Given a transformation algorithm, we alter the original definition of the syntactic logical re-

---

* Most of this work was done while the author was at Research Institute for Mathematical Sciences, Kyoto University.

A. Ohori (Ed.): APLAS 2003, LNCS 2895, pp. 358–375, 2003.

lations so that they relate every pair of a source program and its transformation result. That is, we construct the family of relations satisfying

$$(M, \mathcal{W}[\![M]\!]) \in \Delta_\tau,$$

where M is an arbitrary source expression of type τ and $\mathcal{W}[\![M]\!]$ stands for the transformation result. Then the correctness of the transformation (*i. e.*, the source program and its transformation result behave similarly) follows from the coincidence between the logical relations and the observational equivalence.

There are a few attempts to apply a syntactically formulated relational framework to the correctness proof of program transformation. An example is a boxing transformation on polymorphic values [7,8]. However, the language considered does not have fixpoint recursion. The proof technique in the present paper has a more powerful ability to reason about the observational equivalence in the presence of fixpoint operators (and hence it is sensitive to termination behavior too). Johann [6] exploited the parametricity result induced from the syntactic logical relations to give a formal justification on the shortcut fusion transformation [4], which is a popular transformation algorithm for removing intermediate data structures that are produced between producer/consumer function pairs. The present paper demonstrates that not only the parametricity but also the framework of the syntactic logical relations itself can be a formal basis for arguing the correctness of program transformations.

We show how the syntactic logical relations can effectively constitute a formal correctness proof, through a non-trivial example of program transformation, namely, a *higher-order removal transformation*, which was introduced by the author as a transformation step for removing higher-order functions in a particular class of programs [11]. The major difficulty in giving a correctness proof for this transformation is raised by a *circularity* to be introduced into the structure of the target program. The presence of circularity makes it difficult to show the total correctness of transformation (*i. e.*, the semantics of the whole program is preserved), since there is no base case to induct on the program structure. Using logical relations, however, we can break the circularity and make the induction go through.

Though we employed Pitts' syntactic logical relations, it would be also possible to give the correctness proof using logical relations that are, usually done as such, defined over semantic domains, as Nielsen [10] did in the correctness proof of the general higher-order removal algorithm (*a.k.a.* defunctionalization [15]). However, we prefer Pitts' syntactic approach, since we can avoid technical complications that arise from the domain theoretic approach.

The rest of the paper is organized as follows. Section 2 informally presents the higher-order removal transformation algorithm mentioned above. Section 3 introduces a relational framework for reasoning about observational equivalence of programs based on the syntactic logical relations. Section 4 gives a formal correctness proof of the higher-order removal transformation. Finally Section 5 concludes the paper with discussions on future research topics.

2   The Higher-Order Removal Transformation by Example

Deforestation [19] is a program transformation which removes intermediate data structures that are produced by a function and are immediately consumed by another function. Though notable refinements and improvements on the deforestation algorithm have been proposed [4,16,1,17], it had been long undiscovered how to deforest functions that are defined by means of *accumulating parameters*, which are function arguments passed around throughout a series of recursive calls, as popularly seen in the tail recursive definition of list reverse function. A solution, which is based on the framework of macro tree transducers [2], to this problem was recently proposed by Voigtländer [18]. The author independently developed another one, which was inspired from the composition method for attribute grammars [3].

The program transformation considered in this paper is a higher-order removal transformation, which is a vital step in the latter deforestation algorithm. Let us explain the deforestation process by applying it to an example given in Figure 1. We use Haskell like syntax [5] extended with record syntax: $(l_1{=}M_1, \ldots, l_n{=}M_n)$ expresses a record with labels $l_1, \ldots, l_n$ $(n \geq 0)$ associated with expressions $M_1, \ldots, M_n$, *resp.*, #l M selects the value associated with the field l of record M. $(l_1{::}\tau_1, \ldots, l_n{::}\tau_n)$ represents the type of a record whose label l_i is each associated with a value of type τ_i.

The source program to which deforestation process is applied is the function revflat given in Figure 1(a). It is a composition of a producer function flat and a consumer function rev, which compute the preorder traversal list of leaves of a binary tree and the reversal of list elements, respectively. Though the definition may look verbose, the intention is made clear by removing all the record labels. For example, the definition of flat is equivalent to the following program:

```
flat :: T a → [a] → [a]
flat (Node(t,t')) x0 = flat t (flat t' x0)
flat (Leaf a)     x0 = a:x0
```

We put distinct record labels as the "tags" to uniquely identify the accumulating parameter and the computation result of each different function; h and l are used for tagging the accumulating parameter and the computation result of the function flat, *resp.*; similarly, k and j for those of the function rev. The named record labels are more useful for the purpose of unique identification than the unlabeled tuples.

Figure 2 illustrates the whole deforestation process, which comprises of four subtransformation steps. First, it applies shortcut fusion [4], which is a standard deforestation technique, in order to remove intermediate data structures and to obtain a single recursive function definition. The result is, however, a higher-order function, and we would like to remove this higher-orderedness. For this, we further apply two transformations, which perform type conversions on the higher-order function. They are intended to translate the program into a form

```
data T a = Node (T a,T a) | Leaf a

flat :: T a → (h::[a]) → (l::[a])
flat (Node(t,t')) x0 = (l=#l (flat t (h=#l (flat t' (h=#h x0)))))
flat (Leaf a)     x0 = (l=a:(#h x0))

rev :: [a] → (k::[a]) → (j::[a])
rev (a:t) x0 = (j=#j (rev t (k=a:(#k x0))))
rev []    x0 = (j=#k x0)

revflat :: T a→ [a]
revflat x = #j (rev (#l (flat x (h=[]))) (k=[]))
```

Figure 1(a): Source program

```
rf :: T a → ((hk::[a]) → (hj::[a])) → (lk::[a]) → (lj::[a])
rf (Node(t,t')) x0 = let x2 = rf t' (\y2 -> (hj=#hj (x0 (hk=#hk y2)))) in
                     let x1 = rf t  (\y1 -> (hj=#lj (x2 (lk=#hk y1)))) in
                     \y0 -> (lj=#lj (x1 (lk=#lk y0)))
rf (Leaf a)     x0 = \y0 -> (lj=#hj (x0 (hk=a:(#lk y0))))

revflat :: T a → [a]
revflat x = #lj (rf x (\y -> (hj=#hk y)) (lk=[]))
```

Figure 1(b): Intermediate transformation result

```
rf' :: T a → (hj ::[a], lk::[a]) → (hk::[a], lj ::[a])
rf' (Node(t,t')) x0 = let x2 = rf' t' (hj=#hj x0, lk=#hk x1)
                          x1 = rf' t  (hj=#lj x2, lk=#lk x0)
                      in (lj=#lj x1, hk=#hk x2)
rf' (Leaf a)     x0 = (lj=#hj x0, hk=a:(#lk x0))

revflat :: T a → [a]
revflat x = #lj (rf' x (hj=#hk (rf' x (hj=Ω, lk=[])), lk=[]))
```

Figure 1(c): The result of higher-order removal transformation

Fig. 1. Transformation example

```
flat :: T a → (h::[a]) → (l::[a]),  rev :: [a] → (k::[a]) → (j::[a])
                        ⇓  shortcut fusion
rf :: a T → (h::(k::[a])→(j::[a])) → (l::(k::[a])→(j::[a]))
                        ⇓
rf :: a T→ ((h::(k::[a]))→(h::(j::[a])))→((l::(k::[a]))→(l::(j::[a])))
                        ⇓
rf :: a T → ((hk::[a])→(hj::[a])) → ((lk::[a])→(lj::[a]))
                        ⇓  higher-order removal
rf' :: a T → (hj::[a],lk::[a]) → (hk::[a],lj::[a])
```

Fig. 2. The whole deforestation process

that is suitable as the input to the final higher-order removal transformation step. The intermediate result by these transformations is given in Figure 1(b). (Since the main concern of this paper is in the application of the syntactic logical relations to the correctness proof of a program transformation, we do not go any further on the details of these preceding transformations. The transformation rules for them can be found in [11].)

We notice that, in Figure 1(b), the result of every recursive call of rf t $\cdots$ (where t is either the variable t or t') is bound by a let construct to a variable x_i ($i > 0$) and also that every let bound variable x_i appears, per each constructor case of the definition of rf, once and only once in the form #lj (x_i (lk=M)); We write M_{x_i} for such expression M. The occurrence of the formal function argument x_0 of rf is also linear and it appears in the form #hj (x_0 (hk=M_{x_0})).

The result of applying the higher-order removal transformation is given in Figure 1(c). At the type level, this transformation is understood as a type conversion

from $\sigma_1 = ((\text{hk}::[\text{a}]) \rightarrow (\text{hj}::[\text{a}])) \rightarrow ((\text{lk}::[\text{a}]) \rightarrow (\text{lj}::[\text{a}]))$
to $\sigma_2 = (\text{hj}::[\text{a}],\text{lk}::[\text{a}]) \rightarrow (\text{hk}::[\text{a}],\text{lj}::[\text{a}]).$

Notice that hj and lk, which are the labels of record types occurring at negative positions in the higher-order function type σ_1, constitute the argument type (hj::[a],lk::[a]) of the first-order function type σ_2 and also that hk and lj, which are the labels of records occurring at positive positions in σ_1, constitute the result type (hk::[a],lj::[a]) of σ_2.

$$
\begin{aligned}
\mathcal{W}'[\![H :: T]\!] &= \mathcal{W}'[\![H]\!] :: \mathcal{W}'[\![T]\!] \\
\mathcal{W}'[\![\#lk\ y_0]\!] &= \#lk\ x_0 \\
\mathcal{W}'[\![\#hk\ y_i]\!] &= \#hk\ x_i &(1 \leq i \leq n) \\
\mathcal{W}'[\![\#hj\ (x_0\ (hk = M_{x_0}))]\!] &= \#hj\ x_0 \\
\mathcal{W}'[\![\#lj\ (x_i\ (lk = M_{x_i}))]\!] &= \#lj\ x_i &(1 \leq i \leq n) \\
\mathcal{W}'[\![M]\!] &= M &(\text{otherwise})
\end{aligned}
$$

Fig. 3. Transformation rules for higher-order removal

The higher-order removal transformation on the function rf that respects the above type conversion is formulated as follows. (The transformation on revflat is a bit technical, and is discussed later in Section 4.2.) Every let binding site x_i = rf t ($\backslash y_i$ -> (hj=N_i)) is rewritten to

$$x_i = \text{rf'}\ t\ (\text{hj}=\mathcal{W}'[\![N_i]\!],\ \text{lk}=\mathcal{W}'[\![M_{x_i}]\!]) \tag{1}$$

where $\mathcal{W}'[\![M]\!]$ denotes a transformation on M, which is inductively defined on the structure of M by the rules given in Figure 3. (We only consider a special class of expressions and hence the rules in the figure are sufficient for the transformation.) The linearity in the use of each variable x_i is crucial here for uniquely identifying the expression M_{x_i}. The function value $\backslash y_0$ -> (lj=N_0) returned by the function $\mathtt{rf}$ in Figure 1(b) is transformed similarly but to $(\mathtt{lj}=\mathcal{W}'[\![N_0]\!],$ $\mathtt{hk}=\mathcal{W}'[\![M_{\mathtt{x}_0}]\!])$. To complete the transformation, the sequential let bindings are replaced with a single circular let. The final transformation result is given in Figure 1(c).

The above transformation process (1) is explained as follows. Every recursive call $\mathtt{rf}\ t\ \cdots$, whose result is denoted by a variable $\mathtt{x}_i$ ($i > 0$), is transformed into $\mathtt{rf'}\ t\ R$, where R is a record of type $(\mathtt{hj::[a]},\mathtt{lk::[a]})$ and the value of R at each record label is drawn from the source program as follows: $\mathtt{hj}$ value is set to N_i, which is taken from the $\mathtt{hj}$ field of the record expression returned by the function $\backslash \mathtt{y}_i \to (\mathtt{hj}=N_i)$ (*i. e.*, the second argument to the recursive call); Since every variable $\mathtt{x}_i$ is bound to the result of a recursive call $\mathtt{rf'}t\ \cdots$ (of type $(\mathtt{hk::[a]},\mathtt{lj::[a]})$) in the target program, every application site $\mathtt{\#lj}\ (\mathtt{x}_i\ (\mathtt{lk}=M))$ is rewritten to $\mathtt{\#lj}\ \mathtt{x}_i$, which just refers to the $\mathtt{lj}$ value returned by the recursive call. Also, every occurrence of expression $\mathtt{\#hk}\ \mathtt{y}_i$ is rewritten to $\mathtt{\#hk}\ \mathtt{x}_i$, which just takes the $\mathtt{hk}$ value returned by the recursive call. The transformation for the case $i = 0$ is similarly explained.

The above explanation only alludes to the validity of the transformation from the viewpoint of the type correctness and it tells little about the semantic correctness. It is indeed difficult to give a complete justification on the transformation in a descriptive way. The source of difficulty is that the transformation we consider is a *non-local transformation*, where the result of transformation on a program expression depends on that of another transformation site (*e. g.*, in the transformation rule (1), the transformation result refers to that of another site, namely $\mathcal{W}'[\![M_{\mathtt{x}_i}]\!]$). Even worse, the target program involves a *circularity*, which is introduced by the circular let construct, in its program structure. Due to this circularity, it is even not obvious if the transformation preserves the termination behavior of the source program.

In order to obtain a complete justification, we would need to resort to a formal argument based upon a firm mathematical basis. We notice that the usual inductive argument on the program structure does not work effectively, since there is no base case to induct on the circular structure. In [18], Voigtländer faced this problem in the correctness proof of his deforestation algorithm too. He argued the correctness of each local transformation step only, leaving that of the entire transformation not formally proved.

In the present paper, we employ the syntactic logical relations [14] as the mathematical basis for reasoning about the correctness of the higher-order removal program transformation. For this, we reformulate the syntatic logical relations $\{\Delta_\tau\}_\tau$ so that, every transformation source M and its transformation result, denoted by $\mathcal{W}[\![M]\!]$, are related, *i. e.*, $(M, \mathcal{W}[\![M]\!]) \in \Delta_\tau$. This enables a simultaneous reasoning on different transformation sites: we can induce the relation between the pair of a transformation source and its result (which includes references to the results of transformation on other sites) from the type structure, not resorting to the induction hypothesis on the program structure.

We note that, unlike the usual logical relations, the logical relations formulated as above induce relations between expressions of different types. That is,

Δ_τ is a relation between expressions of type τ and $\mathcal{T}[\![\tau]\!]$, where $\mathcal{T}[\![\cdot]\!]$ is a type conversion function that replaces every type subexpression σ_1 in τ with σ_2. We will discuss the observational equivalence of expressions of different types up to certain contexts that subsume this type mismatch. (See Section 4.2 for the details.)

3   Relational Framework for a Functional Language

This section constructs a relational framework for reasoning about observational equivalence of programs, following the technique developed in [14]. The considered programming language is a simply typed call-by-name functional language.[1] In order to avoid syntactic verbosity, we assume the only recursive data structure is lists. However, the following results are easily generalized to include other data structures such as binary trees.

3.1   The Simply Typed Functional Language

The set of types and language expressions are defined as follows.

Types $\tau ::= \tau \to \tau \mid (l_1 : \tau_1, \ldots, l_n : \tau_n) \mid \tau \; list$
Expressions $M ::= x \mid \lambda x : \tau.M \mid MM \mid \mathbf{fix}\; M$
$\qquad\qquad\quad \mid (l_1 = M_1, \ldots, l_n = M_n)$
$\qquad\qquad\quad \mid \mathbf{match}\; M \; \mathbf{of}\; (l_1 = x_1, \ldots, l_n = x_n) \Rightarrow M$
$\qquad\qquad\quad \mid \mathbf{nil}_\tau \mid M{::}M \mid \mathbf{case}\; M \; \mathbf{of}\; \mathbf{nil} \Rightarrow M, x :: y \Rightarrow M$

Types are either a function type, a record type, or a list type. The set of type expressions are defined inductively, with *unit type* () (the record type which has no record labels) being the base case of induction. We say a type τ is τ'-*free*, if τ has no occurrence of τ' as a type subexpression.

The syntax of the language is an extension of the simply typed λ-calculus with fixpoint operator $\mathbf{fix}\; M$, records $(l_1 = M_1, \ldots, l_n = M_n)$ $(n \geq 0)$, **match**-expression on records, empty list $\mathbf{nil}_\tau$, list constructor $M{::}M$, and **case**-branch on lists. Records are labeled products, where the order of labels is insignificant. Expression $\mathbf{match}\; M \; \mathbf{of}\; (l_1 = x_1, \ldots, l_n = x_n) \Rightarrow M'$ matches a record M against a pattern $(l_1 = x_1, \ldots, l_n = x_n)$ and evaluates M' with binding each x_i to the corresponding element identified by the label l_i (the set of labels $l_1, \ldots, l_n$ is a subset of the labels of the record M).

As usual, a variable occurrence of x in an expression M is said to be *free*, if x is not bound by any binding of λ-, **match**-, and **case**-constructs in M. We write $fv(M)$ to denote the set of free variables in M. An expression M is called *closed* if $fv(M) = \emptyset$. We write $M[x_1/N_1, \ldots, x_n/N_n]$ to represent a *substitution* to expression M whose free occurrences of variables $x_1, \ldots, x_n$ are simultaneously replaced with $N_1, \ldots, N_n$, resp. We assume any substitution is capture-free, i. e., any free variable in N_i's is not bound by the substitution.

---

[1] We consider a monomorphically typed language since parametricity is not the concern of the present paper. The results in the paper can be easily generalized to a polymorphically typed language, however.

$$\frac{}{V \Downarrow V} \qquad \frac{F \Downarrow \lambda x : \tau.M \quad M[x/A] \Downarrow V}{FA \Downarrow V} \qquad \frac{F(\mathbf{fix}\, F) \Downarrow V}{\mathbf{fix}\, F \Downarrow V}$$

$$\frac{M \Downarrow (l_1 = M_1, \ldots, l_n = M_n, \ldots) \quad M'[x_1/M_1, \ldots, x_n/M_n] \Downarrow V}{\mathbf{match}\ M\ \mathbf{of}\ (l_1 = x_1, \ldots, l_n = x_n) \Rightarrow M' \Downarrow V}$$

$$\frac{M \Downarrow \mathbf{nil}_\tau \quad M_1 \Downarrow V}{\mathbf{case}\ M\ \mathbf{of}\ \mathbf{nil} \Rightarrow M_1, x :: y \Rightarrow M_2 \Downarrow V} \qquad \frac{M \Downarrow H :: T \quad M_2[x/H, y/T] \Downarrow V}{\mathbf{case}\ M\ \mathbf{of}\ \mathbf{nil} \Rightarrow M_1, x :: y \Rightarrow M_2 \Downarrow V}$$

Fig. 4. Operational Semantics

$$\frac{\Gamma(x) = \tau}{\Gamma \vdash x : \tau} \qquad \frac{\Gamma, x : \tau \vdash M : \tau'}{\Gamma \vdash \lambda x : \tau.M : \tau \to \tau'} \qquad \frac{\Gamma \vdash F : \tau \to \tau' \quad \Gamma \vdash A : \tau}{\Gamma \vdash FA : \tau'}$$

$$\frac{\Gamma \vdash F : \tau \to \tau}{\Gamma \vdash \mathbf{fix}\, F : \tau} \qquad \frac{\Gamma \vdash M_1 : \tau_1 \quad \cdots \quad \Gamma \vdash M_n : \tau_n}{\Gamma \vdash (l_1 = M_1, \ldots, l_n = M_n) : (l_1 : \tau_1, \ldots, l_n : \tau_n)}$$

$$\frac{\Gamma \vdash M : (l_1 : \tau_1, \ldots, l_n : \tau_n, \ldots) \quad \Gamma, x_1 : \tau_1, \ldots, x_n : \tau_n \vdash M' : \tau}{\Gamma \vdash \mathbf{match}\ M\ \mathbf{of}\ (l_1 = x_1, \ldots, l_n = x_n) \Rightarrow M' : \tau}$$

$$\frac{}{\Gamma \vdash \mathbf{nil}_\tau : \tau\ list} \qquad \frac{\Gamma \vdash M : \tau \quad \Gamma \vdash M' : \tau\ list}{\Gamma \vdash M :: M' : \tau\ list}$$

$$\frac{\Gamma \vdash M : \tau\ list \quad \Gamma \vdash M_1 : \tau' \quad \Gamma, x : \tau, y : \tau\ list \vdash M_2 : \tau'}{\Gamma \vdash \mathbf{case}\ M\ \mathbf{of}\ \mathbf{nil} \Rightarrow M_1,\ x :: y \Rightarrow M_2 : \tau'}$$

Fig. 5. Typing Rules

The formal (call-by-name) operational semantics is given in Figure 4. The *evaluation relation* is expressed by a binary relation $M \Downarrow V$, which reads the expression M is evaluated to V, where V is a *value* that belongs to a subset of expressions defined below.

$$V ::= \lambda x : \tau.M \mid (l_1 = M_1, \ldots, l_n = M_n) \mid \mathbf{nil}_\tau \mid M :: M.$$

The typing rules are defined in the usual way, as given in Figure 5. A *typing judgment* is a ternary relation $\Gamma \vdash M : \tau$, where Γ is a finite map from variables to types, called *type environment*, M is an expression, and τ is a type. We conventionally write a type environment as $x_1 : \tau_1, \ldots, x_n : \tau_n$ $(n \geq 0)$. We write $Exp\,(\tau)$ for the set of closed expressions of type τ, that is, $Exp\,(\tau) = \{M \mid \vdash M : \tau\}$.

In what follows, we assume a few syntactic conventions for brevity.

We write Ω_τ for $\mathbf{fix}\,(\lambda x : \tau.x)$, which is an expression of type τ that diverges under any context. The subscript may be omitted occasionally.

The *field selection* operator $\#l\,M$ is a shorthand for

$$\#l\,M \quad = \quad \mathbf{match}\,M\,\mathbf{of}\,(l = z) \Rightarrow z \qquad (z \text{ is a fresh variable}).$$

Circular let definitions are expressed by combining fixpoint and record operators:

$$\mathbf{let}\ x_1 = M_1; \ldots; x_n = M_n\ \mathbf{in}\ M$$
$$= \quad \mathbf{match}\ (\mathbf{fix}\ (\lambda r : (\overline{x_1} : \tau_1, \ldots, \overline{x_n} : \tau_n).$$
$$\mathbf{match}\ r\ \mathbf{of}\ (\overline{x_1} = x_1, \ldots, \overline{x_n} = x_n) \Rightarrow (\overline{x_1} = M_1, \ldots, \overline{x_n} = M_n)))$$
$$\mathbf{of}\ (\overline{x_1} = x_1, \ldots, \overline{x_n} = x_n) \Rightarrow M$$

where each τ_i is the type of M_i and the variable r and the labels $\overline{x_i}'s$ are fresh.

3.2   The Syntactic Logical Relation

We construct the syntactic logical relations for the simply typed functional language defined above. Due to the page limitation, we omitted proofs and some of the technical details, for which readers are deferred to Pitts' original paper [14].

⊤⊤-closed relations. A *frame stack* is a list of *frames*, written $Id \circ F_n \circ \cdots \circ F_1$ $(n \geq 0)$, where Id represents the empty context, and frames F_i's are either in the form $(-M)$, $(\mathbf{match} - \mathbf{of}\ (l_1 = x_1, \ldots, l_n = x_n) \Rightarrow M)$, or $(\mathbf{case} - \mathbf{of\ nil} \Rightarrow M_1, x :: y \Rightarrow M_2)$. We are interested in only frame stacks $S \in Stack(\tau)$, where $Stack(\tau)$ denotes the set of well-typed frame stacks representing an evaluation context whose argument (i. e., the expression to be filled in the context) has type τ and overall result of computation has type τ' *list* for some type τ'. For the lack of space, we omit the formal typing rules on frame stacks.

$$\frac{S \top M[x/A]}{S \circ (-A) \top \lambda x : \tau.M} \qquad \frac{S \circ (-A) \top F}{S \top FA} \qquad \frac{S \circ (-(\mathbf{fix}\ F)) \top F}{S \top \mathbf{fix}\ F}$$

$$\frac{}{Id \top \mathbf{nil}_\tau} \qquad \frac{S \circ (\mathbf{match} - \mathbf{of}\ (l_1 = x_1, \ldots, l_n = x_n) \Rightarrow M') \top M}{S \top \mathbf{match}\ M\ \mathbf{of}\ (l_1 = x_1, \ldots, l_n = x_n) \Rightarrow M'}$$

$$\frac{S \top M'[x_1/M_1, \ldots, x_n/M_n]}{S \circ (\mathbf{match} - \mathbf{of}\ (l_1 = x_1, \ldots, l_n = x_n) \Rightarrow M') \top (l_1 = M_1, \ldots, l_n = M_n, \ldots)}$$

$$\frac{}{Id \top \mathbf{nil}_\tau} \qquad \frac{S \circ (\mathbf{case} - \mathbf{of\ nil} \Rightarrow M_1, x :: y \Rightarrow M_2) \top M}{S \top \mathbf{case}\ M\ \mathbf{of\ nil} \Rightarrow M_1, x :: y \Rightarrow M_2}$$

$$\frac{S \top M_1}{S \circ (\mathbf{case} - \mathbf{of\ nil} \Rightarrow M_1, x :: y \Rightarrow M_2) \top \mathbf{nil}_\tau}$$

$$\frac{S \top M_2[x/H, y/T]}{S \circ (\mathbf{case} - \mathbf{of\ nil} \Rightarrow M_1, x :: y \Rightarrow M_2) \top H :: T}$$

Fig. 6. Rules for termination relation

A binary relation $S \top M$ is defined inductively, for every $S \in Stack(\tau)$ and $M \in Exp(\tau)$, by the rules given in Figure 6. The relation $S \top M$ reads: the evaluation of M under context S terminates and yields $\mathbf{nil}_{\tau'}$ for some τ'.

Let us write $Rel(\tau, \tau')$ to denote the set of all relations between well-typed expressions that are subsets of $Exp(\tau) \times Exp(\tau')$. Similarly, we write $StRel(\tau, \tau')$ to denote the set of all relations between stack frames that are subsets of $Stack(\tau) \times Stack(\tau')$. We define a pair of complement operators $(-)^\top$ between these two relational domains.

Definition 1. *For any* $r \in Rel(\tau, \tau')$, *we define* $r^\top = \{(S, S') \mid \forall (M, M') \in r. (S \top M \Leftrightarrow S' \top M')\}$. *Also, for any* $s \in StRel(\tau, \tau')$, *we define* $s^\top = \{(M, M') \mid \forall (S, S') \in s. (S \top M \Leftrightarrow S' \top M')\}$.

The two $(-)^\top$ operators together define a Galois connection [13] with respect to inclusion (*i. e.*, $r \subseteq s^\top \Leftrightarrow s \subseteq r^\top$). An important property derived from Galois connections is that the double-negation operators $(-)^{\top\top}$ are a closure operator. That is, they are monotone ($r \subseteq r' \Rightarrow r^{\top\top} \subseteq r'^{\top\top}$), inflationary ($r \subseteq r^{\top\top}$), and idempotent ($r^{\top\top} = (r^{\top\top})^{\top\top}$).

Definition 2. *A relation r is called $\top\top$-closed, if $r = r^{\top\top}$.*

Defining logical relation. For each type constructor, we define a relation constructor, called *action*.

Definition 3 (Actions). *Let $r, r', r_1, \ldots, r_n$ be relations such that $r \in Rel\,(\tau, \tau')$, $r' \in Rel\,(\sigma, \sigma')$, $r_i \in Rel\,(\tau_i, \tau_i')$ ($i = 1, \ldots, n$).*

We define actions $(-) \rightarrow (-) : Rel\,(\tau, \tau') \times Rel\,(\sigma, \sigma') \rightarrow Rel\,(\tau \rightarrow \sigma, \tau' \rightarrow \sigma')$, $(l_1 : (-), \ldots, l_n : (-)) : Rel\,(\tau_1, \tau_1') \times \cdots \times Rel\,(\tau_n, \tau_n') \rightarrow Rel((l_1 : \tau_1, \ldots, l_n : \tau_n), (l_1 : \tau_1', \ldots, l_n : \tau_n'))$, *and* $(-)list : Rel\,(\tau, \tau') \rightarrow Rel\,(\tau\ list, \tau'\ list)$ *as follows.*

$$r \rightarrow r' = \{(F, F') \mid (FA, F'A') \in r' \text{ for all } (A, A') \in r\}$$

$$(l_1 : r_1, \ldots, l_n : r_n) = \{((l_1 = M_1, \ldots, l_n = M_n), (l_1 = M_1', \ldots, l_n = M_n')) \mid$$
$$(M_1, M_1') \in r_1, \ldots, (M_n, M_n') \in r_n\}^{\top\top}$$

$$(r)list = \nu\gamma.\Phi_r(\gamma)$$

In the definition of $(r)list$, $\Phi_r : Rel\,(\tau\ list, \tau'\ list) \rightarrow Rel\,(\tau\ list, \tau'\ list)$ is a function such that $\Phi_r(\gamma) = (\{(\mathbf{nil}_\tau, \mathbf{nil}_{\tau'})\} \cup \{(H, T), (H', T') \mid (H, H') \in r \text{ and } (T, T') \in \gamma\})^{\top\top}$, and $\nu\gamma.F(\gamma)$ denotes a greatest fixpoint of a function F.

The action for list types is well-defined (*i. e.*, the greatest fixpoint exists), since $\top\top$-closure is monotone and hence so is Φ_r.

Definition 4. *The syntactic logical relations $\{\Delta_\tau\}_\tau$ are inductively defined on the structure of type τ by the following construction rules:*

$$\Delta_{\tau \rightarrow \tau'} = \Delta_\tau \rightarrow \Delta_{\tau'}$$
$$\Delta_{(l_1 : \tau_1, \ldots, l_n : \tau_n)} = (l_1 : \Delta_{\tau_1}, \ldots, l_n : \Delta_{\tau_n})$$
$$\Delta_{\tau\ list} = (\Delta_\tau)list$$

The above definition is carefully designed so that each relation Δ_τ is $\top\top$-closed at any type index τ. This, together with the following theorem, justifies the application of the fixpoint operator to expression M of any type $\tau \rightarrow \tau$.

Theorem 1. *[14, Theorem 3.11] Let $r \in Rel\,(\tau, \tau')$ be a $\top\top$-closed relation, and let $F \in Exp\,(\tau \rightarrow \tau)$ and $F' \in Exp\,(\tau' \rightarrow \tau')$ be expressions such that $(FA, F'A') \in r$ for all $(A, A') \in r$. Then, it holds that $(\mathbf{fix}\ F, \mathbf{fix}\ F') \in r$.*

This theorem also gives a justification on the relational reasoning of programs that involve circular let expressions and recursive function definitions, which are a derivative of fixpoint operator.

3.3 Equational Congruence Relation and Its Properties

Let us write $M \sim M'$ to indicate that closed expressions M and M' are related w.r.t. the above logical relations, i. e., $(M, M') \in \Delta_\tau$ for some type τ. The next proposition holds for $\sim$-relation.

Proposition 1. [14, Proposition 4.6] *The relation $\sim$ is a congruence relation, i. e., it is reflexive, symmetric, transitive, and substitutive (i. e., if $fv(M) = \{x_1, \ldots, x_n\}$ and $M_1 \sim M_1', \ldots, M_n \sim M_n'$ then $M[x_1/M_1, \ldots, x_n/M_n] \sim M[x_1/M_1', \ldots, x_n/M_n'])$.*

In order for this proposition to hold for the present language, we need to verify some properties concerning record types. The formal proof is given in a separate paper [12].

In addition to the congruence, several equational properties on $\sim$ can be derived from the so-called *Kleene equivalence*.

Proposition 2. [14, Corollary 3.15] *Let $M, M' \in Exp(\tau)$. M and M' are called* Kleene equivalent, *written $M =_{kl} M'$, if it holds that $\forall V.(M \Downarrow V \Leftrightarrow M' \Downarrow V)$.*

Kleene equivalence respects $\sim$ relation, that is, if $M_1 =_{kl} M_1'$, $M_2 =_{kl} M_2'$, and $M_1 \sim M_2$, then $M_1' \sim M_2'$.

$$(\lambda x : \tau.M)N \sim M[x/N] \qquad \text{fix } F \sim F(\text{fix } F) \qquad \text{let } \mathcal{B} \text{ in } M \sim M\theta$$

$$\#l \, (l = M, \ldots) \sim M \qquad \text{case nil}_\tau \text{ of nil} \Rightarrow M_1, h :: t \Rightarrow M_2 \sim M_1$$

$$\text{case } H :: T \text{ of nil} \Rightarrow M_1, h :: t \Rightarrow M_2 \sim M_2[h/H, t/T]$$

$$\text{let } \mathcal{B} \text{ in } M \sim M\theta \qquad \text{let } \mathcal{B} \text{ in } (\lambda x : \tau.M) \sim \lambda x : \tau.(\text{let } \mathcal{B} \text{ in } M)$$

$$\text{let } \mathcal{B} \text{ in } MN \sim (\text{let } \mathcal{B} \text{ in } M)(\text{let } \mathcal{B} \text{ in } N) \qquad \text{let } \mathcal{B} \text{ in } \#l \, M \sim \#l \, (\text{let } \mathcal{B} \text{ in } M)$$

$$\text{let } \mathcal{B} \text{ in } (l_1 = N_1, \ldots, l_m = N_m) \sim (l_1 = \text{let } \mathcal{B} \text{ in } N_1, \ldots, l_m = \text{let } \mathcal{B} \text{ in } N_m)$$

$$\text{let } \mathcal{B} \text{ in } H :: T \sim (\text{let } \mathcal{B} \text{ in } H) :: (\text{let } \mathcal{B} \text{ in } T)$$

where $\mathcal{B} = x_1 = M_1; \cdots ; x_n = M_n$ and $\theta = [x_1/\text{let } \mathcal{B} \text{ in } M_1, \ldots, x_n/\text{let } \mathcal{B} \text{ in } M_n]$.

Fig. 7. Derived $\sim$-relations

Figure 7 gives several $\sim$-relations derived from Kleene equivalence; $\sim$-relation is stable up to β-reductions, fixpoint unfoldings (and therefore circular let unfoldings), and destructor/constructor pair cancellations (for records and lists); Also, the circular let constructs commute with several other constructs.

Since it has been proved that the syntactic logical relations coincide with the observational equivalence [14, Theorem 4.15], we hitherto reason about observational equivalence of expressions up to $\sim$, using the laws in Proposition 1 and Figure 7.

We notice that, though the present formalization considers list types only, the above results are easily generalized to any polynomial data types, e. g. binary trees. The relations for any polynomial data types can be defined as a greatest fixpoint of a monotone function, likewise in the definition for list types.

4   The Correctness of Higher-Order Removal Transformation

Throughout this section, we write U, X, Y to denote disjoint sets of variables $U = \{u_1, \ldots, u_m\}$, $X = \{x_0, \ldots, x_n\}$, and $Y = \{y_0, \ldots, y_n\}$ $(m, n \geq 0)$. We also fix a list type τ *list*.

We omitted some of the technical details and proofs from this section, due to the page limitation. They can be found in a separate paper [12].

4.1   Definition of the Higher-Order Removal Transformation

Our transformation algorithm applies to a class of expressions of the following form (which is referred to as I, in the rest of the paper):

$$
\begin{aligned}
I \;=\;\; &\lambda x_0 : (hk : \tau \; list) \to (hj : \tau \; list). \\
&\textbf{let } x_n = f_n \; (\lambda y_n : (hk : \tau \; list).(hj = N_n)) \textbf{ in} \\
&\qquad \cdots \\
&\textbf{let } x_1 = f_1 \; (\lambda y_1 : (hk : \tau \; list).(hj = N_1)) \textbf{ in} \\
&\lambda y_0 : (lk : \tau \; list).(lj = N_0)
\end{aligned}
\tag{2}
$$

where $f_1, \ldots, f_n$ $(n \geq 0)$ are variables of type $((hk : \tau \; list) \to (hj : \tau \; list)) \to ((lk : \tau \; list) \to (lj : \tau \; list))$, and $N_1, \ldots, N_n$ are expressions that belong to a particular syntactic class. That is, $N_0 \in Exp_i^{\Gamma_U, X, Y, \pi}((lj : \tau \; list))$ and $N_i \in Exp_i^{\Gamma_U, X, Y, \pi}(hj : \tau \; list)$ $(1 \leq i \leq n)$, where the syntactic class designated by $Exp_i^{\Gamma_U, X, Y, \pi}(\tau)$ is defined as below.

Definition 5. *Let* $\Gamma_U = u_1 : \tau_1, \ldots, u_m : \tau_m$ *be a type environment and* π *be a function* $\{0, \ldots, n\} \mapsto \{0, \ldots, n\}$ *such that* $i > \pi(i)$ *for every* $i = 1, \ldots, n$.

We define a family of set of expressions $\{Exp_i^{\Gamma_U, X, Y, \pi}(\tau)\}_{0 \leq i \leq n}$ *inductively by the following rules (for brevity, we write* $Exp_i(\tau)$ *for* $Exp_i^{\Gamma_U, X, Y, \pi}(\tau)$):

h1 $M \in Exp_i(\tau)$ *whenever* $\Gamma_U \vdash M : \tau$,
h2 $H :: T \in Exp_i(\tau \; list)$ *if* $H \in Exp_i(\tau)$ *and* $T \in Exp_i(\tau \; list)$,
h3 $\#lk \; y_0 \in Exp_0(\tau \; list)$,
h4 $\#hk \; y_i \in Exp_i(\tau \; list)$ $(1 \leq i \leq n)$,
h5 $\#hj \; (x_0 \; (hk = M_{x_0})) \in Exp_{\pi(0)}(\tau \; list)$, *where* $fv(M_{x_0}) \cap X = \emptyset$ *and* $M_{x_0} \in Exp_{\pi(0)}(\tau \; list)$, *and*
h6 $\#lj \; (x_i \; (lk = M_{x_i})) \in Exp_{\pi(i)}(\tau \; list)$ $(1 \leq i \leq n)$, *where* $fv(M_{x_i}) \cap X = \emptyset$ *and* $M_{x_i} \in Exp_{\pi(i)}(\tau \; list)$.

For each i, $Exp_i(\tau)$ represents a syntactically restricted set of expressions of type τ, which possibly contains free variables from U, X, and Y. Each variable $x_i \in X$ has to appear in a function application form (Rules **h5** and **h6**. $\pi(i)$

refers to the index j of expression N_j from which the variable x_i is referenced);
Each variable $y_i \in Y$ must appear with a field selection operator (**h3** and **h4**).
The above expressions can be combined by the list constructor (**h2**).

The expression I is further assumed to meet a *linearity condition*: Each variable $x_i \in X$ occurs once and only once throughout the expressions $N_0, \ldots, N_n$.
(The side condition $i > \pi(i)$ $(i = 1, \ldots, n)$ guarantees that every use of x_i is preceded by the corresponding let binding **let** $x_i = \cdots$.) We intendedly excluded λ-abstractions from the above rules, in order to prevent each unique occurrence of a variable x_i from being applied to the argument that receives varying denotations. This may happen when a λ-expression that abstracts the x_i's application is used in different contexts, e. g., $(\lambda f. \cdots f\, A_1 \cdots f\, A_2)(\lambda z.\#lj\,(x_i(lk = \#lk\,z)))$.

$$
\begin{aligned}
&\mathcal{W}[\![\lambda x_0 : (hk : \tau\ list) \to (hj : \tau\ list). \\
&\quad \textbf{let } x_n = f_n\ (\lambda y_n : (hk : \tau\ list).(hj = N_n))\ \textbf{in} \\
&\qquad \cdots \\
&\quad \textbf{let } x_1 = f_1\ (\lambda y_1 : (hk : \tau\ list).(hj = N_1))\ \textbf{in }\ \lambda y_0 : (lk : \tau\ list).(lj = N_0)]\!] \\
&= \lambda x_0 : (hj : \tau\ list, lk : \tau\ list). \\
&\quad \textbf{let } x_n = f'_n\ (hj = \mathcal{W}'[\![N_n]\!], lk = \mathcal{W}'[\![M_{x_n}]\!]); \\
&\qquad \cdots \\
&\qquad x_1 = f'_1\ (hj = \mathcal{W}'[\![N_1]\!], lk = \mathcal{W}'[\![M_{x_1}]\!]) \\
&\quad \textbf{in }\ (lj = \mathcal{W}'[\![N_0]\!], hk = \mathcal{W}'[\![M_{x_0}]\!])
\end{aligned}
$$

where $\mathcal{W}'$ is the transformation defined in Figure 3, and variables $f_1, \ldots, f_n$ and $f'_1, \ldots, f'_n$ denote recursive function calls to a substructure of the input data type.

Fig. 8. The higher-order removal transformation

The formal definition of the higher-order removal transformation $\mathcal{W}$ is given in Figure 8. It is easy to verify that this transformation is type correct.

Theorem 2. *Let us write* $\sigma_1 = ((hk : \tau\ list) \to (hj : \tau\ list)) \to ((lk : \tau\ list) \to (lj : \tau\ list))$ *and* $\sigma_2 = (hj : \tau\ list, lk : \tau\ list) \to (hk : \tau\ list, lj : \tau\ list)$. *If* $\Gamma_U, f_1 : \sigma_1, \ldots, f_n : \sigma_1 \vdash I : \sigma_1$, *then* $\Gamma_U, f'_1 : \sigma_2, \ldots, f'_n : \sigma_2 \vdash \mathcal{W}[\![I]\!] : \sigma_2$.

4.2   Correctness of Higher-Order Removal Transformation

For the purpose of proving the correctness of the transformation, we reformulate the syntactic logical relations $\{\Delta_\tau\}_\tau$, as we discussed in Section 2. We replace only the relation indexed by $\sigma_1 = ((hk : \tau\ list) \to (hj : \tau\ list)) \to ((lk : \tau\ list) \to (lj : \tau\ list))$ with the relation Θ defined below.

Definition 6. $\Theta \in Rel(((hk : \tau\ list) \to (hj : \tau\ list)) \to ((lk : \tau\ list) \to (lj : \tau\ list)), (hj : \tau\ list, lk : \tau\ list) \to (hk : \tau\ list, lj : \tau\ list))$ *is a relation defined by:*

$(I, J) \in \Theta$ *iff*

(a) $(\#hk\,(J\,(hj = H, lk = L)), \#hk\,(J\,(hj = H', lk = L'))) \in \Delta_{\tau\;list}$ *for all*
$(L, L') \in \Delta_{\tau\;list}$ *and* $H, H' \in Exp\,(\tau\;list),$ *and*

(b) $\left(\begin{array}{c} \#lj\,(J\,(hj = \#hj\,(G'\,(hk = \#hk \\ \#lj\,(I\,G\,(lk = L)), \qquad\qquad (J\,(hj = \Omega_{\tau\;list}, lk = L')))), \\ lk = L')) \end{array} \right) \in \Delta_{\tau\;list}$

for all $(G, G') \in (hk : \Delta_{\tau\;list}) \to (hj : \Delta_{\tau\;list})$ *and* $(L, L') \in \Delta_{\tau\;list}.$

We note that the above modification does retain the original relation Δ_{τ} whenever τ is σ_1-free, *i. e.*, τ is free from occurrences of σ_1. This implies that the observational equivalence of programs of σ_1-free types can be safely reasoned up to $\sim$-relation introduced in Section 3.3. In what follows, we assume τ ranges over the set of σ_1-free types.

We prove that Θ relates the transformation source I and the target $\mathcal{W}[\![I]\!]$.

Proposition 3. *For every expression I of the form (2), it holds that*

$$(I\theta_0, \mathcal{W}[\![I]\!]\theta_0') \in \Theta$$

for any $\theta_0 = [u_1/U_1, \ldots, u_m/U_m, f_1/I_1, \ldots, f_n/I_n]$ *and* $\theta_0' = [u_1/U_1', \ldots, u_m/U_m', f_1'/J_1, \ldots, f_n'/J_n]$ *satisfying* $(U_k, U_k') \in \Delta_{\Gamma_U(u_k)}$ $(1 \leq k \leq m)$ *and* $(I_i, J_i) \in \Theta$ $(1 \leq i \leq n).$

We can prove this proposition basically by induction on the structure of expression, referring to the definition of the relation Θ when we encounter let bound variables. Instead of giving the lengthy proof of this proposition, we explain what are the intentions behind the definition of Θ and how they contribute to establishing the formal proof. (See [12] for the full proof.)

The property (a) of the definition of Θ indicates that the hk value of the record computed by the transformed program $J = \mathcal{W}[\![I]\!]$ depends only on the lk value of the input record and is not affected at all by the input hj value. This means the expression H' for the hj field can be substituted with any other well-typed expression. This property is crucially exploited in the proof in order to break the circularity introduced by the circular let construct: We can suppress the circular references in the transformed program by virtually replacing certain variable references with expressions that do not cause circularity.

The property (b) implies that the lj value, which carries the final answer computed by the original producer/consumer function pair, of the record computed by a single call to I is obtained by using J twice. Computing an lj value by a call to I with G being the initial accumulating parameter is equal to computing an lj value by first calling J to obtain the hk value from the input lk value L', and then by applying J to the pair of the hj value and the input lk value L', where the hj value is obtained by applying G' (an observationally equivalent copy of G) to the hk value computed by the first call of J. This justifies the transformation on $\#lj\,(x_i\,(lk = M_{x_i}))$ by $\mathcal{W}'$.

The total correctness of the higher-order removal transformations is derived from the Proposition 3. Suppose we are given the following expressions $\mathcal{I}$ and $\mathcal{J}$:

$$\mathcal{I} = \lambda f : \tau\ list \rightarrow ((hk : \tau\ list) \rightarrow (hj : \tau\ list)) \rightarrow ((lk : \tau\ list) \rightarrow (lj : \tau\ list)).$$
$$(\lambda x : \tau\ list.\ \mathbf{case}\ x\ \mathbf{of}\ \mathbf{nil} \Rightarrow I_{\mathbf{nil}}, h :: t \Rightarrow I_{h::t}[f_1/f\ t, \ldots, f_n/f\ t])$$
$$\mathcal{J} = \lambda f' : \tau\ list \rightarrow (hj : \tau\ list, lk : \tau\ list) \rightarrow (hk : \tau\ list, lj : \tau\ list)$$
$$(\lambda x : \tau\ list.\ \mathbf{case}\ x\ \mathbf{of}\ \mathbf{nil} \Rightarrow \mathcal{W}[\![I_{\mathbf{nil}}]\!],$$
$$h :: t \Rightarrow \mathcal{W}[\![I_{h::t}]\!][f_1'/f'\ t, \ldots, f_n'/f'\ t])$$

where

- $I_{\mathbf{nil}}$ is an expression of the form (2) with $U = \emptyset$ and $n = 0$ (i. e., no let-bindings), and
- $I_{h::t}$ is an expression of the form (2) with $U = \{h\}$.

In the above, $f\ t$ and $f'\ t$ express recursive calls to the list substructure t. This is generalized to any polynomial data types: E. g., for the case of binary trees instead of lists, the variables f_i's (f_i''s, resp.) would be substituted with either $f\ t$ or $f\ t'$ ($f'\ t$ or $f'\ t'$, resp.), where t and t' are variables representing the two different subtrees of a tree node.

In the present paper, we only prove the observational equivalence between $\mathbf{fix}\,\mathcal{I}$ and $\mathbf{fix}\,\mathcal{J}$, when they are applied to lists of finite length. We notice that the observationally equivalent pairs of expressions of lists of length less than n is characterized by the relation $\Phi_{\Delta_\tau}^n(\emptyset)$, where Φ_r is the function given in Definition 3. This characterization can be also generalized to any polynomial data types, with an appropriate definition of Φ_r.

Theorem 3 (Correctness of transformation). *Let $\mathcal{I}$ and $\mathcal{J}$ be expressions defined as above. It holds that*

$$((\mathbf{fix}\,\mathcal{I})L, (\mathbf{fix}\,\mathcal{J})L') \in \Theta \qquad \text{for every } (L, L') \in \Phi_{\Delta_\tau}^n(\emptyset)\ (n \geq 1).$$

We prove this theorem by induction on the length of lists, where the induction principle is justified by the following lemma.

Lemma 1. *If $(L, L') \in \Phi_{\Delta_\tau}^n(\emptyset)\ (n \geq 1)$, then the following properties hold.*

(i) $L \Downarrow \mathbf{nil}_\tau$ iff $L' \Downarrow \mathbf{nil}_\tau$, and
(ii) if $L \Downarrow H :: T$ then $L' \Downarrow H' :: T'$ for some H' and T' such that $(H, H') \in \Delta_\tau$ and $(T, T') \in \Phi_{\Delta_\tau}^{n-1}(\emptyset)$.
(iii) if $L' \Downarrow H' :: T'$ then $L \Downarrow H :: T$ for some H and T such that $(H, H') \in \Delta_\tau$ and $(T, T') \in \Phi_{\Delta_\tau}^{n-1}(\emptyset)$.

In particular when $n = 1$, if $L \Downarrow V$ and $L' \Downarrow V'$ then $V = V' = \mathbf{nil}_\tau$.

Proof. (of Theorem 3) Proof is by induction on n. If both L and L' diverge, then so do both $(\mathbf{fix}\,\mathcal{I})L$ and $(\mathbf{fix}\,\mathcal{J})L'$. Hence $((\mathbf{fix}\,\mathcal{I})L, (\mathbf{fix}\,\mathcal{J})L') \in \Theta$.

Now we suppose that both L and L' do not diverge. (Non-divergence of one implies that of the other, by lemma 1.) If $n = 1$, then by lemma 1 both L and L' evaluate to $\mathbf{nil}_\tau$. Then we have $(\mathbf{fix}\,\mathcal{I})L \sim I_{\mathbf{nil}}$ and $(\mathbf{fix}\,\mathcal{J})L' \sim \mathcal{W}[\![I_{\mathbf{nil}}]\!]$. Since $(I_{\mathbf{nil}}, \mathcal{W}[\![I_{\mathbf{nil}}]\!]) \in \Theta$ by proposition 3, it follows that $(\mathbf{fix}\,\mathcal{I})L \sim (\mathbf{fix}\,\mathcal{J})L'$.

Suppose $n > 1$. By lemma 1, we have $L \Downarrow H :: T$ and $L' \Downarrow H' :: T'$ for some $(H, H') \in \Delta_\tau$ and $(T, T') \in \Phi_{\Delta_\tau}^{n-1}(\emptyset)$. Then, it holds that

$$(\mathbf{fix}\,\mathcal{I})L \sim I_{h::t}[h/H, f_1/(\mathbf{fix}\,\mathcal{I})T, \ldots, f_n/(\mathbf{fix}\,\mathcal{I})T] \quad \text{and}$$
$$(\mathbf{fix}\,\mathcal{J})L' \sim \mathcal{W}[\![I_{h::t}]\!][h/H', f_1'/(\mathbf{fix}\,\mathcal{J})T', \ldots, f_n'/(\mathbf{fix}\,\mathcal{J})T'].$$

Since $((\mathbf{fix}\,\mathcal{I})T, (\mathbf{fix}\,\mathcal{J})T') \in \Theta$, by induction hypothesis and proposition 3, we have $(\mathbf{fix}\,\mathcal{I})L \sim (\mathbf{fix}\,\mathcal{J})L'$. □

Now we show the total correctness of the higher-order removal transformation using the results in this section. Suppose we are given a recursive definition of function $\mathbf{fix}\,\mathcal{I}$, a function G of type $((hk : \tau\;list) \to (hj : \tau\;list)) \to ((lk : \tau\;list) \to (lj : \tau\;list))$, and lists L and L' of type $\tau\;list$ where L is of finite length. Then, it follows from the property (b) of the relation Θ (Definition 6) that

$$\#lj\,((\mathbf{fix}\,\mathcal{I})\,L\,G\,(lk = L'))$$

is observationally equivalent to

$$\#lj\,((\mathbf{fix}\,\mathcal{J})(hj = \#hj\,(G\,((\mathbf{fix}\,\mathcal{J})(hj = \Omega, lk = L'))), lk = L')).$$

Since the two expressions are related up to $\Delta_{\tau\;list}$, they can substitute for each other under any context.

Applying this to the example in Figure 1 (with regarding $\mathbf{fix}\,\mathcal{I}$ as the recursive function definition of `rf` and also $\mathbf{fix}\,\mathcal{J}$ as that of `rf'`), we obtain

```
revflat x = #lj (rf' x (hj=#hj ((\y -> (hj=#hk y))
                       (rf' x (hj=Ω, lk=[])), lk=[])))
```

The final result in Figure 1(c) follows by a simple calculation. Note that the diverging expression Ω can be substituted with any well-typed list expression, since it does not affect the computation at all (as indicated by the property (a) of Definition 6).

5   Conclusion

We have shown that the framework of syntactic logical relations developed by Pitts [14] can be a powerful device in proving the correctness of program transformation. This was evidenced through a concrete example, a higher-order removal transformation, which is a part of a deforestation algorithm for functions with accumulating parameters.

We believe that the general proof method presented in this paper can apply to the correctness proof of other program transformations. In fact, the two auxiliary transformation processes between the shortcut fusion and the higher-order removal transformation (in Figure 2) can be justified by a similar proof technique. This fact constitutes the complete correctness proof for the deforestation algorithm that was proposed by the author [11], together with a few more technical elaborations on the syntactic condition to be met by the two transformations. The author would like to report this result in a near future.

In Theorem 3, we assumed that the inputs are only finite lists (or finite polynomial data structures, in general). We leave the proof for the inputs of infinite lists open, as we were not able to prove the relation Θ is $\top\top$-closed: If Θ were proved $\top\top$-closed, we would have it as a direct consequence of Theorem 1 without resorting to the induction principle on finite lists. This implies that the $\top\top$-closedness is a key to the question if the composition algorithms for functions with accumulating parameters are valid for infinite data structures. It is folklore in the community of macro tree transducers and attribute grammars that the answer is positive, but there is no formal justification.

The open problem mentioned above raises some technical issues which may be worth investigating. For the relation Θ to be $\top\top$-closed, so must be both of the two properties in Definition 6. Though each property has its own difficulty in showing its $\top\top$-closedness, that of the property (b) seems more fundamental: The problem amounts to showing the $\top\top$-closedness of a relation $\Delta_{\tau\to\tau}$, which is defined for some particular type τ by $\Delta_{\tau\to\tau} = \{(F, F') \mid (FA, F'(F'A')) \in \Delta_\tau$ for all $(A, A') \in \Delta_\tau\}$. An attempt to show this $\top\top$-closedness would be stuck, since we only consider contexts with a single hole whereas in this case we need to reason about contexts with two different holes. It would be interesting to investigate a refinement of Pitts' proof technique for proving (or disproving) this $\top\top$-closedness.

Acknowledgment. I thank Jacques Garrigue for his valuable comments on a draft version. I am also grateful to anonymous referees whose suggestions are helpful for improving the presentation.

References

1. W.-N. Chin. Safe fusion of functional expressions II: Further improvements. *Journal of Functional Programming*, 4(4):515–555, 1994.
2. J. Engelfriet and H. Vogler. Macro tree transducers. *Journal of Computer and System Sciences*, 31:71–146, 1985.
3. H. Ganzinger and R. Giegerich. Attribute coupled grammars. In *Proceedings of the ACM SIGPLAN '84 Symposium on Compiler Construction*, volume 19(6) of *SIGPLAN Notices*, pages 157–170, June 1984.
4. A. Gill, J. Launchbury, and S. Peyton Jones. A short cut to deforestation. In *Proceedings of the Conference on Functional Programming Languages and Computer Architecture*, pages 223–232. ACM Press, June 1993.
5. The Haskell home page. `http://www.haskell.org/`.

6. P. Johann. Short cut fusion: Proved and improved. In *Semantics, Applications, and Implementation of Program Generation, Second International Workshop: SAIG 2001*, volume 2196 of *Lecture Notes in Computer Science*, pages 47–71. Springer Verlag, 2001.
7. X. Leroy. Unboxed objects and polymorphic typing. In *Conference record of the 19th Annual ACM SIGPLAN-SIGACT Symposium on Principles of Programming*, pages 177–188. ACM Press, 1992.
8. Y. Minamide and J. Garrigue. On the runtime complexity of type-directed unboxing. In *Proceedings of the third ACM SIGPLAN International Conference on Functional Programming (ICFP98)*, pages 1–12. ACM Press, 1998.
9. J. C. Mitchell. *Foundations for Programming Languages*. Foundation of Computing Series. The MIT Press, 1996.
10. L. R. Nielsen. A denotational investigation of defunctionalization. Technical Report RS-00-47, BRICS, 2000.
11. S. Nishimura. Deforesting in accumulating parameters via type-directed transformations. In *Informal proceedings of Asian Workshop on Programming Languages and Systems 2002 (APLAS'02)*, 2002. electronic version: http://www.math.kyoto-u.ac.jp/~susumu/papers/aplas02.ps.gz.
12. S. Nishimura. Correctness of a higher-order removal transformation through a relational reasoning. Technical Report Kyoto-Math 2003-06, Kyoto University, 2003. electronic version: http://www.math.kyoto-u.ac.jp/~susumu/papers/aplas03-long.ps.gz.
13. O. Ore. Galois connexions. *Transactions of American Mathematical Society*, 55:493–513, 1944.
14. A. Pitts. Parametric polymorphism and operational equivalence. *Mathematical Structures in Computer Science*, 10(3):321–359, 2000.
15. J. C. Reynolds. Definitional interpreters for higher-order programming languages. *Higher-Order Symbolic Computation*, 11(4):363–397, 1998. Reprint from the Proc. of the 25th ACM National Conference (1972).
16. T. Sheard and L. Fegaras. A fold for all seasons. In *Proceedings 6th ACM SIGPLAN/SIGARCH Int. Conf. on Functional Programming Languages and Computer Architecture, FPCA'93, Copenhagen, Denmark, 9–11 June 1993*, pages 233–242. ACM Press, 1993.
17. A. Takano and E. Meijer. Shortcut deforestation in calculational form. In *Proceedings of the 7th International Conference on Functional Programming Languages and Computer Architecture*, pages 306–313, La Jolla, California, June 1995. ACM SIGPLAN/SIGARCH and IFIP WG2.8, ACM Press.
18. J. Voigtländer. Using circular programs to deforest in accumulating parameters. In K. Asai and W.-N. Chin, editors, *ASIAN Symposium on Partial Evaluation and Semantics-Based Program Manipulation*, pages 126–137. ACM Press, 2002.
19. P. Wadler. Deforestation: transforming programs to eliminate trees. *Theoretical Computer Science*, 73(2):231–248, June 1990.

Extensional Polymorphism by Flow Graph Dispatching

Jun Furuse

INRIA Rocquencourt / LexiFi

Abstract. We propose a new method of run-time instance resolution of generic values of extensional polymorphism, a framework for non-parametric polymorphism in the ML language. For each generic value instance, we dispatch a directed integer graph called *flow*. A flow graph encodes typing witness of a generic value instance, and provides an instruction of selecting one of the overloaded definitions to be evaluated. Thanks to its simple structure, instance resolution is performed much more efficiently than the classical run-time type dispatching.

1 Introduction

Non-parametric polymorphism provides values with type dependent semantics to the ML language. This provides new interesting features which are (of course) impossible in the classical parametric polymorphism: overloading, dynamic typing, generic programming and so on. Such *generic values* are often provided by *run-time type dispatching* mechanism in strongly typed polymorphic functional languages, since under the ML first-order polymorphism, types of values at execution are not always as same as those found at typing, but are just their instances. Therefore, instances of generic values must be passed type contexts for their type dependent semantics in order to resolve their genericity at run-time. This is usually achieved by putting extra abstractions of type arguments called *run-time types* at compilation.

Extensional polymorphism[3] is one of such frameworks for generic values. It provides a simple but powerful way of definition of overloaded values. Selection of overloaded definitions for execution is done by pattern-matching of dispatched run-time types. From the past studies of extensional polymorphism, we have found this run-time type dispatching has a serious semantic problem: sometimes there is no way of calling an overloaded definition, even though it is the only one applicable case in the type context.

In this paper, we propose another new run-time overload resolution for generic values: *flow graph dispatching*. Flow graphs are integer directed graphs which encode typing witness of generic instances efficiently. Not only solving the semantic problem of run-time type dispatching, this simple structure of flow graphs greatly improves the efficiency of overload resolution.

In the rest of this section, we first introduce extensional polymorphism (section 1.1), then we explain the problem of run-time type dispatching in section

A. Ohori (Ed.): APLAS 2003, LNCS 2895, pp. 376–393, 2003.

1.2 and proposes a brief solution using flows in section 1.3. Section 2 and 3 formally introduce the syntax, types and flow graphs of our language. Section 4 and 5 present typing rules and a compilation algorithm using flow dispatching. Related works are compared to our system in section 7.

1.1   Extensional Polymorphism

In extensional polymorphism, an overloaded value is defined by a *generic binding*, a new style of let binding. The following is a definition of overloaded add function for integer and float additions:

```
let add = generic
  | int → int → int ⇒       add_int
  | float → float → float ⇒ add_float
in
    add 1.2 3.4 (* returns 4.6 *)
```

The body of a generic binding consists of a list of *type cases*, type scheme indexed expressions, which are overloaded to one identifier. As let keyword indicates, generic values are treated as ML values as well as the classical parametric polymorphic values. In this sense, extensional polymorphism provides a first-order overloading. For example, it is possible to define generic values in a local context:

```
let double x =
    let add = generic
      | int → int → int ⇒ add_int
      | float → float → float ⇒ add_float
    in
    add x x
in
    double 1, double 1.2 (* returns 2, 2.4 *)
```

This function double is also *generic*: it is a polymorphic function and inherits the genericity of add.

The ML type algebra is extended so that a type can be assigned to each generic value. For example, add's type Σ_{add}:

$$\Sigma_{add} = [\![\text{int} \rightarrow \text{int} \rightarrow \text{int}; \text{float} \rightarrow \text{float} \rightarrow \text{float}]\!]$$

indicates that it is overloaded on two types. The type of double,

$$\Sigma_{double} = \forall \alpha.\{\alpha \rightarrow \alpha \rightarrow \alpha < \Sigma_{add}\} \Rightarrow \alpha \rightarrow \alpha$$

tells that it works like a polymorphic function of type $\forall \alpha.\alpha \rightarrow \alpha$, but the additional part $\{\alpha \rightarrow \alpha \rightarrow \alpha < \Sigma_{add}\}$ called a *constraint* informs that its instantiation to a type $\tau \rightarrow \tau$ is restricted only when $\tau \rightarrow \tau \rightarrow \tau$ is a valid instance of Σ_{add}.

Generic definitions can be recursive to provide recursion on types:

```
let rec print = generic
  | ∀α.α list → unit ⇒
      function [] → () | x::xs → print x; print xs
  | int → unit ⇒ print_int
in ...
```

This **print** recursive generic function recursively calls itself under different types, so that it can print integer lists of any depth.

Type cases are *ordered*: selection of type cases can be controlled by the order of type cases, just like pattern matching. Instances can be overlapped even when one of them is *not* strictly more specific than the others:

```
let get_first_integer = generic
  | ∀α.int * α → int ⇒ fun (x,y) → x
  | ∀α.α * int → int ⇒ fun (x,y) → y
  | ∀αβ.α * β → int ⇒ raise (Failure "there is no int")
```

The above example of **get_first_int** returns not the second, but the first integer when it is instantiated to int * int → int, since the first matched case is prior to the others in multiple matches.

1.2   Run-Time Type Dispatching

In the run-time type dispatching approach, the semantics of overloaded values are given indirectly. A source program is firstly program-transformed (compiled) to a non-generic expression, then the semantics of the source is given as those of compiled expression under the normal ML semantic system. Since the classical ML evaluation is typeless, the type contexts required for generic values must be converted to ML values called *run-time types* and *dispatched* to the compiled generic values by type abstractions and applications. A generic bindings use these dispatched run-time types to select one of overloaded type cases to be executed using pattern matching:

```
let double ty x =
  let add ty = match ty with
                 | int ⇒ add_int | float ⇒ add_float in
  add ty x x
in double int 1, double float 1.2
```

These type abstractions and applications are the same as those of the second order typed lambda calculus, but in general these type operations are attached only where they are necessary for overloaded instance resolutions for efficiency.

Run-time type dispatching is also used for other type-dependent features. *Dynamic typing* is such an application. The compilation of primitives of *dynamic values* [1,8], **dyn** and **coerce** are obtained for free, if we have the type dispatching mechanism:

```
let dyn_comp ty v = (ty,v)
let coerce_comp ty (ty',v) =
  if is_compatible ty ty' then v else raise Error
```

Thus run-time type dispatching for extensional polymorphism looks promising, but it has a serious semantic problem: type case selection by pattern matching cannot support the overlapped instances *correctly*. In some cases, there is no way of selecting correct overlapped instance, even though it is the only one applicable case. To demonstrate this problem we first extend the `print` definition:

```
let rec print = generic
  | ∀α.α list → unit ⇒
       function [] → () | x::xs → print x; print xs
  | int → unit ⇒ print_int
  | ∀α.α list → unit ⇒
          fun _ → print_string "unprintable list"
in ...
```

`print` has a new default case for printing lists: it is intended to print out a message `"unprintable list"` when `print` is applied to a non-integer list, `print ["hello"; "world"]` for example. However, the compilation obtained by type dispatching does not follow this specification:

```
let rec print ty =
  match ty with
  | ty' list ⇒
       function [] → ()
                 | x::xs → print ty' x; print (ty' list) x
  | int ⇒ print_int
  | ty' list ⇒ fun _ → print_string "unprintable list"

print (string list) ["hello"; "world"]
```

The source code `print ["hello"; "world"]` dispatches a run-time type `string list`. The program execution is trapped in the first case, since it matches with the first case, even though the first case cannot print string lists and only the new default case can provide well-defined semantics for `string list → unit`. This ruins the advantage of unique overlapping definitions which are provided by the pattern-match like type case selection semantics of extensional polymorphism.

We *could* add a pattern guard for a workaround this problem, excluding the cases which match at first glance but actually provid no semantics. In this example, the first match case would be rewritten as follows:

```
  | ty' list when print : ty' → unit ⇒ function ...
```

The predicate `print : ty' → unit` in the pattern guard checks whether `print` is well-defined over the type `ty' → unit`. If it is not, for instance when `ty'` is `string`, this case is skipped and the other cases are pattern-matched. This workaround using pattern guards provides better support of overlapped instances, but it cannot be used in practice, since its overhead is too huge. For example printing an integer list with depth n of type `int list`^{n} → `unit`, the pattern guard must prove `print : int list`^{i} → `unit` for all $0 \leq i < n$ *independently*, whose complexity is $O(n^2)$. Therefore, as far as we use the type dispatching, only the realistic solution to this problem is just abandon the overlapping instances. This is not what we want.

1.3 Flow Dispatching

Flow graph dispatching is a solution to the problem of run-time type dispatching. A flow graph (or simply a flow) is a directed integer graph. Each node corresponds with a call of a generic value, and its integer index indicates which type case should be selected and executed among the overloaded definitions. Sub-flows connected to a node are dispatched to the internal generic instances inside the selected type case.

Since flows are complete information of case selections calculated *statically*, selection of overloaded instances at run-time can be ultimately simplified to just array accesses by integer indices obtained from flows. Freed from conditional flow control like type pattern matching at run-time, it is now possible to adopt complex case selection tactics which is more than pattern matching and therefore is performed too costly at run-time: we can avoid the semantic problem of overlap instances of type dispatching by searching execution flows with back-tracking at compile time.

Type cases of a generic value are simply compiled to an array of case definition compilations. For example, plus is converted as follows:

let add = ⟦(fun f → add_int); (fun f → add_float)⟧ in
add.(2) ② 1.2 3.4

Flow graphs instead of run-time types are dispatched to the compilations of generic instances. The index number of the root node is used to select one of overloaded definition compilations. The expression ② graphically represents a flow graph with one node. Its index number 2 is used to select the second element of plus. The postfix operator .(*i*) is an access to the *i*-th member of an array and we suppose the array index starts from 1. The flow graph is also passed to the selected function in the array. In the definition of a derived generic value, sub-flows are dispatched to the internal generic instances. The following is the compilation of double example:

let double = fun f x → add.($index($f.k_{add})) f.k_{add} in
double ①$\xrightarrow{k_{add}}$① 1, double ①$\xrightarrow{k_{add}}$② 1.2

where f.k_{add} is an access to a sub-flow connected by the edge labeled k_{add}. The right node ② connected to the left one is passed to the compilation of plus. $index($f.k_{add})$ returns the index of the right node.

A recursive generic binding is translated to a recursive array definition:

```
let rec print = ⟦(fun f → function
                  | [] → ()
                  | x::xs → print.(index(f.k_p1)) f.k_p1 x;
                            print.(index(f.k_p2)) f.k_p2 xs);
                 (fun f → print_int);
                 (fun f _ → print_string "unprintable list")⟧
```

The compilation of the first type case calls `print` twice recursively. For each, one of sub-flows of `f` is dispatched. Uses of `print` are compiled as follows:

$$
\begin{array}{lll}
\texttt{print 1} & \leadsto & \texttt{print.(2)}\ \textcircled{2}\ \texttt{1} \\
\texttt{print [1;2;3]} & \leadsto & \texttt{print.(1)}\ f_{p1}\ \texttt{[1;2;3]} \\
\texttt{print [[1];[2;3]]} & \leadsto & \texttt{print.(1)}\ f_{p2}\ \texttt{[[1];[2;3]]}
\end{array}
$$

where

$$
f_{p1} = \textcircled{1} \xrightarrow{k_{p2}} \textcircled{2} \quad \text{(with loop } k_{p1}\text{ on } \textcircled{1})
\qquad\qquad
f_{p2} = \textcircled{1} \xrightarrow{k_{p2}} \textcircled{1} \xrightarrow{k_{p2}} \textcircled{2} \quad \text{(with loops } k_{p1}\text{)}
$$

The flows f_{p1} and f_{p2} have loops labelled k_{p1}, which is used to dispatch the passed flow f_{pi} itself to the first internal instance of `print`. This reflects that the type of this instance is equal to the one of whole type case.

The "overlap instance trap" problem of run-time type dispatching disappears using flows:

$$
\texttt{print ["hello"; "world"]} \quad \leadsto \quad \texttt{print.(3)}\ \textcircled{3}\ \texttt{["hello"; "world"]}
$$

Using flows, execution of the above expression is never caught into the first case, but calls the last case as we have intended.

Note that none of the flow operations in these compilations creates new flow graphs. All are deconstruction of flows which will be reduced to simple block references and array accesses and there is no additional memory allocation. This greatly improves the speed of overloaded instance resolution compared to the type dispatching, where new type values can be constructed at run-time.

2   Types and Language

2.1   Types

In order to express non-parametricity of generic values, we first extend the types (figure 1). We use the same type expressions (mono-types) τ as usual, which consist of type variables α and constructors $\mathtt{t}(\tau_1, \ldots, \tau_n)$. Our first extension to the types is the attachment of a set of *constraints* K to a type scheme. In a type scheme, a type expression τ and a constraint set $K = \{k_1, \ldots, k_m\}$ can be abstracted by a set of type variables $\{\alpha_1, \ldots, \alpha_n\}$. These constraints restrict type instantiation of possibly all the quantified type variables at the same time. We introduce a new class of types, *extensional types* Σ for overloaded generic values. Extensional types consist of type arrays and two recursive constructions. A *type array* is a list of type schemes $[\![\sigma_1; \ldots; \sigma_n]\!]$, which lists intuitively the type indices of overloaded definitions. We also introduce μ-abstractions $\mu x.\Sigma$ and μ-variables x. They express the types of recursively defined overloadings, as fixed points of μ-expansions. Recursive variables only appear inside constraints and must be abstracted by some μ-abstractions. A constraint k has the form of type instance predicate $\tau < \Sigma$. They are also used as labels of flow records later.

In our type system, any value, whether generic or not, is associated with an extensional type in type environment. For example, the polymorphic identity

$$
\begin{array}{lll}
\text{Type expressions} & \tau ::= \alpha & \text{Type variables} \\
& \quad | \;\; \mathbf{t}(\tau, \ldots, \tau) & \text{Type constructors} \\
\text{Types schemes} & \sigma ::= \forall \alpha_1 \ldots \alpha_n . K \Rightarrow \tau & \\
\text{Extensional types} & \Sigma ::= [\![\sigma_1; \ldots; \sigma_n]\!] \text{ where } n > 0 & \text{Type arrays} \\
& \quad | \;\; x & \text{Recursive variables} \\
& \quad | \;\; \mu x . \Sigma & \text{Recursive types} \\
\text{Constraint set} & K ::= \{k_1, \ldots, k_n\} \text{ where } n > 0 & \\
\text{Constraints} & k ::= \tau < \Sigma &
\end{array}
$$

Fig. 1. Types

function has an extensional type $[\![\forall \alpha . \emptyset \Rightarrow \alpha \to \alpha]\!]$. To keep visual backward compatibility, we introduce the following abbreviations of extensional types:

$$
\forall \alpha_1 \ldots \alpha_n . \emptyset \Rightarrow \tau \equiv \forall \alpha_1 \ldots \alpha_n . \tau, \qquad \forall . \emptyset \Rightarrow \tau \equiv \tau, \qquad [\![\sigma]\!] \equiv \sigma
$$

These abbreviations also correspond with our compilation strategy: usually a value of type $[\![\sigma_1, \ldots, \sigma_n]\!]$ is compiled to an array of compilations of type $\sigma_1, \ldots, \sigma_n$, but if the extensional type is a singleton array $[\![\sigma]\!]$, the compilation never creates an array, but equal to the compilation of a value of type scheme σ. A value of type scheme $\forall \alpha 1 \ldots \alpha_n . K \Rightarrow \tau$ is usually compiled to a function which takes a flow graph whose record labels are K and returns a value of type τ. But if K is an empty set, this flow abstraction will be omitted.

Here are the extensional types of add, double and print, Σ_{add}, Σ_{double} and Σ_{print} respectively. We will often use them in the rest of this paper:

$$
\begin{aligned}
\Sigma_{\mathrm{add}} &= [\![\mathtt{int} \to \mathtt{int} \to \mathtt{int}; \; \mathtt{float} \to \mathtt{float} \to \mathtt{float}]\!] \\
\Sigma_{\mathrm{double}} &= [\![\forall \alpha . \{k_{\mathrm{add}}\} \Rightarrow \alpha \to \alpha]\!] \text{ where } k_{\mathrm{add}} = \alpha \to \alpha \to \alpha < \Sigma_{\mathrm{add}} \\
\Sigma_{\mathrm{print}} &= \mu x . [\![\forall \alpha . \{k_{\mathrm{p1}}; k_{\mathrm{p2}}\} \Rightarrow \alpha \; \mathtt{list} \to \mathtt{unit} \\
&\qquad\qquad | \; \mathtt{int} \to \mathtt{unit} \; | \; \forall \alpha . \alpha \; \mathtt{list} \to \mathtt{unit}]\!] \\
&\text{where } k_{\mathrm{p1}} = \alpha \; \mathtt{list} \to \mathtt{unit} < x \\
&\qquad\quad k_{p2} = \alpha \to \mathtt{unit} < x
\end{aligned}
$$

For example, an instance of the extensional type Σ_{print} is an instance of either one of type schemes in its array. The instantiation of the first type scheme is one of the parametric scheme $\forall \alpha . \alpha \; \mathtt{list} \to \mathtt{unit}$, but restricted by the constraints k_{p1} and k_{p2}: if $\tau \; \mathtt{list} \to \mathtt{unit}$ is an instance of this scheme, then $\tau \; \mathtt{list} \to \mathtt{unit}$ and $\tau \to \mathtt{unit}$ must be valid instances of x, which represents the extensional type Σ_{print}, the fixed point of this μ-abstracted type array. Thanks to this recursion, all the types of the form $\mathtt{int} \; \mathtt{list} \; \ldots \; \mathtt{list} \to \mathtt{unit}$ is valid instances of Σ_{print}.

The tools for types are extended for extensional types (figure 2). $FV(\Sigma)$ returns the set of free type variables of extensional type Σ. Type substitutions $S(\Sigma)$ affect free type variables inside constraint sets, too. The definition of α-conversions of extensional types is omitted, but is trivially obtained from these definitions. Applying α-conversions when necessary, we suppose all the quantified

$$FV(\alpha) = \{\alpha\}$$
$$FV(\mathbf{t}(\tau_1,\ldots,\tau_n)) = \cup_{i=1}^{n} FV(\tau_i)$$
$$FV(\forall \alpha_1 \ldots \alpha_n.K \Rightarrow \tau) = (FV(\tau) \cup FV(K)) \setminus \{\alpha_1,\ldots,\alpha_n\}$$
$$FV([\![\sigma_1;\ldots;\sigma_n]\!]) = \cup_{i=1}^{n} FV(\sigma_i)$$
$$FV(x) = \emptyset$$
$$FV(\mu x.\Sigma) = FV(\Sigma)$$
$$FV(\{\tau_1 < \Sigma_1, \ \ldots, \ \tau_n < \Sigma_n\}) = \cup_{i=1}^{n}(FV(\tau_i) \cup FV(\Sigma_i))$$

$$S(\forall \alpha_1 \ldots \alpha_n.K \Rightarrow \tau) = \forall \alpha_1 \ldots \alpha_n.S(K) \Rightarrow S(\tau)$$
$$\text{when } \{\alpha_1,\ldots,\alpha_n\} \cap Dom(S) = \emptyset$$
$$S([\![\sigma_1;\ldots;\sigma_n]\!]) = [\![S(\sigma_1);\ldots;S(\sigma_n)]\!]$$
$$S(x) = x$$
$$S(\mu x.\Sigma) = \mu x.S(\Sigma)$$
$$S(\{k_1, \ \ldots, \ k_n\}) = \{S(k_1), \ \ldots, \ S(k_n)\}$$
$$S(\tau < \Sigma) = S(\tau) < S(\Sigma)$$

Fig. 2. Definitions of free type variables and type substitution

variables have different names and there would be no abstract type variable name collisions. The semantics of recursive extensional types are defined as the fixed points of μ-expansions. The μ-expansion Σ' of recursive type $\mu x.\Sigma$ is defined as:

$$\Sigma' \equiv \{x \mapsto \mu x.\Sigma\}(\Sigma)$$

Σ' is obtained from Σ by substitution all the free occurrences x by $\mu x.\Sigma$. We often write $\mu x.\Sigma \xrightarrow{\mu} \Sigma'$ in order to express Σ' is a μ-expansion of $\mu x.\Sigma$. We also suppose automatic α-conversions of μ-abstractions and therefore no collisions of μ-variables.

2.2 Syntax

Our language is an extension of ML with generic binding expressions.

$$e ::= c_\sigma \mid \mathbf{x} \mid \mathbf{fun}\ \mathbf{x} \to e \mid e\ e \mid \mathbf{let}\ (\mathbf{rec})\ \mathbf{x} = e\ \mathbf{in}\ e$$
$$\mid\ \mathbf{let}\ (\mathbf{rec})\ \mathbf{x} = \mathbf{generic}\ \sigma_1 \Rightarrow e_1 \mid \ldots \mid \sigma_n \Rightarrow e_n\ \mathbf{in}\ e$$

Using a generic binding, an ordered list of type-indexed *type case* expressions $\sigma_i \Rightarrow e_i$ can be overloaded to an identifier once and for all: they are not extensible. Explicit annotations of the type indices σ_i are required for type reconstruction of polymorphic recursion of recursive generic bindings. (Type reconstruction is not covered in this paper.) We do not consider overloaded constants in this paper, but it can be easily introduced.

3 Flow Graphs

This section formally redefines generic flow graphs. A *flow graph* f is an integer directed graph whose definition is given in figure 3. Each flow node (n, r) consists

$$\text{Flow graph } f ::= (n, r) \quad \text{Flow nodes}$$
$$| \quad x \qquad \text{Loop variables}$$
$$| \quad \mu x.f \quad \mu\text{-abstractions}$$

$$\text{Flow record } r \equiv \{k_1 = f_1; \; \ldots; \; k_n = f_n\}^\sigma$$

$$\overline{(n, \{k_1 = f_1, \; \ldots, \; k_n = f_n\})} = \ldots$$

$$\overline{\mu x.f} = \quad \begin{matrix} x \\ \overline{f} \end{matrix} \quad : \text{ put a label } x \text{ to the root node of } \overline{f}$$

$$\overline{x} = \quad \longrightarrow \begin{matrix} x \\ n \end{matrix} \quad : \text{ creation of a loop to the node labelled } x$$

Fig. 3. Flow graphs and their graphical representation

of its index number n and a set of edges to other nodes r. A set of edges r is called a *flow record*, since edges in r are labelled by different constraints k_i. As extensional types, flows also have recursive constructions, *flow abstraction* $\mu x.f$ and *flow variable* x. They introduce loops to flow graphs.

Elements of flow nodes are accessed by the following functions:

$$index(n, r) = n \qquad (n, \{k_1 = f_1; \; \ldots; \; k_n = f_n\}^\sigma).k_i^\sigma = f_i$$

Function *index* return the index number of the node. Postfix operator $(.k_i^\sigma)$ provides an access to the node f_i connected at the edge k_i. The type scheme annotation σ to flow records and access operators explicitly tells the set of labels in records. Since the flow record is monomorphic (though its labels contain type variables), a flow record can be represented as an integer array in the actual implementation, sorting the record labels in some lexicographical order, which is given by the annotation σ. Since this type scheme annotation does not play other important roles in this paper, they will be often omitted.

Flow loops are formally defined by the μ-expansions of flow graphs $\mu x.f$, substituting the free occurrences of x in f by $\mu x.f$ itself:

$$\mu x.f \overset{\mu}{\leadsto} \{x \mapsto \mu x.f\} f$$

For example,

$$\text{let } f_{ex} = \mu x.(1, \{k_1 = (2, \{k_3 = x\}); \; k_2 = (3, \{\})), \text{ then}$$
$$f_{ex} \overset{\mu}{\leadsto} (1, \{k_1 = (2, \{k_3 = f_{ex}\}); \; k_2 = (3, \{\}))$$

All the loop variables must be μ-abstracted for the well-definedness of the flows as graphs. We suppose that access functions μ-expand graphs automatically when needed. We continue the above example:

$$f_{ex}.k_1 = (1, \{k_1 = (2, \{k_3 = f_{ex}\}); \; k_2 = (3, \{\})\}).k_1$$
$$= (2, \{k_3 = f_{ex}\})$$

Flows are also represented in a graphical form for easier understanding. The definition of the graphical representation of a flow, $\overline{f}$, is given in figure 3. The leftmost graphical node is called the *root* and corresponds with the out-most flow graph expression. A μ-abstraction $\mu x.f$ attaches a label x to the root of $\overline{f}$ and an internal occurrence of x in f creates a loop to the root of $\overline{f}$. The previous example is expressed graphically as follows:

4   Type Instantiation

We now define the semantics of the extensional types, their type instances in figure 4. The judgement takes the form $M \vdash \tau < \Sigma \rightsquigarrow f$, where M is a finite

$$\text{(inst-scheme)} \quad \frac{\begin{array}{c} \sigma = \forall \alpha_1 \ldots \alpha_n.\{\tau_1 < \Sigma_1, \ \ldots, \ \tau_m < \Sigma_m\} \Rightarrow \tau' \\ \exists S, \ Dom(S) = \{\alpha_1, \ldots, \alpha_n\}, \ S(\tau') = \tau, \\ \forall 1 \leq i \leq m, \ M \vdash S(\tau_i) < S(\Sigma_i) \rightsquigarrow f_i \end{array}}{M \vdash \tau < \sigma \rightsquigarrow \{(\tau_1 < \Sigma_1) = f_1, \ldots, (\tau_m < \Sigma_m) = f_m\}^\sigma}$$

$$\text{(inst-array)} \quad \frac{\exists 1 \leq i \leq n, \ \forall 1 \leq j < i, \ M \vdash \tau \not< \sigma_j, \ M \vdash \tau < \sigma_i \rightsquigarrow r}{M \vdash \tau < [\![\sigma_1; \ldots; \sigma_n]\!] \rightsquigarrow (i, r)}$$

$$\text{(inst-mu)} \quad \frac{(\tau < \mu x.\Sigma) \notin Dom(M) \quad \mu x.\Sigma \xrightarrow{\mu} \Sigma' \quad M \cup \{(\tau < \mu x.\Sigma) \mapsto x\} \vdash \tau < \Sigma' \rightsquigarrow f}{M \vdash \tau < \mu x.\Sigma \rightsquigarrow \mu x.f}$$

$$\text{(inst-cache)} \quad \frac{M(\tau < \mu x.\Sigma) = x}{M \vdash \tau < \mu x.\Sigma \rightsquigarrow x}$$

Fig. 4. Type instantiation and checking algorithm, with flow creation

mapping called a *cache* from constraints to flow loop variables. The instantiation rules also specify the calculation of flows f corresponding to the type instantiations. like Haskell's typing provides its program transformation algorithm.

An instance τ of a type scheme $\sigma = \forall \alpha_1 \ldots \alpha_n.K \Rightarrow \tau'$ is an instance of a parametric polymorphic type $\forall \alpha_1 \ldots \alpha_n.\tau'$, but it must meet the constraint conditions of $K = \{\tau_1 < \Sigma_1, \ldots, \tau_m < \Sigma_m\}$: all the $\tau_i < \Sigma_i$ must be a valid type instantiation under the substitution S, where $S(\tau') = \tau$. Thus type instantiation of all the abstracted type variables $\alpha_1, \ldots, \alpha_n$ can be restricted by the constraints K. An instantiation of a scheme creates a flow record $\{(\tau_1 < \Sigma_1) = f_1, \ldots, (\tau_m < \Sigma_m) = f_m\}^\sigma$ which gathers the flows of instantiations of constraints under S.

An instance of a type array $[\![\sigma_1; \ldots; \sigma_n]\!]$ is defined as an instance of one of σ_i. The corresponding flow is a graph (i, r) where i is the first index number such that $M \vdash \tau < \sigma_i \leadsto r$. This rule corresponds with the type case selection at evaluation: the first match is always used in case of multiple matches. Note that selection is performed using back-tracking, which was practically impossible in run-time type dispatching.

Instantiation of μ-abstracted types $\mu x.\Sigma$ is separated into two parts. If $\tau < \mu x.\Sigma$ is not registered in the cache M, its instance τ is defined in (inst-mu) as an instance of the μ-expansion of $\mu x.\Sigma$ under an extended cache $M \cup \{(\tau < \mu x.\Sigma) \mapsto x\}$, where x is a fresh loop variable. The corresponding flow is μ-abstracted and provides a reference for flow loops. If $\tau < \mu x.\Sigma$ is bound in M, we use (inst-cache) instead, which immediately grants the instantiation and creates a flow loop to $M(\tau < \mu x.\Sigma)$, whose entry node should be installed by (inst-mu).

We say a type expression τ is an instance of an extensional type Σ, when $\emptyset \vdash \tau < \Sigma \leadsto f$ for some flow f, and write $\tau < \Sigma \leadsto f$ or simply $\tau < \Sigma$. For instance, the following is one of valid instantiations of $\Sigma_{\texttt{print}}$:

$$\texttt{int list} \to \texttt{unit} < \Sigma_{\texttt{print}} \quad \leadsto \quad f_{p1} = \quad \text{}$$

An instance checking algorithm of the predicate $\tau < \Sigma$ is directly obtained applying the rules in figure 4 from down to up. Unfortunately, however, this algorithm never terminates for some predicates. More generally speaking, it is not a problem of the checking algorithm: in [3], the predicate $\tau < \Sigma$ itself is proved undecidable under unrestricted uses of (inst-mu). To assure the termination of typing, we have to introduce some restriction to the type system so that recursive extensional types can never μ-expands themselves infinitely in type instantiation. There seem to be two solutions:

- The algorithm is *dynamically* restricted by the maximum numbers of calls of (inst-mu), as in the typing of Hugs extension[7].
- *Static* restriction of the set of extensional types permitted in the system to admissible ones whose type instance check can always terminate in finite steps. If we follow the same admissible condition as proposed in [3], all the extensional type examples in this paper are admissible.

For better interface, we should have the both dynamic and static restrictions in conjunction: the dynamic restriction should be only applied to the non-admissible types.

5   Typing and Compilation

Finally, typing rules are defined in figure 5. Typing rules also specify a program transformation algorithm which provides compilation using flow dispatching. A typing judgment is written as $\Gamma, \mathcal{K} \vdash e : \tau \leadsto e'$. *Typing environment Γ is* a mapping from identifiers to extensional types. *Constraint environment* $\mathcal{K}$ is a finite mapping from constraints to pieces of code which provide accesses to flows, in the case that the flows are not statically computable. The constraints $(\tau < \Sigma)$ in the domain of $\mathcal{K}$ relax type instantiation of generic values of extensional type Σ to τ. Expression e' is the *compilation* of e where generic definitions and their instances are translated into more primitive expressions. We first look the instantiation rules then generalizations. The definitions of the tool functions in the rules are in figure 6.

5.1   Instantiation Rules

We have two rules to instantiate variables, *full* and *partial*.

An instance $\mathbf{x} : \tau$ is called *full instance* under the environment $\Gamma, \mathcal{K}$, when its typing is done by (f-inst). The instance type τ must be a valid instance of extensional type Σ of $\mathbf{x}$ bound in Γ. If we let f be the flow such that $\tau < \Sigma \rightsquigarrow f$, the instance is transformed to an expression $dispatch(\mathbf{x}, \Sigma, f)$. It dispatches the flow f to $\mathbf{x}$ whose extensional type is Σ. The dispatching is different depending on the form of Σ.

If Σ is a type array $[\![\sigma_1, \ldots, \sigma_n]\!]$ with more than one element, the overloaded definitions of $\mathbf{x}$ are compiled to an array of compilations of type $\sigma_1, \ldots, \sigma_n$. We call one of such compilations stored at the position of the index number of the flow, then dispatches the flow itself to the selected compilation. For example, a full instance `print` in the expression `print [1;2;3]` is transformed to the following:

$$dispatch(\texttt{print}, \Sigma_{\texttt{print}}, f_{p1}) = \texttt{print}.(index(f_{p1}))\ f_{p1}$$
$$= \texttt{print}.(1)\ f_{p1}$$

As above, for efficiency, flow accesses are partially evaluated if possible in the compilation phase.

If $\Sigma = [\![\sigma]\!] \equiv \sigma$, the selection of overloaded definitions is not required. If σ has a non-empty set of constraints, we directly dispatch the flow to the variable. For instance, the compilation of `double` in the expression `double 1.2` is as follows:

$$dispatch(\texttt{double}, \Sigma_{\texttt{double}}, (1, \{k_{\texttt{add}} = (2, \{\})\})) = \texttt{double}\ \{k_{\texttt{add}} = (2, \{\})\}$$

If $\Sigma = [\![\sigma]\!]$ and σ's constraint set is empty, σ is a parametric classical type scheme. In such a case, we do not need dispatch the flow. $dispatch(\mathbf{x}, \forall \alpha_1 \ldots \alpha_n.\tau, e)$ simply returns $\mathbf{x}$ itself. Thus the classical non-generic programs are compiled to themselves without any overhead.

Flow dispatch to a value of a μ-abstracted extensional type $\mu x.\Sigma$ is as same as one of Σ.

Another kind of variable instantiation, partial instance by (p-inst) has more relaxed type instantiation than (f-inst): its instance type τ needs not be an exact instance of the corresponding extensional type Σ, but can be an instance of $\lceil \Sigma \rceil$, the *approximation* of Σ. The approximation $\lceil \Sigma \rceil$ is the least general classical ML type scheme which is more general than Σ. In the definition in figure 6,

$$(\text{const}) \ \frac{\tau < \sigma}{\Gamma, \mathcal{K} \vdash c_\sigma : \tau \ \rightsquigarrow \ c_\sigma}$$

$$(\text{f-inst}) \ \frac{\Gamma(\mathbf{x}) = \Sigma \quad \tau < \Sigma \ \rightsquigarrow \ f}{\Gamma, \mathcal{K} \vdash \mathbf{x} : \tau \ \rightsquigarrow \ dispatch(\mathbf{x}, \Sigma, f)}$$

$$(\text{p-inst}) \ \frac{\Gamma(\mathbf{x}) = \Sigma \quad \tau < \lceil \Sigma \rceil \quad (\tau < \Sigma) \in Dom(\mathcal{K})}{\Gamma, \mathcal{K} \vdash \mathbf{x} : \tau \ \rightsquigarrow \ dispatch(\mathbf{x}, \Sigma, \mathcal{K}(\tau < \Sigma))}$$

$$(\text{fun}) \ \frac{\Gamma\{\mathbf{x} : \tau'\}, \mathcal{K} \vdash e : \tau \ \rightsquigarrow \ e'}{\Gamma, \mathcal{K} \vdash \mathbf{fun} \ \mathbf{x} \to e : \tau' \to \tau \ \rightsquigarrow \ \mathbf{fun} \ \mathbf{x} \to e'}$$

$$(\text{app}) \ \frac{\Gamma, \mathcal{K} \vdash e_1 : \tau_1 \to \tau_2 \ \rightsquigarrow \ e_1' \quad \Gamma, \mathcal{K} \vdash e_2 : \tau_1 \ \rightsquigarrow \ e_2'}{\Gamma, \mathcal{K} \vdash e_1 \ e_2 : \tau_2 \ \rightsquigarrow \ e_1' \ e_2'}$$

$$(\text{let}) \ \frac{\begin{array}{c} \Gamma, \mathcal{K} + \mathcal{K}_1 \vdash e_1 : \tau_1 \ \rightsquigarrow \ e_1' \quad \sigma_1, \mathcal{K}_1 = Gen(\Gamma, \mathcal{K} + \mathcal{K}_1, e_1, \tau_1) \\ \text{for some fresh variable } \mathbf{f}, \forall k \in Dom(\mathcal{K}_1), \mathcal{K}_1(k) = \mathbf{f}^{\sigma_1}.k^{\sigma_1} \\ \Gamma\{\mathbf{x} : \sigma_1\}, \mathcal{K} \vdash e : \tau \ \rightsquigarrow \ e' \end{array}}{\Gamma, \mathcal{K} \vdash \mathbf{let} \ \mathbf{x} = e_1 \ \mathbf{in} \ e : \tau \ \rightsquigarrow \ \mathbf{let} \ \mathbf{x} = flowabs(\mathbf{f}, \mathcal{K}_1, e_1') \ \mathbf{in} \ e'}$$

$$(\text{letrec}) \ \frac{\begin{array}{c} \Gamma\{\mathbf{x} : \tau_1\}, \mathcal{K} + \mathcal{K}_1 \vdash e_1 : \tau_1 \ \rightsquigarrow \ e_1' \quad \sigma_1, \mathcal{K}_1 = Gen(\Gamma, \mathcal{K} + \mathcal{K}_1, e_1, \tau_1) \\ \text{for some fresh variable } \mathbf{f}, \forall k \in Dom(\mathcal{K}_1), \mathcal{K}_1(k) = \mathbf{f}^{\sigma_1}.k^{\sigma_1} \\ \Gamma\{\mathbf{x} : \sigma\}, \mathcal{K} \vdash e : \tau \ \rightsquigarrow \ e' \end{array}}{\Gamma, \mathcal{K} \vdash \mathbf{let} \ \mathbf{x} = e_1 \ \mathbf{in} \ e_2 : \tau_2 \ \rightsquigarrow \ \mathbf{let} \ \mathbf{rec} \ \mathbf{x} = flowabs(\mathbf{f}, \mathcal{K}_1, e_1') \ \mathbf{in} \ e'}$$

$$(\text{generic}) \ \frac{\forall 1 \le i \le n, \left\{ \begin{array}{l} \Gamma, \mathcal{K} + \mathcal{K}_i \vdash e_i : \tau_i \ \rightsquigarrow \ e_i' \\ \sigma_i, \mathcal{K}_i = Gen(\Gamma, \mathcal{K} + \mathcal{K}_i, e_i, \tau_i) \\ \text{for some fresh variable } \mathbf{f}, \forall k \in Dom(\mathcal{K}_i), \mathcal{K}_i(k) = \mathbf{f}^{\sigma_i}.k^{\sigma_i} \end{array} \right. \quad \begin{array}{c} \Sigma = \llbracket \sigma_1; \ldots; \sigma_n \rrbracket \quad \Gamma\{\mathbf{x} : \Sigma\}, \mathcal{K} \vdash e : \tau \ \rightsquigarrow \ e' \end{array}}{\begin{array}{c} \Gamma, \mathcal{K} \vdash \mathbf{let} \ \mathbf{x} = \mathbf{generic} \ \lceil \sigma_1 \rceil \Rightarrow e_1 \ | \ \ldots \ | \ \lceil \sigma_n \rceil \Rightarrow e_n \ \mathbf{in} \ e : \tau \\ \rightsquigarrow \ \mathbf{let} \ \mathbf{x} = \llbracket (\mathbf{fun} \ \mathbf{f} \to e_1'); \ \ldots; \ (\mathbf{fun} \ \mathbf{f} \to e_n') \rrbracket \ \mathbf{in} \ e' \end{array}}$$

$$(\text{genericrec}) \ \frac{\forall 1 \le i \le n, \left\{ \begin{array}{l} \Gamma\{\mathbf{x} : \mu x.\Sigma\}, \mathcal{K} + \mathcal{K}_i \vdash e_i : \tau_i \ \rightsquigarrow \ e_i' \\ \sigma_i, \mathcal{K}_i = Gen(\Gamma, \mathcal{K} + \mathcal{K}_i, e_i, \tau_i) \\ \text{for some fresh variable } \mathbf{f}, \forall k \in Dom(\mathcal{K}_i), \mathcal{K}_i(k) = \mathbf{f}^{\sigma_i}.k^{\sigma_i} \end{array} \right. \quad \begin{array}{c} \mu x.\Sigma \xrightarrow{\mu} \llbracket \sigma_1; \ldots; \sigma_n \rrbracket \quad \Gamma\{\mathbf{x} : \mu x.\Sigma\}, \mathcal{K} \vdash e : \tau \ \rightsquigarrow \ e' \end{array}}{\begin{array}{c} \Gamma, \mathcal{K} \vdash \mathbf{let} \ \mathbf{rec} \ \mathbf{x} = \mathbf{generic} \ \lceil \sigma_1 \rceil \Rightarrow e_1 \ | \ \ldots \ | \ \lceil \sigma_n \rceil \Rightarrow e_n \ \mathbf{in} \ e : \tau \\ \rightsquigarrow \ \mathbf{let} \ \mathbf{rec} \ \mathbf{x} = \llbracket (\mathbf{fun} \ \mathbf{f} \to e_1'); \ \ldots; \ (\mathbf{fun} \ \mathbf{f} \to e_n') \rrbracket \ \mathbf{in} \ e' \end{array}}$$

Fig. 5. Typing rules with program transformation

$$\lceil[\![\sigma_1;\dots;\sigma_n]\!]\rceil = antiunif(\lceil\sigma_1\rceil,\dots,\lceil\sigma_n\rceil)$$
$$\lceil\mu x.\Sigma\rceil = \lceil\Sigma\rceil$$
$$\lceil x\rceil = undefined$$
$$\lceil\forall\alpha_1\dots\alpha_n.K \Rightarrow \tau\rceil = \forall\alpha_1\dots\alpha_n.\tau$$

$$dispatch(\mathbf{x}, \forall\alpha_1\dots\alpha_n.\tau, e) = \mathbf{x}$$
$$dispatch(\mathbf{x}, \forall\alpha_1\dots\alpha_n.K \Rightarrow \tau, e) = \mathbf{x}\ e \quad \text{when } K \neq \emptyset$$
$$dispatch(\mathbf{x}, [\![\sigma_1;\dots;\sigma_n]\!], e) = \mathbf{x}.(index(e))\ e \quad \text{when } n > 1$$
$$dispatch(\mathbf{x}, \mu x.\Sigma, e) = dispatch(\mathbf{x}, \Sigma, e)$$

$$flowabs(\mathbf{f}, \emptyset, e) = e$$
$$flowabs(\mathbf{f}, \mathcal{K}, e) = \mathbf{fun\ f} \to e \quad \text{when } \mathcal{K} \neq \emptyset$$

$Gen(\Gamma, \mathcal{K}, e, \tau) =$
  if e is not expansive,
  $\quad \forall\alpha_1\dots\alpha_n.K \Rightarrow \tau,\ \mathcal{K}_{|K}$
  where
  $\quad\{\alpha_1,\dots,\alpha_n\} = FV(\tau) \setminus FV(\Gamma)$
  $\quad K = \{k \in Dom(\mathcal{K}) \mid FV(\{k\}) \cap \{\alpha_i\}_{i=1}^n \neq \emptyset\}$
  otherwise $\tau,\ \emptyset$

Fig. 6. Tool functions for typing and compilation

$antiunif(\sigma_1,\dots,\sigma_n)$ is a function which returns the least general anti-unifier of parametric type schemes $\sigma_1,\dots,\sigma_n$. For example,

$$\lceil\Sigma_{\text{add}}\rceil = \forall\alpha.\alpha \to \alpha \to \alpha \qquad\qquad \lceil\Sigma_{\text{print}}\rceil = \forall\alpha.\alpha \to \mathtt{unit}$$

This relaxed instantiation rule of a value of Σ to τ is only applicable when the constraint $(\tau < \Sigma)$ is bound in the constraint environment $\mathcal{K}$. On the other hand, constraints in the domain of $\mathcal{K}$ must be somehow generalized outside of the typing judgement, that is, the actual type instance checks for the partial instances are postponed to the instantiation of some outer full instances whose definitions use them.

The flow dispatching to a partial instance is not statically known. It must be supplied from the outside via flow diapatching mechanism. Such dispatched flows are stored in the evaluation environment and the constraint environment $\mathcal{K}$ tells how to retrieve such a flow: the flow for a partial instance of Σ to τ is obtained as $\mathcal{K}(\tau < \Sigma)$. Let's consider the typing of $\mathtt{print} : \tau$ under the following conditions:

$$\Gamma(\mathtt{print}) = \Sigma_{\text{print}} \qquad \mathcal{K}(\tau < \Sigma_{\text{print}}) = \mathbf{f}.(\tau < \Sigma_{\text{print}}) \qquad \tau \not< \Sigma_{\text{print}}$$

Since τ is not an instance of Σ_{print}, this instance $\mathtt{print} : \tau$ cannot be a full instance. Since $\mathcal{K}$ contains a binding of $\tau < \Sigma_{\text{print}}$, the expression can be typed by (p-inst):

$$\Gamma, \mathcal{K} \vdash \mathtt{print} : \tau \rightsquigarrow\ dispatch(\mathtt{print}, \Sigma_{\text{print}}, \mathcal{K}(\tau < \Sigma_{\text{print}}))$$
$$= dispatch(\mathtt{print}, \Sigma_{\text{print}}, \mathbf{f}.(\tau < \Sigma_{\text{print}}))$$
$$= \mathtt{print}.(index(\mathbf{f}.(\tau < \Sigma_{\text{print}})))\ \mathbf{f}.(\tau < \Sigma_{\text{print}})$$

5.2   Generalization Rules

Constraints in the bindings of constraint environment can be generalized and integrated into type schemes at type generalization Gen in figure 6. Gen is based on the type generalization in the value polymorphism[12]. It takes an additional argument of a constraint environment $\mathcal{K}$. We filter the domain of $\mathcal{K}$ and gathers all the constraints K which relate with one of abstracted type variables α_i, and attach them as constraints of the generalized type scheme. The function Gen also returns a restriction of the environment $\mathcal{K}$ to K, $\mathcal{K}_{|K}$, which is used in the generalization rules.

The definition clause e_1 of the let expression is typed under an extended constraint environment $\mathcal{K} + \mathcal{K}_1$. The domain of newly added $\mathcal{K}_1$ must be equal to the constraints of generalized type σ_1. This means that for all the partial instances $x : \tau$ of Σ in e_1 generalized by this rule, the constraint $(\tau < \Sigma)$ must appear in both σ_1 and in the domain of $\mathcal{K}_1$. In the compilation of the let binding, the compilation e_1' of e_1 is flow-abstracted as $flowabs(f, \mathcal{K}_1, e_1')$. When the set of generalized constraints is not empty, $flowabs(f, \mathcal{K}, e)$ flow-abstracts e with a fresh variable f. Otherwise, it just returns e without any abstraction. The flows required for the internal partial instances are stored as sub-flows of f. The mapping $\mathcal{K}_1$ is responsible to prepare the appropriate codes to access these sub-flows required in (p-inst). Recall the definition of double as an example:

```
let double = fun x → add x x in ...
```

Typing of the instance add and definition expression are as follows:

$$\Gamma, \mathcal{K} + \{k_{add} \mapsto f.k_{add}\} \vdash add : \alpha \to \alpha \to \alpha \rightsquigarrow add.(index(f.k_{add}))\ f$$
$$Gen(\Gamma, \mathcal{K} + \{k_{add} \mapsto f.k_{add}\}, fun\ x \to add\ x\ x, \alpha \to \alpha) =$$
$$\forall \alpha.\{k_{add}\} \Rightarrow \alpha \to \alpha, \{k_{add} \mapsto f.k_{add}\}$$

From these, the definition of double is compiled to

```
let double = fun f x → add.(index(f.k_add)) f.k_add
```

The recursive version of this rule (letrec) does the almost same thing.

In the rules for generic bindings, overloaded definitions are typed and generalized in the same way as (let). The extensional type of the overloaded identifier $\Sigma = [\![\sigma_1; \ldots \sigma_n]\!]$ is a collection of the type schemes σ_i of these definitions. The body of the binding e is typed under the extended type environment $\Gamma\{x : \Sigma\}$. The compilations of the overloaded definitions are flow-abstracted and packed into an array. The compilation of add in section 1.3 is done in this way.

We have the almost same typing and compilation also in (genericrec), the rule for recursive generic bindings. Differently from its non recursive counterpart, the variable x is bound also in the typing of overloaded definitions, with an extensional type $\mu x.\Sigma$. Unlike normal recursive let, x is polymorphic even inside the definitions. The correction of type schemes from the overloaded definitions must be equal to the μ-expansion of $\mu x.\Sigma$. The compilations of the overloaded definitions are translated to an array of flow-abstracted expressions, which may contain recursive references to the array itself. Now the definition of print is formally compiled as in section 1.3.

6   Possible Extensions

Our typing and compilation have focused on overloading resolutions and ignored
a genericity such as dynamic typing, which requires real type information. For
such features, flows are not directly usable since they are abstracted too much
and are type free. But this is easily fixed by introducing a new construction of
flow node which carries a run-time type instead of an integer index. For example,
the following definition of function `print_then_dyn` and its instance is compiled
using this extended flows: The instance of `print_then_dyn` is applied to a

```
val print_then_dyn : ∀α.{k₁, k₂} ⇒ α → unit
let print_then_dyn x = print x; dyn x in
print_then_dyn [7;8;9];;
```

```
    let print_then_dyn f x =
      print.(index(f.(k₁))) f.(k₁) x; dyn_comp type(f.(k₂)) x in
```

flow graph with a special terminal node with a run-time type `int list`. This
run-time type is delivered to the compilation of the `dyn` primitive via the flow
dispatching mechanism. Here, *type* is a function to obtain the run-time type
from a flow node.

Overloaded values are not extensible for simplicity in this paper, but flow dispatching method can be also used for systems with extensible separate definable
overloaded values: closed local extension is easily implementable as redefinitions
of the array of the compilations of overloaded definitions. Open global extension
seems to be more difficult, since the types and compilation of overloaded values
and flow dispatching for them are not fully computable until link time, when all
the compilation units are available. It is left as a future work how to manage
these informations in separate module compilation environment.

7   Related Works

In the initial study of extensional polymorphism[3], static detection of type failures of generic instances is not by types, but based on abstract interpretation
of programs. Having these information outside of types, their type schemes are
always fully parametric polymorphic. This prevents better type reconstruction
of generic instances. Our extensional types can be regarded as integration of the
abstraction interpretations in the ML type algebra.

Flow dispatching can be considered as a generalisation of Ohori's index number dispatching for compilation of polymorphic records[10]. Our scheme is more
complex due to the arborescent nature of extensional type information.

The structure of flow graphs have some similarities with the dictionaries
used in Haskell[6]. Since we do not manage overloaded values in groups like type
classes, for good comparison, we should suppose that every type-class contains

only one value defined, like System O[9]. Then, a flow can be regarded as an integer index referring to one of the dictionaries belong to a type-class. An identifier occurrence in a dictionary definition corresponds with an integer index in a flow which refers to the corresponding overloaded definition. Dictionary dispatching requires global access of overloaded instance definitions, therefore local overloadings seem to be impossible. For example, Shields and Peyton Jones[11] proposed ML like first-class modules for Haskell, but class instance declarations must be only in the top-level of module implementations which cannot be applied to module functors to keep this globality of dictionaries. On the other hand, since flows are context-free integer graphs, it is not necessary to force the overloaded definitions globally accessible in extensional polymorphism. Local generic definitions are granted.

Types of the languages using dictionary dispatching, have also similarities with our system. The types in System O are written as $\forall\alpha.\pi_\alpha{\Rightarrow}\sigma$ and type instantiation of α is constrained the set of π_α like ours (though a constraint governs only one type variable in System O). Their constraints contain predicates in the form of o : τ, where overloaded identifier names occur instead of their types. This is possible since their overloading definitions are only allowed in the top-level, therefore their names are globally available. The similar notion to our extensional type arrays does not appear in types, but in typing rules: our type arrays $[\![\sigma_1;\ldots;\sigma_n]\!]$ correspond with the multiple bindings of types σ_i to one overloaded symbol of System O in its typing environment. The μ-abstractions of extensional types can be translated to recursive references to overloaded symbols in typing.

The run-time type dispatching is not only used for achieve simple overloading, but is also used to implement other forms of non-parametric polymorphism. Generic Haskell[5] is such an extension which provides overloading over the basic type constructor primitives such as product, sum and basic constant types. Intensional polymorphism[2] is another extension to this direction, mainly targeted to provide various advanced implementation techniques for polymorphic languages such as tag-free GC and unboxed function arguments. Duggan and Ophel[4] propose kinded parametric overloading, an interesting extension which uses the both dictionary and type dispatching methods. Their system has two kinds of overloaded types, open and closed kinds which correspond with open globally extensible overloading by dictionary dispatching, and closed locally defined overloading by type dispatching. These two different dispatching methods can be unified by the flow dispatching hopefully. In the case that static verification of flow analysis is possible, flow passing is also a good alternative dispatching method for these formalization of non-parametric polymorphism.

8   Conclusion

We have developed a new flow graph dispatching mechanism for evaluation of generic values. A flow is an directed integer graph which encodes an evaluation flow, which instructs generic value instances which overloaded definition should be evaluated. Using flow graphs, we could solve serious semantics and efficiency problem of overloading by run-time type dispatching[1]. Flow dispatching is not specific to extensional polymorphism, it is highly possible to improve other formalizations of non-parametric polymorphism.

References

1. Martín Abadi, Luca Cardelli, Benjamin Pierce, and Didier Rémy. Dynamic typing in polymorphic languages. In *Proceedings of the 1992 workshop on ML and its applications*, 1992.
2. Karl Crary, Stephanie Weirich, and J. Gregory Morrisett. Intensional polymorphism in type-erasure semantics. In *International Conference on Functional Programming*, pages 301–312, 1998.
3. Catherine Dubois, François Rouaix, and Pierre Weis. Extensional polymorphism. In *Proceedings of the 22th ACM Conference on Principles of Programming Languages*, January 1995.
4. Dominic Duggan and John Ophel. Open and closed scopes for constrained genericity. volume 275, pages 215–258, 2002.
5. R. Hinze and J. Jeuring. Generic Haskell: Practice and theory. In *Summer School on Generic Programming*, Lecture Notes in Computer Science. Springer-Verlag, 2002.
6. Paul Hudak, Simon Peyton Jones, and Philip Wadler. Report on the programming language Haskell, version 1.2. Technical report, Yale University, 1992.
7. Mark P. Jones and John C. Peterson. Hugs 98: A functional programming system based on haskell 98 - user manual.
8. Xavier Leroy and Michel Mauny. Dynamics in ML. *Journal of Functional Programming*, 3(4):431–463, 1994.
9. Martin Odersky, Philip Wadler, and Martin Wehr. A second look at overloading. In *Functional Programming Languages and Computer Architecture*, pages 135–146, 1995.
10. Atsushi Ohori. A polymorphic record calculus and its compilation. *ACM Transactions on Programming Languages and Systems*, 17(6):844–895, November 1995.
11. MB Shields and SL Peyton Jones. First class modules for Haskell. In *9th International Conference on Foundations of Object-Oriented Languages (FOOL 9), Portland, Oregon*, pages 28–40, January 2002.
12. Andrew K. Wright. Simple imperative polymorphism. *Lisp and Symbolic Computation*, 8(4):343–355, 1995.

---

[1] An experimental implementation as an extension over O'Caml language is available from `http://pauillac.inria.fr/~furuse/generics/`

Register Allocation Based on a Reference Flow Analysis

Dae-Hwan Kim and Hyuk-Jae Lee

School of Electrical Engineering and Computer Science, P.O.Box #054, Seoul National
University, San 56-1, Shilim-Dong, Kwanak-Gu, Seoul, Korea
dhtail@hanmail.net,
hjlee@ee.snu.ac.kr

Abstract. The graph-coloring approach for register allocation has been widely
used but its formulation is too abstract to generate efficient spill code. Recently,
a new register allocation based on the analysis of variable reference flow was
proposed [13]. This register allocation leads to more efficient spill code (i.e,
reduced spill instructions) than the graph-coloring approach, but requires a large
amount of computation. For the trade-off between the computation amount and
code efficiency, this paper proposes two variations of the register allocation
proposed in [13]. The first register allocation technique reduces computation
time by employing a simplified graph-coloring algorithm for variable register
allocation. The second technique generates more efficient code with aggressive
variable flow analysis demanding a large amount of computation than [13].
Experimental results show that the first allocation reduces the amount of spill
code by 22.2 % and the amount of computation by 20.4 % when compared to
the Briggs' allocator. The second allocator improves the efficiency by 6.2 %
with the increase of the computation by 4.6 times when compared to the register
allocation in [13].

1 Introduction

Register allocation is an important compiler optimization that determines whether a
live range is to be stored in a register or in memory. The goal of register allocation is
to store variables in registers as many as possible so that the number of accesses to
memory can be minimized. Because the reduction of accesses to memory leads to the
decrease of execution time, code size and power consumption, extensive research has
been made to improve the efficiency of register allocation [3]-[16].

Register allocation based on graph-coloring has been the dominant approach since
Chaitin first introduced the idea and Briggs improved it later [3], [4], [5], [6], [7],
[14]. In this approach, the register allocation problem is modeled as the coloring
problem of an interference graph of which each node represents a live range and an
edge represents interference of live ranges. Any adjacent live ranges in the graph
interfere each other for register allocation so that they cannot share the same register.
The main contribution of the graph-coloring approach is its simplicity by abstracting
each live range as a single node of an interference graph. However, the simple
abstraction results in the loss of information about program context and, as a result,
degrades the efficiency of register allocation. This is because an edge in the

A. Ohori (Ed.): APLAS 2003, LNCS 2895, pp. 394–409, 2003.

interference graph only indicates that two live ranges interfere at some part of a program but does not specify where and how much they interfere.

In the standard graph-coloring approach, unallocated variables are spilled everywhere (i.e., allocator inserts a store instruction after every definition and a load instruction before every use). This conservative technique obviously generates more spill code than is necessary, because not all references (definitions and uses) of a spilled variable are interfered by allocated variables. One of the recent improvements is the interference region spilling technique proposed by Bergner [3]. In this technique, the allocator inserts spill code only at places relevant to the interference region (i.e., before uses inside an interference region and after definitions that reach an interference region). Thus, the allocator generates far less spill code compared to graph-coloring approach, because even when it is spilled, the variable can share the register outside the interference region.

A variable is called *partially allocated* when some, but not all, references are allocated. The success of register allocation heavily depends on the efficiency of partial allocation. However, interference region spilling still has limitations for efficient partial allocation because it is based on graph-coloring approach. The first limitation comes from the cost model for partial allocation. The cost in [3] is given as the spilling cost of the interference region. However, this cost model does not consider the amount of interference with the unprocessed variables in the coloring stack. The second limitation is due to the allocation order that does not reflect any program context. Considering that the allocated variables prevent unprocessed interfering variables from sharing the register in the interference region, the order of allocation directly affects the performance of register allocation. In the graph-coloring approach, the allocation order is determined by global spill costs. This order does not consider different register pressure at each statement in a program. In addition to the ordering problem, the third limitation lies in the allocation granularity that is too coarse to result in inefficiency. This is because a single node is used to represent the spill cost of a variable, while partial allocation costs are different for the references of a variable.

To overcome the limitations of the graph-coloring approach, a register allocation based on the analysis of a variable reference flow was proposed [13]. In this approach, the allocation is performed at every reference of a variable in the order of a variable reference flow. The benefits (and costs) of various possible register allocations are estimated by tracing the reference sequences and the register with the maximum benefit is allocated. This approach leads to the generation of more efficient code than the graph-coloring approach, but requires a large amount of computation for the analysis of variable reference flow.

This paper proposes two new register allocations that are variations of the technique proposed [13]. The register allocation in [13] consists of two steps, the variable allocation followed by the scratch allocation. The first register allocation proposed in the paper employs the graph-coloring algorithm for variable allocation while using the same technique as in [13] for scratch allocation. The amount of computation is reduced because the graph-coloring approach requires significantly less analysis than the variable allocation in [13]. This reduction is significant because the analysis for variable allocation requires significantly greater computation than that for scratch allocation. The second register allocation employs more aggressive analysis to generate more efficient code with larger computation time than the variable allocation in [13]. Experimental results are provided to show the trade-off relationship between the code efficiency and the computation amount.

The rest of this paper is organized as follows. The review of related work is provided in Section 2. Section 3 introduces the register allocation proposed in [13]. Section 4 explains the proposed register allocation and Section 5 provides experimental results. Conclusions are discussed in Section 6.

2   Related Work

In the graph-coloring approach, an interference graph is generated, where each node represents a variable that competes for a physical register and an edge represents the relation that two corresponding nodes interfere each other such that no two nodes can share the same color. Graph-coloring is performed to assign a color to each node, and then the color is mapped to a physical machine register. If the number of colors is greater than the number of machine registers, some variables are spilled to reduce the register pressure.

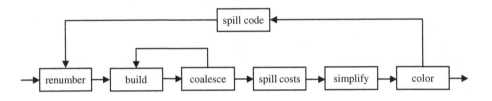

Fig. 1. The flowchart of Briggs' graph coloring

Chaitin [6], [7] at IBM Yorktown firstly abstracted register allocation problem as the graph-coloring problem, and Briggs [4], [5] improved the Chaitin's algorithm in several aspects. Fig. 1 shows the flowchart of the Briggs' algorithm. The role of each stage is as follows. The *renumber* stage identifies and renames each live range. The *build* stage constructs the interference graph. The *coalesce* stage coalesces operands and eliminates copy instructions. The *spill costs* stage estimates spill costs for each live range when the *color* stage cannot allocate a color. It computes the costs of required loads and stores in target machine with each operation weighted by 10^d, where d is the loop-nesting depth. The *simplify* stage determines the allocation ordering of the nodes. It recursively removes unconstrained nodes from the graph, and inserts them onto the allocation stack. If only constrained nodes remain, then it chooses a spill candidate whose estimated spill cost is minimum. In this case, this stage removes a candidate from the stack, and marks it for later spilling. This process is iterated until all nodes are removed. The *color* stage assigns colors to the nodes. It pops the nodes from the stack, and reinserts them into the graph by assigning different colors from adjacent nodes. The *spill code* stage is invoked if any node cannot receive a color. It inserts spill code for the marked live ranges and removes them from the original graph to make the remaining graph colorable.

Main difference from the Chaitin's algorithm is the iterative loop from the *color* stage, not the *simply* stage. Whereas Chaitin's approach would spill a node whose degree is greater than or equal to the number of registers in the *simplify* stage, the Briggs' algorithm optimistically assumes that the node will have a color, and would spill the node for which no color is assigned at the *color* stage. Another difference is the re-materialization in which a value of a variable is recomputed when it is more computationally efficient than reloading.

A significant improvement in the graph-coloring approach is made by Bergner [3]. The main idea is to insert spill code only at the places where a candidate node interferes other nodes allocated with the same color. Due to the increasing number of allocated live ranges and the need for manipulating partially colored live ranges, it consumes much time to renumber and rebuild live ranges.

Load/Store range analysis by Kolte [14] splits each live range into many load/store ranges that form fine granularity candidates of register allocation. These fine granularity candidates are often originated from the same variables, and may require many copy instructions if candidates of the same live ranges are assigned with different registers. In addition, any preprocessing such as live range splitting or fine granularity partitioning does not have coloring information, thus is not as effective as processing during coloring.

Some register allocation approaches focus on the local allocation [9], [11], [12], [16]. These approaches borrow the idea of the OPT page replacement algorithm from operating systems theory. When allocator runs out of registers, the register held by a variable that is to be used at the furthest in the future is preempted. Variable access order within a basic block is analyzed and boundary processing is performed at the entry and at the exit of a basic block to reduce overhead at basic block boundaries. However, contrary to the equal page replacement overhead in operating systems, spill costs for variables are not uniform and the detailed cost model is not given yet. Furthermore in many cases, the next uses are outside the current basic block. Thus this approach does not work well across basic block, and thus fails to generate efficient code.

Goodwin [10] models the register allocation as a 0-1 integer-programming problem. It results in an optimal solution, however it is not practical, because of its complexity in compilation time and excessive memory demands. Another drawback is that it does not work well with many other compiler optimizations such as instruction scheduling, function inlining, and loop unrolling.

3   Fine-Grain Register Allocation Based on a Global Spill Costs Analysis

Kim and Lee in [13] propose a register allocation that improves the efficiency by using information about the flow of variable references of a program. It is a fine-grain approach such that register allocation is performed at every reference of a variable in the order of the variable reference flow. For each reference, the costs of various possible register allocations are estimated by tracing a possible instruction sequence resulting from register allocations. A cost model is formulated to reduce the scope of the trace. This section briefly introduces the register allocation.

```
        a = foo1( );
        b = a + 1;
      foo2(a + b);
        c=foo3();
      foo4(c + 1);
      foo5(c + 2);
      foo6(b + 3);
      foo7(a + 4);
        d = a - b;
```

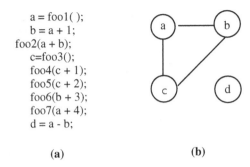

(a)   **(b)**

Fig. 2. Register allocation based on graph-coloring (a) example program (b) interference graph

Consider the program shown in Fig. 2 (a). Register allocation based on graph-coloring constructs the interference graph as shown in Fig. 2 (b) which shows that variables 'a', 'b', and 'c' interfere with each other while 'd' does not have interference with other variables. Assume that only two registers are available, then one variable among 'a', 'b', and 'c' cannot have a register. Variables 'a', 'b', and 'c' are referenced five times, four times, and three times, respectively. Thus, variable 'c' is spilled because it has the minimal spill cost (i.e., has the least number of references). As a result, three memory accesses for variable 'c' are necessary. Considering the reference order of these variables, the graph-coloring approach is not an efficient solution because variable 'c' is consecutively referenced from the fourth to the sixth statements. Thus, it is more efficient to allocate register to variable 'c' while spilling 'a' before the first access of 'c' and reloading it after the last access of 'c'. In this case, only two memory accesses are necessary which is the better result than the graph-coloring approach.

For a given program, the fine-grain approach constructs a varef-graph (variable reference flow graph) that is a partial order of variable references in the program. Each node of this graph represents a variable reference and an edge represents a control flow of the program, i.e., the execution order of the variable references of the program. Note that the execution is only partially-ordered because the complete control flow cannot be decided at compile-time. Fig. 3 shows an example program with the corresponding varef-graph. For illustration, the number of each statement is given in the leftmost column in the program. Each node represents a reference of a variable whose name is given inside the circle. The number to the upper right of the circle is the node number. Note that this number is different from the statement number because one statement can have multiple variable references and consequently have multiple nodes in the varef-graph. In Fig. 3 (b), the reference of variable 'a' at statement (1) is represented by node '1'. The program has two additional references of variable 'a' that are represented by nodes '2' and '5', respectively. Variable 'b' is referenced three times at (3), (4), and (5) and the corresponding nodes are '3', '4', and '6', respectively. Note that statement (5) has references of two variables 'a' and 'b' which are represented by nodes '5' and '6' in the graph, respectively.

(1) a = 1;

(2) **if** (a)
(3)   b = 1;
     else
(4)   b = 2;

(5) **return** a + b;

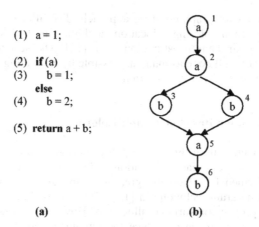

           (a)   (b)

Fig. 3. Variable reference flow graph (varef-graph) (a) example program (b) varef-graph graph

An edge represents a partial execution order of the program. Statement (1) is supposed to be executed first, and the corresponding node '1' is the root node. Statement (2) is supposed to be executed next, and the corresponding node '2' is the successor of node '1'. Statements (3) and (4) are executed next to the statement (2), and therefore the corresponding nodes '3' and '4' are successors of node 2. Statements (3) and (4) must be executed exclusively, and therefore, there is no edge between nodes '3' and '4'. Statements (5) and (6) are executed next in sequence, as shown in the figure.

With the order given by the varef-graph, register allocation is performed at every reference of a variable. The visit order is a modified breadth-first order that is the same as the breadth-first order with the modification that guarantees a successor node to be always visited later than its predecessor. The register allocation continues until all nodes in the varef-graph are visited. When no register is available, the fine-grain allocator preempts a register from previously assigned variable if the preemption reduces the execution cost of a program. To select the register with maximum cost reduction, the preemption cost and benefit are analyzed for all possible registers. The cost estimation often requires large computation with exponential complexity. Thus, a mathematical model for the simple estimation of an approximated cost is derived and a heuristic with a reasonable amount of computation is developed based on the model in [13].

The register allocation consists of two stages. In the first stage, variables are allocated with the number of machine registers. In the second stage, unallocated variables and temporaries called as *scratches* are allocated. From the results of the first stage, the second stage estimates the register allocation benefit, and allocates the register with the maximum benefit.

4 Proposed Register Allocation Techniques

In this section, two heuristics based on the fine-grain register allocation proposed in [13] are proposed. In order to reduce compilation time, the first heuristic combines the fine-grain approach with graph-coloring approach. The allocator performs variable allocation by the graph-coloring allocation, and then performs scratch allocation based on the fine-grain benefit estimation as in [13]. The second heuristic aims to reduce the amount of spill code as many as possible by estimating the costs of various possible allocations to the end of a program.

4.1 Variable Allocation Based on Graph-Coloring

Fig. 4 shows the overall algorithm of the proposed register allocation. The algorithm consists of two steps, the variable allocation and the scratch allocation. The variable allocation is performed based on the graph-coloring approach while scratches are allocated by the fine-grain technique in [13]. The proposed allocator adopts Briggs' graph-coloring approach for variable allocation. However, A major modification to the Briggs' algorithm is made to reduce the amount of computation such that the iteration from the *color* stage to the *renumber* stage is eliminated, whereas the graph-coloring technique iterates the procedure from the *renumber* stage to the *color* stage, until all nodes are colored. It is time-consuming for a graph-coloring allocator to renumber and rebuild the live ranges for spilled variables, especially when enabling a partial coloring. The proposed allocator builds the live ranges only once, therefore, reduces compilation time.

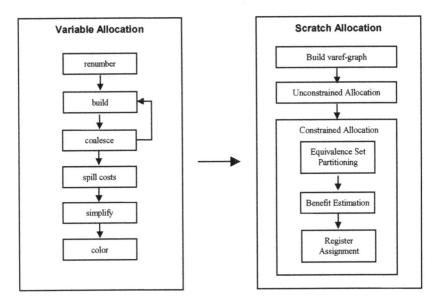

Fig. 4. The flowchart of the first proposed register allocation

After variable allocation, scratch allocation is performed by traversing the varef-graph. Before allocation, nodes corresponding to temporaries are added to the varef-graph. The visit order of the graph is also in the modified breadth-first order. When the allocator visits a scratch node, it allocates a register to the scratch if a free register is available. Those scratches are allocated in the first step of the scratch allocation and called as *unconstrained allocation*. In the second step when available registers are exhausted, the allocator must preempt a register to allocate it for the scratch. Those are called *constrained* scratches. For constrained scratch allocation, the register preemption benefit is computed for all registers as in the fine-grain approach. Then, the register with the maximum benefit is selected. The register allocation continues until all scratch nodes in the varef-graph are visited.

The proposed approach gives the higher priority to variables than temporaries in the register allocation while the Briggs' algorithm does in the opposite way. The Briggs' algorithm guarantees temporaries to be assigned registers while spilling variables for the constrained temporaries. To reduce the complexity of computation, allocation is performed not for each reference but for each live range in the graph-coloring approach. However, the partial allocation benefit is different at each reference. This preference to temporaries makes it difficult to compute the precise partial allocation benefit for variables. When no register is available for a variable, the required spill instructions are computed for the interfering live ranges throughout the program. This computation is overall estimation and does not consider the actual spill cost required at each reference. The lifetime of a temporary is very short compared to that of a variable. Thus, if the variables are allocated before temporaries, the variable can be partially spilled for a temporary, and this spilling occurs only a few references. Then, allocation benefit at each reference can be estimated considering the flow of a program. Thus, it is more computationally convenient and accurate to allocate variables before temporaries. Thus, in the proposed allocator, variables are allocated as the first stage, and then they are partially spilled at the second stage for the lifetimes of temporaries.

In the approach given in Fig. 4, algorithms other than graph-coloring can be used for the variable allocation stage. To improve the efficiency of register allocation, one may use a more complex algorithm with the sacrifice in computation time. The next subsection proposes such a register allocation.

4.2   Fine-Grain Register Allocation Based on Global Benefit Estimation

In the fine-grain approach, the register allocation for one node affects the register allocation for its successors. The complexity increases due to the analysis of all these effects. To reduce the complexity, [13] defines an impact range that models a set of the nodes that are affected by the register allocation for a given node. In [13], the impact range is limited to the next references of a variable that holds a register, and it is called the *first order register allocator* in this paper. Similarly, spill penalty and the preemption penalty of a node are called the *first order spill penalty* and the *first order preemption penalty*, respectively.

Consider the varef-graph shown in Fig. 5 (a). Suppose that the register allocator visits node '2' while node '1' receives register 'r1'. Assume that no register is available for node '2' so that the register allocator needs to decide whether to allocate node '2' or to spill node '2'. Note that this decision affects the register allocation for the successor nodes. This is because the decision for node '2' changes the costs of the nodes whose variable is the same as that of node '2'. Suppose node '2' is determined to be spilled. Then, the next reference of node '2', that is node '4', is likely to be spilled. The spill of node '4' may cause the spill of node '6' which is another reaching definition for node '4'. The spill of node '2' changes the first order spill penalty of node '4', and node '6', and thus decreases the possibility of register allocations for node '4' and node '6'. This increases the possibility of register allocations for node '3', node '5', and node '7'. Consider the case when node '2' preempts a register and is allocaed. It does not decrease the costs of node '4' and node '6', therefore, does not increase the possibility of first order register allocations for node '3', node '5', and node '7'.

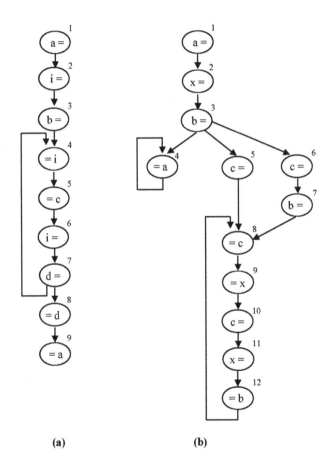

(a)   (b)

Fig. 5. Example varef-graphs for illustrating global benefit estimation

Contrary to the simplification of the first order register allocation, the decision of a register allocation of a node 'n' affects not only the nodes in the impact range but also all the nodes in a program. The decision for a node is either allocation of a register or a spill of a node. To estimate the impact of each case, the first order register allocation is performed to the end of a program, and then the required total spill cost is computed. Among allocation of a register and a spill, the choice that results in the minimum spill code is decided for a node. If the result of a spill of a node is the minimum, no register is allocated to the node.

Fig. 6 shows the flow of the proposed register allocation. It consists of two stages, the variable allocation and the scratch allocation. The variable allocation visits each node in the varef-graph and checks if any register is available. If an available register exists, it assigns the register as in [13]. If no register is available, the allocator needs to decide whether to spill or to preempt. It first spills the node and estimates the cost. For the cost estimation, the first order register allocation is run to the end of the program and counts the number of spill instructions. The next step is to estimate the cost for preemptions. This step needs to be iterated for all available registers. After the spill and preemptions costs are estimated, the register allocation is decided as the choice with the minimum cost. After the variable allocation, the scratch stage is performed in the same way as the first order allocation.

Consider Fig. 5 (b). Assume that the number of registers is two. Let NodeCost(n) be a cost of node 'n'. In general, NodeCost(n) is defined as 10^d where d is the loop depth of 'n' and is zero if 'n' is not inside a loop. Consider the allocations by the first order register allocator. The allocator assigns register 'r1' and 'r2' to node '1' and node '2', respectively, and runs out of registers at node '3'. At node '3', consider the benefit for register 'r1'. The first order preemption penalty is Nodecost(1)+NodeCost(4), which is 11. The first order spill penalty is NodeCost(3)+NodeCost(7)+NodeCost(12), which is 12. Thus, the first order benefit for register 'r1' is 1. For register 'r2', the first order preemption penalty is NodeCost(2)+NodeCost(9)+NodeCost(11), that is 21. The spill penalty is 12. Thus, the first order benefit for register 'r2' is -9. Thus, the first order register allocator preempts register 'r1' and assigns it to a node '3', and the corresponding spill code is inserted at node '1' and node '4' for variable 'a'. Then, at node '5', the first order allocator preempts the register 'r1' and assigns it to node '5', and thus, spills variable 'b' at node '3', node '7', and node '12'. There are no further register preemptions and spills to the end node. Thus, total spill cost generated by the first order allocator is NodeCost(1) + NodeCost(3)+ NodeCost(4) + NodeCost(7) + NodeCost(12), that is 23.

Consider the proposed register allocation. The allocator assigns register 'r1' and 'r2' to node '1' and node '2', respectively, and runs out of registers at node '3'. At node '3', global benefits are estimated for registers 'r1' and 'r2'. Consider the register 'r1' first. Suppose that node '3' preempts 'r1'. With this assumption, the proposed allocator computes the total spill cost when the first order allocator runs to the end node. By the first order allocator, the assigned register 'r1' is preempted at node '5', and there are no further spills to the end of a program. Thus, the total spill cost is 23. Note that this is the same as the result of the first order register allocation in the previous paragraph. Consider the spill of node '3'. The allocator assumes that node '3' is spilled, and computes the total spill cost resulting when the first order allocator runs to the end. In this case, the node '7' and node '12' are also spilled, and there are no further spills. Thus, the total spill cost is 12. Thus, the allocation benefit for register 'r1' is -11. Similarly, the allocation benefit is negative for register 'r2'. As the allocation benefits are negative for all registers, the decision for node '3' is a spill. Proceeding to the end, the proposed allocator determines node '7' and node '12' to be spilled. Thus, the total spill cost of the proposed approach is 12 that are less than that of the first order register allocation, which is 23.

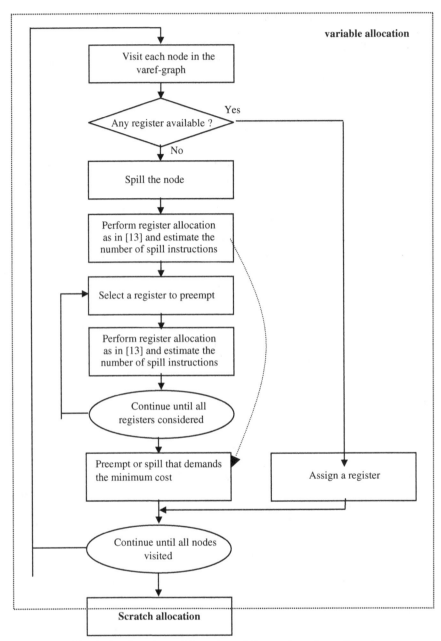

Fig. 6. The flowchart of the proposed fine-grain register allocation

Consider the complexity of the proposed algorithms. For both algorithms, the variable flow graph can be constructed by classical reaching definition analysis in [1], [15]. Consider the time complexity of the proposed scratch allocation. The allocator employs the simplified graph-coloring approach for variable allocation. The time complexity of graph-coloring approach is known as O($n$log$n$) where n is the number of live ranges. The proposed approach does not iterative the coloring algorithm, thus the dominant complexity is in the *simplify* stage and the *color* stage. The time complexity of each stage is known as O(v+e_v) where v is the number of variables that is normally smaller than n, and e_v is the number of edges for variables.

The dominant complexity in the proposed register allocation based on global benefit estimation is in the computation of global benefits. It requires the execution of the algorithm in [13] and the complexity of the algorithm is O(N^2) where N is the number of nodes in the varef-graph. In worst-case, this computation is iterated N times for each node, and thus, the total complexity is O(N^3). In practice, search spaces are localized in the algorithm in [13] because the next reference of a variable is generally located close to the node.

5 Experimental Results

To evaluate the efficiency, the proposed register allocations are implemented in LCC [8] (Local C Compiler) targeting ARM7TDMI processor [2]. For comparison, two more register allocators based on Briggs' algorithm [4], [5] and interference region spilling [3] are also implemented. The reason of choosing these two allocators is that the Briggs' algorithm is a widely used version of the graph-coloring approach while the interference region spilling is one of the best versions of the graph-coloring approach.

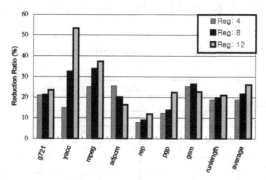

Fig. 7. The ratio of the number of spill instructions generated by the first proposed register allocation and the Briggs' algorithm

Fig. 7 shows the improvements achieved by the first proposed allocation. The vertical axis of the graph represents the ratio of the number of spill instructions generated by the proposed allocator and that by the Briggs' allocator. In counting the number of spill instructions, they are weighted by 10^d if the instructions are inside a loop with nesting depth d. The benchmarks are g721, yacc, adpcm, mpeg, rep, pgp, gsm, and runlength programs. The number of available registers is changed from 4, 8, to 12. With the eight benchmarks, an average of 22.2% improvement is achieved by the proposed allocation over the Briggs' approach. As the number of registers increases from 4, and 8, to 12, the average improvement changes from 18.9%, and 21.7%, to 26.1%, respectively. For a small number of registers, too many spills occur even for the proposed scratch allocation, and consequently, the relative reduction ratio is small. For every benchmark, the proposed allocator spills fewer instructions than Briggs' allocator and the reduction ratio ranges from 7.9% to 53.3%.

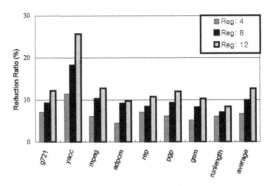

Fig. 8. The ratio of the number of spill instructions generated by the first proposed allocation and interference region spilling

Fig. 8 shows the ratio of improvements achieved by the first proposed allocation compared to the interference region spilling. For the same benchmarks as in Fig. 7, an average of 9.7 % improvements are achieved. It reduces spill instructions by 6.7%, 9.9%, and 12.7% for 4, 8, and 12 registers, respectively. It outperforms in every benchmark.

Table 1. The ratio of compilation time by the first proposed allocation and the Briggs' algorithm

benchmark	number of registers		
	4	8	12
g721	0.67	0.98	1.01
yacc	1.02	1.25	1.15
mpeg	1.65	1.86	1.74
adpcm	0.54	0.60	0.73
rep	0.31	0.59	0.65
pgp	0.34	0.52	0.48
gsm	0.36	0.45	0.54
runlength	0.47	0.58	0.61

The compilation times for both the first proposed allocator and the Briggs' allocator are measured and compared in Table 1. In this table, the first column from the left represents benchmark programs, and the second, the third, and the fourth columns show the ratio of the compilation time of the proposed allocator and the Briggs' allocator when the numbers of registers are 4, 8, and 12, respectively. The ratios of the computation times vary from 0.31 to 1.86. In 17 cases out of 24 combinations, the proposed scratch allocator runs faster than Briggs' allocator. On average, the proposed approach reduces compilation time by 20.4%. The decreases in compilation time are due to the elimination of iteration in graph-coloring approach.

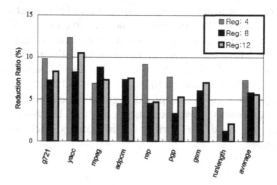

Fig. 9. The ratio of the number of spill instructions generated by the second proposed allocation and the allocator in [13]

Fig. 9 shows the ratio of improvements achieved by the second proposed allocation compared to the first order register allocation in [13]. The experiment is performed for variable allocation. For the same benchmarks as in Fig. 7, an average of 6.2% improvements are achieved. It reduces spill instructions by 7.3%, 5.8%, and 5.6% for 4, 8, and 12 registers, respectively. It outperforms in every benchmark.

Table 2. The ratio of compilation time by the second proposed allocation and the allocator in [13]

benchmark	number of registers		
	4	8	12
g721	12.6	10.6	5.6
yacc	2.7	2.3	1.7
mpeg	3.8	2.1	2.0
adpcm	6.0	6.8	4.4
rep	9.0	6.1	8.5
pgp	2.0	1.4	1.3
gsm	2.3	2.2	1.6
runlength	5.0	3.9	6.5

Table 2 shows the compilation times for both the second proposed allocation and the first order register allocation in [13]. The compilation time of the proposed approach is 4.6 times greater than that for the first order register approach. The ratios of the computation times vary from 1.3 to 12.6. The large increases in compilation time are due to the compilation for the computation of the global benefits when no registers are available for variables.

6   Conclusions

The first register allocator improves the Briggs' allocator by an average of 22.2% and the interference region spilling by 9.7%, respectively. This significant improvement is achieved by analyzing the flow of all references of live ranges. The proposed scratch approach does not rebuild live ranges, so the compilation time is decreased by an average of 20.4% when compared to the Briggs' allocator. The second register allocator improves the efficiency by 6.2% with the increase of the computation amount by 4.6 times when compared to the allocator in [13].

The varef-graph used in the proposed register allocation has a large amount of information such as control flow, execution cost, and load/store identification. This information may be used for further optimizations such as cooperation with instruction scheduling.

References

1.   Aho, A.V., Sethi, R., and Ullman J. D.: Compilers: Principles, Techniques, and Tools. Addison-Wesley Publishing Company, Reading Mass (1986).
2.   Advanced RISC Machines Ltd: ARM Architecture Reference Manual. Document Number: ARM DDI 0100B, Advanced RISC Machines Ltd. (ARM) (1996).
3.   Bergner, P., Dahl, P., Engebretsen, D., and O'Keefe, M.: Spill code minimization via interference region spilling. Proceedings of the ACM PLDI '97 (June 1997), 287–295.
4.   Briggs, P., Cooper, K.D., and Torczon, L.: Rematerialization. Proceedings of the ACM SIGPLAN '92 Conference on Programming Language Design and Implementation, SIGPLAN Notices 27, 7 (June 1992), 311–321.
5.   Briggs, P., Cooper, K.D., Kennedy, K., and Torczon, L.: Coloring heuristics for register allocation. Proceedings of the ACM SIGPLAN '89 Conference on Programming Language Design and Implementation, SIGPLAN Notices 24, 6 (June 1989), 275–284.
6.   Chaitin, G.J.: Register allocation and spilling via coloring. Proceedings of the ACM SIGPLAN '82 Symposium on Compiler Construction, SIGPLAN Notices 17, 6 (June 1982), 98–105.
7.   Chaitin, G.J., Auslander, M.A., Chandra, A.K., Cocke. J., Hopkins, M., and Markstein, P.W.: Register allocation via coloring. Computer Languages 6 (January 1981), 47–57.
8.   Fraser, C.W., and Hanson, D.R.: A Retargetable C Compiler: Design and Implementation. Benjamin/Cummings, Redwood City CA (1995).
9.   Farach, M., and Liberatore, V.: On local register allocation. Proceedings of the 9th Annual ACM-SIAM Symposium on Discrete Algorithms (1998), 564–573.
10. Goodwin, D.W., and Wilken, K.D.: Optimal and near-optimal global register allocation using 0-1 integer programming. Software-Practice and Experience 26, 8 (1996), 929–965.
11. Hsu, W.-C., Fischer, C. N., and Goodman, J.R.: On the minimization of loads/stores in local register allocation. IEEE Transactions on Software Engineering 15, 10 (October 1989), 1252–1260.
12. Kim, D.H.: Advanced compiler optimization for CalmRISC8 low-end embedded processor. Proceedings of the 9th Int. Conference on Compiler Construction, LNCS 1781, Springer-Verlag (March 2000), 173–188.
13. Kim, D.H., and Lee, H.-J.: Fine-Grain Register Allocation Based on a Global Spill Costs Analysis. Proceedings of the 7th Int. Workshop on Software and Compilers for Embedded Systems (Sep 2003).
14. Kolte, P., and Harrold, M.J.: Load/store range analysis for global register allocation. Proceedings of the ACM PLDI '93 (June 1993), 268–277.

15. Mushnick, S. S.: Advanced compiler design and implementation. Morgan Kaufmann, SanFrancisco CA (1997).
16. Proebsting, T. A., and Fischer, C. N.: Demand-driven register allocation. ACM Transactions on Programming Languages and Systems 18, 6 (November 1996), 683–710.

Lazy Stack Copying and Stack Copy Sharing for the Efficient Implementation of Continuations

Tomoharu Ugawa, Nobuhisa Minagawa, Tsuneyasu Komiya, Masahiro Yasugi, and Taiichi Yuasa

Graduate School of Informatics, Kyoto University, Kyoto 606-8501, Japan

Abstract. In order to capture first-class continuations, most stack-based implementations copy contents of the stack to the heap. While various implementation strategies for copying have been proposed, many implementations employ the stack strategy. With this strategy, the entire stack contents is copied to the heap whenever a continuation is captured. This simple strategy is easy to implement and can be used for implementations with foreign language interface. However, this strategy requires a lot of time and memory for creation and invocation of continuations. We propose a lazy stack copying technique. The contents of the stack to copy are preserved on the stack until the function returns that has captured the continuation. So we delay stack copying for the continuation until the function returns. We can avoid stack copying if it is detected that the continuation has become garbage before the function returns. In addition, we propose stack copy sharing, which is realized by using lazy stack copying. We present three models for stack copy sharing. We applied these techniques to Scheme systems and found that the proposed techniques improve runtime and memory efficiency of programs that use first-class continuations.

1 Introduction

A continuation represents the rest of computation. In languages such as Scheme [1,2], continuations can be handled as first-class objects with unlimited extent. In Scheme, the `call/cc` function captures the current continuation, i.e., creates a continuation object which represents the continuation. Then `call/cc` invokes a function with the continuation object as its argument. A continuation object behaves as a function object which takes the value of an expression as its argument. The argument is passed to the rest of the computation as the return value of the `call/cc`.

A continuation is represented by the control stack and some other stacks on a stack-based implementation, in which stack entries for functions are allocated and deallocated in last-in, first-out manner. First-class continuations with unlimited extent allow a function call to return multiple times. This implies that a conventional stack-based implementation requires a special mechanism for implementing first-class continuations.

A. Ohori (Ed.): APLAS 2003, LNCS 2895, pp. 410–426, 2003.

In general, a stack-based implementation may have a control stack and some other stacks such as an object stack and an environment stack. However, it is easy to extend our discussion about a single stack to multiple stacks. So, we concentrate on a control stack below.

The simplest implementation strategy for first-class continuations on a stack-based system is the *stack strategy*. In the stack strategy, when a continuation is captured, a copy of the entire stack is made and stored in the heap as the continuation object. When a continuation is invoked (or *thrown*), the stack is cleared and the continuation object is copied back into the stack.

In the traditional stack strategy, each time `call/cc` is invoked a copy of the stack is made. However, in real programs, most common uses of continuations are non-local exits, which are implemented in C as `longjmp`. If it is detected that a continuation object is used only for a non-local exit, it is not necessary to make a copy of the entire stack, because the contents of the stack is preserved on the stack until the `call/cc` returns. Furthermore, the traditional stack strategy creates multiple copies of a single function frame in the *recapture scenario* defined in [3]. This requires a large amount of heap space and execution time for copying. Using a large amount of heap space for continuation objects increase frequency of garbage collection.

In this paper, we propose *lazy stack copying*, which delays copying of the stack until the function that captured the continuation returns. When the function returns, if it is detected that the continuation object has become garbage, the stack need not be saved in the heap because the continuation will never be thrown later. This improves the performance of programs which use first-class continuations for non-local exits. In the next section we show how lazy stack copying works. In Sect.3 we show the implementation details of *return barrier* which is necessary to implement lazy stack copying. In Sect.4 we propose *stack copy sharing* which can be implemented easily in combination with lazy stack copying. This improves the performance of programs which use first-class continuations in the recapture scenario. In the section, we describe three implementation models for stack copy sharing. We compare these models in Sect.5. In the section, we also discuss overhead and capability to use for compilers and systems using various implementation strategies for first-class continuations. In Sect.6 we evaluate the performance of each model. In Sect.7 we compare our proposal with other work.

2   Lazy Stack Copying

In order to simplify the explanation of lazy stack copying, we first consider the case where `call/cc` is invoked only once during the computation of a program. We discuss the general case where `call/cc` is invoked multiple times, later in this section.

In lazy stack copying, when `call/cc` is invoked, it creates a new continuation object but it does not copy the contents of the stack. Rather, the continuation object contains a pointer to the top of the stack so that the stack can be unwound correctly when the continuation is thrown during the execution of the `call/cc`. When the `call/cc` returns either normally or by throwing the continuation, it *promotes* the continuation object, i.e., it makes a copy of the stack and saves a reference to the copy into the continuation object. This is possible because the contents of the stack at the call of the `call/cc` will be preserved until the `call/cc` returns. After the return of the `call/cc`, the stack contents may be destroyed but the promoted continuation can be thrown any number of times and at any time by using the saved copy of the stack.

The merit of lazy stack copying is that, if it is determined that the continuation will never be thrown after the return of the `call/cc`, then no copy of the stack needs to be made. In order to determine this, we use a conservative but efficient method, based on the fact that if a continuation object is not accessible at all, then it can never be thrown. The continuation object is accessible after the return of the `call/cc` if

1. it is referenced from a global variable,
2. it is referenced from an accessible object in the heap, or
3. it is returned as the return value of the `call/cc`.

Note that even if the continuation object has been stored into a local variable which is allocated on the stack, that stack entry has been popped after the `call/cc` returns. Thus, we do not have to count on references from local variables.

Among the three conditions above, the first two are difficult to check in a reasonable amount of time. Instead, we actually use the following, more conservative conditions:

1'. it has been assigned to a global variable
2'. it has been stored in an object in the heap

In order to check these conditions efficiently, we "mark" the continuation object when it is stored into a global variable or an object in the heap. When the `call/cc` returns, the continuation object is promoted only if it is marked or returned as the value of the `call/cc`.

The write barrier mechanism [4], which is used mainly for garbage collection, can be used for the marking operation. When an object is stored into a global variable or an in-heap object, if the stored object is a continuation object, then it is marked. In addition to the write barrier, we need a *creation time barrier*, which works when a new object is created in the heap. When a newly created object is initialized, if a continuation object is used as the initial value of a slot, then it must be marked.

One of the important features of lazy stack copying is that, if a continuation object is used only for non-local exit, then no stack copy is made in most cases. This is because the continuation is thrown only during the execution of the `call/cc`, and such a continuation object is seldom stored into a global variable or an in-heap object.

Now, let us consider the general case where `call/cc` may be invoked multiple times. We use Fig. 1 to show how throwing or promoting a continuation

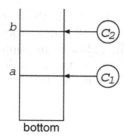

Fig. 1. The control stack and two active continuations.

affects another continuation object. Suppose that `call/cc` was invoked and it created a continuation object c_1. During the execution of the `call/cc`, `call/cc` was invoked again, which created the second continuation object c_2. Figure 1 illustrates the status of the control stack and continuation objects during the execution of the second `call/cc`. We say that there are two *active* continuations and that c_1 is *older* than c_2. We have to pay special attentions to the following cases.

1. When c_2 is promoted:
   The older continuation c_1 may be referenced from the stack region between a and b. If it is, promotion of the younger continuation c_2 may cause a reference from the heap because the contents of the entire stack is copied into the heap. Since it takes time to scan the stack region for a reference to c_1, we conservatively assume that there *is* a reference. There are two ways to handle this case. One is to mark c_1 for later promotion, and the other is to promote c_1 immediately. We chose the second one for the reason mentioned in Sect. 5.
2. When c_1 is thrown:
   If the younger continuation c_2 has been marked for promotion, then it must be promoted immediately. Otherwise, the contents of the stack region between a and b may be destroyed after c_1 is thrown.

In general, there may be n active continuation objects $c_1, c_2, \ldots, c_n$, in the order from the oldest to the youngest, that are not promoted. During the execution of the `call/cc` that created the last c_n, if c_i $(1 \leq i \leq n)$ is thrown, then we promote all marked c_j such that $i \leq j \leq n$. Also, when the last continuation c_n is promoted, we promote all c_j $(1 \leq j \leq n)$.

In order to keep track of the active continuation objects, we use a stack, called "continuation stack". When a new continuation object is created by `call/cc`, it is pushed onto the continuation stack. When a `call/cc` returns normally, the continuation object it created is found at the top of the continuation stack. That continuation object is then popped from the continuation stack. In addition, if the continuation object is marked, then it is promoted and all continuation objects in the continuation stack are promoted if they are not promoted yet.

When a continuation object c is thrown, the continuation stack is scanned. If c is found in the stack, then c and all continuation objects in the stack that are younger than c are popped. In addition, the popped continuations are promoted if they are marked. Furthermore, in case one of the popped continuation object is promoted, all older continuations in the stack are also promoted if not promoted yet.

3 Return Barrier

In this section, we discuss how to detect returns from `call/cc`. We call the detection mechanism a return barrier [5], and call the code driven by the barrier a return barrier code. In a system which is not properly tail recursive, implementation of the return barrier is straightforward. We can place the return barrier code at the end of the `call/cc` function. In the rest of this section, we discuss how to implement the return barrier on proper tail recursive systems.

In proper tail recursive systems, the function invoked by `call/cc` does not return to the `call/cc`, but returns directly to the caller of the `call/cc`. Therefore the barrier code placed at the end of the `call/cc` function would not work. Rather, the barrier code must be executed on return from the function invoked by the `call/cc`.

3.1 Checking All Returns

The simplest implementation of the return barrier is to check whether to execute the barrier code on all returns. However, this causes overhead even if programs do not use `call/cc` since the check is required each time a function returns. Our benchmark result [6] shows that the elapsed time of the call-intensive `tak` benchmark on the SCM [7] with this implementation of the return barrier is 20% longer than that of the original SCM.

3.2 Return Address Replacement

In some systems, tail recursive calls are implemented by reusing function frames. When a function calls another function tail recursively, the function frame for the caller will be reused for the callee. In such systems, the return address of the frame is preserved beyond a tail recursive call. Therefore, we can implement the return barrier by replacing the return address of `call/cc` with the address of the return barrier code. The actual return address may be stored in a separate stack so that the function can return to the caller after execution of the barrier code.

This implementation does not cause overhead to programs that do not use `call/cc`. However, this implementation strongly depends on the structure of the control stack. Systems written in high-level languages such as C would lose their advantage of portability if we implement the return barrier in this way.

3.3   Two Version Evaluators

On interpreter-based systems, we can avoid large overhead and preserve portability by introducing another version of the evaluator which is used only when call/cc invokes a function. This evaluator always executes the return barrier code when it returns. In contrast, the original version need not execute the code. We will show later in this section that a similar technique can be used for compiler-based systems.

The pseudo code of the evaluator is shown in Fig. 2. In the figure, eval_callcc() is the additional evaluator, and eval() is the original version. When eval() evaluates a call of call/cc, it creates a new continuation object, pushes it onto the continuation stack, and invokes eval_callcc() for evaluating the argument of the call/cc. When the eval_callcc() returns, it executes the return barrier code.

Eval_callcc() does not invoke itself even when it evaluates call/cc in a tail position. The reason is that the continuation of the tail recursive call is the same as the last captured continuation. In fact, the evaluator can find the required continuation object at the top of the continuation stack. This feature allows systems to be properly tail recursive. Although eval() invokes eval_callcc() when a function is invoked tail recursively from call/cc, eval_callcc() does not invoke itself any more.

This implementation does not cause overhead to those programs that do no use call/cc. However, the interpreter with two version evaluators requires twice as much stack space as an ordinary interpreter in the worst case. This is because an additional frame of eval_callcc(), which is almost of the same size as a frame of eval(), is allocated onto the stack each time eval() encounters a call/cc. Copying large stacks degrades the performance of programs which cause promotion of continuation objects. This problem can be solved by inlining the body of eval_callcc() at the end of eval() and replacing the call to eval_callcc() with a jump to the inlined code.

The similar technique can be used for compiler-based systems by placing the return barrier code in the call/cc code. In order to attain proper tail recursion, the original code of call/cc should have been written so that it reuses its own stack frame for the function to invoke. The revised code shall work as follows. Before call/cc invokes a function, it checks the return address to see whether the call/cc code was invoked from the call/cc code itself. If so, the code works as the original code. Otherwise, it does not reuse its own stack frame, but allocates a new frame for the function to invoke. By executing the return barrier code on return from the call/cc code, we can obtain the same effect as two version evaluators.

4   Stack Copy Sharing

In the basic lazy stack copying that we described in Sect. 2, stack copies may be duplicated. Some of them can be eliminated by having multiple continuation objects share a single copy.

```
eval_callcc(rator, rands) {
TOP:
    switch(type(rator)) {
    ...
    case CALL_CC:
        rator = first(rands);
        rands = make_rands(contstack_get_top());
        goto TOP; /* tail recursive call */
    ...
    }

    /* place the return barrier code here */

    return val;
}

eval(rator, rands) {
    switch(type(rator)) {
    ...
    case CALL_CC:
        cont = make_continuation();
        contstack_push(cont);
        if ((val = setjmp(cont->jmpbuf)) == 0)
            val = eval_callcc(first(rands), make_rands(cont));
        break;
    ...
    }
    return val;
}
```

Fig. 2. Pseudo code of two version evaluators in C.

For example, in Fig. 1, when c_1 and c_2 are promoted, two stack copies will be created, and both copies contain the contents of the stack region between the bottom and a. If the copy of the region is shared by c_1 and c_2, we can avoid duplicated copies.

It is expected that even after c_1 is promoted, the copy for it be shared with other continuation objects. Suppose that the third continuation object c_3 is created after c_2 is promoted but the call/cc that created c_1 does not return yet. If c_3 is promoted, a stack copy for it will be created. However, the copy does not have to include the stack region between the bottom and a because the region was copied by promotion of c_2.

We propose three models for implementing stack copy sharing in the rest of this section. We compare these models in the next section. In the following, STADDR(c) denotes the address of the stack top when the continuation object c was created.

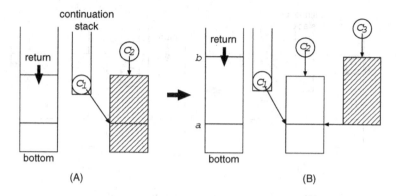

Fig. 3. Promotion in the grafting model.

4.1 Grafting Model

When a continuation is promoted, the grafting model copies the part of the stack that has not been copied and promotes all older continuations by saving appropriate pointers into the continuation objects. In Fig. 3 (A), c_2 is promoted while there is an older continuation object c_1. The grafting model creates a copy (hatched in the figure) of the stack and promotes c_1 as well.

Later, when another continuation object c_3 is being promoted before the call/cc returns that created c_1, a copy (hatched in Fig. 3 (B)) of the stack region between a and b will be made. The copy of the stack region between the bottom and a is shared by three continuation objects.

In general, when a continuation c is promoted, we find the youngest active continuation c' that has already been promoted. Then we copy the region between STADDR(c') and STADDR(c). If there is no such c', we copy the entire stack. In either case, we promote all active continuations that has not been promoted.

Remember that we assume the stack strategy, in which the entire stack will be copied back when a continuation is thrown. In order to avoid duplicated copies, we also have to restore the continuation stack, because the continuation stack is used to determine the stack region that has to be copied. For this purpose, we save the continuation stack into the continuation object when it is created. Note that the cost of this saving operation is little if we implement the continuation stack as a linked list. Saving the continuation stack is necessary also for the other two models.

4.2 Dividing Stack Model

In the grafting model, a continuation may point to the inside of a stack copy. For instance, in Fig. 3 (A), the continuation c_1 point to the middle of the stack copy. Such a situation may complicate the garbage collection. The dividing stack model avoids such a situation by copying the stack into segments. Figure 4 shows

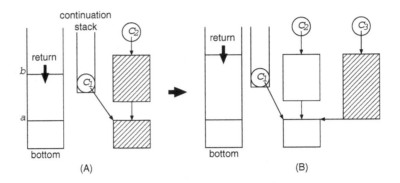

Fig. 4. Promotion in the dividing stack model.

how continuation objects are promoted in the same scenario as in Fig. 3. When the continuation object c_2 is promoted, the contents of the entire stack is copied into two segments (hatched in Fig. 4 (A)). The copy of the stack region between a and b is linked to the copy of the stack region between the bottom and a so that the copy can be written back to the stack when c_2 is thrown. Later, when c_3 is promoted, a new copy (hatched in Fig. 4 (B)) is created. The new copy does not contain the stack region between the bottom and a. Rather, it has a link to the copy of the stack region between the bottom and a, which was created when c_2 was promoted.

In general, there may be n active continuation objects $c_1, c_2, \ldots, c_n$, in the order from the oldest to the youngest. They are stored in the continuation stack. When c_n is promoted, we make a copy of the stack region for each c_j $(1 \leq j \leq n)$ that are not promoted yet. The region for c_j is between STADDR(c_{j-1}) and STADDR(c_j), where STADDR(c_0) is the stack bottom.

4.3   Incremental Dividing Stack Model

In the dividing stack model, when a continuation object is promoted, all the older continuation objects are also promoted. However, we do not have to promote the older continuation objects together because the contents of the stack that an older continuation object requires is preserved on the stack until the call/cc that created it returns. Figure 5 shows how continuation objects are promoted in the incremental dividing stack model. When the continuation object c_2 is promoted, only a copy (hatched in Fig. 5 (A)) of the stack region between a and b is created. The copy has a link to c_1 instead of the copy of the stack region between the bottom and a. C_1 is marked to be promoted later so that the stack region between the bottom and a is copied eventually. Later, when the call/cc that created c_1 returns even normally or by throwing a continuation, a copy (hatched in Fig. 5 (B)) of the region is created.

In general, when a continuation object c is promoted, we copy the stack region between STADDR(c) and STADDR(c'), where c' is the second youngest

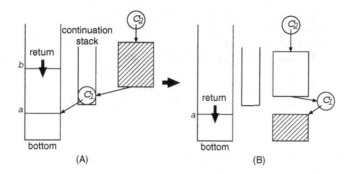

Fig. 5. Promotion in the incremental stack dividing model.

continuation object. Copying of other regions is delayed until c' is promoted. Instead, we mark all active continuation objects for promotion so that the region can be copied later.

5 Discussion

In this section, we discuss lazy stack copying and stack copy sharing in various aspects.

5.1 Comparison of Three Models

Since the stack is large, when we copy the stack, data in cache of CPU are evicted in any model. Furthermore, on some architecture like SPARC, a part of contents of the stack is cached on the registers. On such architectures, we have to write back the contents of such registers onto the stack. This cost of eviction and write back occurs every time the stack is copied. Thus implementations which promote all active continuation objects together decrease the accumulated cost of this kind of cost. The grafting model and the dividing stack model are such implementations. We can also implement the basic lazy stack copying in this way. On the other hand, this cost of the incremental dividing stack model is larger than that of others.

The incremental dividing stack model has an advantage that it delays allocating memory for copies of the stack. This may reduce the number of times of garbage collection because large heap area can be used before copies of the stack are allocated. However, in general, this advantage may contribute little since the heap size is much larger than the stack size.

Because of the above observation, the grafting model looks good. However, in the grafting model, there is a possibility that the garbage collector fails to reclaim memory for continuation objects which is reclaimed in other models. For example, the program shown in Fig. 6 will make an infinite chain of continuation objects shown in Fig. 7 in the model. In the program, when the function 1 is

```
(define k-link #f)
(define (f) (g) (f))
(define (g) (call/cc h))
(define (h Y) (i) (call/cc j) #t)
(define (i) (l k-link) #t)
(define (j Z) (set! k-link Z))
(define (l k-link) (call/cc (lambda (X) X)) #t)
(f)
```

Fig. 6. A sample program which causes memory leak in the grafting model.

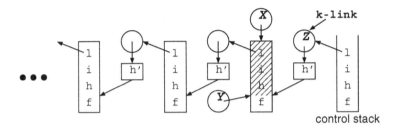

Fig. 7. Chain of continuation objects made by the program in Fig. 6.

invoked, a reference to the object that a global variable k-link holds is passed as an argument. Thus, when the continuation object, say X, that is created in the function l is promoted, the reference is also copied into the stack copy for it. Although the reference to X is discarded immediately, the copy of the stack for X is not discarded since it is shared with the continuation object, say Y, which is created in the function g. Here, an unused reference to the object that was held by the k-link appeared. After that, when the function j is invoked, another continuation object, say Z, is created. Since Y and Z share the stack copy for Y, which is also shared with X, it is referenced from Z indirectly. The reference to Z is stored into the k-link. Next, the function g is invoked again. Then, the reference to Z, which is in the k-link is passed to the function l as its argument. Consequently the chain of the copies of the stack grows.

If the garbage collector can detect unused region of copies of the stack, this problem dose not occur. But this complicates the garbage collector. Furthermore, even if we employ such a garbage collector, the region of stack copy for X and not for Y in the last piece of the chain, which is the hatched region in Fig. 7, is still left unreclaimed.

This problem does not occur in the dividing stack model and the incremental dividing stack model. In those models, the hatched region and the rest of the copy are allocated as separate objects. Thus, the object that has a hatched region is discarded when the continuation object X is discarded.

5.2   Costs of the Write Barrier and the Creation Time Barrier

The write barrier and the creation time barrier are the main overhead. Like `cons`, functions checked by the creation time barrier are frequently used in programs. For example, each time `cons` is invoked, its two arguments are checked. The accumulated cost for the creation time barrier is very high for programs which invokes `cons` many times. The cost of the creation time barrier may be relatively high in compiler-based systems or systems with fast memory allocators. However, actually it is not necessary to check all arguments for `cons`. If it is determined that arguments for `cons` are never continuation objects that have to be marked for promotion, checking the arguments can be omitted. In fact, the check is required only when an argument of a function is passed to `cons` in the body of the function because of the following observations.

- If a continuation object is returned from a function as the return value, it is already promoted.
- If an heap-allocated object is returned from a function, continuation objects referenced by it are already promoted or are marked for promotion.
- If a continuation object is stored into an object or a variable, it is marked for promotion.

Furthermore, it is possible to combine multiple checks for each argument.

We show another technique where the checks performed on creating a closure are reduced. When a closure is created, the creation time barrier checks whether the closure object contains a reference to a continuation object. In simple systems, a closure contains all the local variables and arguments that are accessible from the position where the closure is created. However, if it is detected that a variable is never accessed during a execution of the closure, the variable does not have to be checked. Moreover, such variables do not have to be contained in the closure. In fact, many compiler-based systems exclude such variables from the closure.

5.3   Use with Other Implementation Strategies for First-Class Continuations

There are many implementation strategies [3] for first-class continuations. The *garbage-collection strategy*, which is employed by Standard ML of New Jersey [8, 9], the *spaghetti strategy*, and the *heap strategy* allocate frames in the heap. Thus, such strategies requires almost no cost for capturing continuations. Therefore our proposal is not needed for systems using these strategies. However, [3] says they are not *zero overhead* strategies because they require more machine instructions than an ordinary stack-based implementations to create a single frame, link it to the frame of the caller function, and to dispose the frame.

The *stack/heap strategy* and the *incremental stack/heap strategy*, which will be described in Sect. 7, copy the contents of the stack when `call/cc` is invoked. Thus lazy stack copying works well. In our previous work [6], we applied the

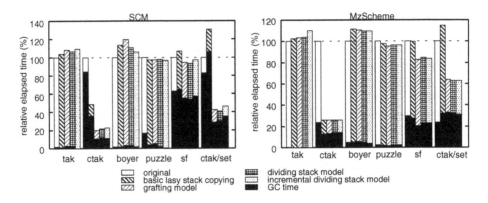

Fig. 8. Relative elapsed times for 6 benchmark programs.

basic lazy stack copying to a system using the incremental stack/heap strategy. Although the incremental stack/heap strategy is an optimized strategy for continuation-intensive programs, we achieved an additional improvement of the efficiency of a continuation-intensive program in the work. On the other hand, stack copy sharing is not needed because these strategies originally shares copies of the stack.

6   Performance Evaluation

We implemented the basic lazy stack copying, the grafting model, the dividing stack model, and the incremental dividing stack model in SCM [7] and MzScheme [10] and ran some benchmark programs on them. Our implementations use a checked optimization techniques in Table 1, not all techniques we described in Sect. 3 and 5.

Figure 8 shows the elapsed times relative to the original systems. The GC time in the figure shows the total time the garbage collector spent. The `ctak` benchmark is a continuation-intensive variation of the call-intensive `tak` benchmark. The `ctak` benchmark makes closures, and SCM encloses all local variables into a closure. Therefore, SCM encloses references to continuation objects even if they are not used in the closure. The `boyer` benchmark is a term rewriting and tautology checking program. It creates many cons cells but no first-class continu-

Table 1. Implemented features.

feature	SCM	MzScheme
two version evaluators	√	√
combining two version evaluators		
static analysis for avoiding the creation time barrier		
reducing the creation time barrier for closures		√

ation. The `puzzle` benchmark creates many first-class continuations, but not so many as `ctak`. These four benchmark programs are in Gabriel benchmarks [11]. The `sf` benchmark is a same-fringe program using coroutines. The `ctak/set` benchmark is almost the same as `ctak`, but it stores every continuation object into a dummy global variable so that all continuation objects are promoted.

Table 2 shows how many bytes are copied for promoting continuation objects (shown in the columns labeled "total size") and how many copies of the stack are made (shown in the columns labeled "number") on SCM. We omit the results on MzScheme because the results are similar. For the `tak` and the `boyer` benchmarks, no continuation object is created in any implementation. Original, basic, grafting, dividing, and incremental in the table represent implementations. They are respectively the original SCM, SCM with the basic lazy stack copying, SCM with the grafting model, SCM with the dividing stack model, and SCM with the incremental dividing stack model. When a copy of the stack is shared among continuation objects, it is counted as 1. On the other hand, when the stack is copied into separate parts, each part is counted as 1.

For benchmarks using first-class continuations, implementations with our proposal create fewer copies of the stack and spend less time than the original implementations with some exceptions. In particular, for the `ctak` and the `ctak/set` benchmarks, the improvements are remarkable. For the `sf` and the `ctak/set` benchmarks, implementations with the basic lazy stack copying spent more time than the original implementations. The reason is that for these benchmarks, all continuation objects are promoted eventually, but none of them are shared. On the other hand, the other implementations reduce the number of stack copies because stack copies are shared.

The results of the `ctak/set` benchmark on systems with the basic lazy stack copying shows that the performance is degraded to large extent. The reason is that the `ctak/set` benchmark is continuation-intensive. Each call to `call/cc` creates an additional frame of `eval_callcc()` on our implementations. Thus the stack grows longer than the original systems. Thus each copy of the stack becomes larger. If these implementations had employed the techniques of the combining two version evaluators, their performance would not degrade so much.

The results of the `ctak` benchmark on SCM with the basic lazy stack copying also need to be explained. SCM creates a closure containing all the accessible local variables. In `ctak`, a reference to a continuation object which is not ac-

Table 2. Total size and the number of the stack copies.

	ctak		puzzle		sf		ctak/set	
	total size	number	total size	number	total size	number	total size	number
original	31922740	47707	7595560	10025	52800944	400008	31022740	47707
basic	15242992	18171	0	0	48800864	400008	43022420	47707
grafting	828120	3539	0	0	30400496	400006	3300308	34302
dividing	828120	13405	0	0	30400496	400008	3300308	47707
incremental	1029180	13405	0	0	33400556	400008	4015898	47707

cessed during a execution of the closure is contained by the closure. Thus, many continuation objects which do not have to be promoted are promoted. A large part of the stack copies can be shared by stack copy sharing. This is the reason why the benchmark results of implementations with stack copy sharing is much better than that without it. On the other hand, MzScheme creates a closure containing only the local variables that will be accessed during a execution of the closure. Thus, the basic lazy stack copying works well.

The `tak` and `boyer` benchmarks makes no continuation objects. For the `tak` benchmark, a little implementation-specific overhead appeared. This overhead arises because we use a simple but inefficient algorithm to check whether continuation objects are enclosed in closures. It is possible to avoid this overhead by replacing the checking algorithm. For the `boyer` benchmark, the creation time barrier for `cons` degrades the performance.

7 Related Work

Lazy allocation [12] is an implementation method that allocates objects on the stack of a high-level language without creating dangling references. In the method, lazy stack copying is done by regarding function frames as objects allocated on the stack. In the method, a copy of the stack is created when a reference to a continuation object is stored into the heap or returned as a return value. To access an object both on the stack and in its copy in the heap in the same manner, a forwarding pointer is employed in the method. Although the solution is described in [12], it also says that lazy allocation does not solve all problems in the high performance implementation of Scheme continuations.

The incremental stack/heap strategy [3] employed in Scheme 48 [13] and in Larceny [14] is an implementation strategy for continuations. In the strategy, each frame of a function is copied to the heap separately. Copies of frames are linked as a list and shared among all continuations that contain the copied frames. The strategy is very efficient for programs which use `call/cc` and causes no overhead to programs without `call/cc`. However, the strategy requires that frames are relocatable since the copy is written back onto a different place from the place it was first allocated in. Because of the restriction, the application area of the strategy is limited.

SOAR [15] is a RISC microcomputer which has many kinds of hardware support for Smalltalk-80 [16]. Smalltalk-80 has a facility to handle first-class continuations called *contexts*. A Smalltalk-80 implementation on SOAR also delays stack copying until the function that created a continuation returns. On the SOAR system, each function frame has a one-bit reference counter [17], which corresponds to the mark for promotion in our proposal. SOAR raises an exception when a reference to a continuation is stored into the heap. The reference counter of each frame is incremented by the exception handler. An exception is also raised when a function returns, if the reference count of its frame is 1.

Continuations can be used to implement multiple threads. The proposed stack copy sharing will improve the performance of multi-threading. However, if continuations are used only for multi-threading, lazy task creation [18] and other techniques specialized for fine grained multi-thread systems [19,20,21] is more efficient.

8   Conclusion

In this paper, we proposed lazy stack copying. Lazy stack copying eliminates many unnecessary stack copying for programs using first-class continuations. We also proposed stack copy sharing. We presented three models for implementing it, and showed that stack copy sharing can be implemented easily in combination with lazy stack copying. These techniques reduce execution time and save memory space for first-class continuations. Our approach can be employed in interpreters written in a high-level languages such as C, which can not access the control stack without restraint. The approach can also be employed in compiler-based systems. We also presented the results of performance measurements of our implementations, which indicate that our approach improves performance of programs that use first-class continuations.

However, the results also show there is some overhead. Our future work includes reducing the overhead by improving our evaluator and by static analysis.

Acknowledgments. This research is supported in part by the 21st century COE program.

References

1. IEEE-1178-1990: IEEE Standard for the Scheme Programming Language. IEEE (1991)
2. Kelsey, R., Clinger, W., Rees, J., eds.: Revised[5] Report on the Algorithmic Language Scheme. In Kelsey, R., Clinger, W., Rees, J., eds.: Higher-Order and Symbolic Computation. Volume 11., Kluwer Academic Publishers (1998)
3. Clinger, W.D., Hartheimer, A.H., Ost., E.M.: Implementation strategies for first-class continuations. In: Higher-Order and Symbolic Computation. Volume 12., Kluwer Academic Publishers (1999) 7–45
4. Jones, R., Lins, R. In: Garbage Collection. JOHN WILEY & SONS (1996)
5. Yuasa, T., Nakagawa, Y., Komiya, T., Yasugi, M.: Return barrier. In: Proceedings International Lisp Conference, San Francisco. (2002, to appear)
6. Ugawa, T., Komiya, T., Yasugi, M., Yuasa, T.: Lazy stack copying for efficient implementation of continuations (in Japanese). In: Nineteenth Conference Proceedings Japan Society for Software Science and Technology, Japan Society for Software Science and Technology (2002)
7. Jaffer, A.: SCM Manual. (2003)
8. Appel, A.W., MacQueen, D.B.: Standard ML of New Jersey. In Wirsing, M., ed.: Third Int'l Symp. on Prog. Lang. Implementation and Logic Programming, New York, Springer-Verlag (1991) 1–13
9. Appel, A.W.: Compiling with Continuations. Cambridge University Press (1992)
10. Flatt, M.: PLT MzScheme: Langurage manual. (2000)

426   T. Ugawa et al.

11. Gabriel, R.: Performance and Evaluation of Lisp Systems. MIT Press (1985)
12. Baker, H.G.: CONS should not CONS its arguments, or, a lazy alloc is a smart alloc. ACM SIGPLAN Notices **27** (1992) 24–34
13. Kelsey, R.A., Rees, J.A.: A tractable Scheme implementation. Lisp and Symbolic Computation **7** (1994) 315–335
14. Clinger, W.D., Hansen, L.T.: Lambda, the ultimate label or a simple optimizing compiler for scheme. In: Proceedings 1994 ACM Conference on Lisp and Functional Programming, ACM Press (1994) 128–139
15. Samples, A.D., Ungar, D., Hilfinger, P.: SOAR: Smalltalk without bytecodes. In: Proceedings OOPSLA '86, ACM SIGPLAN Notices. Volume 21. (1986) 107–118
16. Goldberg, A., Robson, D.: Smalltalk-80: The Language and Its Implementation. Addison-Wesley (1983)
17. Friedman, D.P., Wise, D.S.: The one-bit reference count. BIT **17** (1977) 351–359
18. Mohr, E., Kranz, D.A., Halstead, Jr., R.H.: Lazy task creation: a technique for increasing the granularity of parallel programs. In: Proceedings of the 1990 ACM conference on LISP and functional programming, ACM Press (1990) 185–197
19. Goldstein, S.C., Schauser, K.E., Culler, D.E.: Enabling Primitives for Compiling Parallel Languages. In: Third Workshop on Languages, Compilers, and Run-Time Systems for Scalable Computers. (1995)
20. Taura, K., Yonezawa, A.: Fine-grain multithreading with minimal compiler support - a cost effective approach to implementing efficient multithreading languages. In: SIGPLAN Conference on Programming Language Design and Implementation. (1997) 320–333
21. Chakravarty, M.M.T.: Lazy thread and task creation in parallel graph reduction. Lecture Notes in Computer Science **1467** (1998) 231+

Author Index

Lecture Notes in Computer Science

For information about Vols. 1–2812
please contact your bookseller or Springer-Verlag